Classics in Congressional Politics

edited by

Herbert F. Weisberg
Eric S. Heberlig
Lisa M. Campoli
The Ohio State University

LONGMAN

An imprint of Addison Wesley Longman, Inc.

New York • Reading, Massachusetts • Menlo Park, California • Harlow, England
Don Mills, Ontario • Sydney • Mexico City • Madrid • Amsterdam

Associate Editor: Jennie Errickson
Cover Designer/Manager: Nancy Danahy
Cover Photograph: PhotoDisc, Inc.
Full Service Production Manager: Eric Jorgensen
Senior Print Buyer: Hugh Crawford
Project Coordination, Electronic Page Makeup,
    Text Design, Art Coordination and Studio: WestWords, Inc.
Printer and Binder: The Maple-Vail Book Manufacturing Group
Cover Printer: Coral Graphic Services

For permission to use copyrighted material, grateful acknowledgment is
made to the copyright holders on pp. 453–477, which are hereby made
part of this copyright page.

Library of Congress Cataloging-in-Publication Data
Classics in congressional politics / edited by Herbert F. Weisberg,
    Eric S. Heberlig, and Lisa M. Campoli.
        p.   cm.
    Includes bibliographical references and index.
    ISBN 0-8013-2030-5
        1. United States. Congress.   I. Weisberg, Herbert F.
    II. Heberlig, Eric S., 1970–   . III. Campoli, Lisa M., 1970–   .
    JK1021.C552   1999   98-40538
    328.73—dc21
                                                           CIP

ISBN 0–8013–2030–5

12345678910—MA—01009998

To Our Parents:

Anthony and Lois Campoli,

Dave and Vicki Heberlig

and the memory of Nathan and Jean Weisberg

Contents

Preface

Congress has evolved considerably over the years, but the changes that occurred when the Republicans took back control of the House in 1995 were considered by many to be revolutionary. The study of Congress also has evolved considerably over the years, but the last decade again has witnessed a virtually revolutionary change, with mathematical and formal approaches achieving ascendancy, at least in the journal literature. These two "revolutions" make it important to reconsider the state of this field. How relevant is the classic literature on Congress? What are the continuing questions that have motivated the study of Congress, and how can they inform the continuing study of the national legislature? Our intention in this book is to revisit the classic readings of the field, showing how the continuing questions in the field have informed our contemporary research.

The term "classic" conjures up several images at once: an item of the highest quality, an exemplar, an antique, a definitive piece, and something that is lasting. In referring to scholarly works, a classic is usually all of the above at once: high quality writing that serves as an exemplar, that has been in the literature a long while, that has helped shape the field, and that has withstood the test of time. However, when political scientists look at scholarly pieces that are considered classics, what they see is that these works were important enough to change the direction of later research on the topic. Such works remain of interest even after their specific findings become outdated and after their ideas have been challenged in the later literature because the ideas were something sufficiently provocative to affect the direction of the field for years.

As a result of these considerations, the congressional classics chosen for this book are ones that have affected the directions of legislative research. Therefore, the section introductions will review both the earlier research on each topic and the research that has followed. Of course there always will be disagreements as to exactly which pieces are classics, and there are many more classics in the field than we have space to reprint, but the writings represented in this book do a good job of representing important themes in the legislative literature and significant directions that have emerged in that literature.

In addition to reprinting these classics, we take two steps to emphasize the contemporary relevance of this work. In some sections of the book we have written a short "Contemporary Issue" piece that presents current debates related to the topic of the section, such as showing how the recent arguments on divided government relate to the classic discussions of congressional elections. Also, in several sections we have included a "Contemporary Perspective" reading that demonstrates how the classic questions are addressed in the current scholarly literature.

We focus on seven areas of the congressional literature: legislative change, representation, elections, norms, committees, party leadership, and decision making. Each of these has been an area of considerable research over the years, with later research both building on the early work and challenging that work. Numerous other areas of legislative scholarship certainly could be examined in this same way. We regret only that there is not enough space for us to consider more of these areas.

In discussing these seven areas, we adopt a "controversies" approach, looking for the main controversy underlying the topic and using that debate to organize the discussion. In some areas it is obvious what the main controversy has been, but the literature in some other areas has developed with little regard to a central controversy. In many of these latter areas, the literature examined particular cases (such as a legislative leader, a fight for a leadership position in Congress, or a legislative committee) with little sense of cumulation in terms of how that case relates to a coherent research agenda in the area. We chose what we consider to be the controversy that underlies the literature in such areas, and we show how the literature speaks to that controversy. We hope that thereby we are contributing to building a sense of cumulation for these areas, as well as a clearer sense of what is to be explained in them.

We owe a considerable debt to several people for their assistance in this project. Pam Gordon, Jennie Errickson, and Peter Glovin of Addison Wesley Longman have been very supportive of us in this effort. We also appreciate the many comments of the several readers for the press and Sara Dunlap's able assistance with the manuscript. Herb Weisberg acknowledges a special debt to several generations of graduate students at the University of Michigan and Ohio State University who patiently sat through his legislative behavior seminars in which the ideas underlying this book were developed. Additionally we want to express our appreciation to our instructors and colleagues in this area, principally Herb Asher, Joseph Karlesky, William Keefe, John Kingdon, Warren Miller, Morris Ogul, Kelly Patterson, Samuel Patterson, Randall Ripley, and the late Donald Stokes. Finally our greatest debt is to the Department of Political Science at the Ohio State University, which brought us together and enabled us to work on this project.

A volume of "classics" may seem to imply that the great work in a field already has been done. We hope that readers of this book do not take away that lesson. Congress is ever-changing, and so is our understanding of Congress. The classics give us a basis for building new work on a firm foundation, so that we recognize where we have been as we move on to a higher level of understanding. So, we engage in an exploration of the classics in congressional politics, but with our interest firmly anchored to achievement of new understanding for the future.

INTRODUCTION

Chapter 1

The Study of Congress: Methodologies and the Pursuit of Theory

Like Congress itself, the study of Congress has evolved over the years. As to be expected in any field, the methodologies for studying Congress have become more sophisticated. Even more striking has been the quest for theory, which is in the process of transforming the legislative field. Yet the core research questions in different areas of congressional studies have remained fairly constant over these years. We show in later chapters how the classic writings in the field that we reprint in this book have retained their relevance to the contemporary period. However, understanding these works also requires placing the research on Congress in the context of the development of the field of congressional studies, and that is the focus of this introductory chapter.

THE LEGISLATIVE FIELD

Legislatures are ancient institutions, dating back at least as far as the medieval Spanish Cortes (Holden 1930) and in some senses to the Athenian council and the Boeotian League of ancient Greece and Rome (Beard and Lewis 1932). However, legislatures did not originally have their current range of powers. Most scholars trace the origins of the first representative assemblies to medieval courts (Strayer 1970), and these early legislatures were representative only in the sense that rulers used them as a means by which propertied classes could hear the justification of decisions and give their consent. The men attending these meetings or enlarged sessions of the court were not elected, did not debate issues, and did not cast votes.

The early English parliaments were similarly assemblies of the estates of the realm (particularly the nobility and clergy) called by kings to consent to taxes for their treasuries. Subjects began to employ these assemblies to their own advantage, using them to petition the king for redress of grievances and to obstruct government action by granting less money than the king requested. Only gradually were assemblies transformed into law-making bodies. By the seventeenth century, the English king selected his cabinet and officers from the party with a majority in the parliament. The franchise was slowly extended so that more citizens were able to participate in voting for members of Parliament (Beard and Lewis 1932), and legislatures became the representative bodies that they are today.

The role of legislatures was further expanded by the Founding Fathers when they wrote the Constitution and created a powerful and more independent Congress. Because of the grievances the American colonists had against the British monarchy in which executive power predominated, the authors of the Constitution feared executive power. Therefore, they limited the powers of the new presidency and instituted republican government, in which, as James Madison argued in *Federalist Papers* No. 51, "the legislative authority necessarily predominates." Congress was given great power, which was viewed as appropriate since it was designed to be the branch closest to the people. They gave the Congress a long list of specific powers, such as the power to raise and spend money, as well as a broader grant of power to make all laws "necessary and proper" to exercise the listed responsibilities. Yet the Framers feared the concentration of power in any hands, including the legislature's, so they created a system of separated powers and instituted checks and balances between the branches. Even if its powers were to be checked by the executive and judiciary, the powers of Congress far superseded those of earlier legislatures.

There are still considerable differences in the powers of legislatures. Polsby (1975) distinguishes between two types—the arena legislature and the transformative legislature. The arena legislature is mainly a vehicle for discussion of politics—the executive in those polities makes the fundamental decisions, and the legislature's role is only to discuss those decisions and rubberstamp them. Indeed, on certain government proposals the British parliament can only discuss bills and pass them without amendment, unless it is willing to vote against the government on a motion of confidence and thereby bring down the executive. By contrast, the transformative legislature can change the policy recommendations of the executive. Legislatures in the United States are the epitome of transformative legislatures, with Congress able to ignore presidential proposals and to pass legislation over a presidential veto. As a result of its strong powers, the U.S. Congress has been the focus of considerable scholarly interest.

Legislatures generally and Congress in particular have been studied from a wide variety of perspectives. In the policy arena, people follow how specific bills have become law in order to understand the legislature's intentions or to estimate the chances for passing further legislation on similar topics. Other interests in legislatures tend to be more general. Students of public policy see legislatures as an opportunity to observe policy making in a fairly visible arena. Similarly, students of decision making view legislatures as an instance of real-life decision making in a high-stakes environment. Legislatures fascinate people who study political power since legislatures are places where power is accumulated and exercised. Others study legislatures as representative bodies, and they use the legislature as a focus for examining the interrelations between the public and their elected representatives. The formal rules by which legislatures operate are a focus of attention for scholars who want to study how rules affect outcomes. The nature of the legislature as an institution intrigues scholars who want to apply organizational theory perspectives to public bodies. All these concerns, from the most applied to the most theoretical, are well represented in the legislative literature.

This variety of perspectives that have been applied to the study of legislative politics makes the area fascinating, yet detracts from its sense of unity. Often these approaches have been borrowed from other disciplines. A few examples suffice to demonstrate the variety of approaches that have been used over the years. At one extreme, a military metaphor was used by Gross (1953) to describe the passage of the Employment Act of 1946, with the bill's sponsors being the commanders who strategized and fought the battle to pass the bill. At the opposite extreme, a theatre metaphor has been invoked by Weisberg and Patterson (1998) to understand Congress, with legislators seen as consciously playing to multiple audiences. More conventionally, systems theory has been used to study the roles of legislators (Wahlke et al. 1962), organization theory has been used to study how legislatures develop over time, and rational choice theory has been used to show how institutions can be understood in terms of the strategic actions of purposive actors.

Many fields operate under a single dominant paradigm, a commonly agreed upon framework for research on the topic. There have been attempts to establish such a paradigm in the legislative area; in recent years the rational choice approach has gained particular favor, but no single framework completely dominates the field. The study of legislatures has instead been unified only by the object of interest—the legislature. As a result, research on legislatures has been less cumulative than in some other fields of political science. Yet the fact that so many different types of scholars can come together with an interest in legislatures has given the field a special vitality.

The variety of approaches to studying legislatures has been mimicked by a variety of methods used to study legislatures. There is only a single legitimate way to study topics in some fields, but that has not been the case for legislative studies. Different methodologies have long coexisted in the field, and that situation should be expected to continue. This introductory chapter will set the classic congressional writings into a broader context by recounting the history of the development of the legislative subfield.

EARLY LEGISLATIVE RESEARCH TRADITIONS

The earliest approach to the study of legislatures was institutional. Studies in the nineteenth century generally focused on constitutions and legislative rules, as if reading such documents explained how legislatures function. This legalistic approach fell into disfavor as researchers began to realize that the interesting phenomena in legislatures often did not follow those legalisms. As a result, two new empirical approaches to legislative studies were developed at the end of the nineteenth century—a descriptive tradition and analysis of legislative roll calls.

First, an important descriptive tradition developed in the study of legislative politics, with a focus on observing how the legislature actually works. This descriptive tradition was evidenced by the end of the nineteenth century, in such historical work as Follett's (1896) study of the Speaker of the House and McConachie's (1898) study of congressional committees. The best known of these early empirical works was Woodrow Wilson's ([1885] 1956) study *Congressional Government*. Wilson went past the previous focus on legislative rules to examine how Congress actually worked in practice. His discovery of the importance of committees in the legislative process (see chapter 16 in this book) made it clear that legislative studies could not be limited to formal procedures and had to be more empirically based.

A second methodological tradition began at about the same time—analysis of the roll call record of legislatures. In 1896 Orin Libby issued his "Plea for the Study of Votes in Congress." Within a few years A. Lawrence Lowell (1902) took up that challenge and became the first person to utilize roll call materials in political research with his comparative study of the role of the political party in the American and British legislatures. Lowell's pioneering work was then followed by Stuart Rice's (1928) analysis of consensus and cleavage within and between the parties in legislatures. Herman Beyle (1931) extended Rice's work on the structural properties of legislative parties.

Taken together, the descriptive approach and roll call work were clearly moves toward studying Congress as it actually operates. Both approaches were distinctly atheoretical, focusing on studying Congress as it is without much concern for developing broader generalizations. This early work did, though, have normative and reformist implications which were drawn out after the end of World War II. For example, James McGregor Burns (1949) strung together a series of descriptive case studies explicitly to put *Congress on Trial* and proposed reforms designed to handle its shortcomings, while the documentation of the lower level of party voting in the United States than in Britain helped form the basis of the American Political Science Association's 1950 report *Toward a More Responsible Two-Party System*. However, this reformism proved to be only a temporary direction for the legislative field, which further changed in the 1950s and 1960s in response to intellectual trends in the political science discipline more generally.

LEGISLATIVE RESEARCH IN THE 1950s AND 1960s

The Congress of the 1950s and 1960s has become known as the "textbook Congress," because scholarly descriptions about Congresses of that era became the basis for the description of its normal operation in political science textbooks. Briefly, it was a Congress dominated by senior committee chairs, who were mostly southern conservative Democrats and who had more power than either the official party leaders or the rank-and-file legislators. The process of passing bills was routinized, making it easier for textbooks to describe the locus of power and the bill-passing process.

The 1950s and 1960s were also a period of ferment in political science generally, with the "behavioral revolution" and the subsequent development of the rational choice approach to the study of politics. These two approaches both emphasized the "science" in political science and sought to develop broad theories, though they differed in how they approached theory. These disciplinary trends were naturally echoed in the legislative field.

Behavioral Approach

The behavioral approach to political science that became prominent in the 1950s and 1960s was basically inductive—trying to move to generalizations on the basis of available evidence. These studies focused on the behavior and attitudes of individual actors rather than institutions, and often involved interviews of those political actors and/or quantitative analysis. When behavioralism was applied to the legislative field, many researchers examined congressional committees because of their power in the textbook Congress, along with the roles of committee members and the norms that permitted committee dominance.

Case Studies

The empirical emphasis described above evolved considerably in the 1950s and 1960s. Many of the empirical studies of this era were studies of a single case, but they reflected the desire of behavioralists to develop broader concepts that move toward mid-level theory. As one example of this shift, consider the implications of Woodrow Wilson's discovery of the importance of committees in Congress. Once that insight became part of the conventional wisdom, the research agenda naturally shifted to studying how a committee operates in practice. The influence of the behavioral movement on the study of committees was evident in this work during the 1950s and 1960s, such as Ralph Huitt's (1954) use of the role concept to understand the behavior of members of the House Committee on Banking and Currency, Richard Fenno's (1962, reprinted as chapter 17) borrowing of systems theory from sociology to study how group integration led to consensus in the House Appropriations committee, and John Manley's (1965) study of the Ways and Means committee as a political subsystem of the House.

Behavioral case studies of Congress were often quantitative. This was most evident in Donald Matthews' (1960) masterful study of the U.S. Senate. Matthews provided a comprehensive picture of how the Senate of the 1950s operated, using quantitative evidence on such topics as the social background of senators and the correlates of senatorial effectiveness. He also imported concepts from sociology, as in his chapter (reprinted here as chapter 13) on Senate norms—the mutual expectations of behavior under which the chamber operates.

The case study approach permits rich description of the case being studied. However, it is resource intensive—studying a single case in depth requires a lot of work, and studying several cases so that comparisons can be made requires even more time and effort. Furthermore, the single case approach can just be descriptive, though at its best it is based on theory, as when behavioral legislative research in the 1950s and 1960s was heavily influenced by concepts from sociology. The strongest examples of case study research involve the comparative case approach, which can be based on theoretical perspectives (see especially King, Keohane, and Verba 1994).

Roll Call Analysis

There had been little use of roll call analysis after Rice and Beyle's initial efforts, but the approach was rediscovered in the 1950s and 1960s. Julius Turner (1951a) provided an influential analysis of party voting in Congress, and David Truman (1959) offered an important analysis of the internal structure of party voting patterns. The subsequent development of high-speed computers facilitated large-scale roll call studies. Roll call analysis methods were the subject of several monographs during this period, including MacRae (1958, 1970), Clausen (1964), Anderson, Watts, and Wilcox (1966), and Weisberg (1968). Some of this work is described in more detail in our discussion of decision making in legislatures in chapter 24.

One advantage of the roll call approach is that it does not require the analyst of Congress to go to Washington, D.C., for the actual research. All that is necessary is access to the roll call voting record, which is public data. The drawback of this approach is that it is not altogether clear what roll call data really mean. That is, we know how members voted, but not why. Roll call analysts make assumptions as to the meaningfulness of their data, but different interpretations are possible. For example, early researchers often dealt with roll calls as if they represented the attitudes of the legislators, whereas later researchers regard them more as the public positions that legislators are willing to take for constituents and lobbyists. Again, this interpretation problem will be discussed more in chapter 24.

Interview Studies

A new methodological approach, interviews with legislators, entered the legislative research field in the 1950s. At that time personal interviews were becoming important in studying mass political behavior, so it was a natural extension to start interviewing elites. Two major legislative interviewing studies were conducted in the late 1950s. Wahlke, Eulau, Buchanan, and Ferguson's (1962) comparative state legislature study interviewed legislators in four states using a common interview schedule. The Miller and Stokes (1963) congressional representation study conducted interviews with members of Congress in 1958, supplemented by interviews with their opponents and a national survey of the mass public from their districts (see chapter 6).

Interviews with legislators have varied considerably in their formats (see also Peabody 1969). At one extreme are the very structured interviews with closed-ended questions used by Miller and Stokes in imitation of the structured interviews the University of Michigan's Survey Research Center was taking at the same time with the mass public. At the opposite extreme are the virtually journalistic sessions in which several members of Congress are gathered for recorded round-table discussions, as in Clapp's (1963) study The Congressman. Between these two extremes are semi-structured interviews, such as Kingdon's 1969 interviewing of members of Congress on which his chapter in this book (chapter 25) is based. He had eight questions in mind when he interviewed members about specific votes they had cast. These were very open-ended questions (such as "How did you go about making up your mind?" and "Did you talk to staff people about this?"), and Kingdon even modified the order of questions depending on the flow of the conversation with his respondent.

Interviews are difficult to conduct because of the problem of access. Legislators are very busy people, and it is usually difficult for researchers to gain access to them. The access problem actually varies—access to members of Congress is much more difficult for researchers today than it was in the 1950s, and it is much more severe for Congress than for state legislatures. Researchers often obtain access by going through intermediaries—developing good contacts in the legislature (ideally with the party leaders) who vouch for the authenticity of the researchers and the importance of cooperation with them. Still, interviewing members of Congress requires patience and persistence. Many researchers settle for interviews with staff members, arguing that staff can speak for their members on the topic of the study, but there are real limits on the extent to which staff know the members' actual views.

Formal Theory

Another approach to political science had its beginnings in the 1950s and 1960s—formal theory. Deductive theories were developed, in which the problem being studied is stated in formal (often mathematical) terms and then various conclusions are derived from a set of simplifying assumptions.

Formal theoretical approaches to study of legislatures had their beginnings in abstract work by social choice theorists on voting (Arrow 1951) and committees (Black 1958). Duncan Black's important result of the median voter theorem—that the winning position in a unidimensional committee (a committee in which the conflict is along a single continuum, such as liberal-conservative ideology) is the position of the middle legislator—shaped a lengthy formal theory literature (see also the appendix of MacRae 1958), including work on agenda control and strategic voting. William Riker (1961) showed how the system of voting on pairs of alternatives in legislatures can lead to the paradox of voting in which a majority prefers one alternative to a second, the second to a third, and that third to the first, so that there is no equilibrium position. Riker's (1962) *Theory of Political Coalitions* also spawned a legislative literature on coalition formation and size. Farquharson (1969) focused attention on strategic voting, which again has wide legislative application. Some of these pieces did not discuss Congress directly, but they became the basis of much work on Congress in later decades.

Comparative Legislative Studies

While our emphasis is primarily on the U.S. Congress, it is important to emphasize that no single legislative body can be fully understood in isolation from other legislatures. Thus, an important complement to the research on Congress in the 1950s and 1960s was the development of the field of comparative legislative studies. The result was several empirical studies of legislatures in other countries. For example, Lowell's roll call work applied to the British House of Commons as much as to the Congress. MacRae (1967) and Wood (1968) provided early analyses of voting in the French parliament. Arend Lijphart (1963) and Hayward Alker and Bruce Russett (1965) applied roll call methods to the United Nations General Assembly. Later studies of comparative legislative politics include Hirsch and Hancock (1971), Patterson and Wahlke (1972), Kornberg (1973) and Mezey (1985).

Two special classes of comparative applications should be emphasized: subnational and historical. As to subnational research, the four-state representation study (Wahlke et al. 1962) was an early example of comparative state legislative research, while the Eulau and Prewitt (1973) Bay area study is a rare illustration of comparative studies of city councils. Emphasis on the historical dimension is evident in William Aydelotte's examinations of voting in the British House of Commons in the 1840s and studies by Alexander (1967) and Silbey (1967) of sectional conflict in Congress in the 1800s. Aydelotte's books *Quantification in History* (1971) and *History of Parliamentary Behavior* (1977) are later, important works on quantitative legislative history.

Conclusions

At the end of this time period, Robert Peabody (1969, 3) concluded that "research on Congress has reached an important middle stage in its development." He was writing at the conclusion of two decades that were marked by considerable growth of the congressional research field. Yet the field was still relatively underdeveloped, not yet moving to a theoretical plane. Case study research on Congress was flourishing, Duncan MacRae had contributed his roll call analysis of Congress, major interviewing studies of legislatures had been conducted, and the pioneering formal theory work was written. Legislative politics was blossoming as a field, fostered by the interest of the Social Science Research Council which financed conferences and research on legislatures, by Ralph Huitt's American Political Science Association-sponsored "Study of Congress" which led to the publication of several important books, by the founding of the APSA congressional fellowship program which brought legislative scholars to Washington to work in congressional offices for a year, and by the creation of a Consortium for Comparative Legislative Studies. This was a golden era of congressional studies in which Richard Fenno started his study of committees, Nelson Polsby applied organizational concepts to legislatures, Randall Ripley examined party leadership, and Charles Jones studied congressional parties. The legislative field was ripe to take off, and it did in the next decade.

LEGISLATIVE RESEARCH IN THE 1970S

The Congress of the 1970s became known as the "reform Congress." The power relationships of the textbook Congress were shaken up when northern liberal Democrat reformers changed congressional rules to give more power to subcommittees at the expense of committee chairs (Rieselbach 1977, 1978). The result was increased individualism in Congress, with greater powers for the individual members.

The study of the reform Congress was still heavily behavioral. However, the increased individualism in Congress led to important work in formal theory that modeled Congress from the perspective of the individual legislator.

Behavioral Studies

The behavioral approach still dominated legislative research in the 1970s, but with increased sophistication as compared to the studies of the 1950s and 1960s.

Roll Call Analysis

As chapter 24 will detail, roll call analysis was of central importance to the study of Congress in the 1970s. Clausen (1973) clustered congressional votes taken from 1953 to 1964 by five issue domains and found that voting patterns differed by policy area. Clausen's methods were subsequently used to trace congressional voting patterns across policy domains back through the New Deal (Sinclair 1978, 1982) and into the 1970s (Clausen and Van Horn 1977). Asher and Weisberg (1978, reprinted as chapter 26) also followed members' voting on four issues over time to document the stability and evolution of members' decisions.

Others studied congressional roll call voting using methodologies beyond statistical analyses of votes. Matthews and Stimson (1975) interviewed members of Congress regarding their sources of information in decision making. They then used computer simulations to explore how information diffused across the House (see also Cherryholmes and Shapiro 1969).

Aggregate patterns of congressional voting, rather than the votes of individual members of Congress, also were a subject of study. Brady, Cooper, and Hurley (1979) studied party voting—the degree to which members of the same political party voted together cohesively. Edwards (1976, 1980) examined the degree to which members of Congress supported the positions of the president.

The wide variety of studies produced some quite different explanations of how members of Congress make voting decisions. Weisberg (1978) compared several prominent models of congressional voting statistically, found that they were relatively equally successful in explaining actual votes, and showed that they offered little improvement over simpler models that account for voting just in terms of party and region. His argument raised the hurdles that subsequent roll call studies had to pass in order to be considered successful.

Case Studies

Despite the increasing methodological and statistical focus of research on congressional voting and other topics, case studies continued to be the favored method of studying questions where there were few cases or few ways to "quantify" data. Congressional leadership remained a topic for which case studies dominated. Stewart (1971, reprinted as chapter 21) compared the leadership styles of Senate Majority Leaders Lyndon Johnson and Mike Mansfield. Others, most notably Peabody (1976) and the contributors to Mackaman (1981), documented the politics of leadership transitions and leadership activities in the 1970s.

As chapter 16 details, comparative case studies of committees became important during this period. Fenno (1973) followed his 1960s case studies of single committees with a comparative case study of six House committees. Fenno also shifted his explanations of committee behavior from the sociological systems theories to the economic theories that were increasingly integrated into political science research in the 1970s (see below). In particular, Fenno emphasized the goal orientations of individual members in explaining their choice of committee assignments. Hinckley (1975, reprinted as chapter 18) also employed a comparative committee method, comparing 16 House and Senate committees to examine how differences in the committees' political environments influenced their behavior.

Interview and Observation Studies

Interviews were also a prominent method for studying Congress in the 1970s. Several of the voting studies discussed above relied heavily on interviews, especially the Matthews and Stimson book. Interview-based studies during the decade include Asher's study of the norms of the House (1973b, reprinted as chapter 14). The interview approach was augmented by the application of the participant observation method.

Richard Fenno (1977b, reprinted as chapter 7) innovatively applied the technique of participant observation to the study of congressional representation. Traditional interviews, whether the questions are highly structured or more informal, are conducted in a setting where the question and answer exchange between the interviewer and interviewee are the main activity and focus of attention for both participants. Fenno, instead, went to the legislative districts of members of Congress and followed them around through their activities for several days. Fenno observed. He conversed with the members when they were not occupied with constituents. In his words, he was "soaking and poking—or just hanging around" (1978, xiv). This approach is controversial as it is difficult to prove that the researcher's observations and interpretations can be replicated. Still, this in-depth immersion into the life of a member of Congress led to substantial insights into how members of Congress understand their constituencies and why they interact with their constituents the way they do (see chapter 7).

Fenno's "soaking and poking" changed the way we perceive and study Congress: Activities at home are now seen as essential for understanding activities in Washington. This perspective has become so dominant that it has been adopted by a major textbook on Congress, Davidson and Oleszek's (1998) *Congress and Its Members*. Fenno's insights set the stage for emphasis in the 1980s on the study of legislator-constituent interactions.

Rational Choice Theory

Whereas the congressional literature of the 1950s and 1960s borrowed heavily from sociology, the 1970s were marked by the increasing influence of economics. This was evident in the application of formal theory to Congress, but also in more informal emphasis on the goals of members of Congress. In particular, David Mayhew (1974a) presented a stunningly broad interpretation of Congress based on members having but a single goal: reelection. Similarly, Fenno (1973) grounded his comparative case study of congressional committees on a goal perspective, with members being seen as selecting their committees on the basis of their reelection, policy, and power goals. Fiorina's (1977b) influential study of Congress as part of the Washington establishment was similarly based on the argument that a new breed of members of Congress were motivated by their reelection needs to establish federal programs and then help their constituents with the resultant new bureaucracies. Each of these pieces is based on the notion of "instrumental rationality" where the actions we observe in a legislature are seen as the function of political actors pursuing their own goals.

At the more formal level, several important results with legislative applications were derived in the 1970s. McKelvey (1976) showed that voting cycles are fully chaotic when preferences are not undimensional. Plott and Levine (1978) showed how control of the agenda can determine the decisions of committees.

Fiorina (1974) provided one of the first formal models of constituency influence on voting in Congress, taking into account such considerations as district homogeneity and issue salience. This was soon followed by Shepsle's (1978) modeling of the process of assigning Democrats to House committees. Meanwhile, Weingast (1979) developed a rational choice analysis of the universalism norm under which unanimous coalitions are formed to pass legislation that distributes benefits to congressional districts, suggesting at the end of his article a series of rational choice explanations of other legislative norms. Finally, Shepsle (1979) introduced an important distinction between two sources of equilibria in Congress: the preference-induced equilibrium in which member preferences lead to a solution that defeats all other alternatives, and the structure-induced equilibrium in which institutional arrangements and rules create an equilibrium regardless of member preferences. These works taken collectively refocused congressional studies on the formal rules of the chamber, leading directly to the new institutionalism approach that became important in the 1980s and 1990s.

New Data Sources

Research directions in a field can change for a number of reasons—because of changes in the legislature, innovations in methodology, theoretical developments, and/or new collections of data that allow new domains to be explored. Several important new sources of data were introduced in the 1970s that opened fresh avenues of research into the next decade.

Congressional committees were one major source of new data in the 1970s. The reforms of the 1970s led to members' votes on amendments and legislation in committee being public. These votes have been used to study factional patterns in committees by Parker and Parker (1979) and Unekis and Rieselbach (1984). Also the release of Democrats' committee assignment requests made possible Shepsle's empirical tests of his formal theories of why members seek membership on certain committees (1978). This topic returned to the fore in the 1990s in the debate over the extent to which committees are "outliers" (see chapter 16).

Another new source of data was the result of the Federal Election Campaign Act of 1971 and its 1974 Amendments. These acts required the reporting of campaign contributions and expenditures to the Federal Election Commission, which would make this information publicly available. These data have become the source of Jacobson's (1978, 1980) and many subsequent studies of the impact of campaign spending on congressional election outcomes. They are also the basis for many studies seeking to establish the influence of political action committee (PAC) contributions on votes of members of Congress (see Smith 1995 for a review).

Aggregate election outcomes became a major source of data for studies on congressional elections. Kramer (1971) and Tufte (1975) documented the impact of the national economy and presidential popularity, respectively, on congressional elections. Mayhew (1974b, reprinted as chapter 10) categorized congressional districts by the winner's margin of victory. He found that the number of districts in which congressional races were close, so-called "marginal districts," had decreased over time. Few marginal districts meant that incumbents were safer from electoral defeat than they had been in the past. Mayhew's observation spurred a long line of research devoted to discovering the source of incumbents' electoral "advantage"— and why the marginal districts had "vanished" (e.g., Ferejohn 1977; Fiorina 1977a; Jacobson and Kernell 1983, reprinted as chapter 11).

A final major source of data near the end of this period was the 1978 American National Election Study (ANES) survey. The increased focus on individualism in studies of Congress during this period led to a reorientation of questions in this survey. It introduced new batteries of questions focused on the interactions of constituents and their congressional representatives. The new questions included constituents' knowledge of, attitudes towards, and contacts with their member of Congress. Important works based on these surveys include Jacobson's *Politics of Congressional Elections* (1997), Jacobson and Kernell (1983), Parker and Davidson (1979) on public attitudes toward Congress, and the many studies of the effect of casework activities on members' electoral fortunes (see chapter 5).

Conclusions

Assessing the state of the legislative field just after the 1970s drew to close, Rieselbach (1983) pointed to several "middle-range theories" about specific aspects of Congress but concluded that there was little "grand theory" that encompassed the entire field. He wrote this after a decade that saw the continuation of many of the methods and research questions that had previously occupied legislative scholars, but with developments in methods, theories, and data collection that led to changes in emphases during the decade. The study of congressional voting dominated the 1970s, but at the same time there was greater attention to questions of institutional structure and individual choice driven by formal theories from economics. Increased usage of statistical analysis led to the greater importance of quantifiable data to which theories of legislative behavior can be applied. The legislative studies field also became more institutionalized during this period. By the time the 1970s drew to a close, *Legislative Studies Quarterly* was created as a specialty journal, a Legislative Studies Group was formed that soon became an organized section in the American Political Science Association, and a conference was held on the Mathematical Study of Congress. The legislative subfield was poised to rise to a more mature scientific status.

LEGISLATIVE RESEARCH IN THE 1980s AND 1990s

The Congress of the 1980s and 1990s has become known as the "post-reform Congress."[1] The reforms of the 1970s had worked through the system, and power relationships in Congress changed again when the role of the House Speaker was strengthened and partisanship simultaneously intensified (Davidson 1992; Rohde 1991). Two other important developments in Congress during this period were the prevalence of "divided government" in which one party controlled the presidency and the other party controlled Congress, and the "revolution" that occurred in the House of Representatives when Republicans regained control after the 1994 elections for the first time in 40 years.

As a result of these changes, studies of Congress during this period gave less attention to individual members and greater attention to rules and the role of parties. Research on Congress became more institutional, though a wide array of different approaches was still employed.

Behavioral Studies

Behavioral work on Congress continued in the 1980s and 1990s, but at a diminished pace. Roll call analysis continued as an approach, though its dominance as a focus of study decreased from the 1970s. Roll call studies during the 1980s and 1990s were again notable for their increasing methodological sophistication. In particular, Poole and Rosenthal (1997) published their comprehensive analysis showing how roll call voting in Congress has changed since the beginning of the Republic (see also chapter 24).

Case studies also remained common. For example, the field's understanding of congressional leadership continued to benefit greatly from case studies. Cooper and Brady (1981a) and Sinclair (1982, 1995) were particularly influential studies of party leadership, while committee leadership was the focus of comparative case studies by Strahan (1992), Reeves (1993), and Evans (1991). Comparative case studies were extensively used to study other legislative topics as well, including decision making (Arnold 1990), descriptive representation (Swain 1993), and why individuals run for Congress (Fowler and McClure 1989).

Many of the above case studies also involved intensive interviewing or, more broadly, soaking and poking. Fenno (1996) continued his work on representation but shifted from following around members of the House to following around Senators. Senators proved to be popular interviewees as Sinclair (1989) and Harris (1993) used them as sources for their studies of the changes in the contemporary U.S. Senate. Hall's interviews with congressional staffers were the source of his unique data on the "informal," behind-the-scenes participation of members of Congress in the development of legislation (1987, 1996).

The New Institutionalism

In the 1980s and 1990s, rational choice theories were increasingly applied to understanding legislatures, so much so that some feel that it has become the dominant paradigm in the field. Ordeshook (1986) explains that a formal approach to political science is appropriate because political science is concerned with the actions and decisions that individuals take within institutions such as legislatures. These institutions are human creations established and designed to meet human purposes such as inducing people to make specific choices or leading them to avoid choices that they might make under another institutional arrangement (Ordeshook 1986, 243). Institutions endure or end because they meet individual goals or fail to do so. A formal approach to legislatures therefore might involve studying institutional outcomes to explain institutional survival and failure, or studying how institutions affect individual choice to learn why particular institutions are selected.

As Shepsle (1985) observes, rational choice approaches to legislatures involve equilibrium theories (the study of voting rules, addressed here in Part IV), incidence analysis (how policy choices affect constituencies), and theories of agency (formalization of incentive structures linking principal to agent, addressed here in Part V). In the early 1980s, scholars began building on the earliest applications of formal models to legislatures in order to describe Congress and its structures in greater depth. These models relied on spatial modeling and a "politics-of-distribution" perspective to suggest ways "in which institutional structure channeled expressions of legislative self-interest" (Shepsle and Weingast 1995, 8). Instead of simple majority rule voting, congressional activity was now seen in terms of ongoing strategic interactions in a context of fixed institutional arrangements (see Part IV).

Models of the late 1980s were distinguished by their consideration of changing institutional arrangements and imperfect information in Congress (see Shepsle and Weingast 1995). For example, committees (see Part V) were modeled as issue specialists which would gather information to improve chamber output, given the correct incentives (Gilligan and Krehbiel 1989; Krehbiel 1991). Legislative leaders (see Part VI) were seen as agents selected to coordinate party activities as a solution to members' collective dilemmas in the pursuit of individual goals (Rohde 1991; Cox and McCubbins 1993). Delegation and control relationships (Kiewiet and McCubbins 1991) were introduced as part of the congressional context as well as the larger institutional context in which Congress operates.

A number of important works have developed from this approach. Most notably, Cox and McCubbins (1993) applied the economic concept of cartels to reinterpret the role of congressional parties. They argue that these parties are "legislative cartels" that have usurped the power to make the rules controlling the passage of legislation, thereby considerably challenging usual views of weak congressional parties.

Even studies that are not explicitly formal in their approach increasingly make use of the concepts developed in this work. The notion of legislators as purposive actors pursuing a limited number of goals is pervasive in the field, from studies of leadership of legislative committees (Evans 1991) to studies of the leadership of the congressional parties (Sinclair 1995) and Sinclair's (1989) comprehensive study *The Transformation of the U.S. Senate*. The best of these studies exemplify how our abstract theorizing must be based on rich descriptive work, so that theories incorporate our best understanding of Congress.

The new institutionalist approach to Congress became the basis of a reader on Congress (McCubbins and Sullivan 1987). While many view rational choice as the long-awaited shift to a more theoretical field of legislative study, Green and Shapiro (1994) have attacked rational choice, arguing that the presumption of universalism—that it can be employed in many institutional contexts—is unrealistic and results in methodologically flawed research. They are particularly critical of abstract social choice work and experimental approaches as applied to legislatures, feeling that the modelers reject data that are discordant with their theories rather than rejecting theories that do not fit the data. Yet even Green and Shapiro admit that some applications of rational choice theory—for example studies of congressional committees (Cox and McCubbins 1993; Kiewiet and McCubbins 1991; Krehbiel 1991)—show a greater commitment to empirical testing. In the end, they conclude (197) that "whether rational choice scholarship will in the future contribute significantly to the study of legislative politics depends on the degree to which empirical inquiries can overcome methodological infirmities" such as testing propositions involving variables which have causal order problems and obtaining reliable measures of legislative constructs.

As shall be seen in later chapters, the formal theory approach has been one source of a resurgence of the institutional approach to studying legislatures. The formal theory work has brought back an interest in the institution itself and how its rules affect its functioning. In part this approach developed because of perceived weaknesses in other approaches. Empirical case studies were generally atheoretical, many roll call analyses seemed to be merely methodological exercises, and interview studies often focused more on the individual legislator than on the legislature. The "neo-institutional" approach was therefore useful in making sure that the legislative institution was again the object of attention—though many would instead argue that researchers have long studied legislative institutions and it was only the neo-institutionalists who had temporarily forgot the proper object of study.

It is important to note that the new institutionalism is broader than the formal variety. "Historical institutionalism" is a distinct stream of work in comparative politics that studies how political struggles are affected by their institutional settings. It focuses particularly on "intermediate-level institutions" such as party structures and policy networks. Rather than emphasize strategies and choices as rational choice work does, this form of institutionalism examines goals as they are shaped by institutional context. Goals, strategies, and preferences are seen as things to explain, particularly as they are influenced by institutions (Thelen and Steinmo 1992). Some studies of the historical development of Congress fall directly under this new institutionalism rubric.

Historical Data

With the renewed focus on Congress as a rule-based institution, there has been attention to how the institution and its rules have changed over time. This increased use of longitudinal perspectives on Congress has led to greater mining of archival data. For example, Steven Smith (1989; Bach and Smith 1988) documented the changing use of House and Senate rules by counting of the usage of various procedural tools across selected Congresses for 30 years. Hibbing (1991) gathered four decades' worth of data—including election records, party and committee leadership positions, votes, legislative participation, and district activities—to examine how the careers of House members evolve over time. Baumgartner and Jones's studies of committee jurisdiction and agenda change (1993; Jones, Baumgartner, and Talbert 1993) were based on their coding of 40 years of committee hearings on pesticides, drug abuse, tobacco, and nuclear power. The committee outlier debate (see chapter 16) has also relied on years of committee assignments and voting records to compare the behavior of committee and non-committee members.

Along similar lines, increased attention has been given to the historical development of Congress and its rules. Swift (1996), for example, has examined the development of the Senate as an institution, while Binder and Smith (1997) have analyzed the Senate filibuster in its historical perspective.

Divided Government

The development of legislative research depends on changes in social science methods and theories, but also on changes in the political context of legislatures (Eulau 1985, 7). Two features of the congressional context in the 1980s and 1990s have significant implications for the legislative literature. First, much of this period was marked by divided government, with one party controlling the White House and the opposite party controlling one or both chambers of Congress. While this was not unprecedented historically, there was little research on divided government until this period (see the Contemporary Response following chapter 8). Then came the 1994 Republican takeover of the House of Representatives for the first time in 40 years. The immediate changes in congressional operations made by the new Republican majorities has naturally led to research on congressional committees, parties, and leadership. More fundamentally, Republican leadership of Congress will provide an opportunity to examine the generalizability of many of the conclusions from all arenas of congressional scholarship. Republican management of Congress will help us determine what patterns of behavior are truly basic to congressional life versus what behaviors were peculiar to the Democratic-controlled Congress.[2] Where relevant throughout the book, we will note the potential impact of Republican control on the congressional literature.

Conclusions

Two important series of review articles were published in *Legislative Studies Quarterly* in the 1980s and 1990s. The first set was published together as the *Handbook of Legislative Research* (Loewenberg, Patterson, and Jewell 1985). The *Handbook* is an impressive collection of research findings, but it makes little attempt to combine the separate pieces into an overarching theory. By contrast, the second set, which became the basis of a book on *Positive Theories of Congressional Institutions* (Shepsle and Weingast 1995), demonstrated the development of theory across wide expanses of the legislative field. The field has changed greatly from its original atheoretical beginnings. There is still a focus on individual legislators, as there had been in the earlier behavioral period and during the reform Congress, but there is also renewed concentration on the legislative institution. The pursuit of theory in the legislative field may finally be on the verge of victory.

ORGANIZATION OF THE BOOK

The remainder of the book is organized around a series of substantive controversies. Our goal is to illustrate how the evolution of the study of politics has affected and changed our understanding of these substantive areas. Our introductory chapters emphasize the major studies, methodologies, and debates in each of these legislative subfields. Some studies are then reprinted as "classics" because they best exemplify the major approaches to study or the substantive "sides" of the debate in the subfield.[3] In many cases, these articles also stand as pivotal in changing the direction of study, theoretically or methodologically, and in contributing new insights to our understanding of legislative politics.

Of course, we could have chosen other topics, but we believe those we have chosen are the most grounded and developed throughout the evolving empirical literature. Inevitably, there are other subjects that are worthy of discussion that we do not have the space to include. Indeed, the variety and richness of substantive questions as well as approaches to study are the most salient strengths of the field of legislative politics.

While our introductory chapters define the "sides" of substantive debate and trace the evolution of the subfields to the present, we also accentuate the current relevance of the questions studied in these fields by including "Contemporary Issue" and "Contemporary Response" sections. To the extent that these contemporary articles trigger new questions and ideas for studying legislative politics in the minds of our readers, so much the better.

NOTES

1. Davidson (1992) dates the reform period in Congress as 1965–78, with the postreform period starting with the Congress that followed Democratic losses in the House in the 1978 midterm election, but it is more convenient to date the intellectual trends in the congressional literature by way of sets of decades.
2. As of our writing, it is too early to draw definite conclusions about the patterns of behavior and operation of the Republican Congress. The 104th Congress was dominated by the Contract with America and highly confrontational budget showdowns (Weisberg and Patterson 1998). However, the 105th Congress operated much more like the traditional Democratic Congresses documented in the political science literature.
3. In reprinting these chapters, we use the authors' original text as much as possible, except for some editing due to length considerations. This decision means that gender-specific language is used in many of the readings because that was the norm when they were written.

PART I

LEGISLATIVE DEVELOPMENT

Chapter 2

How Do Legislatures Develop?

Legislatures change. That is a simple fact of legislative life. After all, legislatures are institutions, and institutions inevitably change over time. The key question is how these changes in legislatures should be interpreted. Some changes are part of explicitly political processes, such as reform cycles. Other changes occur more subtly and are more likely to be noticed by outside observers or historians than participants. Are these changes that occur part of an inherent process? Or are they more random? Are they linear? Or are they cyclical?

The congressional changes of the last two centuries are good examples of legislative change. For one thing, the careerism that typified the twentieth-century Congress was not present in the nineteenth century. Members typically served a term or two and then returned to their home district; many districts followed a "rotation" system with members being expected to serve only short periods and then give someone else a chance (Kernell 1977).

Another major change involves party leadership in Congress. By the end of the nineteenth century the House party leaders had become all-powerful, but a revolt against the Speaker in 1910 led to power shifting—first to the party caucus in the 1910s, next to the committee chairs by the 1950s, and then to subcommittees after reforms in the early 1970s. Meanwhile, the party leaders' powers have increased since the 1980s, though these powers remain much less than those of party leaders a century earlier.

A third important change involves the choice of committee chairs. Party leaders selected chairs in the nineteenth century, but after the 1910 revolt the seniority system became important, with the member of the majority party with the longest consecutive service on the committee becoming chairman. Reforms in the 1970s led to the possibility of party caucus votes on committee chairs at the start of each Congress, while reforms in the 1990s permit caucus votes on committee chairs in midsession.

These changes in careerism, party leadership, and committee leadership are actually interrelated. At one level, seniority could not be an important consideration in the nineteenth century before careerism existed and when party leaders exerted full power. Beyond this, many scholars would view these changes in broader perspective, treating them as instances of broad change processes through which legislatures progress. However, there is controversy as to the nature of these change processes.

Legislative scholars of the first half of the twentieth century did not pay much attention to historical changes in Congress. That situation changed in the 1960s, first with a widely circulated but then unpublished manuscript by H. Douglas Price (see Price 1977 for a published example of his work on this topic) and then with an influential article by Nelson Polsby (1968) that is reprinted in this section. Yet the "institutionalized" Congress described by Polsby continued to change. A reform phase in the early 1970s increased the powers of subcommittees at the expense of congressional committees. The "postreform Congress" (Davidson 1992) was dominated by entrepreneurial members who were intent on engaging in individualistic legislative activism. The Congress of the late 1980s and 1990s was a more partisan Congress, operating in an environment dominated by budget deficits, ideologically polarized divided government, and homogeneous parties both in Congress and in constituencies. Perhaps because of these dramatic changes and because of calls by congressional scholars to be more sensitive to the time-bound nature of many congressional studies (Cooper and Brady 1981b), considerable attention has been paid to describing how Congress has changed since the 1960s and explaining why these changes occurred (e.g., Shepsle 1989; Sinclair 1989; Rieselbach 1994; Rohde 1991).

Polsby's classic article altered how we look at change in Congress. It treats congressional change as the natural development of an institution. Congress changes in the same way and in response to the same forces as do other social institutions. His views led to the application of his "institutionalization" concept to the development of a variety of legislatures around the world. An opposing view of congressional change is that change is based on reforms engineered by the members of the institution themselves. This view sees members of Congress as driven by certain goals. When the attainment of these goals is threatened, members will reform the institution so that it again facilitates their goal achievement. While the external environment may provide incentives for members to work towards institutional change, the focus here is on the motives and activities of the individual members.

LEGISLATIVE CHANGE AS INSTITUTIONALIZATION

Political scientists usually treat legislatures as political bodies, but sociologists instead regard them as instances of institutions. Additionally, sociologists observe many common elements in institutions and how they change (see Eisenstadt 1964 for an early sociological treatment of institutionalization). To take one definition (Huntington 1968, 12), institutions are "stable, valued, recurring patterns of behavior," while "institutionalization" is "the process by which organizations and procedures acquire value and stability."

Polsby (1968, reprinted here as chapter 3) provides an interpretation of the change in Congress as a case of institutionalization. He does not actually define institutionalization as a general term, but instead lists three criteria for institution-alized organizations: autonomy, complexity, and universalism. He then determines the extent to which Congress meets each criterion. Autonomy is the extent to which Congress is differentiated from its environment. He measures autonomy by the decrease in membership turnover and the changes in career trajectories of House Speakers. Internal complexity, or the division of labor within Congress, is measured by the increase of committee independence, the increase in the number and diversity of party leadership positions, and the expanding amount of resources devoted to internal House management. Polsby's final criterion of institutionaliza-tion is universalistic decision making, where the application of rules becomes auto-matic rather than discretionary. The growth in the use of the seniority rule for committee assignments is part of the evidence for universalism. The article ends with a brief discussion of the causes and consequences of institutionalization, but these are virtual afterthoughts to the main documentation and interpretation of changes that have occurred in Congress.

A technical question concerns how well Polsby has measured his three criteria for institutionalization. This piece has led to a cottage industry of scholars who seek better measures of his indicators, including workload, complexity, and autonomy of subunits. One positive result of this work is a focus on measuring organizational aspects of legislative performance. Legislative performance is diffi-cult to measure, and Polsby's work usefully turned attention to measurement issues.

Alternative Interpretations of Institutionalization

An important issue is whether Polsby is correct in labeling these changes as insti-tutionalization. Might these same changes reflect some other pattern? To be provocative, might they instead be a case of fossilization or ossification or petrifica-tion? In other words, the institutionalization term is not value-neutral. It makes the changes in the legislature seem both inevitable and positive, where a term like "ossification" would instead make the changes seem negative. Instead of regarding the longer tenure in office and similar indicators as evidence of the autonomy of Congress, Huntington (1965a) views them as showing the increased insulation of Congress. This also points out how these changes can be seen as making it harder for groups to penetrate the system and affect government policy.

Professionalization is a similar legislative change concept used in the state leg-islature literature (Rosenthal 1996). Legislatures in most U.S. states could have been viewed as amateur up through the 1950s: They met only a few months every other year, legislators received low pay, and there were few staff resources. Legislators generally held other jobs during the time the legislature was not in ses-sion. Subsequently, most state legislatures began meeting more months every year with higher pay and more staff. As the job of being a legislator became full-time, outside income was limited and legislators developed expertise. The legislators became professionals and the legislatures became professional. The professional-ization term sounds objective and value-neutral, but it is not. It makes the changes in the legislature seem appropriate and positive. After all, a professional legislature sounds more competent than an amateur body. However, some people would argue that it is better to have regular citizens serve as legislators than professional politicians. Indeed, by the 1990s a majority of the public became dissatisfied with legislatures that seemed too institutionalized and professional, leading to the movement to limit the number of terms of legislators (see the Contemporary Issue at the end of this chapter). The point is that our use of terms to describe change processes includes subtle evaluations of those change processes because the terms each have their own connotations. Terms like professionalization and institutionalization not only describe change processes but also implicitly evaluate those processes, and we need not accept those evaluations even if we agree that the changes have occurred.

Another way to think about legislative change is in terms of how adaptable the institution is. Some institutions are flexible, being able to adapt readily to relevant changes in their external environments, while others are too rigid to change quickly. In a sense, this distinction would present a second dimension to Polsby's concern with institutionalization—the pace of change in the organization as distinct from the direction of that change. Legislatures are not the most flexible of institutions, but they certainly vary in terms of how fast they can change. For example, the fact that the entire membership of the U.S. House of Representatives is up for election every two years means that chamber can change relatively quickly. By contrast, only a third of the U.S. Senate is elected every two years, which slows the pace of change in that chamber. Furthermore, its rules permit a filibuster supported by two-fifths plus one of its members to prevent a vote on a bill, making it even harder to produce change in the Senate. Correspondingly, the House adopts new rules at the beginning of each Congress, while the Senate considers itself a continuous body operating under the same rules until they are amended. This contrast between the two chambers became very visible in 1995 and 1996 when the Republican party gained control of both chambers for the first time since the early 1950s but the large policy changes passed by the House were routinely moderated and stalled in the Senate.

Institutionalization has also been studied for some non-U.S. legislatures (Gerlich 1973; Sisson 1973). The institutionalization topic clearly developed out of a concern with modernization, making studies of how new legislatures develop particularly relevant. Opello (1986) has used the Polsby approach to comment on the Portuguese parliament. He finds Portugal's decade-old Assembly of the Republic lacking with respect to the Polsby criteria, especially in terms of its autonomy. As a result, it is a "minimal legislature," lacking the identity that could give it esprit de corps and make membership in it a source of gratification to legislators. O'Brien (1994) has studied China's National People's Congress. While that body has not yet achieved the autonomy required for institutionalization, it is becoming embedded into the governmental system. O'Brien argues that a legislature achieves "embeddedness" as its jurisdiction is expanded and its capacity is increased. He finds that support by the executive was essential for the National People's Congress to achieve embeddedness. O'Brien's work is particularly significant in suggesting that the full institutionalization concept may not be appropriate for studying new legislatures.[1]

Nonlinear Legislative Change

Another natural question is whether "deinstitutionalization" can also occur in a legislature. The seniority reforms in the 1970s and the term limit movement in the 1990s reverse some of the trends that Polsby reported, and these reversals seem to counter the notion of institutionalization. Polsby himself discusses this issue in one of his last paragraphs where he recognizes that decay has sometimes occurred in the institutional structure of Congress. Yet he clearly feels that institutions resist decay, and his examples of decay are ones that were only temporary setbacks to the major trends he described.

Specifically, let us examine the seniority rule, which Polsby takes as an example of the move to universalistic procedures in the House. Under the strict seniority rule, the member of the majority party with the greatest consecutive service on the committee is chosen as chair. Polsby shows how the seniority violation rate fell from 60% in the 1881–89 period to less than 1% in the 1951–63 period. It remained below 1% from 1965–74 but rose to 3% in 1975–96. The overall rate of violation of seniority in this period is still quite low compared to the 60% of the 1881–89 era, but much higher than the low point of 1951–74. Seniority violations have increased since the reforms for all committee appointments, not just chairs (Cox and McCubbins 1993, chapter 2). House committee chairs are no longer chosen by a strictly universalistic procedure. This is a case where the numbers convey a faulty impression: The rate of seniority violation is low enough to suggest that universalistic procedures still predominate, but the violation rate understates the importance of having modified the seniority rule. The effect of modifying the rule has been to make the chairs more responsive to the party caucus, in that the chairs realize that they can be deposed if they wander too far away from caucus wishes. The caucus votes on chairs, and those chairs receiving significant numbers of negative votes usually have learned from the opposition. Modification of the seniority rule has led to changes in the expectations for committee chairs, even if the number of seniority violations remains low.

Hibbing (1988) provides a counterexample to Polsby in his application of Polsby's approach to the British House of Commons. Hibbing argues that focusing on current legislative rules leads to overstating the case for institutionalization, since those current rules often replaced earlier rules that were more universalistic. Hibbing's best example involves debate in the House of Commons. The current Question Time procedure for backbenchers to ask questions of government ministers can be seen as the epitome of a universalistic procedure. However, the previous rule was that debate must pertain to the motion being debated by the House, and that rule was as universalistic as the current Question Time procedure. Hibbing ends up doubting that institutionalization is unidirectional. He instead argues that the flow of change depends on the time frame and the indicators employed. Hibbing further argues that environmental arguments tend to be overly unidirectional (society is seen as becoming more complex so corresponding legislative change is seen as monotonic), while organizational theory can be more flexible in this regard.

Organizational Theory Perspectives

Polsby's institutionalization article does a far more complete job of describing changes in Congress and discussing their implications than in treating the causes of these changes (though no single article can be expected to cover all aspects of a topic). As it turns out, the causes of these changes can be discussed in an organizational theory framework that is fully compatible with Polsby's institutionalization argument. Organization theory explains legislative processes using such factors as the external environment, organizational patterns (such as centralization), and internal needs (such as expertise). In particular, organization theory gives more explicit attention to the role of the external environment in producing legislative changes than Polsby does.

A few studies have applied organization theory to legislatures. Froman (1968b) provided an early suggestion of the importance of organization theory for studying legislatures, linking characteristics of Congress to features of the general political setting. Cooper (1977) has since applied organization theory to Congress more systematically, showing how environmental factors affect Congress. He presents general propositions from organization theory regarding environment, performance, structure, and adaptation and then applies each to Congress. Cooper argues that congressional change is a result of demand strain (pressures to solve pressing social problems), structural strain (conflicts between congressional divisions of labor), the motivational needs of individual members, and the necessity of integrating demands and information in order to produce public policy. Hedlund (1985) gives an excellent review of applications of organizational theory to legislatures.

One common aspect of the explanations of legislative change reviewed in this section is that they are at the macro level. They treat change at the level of the organization that is changing. Some of the explanations view change as inevitable, and others view it as due to other macro-level phenomena (such as changes in the legislature's external environment). Yet these explanations are similar in looking for patterns but not focusing on the individual legislators who were responsible for the changes.

LEGISLATIVE CHANGE AS GOAL-BASED REFORM

In contrast to the macro-level explanations of legislative change reviewed in the section above, many scholars view legislative change as due to the goal-seeking behavior of individual legislators. From this perspective, legislative change is seen as the result of political reforms that occur because many legislators find they cannot accomplish their individual goals under the old rules and procedures of the legislature. Also, as the membership of Congress changes or the political incentives for goal achievement change, members modify institutional structures to facilitate their goal attainment. Institutional change is member-directed.

As will be evident in many sections of this book, dramatic gains in understanding the behavior of legislators have been made by postulating a very small number of legislators' goals and examining the operation of the legislature through those goals. While there are different perspectives on what the most important goals of members of Congress are, scholars using this approach agree that analyzing the way Congress operates and evolves should be based on understanding the way the members themselves want the institution to operate and evolve. This approach is somewhat controversial, but many legislative researchers would consider it the crucial insight of the field in the past half century.

Reelection as the Goal

The most parsimonious version of this approach is from a book by David Mayhew (1974a). Mayhew portrays a Congress made up of legislators with but a single concern—reelection. Mayhew uses the single reelection goal as a way of deducing how members of Congress would behave in office and how they would structure the institution in order to facilitate goal achievement. Specifically, members would engage in three activities to help themselves win reelection: advertising (making sure their constituents know their names, as by sending out congratulations cards for high school graduations), credit claiming (taking personal credit for desirable government actions, such as projects in their districts), and position taking (taking positions on issues of concern to constituents or interested groups). From postulating this single goal, Mayhew is able to deduce a system that operates in a manner very similar to how the U.S. Congress operates.

Mayhew (81–82) argues that ". . . the organization of Congress meets remarkably well the electoral needs of its members. To put it another way, if a group of planners sat down and tried to design a pair of American national assemblies serving members' electoral needs year in and year out, they would be hard pressed to improve on what exists." The congressional office, "part management firm, part political machine," (84) allows members to service constituent needs and use the franking privilege (free congressional mail) as means for members to advertise themselves in their districts. Congressional committees provide opportunities for position taking and delivering benefits (e.g., pork barrel projects) to constituents. And, because committees divide congressional labor, they give members the ability to claim credit believably for committee products. Mayhew also saw weak congressional parties as facilitating member reelection goals: Weak parties allowed members to take whatever positions were necessary to be reelected, regardless of the party agenda. Thus, Congress is organized in a manner that facilitates members' achievement of their reelection goals.

According to the reelection goal perspective, legislative reform would be explained by arguing that members accept the rules, procedures, and organization of a legislative chamber so long as the rules, procedures, and organization do not hinder their reelection attempts. When enough members feel that their reelection chances would be enhanced by different rules, then legislative reforms are enacted.

In this vein, Katz and Sala (1996) argue that changes in committee assignment practices at the turn of the century consistent with a shift to careerism were a result of changed electoral incentives in the 1890s. Before that era, voters were given ballots by their party which they were expected to cast publicly, but the introduction of the Australian ballot in the 1890s allowed each member of Congress to be voted on individually. Thus, members of Congress had greater need to use their activity in Congress to create voters loyal to them personally, and they were willing to make institutional changes that would facilitate this. The ballot changes led to greater incentives for stable committee assignments so members could develop the policy expertise to claim credit for committee products and to take more credible positions on the committee's policy issues. Stable committee assignments allowed for seniority to become the primary means of selecting committee chairs.

More contemporary reforms also can be attributed to electoral motives. Shepsle (1989) argues that as House districts became less homogeneous during the 1960s due to court-ordered redistricting, members had to find new ways of appealing to more diverse constituencies. Increased staff and office resources provided members with the ability both to travel home often and service constituent needs and to be involved more widely in the legislative process. This allowed members to become legislative "entrepreneurs"—able to get involved on any issues that might be of interest to constituents or interest groups regardless of committee assignments. Members could thereby create personal followings independent of party fortunes, and therefore they were better able to cope flexibly with the demands of a diverse constituency. Similarly, Sinclair (1989) argues that the electoral insecurity of newly elected liberal Democratic senators in the 1960s was a key reason behind the expansion of the number of subcommittees, modification of the cloture rule (filibusters could be ended with 60 votes rather than two-thirds), and the Legislative Reorganization Act of 1970 which limited members to service on one prestige committee and limited each member to one subcommittee chair per major committee. Thus, electoral considerations have played primary roles in creating institutional change in both the House and the Senate.

Mayhew's book has been very influential in the subsequent literature on Congress. In particular, proponents of a rational-choice approach to studying legislatures find its goal-based approach useful, even though Mayhew's work is not actually mathematical. For example, Fiorina (1977b) used a similar reelection-based model to account for the growth in the federal bureaucracy. The single-goal approach of Mayhew is simplistic, though it is amazing how much Mayhew can explain with just the single goal. So many of the changes in Congress that appear inevitable when viewed through the lens of institutionalization are seen to be clear effects of legislative reforms due to the reelection goal.

Still, the notion of legislators as solely reelection-motivated is controversial. On the one hand, members are clearly interested in reelection. But to emphasize that goal exclusively would be something like understanding human behavior through emphasizing the goal of breathing. These maintenance goals are essential for survival (political survival in one case, personal survival in the other), but the activities that go beyond maintenance needs are generally more interesting. Also, the reelection emphasis fits well with Joseph Schlesinger's (1966) discussion of the static ambition of politicians who are content to stay in their current offices, but it misses discrete ambition (which admits that some legislators are content to serve a short time and then voluntarily retire). This has led to several studies of voluntary retirements from Congress (Hall and Van Houweling 1995; Herrick, Moore, and Hibbing 1994).

Another drawback to the Mayhew approach is that it comes close to being one that cannot be disproved. It is hard to imagine any legislative circumstance that could not be interpreted as due to a reelection motive, making the approach virtually tautological. Still, a few researchers have found evidence to the contrary. In chapter 4 in this section, Dodd (1977) argues against reelection being an all-consuming goal, in that members would spend most of their time in their districts seeking reelection rather than in Washington if that were the primary goal of legislators. Krehbiel (1991) also argues that most bills passed by Congress lack a constituency dimension. If reelection alone is too narrow a goal to explain legislators' behavior, then we need to look beyond it to explain members' motivations for congressional reform.

Power as the Goal

Other writers have employed a goal approach without accepting Mayhew's emphasis on the reelection goal. As seen in chapter 4, Dodd (1977) has also followed a single-goal approach, but with the quest for personal power as that goal. He recognizes the importance of reelection, but only as instrumental to remaining in Congress to achieve power goals. Dodd sees Congress as organized in a manner conducive to the fulfillment of members' power goals: Power is decentralized to committees and subcommittees where members have substantial ability to influence the policies they care about most. Members spend most of their time in committee rather than giving symbolic speeches on the floor or doing constituent work in their offices. Once they are electorally secure, members seek seats on the policy and power committees where they can have influence over important national legislation.

To Dodd, legislative changes occur when enough members find reforms useful for enhancing their power positions. For example, the dominance of committee chairs in the 1950s and 1960s did not give new members of Congress enough power, so these new members supported reforms of the seniority system that shifted power from committee chairs to subcommittee chairs. Dodd develops a cyclical theory of congressional reform based on the importance of the power goal of legislators. Any distribution of power advantages some actors over others, which provides the motivation to support legislative reform movements. Reforms occur in a cyclical manner since reforms establish new power balances which eventually disadvantage enough legislators that they enact further reforms.

In particular, Dodd argues that reform cycles are based on congressional interactions with the president. Members desire to have an individual impact, but this exacerbates Congress's tendency towards fragmentation. When Congress is unable to propose and pass coherent policy, the president is advantaged. At the same time, a fragmented Congress is less able to act as an effective check on the president. So members realize that for Congress, and hence themselves individually, to be effective and have a policy impact, they must challenge presidential dominance. To do this, they allow for greater centralization of power to the congressional party leadership in order to propose and pass policy more responsibly and to act as a more effective check against an aggressive president. This argument places legislative change directly in the political realm, viewing change as political reform rather than as part of Polsby's seemingly inevitable institutionalization process. This piece by Dodd has not affected the congressional research literature as much as the Polsby article did, but it is an important argument for the ways in which member goals can affect the institutional structure of Congress as well as a demonstration of how legislators can be seen as pursuing goals other than reelection.

Where Dodd focuses on power in their chamber as a goal of members of Congress, Schlesinger's (1966) concept of "progressive ambition" emphasizes that some members also seek power positions beyond their chamber. Many members of the U.S. House of Representatives are interested in moving up to the Senate, while many members of that body are interested in moving up to the presidency or other offices. Rohde (1979, see chapter 9 in this book) has developed a path-breaking view of progressive ambition as being manifested as a function of opportunities (such as open Senate seats) and the legislator's willingness to bear risk (as evidenced by whether the member originally sought office by opposing an incumbent or waiting until there was a vacant House seat).

Multiple Goals

In contrast with the single goal emphasis of Mayhew and Dodd, other scholars have written of three goals. Fenno (1973) speaks of policy goals in addition to the reelection and power goals that have already been discussed. Members with policy goals are concerned with enacting what they consider good public policy in areas of importance to them. As described in chapter 16 of this book, Fenno argues that legislators with different goals tend to serve on different types of committees in Congress.[2]

Policy goals can also lead to legislative reform. Members motivated by policy goals will push reforms when the rules and procedures of the chamber prevent them from passing the policy changes they favor. For example, civil rights proponents in the Senate pushed through a weakening of the vote required to stop a filibuster when they saw Southern anti–civil rights forces repeatedly stopping civil rights bills through sustained filibusters. Similarly, members who were concerned with the nation's large budget deficits in the 1980s changed congressional procedures for considering the budget so as to make it harder for Congress to be fiscally irresponsible.

The goals of members can change over time as new members are elected to Congress or as incumbent members adapt to an evolving political environment. For example, more activist and liberal members were a driving force behind reforms in the 1970s that strengthened the House Democratic party leadership, weakened committee chairs (Cox and McCubbins 1993; Rohde 1991), and led to a breakdown of apprenticeship norms in the Senate (Sinclair 1989). Applying Fenno's threefold goal typology to the motives of the 1970s reformers, policy goals are apparent in the desire of liberals to strengthen a party leadership they believed would eventually aggressively support their liberal agenda; power goals are apparent in the weakening of committee chairs in order to allow for greater individual member participation in the legislative process; and reelection goals are apparent in the belief of members that being more visibly active in the legislative process would help them advertise, claim credit for their accomplishments, and take positions on a variety of salient issues. Similarly, in the 1980s Republicans frustrated with being the "permanent minority" strengthened their leadership institutions in order to highlight their differences with the Democrats and to make the issue appeals to the public they thought were necessary to eventually become the majority party (Connelly and Pitney 1994). Once they were the majority, they would have greater ability to participate legislatively and could implement the conservative policy they desired.

The possibility of goal change also suggests examining the ways in which legislators' goals evolve over their tenure in office. Thus Fenno (1978, chapter 6) distinguishes between an initial expansionist phase of legislative careers in which the newly elected members emphasize the reelection goal as they reach out to increase their vote totals, and a later protectionist phase in which members pursue their policy or power goals while seeking just to maintain their electoral base. Dodd also speaks of different career stages in chapter 4. The Fenno and Dodd suggestions have also led to attention to legislative careers, particularly Hibbing's (1991) systematic study of how formal positions in the House, voting rates, legislative activity, and district activity change through increased tenure in office.

Finally, in addition to individual goals, there can exist collective goals. Members of the minority share the collective goal of achieving majority status, so that they have the power that accompanies that status. Members of the majority party share the collective goal of passing a legislative program in a responsible manner, so that the public sees them as deserving to remain in power. In the following section, we will consider collective goals and other macro-level factors in Congress.

Macro-Level Incentives

The focus of this section has been on micro-level goals of legislators, but it is also appropriate to point to macro-level considerations that affect political reform. For example, the partisan composition of the legislature provides a context that may facilitate or retard reform efforts. There was much talk of legislative reform in the 103rd Congress of 1993–94, but the Democratic majority was too internally divided to pass reforms, particularly ones that challenged the power of Democratic committee and subcommittee leaders. By contrast, the Republican House majority in the 104th Congress of 1995–96 viewed itself as having a reform mandate and wanted to redress the grievances they had built up in 40 years of being in the minority. Their ability to pass reforms was enhanced by the many Republican freshmen who were not wedded to the "old ways" of doing business in Congress. Examining earlier historical periods, Binder's (1995, 1996) work on House rules changes and Binder and Smith's (1997) book on the Senate filibuster also view rules reform as based on narrow calculations of partisan and political advantage rather than on the refinement of rules to achieve universalism or some other neutral ideal.

Other macro-level considerations, and the ways in which they interact with micro-level considerations, are elaborated by Swift (1996) in her description of "reconstitutive" changes in the early Congresses. She defines reconstitutive change as "rapid, marked, and enduring shift in the fundamental dimensions of the institution" (4), with such change depending on the congressional agenda, voters, political parties, the chamber's view of its beliefs about its role, and the existence of a group of members leading the reconstitution. She illustrates this concept with the changes in the Senate from 1787 to 1841 when the Senate became an important body rather than just an ancillary upper chamber. New issues, new voters, and domination of the Democratic-Republican party during the "Era of Good Feelings" provided the external stimuli for change in the Senate. Greater consensus about the role of the Senate as a democratic institution and greater concern with sectional representation could indicate changed goals of senators. Last, internal leadership for these changes in the Senate was necessary to take advantage of the "window of opportunity" and constitutes the type of political reform movement apparent in other reform-based changes in Congress.

Change in contemporary Congresses can similarly be understood as an interaction between member goals and macro-level changes in the political environment. Sinclair (1995) argues that strengthened congressional party leadership institutions in the 1980s were the result of individual Democratic members of Congress being inhibited in their ability to achieve their goals of policy activism in a political environment dominated by high budget deficits and an ideologically opposed president. In order to pass budgets or pass any significant policies, members had to delegate power to the party leadership for negotiated settlements with the president. At the same time, with white Southerners increasingly shifting to the Republican party and Southern Democrats increasingly relying on the votes of African-Americans, the parties became more homogeneous ideologically (Rohde 1991, reprinted here as chapter 23). This external change decreased the cost to individual members of an active leadership, as the leadership could now act to promote the policy preferences of the party as a whole without endangering the electoral fortunes of any party faction.

In the 1990s, public opinion towards Congress as an institution was an important incentive pushing congressional change (Rieselbach 1995). While individual members of Congress succeeded spectacularly in terms of being reelected in the 1980s, public attitudes towards Congress as an institution were quite negative. While this is nothing new (e.g., Fenno 1975), the high rates of reelection, in combination with a new term limits movement, fueled public perceptions that Congress was unresponsive and unaccountable. Displays of questionable ethics resulting in the resignation of Speaker Jim Wright, the Keating Five savings and loan scandal, and the House Bank check-bouncing scandal provided more concrete evidence of a Congress out of touch and out of control. Congress responded to the ethical clouds by eliminating honoraria (the acceptance of speaking fees from interest groups) in exchange for a salary increase, closing the House Bank, and cutting back on the franking privilege and other perquisites. They also created a Joint Committee on the Organization of Congress in order to propose ways to streamline the committee system and legislative process so that Congress could be more responsive. In 1995, the new Republican majority, especially in the House, further sought to assuage public anger by making Congress obey the same laws as the private sector (e.g., workplace safety, hiring, and wage rules), cutting its own committees and staff as a sign of reining in a Congress that was seen as bloated and spendthrift, and voting on the ten planks of the Contract with America in order to demonstrate their responsiveness and accountability.

From the goal perspective, external changes help produce institutional change by bringing in new members with a different distribution of goals from the existing membership or by changing the political incentives towards which goal-oriented members must work. Yet it is the initiative of members themselves that produces the change, and the nature of the change is determined by what best meets their needs, rather than an automatic evolutionary response to changes in the external environment. Political leaders seek reforms for their own career goals and policy reasons, thus providing the mechanism for legislative change.

It should be emphasized that some controversy surrounds the use of the modified goal approach. Mayhew would look at the multiple goal emphasis of the past several pages and respond that all that matters is reelection. Policy goals matter only to the extent that they help satisfy reelection constituencies, or at least donors to reelection campaigns. Power goals matter only to the extent to which they impress reelection constituencies, or at least help gain support from donors to reelection campaigns. The institutionalization argument of the first half of this chapter would not even find the reelection goal of much interest. Its supporters would contend that institutionalization occurs regardless of legislators' goals, and that the process might at most accelerate, slow down, or be temporarily reversed depending on member goals and reform movements, but that the trend towards autonomy, complexity, and universalism are long-term patterns that prevail at the macro level in all organizations.

CONCLUSION

The time dimension is one of the most important aspects of legislative research, as was emphasized in Cooper and Brady's (1981b) influential review article of "diachronic" analyses of Congress. Cooper and Brady called for more attention to the impact of time on studies of Congress, arguing that the discipline's conclusions regarding the nature of Congress were not generalizable unless they held across time. But as Mezey (1993, 354) has reminded us, it is far easier to describe legislative change than to explain it. We may be able to find some regularities to change processes in legislatures, but already it is clear that change processes can take many shapes. Similarly, many different political processes can lead to legislative changes.

The two halves of this chapter contrasted a macro view of legislatures that looks at trends over time at the organizational level with a more micro view that emphasizes the personal ambitions of legislators. Each of these approaches has strong advocates, but juxtaposing them in this way is a reminder of how both provide useful insights. One way to reconcile the two would be to view the micro-level goals discussed in the second half of this chapter as the way to explain the macro-level changes discussed in the first half, even though these organizational theory and rational choice perspectives have developed quite separately from one another.

The multiple goal focus is more realistic than the single goal focus of Mayhew and Dodd. The importance of reelection to politicians is obvious on its face, and that fact is critical to understanding legislatures. Yet, it is important to study the causes and effects of legislators not seeking reelection as well as to recognize that other goals may also matter. Similarly power can be an important motivating force, but politics is more than the raw pursuit of power. Few people are motivated only by a single goal, and greater complexity to our theories should help us better understand the behavior we are studying.

The goal perspective is vital to understanding the recent literature on congressional change. It gives considerable theoretical leverage in explaining why congressional change occurs and why it occurs in the way it does. Yet the same reforms can be interpreted differently in support of different goals. For example, weakening committees and allowing wider legislative activism for individual members can be interpreted as consistent with electoral, policy, and power goals. This points to the difficulty of explaining change after the fact in a falsifiable manner, but we are not yet at the stage of being able to predict legislative change from a goal perspective.

In any case, it is important to recognize that member goals are not formed in a vacuum. They are based on political incentives and the political environment outside Congress. While there may not be "natural" processes of legislative change, it is important to understand how reforms pushed by individual members are influenced by changing circumstances outside Congress. Changing issue agendas, changing emphases by interest groups, and changes in the presidency, media, and political parties can all affect member goals.

Legislatures inevitably change. This change can be seen as part of an evolutionary process common to many other institutions and organizations, but this change is very much the result of members pursuing their goals under changing political contexts. Political conditions will keep changing, and, as a result, Congress and other legislatures will change further. The precise contours of these changes cannot be foreseen at the moment, but a description of any legislature as a static institution should never be accepted.

NOTES

1. Polsby (1975) proposes a separate distinction between legislatures based on their ability to develop laws, distinguishing between transformative legislatures which can transform proposals into laws, and arenas (like the British Parliament) which can debate but not modify executive proposals.
2. Goodman et al. (1986) show that state legislators have several more goals, especially constituency service as a goal in its own right, and they emphasize that legislators often have multiple goals.

CONTEMPORARY ISSUE

Term Limits

Recent efforts to limit lawmakers' terms of office present a compelling example of legislative change. These efforts are also strong evidence of the public's dissatisfaction with the institutionalization of U.S. legislatures and the careerism of U.S. legislators. Public confidence in Congress was indeed low in the late 1980s and early 1990s (Kimball and Patterson 1997; Patterson and Monson 1999). Term limits became an attractive reform to many voters because this reform would result in the removal of large numbers of incumbents at once. Although the Supreme Court in 1995 struck down all efforts by states to impose term limits on members of Congress, term limitations have been enacted for several state legislatures.[1]

Should members of Congress ever be limited in the number of terms they may serve, the trend toward careerism in Congress and the resulting reliance on the seniority system (as in committee chair selection) would be greatly affected, as might aspects of congressional elections and representation. In the following essay, we examine term limits as a possible source of change in Congress—their history, current efforts to enact them, the forms term limits can take—and, most important, their consequences for legislative organization, behavior, and policy making. The consequences of term limits for elections and representation are discussed in chapter 8.

HISTORY OF TERM LIMITS

Limiting legislator's terms of office is perhaps the modern counterpart of rotation in office. The notion that citizens should serve in public office for only a limited term and then return to private life originated as a principle of democratic theory in ancient Greece and Rome and influenced institutional arrangements throughout recorded history as a means of preventing political corruption and tyranny. Governments employed rotation in office to enhance political representation and promote wider participation in political decision making.

Based on such historical perspectives, Petracca (1992) suggests that term limitations were an important component of U.S. democracy until the turn of the century and argues that the contemporary debate over limiting legislative terms actually represents a return to the democratic creed articulated by Antifederalists at the Constitutional Convention in 1787. Although not adopted formally, rotation in office was considered to be a norm in legislative behavior and reached its zenith during the Jacksonian era.

Jackson responded to the public's desire for a more participatory democracy by extending rotation to administrative offices. He defended this action by claiming that all citizens were capable of holding public office and that limited terms lessened the chance that officials familiar with government would be tempted to engage in bureaucratic corruption. Although Jackson succeeded in restoring a measure of public faith in government, his creation of the spoils system contributed to the decline of rotation in office as a norm. As the spoils system (in which officeholders were able to employ their political supporters in patronage positions regardless of merit) led to political corruption, reformers, particularly Progressives, sought to abolish it and they attacked the practice of rotation in office as well.

Petracca's additional explanations for rotation's decline echo Polsby's process of institutionalization. Political power decentralized as the House of Representatives institutionalized; as a result, serving in Congress became more attractive as a career. A growing norm of professionalism extended to politics and made this legislative careerism acceptable. Further, Petracca argues, careerism became associated with effective governance. As political affairs grew more complicated, the bureaucracy grew and political expertise was valued.

PUBLIC SUPPORT FOR ENACTMENT

Affairs of state remain complicated, but many observe that there is little contemporary regard for political expertise. The term-limits "movement" gained wide public support in 1988, a time when Democrats were though to have permanent majority status in Congress and incumbents seemed invulnerable when they ran for reelection. In 1990, public confidence in Congress remained at the low level reported almost 20 years earlier, following Watergate. Fifteen percent of the public had "a great deal of confidence" in Congress and 59% had "only some" confidence (Sundquist 1992). Speaker Jim Wright (D-TX) and Democratic Whip Tony Coelho (CA) resigned following scandals in 1989 and the voters were purportedly ready to "throw the (elected) rascals out."

In an abstract sense at least, voters were ready to do just that. Seventy percent of voters supported term limits, though 96% of congressional incumbents were reelected in 1990 (Sundquist 1992). Sundquist attributes this irony to voters' satisfaction with their own representative and frustration with Congress as a whole. Term limits, then, were a means of ridding Congress of the members voters themselves could not vote out of office (Fenno 1975; Hibbing and Theiss-Morse 1995; Parker and Davidson 1975). In this climate of opinion, the term-limit movement of the late 1980s and early 1990s was very successful in enacting limits for state legislators.

CONSEQUENCES OF LEGISLATIVE TERM LIMITS

Because discussions of term limits often rely on normative perspectives, the conclusions reached reveal more about the views of who is making the argument than about term limits' effects. In actuality, much of the literature on term limits' effects is speculative and related to electoral competition.

Proponents value term limits as means of unseating entrenched incumbents and creating legislative turnover. For them, more open-seat elections place members "closer to the public" and thereby improve representation. They believe that term limits will result in a citizen legislature in which members are better able to act on difficult policy issues such as the budget deficit and entitlements because members will lack incentives to cater to constituents or special interests. George Will (1995), one of the most vocal proponents of term limits, goes so far as to argue that term limits would eliminate careerism as a motive for running for office and would weaken the influence of lobbyists. Ultimately, term-limit proponents foresee a period of policy innovation with decreased influence of interest groups.

Among opponents, however, there is a fear that term limits would result in amateur legislators at the mercy of professional lobbyists and staff, who would become the repositories of legislative expertise and institutional memory. Based on his study of House members' career patterns, Hibbing (1991) finds a gap between the legislative contributions of junior and senior members. He argues against term limits because his research reveals the more senior members to be more active and expert in the legislative process. Opponents also argue that even if members were prevented from seeking reelection, they would seek to marshal support and resources to run for higher office. Such candidates would not only remain ambitious, but would be less experienced as they assume positions of greater responsibility. Finally, even if these candidates choose not to run for higher office, they could enter the private sector and begin careers as lobbyists. Such a trend might create a revolving door with retired legislators lobbying their former colleagues or staff. Taking another tack, other term-limit opponents argue that term limits make serving in Congress less attractive to people who desire careers in public service. For example, Ornstein (1995) argues that term limits harness the very ambition that drives the U.S. political system by bringing people to run for office.

On balance, the picture is not as bleak as term-limit opponents forecast and the power of incumbency might be overstated by proponents of term limits. The conventional wisdom in the political science literature is that term limits would alter the electoral connection, first affecting the types of candidates elected to office and then changing the legislature itself. For example, some fear that term limits would lead to legislators with a short-run time perspective who produce poor public policy. However, after examining the research on the topic, Cain (1996) concludes that whatever impact term limits might have will vary with the type of legislature on which they are imposed as well as with the length of the term limit itself. Professionalized legislatures will be affected more than nonprofessional bodies; governments with division of power will experience greater effects than those in which a single branch of government dominates; and finally, term limits establishing very short terms of service will have greater impact than those that exceed the average rate of turnover.

Even more positive in their assessment are Glazer and Wattenberg (1996), who argue for the importance of political innovation. They posit that by limiting legislators' concerns for reelection to current office and increasing incentives to seek higher office, term limits will motivate legislators to address important policy issues first. Based on microeconomic reasoning, they also argue that term limits will reduce the influence of special interests. For them, term limits will result in short-term politicians who exercise less influence over bureaucrats. Interest groups will be less able to access the bureaucracy through such legislators and former legislators hired by special interests will be less effective as lobbyists because few of their colleagues will remain in the legislature.

One of the few studies based on actual data is Carey, Niemi, and Powell's (1998) survey of state legislators. They find that enacted term limits affect institutions and behavior even before preventing an incumbent from serving an additional term. Term limits decrease the amount of time spent on pork-barrel projects and heighten the priority of state needs relative to those of legislators' districts. They also find no systematic differences in the composition of legislatures in term-limit and non-term-limit states. Moreover, they conclude that term limits appear to have redistributed power from majority party leaders to governors and legislative staff.

Ultimately, scholars urge caution in forecasting the consequences of legislative term limits. Both proponents and opponents of such measures have latched on to contradictory propositions. Even term limits' effect on legislative organization is in doubt. Cohen and Spitzer (1992), for example, note that the committee system and the seniority system now provide the basis of an increasing reward structure in Congress. Term limits will flatten the reward structure to members over the course of their legislative careers. The power of junior legislators will increase and that of senior members will decrease. As a result, members' incentives to cooperate with constituents will be undermined, as they would no longer gain power with increased tenure.

Under term limits, seniority and the committee system lose some appeal as organizational devices, so term limits might ultimately have a ripple effect on Congress that influences important aspects of the legislative process. However, Cohen and Spitzer also note that term limits might lead to internal institutional changes in legislatures that act to countervail commonly expected trends, in which case term limits may not alter the seniority system as much as otherwise might be the case.

FUTURE PROSPECTS FOR OBSERVANCE OF TERM LIMITS

Political reforms, however well-meant they are, always have unintended consequences. If adopted in such a manner as to pass constitutional muster, term limits would certainly change the operation of Congress, and in ways that even the most astute analysts cannot fully assess in advance. In any case, the future of the term-limits movement seems very much in doubt at this time. The term-limit movement developed in the late 1980s when House Democrats seemed to be staying in Congress forever without solving such national problems as the budget deficit, but political observers suggest that the public is now, at least momentarily, less angry with Washington.

Furthermore, considerable change in personnel occurred in Congress in the early 1990s even without term limits. Several members retired after the investigation of overdrafts at the House bank and other high-profile Congressional scandals. Several Democrats retired after the election of a Republican Congress took away their chance to become committee heads. At the same time, there was an increased tendency for younger members to leave Congress voluntarily, in order to spend time with their families or to pursue other careers. The net result is that is majority of the members of the 105th Congress (1997–98) were first elected after 1990. These events strengthen the view that voters are sovereign. Voters' decisions to reelect or oust incumbents are sufficient to create electoral change, and circumscribing their alternatives may be unnecessary. Thus, ironically, the term-limit movement may have achieved its goal without the official enactment of the reform that it promoted.

Still, enough members of Congress are unwilling to leave voluntarily to keep the term-limit movement alive. Indeed, some legislators who once pledged to quit after serving a few terms have reneged on their promises.[2] Republicans do not want to relinquish their majority party status any more than Democratic members once did, and several members who once supported term limits now conveniently claim that they did not realize how much their constituents would benefit from their accumulation of seniority in Congress. Some members who were elected on a pledge to leave office voluntarily after a few terms have voted against constitutional amendments on the topic.[3] Several interest groups, particularly U.S. Term Limits and Americans for Limited Terms, remain committed to imposing term limits, by supporting candidates who pledge to retire voluntarily and who promise to support a constitutional amendment. Yet all of this shows the difficulty of imposing internal reforms on a legislature through external pressures. It is hard to turn the hands back on the clock of institutionalization.

NOTES

1. In addition to term limitations for state legislators, a form of term limits exists for many governors and the president. Efforts to enact term limitations for members of Congress have been unsuccessful thus far, however.

In 1994, the Arkansas Supreme Court heard a challenge to that state's term limit rule (*U.S. Term Limits, Inc.* v. *Hill*, 1994). Although the court upheld the portions of the law that applied to state legislators, state-imposed term limits for members of Congress were struck down. In deciding whether a term-limit amendment to the Arkansas constitution violated the U.S. constitution, the U.S. Supreme Court did in fact strike down all term limits imposed by states on their representatives to the U.S. Congress (*U.S. Term Limits, Inc.* v. *Thornton*, 1994).

In their 1994 Contract with America, congressional Republicans pledged to bring a term-limit constitutional amendment to a vote and argued that term limits were needed to build electoral competition and ensure congressional turnover, but it appears that some Republicans experienced a change of heart once their party gained majority status. Term limits now do exist for committee chairs and the Speaker, however. Chairs are limited to six years of service, the Speaker to eight.

In 1995, Speaker Gingrich realized that a constitutional amendment to limit the terms of members had little chance of passage and began to explore other ways to enact term limits. One proposal would have permitted states to set their own term limits.

2. Katharine Q. Seelye, 1998, "Term-Limits Advocates Take a Bad Thrashing," *New York Times*, 21 May, p. A12 (National edition). Seelye reports that Rep. George Nethercutt (R-WA), Rep. Scott McInnis (R-CO), Rep. William Goodling (R-PA), and Sen. Alfonse D'Amato (R-NY) have reconsidered their pledges.

3. An extreme instance is William Goodling (R-PA) who pledged in 1994 to step down in 1996, was reelected in 1996 after announcing his support for a constitutional amendment to impose term limits, subsequently voted against such constitutional amendments on six occasions, and then pledged in 1998 that he would not seek reelection in 2000.

Chapter 3

The Institutionalization of the U.S. House of Representatives

NELSON W. POLSBY

Most people who study politics are in general agreement, it seems to me, on at least two propositions. First we agree that for a political system to be viable, for it to succeed in performing tasks of authoritative resource allocation, problem solving, conflict settlement, and so on, in behalf of a population of any substantial size, it must be institutionalized. That is to say, organizations must be created and sustained that are specialized to political activity (see Huntington 1965b for a summary). Otherwise, the political system is likely to be unstable, weak, and incapable of servicing the demands or protecting the interests of its constituent groups. Secondly, it is generally agreed that for a political system to be in some sense free and democratic, means must be found for institutionalizing representativeness with all the diversity that this implies, and for legitimizing yet at the same time containing political opposition within the system (Chambers 1967; Dahl 1966).

Our growing interest in both of these propositions, and in the problems to which they point, can begin to suggest the importance of studying one of the very few extant examples of a highly specialized political institution which over the long run has succeeded in representing a large number of diverse constituents, and in legitimizing, expressing, and containing political opposition within a complex political system—namely, the U.S. House of Representatives. . . .

The operational indices I am about to suggest which purport to measure empirically the extent to which the U.S. House of Representatives has become institutionalized may strike the knowledgeable reader as exceedingly crude; I invite the ingenuity of my colleagues to the task of suggesting improvements.

For the purposes of this study, let us say that an institutionalized organization has three major characteristics: 1) it is relatively well-bounded, that is to say, differentiated from its environment. Its members are easily identifiable, it is relatively difficult to become a member, and its leaders are recruited principally from within the organization. 2) The organization is relatively complex, that is, its functions are internally separated on some regular and explicit basis, its parts are not wholly

Source: *American Political Science Review* (1968) 62:144–68. Reprinted by permission of the publisher.

interchangeable, and for at least some important purposes, its parts are interdependent. There is a division of labor in which roles are specified, and there are widely shared expectations about the performance of roles. There are regularized patterns of recruitment to roles, and of movement from role to role. 3) Finally, the organization tends to use universalistic rather than particularistic criteria, and automatic rather than discretionary methods for conducting its internal business. Precedents and rules are followed; merit systems replace favoritism and nepotism; and impersonal codes supplant personal preferences as prescriptions for behavior.

Since we are studying a single institution, the repeated use of words like "relatively" and "tends" in the sentences above refers to a comparison of the House of Representatives with itself at different points in time. The descriptive statement: "The House of Representatives has become institutionalized over time" means then, that over the life span of this institution, it has become perceptibly more bounded, more complex, and more universalistic and automatic in its internal decision making. But can we find measures which will capture enough of the meaning of the term "institutionalization" to warrant their use in an investigation of the process at work in the U.S. House of Representatives?

THE ESTABLISHMENT OF BOUNDARIES

One aspect of institutionalization is the differentiation of an organization from its environment. The establishment of boundaries in a political organization refers mostly to a channeling of career opportunities. In an undifferentiated organization, entry to and exit from membership is easy and frequent. Leaders emerge rapidly, lateral entry from outside to positions of leadership is quite common, and persistence of leadership over time is rare. As an organization institutionalizes, it stabilizes its membership, entry is more difficult, and turnover is less frequent. Its leadership professionalizes and persists. Recruitment to leadership is more likely to occur from within, and the apprenticeship period lengthens. Thus the organization establishes and "hardens" its outer boundaries.

Such measures as are available for the House of Representatives unmistakably show this process at work. In the eighteenth and nineteenth centuries, the turnover of representatives at each election was enormous. Excluding the Congress of 1789, when of course everyone started new, turnover of House members exceeded 50% in fifteen elections—the last of which was held in 1882. In the twentieth century, the highest incidence of turnover (37.2%—almost double the twentieth century median) occurred in the Roosevelt landslide of 1932—a figure exceeded 47 times— in other words almost all the time—in the eighteenth and nineteenth centuries. As Figure 3.1 makes clear, there has been a distinct decline in the rate at which new members are introduced into the House. Figure 3.2 makes a similar point with data that are partially independent; they show that the overall stability of membership, as measured by the mean terms of members (total number of terms served divided by total number of representatives) has been on the rise.

These two figures provide a fairly good indication of what has happened over the years to rank-and-file members of the House. Another method of investigating the extent to which an institution has established boundaries is to consider its leaders, how they are recruited, what happens to them, and most particularly the extent to which the institution permits lateral entry to and exit from positions of leadership.

The classic example of lateral movement—possibly the most impressive such record in U.S. history—is of course contained in the kaleidoscopic career of Henry Clay, seventh Speaker of the House. Before his first election to the House, Clay had already served two terms in the Kentucky House of Representatives, and had been sent by the legislature to the U.S. Senate for two nonconsecutive short terms. Instead of returning to the Senate in 1811, he ran for the Lexington seat in the U.S. House and was elected. He took his seat on March 4, 1811, and eight months later was elected Speaker at the age of 34. Three years later, he resigned and was appointed a commissioner to negotiate the Treaty of Ghent with Great Britain. The next year, he returned to Congress, where he was again promptly elected Speaker. In 1820 he resigned once again and left public office for two years. But in 1823 he returned to the House, served as Speaker two more terms, and then resigned again, to become Secretary of State in John Quincy Adams' cabinet. In 1831, Clay became a freshman Senator. He remained in the Senate until 1844, when he resigned his seat. Five years later he reentered the Senate, this time remaining until his death in 1852. Three times (in 1824, 1832, 1844) he was a candidate for president (Follett 1896; Mayo 1937; Mooney 1964; Van Deusen 1937).

Clay's career was remarkable, no doubt, even in a day and age when the boundaries of the House of Representatives were only lightly guarded and leadership in the House was relatively open to lateral entry. But the point to be emphasized here

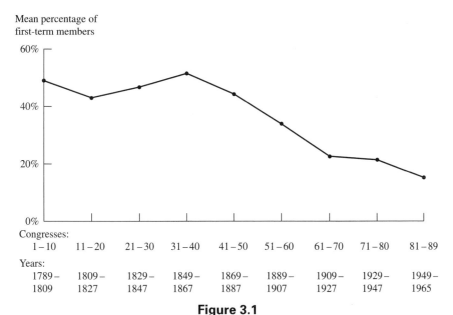

Figure 3.1

The establishment of boundaries: Decline in percentage of first term members, U.S. House of Representatives, 1789–1965.

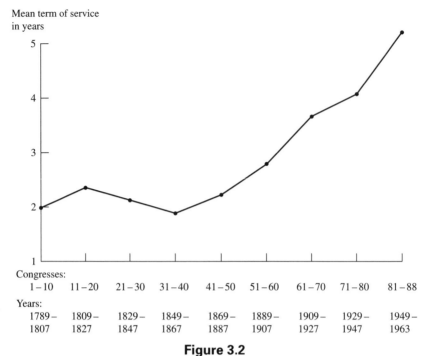

Figure 3.2
The establishment of boundaries: Increase in terms served by incumbent members of the U.S. House of Representatives, 1789–1965.

is that Clay's swift rise to the speakership is only slightly atypical for the period before the turn of the twentieth century.

There has been a change over time in the seniority of men selected for the speakership. Before 1899, the mean years of service of members selected for the speakership was six; after 1899, the mean rises steeply to 26. Figure 3.3 and Table 3.1 summarize the gist of the finding in compact form.

Just as nineteenth-century Speakers arrived early at the pinnacle of House leadership, many left early as well and went on to other things: freshmen Senators, state legislators, Cabinet members, and judges in the state courts. One became president of the United States, one a justice of the Supreme Court, one a minister to Russia, one the mayor of Auburn, New York, and one the receiver-general of the Pennsylvania land office. Indeed, of the first 27 men to be Speaker, during the first 86 years of the Republic, *none* died while serving in the House of Representatives. In contrast [as of 1968], of the last Speakers, six died while serving, and of course one other sits in the House today. Figure 3.4 gives the relevant information for all Speakers.

The importance of this information about Speakers' careers is that it gives a strong indication of the development of the speakership as a singular occupational specialty. In earlier times, the speakership seems to have been regarded as a position of political leadership capable of being interchanged with other, comparable

Mean years of prior
service by Speakers

Figure 3.3

The establishment of boundaries: Mean years served in Congress before first
becoming Speaker by 20-year intervals.

Table 3.1

**The establishment of boundaries:
Summary of years served in Congress
before first selection as Speaker**

	Before 1899	1899 and after
8 years or less	25	0
9–14 years	8	0
15–20 years	0	2
21–28 years	0	10
	33 Speakers	12 Speakers

positions of public responsibility—and indeed a high incidence of this sort of interchange is recorded in the careers of nineteenth-century Speakers. That this sort of interchange is most unusual today suggests—as do the other data presented in this section—that one important feature in the development of the U.S. House of Representatives has been its differentiation from other organizations in the political system, a stabilization of its membership, and a growing specialization of its leaders to leadership of the House as a separate career.

The development of a specifically House leadership, the increase in the overall seniority of members, and the decrease in the influx of newcomers at any

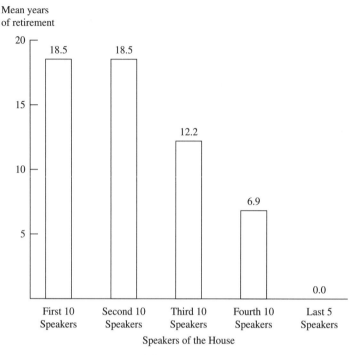

Speakers of the House

Figure 3.4
The establishment of boundaries: Emergence of careers specialized to House leadership.

point in time have the effect not only of separating the House from other organizations in the political system, but also of facilitating the growth of stable ways of doing business within the institution, as we shall see shortly.

THE GROWTH OF INTERNAL COMPLEXITY

. . . Briefly, the growth of internal complexity can be shown in three ways: in the growth in the autonomy and importance of committees, in the growth of specialized agencies of party leadership, and in the general increase in the provision of various emoluments and auxiliary aids to members in the form of office space, salaries, allowances, staff aid, and committee staffs.

A wholly satisfactory account of the historical development of the House committee system does not exist. But perhaps I can swiftly sketch in a number of plausible conclusions from the literature.

From the perspective of the present-day United States, the use of standing committees by Congress is scarcely a controversial issue.[1] Yet, in the beginning the House relied only very slightly upon standing committees. Instead of the present-day system, where bills are introduced in great profusion and automatically shunted to one or another of the committees whose jurisdictions are set forth in the rules, the practice in the first, and early Congresses was for subjects to be debated initially in the whole House and general principles settled upon, before they were parceled out for further action—fact-finding, detailed consideration or the proposal of a bill—to any one of four possible locations: an officer in the Executive Branch, a Committee of the Whole, a Select Committee formed ad hoc for the reception of a particular subject, or a standing committee. Generally, one of the alternatives to standing committees was used. . . .

It is difficult to disentangle the early growth of the standing committee system from concurrent developments in the party system. For as Alexander Hamilton took control of the administration of George Washington, and extended his influence toward men of like mind in Congress, the third alternative to standing committees—reference to a member of the Executive Branch—became an important device of the Federalist majority in the House. . . .

In the first two Congresses Hamilton is said to have used the Federalist caucus to guide debate in the Committee of the Whole, and also to have arranged for key financial measures to be referred directly to himself for detailed drafting (Harlow 1917, 120–50). This practice led, in the Second Congress, to sharp clashes with followers of Jefferson, who

> made it perfectly clear that if they should ever get the upper hand in Congress, they would make short work of Hamilton, and restore to the House what they considered to be its constitutional authority over finance (Harlow 1917, 151).

The Republicans did in fact gain the upper hand in the Third Congress (elected in 1792) and they restored detailed power over finances to the Committee of the Whole. This did not work satisfactorily, however, and in the Fourth Congress a Committee on Ways and Means was formed. Harlow says:

> The appointment of . . . standing committees, particularly . . . Ways and Means, was in a way a manifestation of the Republican theory of government. From their point of view, the members of the House, as the direct representatives of the voters, ought to be the mainspring of the whole system. Hitherto, the Federalists had sold their birthright by permitting the executive to take a more active part in the government than was warranted by the Constitution. The Republicans now planned to bring about the proper balance between the different branches, by broadening at once the scope of the operations of the House, and restricting the executive. It was the better to enable the House to take its assigned part that the new type of organization was worked out. Just as the heads of departments were looked upon as agents of the executive, so the committees would be considered as the agents of the House (Harlow 1917, 157–158).

During the presidency of Thomas Jefferson, committees were constituted and employed as agents of the president's faction in Congress which was in most matters actively led by the president himself. Binkley says:

> . . . When the House of Representatives had elected its Speaker and the committee chairmen had been appointed it was apparent to the discerning that lieutenants of the president had not appointed them, but his wishes, confidentially expressed, had determined them just as surely as if he had formally and publicly nominated them. Here was

the fulfillment of Marshall's prediction that Jefferson would "embody himself in the House of Representatives" (Binkley 1962, 64).

. . . In essence, by the early years of the nineteenth century, the House committee system had passed through two distinct phases: the no-committee, Hamiltonian era, in which little or no internal differentiation within the institution was visible; and a Jeffersonian phase, in which factional alignments had begun to develop—these were exploited by the brilliant and incessant maneuverings of the president himself, who selected his lieutenants and confidants from the ranks of Congress ad hoc, as political requirements and opportunities dictated. During this period a small number of standing committees existed, but were not heavily relied upon. Their jurisdictions were not so securely fixed that the Speaker could not instead appoint select committees to deal with business that ought to have been sent to them (Binkley 1949).

The advent of Henry Clay and the victory of the War Hawk faction in the elections of 1810 brought the committee system to its third phase. Clay for the first time used the Speaker's prerogative of appointment of members to committees independently of presidential designs. There is some question whether Clay's appointment policies were calculated to further his policy preferences or merely his popularity (and hence his presidential ambitions) within the factionally divided House (Young 1966), but there seems no reason to doubt that Clay won for the speakership a new measure of independence as a power base in the American political system. Under Clay five House committees were constituted to oversee expenditures in executive departments, the first major institutionalization of the congressional function of oversight. William N. Chambers (1963) writes:

> [By] 1814 the committee system had become the dominant force in the chamber. Thus effective power was exercised not by the president, as had been the case with Jefferson, but by factional congressional leaders working through the speakership, the caucus, and the committees.

For the next 100 years the committee system waxed and waned more or less according to the ways in which committees were employed by the party or faction that dominated the House and elected the Speaker. Figures from the latter decades of the nineteenth century testify amply to the leeway afforded Speakers—especially new ones—in constituting committees regardless of their prior composition (Polsby, Gallaher, and Rundquist 1969). In part, it was Speaker Cannon's increasing use of this prerogative in an attempt to keep control of his fragmenting party that triggered the revolt against his speakership in 1910–11, and that led to the establishment of the committee system as we know it today (Chiu 1928).

Under the fourth, decentralized, phase of the committee system, committees have won solid institutionalized independence from party leaders both inside and outside Congress. Their jurisdictions are fixed in the rules: Their composition is largely determined and their leadership entirely determined by the automatic operation of seniority. Their work is increasingly technical and specialized, and the way in which they organize internally to do their work is entirely at their own discretion. Committees nowadays have developed an independent sovereignty of their own, subject only to very infrequent reversals and modifications of their powers by House party leaders backed by large and insistent majorities.

To a degree, the development over the last 60 years of an increasingly complex machinery of party leadership within the House cross-cuts and attenuates the independent power of committees. Earlier, the leading faction in the House elected the Speaker and the Speaker in turn distributed the chairmanships of key committees to his principal allies and opponents. Thus the work of the House was centralized to the extent that the leading faction in the House was centralized. But differences of opinion are not uncommon among qualified observers. The Jeffersonian era, for example, is widely regarded as a high point of centralization during the nineteenth century. Harlow (1917) reports:

> From 1801 to 1808 the floor leader was distinctly the lieutenant of the executive. William B. Giles, who was actually referred to as "the premier, or prime minister," Caesar A. Rodney, John Randolph of Roanoke, and Wilson Cary Nicholas all held that honorable position at one time or another. It was their duty to look after party interests in the House, and in particular to carry out the commands of the president. The status of these men was different from that of the floor leader of today. . . . They were presidential agents, appointed by the executive, and dismissed at his pleasure.

. . . After Jefferson, the Speaker became a power in his own right; not infrequently he was a candidate for the presidency himself, and the House was more or less organized around his, rather than the president's, political interests. There was no formal position of majority leader; the leading spokesman for the majority party on the floor was identified by personal qualities of leadership and by the favor of the Speaker (or in the Jeffersonian era, of the president) rather than by his institutional position (Ripley 1967; Young 1966).

Later, however, the chairman of the Ways and Means Committee—a key post reserved for the chief lieutenant of the Speaker—became de facto floor leader, a natural consequence of his responsibilities in managing the tariff bills that were so important in nineteenth-century congressional politics. Occasionally the chairman of the Committee on Appropriations was the de facto leader, especially during periods of war mobilization, when the power of the House in the political system was coextensive with the power of the purse.[2] In the last part of the nineteenth century, however, the Committee on Appropriations was temporarily dismantled, and the chairman of [the] Ways and Means Committee began to receive the formal designation as party leader.

The high point of the Ways and Means chairman's power came in the aftermath of the 1910 revolt against the Speaker. The power of committee appointments was for Democrats lodged in the Ways and Means Committee. Chairman Oscar Underwood, in cooperation with President Wilson, for a time (1911–1915) eclipsed the Speaker and the committee chairmen by operating the majority party by caucus (Brown 1922; Davis 1911).

But Underwood's successor as Chairman of Ways and Means, Claude Kitchin (majority leader 1915–19), disapproved of Wilson's war policies; this made it cumbersome and impractical for the leader of the majority on the floor and in caucus to hold this job by virtue of what was becoming an automatic succession through seniority to the chairmanship of Ways and Means. A separation of the two roles was effected after the Democrats became the minority in 1919 (Arnett 1937; Hasbrouck 1927; Ripley 1967). Ever since then, the majority leader's job has existed as a full-time position; the incumbent now holds a nominal, junior committee post but he rarely attends committee meetings. At the same time, the majority leader has become less of a president's man, and the caucus is now dormant as an instrument of party leadership—although it now sometimes becomes a vehicle, especially at the opening of Congress, for the expression of widespread dissatisfaction by rank-and-file House members. Thus, while binding votes on policy matters have not been put through the caucus by party leaders, the Republican caucus has three times in recent years deposed party leaders and the Democratic caucus has deprived three of its members of their committee seniority.

Formally designated party whips are, like the differentiated post of majority leaders, an innovation principally of the twentieth century. The first whips date back to just before the turn of the century. In the early years, the designation seems to have been quite informal, and it is only recently that an elaborate whip system, with numerous deputies, a small staff, and formal procedures for canvassing members, has been established by both parties in the House (Ripley 1964).

Thus, we can draw a contrast between the practices of recent and earlier years with respect to formal party leaders other than the Speaker:

1. Floor leaders in the twentieth century are officially designated; in the nineteenth, they were often informally designated, indefinite, shifting or even competitive, and based on such factors as personal prestige, speaking ability, or presidential favor (see Alexander 1916, 111–14).
2. Floor leaders in recent years are separated from the committee system and elected by party members; earlier they were prominent committee chairmen who were given their posts by the Speaker, sometimes as a side-payment in the formation of a coalition to elect the Speaker (Alexander 1916, 110).
3. Floor leaders today rely upon whip systems; before 1897 there were no formally designated whips.

A third indicator of the growth of internal organization is the growth of resources assigned to internal House management, measured in terms of personnel, facilities, and money. Visitors to Washington are not likely to forget the sight of the five large office buildings, three of them belonging to the House, that flank the Capitol. The oldest of these on the House side was built just after the turn of the century, in 1909, when a great many other of our indices show significant changes.

. . . The only major contemporary study we have of congressional staff speaks of present "tendencies toward overexpansion of the congressional staff," and says that "Three-fourths of the committee aides interviewed" thought that professional staffs of committees were sufficiently large to handle their present work load (Kofmehl 1962; see also Patterson 1967; Rogers 1941).

Needless to say, that work load has grown, and, though it is impossible to say precisely by how much, congressional staffs have grown as well. This is roughly reflected in figures that are more or less comparable over time on that portion of the legislative budget assigned to the House. These figures show the expected increases. However, except for the jump between 1945 and 1946, reflecting the new provisions for staff aid of the Legislative Reorganization Act, the changes in these figures over time are not as abrupt as is the case with other of our time series. Nor would changes over time be even as steep as they are in Table 3.2 if these figures were corrected for changes in the purchasing power of the dollar. So we must regard this indicator as weak, but nevertheless pointing in the expected direction.

FROM PARTICULARISTIC AND DISCRETIONARY TO UNIVERSALISTIC AND AUTOMATED DECISION MAKING

The best evidence we have of a shift away from discretionary and toward automatic decision making is the growth of seniority as a criterion determining committee rank and the growth of the practice of deciding contested elections to the House strictly on the merits.

The literature on seniority presents a welter of conflicting testimony. Some commentators date the seniority system from 1910 (Galloway 1946; Goodwin 1959), others say that seniority as a criterion for determining the committee rank of members was in use well before (Chiu 1928; Hinds 1909; Pollock 1925). Woodrow Wilson's classic account of *Congressional Government* in 1885 pays tribute both to the independence of the committees and their chairman and to the absolute discretion of the Speaker in the committee appointment process (Wilson [1885] 1956, 82, 85–86). It is clear that the Speaker has no such power today. In another paper my colleagues and I present a detailed preliminary tabulation and discussion on the extent to which seniority in its contemporary meaning was followed in the selection of committee chairmen in the most recent 40 Congresses (Polsby, Gallaher, and Rundquist 1969). The central finding for our present purposes (summarized in Figure 3.5) is that the seniority system—an automatic, universally applied, nondiscretionary method of selection—is now always used, but that formerly the process by which chairmen were selected was highly and later partially discretionary.

The figures for before 1911 can be interpreted as indicating the use of the Speaker's discretion in the appointment of committee chairmen. After 1911, when committee appointment powers are vested in committees on committees, the figures principally reflect the growth of the norm that no one man should serve as chairman of more than one committee. Congressmen often sat on a large number of committees, and senior men rose to the top of more than one committee, but allowed less senior men to take the chair, much as the custom presently is in the U.S. Senate. After 1946, when the number of committees was drastically reduced, this practice died out, and a strictly automated system of seniority has asserted itself.

The settlement of contested elections on some basis other than the merits seems in earlier years to have been a common phenomenon. . . . A journalist

Table 3.2
The growth of internal complexity: Expenditures made by the House of Representatives

Fiscal Year	Expenditures (1000s dollars)	Fiscal Year	Expenditures (1000s dollars)	Fiscal Year	Expenditures (1000s dollars)
1872	1,952	1905	3,367	1935	8,007
1873	3,340	1906	3,517	1936	8,377
1874	2,687	1907	3,907	1937	8,451
		1908	4,725	1938	8,139
1875	2,030	1909	5,005	1939	8,615
1876	2,201				
1877	2,232	1910	4,897	1940	9,375
1878	2,183	1911	5,066	1941	9,511
1879	2,230	1912	4,741	1942	9,678
		1913	5,148	1943	9,361
1880	2,137	1914	5,012	1944	10,944
1881	2,191				
1882	2,188	1915	5,081	1945	11,660
1883	2,339	1916	4,917	1946	14,243
1884	2,405	1917	5,400	1947	16,012
		1918	5,331	1948	18,096
1885	2,466	1919	5,304	1949	18,110
1886	2,379				
1887	2,232	1920	7,059	1950	20,330
1888	2,354	1921	6,510	1951	21,053
1889	2,416	1922	6,001	1952	23,474
		1923	6,588	1953	23,662
1890	2,567	1924	6,154	1954	23,660
1891	2,520				
1892	2,323	1925	7,761	1955	26,610
1893	2,478	1926	7,493	1956	34,587
1894	2,844	1927	7,526	1957	36,738
		1928	7,623	1958	39,524
1895	2,945	1929	7,813	1959	43,882
1896	2,843				
1897	3,108	1930	8,260	1960	44,207
1898	2,948	1931	8,269	1961	47,324
1899	3,063	1932	8,310	1962	50,295
		1933	7,598	1963	52,983
1900	2,981	1934	7,154	1964	55,654
1901	3,066				
1902	3,088			1965	58,212
1903	3,223			1966 (est.)	65,905
1904	3,247			1967 (est.)	70,883

Source: U.S. Executive Office of President. Bureau of the Budget. *The Budget of United States Government.* Annual Volumes for 1921–1967. Washington: U.S. Government Printing Office.

U.S. Treasury Department. *Combined Statement of Receipts, Expenditures and Balances of the United States Government.* Annual Volumes for 1872–1920. Washington: U.S. Government Printing Office.

Average percentage
of committees on
which seniority
was violated

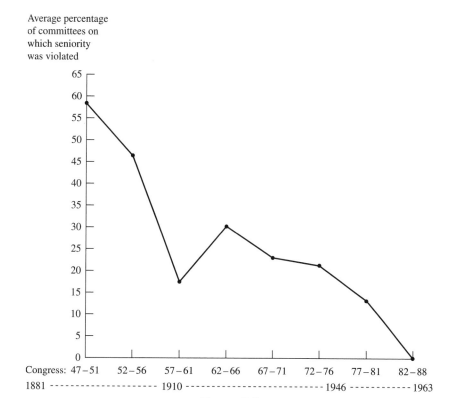

Congress: 47–51   52–56   57–61   62–66   67–71   72–76   77–81   82–88
1881 -------------------- 1910 -------------------------- 1946 ----------- 1963

Figure 3.5
The growth of universalism: Decline in violations of seniority, committee chairmen,
U.S. House of Representatives, 1881–1963.

writing at the beginning of the twentieth century summarizes the situation as he
had encountered it over a twenty-year period:

> It may be said . . . that there is no fairness whatever exercised in . . . contests for seats,
> especially where the majority needs the vote for party purposes. Hundreds of men
> have lost their seats in Congress, to which they were justly entitled upon all fair, rea-
> sonable, and legal grounds, and others put in their places for purely partisan reasons.
> This has always been so and doubtless will continue so. . . . (Stealey 1906, 147).

In fact, it has not continued so; nowadays, contested elections are settled with
much more regard to due process and the merits of the case than was true
throughout the nineteenth century. By 1926, a minority member of the
Committee on Elections No. 1 could say:

> In the eight years I have served on Elections Committees and six years upon this
> Committee, I have never seen partisanship creep into that Committee but one time.
> There has not been any partisanship in the Committee since the distinguished gen-
> tleman from Utah became Chairman of that Committee. A Democrat was seated the
> last time over a Republican by this Committee, and every member of the Committee
> voted to seat that Democrat (quoted in Hasbrouck 1927, 40).

This quotation suggests a method by which the development of universalistic criteria for settling contested House elections can be monitored, namely, measuring the extent to which party lines are breached in committee reports and in voting on the floor in contested cases. I have made no such study, but on the basis of the accumulated weight of contemporary reports such as I have been quoting, I predict that a time series would show strict party voting in the nineteenth century, switching to unanimity or near-unanimity, in most cases, from the early years of the twentieth century onward.

Attempts to establish legal precedents for the settlement of contested elections date from the recommendations of the Ames Committee in 1791. In 1798 a law was enacted prescribing a uniform mode of taking testimony and for compelling the attendance of witnesses. This law was required to be renewed in each Congress and was allowed to lapse in 1804. Bills embodying similar laws were proposed in 1805, 1806, 1810, 1813, and 1830. Not until 1851 was such a law passed, which provided for the gathering of testimony forming the bases of the proofs of each contestant's claim, but not for rules concerning other aspects of contested elections. More significant, however, was a clause permitting the House to set the law aside in whole or in part in specific cases, which apparently the House availed itself of with some regularity in the nineteenth century. With a few modifications this law is still in effect.[3]

The absolute number of contests shows a decrease in recent decades, as does the number of contests in relation to the number of seats. This suggests that the practice of instigating contests for frivolous reasons has passed into history; contemporary House procedures no longer hold out the hope of success for such contests. Figure 3.6 gives the figures, by decades (Rovere 1965).

There is today, certainly, no wholesale stealing of seats. If any bias exists in the system, it probably favors the protection of incumbents irrespective of party,[4] and hence (we may surmise not incidentally) the protection of the boundaries of the organization.

CAUSES, CONSEQUENCES, CONCLUSIONS

It seems reasonable to conclude that one of the main long-run changes in the U.S. House of Representatives has been toward greater institutionalization. Knowing this, we may wish to ask, at a minimum, these three questions: What caused it? What follows from it? What can this case tell us about the process in general? It is not from lack of space alone that our answers to each of [these] three questions will be brief and highly speculative.

Not much, for example, is known about the causes of institutionalization. The best theoretical guess in the literature is probably Durkheim's: "The division of labor varies in direct ratio with the volume and density of societies, and, if it progresses in a continuous manner in the course of social development, it is because societies become regularly denser and generally more voluminous" (1947, 262). "Density" in at least some sense is capable of being operationalized and measured separately from its institutional consequences. For present pur-

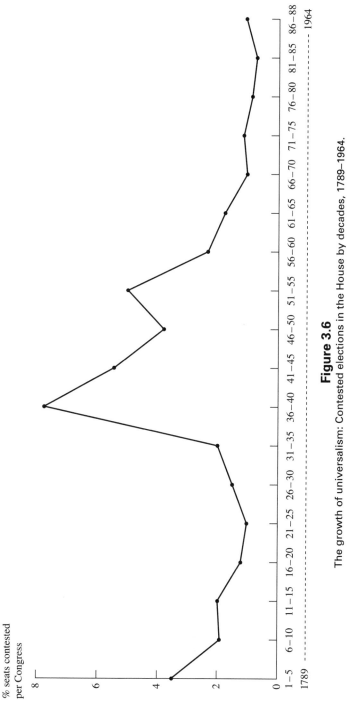

Figure 3.6

The growth of universalism: Contested elections in the House by decades, 1789–1964.

poses, the proposition can probably be rendered as follows: As the responsibilities of the national government grew, as a larger proportion of the national economy was affected by decisions taken at the center, the agencies of the national government institutionalized (cf. Young 1966, 252–53). Another, complementary, translation of the density theorem would be that as organizations grow in size, they tend to develop internally in ways predicted by the theory of insitutionalization. Size and increasing workload seem to me in principle measurable phenomena (Galloway 1961; Hall, Haas, and Johnson 1967). Size alone, in fact, seems almost too easy. Until a deliberative body has some minimum amount of work to do, the necessity for interaction among its members remains slight, and, having no purpose, coordination by means of a division of labor, rules and regulations, precedents and so on, seem unlikely to develop. So a somewhat more complicated formula has to be worked out, perhaps relating the size of an organization to the amount of work it performs (e.g., number of workdays per year, number of full-time as opposed to nominal members, number of items considered, number of reports rendered) before the strength of "density" and "volume" can be tested as causes of the process of institutionalization.

A discussion of the consequences of the House's institutionalization must be equally tentative. It is hard—indeed for the contemporary observer, impossible—to shake the conviction that the House's institutional structure does matter greatly in the production of political outcomes. A recent popular account begins:

> A United States Congressman has two principal functions: to make laws and to keep laws from being made. The first of these he and his colleagues perform only with sweat, patience and a remarkable skill in the handling of creaking machinery; but the second they perform daily, with ease and infinite variety (Bendiner 1964, 15).

No observer who focuses upon policy results, or who cares about the outputs of the American legislative process, fails to note the "complicated forms and diversified structure" which "confuse the vision, and conceal the system which underlies its composition" (Wilson [1885] 1956). All this is such settled knowledge that it seems unnecessary to mention it here. Still, it is important to stress that the very features of the House which casual observers and freshman legislators find most obstructive are principal consequences of (among other things) the process we have been describing.[5]

It is, however, not merely the complexity or the venerability of the machinery that they notice. These, in our discussion so far, have been treated as defining characteristics rather than consequences of institutionalization. What puzzles and irks the outside observer is a partial displacement of goals, and a focus of resources upon internal processes at the expense of external demands, that come as a consequence of institutionalization. This process of displacement is, of course, well known by social theory in other settings (see Blau 1964; Selznick 1953). A closer look at the general character of this displacement is bound to suggest a number of additional consequences.

For example, representatives may find that the process of institutionalization has increased their incentives to stay within the system. For them, the displacement of resources transforms the organization from a convenient instrument for the pursuit of social policies into an end value itself, a prime source of gratification, of status and power (Selznick 1957).

The increasing complexity of the division of labor presents an opportunity for individual representatives to specialize and thereby enormously increase their influence upon a narrow range of policy outcomes in the political system at large. Considered separately, the phenomenon of specialization may strike the superficial observer as productive of narrow-minded drones. But the total impact of a cadre of specialists operating over the entire spectrum of public policies is a formidable asset for a political institution; and it has undoubtedly enabled the House to retain a measure of autonomy and influence that is quite exceptional for a twentieth-century legislature.[6]

Institutionalization has, in the House, on the whole meant the decentralization of power. This has created a great many important and interesting jobs within the House, and thus increased the attractiveness of service therein as a career. Proposed reforms of Congress which seek to move toward a recentralization of congressional power rarely consider this fact. . . .

Thus we can argue that, along with the more obvious effects of institutionalization, the process has also served to increase the power of the House within the political system and to spread somewhat more widely incentives for legislators to participate actively in policy making.

A final possible consequence of institutionalization can be suggested: that the process tends to promote professional norms of conduct among participants. Indeed, something like these norms are built into the definition of institutionalization by some commentators (see Gerth and Mills 1946; Weber 1947). . . .

In fact, there is coming to be a sizeable body of literature about the norms of professional legislative conduct. Time and again, the norms of predictability, courtesy, and reciprocity are offered by professional legislators as central to the rules of the legislative game (Fenno 1962; Huitt 1961b; Kornberg 1964; Masters 1961; Matthews 1959; Wahlke et al. 1962). Thus, we can suggest a hypothesis that the extent to which these norms are widely applied in a legislative body is a direct function of that body's structural institutionalization. Appropriate tests can be made cross-sectionally, by comparing contemporary legislatures that vary with respect to boundary maintenance, internal complexity, and universalistic-automated internal decision making. Historically, less satisfactory tests are possible, since a number of vagaries enter into the determination of what is recorded and what is not, and since antecedent factors may account for both structural and normative institutionalization. This makes it hard to estimate the dispersion and importance of norms of conduct.

Nevertheless, the history of the House does suggest that there has been a growth in the rather tame virtue of reciprocity, courtesy, and predictability in legislative life since the turn of the century. Clem Miller describes human relations in the House of today:

> One's overwhelming first impression as a member of Congress is the aura of friendliness that surrounds the life of a congressman. No wonder that "few die and none resign." Almost everyone is unfailingly polite and courteous. Window washers, clerks, senators—it cuts all ways. We live in a cocoon of good feeling . . . (Miller 1962, 93).

No doubt there are breaches in the fabric of good fellowship, mostly unpublicized, but the student of Congress cannot refrain even so from comparing this testimony with the following sampling of nineteenth-century congressional conduct:

> Upon resuming his seat, after having replied to a severe personal arraignment of Henry Clay, former Speaker White, without the slightest warning, received a blow in the face. In the fight that followed a pistol was discharged wounding an officer of the police. John Bell, the distinguished Speaker and statesman, had a similar experience in Committee of the Whole (1838). The fisticuffs became so violent that even the Chair would not quell it. Later in the day both parties apologized and "made their submissions." On February 6, 1845, Edward J. Black, of Georgia, "cross over from his seat, and coming within the bar behind Joshua R. Giddings as he was speaking, made a pass at the back of his head with a cane. William H. Hammett, of Mississippi, threw his arms round Black and bore him off as he would a woman from a fire. . . ."
>
> "These were not pleasant days," writes Thomas B. Reed. "Men were not nice in their treatment of each other" (Alexander 1916, 115–16).[7]

Indeed they were not: Nineteenth-century accounts of Congressional behavior abound in passages like these. There is the consternation of members who put up with the presence on the floor of John Randolph's hunting dogs (Cutler and Cutler 1888; Mayo 1937). There is the famous scene on May 22, 1851, when Representative Preston Brooks of South Carolina entered the U.S. Senate and beat Senator Charles Sumner senseless with a cane,[8] and the record contains accounts of more than one such occasion:

> When Matthew Lyon, of Kentucky, spat in his face, [Roger] Griswold [of Connecticut, a member 1795–1805] stiffened his arm to strike, but remembering where he was, he coolly wiped his cheek. But after the House by its vote failed to expel Lyon, he "beat him with great violence," says a contemporary chronicle, "using a strong walking-stick" (Alexander 1916, 111–12).

With all the ill will that the heat of battle sometimes generates currently, the House has long since left behind the era of guns and dogs, canings and fisticuffs, that occupied so much of the nineteenth-century scene. No doubt this reflects general changes in manners and morals, but it also reflects a growth in the value of the House as an institution capable of claiming the loyalty and good behavior of its members. The best test of the hypothesis, to be sure, remains the cross-sectional one. If American state legislatures, for example, can be found to differ significantly with respect to structural institutionalization, they may also be found to vary concomitantly with respect to the application of the norms of professional legislative life.

Finally, the study of the institutionalization of the House affords us a perspective from which to comment upon the process in general. First, as to its reversibility. Many of our indicators show a substantial decay in the institutional structure of the House in the period surrounding the Civil War. In sheer numbers, the House declined from 237 members in the Congress of 1859 to 178 in the Congress of 1861; not until a decade later did the House regain its former strength. Frivolous contests for seats reached a height in this period, and our rank-and-file boundary measures reflect decay as well. It may be true, and it is certainly amusing, that the strength of the British Admiralty grows as the number of ships declines (Parkinson 1957, 39), but that this illustrates an inflexibly narcissistic law of institutional growth may be doubted. As institutions grow, our expectations about the displacement of resources inward do give us warrant to predict that they will resist decay, but the indications of curvilinearity in our present findings give us ample warning that institutions are also continuously subject to environmental influence and their power to modify and channel that influence is bound to be less than all-encompassing.

Some of our indicators give conditional support for a "take-off" theory of modernization. If one of the stigmata of the take-off to modernity is the rapid development of universalistic, bounded, complex institutional forms, the data presented here lend this theory some plausibility. The "big bang" seems to come in the 1890–1910 period, on at least some of the measures.

In conclusion, these findings suggest that increasing hierarchical structure is not a necessary feature of the institutionalization process. Organizations other than bureaucracies, it seems clear, also are capable of having natural histories which increase their viability in the modern world without forcing them into uniformly centralized patterns of authority.

NOTES

1. It certainly is, on the other hand, in the present-day United Kingdom, where purely legislative committees are regarded as a threat to the cohesion of the national political parties because they would give the parliamentary parties special instruments with which they could develop independent policy judgments and expertise and exercise oversight over an executive, which is, after all, not formally constituted as a entity separate from Parliament. Thus committees can be construed as fundamentally inimical to unified Cabinet government. For an overview see Crick (1965a, 1965b); and Hill and Whichelow (1964), especially pp. 64–82.
2. From 1865 to 1869, for example, Thaddeus Stevens left the chairmanship of Ways and Means (a post he had held 1861–65) to become chairman of the new Committee on Appropriations. See McCall (1899, 259–60). McCall says, oddly, that at the time the Appropriations Committee was not very important, but this is hard to credit. From 1895 to 1899, Joseph G. Cannon was floor leader and chairman of Appropriations. See Taylor (1941).
3. See U.S., *Revised Statutes of the United States*, Title II, Ch. 8, Sections 105–130, and Dempsey (1956, 55–60). For indications of attempts to routinize the process of adjudication by setting up general criteria to govern House disposition of contested elections, see two 1933 cases: *Gormley v. Goss* (House Report 893, 73rd Congress; see also 78 *Congressional Record*, 4035, 7087, April 20, 1934) and *Chandler v. Burnham* (House Report 1278, 73rd Congress; see also 78 *Congressional Record*, 6971, 8921, May 15, 1934).
4. See, e.g., the assignment of burden of proof in *Gormley v. Goss* and *Chandler v. Burnham* (as cited in endnote 3).
5. This is not to say, however, that the policy output of the House is exclusively determined by its level of institutionalization. The Eighty-eighth, Eighty-ninth, and Ninetieth Congresses all represent more or less equivalent levels of institutionalization, yet their policy outputs varied greatly.

6. This position disagrees with Sidney Hyman, "Inquiry into the Decline of Congress," *New York Times Magazine,* January 31, 1960. For the argument that twentieth-century legislatures are on the whole weak see Truman (1959, 1–10; 1965, 1–4; 1966, 84–96). For the beginning of an argument that the U.S. Congress may be an exception, see Polsby (1964, 2, 31–32, 47–115).
7. The internal quotations are from John Quincy Adams' *Diary* and from an article by Reed in the *Saturday Evening Post,* December 9, 1899.
8. A motion to expel Brooks from the House for his act was defeated, but soon thereafter Brooks resigned anyway. He was subsequently reelected to fill the vacancy caused by his resignation. See *Biographical Directory of the American Congress, 1774–1961* (Washington: Government Printing Office, 1961), 604.

Chapter 4

Congress and the Quest for Power

LAWRENCE C. DODD

The postwar years have taught students of Congress a very fundamental lesson: Congress is a dynamic institution. The recent congressional changes picture an institution that is much like a kaleidoscope.... The appreciation and understanding of the moving image requires not only comprehending the role of each colorful geometric object in a specific picture, nor developing a satisfactory interpretation of the principles underlying a specific picture or change in specific aspects of the picture, but grasping the dynamics underlying the structural transformations themselves. So it is with Congress. To understand and appreciate it as an institution we must focus not only on particular aspects of internal congressional structure and process, nor on changes in particular patterns. We must seek to understand the more fundamental dynamics that produce the transformations in the congressional mosaic....[1]

As with politicians generally, members of Congress enter politics in a quest for personal power. This quest may derive from any number of deeper motives: a desire for ego gratification or for prestige, a search for personal salvation through good works, a hope to construct a better world or to dominate the present one, or a preoccupation with status and self-love. Whatever the source, most members of Congress seek to attain the power to control policy decisions that impose the authority of the state on the citizenry at large.

The most basic lesson that any member of Congress learns on entering the institution is that the quest for power by service within Congress requires reelection. First, reelection is necessary in order to remain in the struggle within Congress for "power positions."[2]...

Because reelection is so important, and because it may be so difficult to ensure, its pursuit can become all-consuming. The constitutional system, electoral laws, and social system together have created political parties that are weak coalitions. A candidate for Congress normally must create a personal organization

Source: *Congress Reconsidered,* ed. Lawrence C. Dodd and Bruce I. Oppenheimer (Washington: CQ Press, 1977) pp. 269–307. Reprinted by permission of the author.

rather than rely on her or his political party. The "electoral connection" that intervenes between the desire for power and the realization of power may lead members to emphasize form over substance, position taking, advertising, and credit claiming rather than problem solving. In an effort to sustain electoral success, members of Congress may fail to take controversial and clear positions, fail to make hard choices, fail to exercise power itself (Mayhew 1974a, 32–77). Yet members of Congress generally are not solely preoccupied with reelection. Most members have relatively secure electoral margins. This security stems partially from the fact that members of Congress *are* independent of political parties and are independent from responsibility for selecting the executive, and thus can be judged more on personal qualities than on partisan or executive affiliations. Electoral security is further reinforced because members of Congress personally control financial and casework resources that can help them build a loyalty from their constituents independent of policy or ideological considerations. The existence of secure electoral margins thus allows members to devote considerable effort toward capturing a "power position" within Congress and generating a mystique of special authority that is necessary to legitimize a select decision-making role for them in the eyes of their nominal peers.

The concern of members of Congress with gaining congressional power, rather than just securing reelection, has had a considerable influence on the structure and life of Congress. Were members solely preoccupied with reelection, we would expect them to spend little time in Washington and devote their personal efforts to constituent speeches and district casework. One would expect Congress to be run by a centralized, efficient staff who, in league with policy-oriented interest groups, would draft legislation, investigate the issues, frame palatable solutions, and present the members with the least controversial bills possible. Members of Congress would give little attention to committee work, and then only to committees that clearly served reelection interests. The primary activity of congresspeople in Congress, rather, would be extended, televised floor debates and symbolic roll call votes, all for show. Such a system would allow the appearance of work while providing ample opportunity for the mending of home fences. Alternatively, were only a few members of Congress concerned about power, with others concerned with reelection, personal finances, or private lives, one might expect a centralized system with a few leaders exercising power and all others spending their time on personal or electoral matters.

Virtually all members of the U.S. Congress are preoccupied with power considerations. They are unwilling—unless forced by external events—to leave the major decisions in either a centralized, autonomous staff system or a central leadership. Each member wants to exercise power—to make the key policy decisions. This motive places every member in a personal conflict with every other member: To the extent that one member realizes her or his goal personally to control all key decisions, all others must lose. Given this widespread power motive, an obvious way to resolve the conflict is to disperse power—or at least power positions—as widely as possible. One logical solution, in other words, is to place basic policy-making responsibility in a series of discrete and relatively autonomous committees and subcommittees, each having control over the decisions in a specified jurisdictional area.

Each member can belong to a small number of committees and, within them, have a significant and perhaps dominant influence on policy. Although such a system denies every member the opportunity to control all policy decisions, it ensures that most members, particularly if they stay in Congress long enough to obtain a sub-committee or committee chair, and if they generate the mystique of special authority necessary to allow them to activate the power potential of their select position, can satisfy a portion of their power drive.

Within Congress, as one would expect in light of the power motive, the funda-mental structure of organization is a committee system. Most members spend most of their time not in their district but in Washington, and most of their Washington time not on the floor in symbolic televised debate but rather in the committee or subcommittee rooms, in caucus meetings, or in office work devoted to legislation.[3] While the staff, particularly the personal staff, may be relegated to casework for constituents, the members of Congress sit through hearing after hearing, debate after debate, vote after vote seeking to shape in subcommittee, committee, and floor votes the contours of legislation. This is not to suggest, of course, that members of Congress do not engage in symbolic action or personal casework and do not spend much time in the home district; they do, in their effort at reelection. Likewise, staff do draft legislation, play a strong role in committee investigations, and influence the direction of public policy; they do this, however, largely because members of Congress just do not have enough time in the day to fulfill their numerous obligations. Seen in this perspective, Congress is not solely, simply, or primarily a stage on which individuals intentionally and exclusively engage in meaningless charades. Whatever the end product of their effort may be, members of Congress have actively sought to design a congressional structure and process that would maximize their ability to exercise personal power within Congress and, through Congress, within the nation at large. . . .

Because an essential type of legislative authority is associated with each con-gressional committee, members find that service on any committee can offer some satisfaction of their power drive. There are, nevertheless, inherent differences in the power potential associated with committees, differences that are tied to the varia-tion in legislative function and in the comprehensiveness of a committee's decisional jurisdiction. This variation between committees is sufficient to make some commit-tees more attractive as a place to gain power. Because members are in a quest for power, not simply reelection, they generally will seek to serve on committees whose function and policy focus allow the broadest personal impact on policy. . . .

Because of the constraints operating within a system of committee govern-ment, congressional careers reflect a set of stages. The first stage entails an emphasis on shoring up the electoral base through casework, serving on con-stituent-oriented reelection committees, and gaining favor within Congress by serving on the housekeeping committees. Of course, the first stage is never fully "completed": there is never a time at which a member of Congress is "guaranteed" long-term reelection or total acceptance within Congress, so both constituent and congressional service are a recurring necessity. But a point is normally reached—a point defined by the circumstances of the member's constituency, the opportuni-ties present in Congress, and the personality and competence of the member—

when he or she will feel secure enough, or perhaps unhappy enough, to attempt a move to a second stage. In the second stage members broaden their horizons and seek service on key policy committees that draft important legislation regulating such national policy dimensions as interstate commerce, education, or labor. In this stage, representatives begin to be "legislators," to preoccupy themselves with national policy matters. Because of the limited number of positions on power committees, many members will spend most, perhaps the rest, of their career in this stage, moving up by committee seniority to subcommittee and committee chairs on the policy committees. As they gain expertise in the specific policy area, and create a myth of special personal authority, they will gain power in some important but circumscribed area of national policy. For members who persist, however, and/or possess the right attributes of electoral security and personal attributes, a third stages exists: service on a power committee—Rules, Ways and Means, or Finance, Appropriations, and, in the Senate, Foreign Relations. Service on these committees is superseded, if at all, only by involvement in a fourth stage: service in the party leadership as a floor leader or Speaker. Few individuals ever have the opportunity to realize this fourth and climactic step; in a system of committee government, in fact, this step will be less sought and the battles less bitter than one might expect,[4] considering the status associated with them, because power will rest primarily in committees rather than in the party. Although party leadership positions in a system of committee government do carry with them a degree of responsibility, particularly the obligation to mediate conflicts between committees and to influence the success of marginal legislation on the House floor, members will generally be content to stay on a power committee and advance to subcommittee and committee chair positions rather than engage in an all-out effort to attain party leadership positions.

This career path, presented here in an idealized and simplified fashion, is a general "power ladder" that members attempt to climb in their quest for power within Congress. Some members leave the path voluntarily to run for the Senate (if in the House), to run for governor, to serve as a judge, or to serve as president. Some for special reasons bypass one or another stage, choose to stay at a lower rung, are defeated, or retire. Despite exceptions, the set of stages is a very real guide to the long-term career path that members seek to follow. Implicit within this pattern is the very real dilemma discussed earlier: Progress up the career ladder brings with it a greater opportunity for significant personal power, but also greater responsibility. As members move up the power ladder, they move away from a secure world in which reelection interest can be their dominant concern and into a world in which concerns with power and public policy predominate. They take their chance and leave the security of the reelection stage because of their personal quest for power, without which reelection is a largely meaningless victory. . . .

As a form of institutional organization, committee government posseses certain attributes that recommend it. By dividing policy concerns among a variety of committees it allows members to specialize in particular policy areas; this division provides a congressional structure through which the members can be their own expert advisers and maintain a degree of independence from lobbyists or outside specialists. Specialization also provides a procedure whereby members can become acquainted with particular programs and agencies and follow their behavior over a period of years, thus allowing informed oversight of the implementation of public policy. The dispersion of power implicit in committee government is important, furthermore, because it brings a greater number of individuals into the policy-making process and thus allows a greater range of policy innovation. In addition, as stressed above, committee government also serves the immediate power motive of congresspeople by creating so many power positions that all members can seek to gain power in particular policy domains.

Despite its assets, committee government does have severe liabilities, flaws that undermine the ability of Congress to fulfill its constitutional responsibilities to make legislative policy and oversee the implementation of that policy. First, committee government by its very nature lacks strong, centralized *leadership,* thereby undermining its internal decision-making capacity and external authority. . . . Closely related to the lack of leadership is a lack of *fiscal coordination.* . . . A third detriment associated with committee government, and one that is exacerbated by the absence of leadership and committee coordination, is the lack of *accountability* and *responsibility.* . . . The lack of accountability and the damage to Congress's popular support are augmented by a fourth characteristic of committee government—a tendency toward *insulation* of congressional decision making. . . .

Finally, committee government undermines the ability of Congress to perform that one function for which committee government would seem most suited—aggressive oversight of administration. According to the classic argument, the saving grace of committee government is that the dispersion of power and the creation of numerous policy experts ensure congressional surveillance of the bureaucracy. Unfortunately, this argument ignores the fact that the individuals on the committees that pass legislation will be the very people least likely to investigate policy implementation. They will be committed to the program, as its authors or most visible supporters, and will not want to take actions that might lead to a destruction of the program. . . . Members of Congress are unwilling to resolve this problem by creating permanent and powerful oversight committees because such committees, by their ability to focus attention on problems of specific agencies and programs, would threaten the authority of legislative committees to control and direct policy in their allotted policy area. Committee government thus allows a *failure of executive oversight.*

In the light of these five problems, the irony of committee government is that it attempts to satisfy members' individual desires for personal power by dispersing internal congressional authority so widely that the resulting institutional impotence cripples the ability of Congress to perform its constitutional roles, thereby dissipating the value of internal congressional power. Members of Congress thus are not only faced with the daily dilemma of balancing reelection interests with their efforts at upward power mobility within Congress; their lives are also complicated by a cruel paradox, the ultimate incompatibility of widely dispersed power within Congress, on the one hand, and a strong role for Congress in national decision making, on the other. This inherent tension generates an explosive dynamic within Congress as an organization and between Congress and the executive.

In the short run, as members of Congress follow the immediate dictates of the personal power motive, they are unaware of, or at least unconcerned with, the long-term consequences of decentralized power; they support the creation of committee government. The longer committee government operates, the more unhappy political analysts and the people generally become with the inability of Congress to make national policy or ensure policy implementation. . . . Slowly at first, presidents take over the roles of chief legislator, chief budgetary officer, overseer of the bureaucracy, chief tribune, and protector of the people. Eventually the president's role in these regards becomes so central that he feels free to ignore the wishes of members of Congress, even those who chair very important committees, and impose presidential policy on Congress and the nation at large.

The coming of a strong, domineering, imperial president who ignores Congress mobilizes its members into action. They see that their individual positions of power within Congress are meaningless unless the institution can impose its legislative will on the nation. They search for ways to regain legislative preeminence and constrain the executive. Not being fools, members identify part of the problem as an internal institutional one and seek to reform Congress. Such reform efforts come during or immediately following crises in which presidents clearly and visibly threaten fundamental power prerogatives of Congress. The reforms will include attempts to provide for more centralized congressional leadership, fiscal coordination, congressional openness, better oversight mechanisms, clarification of committee jurisdictions, procedures for policy coordination, and procedures to encourage committee accountability. Because the quest for personal power continues as the underlying motivation of individual members, the reforms are basically attempts to strengthen the value of internal congressional power by increasing the power of Congress vis-à-vis the executive. The reform efforts, however, are constrained by consideration of personal power prerogatives of members of Congress. The attempt to protect personal prerogatives while centralizing power builds structural flaws into the centralization mechanisms, flaws that would not be present were the significance of congressional structure for the national power of Congress itself the only motive. The existence of these flaws provides the openings through which centralization procedures are destroyed when institutional crises pass and members again feel free to emphasize personal power and personal careers. In addition, because policy inaction within Congress often will be identified as the immediate cause of presidential power aggrandizement, and because policy immobilism may become identified with key individuals or committees that have obstructed particular legislation, reform efforts also may be directed toward breaking up the authority of these individuals or committees and dispersing it among individuals and committees who seem more amenable to activist policies. This short-term dispersal of power, designed to break a legislative logjam (and, simultaneously, to give power to additional individuals), will serve to exacerbate immobilism in the long run when the new mechanisms of centralization are destroyed.

Viewed in a broad historical perspective, organizational dynamics within Congress, and external relations of Congress to the president, have a "cyclical" pattern. At the outset, when politicians in a quest for national power first enter Congress, they decentralize power and create committee government. Decentralization is followed by severe problems of congressional decision making, presidential assumption of legislative prerogatives, and an eventual presidential assault on Congress itself. Congress reacts by reforming its internal structure: Some reform efforts will involve legislation that attempts to circumscribe presidential action; other reforms will attempt to break specific points of deadlock by further decentralization and dispersal of congressional authority; eventually, however, problems of internal congressional leadership and coordination will become so severe that Congress will be forced to undertake centralizing reforms. As Congress moves to resolve internal structural problems and circumscribe presidential power, presidents begin to cooperate so as to defuse the congressional counterattack; to do otherwise would open a president to serious personal attack as anticongressional and thus antidemocratic, destroying the presidency's legitimizing myth as a democratic institution and identifying presidential motivations as power aggrandizement rather than protection of the Republic. As the immediate threat to congressional prerogatives recedes, members of Congress (many of whom will not have served in Congress during the era of institutional crisis) become preoccupied with their immediate careers and press once again for greater power dispersal within Congress and removal of centralizing mechanisms that inhibit committee and subcommittee autonomy. Decentralization reasserts itself and Congress becomes increasingly leaderless, uncoordinated, insulated, unresponsive, unable to control executive agencies. Tempted by congressional weakness and hounded by cries to "get the country moving," the executive again reasserts itself and a new institutional crisis eventually arises. . . .

NOTES

1. The approach presented here has been influenced particularly by the work of Fenno (1973), Huntington (1965a), and Mayhew (1974a).
2. By the power positions I mean those formal positions within the congressional institution that carry with them the legal authority over such prerogatives as parliamentary procedure, financial and staff resources, information collection and dispersal, and agenda setting, that are amenable to the control of policy making in a legislative assembly.
3. A survey conducted during the Eighty-ninth Congress under the auspices of the American Political Science Association's Study of Congress found that the average congressperson spent only 5.6 days per month in the home district while Congress was in session (a phenomenon that increasingly covers the calendar year). Although the figure demonstrates that members do take care to return home (a fact that Fenno's research shows is partially related to the location of the family home), members clearly devote *most* of their time to work in Washington. See Tacheron and Udall (1970, 303–4) and Fenno (1977b).
4. See Peabody (1976). I am struck in Peabody's discussion by the small number of leadership challenges, the lack of really bitter struggles, and the short amount of time and small amount of resources put into leadership battles.

PART II

REPRESENTATION

Chapter 5

What Is Representation?

One of the many reasons that legislatures are important to study is that they are representative bodies. But what is meant by "representation"? In what senses do legislators represent? And in what senses are legislators representative?

Representation is not explicitly mentioned in the Constitution. Still, the Founders considered it an important duty stemming from members' election to office. Several of the *Federalist Papers* are concerned specifically with justifying how a small Congress will represent a large public. Yet they did not foresee the conflict between representation and law making which many critics view as the dilemma of the modern Congress.

This is the only controversy reviewed in this book that is about definitions, but it would be naive to view the debate as totally a matter of definitions. It is also an empirical debate, as to how prevalent different forms of representation are and what their consequences are for the legislator and for the constituent. Additionally it is a normative debate, with some writers considering certain forms of representation less appropriate than others. Thus, this controversy transcends simple definitional matters.

One of the most thorough treatments of representation is Hanna Pitkin's (1967) definitional study *The Concept of Representation*. She starts with formalistic views of representation in terms of authorization (having been selected by the public) and accountability (having to be reelected in order to stay in office). However, she quickly moves to other meanings of the term, particularly "standing for" another person or "acting for" another person. These further meanings of representation will be discussed below in the context of the general literature in the field.

The original view was that legislators represent their constituents on policy issues. That sounds fairly simple, but it has become a fairly complicated matter, with many distinctions having been drawn over the years. The later view is that representation goes beyond issues. Many legislative scholars now regard representation as involving both issues and other matters, but they would still disagree as to whether each type is equally desirable.

REPRESENTATION OF CONSTITUENTS ON POLICY ISSUES

One early view was that representatives are chosen to represent their constituents on the issues. Pitkin (1967) describes this as the representative "acting for" the represented, as their substitute since they are not present. However, does this mean doing what the constituents want to be done? Or does it mean representing their interests? This distinction is termed the "style" of representation (Wahlke et al. 1962). It is usually summarized in a famous quote by Edmund Burke, a member of the British House of Commons in the 1700s. Burke was faced with a vote in which his constituents from Bristol wanted him to vote one way but in which he felt that a vote the other way was in their best interest. Was he to vote their desires or his conscience? Was he to represent their wills or their interests? In modern terms, was he an instructed "delegate" whose job is to follow the constituent mandate, or a "trustee" who was chosen to exercise his independent judgment?[1] Faced with this dilemma, Burke eloquently argued in his "Speech to the Electors of Bristol":

> Certainly, Gentlemen, it ought to be the happiness and glory of a representative to live in the strictest union, the closest correspondence, and the most unreserved communication with his constituents. Their wishes ought to have great weight with him; their opinions high respect; their business unremitted attention. It is his duty to sacrifice his repose, his pleasure, his satisfactions, to theirs—and above all, ever, and in all cases, to prefer their interest to his own.
>
> But his unbiased opinion, his mature judgment, his enlightened conscience, he ought not to sacrifice to you, to any man, or to any set of men living. . . . Your representative owes you, not his industry only, but his judgment; and he betrays, instead of serving you, if he sacrifices it to your opinion. . . .
>
> Parliament is not a congress of ambassadors from different and hostile interests, which interests each must maintain, as an agent and advocate, against other agents and advocates; Parliament is a deliberative assembly of one nation, with one interest—that of the whole—where not local purposes, not local prejudices, ought to guide, but the general good, resulting from the general reason of the whole. You choose a member, indeed; but when you have chosen him, he is not a member of Bristol, but he is a member of Parliament (Burke 1948, 39–41).

In the end, Burke decided to be a trustee, following his own judgment even if that meant voting against the instructions of his district. Regardless of the eloquence of his speech, Burke was defeated at the next election. His Bristol constituents apparently decided they did not want their representative to vote against their expressed desires.

Burke's dilemma of representing constituents on issues was central to the early empirical work on representation in the 1950s. There were actually two important studies of that era. One was the Wahlke, Eulau, Buchanan, and Ferguson study of representation in four state legislatures (1962). The researchers interviewed 474 legislators in California, New Jersey, Ohio, and Tennessee in 1957, focusing on their perceptions of their roles. They make an important distinction between the "style" and the "focus" of representation. The style dimension, as just described, involves how representation occurs—whether the member is a delegate or a trustee. They also added a third category, an in-between "politico" category for the member whose self-description is sometimes an instructed delegate and other times a Burkean trustee. A politico may switch between delegate and trustee role in different situations, or may voice both roles simultaneously, which could entail role conflict. The focus dimension involves what constituency the representative is representing. This usually involves "areal roles"—for state legislators whether they are representing their district or the whole state, or for national legislators whether they are representing their district or the whole nation. These two dimensions are intended to be separate from one another. That is, a representative whose style is that of a delegate could follow the desires of the district or of the state/nation. Similarly, a representative whose style is that of a trustee could do what he or she would consider in the best wishes of the district or of the state/nation.

This research on representational styles led to numerous studies. It became fashionable to interview legislators and classify their responses in terms of these style and focus dimensions. What is less clear, however, is how valid the responses are. In other words, responses might show more about what legislators feel are appropriate answers to these questions than what their actual representational roles are. After all, legislators cannot be expected to say that they ignore their constituents' wishes across the board because they feel they know more than their constituents do (though they may admit that this happens on an occasional issue). Similarly legislators may not want to state that they never exercise any free judgment but just do exactly what their constituents want on every matter. The usual questions used to measure representational style are actually very broad ("How would you describe the job of being a legislator—what are the most important things you should do here? Are there any important differences between what you think this job is and the way your constituents see it?"), but a short answer to this question might not reveal the full nuance of representational roles.

The other major empirical study of the 1950s was the 1958 Miller and Stokes representation study (1963, reprinted here as chapter 6). This was part of the National Election Study (NES) series which scholars at the University of Michigan's Survey Research Center were starting in the 1950s. After major presidential election studies in 1952 and 1956, they decided to mount a major study of the 1958 congressional campaign. A survey of constituents was augmented by surveys of incumbent members of Congress and congressional candidates in the districts that were part of their national sample. Miller and Stokes were the first to attempt to link actual constituent opinions to the behavior of the district's legislator—and by defining representation in terms of issue agreement between legislators and constituents, substantive representation was the dominant operational definition of representation for years in empirical research.

Miller and Stokes used an inventive research design. They asked the mass electorate a set of issue questions, and then they developed parallel questions for the members of Congress and the congressional candidate surveys. Furthermore, they asked the members and candidates for not only their own attitudes but also their perceptions of the district attitude. They examined several different issues by including questions that separately measured attitudes on social welfare issues, on civil rights, and on foreign policy. Finally, they analyzed congressional votes in these three separate issue domains to see how legislators voted in each area.

Miller and Stokes found different representation styles for the three different issue areas. Social welfare was an area in which party predominated. Liberal districts tended to elect Democrats, while conservative districts tended to elect Republicans. Democrats in Congress tended to vote liberal on these issues while Republicans tended to vote conservative. This is a case of party voting due to shared values rather than to disciplined parties per se. By contrast, civil rights was an area in which the delegate model held. The major division on civil rights was regional. Members from the South knew their districts opposed civil rights and they voted against it; members from the north knew their districts were more favorable and they voted more favorably. Finally, neither model held for foreign affairs. Instead, this area seemed to be an area of executive dominance. Trustees were prepared to recognize the president's greater expertise in this area and were often prepared to defer to his expertise. Of course these results are very dated by now, but it is easy to imagine that these different types of representation might still apply today in different issue areas.

The policy implications are also important to recognize. Members of a legislature can have flexibility in some areas to act as trustees because they act as delegates in other areas. This argument has been made by others, as when Fenno (1978) emphasized that a legislator's home style is used to earn constituents' trust, so that the member is permitted to exercise her or his own judgment in some areas. Stokes and Miller (1962) also found that the public knew little about what the representative was doing, and they argued that gave members considerable flexibility—they could act as trustees because they knew no one was watching. However, that position might not hold today, with interest groups watching closely and communicating to constituents when the member strays from their positions.

It should be added that the Miller and Stokes methodology became very controversial. For one thing, the estimates of constituent opinions were based on an average of less than twenty respondents per district, with some districts having just a handful of respondents. The analysis was based on a sophisticated statistical "path analysis," but many later researchers have disagreed with aspects of that analysis. For example, the Miller and Stokes conclusions are based on the correlations among the different variables in their model, but correlations only test whether the districts that are more liberal on one variable are more liberal on the other rather than measuring more directly the extent to which opinions match. Still, their basic result that representation can be different in different issue areas remains an important point.

Fenno (1978) turned to the question of what a constituency actually is—and in doing so redefined our conceptualization of the legislator-constituent relationship. Although we generally use the notion of the "geographic constituency," all people who live within the geographic boundaries of the district as drawn by the state legislature, Fenno points out that there are three further constituencies inside the physical district. If the geographic constituency is defined legally, the other constituencies are defined politically—based on the types of constituents who support the member of Congress. The "reelection constituency" consists of the constituents whom the member of Congress believes vote for him or her. The "primary constituency" is the loyalists who support the member of Congress with intensity, and regardless of the quality of the challenger. The primary constituency provides many of the volunteers and contributors to the candidate's campaigns. Finally, the "personal constituency" is the "intimates," the member's closest friends in the district. These are the old pals whom the member sees on most every visit back home, and members would have a hard time explaining to these pals a vote that goes against his or her usual pattern. The legislator's view of his or her constituency can thus be viewed as a set of concentric circles, with the geographic constituency as the outside circle and the personal constituency as the inner circle, closest to the representative. The closer the constituents are to the "intimates," the easier time the member has building rapport and feeling "at home." Thus, the legislator can most easily "represent" those closest to him or her politically.

Generally, members of Congress seek to convince their constituents that they represent them regardless of the extent to which they agree on specific issues. Fenno (1977, reprinted here as chapter 7) argues that representatives develop a "home style," a way of presenting themselves to their districts. We all "present our selves" to others. In this case, legislators adopt a presentation style that builds the trust of their constituents. They do this by attempting to convey a sense of qualification, identification, and empathy in their presentation of self. The legislator's message of identification is that "I am one of you." The message of empathy is that the representative understands constituents' problems. Their message of qualification is that they are competent to address their constituents' needs in Washington. With enough trust, the member creates flexibility to vote her or his own judgment. To maintain trust, members of Congress develop ways to explain their Washington activity, including committees and floor voting, to constituents. In sum, the representative's message is that he or she is making the same decisions the constituents would if they were in Washington—to blur the distinctions between voting as a trustee and a delegate.

Fenno also made a distinction between the relative homogeneity or heterogeneity within the constituencies based on the amount of diversity or conflict the member of Congress sees in the district. Others also have made this distinction and have hypothesized that more heterogeneous districts would be more difficult to represent due to the variety of demands from different groups of constituents. However, those who have studied the relationship between district diversity and the electoral margins of the representative have found no relationship (Bond 1983; Fiorina 1974). Similarly, Krasno (1994) finds that senators from more diverse states are evaluated as favorably as senators from more homogeneous states, suggesting that senators have little difficulty building coalitions across heterogeneous constituents. Krasno also finds that the size and heterogeneity of the state bear little relationship to senators' probability of reelection, particularly recently.

Although studies of policy representation traditionally have focused on the correlation between constituents' and legislators' opinions in the voting context, issue representation can occur in other aspects of policy making. Members often attempt to secure committee and subcommittee assignments that will allow them to serve their constituents (Fenno 1973; Shepsle 1978). Chapter 16 will explore committee assignments and the implications of "self-selection" to committees in detail.

Members of Congress also can represent their constituents on policy through choices regarding how to allocate their time and effort in developing legislation. Browne (1995) finds that constituents are the most prominent source of inspiration for legislation in agriculture and related domains. Members of Congress are more likely to get their ideas for legislation from constituents rather than interest groups, bureaucrats, or other "experts." Hall (1987, 1996) demonstrates that district interests affect the extent to which members of Congress are personally involved in subcommittee, committee, and floor activities. He shows few members participate in developing most legislation, but that members are more active when their district is affected by the legislation. Hall finds that the presence of district interests have a somewhat greater impact on formal participation in public arenas, where behavior is visible, but that district interests also influence members' levels of informal involvement, such as participation in behind the scenes negotiations. The "trustee vs. delegate" debate is still relevant though. Members' personal policy interests and priorities also exert a substantial impact on legislative participation. Members get involved in legislation on issues that they care about regardless of its effect on their constituents.

Although discussions of representation traditionally focused on the extent to which legislators advocated the policy preferences of their constituents in government, other conceptions of representation include additional facets of the legislator-constituent relationship. These alternative conceptions include legislative activities other than voting, such as doing casework, interacting personally with constituents, and speaking for citizens beyond the geographic boundaries of a congressional district. In recent years, political scientists have increasingly studied these nonpolicy aspects of representation. Whether studying alternative forms of representation has increased our understanding of the relationships between legislators and constituents is not controversial. What remains controversial is whether these alternative forms of representation are "legitimate": whether legislators' emphasis on them detracts from substantive representation, makes it more difficult for citizens to express their policy preferences through their legislators, and concurrently, makes it more difficult to hold legislators accountable for government policy.

REPRESENTATION BEYOND ISSUES

An expansive perspective on representation is that of Eulau and Karps (1977), who define four separate components of representation. Policy representation is issue-based agreement, discussed above. Service representation involves doing constituent service, such as casework. Allocation representation involves obtaining projects that help the district, making pork-barrel activities a form of representation. Symbolic representation involves building trust through symbolic measures.

To the extent that service, allocation, and symbolic responsiveness are seen as aspects of representation, representation is broader than representing constituents on issues.

The Eulau and Karps emphasis on different forms of responsiveness is congruent with other theoretical strains in the literature. First, Fenno's notion of home styles (1978) fits well with it, because some members choose nonpolicy home styles, such as a constituency service role. Also, they are compatible with Mayhew's description of three activities that members do to get reelected (1974a): advertising, credit claiming, and position taking. Credit claiming closely relates to service and allocation responsiveness, since the member who does casework or brings home pork claims credit for these actions.

To organize our discussion of alternative conceptions of representation, in Table 5.1 we have constructed a typology based on two dimensions: 1) the amount of emphasis on policy agreement between legislators and constituents, and 2) whether representation occurs only between legislators and constituents in their geographic district or whether legislators can appropriately represent others as well. This dimension is similar to the "areal" role discussed previously (Wahlke et al. 1962). The traditional conception of issue representation is based on the legislator's policy agreement with constituents in his or her district. Though Eulau and Karps' service and allocational representation share an emphasis on activities benefiting constituents in the district, they do not emphasize policy agreement. Nor is symbolic representation based on policy. It is based on the trust built by group identifications and shared goals and symbols that reach beyond a legally defined geographic district. Similarly, descriptive representation's concern with the extent to which legislative representation parallels the demography of the country is based on neither districts nor policy. Finally, collective representation emphasizes whether the policy preferences of the nation as a whole are the product of congressional action. As such, its policy emphasis is high, but its district emphasis is low.

Service/Allocational Representation

Service and allocational representation, including legislators' casework and pork-barrel activities for constituents in their districts, started to receive considerable attention in the literature during the 1970s. Fiorina (1977a) sought to explain the increased electoral safety of congressional incumbents and hypothesized that legislators' increased attention to constituency service was the cause. He charged that

Table 5.1

A typology of conceptions of representation

		District-based conception	
		Yes	No
Policy content	High	Policy/Issue	Collective
	Low	Service/Allocational	Symbolic/Descriptive

members of Congress intentionally create programs that do not work (and thus increase the size of the federal bureaucracy) so that they can reap the benefits of protecting constituents from bureaucrats in addition to the benefits of establishing the program in the first place. Either serves the legislator's interest in reelection by creating grateful constituents. Fiorina's hypotheses opened a new and substantial avenue of congressional research on the effects of legislators' casework activities.

There may be several motives for engaging in service activities, including a feeling of duty or the desire to be helpful, but few would argue that legislators do not also expect an electoral payoff. Constituents who have been helped by their representative, or who know others who have been helped, are thought to support their benefactor loyally in the voting booth. Such service is thought to be especially effective in today's candidate-centered politics—service can be used as a way of attracting independent and split-ticket voters in a weak party era (Parker 1986). Indeed, casework and getting projects for the district (pork barreling) are perceived by constituents to be important parts of the job and are almost uniformly viewed as a reason to support their representatives (Cain, Ferejohn, and Fiorina 1987; Krasno 1994).

Evidence to support the thesis of electoral impact has been surprisingly mixed. Johannes and McAdams (1981) studied a sample of congressional offices and found that members doing more service were not elected by larger margins. In a cross-time study, Hibbing (1991) found that changes in constituent service were unrelated to electoral support. Krasno (1994) confirms that constituent service has no impact on voting for the incumbent in House elections, but finds that it has a larger impact on voting for senators. In the most thorough analysis of the subject, Cain, Ferejohn, and Fiorina (1987) find that the effects of constituent service are indirect: Service affects constituents' perception of the legislator, and perceptions influence their votes. Still, the measurement of the effects of service on voting is limited by various methodological considerations, such as the difficulty in measuring the amount of service done by a member of Congress. Furthermore, as Fiorina (1981) has argued, members anticipating a close election may increase their casework activity, thereby increasing their vote and depressing the apparent electoral impact of the service activity in a single election. Also, variation in service is restricted—service is done by all members and none is willing to stop so that political scientists can conduct a field experiment to measure the electoral effects of not doing constituent service.

Pork-barrel activities are also relevant to district service. Stein and Bickers (1995) find that legislators elected by small margins in open seat districts are the members of Congress most likely to increase the number of grants sent to their districts. The increase in grants can help to ward off quality challengers. They find that like the impact of service, the electoral impacts of pork projects are indirect. Projects are likely to be noticed by interest groups and the most attentive constituents, not by voters in general. Thus, the member's success in gaining projects influences the votes of only those aware of the projects.

It is important to consider whether these forms of service representation are desirable. The affirmative argument is that it is necessary for constituents to have people intercede with the government bureaucracy for them, and legislators (whether federal, state, or city) will get more attention from the bureaucracy than constituents will get by themselves. The counterargument is that this allows members to build relationships with constituents on the basis of nonpolicy matters, which inevitably takes away from the extent of issue representation.

Similarly, there is a normative question of the desirability of allocational responsiveness. Each district clearly wants to have resources allocated to it and wants its representative to help create jobs in the district. It is possible to put together coalitions in support of bills that provide such allocations to many districts. However, the effect is to impose costs on all taxpayers. This gives representatives an incentive to vote for bills that help their districts while hurting the nation. Budget deficits result in part from this problem—Congress passes more projects than are efficient for the nation even if they help many individual districts.

Symbolic/Descriptive Representation

Another form of nonissue representation is symbolic representation. Pitkin (1967) uses this term to point out that representatives are symbols. Just as a flag becomes a symbol of a nation and a constitutional monarch becomes a symbol of a government, so a legislator can be a symbol that represents the public. Legislatures clearly perform a symbolic function when they legitimize legislation by passing it. This symbolic function is further emphasized by the various ritualistic actions involved in the legislative day such as the morning prayer, approval of the record of the previous day, and the formal terms of address used on the floor.

The concept of symbolic representation implies that representation can go beyond the geographic district. Even Fenno's four concentric circles (1977) assume that the relevant constituents are always internal to the geographic district. However, that is not necessarily the case. When African-American representatives represent African-Americans nationally, even those outside of their districts, representation is not geographically tied. When members get money for reelection from interest groups that are external to their district (and are tied more to their committee assignments than to their district makeup), representation is not geographically tied. The political science literature has not thoroughly examined the extradistrict aspects of representation, but it would be naive to treat representation as solely district-based.

The symbolic aspect of representation is similar to Pitkin's notion of "standing for" another person as representation. One form of such representation may be what Pitkin (1967) terms "descriptive representation." Descriptive representation occurs when the legislative assembly matches the general population in relevant respects. For example, a legislature would be descriptively representative of the population in terms of gender if just over half the legislature is female, matching the proportion in the population. Descriptive representation is rare in legislatures. Perhaps the closest occurred under the Supreme Soviet in the former U.S.S.R. when it was set up, at least in theory, so that its proportion of worker members matched the national proportion of workers, farmers matched the national proportion of farmers, and so on. The U.S. system does not emphasize descriptive likeness, but there is still considerable attention paid to the demographics of

Congress. The growth in the number of female legislators over the years is traced in the popular press as well as academic papers. Similarly there is attention to the growth in the numbers of African-American and Hispanic members. The religious affiliations of members of Congress are also widely reported, as are their educational and income levels. We might not expect Congress to match the U.S. public demographically, but we do note when there are large disparities. And the extent to which legislative districts should be drawn to promote the election of members of groups who have been historically underrepresented due to discrimination, particularly racial minorities, has been the subject of intense battles in Congress and the Supreme Court over the years (see the contemporary response on majority-minority districts following this chapter). Even districting, of course, cannot be used to increase the descriptive representation of women or of other groups that are not geographically concentrated.

Traditionally, Congress and state legislatures have been the bastion of the highly educated, mature, white male. Although women and minorities have increased their representation in recent years, they are still "underrepresented" in legislatures with respect to their share of the population in the United States. The debate surrounding descriptive representation is over to what extent different social groups need to have their members holding public office in order for that group's substantive "interests" to be protected. Put another way, does it make a difference to have legislators from different social groups and social backgrounds?

This brings the discussion back to the topic of policy representation. Most fundamentally, is policy representation of minority groups sufficient when they are underrepresented descriptively? Some empirical data can be mustered to assess the extent to which the policy views of minorities are accurately represented by nonminority legislators, but this is also a normative question that leads quickly to vigorous political debates.

Some have argued that policy representation can occur without accurate descriptive representation. In particular, in her study of African-American members of Congress, Swain (1993) questions whether descriptive and symbolic representation should take precedence over policy or service representation. She argues that whites who represent districts where a majority of constituents are minorities can vote in ways that reflect the "interests" of their minority constituents and can be assertive in servicing the needs of their minority constituents. Several facets of her argument are controversial, however. For example, how should one conceive of the substantive "interests" of a group of people? How should we test legislators' responsiveness to constituents? Further, while asserting that factors other than race play critical roles in the substantive representation of African Americans, she does not include the race of legislators in the statistical models in which she tests this hypothesis.

Nevertheless, other political scientists have made arguments similar to Swain's. Cameron, Epstein, and O'Halloran (1996) find that African-American voters do not have to be a majority in a congressional district in order to elect African-American representatives or for their substantive policy preferences to be represented by white legislators. Furthermore, to the extent that African-American voters are packed into majority-minority districts, their overall level of substantive representation declines as hostile Republicans are more likely to be elected in the neighboring old districts from which African-American voters are removed—districts that used to be represented by moderate white Democrats. Similarly, Hero and Tolbert (1995) have found that Hispanic members of Congress and those from districts with high numbers of Hispanic constituents do not have distinctive voting patterns—both tend to vote with their respective political parties. Thus, they conclude that representation of Hispanics occurs through the parties.

Greater differences have been found when studying representation and gender. Women legislators have been found to vote differently than men (see Thomas 1994 for a review). Male and female state legislators also have different priorities, with women tending to give greater priority to women's, children's, and family issues, and men giving greater priority to business issues (Thomas 1994). Relatedly, Hall (1996) finds that women, minority, and older members of Congress are more likely to participate in the legislative process on issues that "evoke" the shared interest of the group.

Male and female legislators may differ in other ways as well. Kathlene (1994) finds that in the Colorado legislature, male legislators are more aggressive in speaking in committee than female legislators, including on "women's issues" and on committees where the chair is female and a majority of members are female. In fact, she finds that as the proportion of female legislators on a committee increases male legislators become more aggressive. This suggests that merely increasing the number of women in legislatures may not be sufficient to assure that women legislators are "heard." Kathlene (1995) also finds that there can be gender differences among legislators in the perception of social problems and their solutions. This also implies that some policy views of women cannot fully be incorporated without more women in legislatures.

There are other ways in which groups may be represented in Congress. Legislative caucuses, also called Legislative Service Organizations (LSOs), have been institutional mechanisms in Congress for the promotion of group interests and agenda items (see Stevens, Mulhollan, and Rundquist 1981). Caucuses provide a way to represent interests that are not geographically tied to single congressional districts. Caucuses have been formed on a wide variety of topics, from social-demographic groups such as the Black, Hispanic and Women's Caucuses, to ideological interests or party factions such as the liberal Democratic Study Group, to regional groups such as the Northeast-Midwest Congressional Coalition and Sunbelt Caucus, to industry-based groups (the Steel Caucus) and many issue-related groups in between. Some of these groups are very informal, while others received financial support from Congress until 1995. The new Republican majority ended this funding, forcing caucuses to work out of the offices of individual members of Congress, find outside financial support, or close.

Collective Representation

The final form of representation to consider is collective representation. Like descriptive representation, this perspective emphasizes that representation can go beyond district-based constituents. Weissberg (1978) contrasts the usual "dyadic" view of representation in which legislators represent their constituents with a more "collective" view. Given diverse constituencies, it is impossible for a member of Congress to represent all constituents equally on their issue positions and according to their descriptive characteristics.[2] Collective representation occurs when the proportion of conservatives in a legislature is close to the national proportion of conservative voters, even if a particular conservative voter does not have a conservative legislator from her district. Using sampling theory, Weissberg makes the provocative argument that random selection of representatives, or even random voting by legislators, will produce policy that reflects public opinion at least as accurately as when legislators attempt to vote their constituents' preferences on a district-by-district basis. This claim is controversial because it means that legislators need not be attuned to the preferences of constituents in their districts in order for constituents to have their policy views represented.

Political parties can be one means for achieving collective representation (Hurley 1989). Even though a Republican constituent may have a Democratic representative, she may be represented through the activities of the Republican party in Congress. According to the responsible party model often used to describe parties in European parliaments, political parties propose programs during campaigns, have candidates who run for office on the basis of the party program, and, once in office, cohesively support the party agenda to pass it into law and implement it. Voters would then hold the majority party responsible for its performance in office and the results of its program. Though congressional parties in the United States rarely follow this model, the Republicans' Contract with America in 1994 and efforts to pass it through the House of Representatives in 1995 are as close an approximation as we usually see. Certainly the Republican leadership took the opportunity provided by their unexpected takeover of the majority status in Congress to claim an electoral mandate from the public to implement the Contract. In addition, though most political scientists support the view that members' electoral success has become quite independent of their party's, and even of their party's presidential candidate, Cox and McCubbins (1993) provide evidence that "party swings" in the member's share of the vote do occur. The loss of congressional seats by the president's party in midterm elections also can be interpreted as a referendum on his or her party's collective performance.

We can also consider collective representation in terms of whether Congress represents the nation as a whole. Page and Shapiro (1983) find that changes in public opinion on specific issues are congruent with changes in policy in a plurality of cases. However, in just over half the cases the change in policy may have occurred prior to the change in public opinion. Stimson, MacKuen, and Erikson (1995), using more sophisticated methodologies, find that policies passed by Congress do tend to follow broad ideological shifts in public opinion, which they label "public mood." In addition, they examine mechanisms through which public opinion change influences policy. Interestingly, the mechanisms differ between the House and Senate. In the Senate, policy change is largely the result of membership turnover caused by elections. In the House, policy change is not mediated by election results; members of the House engage in "rational anticipation" of the electoral consequences of public opinion change, and adjust policy votes so as not to risk electoral retribution from voters.

Yet collective representation potentially can conflict with other facets of representation. For example, what happens when the party agenda conflicts with the desires of constituents in the district? Though members of Congress typically abandon the party position when it conflicts with the intense desires of constituents (Kingdon 1989), at times legislators have been known to cast risky votes in support of their party. One recent, high-profile example was freshman Democrat Marjorie Margolies-Mezvinsky's dramatic, last-minute provision of the critical 218th vote for House passage of President Clinton's budget deficit reduction package in 1993. She voted with her party despite her campaign promise not to vote to raise taxes on her wealthy suburban Philadelphia constituents. Her placement of party over constituency on this high-profile vote contributed to her defeat in the 1994 election. Thus, although issues such as deficit reduction, free trade, gun control, or fewer military bases may be broadly popular, often members of Congress feel constrained to vote against them in the face of intense opposition in their district.

CONCLUSION

Attempts to understand the nature of representation have long been central to the study of legislatures. What types of interactions between legislators and constituents should be considered part of representation? Are some types of interactions more legitimate than others? To what extent should representation be based on the needs and desires of constituents in a geographical legislative district as opposed to individuals or groups dispersed across many districts or even the country as a whole? As this chapter has detailed, scholars have developed many ways to conceptualize the relationships between legislators and their constituents that have placed varying degrees of emphasis on policy agreement and district-based constituencies.

Legislators themselves see variety in their responsibilities. When members of Congress are asked the duties of their job (Davidson and Oleszek 1998, chapter 5), 87% respond legislation, 79% answer constituent services, 43% describe an educational role, 26% mention representation, and 11% give the politico role. On the one hand, multiple aspects of representation are meaningful. Policy is important, but so is nonpolicy representation. In particular, service seems to be as important as policy. On the other hand, this does not mean that nonpolicy representation should be seen as a substitute for policy responsiveness. Nonpolicy responsiveness may be important to voters, but this does not increase the effectiveness of legislatures as institutions.

Like their legislators, constituents view both policy and service representation as important. When asked what activities are important for their legislators to undertake, no one activity dominates. Constituents respond: keeping in touch (30%), policy (17%), protecting the district (15%), and oversight (15%) (Cain, Ferejohn, and Fiorina 1987). When asked what they like or dislike about their incumbent representative, constituents overwhelmingly mention policy issues.

However, policy mentions are rather evenly split between positive and negative comments; comments regarding casework and pork barreling tend to be positive only (Krasno 1994). This is consistent with Mayhew's argument (1974a) that legislators will emphasize credit-claiming activities (casework and pork) over position taking, since credit claiming creates only friends, while position taking can create both friends and enemies. In a study of a single congressional district, Serra and Moon (1994) found that both casework and policy agreement affect constituents' votes. This supports that notion that legislators benefit by paying attention to both types of representation.

Although we might expect that members of the Senate and House would differ in their representational behavior due to differences in the size and diversity of their constituencies, there is little contemporary evidence to support this argument. Krasno (1994) finds constituents have similar expectations for job performance for senators and representatives, contact them for similar reasons, and evaluate their performance in similar ways (though policy positions are somewhat more important for senators). In fact, in small states, constituents report more contacts with their individual senators than with their representative (Oppenheimer 1996). The similarity in how senators and representatives perform their representation duties fits with the view that the U.S. bicameral system is structured so that people have *two* agents working toward the *single* end of representing the public interest.

It is clear that representation extends beyond policy matters, but an important question is whether this is desirable. To Fiorina (1977) in particular, the nonpolicy aspects of representation seem less than legitimate. Nonpolicy representation allows legislators to be reelected regardless of how well they represent constituencies on issues. Voters see their legislators as effective in casework or in bringing pork-barrel projects to the district and reelect members on that basis without caring about policy matters. This makes incumbents safer at reelection time, which in turn makes Congress less responsive to attitudinal changes in the electorate. Changes in public attitudes are less completely captured by changes in the composition of Congress if these nonpolicy activities help make members immune to policy shifts in the electorate.

At the same time, constituents clearly want assistance from their legislators in dealing with government and want legislators to help provide jobs and federal projects in the district. Shouldn't voters themselves decide the relative weight to give to policy versus nonpolicy representation? In addition, evidence presented by Page and Shapiro (1983) and Stimson, MacKuen, and Erikson (1995) suggests that policy change is responsive to changes in public opinion even without substantial membership turnover. Legislators who feel "unsafe at any margin" (Mann 1978) are likely to engage in service activities as well as anticipate constituent reaction to legislative votes in order to maintain electoral support from constituents.

Given the classic status of this debate, we do not intend to resolve it here. Rather, it is important to note interaction between the normative debate and the questions political scientists seek to study. As this chapter points out, normative debates lead us to research questions; our research findings provide evidence and analysis that inform, and fuel, the debates. If anything is clear from these debates, it is that how we conceive and study representation very much affects our understanding of legislatures, legislators, and constituents.

NOTES

1. Pitkin (1967) includes the trustee and delegate as two aspects of representation as "acting for."
2. Weissberg's conception of collective representation includes "descriptive" representation discussed above, which has low policy content. Here we emphasize the policy-related aspects of collective representation.

CONTEMPORARY ISSUE:

Districting and Majority-Minority Districts

Since the Supreme Court ordered that legislative districts must be as equal as possible in terms of the number of individuals who reside in them in order to assure the standard of "one person, one vote" (*Wesberry* v. *Sanders* 1964), redistricting has been a salient political battle after the census is taken each decade. Some states lose seats in Congress due to population declines and must combine existing districts; other states gain seats due to population increases and must carve additional districts out of the old. All states, save those with a single at-large district, must redraw district lines to adjust for internal population shifts. The courts seek to protect various goals in this process, among them the "one person, one vote" standard, natural community boundaries, the compactness and contiguity of districts, and fairness to various social groups including ethnic groups and political parties (Butler and Cain 1992, 65–66). As often happens in politics, these goals come into conflict and politicians and the courts struggle over the extent to which some goals should be prioritized over others.

In particular, one of the major sources of controversy in the districting process has been the extent to which the federal government should protect the opportunity of minority groups to elect officials of their group. The Voting Rights Act of 1965 declared that districting arrangements were illegal if they were intentionally drawn to dilute minority voting strength. Previously, rather than assigning a region with a high concentration of African Americans its own legislative district in order to allow for the potential election of an African-American legislator, Southern segregationists divided African-American communities into multiple legislative districts where white voters were the majority. This practice was not ended with the Voting Rights Act, however, since it was difficult to prove the "intent" to divide minority voters.

Congress responded with the Voting Rights Amendments of 1982, which stated that districting plans that had the effect of diluting minority voting strength could be overturned. To enforce this provision, the Justice Department required states to maximize the number of districts in which minority voters would outnumber whites—called "majority-minority" districts. This strategy was used to produce a dramatic increase in the number of majority-minority districts in 1992: fifteen new black-majority districts, for a total of 32; and nine new Latino-majority districts, for a total of 20.

Because minority voters often do not live in geographically concentrated tracts where a district could be easily drawn (e.g., African Americans in the rural South), districting commissions often had to create bizarrely shaped districts, zigzagging across the state to pick up enough pockets of minority voters to make them the majority in the district. The Twelfth Congressional District of North Carolina, for example, follows Interstate 85 for 160 miles from Durham to Charlotte, reaching out to incorporate African-American neighborhoods along the way. The district is so narrow at some points, one candidate joked, "I love this district because I can drive down I–85 with both car doors open and hit every person in the district."[1] The end result is that these districts contain a sufficient number of minority voters, but often divide towns and other natural communities.

White voters challenged a number of these oddly shaped majority-minority districts. The Supreme Court, too, reacted with skepticism. In *Shaw* v. *Reno* (1993), the Court objected to districts that abandoned standards of compactness and contiguity for the sole purpose of helping elect minorities to office. In *Miller* v. *Johnson* (1995), the Court went further, ruling that districts drawn with the intent of electing a minority representative are unconstitutional. The drawing of district lines must be done in a color-blind fashion. In separate cases, the Court ordered that a number of these districts be redrawn. However, the Court has never ordered gerrymandered districts designed to favor one political party to be redrawn, despite declaring this practice unconstitutional in *Davis* v. *Bandemer* (1986).

Before 1992, many Southern states, despite having large populations of African Americans, had not elected minority representatives since Reconstruction. For example, North Carolina, before electing two African Americans from majority-minority districts, had never elected an African-American member of Congress although African Americans constituted 20% of its population (Canon, Schousen, and Sellers 1994). Hadley and Grofman (1994) document that the increase in the election of African-American officials in the South has been due to federally imposed redistricting rather than changes in voting behavior.

At the same time, aggregating minority voters into one district necessarily removes them from surrounding districts. The result may be that the majority-minority district elects a minority representative but also that representatives in neighboring districts now have less electoral pressure to represent the interests of minority voters. Overby and Cosgrove (1996) studied white incumbents who returned after the 1992 redistricting. They concluded that the policy representation as well as descriptive representation of African Americans is affected by districting. Especially for Southern Democrats, voting records became less liberal as African-American voters were removed from their districts (cf. Whitby 1997). Lublin (1997) notes that increasing the number of minority representatives in Congress increases the number of liberal votes, but to the extent that minorities are replacing white Democrats does not increase the probability that legislation they favor will pass.

Relatedly, if the votes of African Americans are necessary for moderate Democrats to win congressional seats in the South, removing those voters increases the probability that conservative Republicans will be elected. Hill (1995) and Lublin (1997) provide evidence that this occurred due to the 1992 redistricting. For example, the Georgia congressional delegation changed from nine Democrats and one Republican to eight white Republicans and three African-American Democrats between 1992 and 1994.

Yet there is disagreement regarding whether minority voters would obtain better policy representation even if they had less descriptive representation in a system without majority-minority districts. Swain (1993) argues that minorities would not necessarily achieve better representation since white Democrats vote in the interest of African Americans. Whitby (1997) presents evidence that the relationship between the descriptive and policy representation of African Americans is conditional. First, it depends on whether the votes are on final passage of legislation or on amendments. White Democrats represent African Americans on final passage votes at high levels (i.e., vote liberally), but are less likely to represent African Americans on amendments. Presumably votes on amendments are less visible to constituents. African-American representatives, on the other hand, are consistent. Whitby also finds that the degree to which white legislators represent African Americans on issues depends on the congressional agenda. In some years, civil rights issues are very consensual and are supported by wide margins of both African Americans and white legislators. However, in years when the congressional civil rights agenda is more divisive, African-American representatives are more likely than whites to represent black interests (i.e., vote liberally). Thus, to the extent that we can define the policy representation of African-American constituents based on voting records (particularly defined as voting in a consistently liberal manner), policy representation may indeed be facilitated by descriptive representation.

The continued use of redistricting as a means of increasing minority representation is likely to diminish in its effectiveness even if it remains legal. A region must have a critical size of minority voters for redistricting to be a relevant tool (Butler and Cain 1992, 134–35), and after 1992, fewer areas meet this condition. Moreover, districting does nothing to increase the representation of groups that are not geographically concentrated, such as women. Thus, some have suggested alternative structures for congressional districts in order to increase minority representation. Neither of the methods we discuss are allowed under current law.

One is to shift to a system of proportional representation (PR) used in some European countries. In a PR system, candidates are elected to the legislature based on their party's or group's share of the vote nationally (or perhaps by state). This contrasts with our single-seat, "winner-take-all" system. The current system may discourage the election of minority candidates since members of this group do not have the votes to elect one of their own without the assistance of voters from the majority group. A PR system could mandate that citizens are represented descriptively based on a group characteristic such as race or gender. For example, if African-American candidates received 20% of the vote, they would receive their proportional share of the seats in the legislature, 20%. However, such a system would detract from local district representation (e.g., policy and service) and there would be substantial disagreement regarding which types of groups should be eligible for proportional representation (political parties, the working class, people with disabilities?).

Another method is "cumulative voting" (see Guinier 1994). In this system, larger districts would elect more than one representative and voters would cast a number of votes equal to the number of congressional seats apportioned to the district. But voters can cast their multiple votes for the same candidate—cumulating their votes for one candidate. In this way, minority voters do not have to be the majority in the district to elect a minority representative: Assuming the minority has a relatively sizable presence in the district, if they cast a large proportion of their votes for a single minority candidate, he or she is likely to win one of the district's seats. Even if majority voters do not support the minority candidate, they are likely to split their votes among several majority candidates, allowing the accumulated votes of minority voters to elect the minority candidate to one of the seats. Of course, candidates could still build coalitions of both majority and minority group members. Supporters note that cumulative voting helps achieve representation for all types of political minorities, including Republicans in Democratic regions and women, not just racial minorities. Opponents argue that cumulative voting assumes that candidates will not create cross-racial coalitions to win office (Swain 1993), and in fact, may discourage it by asking minority voters to cast all their votes only for minority candidates. Cumulative voting also would seem to violate the Supreme Court's "one person, one vote" standard, since an individual can cast multiple votes for the same candidate. Others fear that this system is too complicated for the average voter to understand and would not work in practice.

Though the adoption of proportional representation or cumulative voting is very unlikely, these debates focus our attention on the meaning of representation, the relationship between electoral structures and representation, the normative and constitutional values involved in making "technical" decisions of drawing district boundaries, and the difficulties of trying to "represent" all citizens equally in a republican government.

NOTE

1. Quoted in Ronald Smothers, 1992, "Two Strangely Shaped Hybrid Creatures Highlight North Carolina's Primary," *New York Times,* 3 May, National edition, p. A28.

Chapter 6

Constituency Influence in Congress

WARREN E. MILLER AND DONALD E. STOKES

Substantial constituency influence over the lower house of Congress is commonly thought to be both a normative principle and a factual truth of American government. From their draft constitution we may assume the Founding Fathers expected it, and many political scientists feel, regretfully, that the Framers' wish has come all too true.[1] Nevertheless, much of the evidence of constituency control rests on inference. The fact that our House of Representatives, especially by comparison with the House of Commons, has irregular party voting does not of itself indicate that congressmen deviate from party in response to local pressure. And even more, the fact that many congressmen *feel* pressure from home does not of itself establish that the local constituency is performing any of the acts that a reasonable definition of control would imply.

CONSTITUENCY CONTROL IN THE NORMATIVE THEORY OF REPRESENTATION

Control by the local constituency is at one pole of *both* the great normative controversies about representation that have arisen in modern times. It is generally recognized that constituency control is opposite to the conception of representation associated with Edmund Burke. Burke wanted the representative to serve the constituency's *interest* but not its *will*, and the extent to which the representative should be compelled by electoral sanctions to follow the "mandate" of his constituents has been at the heart of the ensuing controversy as it has continued for a century and a half.[2]

Constituency control also is opposite to the conception of government by responsible national parties. This is widely seen, yet the point is rarely connected with normative discussions of representation. Indeed, it is remarkable how little

Source: *American Political Science Review* (1963) 57:45–57. Reprinted by permission of the publisher.

attention has been given to the model of representation implicit in the doctrine of a "responsible two-party system." . . .

The conception of representation implicit in the doctrine of responsible parties shares the idea of popular control with the instructed-delegate model. Both are versions of popular sovereignty. But "the people" of the responsible two-party system are conceived in terms of a national rather than a local constituency. Candidates for legislative office appeal to the electorate in terms of a *national* party program and leadership, to which, if elected, they will be committed. Expressions of policy preference by the local district are reduced to endorsements of one or another of these programs, and the local district retains only the arithmetical significance that whichever party can rally to its program the greater number of supporters in the district will control its legislative seat.

No one tradition of representation has entirely dominated U.S. practice. Elements of the Burkean, instructed-delegate, and responsible party models can all be found in our political life. Yet if the American system has elements of all three, a good deal depends on how they are combined. Especially critical is the question whether different models of representation apply to different public issues. Is the saliency of legislative action to the public so different in quality and degree on different issues that the legislator is subject to very different constraints from his constituency? Does the legislator have a single generalized mode of response to his constituency that is rooted in a normative belief about the representative's role or does the same legislator respond to his constituency differently on different issues? More evidence is needed on matters so fundamental to our system.

AN EMPIRICAL STUDY OF REPRESENTATION

To extend what we know of representation in the American Congress the Survey Research Center of The University of Michigan interviewed the incumbent congressman, his nonincumbent opponent (if any), and a sample of constituents in each of 116 congressional districts, which were themselves a probability sample of all districts.[3] These interviews, conducted immediately after the congressional election of 1958, explored a wide range of attitudes and perceptions held by the individuals who play the reciprocal roles of the representative relation in national government. The distinguishing feature of this research is, of course, that it sought direct information from both constituent and legislator (actual and aspiring). To this fund of comparative interview data has been added information about the roll call votes of our sample of congressmen and the political and social characteristics of the districts they represent.

Many students of politics, with excellent reason, have been sensitive to possible ties between representative and constituent that have little to do with issues of public policy. For example, ethnic identifications may cement a legislator in the affections of his district, whatever (within limits) his stands on issues. And many congressmen keep their tenure of office secure by skillful provision of district benefits ranging from free literature to major federal projects. In the full study of which this analysis is part we have explored several bases of constituency support that have little to do with policy issues. Nevertheless, the question [of] how the representative should make up his mind on legislative issues is what the classical arguments over representation are all about, and we have given a central place to a comparison of the policy preferences of constituents and representatives and to a causal analysis of the relation between the two.

. . . Far from looking over the shoulder of their congressmen at the legislative game, most Americans are almost totally uninformed about legislative issues in Washington. At best the average citizen may be said to have some general ideas about how the country should be run, which he is able to use in responding to particular questions about what the government ought to do. . . .

What makes it possible to compare the policy preferences of constituents and representatives despite the public's low awareness of legislative affairs is the fact that congressmen themselves respond to many issues in terms of fairly broad evaluative dimensions. Undoubtedly policy alternatives are judged in the executive agencies and the specialized committees of the Congress by criteria that are relatively complex and specific to the policies at issue. But a good deal of evidence goes to show that when proposals come before the House as a whole they are judged on the basis of more general evaluative dimensions (MacRae 1958). For example, most congressmen, too, seem to have a general conception of how far government should go in the area of domestic social and economic welfare, and these general positions apparently orient their roll call votes on a number of particular social welfare issues.

It follows that such a broad evaluative dimension can be used to compare the policy preferences of constituents and representatives despite the low state of the public's information about politics. In this study three such dimensions have been drawn from our voter interviews and from congressional interviews and roll call records. As suggested above, one of these has to do with approval of government action in the social welfare field, the primary domestic issue of the New Deal-Fair Deal (and New Frontier) eras. A second dimension has to do with support for American involvement in foreign affairs, a latter-day version of the isolationist-internationalist continuum. A third dimension has to do with approval of federal action to protect the civil rights of Negroes.[4]

Because our research focused on these three dimensions, our analysis of constituency influence is limited to these areas of policy. No point has been more energetically or usefully made by those who have sought to clarify the concepts of power and influence than the necessity of specifying the acts *with respect to which* one actor has power or influence or control over another (Dahl 1957). Therefore, the scope (Lasswell and Kaplan 1950, 71–73) or range (Cartwright 1959, 183–220) of influence for our analysis is the collection of legislative issues falling within our three policy domains. We are not able to say how much control the local constituency may or may not have over *all* actions of its representative, and there may well be pork-barrel issues or other matters of peculiar relevance to the district on which the relation of congressman to constituency is quite distinctive. However, few observers of contemporary politics would regard the issues of government provision of social and economic welfare, of American involvement in world affairs, and of federal action in behalf of the Negro as constituting a trivial range of action. Indeed, these domains together include most of the great issues that have come before Congress in recent years.

In each policy domain we have used the procedures of cumulative scaling, as developed by Louis Guttman and others, to order our samples of congressmen, of opposing candidates, and of voters. In each domain congressmen were ranked once according to their roll call votes in the House and again according to the attitudes they revealed in our confidential interviews. These two orderings are by no means identical, nor are the discrepancies due simply to uncertainties of measurement.[5] Opposing candidates also were ranked in each policy domain according to the attitudes they revealed in our interviews. The nationwide sample of constituents was ordered in each domain, and by averaging the attitude scores of all constituents living in the same districts, whole constituencies were ranked on each dimension so that the views of congressmen could be compared with those of their constituencies. Finally, by considering only the constituents in each district who share some characteristic (voting for the incumbent, say) we were able to order these fractions of districts so that the opinions of congressmen could be compared with those, for example, of the dominant electoral elements of their districts.

In each policy domain, crossing the rankings of congressmen and their constituencies gives an empirical measure of the extent of policy agreement between legislator and district. In the period of our research this procedure reveals very different degrees of policy congruence across the three issue domains. On questions of social and economic welfare there is considerable agreement between representative and district, expressed by a correlation of approximately 0.3. This coefficient is, of course, very much less than the limiting value of 1.0, indicating that a number of congressmen are, relatively speaking, more or less "liberal" than their districts. However, on the question of foreign involvement there is no discernible agreement between legislator and district whatever. Indeed, as if to emphasize the point, the coefficient expressing this relation is slightly negative (−0.09), although not significantly so in a statistical sense. It is in the domain of civil rights that the rankings of congressmen and constituencies most nearly agree. When we took our measurements in the late 1950s the correlation of congressional roll call behavior with constituency opinion on questions affecting the Negro was nearly 0.6.

The description of policy agreement that these three simple correlations give can be a starting point for a wide range of analyses. For example, the significance of party competition in the district for policy representation can be explored by comparing the agreement between district and congressman with the agreement between the district and the congressman's nonincumbent opponent. Alternatively, the significance of choosing representatives from single-member districts by popular majority can be explored by comparing the agreement between the congressman and his own supporters with the agreement between the congressman and the supporters of his opponent. Taking *both* party competition and majority rule into account magnifies rather spectacularly some of the coefficients reported here. This is most true in the domain of social welfare, where attitudes both of candidates and of voters are most polarized along party lines. Whereas the correlation between the constituency majority and congressional roll call votes is nearly +0.4 on social welfare policy, the correlation of the district majority with the nonincumbent candidate is −0.4. This difference, amounting to almost 0.8, between these two coefficients is an indicator of what the dominant electoral element of the constituency gets on the average by choosing the congressman it has and excluding his opponent from office.[6]

These three coefficients are also the starting point for a causal analysis of the relation of constituency to representative, the main problem of this paper. At least on social welfare and Negro rights a measurable degree of congruence is found between district and legislator. Is this agreement due to constituency influence in Congress, or is it to be attributed to other causes? If this question is to have a satisfactory answer the conditions that are necessary and sufficient to assure constituency control must be stated and compared with the available empirical evidence.

THE CONDITIONS OF CONSTITUENCY INFLUENCE

Broadly speaking, the constituency can control the policy actions of the representative in two alternative ways. The first of these is for the district to choose a representative who so shares its views that in following his own convictions he does his constituents' will. In this case district opinion and the congressman's actions are connected through the representative's own policy attitudes. The second means of constituency control is for the congressman to follow his (at least tolerably accurate) perceptions of district attitude in order to win reelection. In this case constituency opinion and the congressman's actions are connected through his perception of what the district wants.[7]

These two paths of constituency control are presented schematically in Figure 6.1. As the figure suggests, each path has two steps, one connecting the constituency's attitude with an "intervening" attitude or perception, the other connecting this attitude or perception with the representative's roll call behavior. Out of respect for the processes by which the human action achieves cognitive congruence we have also drawn arrows between the two intervening factors, since the congressman probably tends to see his district as having the same opinion as his

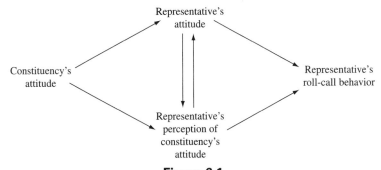

Figure 6.1
Connections between a constituency's attitude and its representative's roll-call behavior.

own and also tends, over time, to bring his own opinion into line with the district's. The inclusion of these arrows calls attention to two other possible influence paths, each consisting of *three* steps, although these additional paths will turn out to be of relatively slight importance empirically.

Neither of the main influence paths of Figure 6.1 will connect the final roll call vote to the constituency's views if either of its steps is blocked. From this, two necessary conditions of constituency influence can be stated: *First,* the representative's votes in the House must agree substantially with his own policy views or his perceptions of the district's views, and not be determined entirely by other influences to which the congressman is exposed; and, *second,* the attitudes or perceptions governing the representative's acts must correspond, at least imperfectly, to the district's actual opinions. It would be difficult to describe the relation of constituency to representative as one of control unless these conditions are met.[8]

Yet these two requirements are not sufficient to assure control. A *third* condition must also be satisfied: The constituency must in some measure take the policy views of candidates into account in choosing a representative. If it does not, agreement between district and congressman may arise for reasons that cannot rationally be brought within the idea of control. For example, such agreement may simply reflect the fact that a representative drawn from a given area is likely, by pure statistical probability, to share its dominant values, without his acceptance or rejection of these ever having been a matter of consequence to his electors.

EVIDENCE OF CONTROL: CONGRESSIONAL ATTITUDES AND PERCEPTIONS

How well are these conditions met in the relation of American congressmen to their constituents? There is little question that the first is substantially satisfied; the evidence of our research indicates that members of the House do in fact vote both their own policy views and their perceptions of their constituents' views, at least on issues of social welfare, foreign involvement, and civil rights. If these two intervening factors are used to predict roll call votes, the prediction is quite successful. Their multiple correlation with roll call position is 0.7 for social welfare, 0.6 for foreign involvement, and 0.9 for civil rights; the last figure is especially persuasive. What is more, both the congressman's own convictions and his perceptions of district opinion make a distinct contribution to his roll call behavior. In each of the three domains the prediction of roll call votes is surer if it is made from both factors rather than from either alone.

Lest the strong influence that the congressman's views and his perception of district views have on roll call behavior appear somehow foreordained—and, consequently, this finding seem a trivial one—it is worth taking a sidewise glance at the potency of possible other forces on the representative's vote. In the area of foreign policy, for example, a number of congressmen are disposed to follow the administration's advice, whatever they or their districts think. For those who are, the multiple correlation of roll call behavior with the representative's own foreign policy views and his perception of district views is a mere 0.2. Other findings could be cited to support the point that the influence of the congressman's own preferences and those he attributes to the district is extremely variable. Yet in the House as a whole over the three policy domains the influence of these forces is quite strong.

The connections of congressional attitudes and perceptions with actual constituency opinion are weaker. If policy agreement between district and representative is moderate and variable across the policy domains, as it is, this is to be explained much more in terms of the second condition of constituency control than the first. The representative's attitudes and perceptions most nearly match true opinion in his district on the issues of Negro rights. Reflecting the charged and polarized nature of this area, the correlation of actual district opinion with perceived opinion is greater than 0.6, and the correlation of district attitude with the representative's own attitude is nearly 0.4, as shown by Table 6.1. But the comparable correlations for foreign involvement are much smaller—indeed almost negligible. And the coefficients for social welfare are also smaller, although a detailed presentation of findings in this area would show the representative's perceptions and attitudes are more strongly associated with the attitude of his or her electoral *majority* than they are with the attitudes of the constituency as a whole.

Knowing this much about the various paths that may lead, directly or indirectly, from constituency attitude to roll call vote, we can assess their relative importance. Since the alternative influence chains have links of unequal strength, the full chains will not in general be equally strong, and these differences are of great importance in the relation of representative to constituency. For the domain of civil rights Figure 6.2 assembles all the intercorrelations of the variables of our system. As the figure shows, the root correlation of constituency attitude with roll call behavior in this domain is 0.57. How much of this policy congruence can be accounted for by the influence path involving the representative's attitude? And how much by the path involving his perception of constituency opinion? When the intercorrelations of the system are interpreted in the light of what we assume its causal structure to be, it is influence passing through the congressman's perception of the district's views that is found to be preeminently important.[9] Under the least favorable assumption as to its importance, this path is found to account for more than twice as much of the variance of roll call behavior as the paths involving the representative's own attitude.[10] However, when this same procedure is applied to

Table 6.1
Correlations of constituent attitudes

Policy domain	Correlation of constituency attitude with	
	Representative's perception of constituency attitude	Representative's own attitude
Social welfare	.17	.21
Foreign involvement	.19	.06
Civil rights	.63	.39

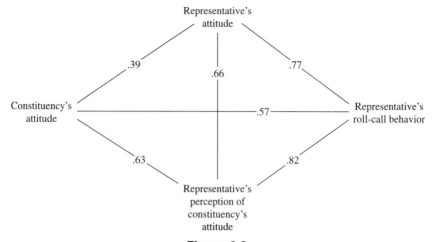

Figure 6.2
Intercorrelations of variables pertaining to civil rights.

our social welfare data, the results suggest that the direct connection of constituency and roll call through the congressman's own attitude is the most important of the alternative paths.[11] The reversal of the relative importance of the two paths as we move from civil rights to social welfare is one of the most striking findings of this analysis.

EVIDENCE OF CONTROL: ELECTORAL BEHAVIOR

Of the three conditions of constituency influence, the requirement that the electorate take account of the policy positions of the candidates is the hardest to match with empirical evidence. Indeed, given the limited information the average voter carries to the polls, the public might be thought incompetent to perform any task of appraisal. Of constituents living in congressional districts where there was a contest between a Republican and a Democrat in 1958, less than one in five said they had read or heard something about both candidates, and well over half conceded they had read or heard nothing about either. And these proportions are not much better when they are based only on the part of the sample, not much more than half, that reported voting for Congress in 1958. The extent of awareness of the candidates among voters is indicated in Table 6.2. As the table shows, even of the portion of the public that was sufficiently interested to vote, almost half had read or heard nothing about either candidate.

Just how low a hurdle our respondents had to clear in saying that they had read or heard something about a candidate is indicated by detailed qualitative analysis of the information constituents *were* able to associate with congressional candidates. Except in rare cases, what the voters "knew" was confined to diffuse evaluative judgments about the candidate: "he's a good man," "he understands the problems," and so forth. Of detailed information about policy stands not more

Table 6.2

Awareness of congressional candidates
among voters, 1958

Read or heard something about incumbent*				
		Yes	No	
Read or heard something about nonincumbent	Yes	24	5	29
	No	25	46	71
		49	51	100%

*In order to include all districts where the House seat was contested in 1958 this table retains ten constituencies in which the incumbent congressman did not seek reelection. Candidates of the retiring incumbent's party in these districts are treated here as if they were incumbents. Were these figures to be calculated only for constituencies in which an incumbent sought reelection, no entry in this four-fold table would differ from that given by more than 2%.

than a chemical trace was found. Among the comments about the candidates given in response to an extended series of free-answer questions, less than 2% had to do with stands in our three policy domains; indeed, only about three comments in every hundred had to do with legislative issues of *any* description.[12]

This evidence that the behavior of the electorate is largely unaffected by knowledge of the policy positions of the candidates is complemented by evidence about the forces that *do* shape the voters' choices among congressional candidates. The primary basis of voting in American congressional elections is identification with party. . . . What is more, traditional party voting is seldom connected with current legislative issues. As the party loyalists in a nationwide sample of voters told us what they liked and disliked about the parties in 1958, only a small fraction of the comments (about 15%) dealt with current issues of public policy (Stokes and Miller 1962).

Yet the idea of reward or punishment at the polls for legislative stands is familiar to members of Congress, who feel that they and their records are quite visible to their constituents. Of our sample of congressmen who were opposed for reelection in 1958, more than four-fifths said the outcome in their districts had been strongly influenced by the electorate's response to their records and personal standing. Indeed, this belief is clear enough to present a notable contradiction: Congressmen feel that their individual legislative actions may have considerable impact on the electorate, yet some simple facts about the representative's salience to his constituents imply that this could hardly be true.

In some measure this contradiction is to be explained by the tendency of congressmen to overestimate their visibility to the local public, a tendency that reflects the difficulties of the representative in forming a correct judgment of constituent opinion. The communication most congressmen have with their districts inevitably puts them in touch with organized groups and with individuals who are relatively well informed about politics. The representative knows his constituents mostly from dealing with people who *do* write letters, who *will* attend meetings, who *have* an interest in his legislative stands. As a result, his sample of contacts with a constituency of several hundred thousand people is heavily biased: Even the contacts he apparently makes at random are likely to be with people who grossly overrepresent the degree of political information and interest in the constituency as a whole.

But the contradiction is also to be explained by several aspects of the representative's electoral situation that are of great importance to the question of constituency influence. The first of these is implicit in what has already been said. Because of the pervasive effects of party loyalties, no candidate for Congress starts from scratch in putting together an electoral majority. The congressman is a dealer in increments and margins. He starts with a stratum of hardened party voters, and if the stratum is broad enough he can have a measurable influence on his chance of survival simply by attracting a small additional element of the electorate—or by not losing a larger one. Therefore, his record may have a very real bearing on his electoral success or failure without most of his constituents ever knowing what that record is.

Second, the relation of congressman to voter is not a simple bilateral one but is complicated by the presence of all manner of intermediaries: the local party, economic interests, the news media, racial and nationality organizations, and so forth. Such is the lore of American politics, as it is known to any political scientist. Very often the representative reaches the mass public through these mediating agencies, and the information about himself and his record may be considerably transformed as it diffuses out to the electorate in two or more stages. As a result, the public—or parts of it—may get simple positive or negative cues about the congressman which were provoked by his legislative actions but which no longer have a recognizable issue content.

Third, for most congressmen most of the time the electorate's sanctions are potential rather than actual. Particularly the representative from a safe district may feel his proper legislative strategy is to avoid giving opponents in his own party or outside of it material they can use against him. As the congressman pursues this strategy he may write a legislative record that never becomes very well known to his constituents; if it doesn't win votes, neither will it lose any. This is clearly the situation of most Southern congressmen in dealing with the issue of Negro rights. By voting correctly on this issue they are unlikely to increase their visibility to constituents. Nevertheless, the fact of constituency influence, backed by potential sanctions at the polls, is real enough.

That these potential sanctions are all too real is best illustrated in the election of 1958 by the reprisal against Representative Brooks Hays in Arkansas's Fifth District (Silverman 1962). Although the perception of Congressman Hays as too moderate on civil rights resulted more from his service as intermediary between the White House and Governor Faubus in the Little Rock school crisis than from his record in the House, the victory of Dale Alford as a write-in candidate was a striking reminder of what can happen to a congressman who gives his foes a powerful issue to use against him. The extraordinary involvement of the public in this race can be seen by comparing how well the candidates were known in this constituency with the awareness of the candidates shown by Table 6.2 above for the

Table 6.3

Awareness of congressional candidates
among voters in Arkansas Fifth District, 1958

		Read or heard something about Hays		
		Yes	No	
Read or heard something about Alford	Yes	100	0	100
	No	0	0	0
		100	0	100%

country as a whole. As Table 6.3 indicates, not a single voter in our sample of Arkansas's Fifth District was unaware of either candidate.[13] What is more, these interviews show that Hays was regarded both by his supporters and his opponents as more moderate than Alford on civil rights and that this perception brought his defeat. In some measure, what happened in Little Rock in 1958 can happen anywhere, and our congressmen ought not to be entirely disbelieved in what they say about their impact at the polls. Indeed, they may be under genuine pressure from the voters even while they are the forgotten men of national elections.

CONCLUSION

Therefore, although the conditions of constituency influence are not equally satisfied, they are met well enough to give the local constituency a measure of control over the actions of its representatives. Best satisfied is the requirement about motivational influences on the congressman: Our evidence shows that the representative's roll call behavior is strongly influenced by his own policy preferences and by his perception of preferences held by the constituency. However, the conditions of influence that presuppose effective communication between congressman and district are much less well met. The representative has very imperfect information about the issue preferences of his constituency, and the constituency's awareness of the policy stands of the representative ordinarily is slight.

The findings of this analysis heavily underscore the fact that no single tradition of representation fully accords with the realities of American legislative politics. The American system *is* a mixture, to which the Burkean, instructed-delegate, and responsible party models all can be said to have contributed elements. Moreover, variations in the representative relation are most likely to occur as we move from one policy domain to another. No single, generalized configuration of attitudes and perceptions links representative with constituency but rather several distinct patterns, and which of them is invoked depends very much on the issue involved.

The issue domain in which the relation of congressman to constituency most nearly conforms to the instructed-delegate model is that of civil rights. This conclusion is supported by the importance of the influence path passing through the representative's perception of district opinion, although even in this domain the sense in which the constituency may be said to take the position of the candidate into account in reaching its electoral judgment should be carefully qualified.

The representative relation conforms most closely to the responsible party model in the domain of social welfare. In this issue area, the arena of partisan conflict for a generation, the party symbol helps both constituency and representative in the difficult process of communication between them. On the one hand, because Republican and Democratic voters tend to differ in what they would have government do, the representative has some guide to district opinion simply by looking at the partisan division of the vote. On the other hand, because the two parties tend to recruit candidates who differ on the social welfare role of government, the constituency can infer the candidates' position with more than random accuracy from their party affiliation, even though what the constituency has learned directly about these stands is almost nothing. How faithful the representation of social welfare views is to the responsible party model should not be exaggerated. Even in this policy domain, American practice departs widely from an ideal conception of party government (see Stokes and Miller 1962). But in this domain, more than any other, political conflict has become a conflict of national parties in which constituency and representative are known to each other primarily by their party association.

It would be too pat to say that the domain of foreign involvement conforms to the third model of representation, the conception promoted by Edmund Burke. Clearly it does in the sense that the congressman looks elsewhere than to his district in making up his mind on foreign issues. However, the reliance he puts on the president and the administration suggests that the calculation of where the public interest lies is often passed to the executive on matters of foreign policy. Ironically, legislative initiative in foreign affairs has fallen victim to the very difficulties of gathering and appraising information that led Burke to argue that Parliament rather than the public ought to hold the power of decision. The background information and predictive skills that Burke thought the people lacked are held primarily by the modern executive. As a result, the present role of the legislature in foreign affairs bears some resemblance to the role that Burke had in mind for the elitist, highly restricted *electorate* of his own day.

NOTES

1. To be sure, the work of the Federal Convention has been supplemented in two critical respects. The first of these is the practice, virtually universal since the mid-nineteenth century, of choosing representatives from single-member districts of limited geographic area. The second is the practice, which has also become virtually universal in our own century, of selecting party nominees for the House by direct primary election.

2. In the language of Eulau et al. (1959), we speak here of the "style," not the "focus," of representation. An excellent review of the mandate-independence controversy is given by Hanna Fenichel Pitkin (1961). For other contemporary discussions of representation, see de Grazia (1951) and Fairlie (1940).

3. It will be apparent in the discussion that follows that we have estimated characteristics of whole constituencies from our samples of constituents living in particular districts. In view of the fact that a sample of less than 2,000 constituents has been divided among

116 districts, the reader may wonder about the reliability of these estimates. After considerable investigation we have concluded that their sampling error is not so severe a problem for the analysis as we had thought it would be. Several comments may indicate why it is not.

To begin with, the weighting of out sample of districts has increased the reliability of the constituency estimates. The correct theoretical weight to be assigned each district in the analysis is the inverse of the probability of the district's selection, and it can be shown that this weight is approximately proportional to the number of interviews taken in the district. The result of this is that the greatest weight is assigned the districts with the largest number of interviews and, hence, the most reliable constituency estimates. Indeed, these weights increase by half again the (weighted) mean number of interviews taken per district. To put the matter another way: The introduction of differential weights trades some of our sample of congressional districts for more reliable constituency estimates.

Our investigation of the effect of the sampling variance of the constituency estimates is quite reassuring. When statistics computed from our constituency samples are compared with corresponding parameter values for the constituencies, the agreement of the two sets of figures is quite close. For example, when the proportions voting Democratic in the 116 constituencies in 1958, as computed from our sample data, are compared with the actual proportions voting Democratic, as recorded in official election statistics, a product moment correlation of 0.93 is obtained, and this figure is the more impressive since this test throws away nonvoters, almost one-half of our total sample.

4. The content of the three issue domains may be suggested by some of the roll call and interview items used. In the area of social welfare these included the issues of public housing, public power, aid to education, and government's role in maintaining full employment. In the area of foreign involvement the items included the issues of foreign economic aid, military aid, sending troops abroad, and aid to neutrals. In the area of civil rights the items included the issues of school desegregation, fair employment, and the protection of Negro voting rights.

5. That the representative's roll call votes can diverge from his true opinion is borne out by a number of findings of the study (some of which are reported here) as to the conditions under which agreement between the congressman's roll call position and his private attitude will be high or low. However, a direct confirmation that these two sets of measurements are not simply getting at the same thing is given by differences in attitude-roll call agreement according to the congressman's sense of how well his roll call votes have expressed his real views. In the domain of foreign involvement, for example, the correlation of our attitudinal and roll call measurements was .75 among representatives who said that their roll call votes had expressed their real views fairly well. But this correlation was only .04 among those who said that their roll call votes had expressed their views poorly. In the other policy domains, too, attitude-roll call agreement is higher among congressmen who are well satisfied with their roll call votes than it is among congressmen who are not.

6. A word of caution is in order, lest we compare things that are not strictly comparable. For obvious reasons, most nonincumbent candidates have no roll call record, and we have had to measure their policy agreement with the district entirely in terms of the attitudes they have revealed in interviews. However, the difference of coefficients given here is almost as great when the policy agreement between the incumbent congressman and his district is also measured in terms of the attitudes conveyed in confidential interviews.

7. A third type of connection, excluded here, might obtain between district and congressman if the representative accedes to what he thinks the district wants because he believes that to be what a representative *ought* to do, whether or not it is necessary for reelection. We leave this type of connection out of our account here because we conceive an influence relation as one in which control is not voluntarily accepted or rejected by someone subject to it.

8. It scarcely needs to be said that demonstrating *some* constituency influence would not imply that the representative's behavior is *wholly* determined by constituency pressures. The legislator acts in a complex institutional setting in which he is subject to a wide variety of influences. The constituency can exercise a genuine measure of control without driving all other influences from the representative's life space.

9. We have done this by a variance-component technique similar to several others proposed for dealing with problems of this type. See especially Simon (1954), Blalock (1961), and the almost forgotten work of Wright (1920). Under this technique a "path coefficient" (to use Wright's terminology, although not his theory) is assigned to each of the causal arrows by solving a set of equations involving the correlations of the variables of the model. The weight assigned to a full path is then the product of its several path coefficients, and this product may be interpreted as the proportion of the variance of the dependent variable (roll call behavior, here) that is explained by a given path. . . .

The two limiting models with their associated systems of equations and the formulas for computing the relative importance of the three possible influence paths under each model are given below.

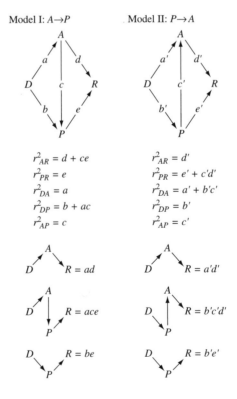

Model I: $A \rightarrow P$

$$r^2_{AR} = d + ce$$
$$r^2_{PR} = e$$
$$r^2_{DA} = a$$
$$r^2_{DP} = b + ac$$
$$r^2_{AP} = c$$

$R = ad$

$R = ace$

$R = be$

Model II: $P \rightarrow A$

$$r^2_{AR} = d'$$
$$r^2_{PR} = e' + c'd'$$
$$r^2_{DA} = a' + b'c'$$
$$r^2_{DP} = b'$$
$$r^2_{AP} = c'$$

$R = a'd'$

$R = b'c'd'$

$R = b'e'$

10. By "least favorable" we mean the assumption that influence goes only from the congressman's attitude to his perception of district attitude (Model I) and not the other way round. Under this assumption, the proportions of the variance of roll call behavior accounted for by the three alternative paths, expressed as proportions of the part of the variance of roll call votes that is explained by district attitude, are these:

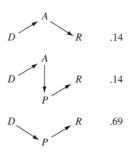

Inverting the assumed direction of influence between the congressman's own attitude and district attitude (Model II) eliminates altogether the effect that the representative's attitude can have had on his votes, independently of his perception of district attitude.

11. Under both Models I and II the proportion of the variance of roll call voting explained by the influence path involving the representative's own attitude is twice as great as the proportion explained by influence passing through his perception of district attitude.

12. What is more, the electorate's awareness of Congress as a whole appears quite limited. A majority of the public was unable to say in 1958 which of the two parties had controlled the Congress during the preceding two years. Some people were confused by the coexistence of a Republican President and a Democratic Congress. But for most people this was simply an elementary fact about congressional affairs to which they were not privy.

13. The sample of this constituency was limited to 23 persons of which 13 voted. However, despite the small number of cases the probability that the difference in awareness between this constituency and the country generally is the result only of sampling variations is much less than one in a thousand.

Chapter 7

U.S. House Members in Their Constituencies: An Exploration

RICHARD F. FENNO, JR.

Despite a voluminous literature on the subject of representative–constituency relationships, one question central to that relationship remains underdeveloped. It is: what does an elected representative see when he or she sees a constituency? And, as a natural follow-up, what consequences do these perceptions have for his or her behavior? The key problem is that of perception. And the key assumption is that the constituency a representative reacts to is the constituency he or she sees. The corollary assumption is that the rest of us cannot understand the representative-constituency relationship until we can see the constituency through the eyes of the representative. These ideas are not new. They were first articulated for students of the United States Congress by Lewis Dexter (1957, 1969). Their importance has been widely acknowledged and frequently repeated ever since. But despite the acceptance and reiteration of Dexter's insights, we still have not developed much coherent knowledge about the perceptions members of Congress have of their constituencies.

A major reason for this neglect is that most of our research on the representative-constituency linkage gets conducted at the wrong end of that linkage. Our interest in the constituency relations of U.S. senators and representatives has typically been a derivative interest, pursued for the light it sheds on some behavior—like roll-call voting—in Washington. When we talk with our national legislators about their constituencies, we typically talk to them *in Washington* and, perforce, in the Washington context. But that is a context far removed from the one in which their constituency relationships are created, nurtured, and changed. And it is a context equally far removed from the one in which we might expect their perceptions of their constituencies to be shaped, sharpened or altered. . . . As a research strategy, therefore, it makes some sense to study our representatives' perceptions of their constituencies while they are actually in their constituencies—at the constituency end of the linkage.

Source: *American Political Science Review* (1977) 71:883–917. Reprinted by permission of the publisher.

Since the fall of 1970, I have been traveling with some members of the House of Representatives while they were in their districts, to see if I could figure out—by looking over their shoulders—what it is they see there. These expeditions, designed to continue through the 1976 elections, have been totally open-ended and exploratory. I have tried to observe and inquire into anything and everything the members do. Rather than assume that I already know what is interesting or what questions to ask, I have been prepared to find interesting questions emerging in the course of the experience. The same with data. The research method has been largely one of soaking and poking—or, just hanging around. This paper, therefore, conveys mostly an impressionistic feel for the subject—as befits the earliest stages of exploration and mapping.

As of June 1976, I had accompanied 14 sitting House members, two House members-to-be and one House member-elect in their districts—for a minimum of two, a maximum of ten, and an average of five days each—sometimes at election time, sometimes not. In 11 cases I have accompanied the member on more than one trip; in six cases I have made only one trip. Since I am a stranger to each local context and to the constellation of people surrounding each member, my confidence in what I see and hear increases markedly when I can make similar observations at more than one point in time. In ten cases I have supplemented my trips to the district with a lengthy interview in Washington. In the district, I reconstruct my record from memory and from brief jottings, as soon after the event as is feasible. In Washington, I take mostly verbatim notes during the interview and commit them to tape immediately thereafter.

I have tried to find a variety of types of members and districts, but I made no pretense at having a group that can be called representative, much less a sample. The 17 include nine Democrats and eight Republicans. Geographically, three come from two Eastern states; six come from five Midwestern states; three come from three Southern states; five come from three far Western states. . . . There is some variation among them in terms of ideology, seniority, ethnicity, race, sex,[1] and in terms of safeness and diversity of district. But no claim is made that the group is ideally balanced in any of these respects.

PERCEPTIONS OF THE CONSTITUENCY

The District: The Geographical Constituency

What then do House members see when they see a constituency? One way they perceive it—the way most helpful to me so far—is as a nest of concentric circles. The largest of these circles represents the congressman's broadest view of his constituency. This is "the district" or "my district." It is the entity to which, from which, and in which he travels. It is the entity whose boundaries have been fixed by state legislative enactment or by court decision. It includes the entire population within those boundaries. Because it is a legal entity, we could refer to it as the legal constituency. It captures more of what the congressman has in mind when he conjures up "my district," however, if we label it the *geographical constituency*. We retain the idea that the district is a legally bounded space and emphasize that it is located in a particular place. . . .

[W]hen you ask a congressman, "What kind of district do you have?", the answer often begins with, and always includes, a geographical, space-and-place, perception. Thus, the district is seen as "the largest in the state, 28 counties in the southeastern corner" or "three layers of suburbs to the west of the city, a square with the northwest corner cut out." If the boundaries have been changed by a recent redistricting, the geography of "the new district" will be compared to that of "the old district."

If one essential aspect of "the geographical constituency" is seen as its location and boundaries, another is its particular internal makeup. And House members describe their districts' internal makeup using political science's most familiar demographic and political variables—socioeconomic structure, ideology, ethnicity, residential patterns, religion, partisanship, stability, diversity, etc. Every congressman, in his mind's eye, sees his geographical constituency in terms of some special configuration of such variables. For example,

> Geographically, it covers the northern one-third of the state, from the border of (state X) to the border of (state Y), along the Z river—22 counties. The basic industry is agriculture—but it's a diverse district. The city makes up one-third of the population. It is dominated by the state government and education. It's an independent-minded constituency, with a strong attachment to the work ethic. A good percentage is composed of people whose families emigrated from Germany, Scandinavia and Czechoslovakia. I don't exactly know the figures, but over one-half the district is German. And this goes back to the work ethic. They are a hardworking, independent people. They have a strong thought of "keeping the government off my back, we'll do all right here." That's especially true of my out-counties.

Some internal configurations are more complex than others. But, even at the broadest level, no congressman sees, within his district's boundaries, an undifferentiated glob (Matthews and Stimson 1975, 28–31). And we cannot talk about his relations with his "constituency" as if he did. . . .

. . . [M]embers of Congress do think in terms of the homogeneity or heterogeneity of their districts—though they may not always use the words.

> It's geographically compact. It's all suburban—no big city in the accepted sense of the word and no rural area. It's all white. There are very few blacks, maybe 2%. Spanish surnamed make up about 10%. Traditionally, it's been a district with a high percentage of home ownership. . . . Economically, it's above the national average in employment . . . It's not that it's very high income. Oh, I suppose there are a few places of some wealth, but nothing very wealthy. And no great pockets of poverty either. And it's not dominated by any one industry. The X County segment has a lot of small, clean, technical industries. I consider it very homogeneous. By almost any standard, it's homogeneous. . . .

Because it is a summary variable, the perceived homogeneity-heterogeneity characteristic is particularly hard to measure; and no metric is proposed here. Intuitively, both the number and the compatibility of significant interests within the district would seem to be involved. The greater the number of significant interests—as opposed to one dominant interest—the more likely it is that the district will be seen as heterogeneous. But if the several significant interests were viewed as having a single lowest common denominator and, therefore, quite compatible, the district might still be viewed as homogeneous. One indicator, therefore, might be the ease with which the congressman finds a lowest common denominator of interests for some large proportion of his geographical constituency.[2] . . . All we can say is that the less actual or potential conflict he sees among district interests, the more likely he is to see his district as homogeneous. Another indicator might be the extent to which the geographical constituency is congruent with a natural community. Districts that are purely artificial (sometimes purely political) creations of districting practices, and which pay no attention to preexisting communities of interest are more likely to be heterogeneous (see Stokes and Miller 1962). Preexisting communities or natural communities are more likely to have such homogenizing ties as common sources of communication, common organizations, and common traditions.

The Supporters: The Reelection Constituency

Within his geographical constituency, each congressman perceives a smaller, explicitly political constituency. It is composed of the people he thinks vote for him. And we shall refer to it as his *reelection constituency.* As he moves about the district, a House member continually draws the distinction between those who vote for him and those who do not. "I do well here"; "I run poorly here." "This group supports me"; "this group does not." By distinguishing supporters from non-supporters, he articulates his baseline political perception.

House members seem to use two starting points—one cross-sectional and the other longitudinal—in shaping this perception. First, by a process of inclusion and exclusion, they come to a rough approximation of the upper and lower ranges of the reelection constituency. That is to say, there are some votes a member believes he almost always gets; there are other votes he believes he almost never gets. One of the core elements of any such distinction is the perceived partisan component of the vote—party identification as revealed in registration or poll figures and party voting. "My district registers only 37% Republican. They have no place else to go. My problem is, how can I get enough Democratic votes to win the general election." Another element is the political tendencies of various demographic groupings.

> My supporters are Democrats, farmers, labor—a DFL operation—with some academic types. . . . My opposition tends to be the main street hardware dealer. I look at that kind of guy in a stable town, where the newspaper runs the community—the typical school board member in the rural part of the district—that's the kind of guy I'll never get. At the opposite end of the scale is the country club set. I'll sure as hell never get them, either.

Starting with people he sees, very generally, as his supporters, and leaving aside people he sees, equally generally, as his nonsupporters, each congressman fashions a view of the people who give him his victories at the polls.

The second starting point for thinking about the reelection constituency is the congressman's idea of who voted for him "last time." Starting with that perception, he adds or subtracts incrementally on the basis of changes that will have taken place (or could be made by him to take place) between "last time" and "next time." It helps him to think about his reelection constituency this way because that is about the only certainty he operates with—he won last time. And the process by which his desire for reelection gets translated into his perception of a reelection constituency is filled with uncertainty. At least that is my strong impression. House members see reelection uncertainty where political scientists would fail to unearth a single objective indicator of it. . . .

Of all the many sources of uncertainty, the most constant—and usually the greatest—involves the electoral challenger. For it is the challenger who holds the most potential for altering any calculation involving those who voted for the congressman "last time." "This time's" challenger may have very different sources of political strength from "last time's" challenger. Often, one of the major off-year uncertainties is whether or not the last challenger will try again. While it is true that House members campaign all the time, "the campaign" can be said to start only when the challenger is known. At that point, a redefinition of the reelection constituency may have to take place. If the challenger is chosen by primary, for example, the congressman may inherit support from the loser (Johnson and Gibson 1974). . . . The shaping of perceptions proceeds under conditions of considerable uncertainty.

The Strongest Supporters: The Primary Constituency

In thinking about their political condition, House members make distinctions within their reelection constituency—thus giving us a third, still smaller concentric circle. Having distinguished between their nonsupporters and their supporters, they further distinguish between their routine or temporary supporters and their very strongest supporters. Routine supporters only vote for them, often merely following party identification; but others will support them with a special degree of intensity. Temporary supporters back them as the best available alternative; but others will support them regardless of who the challenger may be. Within each reelection constituency are nested these "others"—a constituency perceived as "my strongest supporters," "my hard core support," "my loyalists," my true believers," "my political base." We shall think of these people as the ones each congressman believes would provide his best line of electoral defense in a primary contest, and label them *the primary constituency* (Snowiss 1966). It will probably include the earliest of his supporters—those who recruited him and those who tendered identifiably strong support in his first campaign—thus, providing another reason for calculating on the basis of "last time." From its ranks will most likely come the bulk of his financial help and his volunteer workers. From its ranks will least likely come an electoral challenger.

A protected congressional seat is as much one protected from primary defeat as from general election defeat. And a primary constituency is something every congressman must have.

> Everybody needs some group which is strongly for him—especially in a primary. You can win a primary with 25,000 zealots. . . . The most exquisite case I can give you was in the very early war years. I had very strong support from the anti-war people. They were my strongest supporters and they made up about 5% of the district.

The primary constituency, I would guess, draws a special measure of a congressman's interest; and it should, therefore, draw a special measure of ours. But it is not easy to delineate—for us or for them. Asked to describe his "very strongest supporters," one member replied, "That's the hardest question anyone has to answer." The primary constituency is more subtly shaded than the reelection constituency, where voting provides an objective membership test. Loyalty is not the most predictable of political qualities. . . . Despite some difficulty, most members—because it is politically prudent to do so—make some such distinction, in speech or in action or both. By talking to them and watching them, we can begin to understand what those distinctions are.

Here are two answers to the question, "who are your very strongest supporters?"

> My strongest supporters are the working class—the blacks and labor, organized labor. And the people who were in my state legislative district, of course. The fifth ward is low-income, working class and is my base of support. I grew up there; I have my law office there; and I still live there. The white businessmen who are supporting me now are late converts—very late. They support me as the least of two evils. They are not a strong base of support. They know it and I know it.
>
> I have a circle of strong labor supporters and another circle of strong business supporters. . . . They will "fight, bleed and die" for me, but in different ways. Labor gives you the manpower and the workers up front. You need them just as much as you need the guy with the two-acre yard to hold a lawn party to raise money. The labor guy loses a day's pay on election day. The business guy gets his nice lawn tramped over and chewed up. Each makes a commitment to you in his own way. You need them both.

Each description reveals the working politicians' penchant for inclusive thinking. Each tells you something about a primary constituency, but each leaves plenty of room for added refinements.

. . . Like other observers of American politics, I have found this idea of "at homeness" a useful one in helping me to map the relationship between politicians and constituents (Frady 1969; White 1961, 1973)—in this case the perception of a primary constituency. House members sometimes talk in this language about the groups they encounter.

> I was born on the flat plains, and I feel a lot better in the plains area than in the mountain country. I don't know why it is. As much as I like Al [whom we had just lunched with in a mountain town], I'm still not comfortable with him. I'm no cowboy. But when I'm out there on that flat land with those ranchers and wheat farmers, standing around trading insults and jibes and telling stories, I feel better. That's the place where I click.

It is also the place where he wins elections—his primary constituency. "That's my strong area. I won by a big margin and offset my losses. If I win next time, that's where I'll win it—on the plains." Obviously, there is no one-to-one relationship between the groups with whom a congressman acts and feels most at home and his primary constituency. But it does provide a pretty good unobtrusive clue.[3] So I found myself fashioning a highly subjective "at homeness index" to rank the degree to which each congressman seems to have support from and rapport with each group. . . .

The Intimates: The Personal Constituency

Within the primary constituency, each member perceives still a fourth, and final, concentric circle. These are the few individuals whose relationship with him is so personal and so intimate that their relevance to him cannot be captured by their inclusion in any description of "very strongest supporters." In some cases they are his closest political advisers and confidants. In other cases, they are people from whom he draws emotional sustenance for his political work. We shall think of these people as his *personal constituency.*

One Sunday afternoon, I sat in the living room of a congressman's chief district staff assistant watching an NFL football game—with the congressman, the district aide, the state assemblyman from the congressman's home county, and the district attorney of the same county. Between plays, at halftime and over beer and cheese, the four friends discussed every aspect of the congressman's campaign, listened to and commented on his taped radio spots, analyzed several newspaper reports, discussed local and national personalities, relived old political campaigns and hijinks, discussed their respective political ambitions. Ostensibly they were watching the football game; actually the congressman was exchanging political advice, information, and perspectives with three of his six or seven oldest and closest political associates.

. . . The personal constituency is, doubtless, the most idiosyncratic of the several constituencies. Not all members will open it up to the outside observer. Nine of the 17 did, however; and in doing so, [they] usually revealed a side of [their] personality not seen by the rest of [their] constituencies. "I'm really very reserved, and I don't feel at home with most groups—only with five or six friends," said [one of] the congressmen after the football game. The relationship probably has both political and emotional dimensions. . . .

In sum, my impression is that House members perceive four constituencies—geographical, reelection, primary, and personal—each one nesting within the previous one.

POLITICAL SUPPORT AND HOME STYLE

What, then, do these perceptions have to do with a House member's behavior? Our conventional paraphrase of this question would read: What do these perceptions have to do with behavior at the other end of the line—in Washington? But the concern that disciplines the perceptions we have been talking about is neither first nor foremost a Washington-oriented concern. It is a concern for political support at home. It is a concern for the scope of that support—which decreases as one moves from the geographical to the personal constituency. It is a concern for the stability of that support—which increases as one moves from the geographical to the personal constituency. And it ultimately issues in a concern for manipulating scopes and intensities in order to win and hold a sufficient amount of support to win elections. Representatives, and prospective representatives, think about their constituencies because they seek support there. They want to get nominated and elected, then renominated and reelected. For most members of Congress most of the time, this electoral goal is primary. It is the prerequisite for a congressional career and, hence, for the pursuit of other goals. And the electoral goal is achieved—first and last—not in Washington but at home. . . .

Our Washington-centered research has caused us systematically to underestimate the proportion of their working time House members spend in their districts. As a result, we have also underestimated its perceived importance to them. . . . A survey conducted in 419 House offices covering 1973 indicates that the average number of trips home (not counting recesses) was 35 and the number of days spent in the district during 1973 (counting recesses) was 138.[4] No fewer than 131, nearly one-third, of the 419 members went home to their districts *every single weekend*. Obviously the direct personal cultivation of their various constituencies takes a great deal of their time; and they must think it is worth it in terms of winning and holding political support. If it is worth *their* time to go home so much, it is worth *our* time to take a commensurate degree of interest in what they do there and why.

As they cultivate their constituencies, House members display what I shall call their *home style*. When they discuss the importance of what they are doing, they are discussing the importance of *home style* to achievement of their electoral goal. At this stage of the research, the surest generalization one can make about home style is that there are as many varieties as there are members of Congress. "Each of us has his own formula—a truth that is true for him," said one. It will take a good deal more immersion and cogitation before I can improve upon that summary comment. At this point, however, three ingredients of home style appear to be worth looking at. They are: first, the congressman's allocation of his personal resources and those of his office; second, the congressman's presentation of self; and third, the congressman's explanation of his Washington activity. Every congressman allocates, presents, and explains. The amalgam of these three activities for any given representative constitutes (for now, at least) his home style. His home style, we expect, will be affected by his perception of his four constituencies.

HOME STYLE: ALLOCATION OF RESOURCES

Every representative must make a basic decision with regard to his home style: "How much and what kinds of attention shall I pay to home?" Or to put it another way: "Of all the resources available with which to help me do my job, which kinds and how much of each do I want to allocate directly to activity in the district?" There are, of course, many ways to allocate one's resources so that they affect the district. Our concern is with *resources allocated directly to the district*. Of these, we propose to look first, at the congressman's *time* and second, at the congressman's *staff*. The congressman's decision about how much time he should spend physically at home and his decision about how much of his staff he should place physically in the district are decisions which give shape to his home style.

Of all the resources available to the House member, the scarcest and most precious one, which dwarfs all others in posing critical allocative dilemmas, is his time. Time is at once what the member has least of and what he has the most control over. When a congressman divides up his time, he decides by that act what kind of congressman he wants to be. He must divide his time in Washington. He must divide his time at home. The decision we are concerned with here is the division of his time between Washington and home. When he is doing something at home, he must give up doing some things in Washington, and vice versa. So he chooses and he trades off; and congressmen make different allocative choices and different allocative trades. In this section, we shall focus on the frequency with which various congressmen returned to their districts in 1973. . . . The most important of . . . choices [of how to allocate resources] are choices about how to use his staff. And among the key choices about staff is how to allocate them between Washington and the district. . . .

For 1973, it should be noted, each member was allowed a maximum of 16 staff members and a maximum payroll of $203,000. And for the two-year period 1973–74 (the Ninety-third Congress) each member was reimbursed for 36 round trips to his district. Members were not, of course, required to use any of these allowances to the maximum. . . .

[A] House member's decision on how to allocate his time between home and Washington is affected: (1) by his seniority, if it is very low or very high [Table 7.1]; (2) by the distance from Washington to home, if that distance is very long or very short [Table 7.2]; and (3) by the place where his family is located, whether his family moves to Washington or remains in the district [Table 7.3]. A congressman's electoral margin, objectively measured, has little effect on his time allocations [Table 7.4]. How, if at all, these factors are interrelated, and how strongly each factor contributes to the allocative pattern are matters for later analysis.

Members of Congress also decide what kind of staff presence they wish to establish in the district. Here, too, we find great variation. On the percentage of total staff expenditure allocated to district staff, the range, in 1973, went from 0% to 81%. We might think that a member who decides to give a special degree of personal attention to "home" would also decide to give a special degree of staff attentiveness to "home." But the relationship between the two allocative decisions does not appear to be strong. Using percentage of total staff expenditure on district staff (as we shall throughout this section) as the measure of dis-

Table 7.1
Trips home and seniority

| Seniority | Frequency of trips home | | | |
	Low (0–23)	Medium (24–42)	High (43+)	Total
Low (1–3 terms)	34 (22%)	44 (28%)	78 (50%)	156 (100%)
Medium (4–7 terms)	43 (28%)	59 (38%)	52 (34%)	154 (100%)
High (8+ terms)	52 (48%)	26 (24%)	31 (28%)	189 (100%)
	129	129	161	419
Mean seniority	7.0 terms	5.0 terms	4.7 terms	

Note: Gamma = −.30

Table 7.2
Trips home and region

| Region | Frequency of trips home | | | Total |
	Low (0–23)	Medium (24–42)	High (43+)	
East	5 (5%)	20 (20%)	76 (75%)	101 (100%)
South	36 (35%)	32 (30%)	36 (35%)	104 (100%)
Border	9 (26%)	10 (29%)	16 (45%)	35 (100%)
Midwest	29 (28%)	47 (44%)	30 (28%)	106 (100%)
Far West	50 (69%)	20 (27%)	3 (4%)	73 (100%)
	129	129	161	419

Regions:

East: Connecticut, Maine, Massachusetts, New Hampshire, New Jersey, New York, Pennsylvania, Rhode Island, Vermont

South: Alabama, Arkansas, Florida, Georgia, Louisiana, Mississippi, North Carolina, South Carolina, Tennessee, Texas, Virginia

Border: Delaware, Kentucky, Maryland, Missouri, Oklahoma, West Virginia

Midwest: Illinois, Indiana, Iowa, Kansas, Michigan, Minnesota, Nebraska, North Dakota, Ohio, South Dakota, Wisconsin

Far West: Alaska, Arizona, California, Colorado, Hawaii, Idaho, Montana, Nevada, New Mexico, Oregon, Utah, Washington, Wyoming

Table 7.3
Trips home and family residence

| Family residence | Frequency of trips home | | | Total |
	Low (0–23)	Medium (24–42)	High (43+)	
Washington area	87 (41%)	89 (42%)	37 (17%)	213 (100%)
District	3 (4%)	6 (8%)	69 (88%)	78 (100%)
Unmarried	5 (14%)	12 (32%)	20 (54%)	37 (100%)
	95	107	126	328

Table 7.4
Trips home and electoral margin

| Election margin (1972) | Frequency of trips home (1973) | | | Total |
	Low (0–23)	Medium (24–42)	High (43+)	
Less than 55%	21 (29%)	28 (38%)	24 (33%)	73 (100%)
55–60%	18 (32%)	18 (32%)	20 (36%)	56 (100%)
61–65%	22 (27%)	17 (20%)	44 (53%)	83 (100%)
More than 65%	68 (33%)	66 (32%)	73 (35%)	207 (100%)
	129	129	161	419

Note: Gamma = −0.3

trict staff strength, we find a very weak correlation (Pearson's r = .20) between a congressman's decision on that matter and the number of trips he takes home. Table 7.5 clusters and cross-tabulates the two allocative decisions. For our measure of district staff strength we have divided the percentage of expenditures on district staff into thirds. The lowest third ranges from 0 to 22.7%; the middle third ranges from 22.8 to 33.5%; the highest third ranges from 33.6 to 81%. The cross-tabulation also shows a pretty weak overall relationship. For now, therefore, we shall treat the two decisions as if they were made independently of one another and, hence, are deserving of separate examination.

What kinds of members, then, emphasize the value of a large district staff operation? Once again, it turns out, they are not members in special electoral trouble. Table 7.6 displays the total lack of any discernible impact of electoral situation (objectively measured) on district staff strength. Nor, as indicated in Table 7.7, does seniority make any difference in staff allocative decisions. That it does not adds strength to the idea that the relationship between seniority and home visits discovered earlier is accounted for—as we have suggested—by career-and-goal factors rather than by electoral factors.

The other variables discussed earlier—family residence and distance—do not have the obvious implications for staff allocation that they have for the member's own time dilemmas. It might be that if his family is in the district, and if he plans to be home a lot, a congressman might decide to have a big district staff operation to

Table 7.5
Trips home and district staff expenditures

District staff expenditures	Frequency of trips home			
	Low (0–23)	Medium (24–42)	High (43+)	Total
Lowest 1/3	53 (39%)	42 (31%)	40 (30%)	135 (100%)
Middle 1/3	42 (30%)	55 (40%)	41 (30%)	138 (100%)
Highest 1/3	31 (23%)	32 (23%)	75 (54%)	138 (100%)
	126	129	156	411

Note: Gamma = −.28

Table 7.6
District staff expenditures and electoral margin

Electoral margin 1972	District staff expenditures (1973)			
	Lowest 1/3	Middle 1/3	Highest 1/3	Total
Less than 55%	20 (27%)	28 (38%)	26 (35%)	74 (100%)
55–60%	20 (36%)	20 (36%)	16 (28%)	56 (100%)
61–65%	24 (29%)	29 (35%)	29 (35%)	82 (100%)
More than 65%	72 (36%)	61 (30%)	68 (34%)	201 (100%)
	136	138	139	413

Note: Gamma = −0.4

Table 7.7

District staff expenditures and seniority

Seniority	District staff expenditures			Total
	Lowest 1/3	Middle 1/3	Highest 1/3	
Low (1–3 terms)	44 (29%)	54 (35%)	56 (36%)	155 (100%)
Medium (4–7 terms)	44 (29%)	56 (37%)	51 (34%)	151 (100%)
High (8+ terms)	47 (44%)	28 (26%)	32 (30%)	107 (100%)
	136	138	139	413

Note: Gamma = −.13

Table 7.8

District staff expenditures and family residence

Family residence	District staff expenditures			Total
	Lowest 1/3	Middle 1/3	Highest 1/3	
Washington area	85 (40%)	77 (37%)	48 (23%)	210 (100%)
District	21 (28%)	17 (23%)	37 (49%)	75 (100%)
Unmarried	8 (22%)	10 (28%)	18 (50%)	36 (100%)
	114	104	103	321

work with him there. That supposition receives some support in Table 7.8. Another possibility is that members might decide to use a strong district staff to compensate for their lack of personal attention via trips home. However, this idea is not supported in Table 7.8, nor in Table 7.9, which seeks to uncover regional and distance patternings of district staffs. Representatives who live nearest to Washington (East) and who tend to go home the most do tend to have large district staffs. But representatives who live farthest away and tend to go home the least show only a slight tendency to compensate by allocating heavy expenditures to their district staffs.

Table 7.9, however, does reveal some regional allocation patterns that did not appear when we looked for regional patterns in home visits. Region, it appears, captures a good deal more than distance, particularly in relation to staff allocations. The Southern and border regions emerge with distinctive patternings here. To a marked degree, House members from these two areas eschew large staff operations in their districts. Scanning our two regional tabulations (Table 7.8 and 7.9), we note that every region save the Midwest reveals a noteworthy pattern of resource allocation. In the East we find high frequency of home visits and large district staffs; in the Far West, we find a low frequency of home visits; in the Southern and border regions, we find small district staffs. Again, the two types of allocative decisions appear to be quite distinct and independent. Region, we tentatively conclude, has a substantial affect on home style.

. . . Home style is, then, partly a matter of place—i.e., it is affected by the nature of the congressman's geographical constituency. That constituency is, after all, the closest thing to a "given" in his nest of perceptions. But home style is also partly a matter of individual choice. And in this respect, it can be affected by his

Table 7.9
District staff expenditures and region

Region	District staff expenditures			
	Lowest 1/3	Medium 1/3	Highest 1/3	Total
East	16 (16%)	31 (31%)	52 (53%)	99 (100%)
South	47 (46%)	36 (35%)	19 (19%)	102 (100%)
Border	18 (55%)	8 (24%)	7 (21%)	33 (100%)
Midwest	39 (37%)	34 (32%)	33 (31%)	106 (100%)
Far West	16 (22%)	29 (40%)	28 (38%)	73 (100%)
	136	138	139	413

Regions:

East: Connecticut, Maine, Massachusetts, New Hampshire, New Jersey, New York, Pennsylvania, Rhode Island, Vermont

South: Alabama, Arkansas, Florida, Georgia, Louisiana, Mississippi, North Carolina, South Carolina, Tennessee, Texas, Virginia

Border: Delaware, Kentucky, Maryland, Missouri, Oklahoma, West Virginia

Midwest: Illinois, Indiana, Iowa, Kansas, Michigan, Minnesota, Nebraska, North Dakota, Ohio, South Dakota, Wisconsin

Far West: Alaska, Arizona, California, Colorado, Hawaii, Idaho, Montana, Nevada, New Mexico, Oregon, Utah, Washington, Wyoming

perception of his other three constituencies. That, indeed, is what we expect to find as we move to discuss the other elements of home style.

HOME STYLE: PRESENTATION OF SELF

Most House members spend a substantial proportion of their working time "at home." Even those we placed in the "low frequency" category return to their districts more often than we would have guessed—over half of them go home more than once (but less than twice) a month.[5] What, then, do they do there? Much of what they do is captured by Erving Goffman's idea of *the presentation of self* (1959). That is, they place themselves in "the immediate physical presence" of others and then "make a presentation of themselves to others.". . .

In all such encounters, says Goffman, the performer will seek to control the response of others to him by expressing himself in ways that leave the correct impressions of himself with others. His expressions will be of two sorts—"the expression that he gives and the expression that he gives off." The first is mostly verbal; the second is mostly nonverbal. Goffman is particularly interested in the second kind of expression—"the more theatrical and contextual kind"—because he believes that the performer is more likely to be judged by others according to the nonverbal than the verbal elements of his presentation of self. Those who must do the judging, Goffman says, will think that the verbal expressions are more controllable and manipulable by the performer; and they will, therefore, read his nonverbal "signs" as a check on the reliability of his verbal "signs." . . .

Goffman does not talk about politicians; but politicians know what Goffman is talking about. Goffman's dramaturgical analogues are appropriate to politics because politicians, like actors, perform before audiences and are legitimized by their audiences. The response politicians seek from others is *political support.* And the impressions they try to foster are those that will engender political support. House member politicians believe that a great deal of their support is won by the kind of individual self they present to others, i.e., to their constituents. More than most people, they believe that they can manipulate their "presentation of self." . . . In the member's own language, constituents want to judge you "as a person." The comment I have heard most often from the constituents of my representatives is: "He's a good man," or "She's a good woman," unembossed by qualifiers of any sort. Constituents, say House members, want to "size you up" or "get the feel of you" "as a person," or "as a human being." And the largest part of what members mean when they say "as a person" is what Goffman means by "expressions given off."

So members of Congress go home to present themselves "as a person". . . . The representative's word for these supportive inferences is *trust.* It is a word they use a great deal. If a constituent trusts a House member, the constituent says something like: "I am willing to put myself in your hands temporarily; I know you will have opportunities to hurt me—though I may not know when those opportunities occur; I assume that you will not hurt me and I'm not going to worry about your doing so until it is proven beyond any doubt that you have betrayed that trust." The ultimate response members of Congress seek is political support; but the instrumental response they seek is trust. The presentation of self—what is "given" in words and "given off" as a person—will be calculated to win trust. "If people like you and trust you as an individual," members often say, "they will vote for you." So trust becomes central to the congressman-constituent relationship. . . .

Trust is, however, a fragile relationship. It is not an overnight or a one-time thing. It is hard to win; and it must be constantly renewed and rewon. So it takes an enormous amount of time to build and maintain constituent trust. That is what House members believe. That is why they spend so much of their working time at home. Much of what I have observed in my travels can be explained as a continuous and continuing effort to win (for new members) and to maintain (for old members) the trust of their various constituencies. Most of the communication I have heard and seen is not overtly political at all. It is, rather, part of a ceaseless effort to reinforce the underpinnings of trust in the congressman or congresswoman "as a person." Viewed from this perspective, the archetypical constituent question is not "what have you done for me lately" but "how have you looked to me lately." House members, then, make a strategic calculation that helps us understand why they go home so much. Presentation of self enhances trust; enhancing trust takes time; therefore, presentation of self takes time.

Of the "contextual," "expressions given off" in the effort to win and hold constituent trust, three seem particularly ubiquitous. First, the congressman conveys to his constituents a sense of his *qualification.* Contextually and verbally, he gives them the impression that "I am qualified to hold the office of United States Representative." "I understand the job and I have the experience necessary to do a good job." "I can hold my own—or better—in any competition inside the

House." All members try to convey their qualifications. But it is particularly crucial that any nonincumbent convey this sense of being "qualified." For him, it is the threshold impression—without which he will not be taken seriously as a candidate for Congress. Qualification will not ensure trust, but it is at least a precondition.

Second, the congressman conveys a sense of *identification* with his constituents. Contextually and verbally he gives them the impression that "I am one of you." "I think the way you do and I care about the same things you do." "You can trust me because we are like one another." The third is a sense of *empathy* conveyed by the congressman to his constituents. Contextually and verbally, he gives them the impression that "I understand your situation and I care about it." "I can put myself in your shoes." "You can trust me because—although I am not one of you—I understand you." Qualification, identification, and empathy are all helpful in the building of constituent trust. To a large degree, these three impressions are conveyed by the very fact of regular personal contact at home. . . . Thus do decisions about the allocation of resources affect the frequency of and opportunity for the presentation of self.

Once he is home, what kind of a presentation does he make there? How does he decide what presentation to make? How does he allocate his time among his perceived constituencies? How does he present himself to these various constituencies? What proportion of competence, identification, or empathy (or other expressions) does he "give off"? In short, what kinds of home styles are presented; and how do they differ among House members? I shall work toward an answer to these questions by discussing the styles of two representatives.

Presentation of Self: A Person-to-Person Style

While it is probably true that the range of appropriate home styles in any given district is large, it is also probably true that in many geographical constituencies there are distinct limits to that range. Congressman A believes there is a good "fit" between his kind of district and his kind of home style. He thinks of his geographical constituency as a collection of counties in a particular section of his state—as Southern, rural, and conservative. And he believes that certain presentations of self would not be acceptable there. "I remember once," he told a small group at dinner before a college lecture,

> when I was sitting in the House gallery with a constituent listening to Congressman Dan Flood speak on the floor. Dan is a liberal from Wilkes Barre, Pennsylvania. He is a former Shakespearean actor and his wife is a former opera singer. Dan was wearing a purple shirt and a white suit; and he was sporting his little waxed moustache. My constituent turned to me and asked, "what chance do you think a man like that would have of getting elected in our district?" And I said, "Exactly the same chance as I would have of getting elected in Wilkes Barre, Pennsylvania."

The expressions "given off" by a former actor with a purple shirt, a white suit, and a waxed moustache would be suicidal in Congressman A's district.

. . . Congressman A sees his geographical constituency as a homogeneous, natural community. And he thinks of himself as totally at one with that community— a microcosm of it. Three generations of his family have lived there and served as its leaders and officeholders. He himself held two elective offices within the district before running for Congress. He has been steeped in the area he represents.

> I should write a book about this district—starting with the Indians. It's a very historic district and a very cohesive district—except for Omega County. Nobody knows it like I do.
>
> One thing that ties the district together is the dominance of the textile industry and the dependence of the people of the district—employer and employee—on the textile industry. . . . If I were hostile to the textile industry, it would be fatal. But that could never happen because I feel so close to the textile industry.
>
> I represent a district in which my constituents and I have total mutual confidence, respect and trust—95%, nearly 100%.

Congressman A feels a deep sense of identification with his constituents. It is this sense of identification that he conveys—verbally and nonverbally—when he presents himself to them.

"In my state," he says, "only a person-to-person campaign will work." So, when he goes home, he "beats the bushes," and "ploughs the ground," in search of face-to-face contact with the people of his district. . . . In each encounter, he reaches (if the other person does not provide it) for some link between himself and the person he is talking with—and between that person and some other person. There is no conversation that does not involve an elaboration of an interpersonal web and of the ties that bind its members one to the other. In the forefront, always, are ties of family: Congressman A possesses an encyclopedic memory for the names and faces, dates and places of family relations. . . . He continually files, sorts, arranges and rearranges his catalogues of linkages—person-to-person, place to place, event to event, time to time. . . .

The expression he tries to give off in all his person to person dealings is that he knows them, that they know him "as a person," that they are all part of the same community, and that his constituents, therefore, have every reason to make favorable inferences about him. "They know me," he says, "and they trust me."

. . . When asked to describe "his very strongest supporters," he explained: "My strongest supporters are the people who know me and whom I have known and with whom I have communicated over the years. . . in my oldest counties, that means 30–40 years." He does not perceive his primary constituency in demographic terms but in terms of personal contacts. In a district seen as homogeneous there are few benchmarks for differentiation. . . . His primary constituency, as may be the case in homogeneous districts, is quite amorphous—as demographically amorphous as V. O. Key's classic "friends and neighbors" victory pattern (1949). But it is sizeable enough and intense enough to have protected Congressman A, for a considerable number of terms, from any serious primary challenge.

Congressman A does not come home a lot, falling into our low-frequency category (0–23) of trips home. He spent 80 working days there in 1973. When he does, he spends most of his time where it is strategically profitable (and personally comfortable)—with his primary constituency. There, he reinforces his ties to the group of greatest importance to him in his traditionally one-party district.

. . . He has a small district staff—three people, one full-time office, and one half-time office—and when he is home, he is as apt to pick up someone's personal problems and jot them down on the back of an envelope as he tours around as he is to find out about these problems from his district aides. Congressman A, at home, is a virtual one-man band. His home style is one of the hardest to delegate to others; and he has no inclination to do so.

He allocates relatively little of his time to his larger reelection constituency. Omega County, singled out earlier as out of the district's mold, is not rural, is populated heavily by out-of-staters, and has experienced rapid population growth. Congressman A admits he does not feel "at home" there. Yet he still gets a sizeable percentage of Omega County's votes—on grounds of party identification. He explained why he didn't spend time among these reelection constituents.

> It is so heterogeneous, disorganized, and full of factions. . . . I don't spend very much time there. Some of my good friends criticize me and say I neglect it unduly. And they have a point. But I can get 50% of the vote without campaigning there at all; and I couldn't get more than 75% if I campaigned there all the time. If I did that, I would probably lose more votes than I gained, because I would become identified with one of the factions, and half the people would hate me. On top of that, I would lose a lot of my support elsewhere in the district by neglecting it. It's just not worth it.

There is another reason besides time costs and political benefits. It is that Congressman A's home style is totally inappropriate for Omega County, and he avoids the personal unpleasantness that would be involved in trying to campaign there. Strategically, Congressman A will accept any increment of support he can get beyond his primary constituency. ("The black people who know me know that I will help them with their problems.") But he allocates very little of his time to the effort.

Congressman A's presentation of self places very little emphasis on articulating issues. . . . [H]e was clearly least "at home" at a college, in a lecture-plus-question-and-answer format. He accepts invitations of this sort to discuss issues. But he does nothing to generate such engagements; nor does he go out of his way to raise issues in his dealings with others at home. On the single occasion when he broke this pattern, he tested out his potentially controversial position with his primary constituents (i.e., the American Legion post in his home town), found it to be acceptable, and articulated it often thereafter. Congressman A's home style does, however, take place *within an issue context*. There is widespread agreement in the district, and very strong agreement within his primary constituency, on the major issues of race, foreign aid, government spending and social conservatism. The district voted for George Wallace in 1968. Thus while Congressman A's home style is apparently issueless, it may depend for its very success on an underlying issue consensus.

There are, therefore, strategic reasons as well as personal reasons for Congressman A not to focus heavily on specific issues. To do so would be unnecessary and potentially divisive. Congressman A is protective of his existing constituency relations and will not want to risk alienating any of his support by introducing or escalating controversy of any kind. He is a stabilizer, a maintainer. . . . If he gets into electoral difficulty, Congressman A will resort not to a discussion of "the issues," but to an increased reliance on his person-to-person home style. And, so long as his strategic perceptions are accurate, he will remain a congressman.

Presentation of Self: An Issue-Oriented Style

If Congressman B's geographical constituency places any constraints on an appropriate home style, he is not very aware of them. He sees his district as heterogeneous.

> It is three worlds: three very different worlds. . . . It has a city—which is an urban disaster. It has suburbs—the fastest growing part of the district. . . . It has a rural area which is a place unto itself.
> We spent all afternoon talking to the Teamsters in the city; and then we went to a cocktail party in a wealthy suburb. That's the kind of culture shock I get all the time in this district—bam! bam! bam!

The "three worlds" are not just different. They are also socially and psychologically separated from one another.

> Actually the people in the three worlds don't know the others are even in the district. They are three separate worlds. In the city, they call it the city district; in the rural area, they call it their district. And both of them are shocked when they are told that they each make up only one-quarter of the district.

The other half are the suburbs—which are themselves very disparate. A few suburbs are linked to the city; most are not. Some are blue collar; others are affluent. Some are WASP; others are ethnic. The district is, then, perceived not only as diverse and artificial, but as segmented as well. The possibilities for an acceptable presentation of self would seem to be limitless.

Congressman B's past associations in the district do not incline him toward a style peculiar to any one of "the three worlds." His district ties are not deep; he is a young man who went to college, worked and got his political feet wet outside his district and his state. Nor are the ties strong: He grew up in a suburb in which he probably feels less "at home" ("We lost that stupid, friggin' town by 1,000 votes last time.") than anywhere in the district. When he first thought about running, he knew nothing about the district. "I can remember sitting in the living room here, in 1963, looking at the map of the district, and saying to myself, 'X? Y? I didn't know there was a town called X in this district. Is there a town called Y?' I didn't know anything about the district." Furthermore, he didn't know any people there. "We started completely from scratch. I was about as little known in the district as anyone could be. In the city, I knew exactly two people. In the largest suburb, I didn't know a single person." He has (unlike Congressman A) absolutely no sense that "only a person like myself" can win in his district. Indeed, he thinks the opponent he first defeated was better suited to the district and should have won the election. "If I were he, I'd have beaten me." In terms of a geographical constituency and an individual's immersion in it, it is hard to imagine two more different perceptions of me-in-the-constituency than those of Congressman A and Congressman B.

Congressman B has not been in office very long. Not only did he begin from scratch, but he has been scratching ever since. He lost his first race for Congress; he succeeded in his second; and he now represents an objectively (and subjectively) marginal district. His entire career has been spent reaching out for political support. As he has gone about identifying and building first a primary and then a reelection constituency, he has simultaneously been evolving a political "self" and methods of presenting that "self" to them.

His earliest campaign promises were promises about the allocation of resources. He pledged to return to the district every week and to open three district offices, one in each of the "three worlds." These commitments about home style were contextually appropriate, if not contextually determined. For a candidate who neither knew nor was known in the district, pledges of attentiveness would seem almost mandatory. Furthermore, they allowed him to differentiate his proposed style from that of the incumbent—who was not very visible in the district and who operated one office there staffed by two people. Also, these pledges allowed him to embroider his belief that "a sense of distance has developed between the people and the government," necessitating efforts to "humanize" the relationship. And finally, his pledges gave him a lowest common denominator appeal based on style to a district with palpably diverse substantive interests. In 1973, Congressman B made 30 trips home, spent 109 working days there, operated three district offices and assigned one-half of his total staff of fourteen to the district. Promises have turned into style. "We have given the impression of being hardworking—of having a magic carpet, of being all over the place. It's been back-breaking, but it's the impression of being accessible."

Congressman B's actual presentation of self, i.e., what he does when he goes home, has evolved out of his personal interests and talents. He was propelled into active politics by his opposition to the Vietnam War. And his political impulses have been strongly issue-based ever since. He is severely critical of most of what has gone on in American public life for the last ten years. And he espouses a series of programmatic remedies—mostly governmental—for our social ills. . . .

Congressman B presents himself. . . in public, as a practitioner of an open, issue-based, and participatory politics. It was his antiwar stand particularly, and his issue orientation generally, that attracted the largest element of his primary constituency. These were the antiwar activists—young housewives, graduate students, and professionals—who created, staffed, and manned the large volunteer organization that became his political backbone. . . . Lacking a natural community to tie into and lacking any widespread personal appeal (or basis for such), Congressman B turned to the only alternative basis for building support—an organization. The "strongest supporters" in his organization did not support him because they knew him or had had any previous connection with him. The bond was agreement on the central issues and on the importance of emphasizing the issues. That agreement was the only "qualification" for the office that mattered to them. Within this group, the sense of identification between candidate and supporters was nearly total. He was "one of them." They trusted him. And they, with some trade union help (especially financial), gave him a victory in his initial primary.

In reaching for broader electoral support, Congressman B has been guided, in addition to his commitment to "the issues," by a personal penchant for talking about them. That is, he is an exceptionally verbal person; and he has evolved a suitably verbal home style. He places special emphasis on articulating, explaining, discussing, and debating issues. In each campaign (whether he be challenger or incumbent) he has pressed for debates with his opponent; and his assessment of his opponents focuses on their issue positions and their verbal facility. ("He's very conservative and, I understand, more articulate than the last guy. I felt sorry for him; he was so slow.")

In his first two campaigns the main vehicle for presenting himself to his prospective election-reelection constituency was "the coffee." He would sit in a living room or a yard, morning, afternoon, and evening (sometimes as often as eight or ten times each day) with one or two dozen people, stating his issue positions, answering their questions, and engaging in give and take. At the verbal level, the subject was substantive problems. But Congressman B knew that expressions "given off" were equally important.

> People don't make up their minds on the basis of reading all our position papers. We have 26 of them, because some people are interested. But most people get a gut feeling about the kind of human being they want to represent them.

Thus, his display of substantive knowledge and his mental agility at "the coffees" would help convey the impression that "as a human being" he was qualified for the office. And, not relying wholly on these expressions given off, he would remind his listeners, "No congressman can represent his people unless he's quick on his feet, because you have to deal with 434 other people—each of whom got there by being quick on his feet." Coffees were by no means the only way Congressman B presented himself. But it was his preferred method.

. . . Once in office, he evolved a natural extension of the campaign coffee—a new vehicle which allowed him to emphasize, still, his accessibility, his openness and his commitment to rational dialogue. It is "the open meeting," held twice a year, in every city and town in the district—nearly 200 in each session of Congress. Each postal patron gets an invitation to "come and 'have at' your congressman." And, before groups of four to 300, in town halls, schools, and community centers, he articulates the issues in a question and answer format. The exchanges are informative and wide-ranging; they are punctuated with enthusiasm and wit. The open meetings, like the coffees, allow Congressman B to play to his personal strengths—his issue interests and his verbal agility. In the coffees, he was concerned with conveying threshold impressions of qualification, and his knowledge and status reinforce that impression in the open meetings. But in the open meetings, he is reaching for some deeper underpinnings of constituent trust. He does this with a presentation of self that combines identification and empathy. "I am not exactly one of you," he seems to tell them, "but we have a lot in common, and I feel a lot like you do." He expresses this feeling in two ways.

One expression "given" and "given off" in the open meetings is the sense that the give-and-take format requires a special kind of congressman and a special kind of constituency and involves them, therefore, in a special kind of relationship. In each meeting I attended, his opening remarks included two such expressions.

> One of the first pieces of advice I got from a senior member of my party was: "Send out lots of newsletters, but don't mention any issues. The next thing you know, they'll want to know how you vote." Well, I don't believe that.
>
> My colleagues in Congress told me that the questionnaires I sent you were too long and too complicated and that you would never answer it. Well, 5,000 have been filled out and returned already—before we've even sent them all out.

At the same time that he exhibits his own ability to tackle any question, explain any vote, and debate any difference of opinion, he massages the egos of his constituents by indicating how intelligent, aware, and concerned they are to engage with him in this new, open, rational style of politics. . . .

A second, related, expression "given off" is the sense that Congressman B, though he is a politician, is more like his constituents than he is like other politicians. It is not easy for him to convey such an impression, because the only thing his potential reelection constituents know about him is that he is a politician. They do not know him from any prior involvement in a community life. So he works very hard to bind himself to his constituents by disassociating himself from "the government" and disavowing his politician's status. He present himself as an antipolitician, giving off the feeling that, "I'm just as fed up with government and the people who run it as you are." Since he is a congressman-politician, he is unrelentingly harsh in his criticism of Congress and his fellow legislators.

> As you know, I'm one of the greatest critics of Congress. It's an outrageous and outmoded institution.
> All Congress has ever done since I've been in Congress is pass the buck to the president and then blame him for what goes wrong. . . . Congress is gutless beyond my power to describe to you. . . .

A politician seeking to convey the impression that he is not a politician, Congressman B hopes to build constituent trust by inviting them to blend their cynicism with his.

The presentation of self—an accessible, issue-oriented, communicative antipolitician—at the open meetings is a lowest common denominator presentation. It can win support in each of "the three worlds" without losing support in any. For it is the style, not the issue content, that counts most in the reelection constituency. Congressman B is completely comfortable in the setting. "That was fun," he says after each open meeting. And, occasionally, "it's more fun when there's some hostility." But it is the format more than the audience that makes him feel really "at home." He is not a person-to-person campaigner. . . . He, on the other hand, keeps his distance from the personal problems of his constituents, inviting them to talk with the staff members who accompany him to the open meetings. Of course, he meets people face-to-face—all the time. But he does not know or seek out much about them as individuals, not much that would build anything more than a strictly political connection. An aptitude for names and faces, a facility with tidbits of personal information and small talk, an easy informality in face-to-face relations—these are not his natural personal strengths. But they are not the keys to his success with his reelection constituency. He has evolved a home style that does not call for person-to-person abilities in large supply.

The open meetings remain the centerpiece of his home style. "They are the most extraordinary thing we've ever done, and the most important." He sees them as vehicles which help him reach out to and expand his reelection constituency. For he remains a builder instead of a stabilizer in his constituency relations.

> Politically, these open meetings are pure gold. Fifty may come, but everybody in town
> gets an invitation. . . . I do know that none of our loyalists come to the meetings. They
> know the meetings are nonpartisan. Maybe one or two of them will show up, but
> mostly they are new faces.

They have given him entree into the least supportive, rural areas of his district, where he recruits support and neutralizes the more intense opposition. At
first, he says, "in some of these towns they didn't know what to say to a Democrat.
They probably hadn't met one except for people who fixed their toilets." Yet at the
open meetings, "we've had better turnouts, proportionately, in the rural area."
"And we get a lot of letters from people there who say they disagree with us but
respect our honesty and independence." In time—but only in time—interest and
respect may turn into the supportive inferences that connote trust.

But as Congressman B spends more and more of his time at home cultivating
an expanding reelection constituency, his oldest and strongest supporters have felt
neglected. So Congressman B has a more complex strategic problem, in terms of
allocating his time, than Congressman A.

> When we began, we had the true believers working their hearts out. It was just like a
> family. But the more you gain in voters, and the more you broaden your constituency,
> the more the family feels hurt. Our true believers keep asking me, "Why don't you drink
> with us?" "Why don't you talk to me personally anymore?" I have to keep talking to
> them about the need to build a larger majority. I have to keep telling them that politics
> is not exclusive; it is inclusive. It is not something that can be done in the living room.

The true believers are not threatening a total loss of support; but declining
enthusiasm would present a serious support problem. One way Congressman B
may deal with the problem is to come home more, so that he can give the necessary
time to the true believers. He does come home more than Congressman A, perhaps partly because his strategic problems at home require it. Still, Congressman B
emphasizes identifying and building support beyond the primary constituency in
"the three worlds." And he finds the open meetings the most effective (and most
comfortable) vehicle for him. "What more could anyone ask," he says, "than to have
the congressman come to their town personally?" His primary constituents do ask
something more. And, so long as he gives it to them, he will remain a congressman.

Presentation of Self: Constituency Constraints and Constituency Careers

Our description of the person-to-person and the issue-oriented styles is exemplary,
not exhaustive.[6] Speculatively, however, presentation of self would seem to be
explainable by three kinds of factors—*contextual, personal, and strategic.*

Contextually, a representative thinks about his constituency relations in terms of
me-in-the-constituency. That perception predates his service in Washington and
cannot be understood by drawing inferences from his Washington behavior. Part of
the content of that perception involves a sense of fit—a good fit as in the case of
Congressman A, a nonfit as in the case of Congressman B, and a bad fit as in the case
of one congressman (not in my group) who refers to his district as "outer Mongolia."

A congressman's sense of fit will, in turn, be affected by whether he sees the district as homogeneous or heterogeneous. Good fits are more likely in homogeneous districts. But the reverse side of the coin is that home styles are more likely to be imposed upon the congressman in homogeneous districts. If Congressman A did not represent his district, someone who performed similarly at home probably would. In a heterogeneous district—Congressman B's case—home style is much more a matter of individual choice, and is more likely to be imposed by the congressman on his district. Thus, . . . we would expect to find the most idiosyncratic patterns appearing in the most heterogeneous districts. Homogeneous districts, in sum, impose more stylistic constraints on a congressman than do heterogeneous districts.

A second contextual impact on the presentation of self, however, may produce contrary tendencies. Once a congressman has imposed a particular presentational style upon his district, his successors may feel constrained to continue that style. That is, a congressman's home style may be influenced by the previous congressman's home style. Congressman B deliberately chose a style that contrasted with his predecessor's in order to help develop an identifiable political self. It is equally plausible (and it happened in my group) that expectations about style could be so strongly implanted in the district by a predecessor, that the new congressman dare not change. Similarly, a choice of home style by imitation or by contrast can occur with reference to a neighboring congressman—if the congressman choosing a style has reason to believe that some of his constituents are likely to compare him to that neighbor. Regardless of district makeup, then, under certain conditions one congressman's style may be shaped by the style of another congressman, past or present.

From the cases of representatives A and B, it seems clear that the presentation of self is also shaped by each individual's inclinations and talents. Every congressman has some latitude in deciding how to present himself "as a person." That is not to say that House members *like* to do all the things they do at home. More members than I would have expected described themselves as "shy," "reserved," or "not an extrovert." But they go home and present themselves anyway. And they try to do what they are most comfortable doing and try not to do that which they are most uncomfortable doing. Congressman A seeks out person-to-person relationships, but does not encourage issue-oriented meetings. Congressman B seeks out issue-oriented meetings, but does not encourage person-to-person relationships. Experience, interest, abilities—all the personal attributes of a congressman's self—help shape his presentation of that self to others.

Strategically, each congressman must decide how he will allocate his time when he is at home. And it is of some help to think of this strategic problem in terms of his perceived constituencies. From our two cases, we might generalize that a man in a homogeneous district will spend most of his time with his primary constituency. Homogeneous districts are most likely to be perceived as protected in the general election, so that the strategic problem is to hold sufficient primary constituency support to ward off a primary challenger. By the same token, the primary constituency in a homogeneous district is probably more amorphous and less easily defined than it is in a heterogeneous district. Thus a concentration of effort in the primary constituency does not mean that any less time will be required to cultivate it.

By contrast, in a district perceived to be both heterogeneous and electorally unprotected, the congressman will spend relatively more time in his reelection constituency. But he faces a problem of balance. He will play "the politics of inclusion" by spending time expanding his reelection constituency, partly on the assumption that his strongest supporters have no inclination to go elsewhere. Yet he cannot neglect the primary constituency unduly, since their loyalty and intensity of commitment are necessary to sustain a predictably difficult election campaign. He may, of course, be able to allocate resources other than his time, i.e., votes, to keep his primary constituency content (Fiorina 1973). But there is every evidence from my experience that the congressman's strongest supporters are more—not less—demanding of the congressman's time than his other constituencies.

A strategic problem in allocating time, alluded to briefly in discussing Congressman B, involves the presentation of self to one's strongest opponents—to the people each congressman believes he "will never get." House members handle the problem differently. But most of them will accept (and some will solicit) opportunities to present themselves before unfriendly constituents. The strategic hope is that displaying themselves "as a person" may reduce the intensity of the opposition . . . Any time spent cooling the ardor of the opposition is time usefully spent, for it may mean less intense support for the challenger. Functionally, the same accents used in presenting one's self to supporters apply to a presentation to opponents—the emphasis on qualification, the effort at identification, the projection of empathy. In other words, the process of allaying hostility differs little from the process of building trust. That makes it easier for House members to allocate some time—probably minor—to a strategy of neutralization.

Students of Congress are accustomed to thinking about a congressman's *career in the House*—his early adjustments, his rise in seniority, his placement on the ladders of committee and party, the accumulation of his responsibilities, the fluctuations of his personal "Dow Jones Average." But House members also pursue a *career in the constituency.* Congressman B's evolution from "scratch" to a concern with his primary constituency to a concern with his reelection constituency gives evidence of such a constituency career. He was as much a newcomer in the district as newcomers are (or were) purported to be in the House. He had to work out an appropriate home style there just the way each new House member adapts to the House as an institution. Congressman B has been, and is, in the expansionist phase of his career, continually reaching out for increments of support. Congressman A, by comparison, is in a more protectionist phase of his constituency career. He believes that he has, over a considerable period of time, won the trust of his constituents (i.e., his primary constituents). He is working mainly to reinforce that trust; to protect the support he already has. Congressman B does not talk about constituent trust; he never says, "my constituents trust me." His presentation of self is designed to build trust, but, as we have said, it takes time.

The idea of a career in the constituency helps to highlight an important fact about the congressman as an elective politician. As any textbook treatment of incumbency tells us, the congressman is a particularly long-lived political species. He has been making or will make presentations of self to his constituents *for a long time.* . . . A congressman's political support will depend especially heavily upon his presentation of self. That, of course, is precisely what House members themselves tell us whenever we have asked. They tell us that their "personal record and standing" or their "personalities" are more important in explaining their election than "issues" or "party identification" (Leuthold 1968; Stokes and Miller 1962)." They tell us, in other words, that their home style—especially their presentation of self—is the most important determinant of their political support. The idea of a lengthy constituency career helps us understand why this might be true. For it makes home style into a durable, consistent long-term factor in congressional electoral politics. In any congressional electoral analyses patterned after our presidential electoral analyses, home style may have to be elevated to a scholarly status heretofore reserved only for party identification and issue voting.

HOME STYLE: EXPLANATION OF WASHINGTON ACTIVITY

When members of Congress are at home, they do something that is closely allied with, yet separable from, the presentation of self to their constituencies. They explain what they have done in Washington. For some House members, their Washington activities are central to their presentation of self. One congressman, for example, routinely began every speech before every district group as follows:

> I have represented this district for the last 20 years. And I come to you to ask for a two-year renewal of my contract. I'm running because I have a 20-year investment in my job and because I think you, as my constituents, have an investment in my seniority. In a body as large as the House of Representatives with 435 elected, coequal members, there has to be a structure if we're ever going to get anything done. And it takes a long time to learn that structure, to learn who has the power and to learn where to grease the skids to get something done. I think I know the structure and the people in the House better than any newcomer could. And I believe I can accomplish things for you that no newcomer could.

He wants his constituents to see him "as a person" in terms of his importance in Washington. By contrast, neither Congressman A nor Congressman B makes his Washington activity central to his presentation of self. But whether or not his behavior in Washington is central to his presentation of self, every House member spends some time at home explaining and justifying his Washington behavior to his various constituencies. He tells them what he has done and why. What he says, how he says it, and to whom can be viewed as a distinctive aspect of his home style.

The objective of every congressman's explanations—our usage of *explanation* incorporates the idea of *justification* as well—is political support. And just as a congressman chooses, subject to constraints, a presentational style, so too does he choose, subject to constraints, an explanatory style. When most people think of explaining what goes on in Washington to constituents, they think of explaining votes. But we should conceptualize the activities subject to explanation more broadly than that. A House member will explain any part of his activity in

Washington if he thinks that part of his activity is relevant to the winning and holding of support at home. Just what kinds of behavior he thinks his various constituencies want or need to have explained to them is an empirical matter; but one which bulks especially large among my representatives is their effectiveness (or lack of it) inside the House on behalf of their constituencies. Often this explanation of one's internal influence also entails a more general explanation of the workings of Congress. . . .

The range of possible activities requiring a home explanation extends well beyond voting. Still, voting is the Washington activity we most easily recognize; and we can make most of our comments in that context. From John Kingdon's splendid discussion of "explaining" (1973, 46–53), we know that, at the time they decide to vote, House members are very aware that they may be called upon to explain their vote to some of their constituents. Moreover, says Kingdon, the anticipated need to explain influences their decision on how to vote. They may cast a certain vote only if and when they are convinced that they have a satisfactory explanation in hand. Or they may cast a certain vote because it is the vote least likely to require an explanation. Kingdon is interested in finding out why members of Congress vote the way they do. But along the way, he helps make the case for finding out why members of Congress explain the way they do. For, if the anticipated need to explain has the effect on voting that Kingdon suggests—i.e., if it makes voting more complicated and more difficult than it otherwise would be— then the act of explaining must be as problematical for House members as the act of voting. House members believe that they can win and lose constituent support through their explanations as well as through their votes. To them, therefore, voting and explaining are interrelated aspects of a single strategic problem. If that is the way House members see it, then it might be useful for political scientists to look at it that way, too—and to spend a little less of our time explaining votes and a little more of our time explaining *explanations.*

Members are, of course, called upon to vote much more often than they are called upon to explain. That is, they are never called upon to explain all their votes. Their uncertainty about which votes they will have to explain, however, leads them to prepare explanations for more votes than they need to, the need being enforced on them by dissatisfied constituents and, primarily, by the electoral challenger. The challenger, particularly, controls the explanatory agenda—or, better, tries to do so. All the uncertainty that the challenger produces for the perception of constituency, the challenger also brings to the problem of explanation.

Representatives will strike different postures regarding the need to explain. Some will explain their votes only when they feel hard pressed by constituents and/or challenger to do so. They will follow the congressional adage that "if you have to explain, you're in trouble." And their explanatory practices, if not their voting practices, will be calculated to keep them out of trouble. Other members bend over backward to explain every vote that any constituent might construe as controversial—sometimes well in advance of the vote. It is our hunch that the more issue-oriented a congressman's presentation of self, the more voluminous will be his explanations. Our Congressman B, for example, produces a heavy volume of explanation. "We have explained every difficult vote. Anyone who gives a twit about how I vote has the opportunity to know it. We have explained our votes on all the toughies." Given his presentational style, it is hard to see him adopting any other explanatory style. In both cases, the content of what he says is less important than the fact that he says it—i.e., than his style.

I shall resist the temptation to spell out all the possible relationships between the presentational and explanatory aspects of home style. But it seems obvious that they exist. We would, at the least, expect to find a "strain toward compatibility" operating between the two. And we would expect to find the presentation of self— as the centerpiece of home style—to be the more controlling aspect in the relationship. We would further expect both aspects of home style to be influenced by the same constituency constraints. For example, we would expect the broadest perception of me-in-the-constituency—the sense of fit the congressman has with his various constituencies—to underlie the choice of explanatory styles, just as it underlies the choice of presentational styles.

. . . There probably are, in every district, one or two issues on which the congressman is constrained in his voting by the views of his reelection constituency. (Whether he *feels* constrained—which depends on whether or not he agrees with those constituent views—is beside the point.) But on the vast majority of votes, a congressman can do as he wishes—provided only that he can, if and when he needs to, explain his vote to the satisfaction of interested constituents. The ability to get his explanations accepted at home is, then, the essential underpinning of his voting leeway in Washington. Thus the question arises, how can the congressman act so as to increase the likelihood that his explanations will be accepted at home? And the answer the House members give is: He can win and hold constituent trust. The more your various constituencies trust you, House members reason, the less likely they are to require an explanation of your votes and the more likely they are to accept your explanation when they do require it. The winning of trust, we have said earlier, depends largely on the presentation of self. Presentation of self, then, not only helps win votes at election time; it also makes voting in Washington easier. So congressmen make a strategic calculation. Presentation of self enhances trust; trust enhances the acceptability of explanations; the acceptability of explanations enhances voting leeway; therefore, presentation of self enhances voting leeway.

When I asked Congressman C if he wasn't more liberal than his district, he said:

Hell, yes, but don't quote me on that. It's the biggest part of my problem—to keep people from thinking I'm a radical liberal.

. . . Later still, he mused out loud about how he managed this problem.

It's a weird thing how you get a district to the point where you can vote the way you want to without getting scalped for doing it. I guess you do it in two ways. You come back here a lot and let people see you, so they get a feel for you. And, secondly, I go out of my way to disagree with people on specific issues. That way, they know you aren't trying to snow them. And when you vote against their views, they'll say, "Well, he's got his reasons." They'll trust you. I think that's it. If they trust you, you can vote the way you want to and it won't hurt.

. . . As a final note, two general patterns of explanation deserve mention. One I had expected to find but have not, and one I had not expected to find but have. Both invite further research. In view of the commonly held notion that elective politicians "talk out of both sides of their mouths" (which Goffman (1959, 136) discusses in terms of performances before "segregated audiences"),[7] I had expected to find members of Congress explaining their activity somewhat differently to their various constituencies. The likelihood seemed especially strong in heterogeneous districts, where the opportunity and temptation would be greatest. But I have found little trace of such explanatory chameleons in my travels. The House members I observed give the same explanations for their Washington activity before people who disagree with them as before people who agree with them—before nonsupporters as well as supporters, from one end to the other in the most segmented of districts. . . . Their presentation of self may vary from group to group in the sense that the basis for demonstrating identification or empathy will have to differ from group to group. As they reach out to each group in a manner appropriate to that group, they may take on some local coloration; and they may tailor their subject matter to fit the interests of their audience. However, they rarely alter their explanations of their Washington activity in the process.

An explanatory pattern I had not expected to find was the degree to which the congressman at home explains his Washington activity by disassociating it from the activity of his colleagues and of Congress as a whole. I had assumed that home styles would be highly individualized. And I should not have been surprised, therefore, when I heard every one of my 17 members introduced at home as "the best congressman in the United States." But I was not prepared to find each of them polishing this individual reputation at the expense of the institutional reputation of the Congress (Fenno 1975). In explaining what he was doing in Washington, every one of my House members took the opportunity to portray himself as "different from the others"—the other being "the old chairmen," "the inexperienced newcomers," . . . and so on. The diversity of the House provides every member with plenty of collegial villains to flay before supportive constituents at home. Individual members do not take responsibility for the performance of Congress; rather each portrays himself as a fighter against its manifest shortcomings. Their willingness, at some point, to stand and defend their votes contrasts sharply with their disposition to run and hide when a defense of Congress is called for. Congress is not "we"; it is "they." And members of Congress run *for* Congress by running *against* Congress. Thus, individual explanations carry with them a heavy dosage of critical commentary on Congress.

CONCLUSION: POLITICAL SUPPORT, HOME STYLE, AND REPRESENTATION

"A congressman has two constituencies," Speaker Sam Rayburn once said. "He has his constituents at home and he has his colleagues here in the House. To serve his constituents at home, he must serve his colleagues here in the House." For over 20 years, political scientists have been researching the "two constituencies."

Following the thrust of Rayburn's comment, we have given lopsided attention to the collegial constituency on Capitol Hill. And we have neglected the constituency at home. Knowing less than we might about one of the two constituencies, we cannot know all that we should about the linkage between them. This chapter argues for opening up the home constituency to more political science investigation than it has received. It suggests that students of Congress pay more attention to "home" as a research focus and a research site. . . .

While this chapter has not dwelled directly on the topic of representation, our exploration has implications for the family of questions, both descriptive and normative, raised by studies of representation. . . . A more inclusive, process-oriented view of representation has the effect of making it less exclusively a policy-centered subject. Traditionally, representation has been treated mostly as a structural relationship in which the congruence between the policy preferences of the represented and the policy decisions of the representative is the measure of good representation. The question we normally ask is: "How well does Representative X represent his or her district?" And we answer the question by matching and calibrating substantive policy agreement. But our view here is that there is an intertwining question: "How does Representative X carry his or her district?" To answer that question, we shall need to consider more than policy preferences and policy agreements. We shall need to consider the more encompassing subject of home style and the constituent trust generated by home style. We shall need to entertain the possibility that constituents may want good access as much as good policy from their representative. . . . The point is not that policy preferences are not a crucial basis for the representational relationship. They are. The point is that we should not start our studies of representation by assuming they are the *only* basis for a representational relationship. They are not.

. . . [T]his chapter asks that we entertain the. . . view that the Washington and the home activities can be mutually supportive. Time spent at home can be time spent developing leeway for activity undertaken in Washington. And it may be that leeway in Washington should be more valued than the sheer number of contact hours spent there. It may be, then, that the congressman's effectiveness in Washington is vitally influenced by the pattern of support he has developed at home and by the allocational, presentational, and explanatory styles he displays there. To put the point more strongly, perhaps we cannot understand his Washington activity without first understanding his perception of his constituencies and the home style he uses to cultivate their support.

No matter how supportive of one another their Washington and home activities may be, House members still face constant tension between them. Members cannot be in two places at once. They cannot achieve legislative competence and maintain constituency contact, both to an optimal degree. . . . Thus, our focus on home activity may help us understand some changing characteristics of House members.

Our professional neglect of the home relationship has probably contributed to a more general neglect of the representational side of Congress's institutional capabilities. At least it does seem to be the case that the more one focuses on the home activities of its members, the more one comes to appreciate the representative strengths and possibilities of Congress. Congress *is* the most representative of our national political institutions (Fenno 1977a). It mirrors much of our national diversity, and its members maintain contact with a variety of constituencies at home. While its representative strengths surely contribute to its deserved reputation as our slow institution, the same representative strengths give it the potential for acquiring a reputation as our fair institution. In a period of our national life when citizen sacrifice will be called for, what we shall be needing from our political institutions are not quick decisions, but fair decisions. Some of the recent internal congressional reforms [of 1975] have increased the potential for both representativeness and fairness. They have increased the equality of representation by distributing influence more broadly inside Congress. They have increased the visibility of representation by opening up congressional proceedings to public view. This is by no means all that is needed. But it is enough to place an added obligation on the members of Congress to educate their constituencies in the strengths as well as the weaknesses of the institution. Members should participate in consensus building in Washington; they should accept some responsibility for the collective performance of Congress; and they should explain to their constituents what an institution that is both collective and fair requires of its individual members.

The evidence of this study indicates that members have the leeway to educate their constituents if they have the will to do so. The evidence of this study also shows that they may not have that will. Instead, they often seek support and trust for themselves by encouraging a lack of support and trust in the Congress. By refusing to accept responsibility for an institutional performance, they simultaneously abdicate their responsibility to educate their constituents in the work of the institution. Instead of criticizing House members for going home so much, we should criticize them for any failure to put their leeway to a constructive purpose—during the legislative process in Washington and during the explanatory process at home. The trust of his, or her, supportive constituents should be viewed by a House member as his, or her, working capital—not just to be hoarded for individual benefit but to be drawn on, occasionally, for the benefit of the institution. So long as House members explain themselves but not the institution, they help sustain (wittingly or unwittingly) the gap between a 10% approval level for Congress and a 90% reelection record for themselves. If this imbalance seems unhealthy for both Congress and the Republic, we have yet another justification for an increased scholarly attentiveness to our House members at home.

NOTES

1. The group contains 16 men and one woman. In the title of the paper and in the introduction, I have deliberately employed the generic language "House member," "member of Congress," "representative," and "his or her" to make it clear that I am talking about men and women. And I have tried to use the same language wherever the plural form appears in the paper. That is, I have tried to stop using the word "congressmen." In the body of the paper, however, I shall frequently and deliberately use "congressman" and "his" as generic terms. Stylistically, I find this a less clumsy form of

the third person singular than "congressperson" followed always by "his or her." This usage has the additional special benefit, here, of camouflaging the one woman in the group. Where necessary, I have used pseudonyms for these 17 members in the text.

2. Marginal districts probably tend to be heterogeneous. Safe district probably are both heterogeneous and homogeneous. On the relationship of electoral conditions to homogeneity and heterogeneity, I owe a lot to my conversations with Morris Fiorina. See Fiorina (1974a) and Miller (1964).

3. On recent trips, wherever possible, I have also asked each congressman at the end of my visit, to rank order the events of the visit in terms of their "political importance" to him and in terms of the degree to which he felt "at home" or "comfortable" in each situation.

4. These surveys will be described in the next section of the paper. We shall not, however, again use the figures on total numbers of days spent in the district. They seem less reliable than the others, when checked against the few cases in which I have the complete record. Also, it should be noted that the number of cases for which the total number of days was collected was 401.

5. Fifty-six percent, or 72 of 129.

6. The two styles are most common among my group. They may be the most common among all representatives. In his study of representation, Peterson (1970) uses two very similar analytical categories, "particularistic representation" (person-to-person) and "universalistic representation" (issue-oriented). Other styles [are] elaborated in Fenno (1978).

7. A possible pattern of explanation requiring further research is that members explain their activities in different policy areas to distinctive groups in the constituency. See Clausen (1973), especially his discussion of a special foreign policy constituency (225–226).

PART III

ELECTIONS

Chapter 8

How Do Candidacies Affect Elections?

Elections are basic to a legislature and central to democracy. Members are first chosen and then have to face the electorate again to stay in office. Citizens thus give their representatives the authority to govern when they are first elected and then hold them accountable at the next election. Elections also determine the composition and partisan balance of a legislature, and thereby suggest a general direction for policy and decision making.

The decisions of individuals to run for office and to run for reelection are at the heart of elections. In justifying the American Constitution, Madison wrestled in *The Federalist Papers* with how candidacies relate to democracy. He saw this as crucial, writing (*Federalist* No. 57) that "the aim of every political constitution is, or ought to be, first to obtain for rulers men who possess most wisdom to discern, and most virtue to pursue, the common good of the society; and in the next place, to take the most effectual precautions for keeping them virtuous whilst they continue to hold their public trust." He regarded frequent elections as a partial solution to these twin problems, but recognized that only transforms the question into the characteristics of those who run for office. Madison argued that the answer to this question rests in the legislator's selfish ambition: ". . . those ties which bind the representative to his constituents are strengthened by motives of a more selfish nature. . . . Duty, gratitude, interest, ambition itself, are the cords by which they [legislators] will be bound to . . . the great mass of the people."

The research literature on congressional elections has picked up these themes. Topics that have been examined include the demographic characteristics of candidates and the reasons that people become active in politics. However, the fundamental theoretical development has been the recognition that candidacies involve ambition and strategy. Even so, many aspects of candidacies remain understudied (see especially Fowler 1993).

The decisions, personal attributes, and political skills of individual candidates all affect election outcomes. On the one hand, a candidate who decides to run for office against a sitting member of Congress fosters competition. Her candidacy, prompted by her favorable assessment of the political context, could be enhanced if she reflects the partisan and sociodemographic composition of the district better than the incumbent (personal attributes) and if she mobilizes groups of voters to form an electoral coalition by effectively presenting a case for her election to office (political skills). At the same time, the incumbent affects the election's outcome through his own decisions, personal attributes, and political skills. Moreover, he benefits from the resources available to him as a result of his incumbency as well as from voters' familiarity with him and his performance in Congress.

In this sense, legislative elections involve an interplay between forces of continuity and change as well. Incumbents have a considerable advantage, though one that can sometimes be offset by a quality challenger. Quality challengers provide accountability, introduce new ideas for policy change, keep incumbents responsive, and foster party competition. Elections can provide the change in a legislature that leads to a new majority to pass a bill that was previously stalled, though most often elections create only smaller changes.

As we have explored in chapter 5, the literature of the 1960s and 1970s focused on representation, with increasing sophistication as to how that term was to be understood. The literature of the 1980s and 1990s has shifted to elections, as if voting in legislative elections has to be better understood before representation can itself be studied at greater depth. This chapter reviews how the focus of election studies changed over time. We begin by exploring one important approach to understanding elections from the candidates' perspective—ambition theory. We then examine the two competing elements in elections—the incumbent and the challenger. The early literature focused on understanding the incumbency advantage, whereas later research has turned more to the strategic decisions of challengers. Finally, we use this discussion to comment on the effects of term limits on the electoral connection.

AMBITION AND STRATEGY

Perhaps the most basic question with which to begin is how and why do candidates choose to run? What are their considerations? Although we will address the differences between incumbents and challengers in short order, our subject for now is the decision to run more generally. The central concept of such discussions is political ambition (Schlesinger 1996)—the desire of people to achieve political office and power. In a representative democracy, voters must have the option of replacing unsatisfactory officeholders. Without ambitious people willing to assume office, there is no supply of candidates from which to choose a new officeholder and therefore no competition in elections and ultimately, no accountability of elected officials. As Fowler (1993) concludes, a legitimate regime requires a supply of candidates willing to link citizens to their government.

It is useful to begin by contrasting two models of elections: party-centered and candidate-centered elections. In party-centered elections, candidates run on the basis of their party ties and citizens vote on the basis of their party identification. The parties themselves recruit candidates, and the candidates are generally beholden to the parties. This is a fair description of U.S. politics during the era of urban party machines in the early 1900s when party bosses could choose their candidates. By contrast, in candidate-centered elections, candidates run on their own. With much of the electorate considering themselves politically independent, candidates run their own campaign advertisements designed to show their independence from their parties. This is the system that developed with the advent of political primaries, which allowed candidates to be nominated without the endorsement of party leaders. Candidate ambition obviously matters much more in the current era of candidate-centered elections than it did when elections were party-centered.

The shift to candidate-centered elections has also greatly affected campaign financing. Political parties were crucial to campaign funding in the era of party-centered elections. Now candidates have to generate their campaign money themselves. Some candidates can finance their campaigns themselves, but most must raise that money from donors. The result is what Herrnson (1995) has described as two campaigns for Congress: the campaign for funds and the campaign for votes. House campaigns are especially dependent on political action committees (PACs) because of members' relatively short terms in office. Senators are also dependent on PACs, but less so than representatives, because their longer term insulates them from funding pressures until the campaign approaches and because more are millionaires who are able to self-finance much of their campaign. The facts of life of campaign financing are sufficient to discourage many potential challengers.

If the candidates from whom the voters can choose are mainly self-selected, it is then essential to understand why some potential candidates decide to run for public office. Ambition theory states that in deciding to run, potential candidates assess the costs and benefits of their options and act in a way that furthers their political ambitions. As Kazee (1994) notes, "the decision to run results primarily from a matching of individual ambition and the context of opportunities available to the potential candidate" (7). The theory assumes that all politicians are ambitious (Schlesinger 1966) and are rational decision makers (Fowler 1993).

Ambition theory implies that, once in office, politicians will run for higher office if these positions can be obtained with acceptable cost and risk (Black 1972; Rohde 1979). We reprint the chapter by Rohde (chapter 9) because it so clearly lays out and tests this theory. It spells out the cost-benefit calculations involved when members of the House decide to run for the Senate or for a governorship. It is hypothesized that members take into account the value of the higher office, the likelihood of winning that office, and the value of their current House seat. Additionally, Rohde argues that some politicians are more willing to take risks, and he tests the role of this factor too in the differential rates at which members of the House seek higher offices. Not only does Rohde claim that these are relevant factors, but he also operationalizes each one and empirically tests its importance.

Rohde shows the circumstances under which members of the House are most likely to seek higher office, but he does not directly address the emergence of candidates for the House itself. Jacobson and Kernell (1983) clarify the strategic considerations involved in the initial decision to run for Congress, while providing a solution to an important puzzle in the congressional voting literature. Their basic premise is that potential candidates act strategically and are more likely to run for office when the candidates consider national conditions to be most favorable for their political party.

Consider the following puzzle. On the one hand, early studies of individual voting decisions had generally failed to find a relationship between a person's economic situation and his or her congressional vote (e.g., Fiorina 1978). Yet Kramer (1971) and Tufte (1975) had shown the importance of the economy at the aggregate level, with the president's party doing better in years when the economy was performing well. Indeed, Tufte (1975) had concluded that the national division of votes in midterm congressional elections can be explained as a function of the change in per capita, real disposable income in the year prior to the election and the president's job-performance rating in the September before the election. He conclusively demonstrates that national politics and the economy shape election outcomes. But how can Tufte's result coexist with the lack of relationship between a person's economic situation and his or her vote? That is the puzzle that Jacobson and Kernell help explain.

As illustrated in the selection from their book that is reprinted here as chapter 11, Jacobson and Kernell posit that politicians' decisions to run reflect the national political context. They argue that candidates and the political elites involved in recruiting and funding candidates serve as a link between national-level conditions and voters' individual voting decisions. That is, the national context influences the decision to run for office or contribute to a congressional campaign. These elite decisions therefore shape the choices presented to voters, who are more likely to support quality candidates who are running organized and well-funded campaigns. Ultimately, then, even voters who are unaware of campaign issues or the national political context are likely to vote in a way that reinforces that context. Their voting decisions reflect the advantages that the political party favored by the present political climate is likely to enjoy.

The state of the economy is one important component of the national context, along with scandals that make the president's party look bad. Strategic politicians consider these factors when deciding whether it is the right year for them to run for Congress. As a result, the president's party is likely to attract stronger candidates and do better in years when the economy is stronger, while the opposition party is likely to attract stronger candidates when the economy is weaker. Thus Jacobson and Kernell's argument can explain the puzzle of economic voting—how Kramer and Tufte could find a relationship between the state of the economy and congressional voting results even if other studies show that individual voters do not vote on the basis of their own economic well-being. Ambitious politicians behaving in a strategic manner provide the explanatory mechanism.[1]

Scandals also can discourage strategic politicians from running in years when they are unlikely to win. Thus, the investigation of President Clinton's relationship with Monica Lewinsky probably discouraged some strong potential Democratic candidates from running in 1998. Still, the strong economy and President Clinton's popularity allowed the Democrats to gain five House seats in the 1998 election.

Ambition theory is not without shortcomings, however. As Fowler (1993) notes, little is understood about the origins of political ambition or how it develops. Schlesinger (1966) distinguished among three kinds of ambition for politicians. All politicians are assumed to desire higher office and therefore exhibit "progressive ambition." However, in some situations a politician who holds public office decides to leave politics (discrete ambition), perhaps to spend more time with his family or to pursue a lucrative career in the private sector. In other situations, a politician might be content to remain in a single office (static ambition), as when senior members of Congress run for reelection in order to maintain the power on committees that their seniority has earned them. Scholars often neglect to examine the political careers of those who display discrete or static ambition, studying mainly the instances of progressive ambition. Moreover, scholars have not fully explored the interactions between ambition and context (Fowler 1993). Prewitt (1990) argues that ambition is actually the interaction of a politician's changing self-image (such as the realization that she has become sufficiently well known to run for higher office) and the opportunities that a changing political context presents to her.

Although ambition theory is an imperfect lens through which to view the decision to run, it remains a powerful heuristic, an approach that reveals a great deal about congressional candidates' choices and goals. This topic might have been less important a century ago when political parties were stronger and dominated the political landscape. Elections today, however, are candidate-centered rather than party-centered. Both parties recognize the importance of candidate recruitment, while those who aspire to public office are frequently derided for being "self-selected" to govern. In this situation, congressional scholars would do well to learn more about political careers and what makes for political aspirations. If for no other reason, researching who runs and why will reveal critical information about who wins office and the qualities that members of Congress possess.

ELECTIONS AS REFERENDA ON INCUMBENTS

Congressional election scholars often focus on members' efforts to remain in office. That is, much of what is known about congressional elections is based on studies of incumbency. The importance of individual candidates and campaigns has increased to fill the gap left by declining or decentralized political parties. Incumbent officeholders, armed with the resources of their offices, have thrived in this setting and their electoral advantages, measured by electoral margins of victory, has increased.

The importance of studying incumbents cannot be overstated, particularly given how successful members have become at making a career on Capitol Hill. House reelection rates from 1946 to 1996 ranged from 83% to 98%. Senators are slightly less successful than their House counterparts in being reelected (Senate reelection rates ranged from 64% to 96% for that time period but varied more dramatically from election to election), in spite of the comparably greater resources that incumbent senators enjoy. Congressional turnover is more a result of retirements than of incumbents' defeats.

The early survey studies of congressional elections served to reinforce the importance of incumbency. The 1958 National Election Study that Miller and

Stokes analyze in chapter 6 included questions on whether the respondents had read or heard anything about the congressional candidates in their districts. The level of information was low, with less than half of the actual voters having read or heard anything about either candidate (Stokes and Miller 1962). The ability to recall the names of the candidates was also low. Knowledge of which party controlled Congress was at an equally dismal level. Congressional elections became viewed as low information settings in which voters are likely to know only a few basic facts about a candidate—party, simple demographics (especially gender and race), and incumbency.

From this perspective, congressional elections can be considered referenda on whether to retain the incumbents in office. Understanding congressional elections becomes a matter of understanding the incumbency advantage—how it is defined and measured, and what it reveals about the ambitious members who try to retain their seats in Congress.

Once in office, the member attempts to represent constituents effectively. Members' efforts to gain the attention and recognition of their constituents through legislative activity, service, and personal interaction serve the electoral connection. As discussed in chapter 5, there are several studies that examine whether these efforts increase the electoral safety of members (e.g., Johannes and McAdams 1981 versus Fiorina 1981). However, additional research indicates that the political context might condition the impact that service and constituents' attention could have on election outcomes (King 1991; Parker 1986). Just as the political context might disadvantage a candidate's political party and make the candidate less likely to run for office (Jacobson and Kernell 1983), an unfavorable political climate might matter less to reelection when the member has created an attentive constituency through service.

It is little surprise, then, that the subject of incumbency has been the focus of a great deal of attention. However, there was an important shift in the study of this topic when Mayhew (1974b) discovered a consequential change in electoral outcomes. Reprinted here as chapter 10, Mayhew observed incumbent margins of victory and found that most incumbents were no longer experiencing difficult reelection contests. House districts previously won by narrow majorities and classified as "marginal" were "vanishing." This work has led to many articles that try to explain why the marginals vanished.

Mayhew argues that given the same amount of candidate information in each election, voters were behaving in much the same way in 1966 as they did in 1958, but that in 1966, incumbents were better able to disseminate information about their reelection campaigns. That is, for Mayhew, aggregate changes in voter behavior were caused by a shift in the marginal distributions of voters across informational categories. He further speculates that such changes were due to an increasing use of incumbent privileges such as franking and incumbents' growing skill in campaigning. Ultimately, Mayhew's study rests on the premise that an increase in a candidate's visibility will increase that candidate's share of the vote. Scholars such as Ferejohn (1977) question whether incumbents' efforts to increase their visibility had an effect on their share of the vote, but in any case, incumbents' use of institutional resources does not hinder voters' awareness of other candidates.

What is the incumbency effect, then, and how should it be measured? Incumbency itself is perhaps best described as the advantage of office and the sources of such advantage are many. First, the institutional context of Congress benefits members as they pursue reelection strategies. Under a decentralized committee system, members can specialize in issues that benefit their constituents, and members' norms of deference and reciprocity lead members to defer to the requests of fellow members for district benefits. Weak party discipline also facilitates members' reelection efforts in that members can easily "vote the district," not the party. The more tangible spoils of office facilitate member reelection as well. Members are given allowances to employ large personal staffs, to travel home to the district, to run their offices, and to communicate with constituents. Furthermore, these benefits add to each member's name recognition among constituents and permit members to serve their constituents as a sort of ombudsman (Ferejohn 1977; McAdams and Johannes 1987). Fiorina (1977a) argued that the benefits of office grew to become the assets of reelection as explained in chapter 5.

Scholars then began to engage in developing various measures of how much of a candidate's margin of victory was explained by that candidate's incumbency status. These studies attempt to distinguish between votes received due to partisan affiliation or issues and the "personal vote" received on the basis of individual activities. One approach to measurement utilizes regression analysis and survey data in order to examine how much of the variance in voting can be explained by voters' attitudes toward a candidate in contrast to long-term variables such as partisanship. Cain, Ferejohn, and Fiorina (1987) find evidence of a "personal vote" for incumbents, but further efforts to identify the personal vote component of the incumbency advantage have yielded only mixed results. Other scholars have engaged in analyses of election returns in an effort to measure the incumbency effect (Alford and Hibbing 1981; Cover and Mayhew 1977; Garand and Gross 1984). These studies center on the "sophomore surge" (whether incumbency can explain an increased margin of victory for members first seeking reelection to a seat first won in an open-seat race) and the "retirement slump" (the difference between the vote share last won by a retiring member and the vote share won by his party's candidate to succeed him in the resulting open-seat campaign in that district).

Gelman and King (1990) take issue with incumbency effect measures based only on open seat contests or elections involving members who have served one term. They offer an alternative measure of the incumbency effect that they describe as an unbiased estimate, in that they include data from all contested races and control for previous votes and the partisan history of seats. This method results in a higher estimate of the incumbency advantage than found in previous studies. Gelman and King conclude that since 1900 the average advantage of House incumbents has been approximately two percentage points. This may seem small, but it is certainly enough to tip a close election to the incumbent.

Is the incumbency effect or the activities of members in office much ado about nothing, then? Not really. In a general sense, members engage in these activities and develop a "home style" because they believe that such efforts make a difference in election outcomes (see chapter 7). For example, members value each activity differently. Measuring this effect is a difficult matter, yet evidence suggests that efforts to engage in representative behavior do pay off.

ELECTIONS AS CONTESTS BY CHALLENGERS

If earlier literature saw incumbents as invulnerable, scholarly consensus gradually shifted. Mann (1978) emphasizes that members of Congress see their colleagues defeated and so they never view their own races as fully safe. Congressional election survey data were also reevaluated. Analysis of the 1978 National Election Study (Mann and Wolfinger 1980) showed that voters were able to recognize the names of congressional candidates, with the visibility and reputation of the challenger having important effects. With these observations, research eventually turned from incumbents to their challengers. From this perspective, congressional elections are close contests when there are effective challengers. Understanding congressional elections becomes a matter of understanding the mechanisms leading to the emergence of strong challengers.

Earlier we spoke of the strategic considerations of the decision to run for office. How might a potential candidate's decision to run be influenced by the presence of an incumbent? Potential candidates are particularly attracted to races when there are economic or partisan conditions working in their favor. Incumbent scandals make challenges more likely as well. Based on ambition theory, however, potential candidates are unlikely to challenge strong incumbents. The costs are too great and a loss is more likely than not. In theory, potential challengers currently holding other offices are even less likely to challenge incumbents. For them the costs of running are even greater; they are unlikely to sacrifice their current offices or risk their political careers on races they stand little chance of winning. The irony is that these current officeholders—experienced politicians—are the potential challengers who have the best chance of unseating incumbents. Ultimately, the strategic decisions of challengers serve to keep incumbents in office. Jacobson (1990) concludes that incumbent success is largely attributable to inexperienced challengers who lack the issues and the adequate funding that make for a competitive election. Similarly, Krasno (1994) argues that Senate elections are more competitive than those in the House because Senate challengers are more likely than House challengers to be experienced politicians who wage credible campaigns against incumbents.

Both Jacobson and Krasno's findings are examples of what has come to be known as the "quality challenger hypothesis." Using a parsimonious binary measure of challenger quality—whether the challenger previously held elected office—Jacobson concludes that Democrats were controlling Congress in the 1980s because they were fielding more experienced candidates than the Republicans. Jacobson's measure is one of many, the most recent being offered by Squire. Squire (1992) uses a six-point measure based on previous office held and an indicator based on media reports of the candidates' media skills.

Yet inexperienced challengers are not necessarily weak ones. Canon (1990) pointed out that not all challengers are the same. Candidates who are already celebrities, such as ex-athletes, ex-astronauts, ex-actors, and ex-local television personalities, should be considered strong challengers even if they have not previously held political office. Accordingly, Green and Krasno (1988) construct a challenger quality measure that also includes individual qualities such as celebrity or occupational status, previous runs for office, and party activism.

Interestingly, none of the challenger quality studies are concerned with the role of campaign professionals such as consultants. Scholars find that primary election winners are more likely than losers to have had the consultation and encouragement of party leaders. In particular, Herrnson (1992) finds that campaign professionalism affects campaign fundraising even when controls are introduced to factor out the impact of money on professionalism. However Herrnson's work on candidate use of campaign consultants and the national party organizations' training of candidates has not been incorporated in measures of campaign quality.

Another appropriate measure of challenger quality is money. Jacobson (1980, 1985, 1990) demonstrates that the amount of money challengers spend affects election outcomes. Paradoxically, the more an incumbent spends, the more likely the incumbent is to lose. Jacobson's explanation is that the more challengers spend, the more incumbents must spend, and it is the incumbent facing a well-funded challenger who is most likely to lose. Challengers are well funded only if they are thought to have a good chance to win and interest groups are more likely to view the challenger's chances as favorable if the candidate has had previous political experience and is in an electoral situation that appears to offer hope of success. Thus, there is a cycle for challengers that is reinforced by the behavior of political elites such as campaign contributors and journalists. Quality challengers attract money and attention from the media, which in turn leads to a greater perception of their viability as challengers and ultimately to more money and attention. This process was examined by Westlye (1992), who analyzed *Congressional Quarterly* preelection summaries of races. He concludes that candidates determine how competitive Senate elections are—their personal attributes attract media attention and elite support, both of which make for a hard-fought election.

For the strongest or highest quality challengers, the decision to run against an incumbent is strongly influenced by context. McAdams and Johannes (1987) conclude that an incumbent's constituency attentiveness is less important to a challenger's decision to run than the incumbent's ideological position. Moderate incumbents are best able to deter challengers. High quality challengers are also deterred by the campaign war chests of incumbents (Box-Steffensmeier 1996). And while strategic challengers must take advantage of circumstances such as a poor economy or an administration scandal, favorable national conditions are not sufficient for a viable challenge to an incumbent. Studies have shown that strong challengers are better able than weak ones to capitalize on a favorable political context (Jacobson and Kernell 1990) and that district-level factors may have the more consistent impact on the emergence of quality challengers (Krasno and Green 1988).

While our emphasis in this section has been on challengers and their quality, similar considerations apply in open-seat races. The ideal time for a quality candidate to seek the seat is when an incumbent decides to retire. Typically this is true for the strongest candidates from both parties. Rohde would view this as a low-risk opportunity for potential candidates. The number of open seat races in Congress is typically small (20–40 in the 1980s), though there was a considerable increase in 1992 when 65 members retired, due mostly to three factors: redistricting, the House Bank scandal, and the fact that 1992 was the last year they could keep unspent campaign funds for personal use. Each party seeks to retain its open seats, while the other party sees them as their best opportunity to gain seats (especially if national short-term forces, such as the economy, operate in the party's favor).

TERM LIMITS AND THE ELECTORAL CONNECTION

As we consider incumbents and challengers, an underlying question is how effective are elections as instruments for creating representation? Although there is a considerable literature on whether elections matter,[2] another way to examine this issue is to ask if the process or act of representation suffers when the electoral connection is severed. Arguably, members not able to run for reelection might be viewed as less obliged to represent constituents as faithfully as they had previously, if not on all issues, then on some particularly salient or controversial questions. If reelection incentives no longer drive legislative behavior, what does and with what consequences?

The electoral connection can be severed when members choose to retire or when limits are imposed on the number of terms that members may serve. (For a discussion of term limits see the Contemporary Issue that follows chapter 2.) There is a somewhat extensive literature on member behavior when the reelection incentive is absent. Scholars have attempted to study the effects of term limits by studying groups of retiring legislators based on the notion that the performance of such legislators should suggest how legislators might behave if reelection is prohibited. Herrick, Moore, and Hibbing (1994) find that term limits should decrease overall legislative activity such as bills sponsored or amendments offered, as well as decrease attention to constituents. They also suggest that term limits should encourage members' issue specialization, making for a more focused legislative agenda. A related vein of research concerns how members' behavior varies with their seniority. In his study of careers in the House, Hibbing (1991) uses longitudinal data to conclude that representatives' roll-call behavior becomes less liberal with tenure, as well as less extreme and less supportive of their party. Additionally, longstanding members tend to participate in roll-call votes less frequently.

More frequent turnover of legislators could also yield greater change in the policy content of legislation. As Asher and Weisberg argue in chapter 26, members of Congress frequently adopt long-term voting positions on public policy issues. Members can change their positions ("conversion"), but that seems to be rare. Policy change instead depends to a large extent on the infusion of new members to the legislature ("membership replacement"). Replacement is a particularly effective dynamic for policy change when there is a massive shift in the partisan composition of the chamber, as when the liberal "Great Society" was enacted after a large number of new Democrats were elected in 1964 and when the conservative "Contract with America" was largely passed by the House after a large number of new Republicans were elected in 1994. Term limits would obviously increase the rate of membership replacement, though not necessarily leading to the policy changes that accompany shifts in partisan composition. Although there is scholarly support for that notion that turnover can help produce policy change (e.g., Brady and Sinclair 1984), there are few examples of institutional turnover on such a frequent basis.

Scholars do examine directly whether term limits are sufficient to create electoral change or improve the quality of representation. Gerber and Lupia (1996) use game theory to examine incentives for responsive legislators. They posit that even if term limits increased electoral competition, that increase is neither necessary nor sufficient to result in greater member responsiveness. They suggest that reformers seeking a more responsive membership should advocate increased voter awareness and knowledge. Moncrief, Thompson, Haddon, and Hoyer (1992) examine state legislators' tenure in office and conclude that most term-limit proposals would eliminate only a small portion of the incumbency distribution and therefore have only a limited effect on overall legislative tenure in the states. At the congressional level, Reed and Schansberg (1994) and Gilmour and Rothstein (1994) both develop estimates of term limits' impact on party balance and turnover. Both models predict Republican gains, but the authors caution that partisan implications are likely to be modest. Such efforts are fraught with difficulty because the enactment or threat of term limits can easily alter model parameters such as retirement rates. Finally, Grofman and Sutherland (1996) contend that term limits could unintentionally decrease electoral competition by offering incentives for quality challengers to delay running until a seat opens through forced retirement.

Compelling comparative evidence on the effects of legislative term limits also exists, however. John Carey studies the effects of constitutionally limited legislative terms in Costa Rica, the only long-term democracy to impose term limits on legislators, and challenges the claims that term-limit advocates in the United States make about political careers, pork-barrel politics (relations with voters), and the efficacy of political parties in enacting legislative programs (party cohesion). Ultimately, he concludes that the effects of term limits vary with the electoral system on which term limits are imposed, the resources available to party leaders, and consequently, the career paths open to former legislators. For Carey, term limits do not eliminate political careerism or produce more altruistic legislators; they only redirect members' ambitions by "legally severing their direct dependence on voters for career advancement" (Carey 1996, 198).

Based on his research, Carey argues that without the existence of a direct electoral connection, legislative representation depends on the parties' ability to control members' political careers. In nations with different electoral rules where political parties enjoy greater resources, these resources can be used to control members' access to other political positions and a kind of collective electoral connection can exist because parties can be subject to the electoral review of voters. In the United States with its candidate-centered politics, however, term limits would be more likely to weaken party control in this regard and undermine electoral accountability. Carey's study of term limits in Costa Rica even suggests that term limits do not guarantee the elimination of particularistic activities. Because Costa Rican political parties are capable of controlling postlegislative careers, politicians tend to respond to this pressure by meeting party demands to engage in pork barreling and constituent service work.

For members of Congress, postlegislative career prospects are somewhat different. Herrick and Nixon (1994) examine the career patterns of former House members who left Congress between 1971 and 1992. Based on their survey data, they find that although only 27% of former members immediately assumed positions in the bureaucracy or as lobbyists, those who were forced out of office were more likely than not to have done so. They conclude that reforms intended to increase turnover in Congress are unlikely to alter the motives of politicians, but quite likely to affect politics outside Congress. That is, congressional term limits only would exacerbate the problem of a "revolving door" leading to lobbying and the bureaucracy.

Although the various proposals to enact term limits for legislators seem to produce unusually divided opinion, the preceding discussion of term limits illustrates the importance of the electoral connection between representatives and the represented. Members' wishes to be reelected affect their behavior and their representational behavior affects the decisions of their constituents as well as the decisions of their electoral rivals.

CONCLUSION

In this chapter we have emphasized the ways in which the literature addresses how candidacies affect elections. Incumbents' efforts to create an attentive constituency and the resulting incumbency effect in outcomes constitute one half of the equation, while decisions by potential challengers to run provide the other half.

The literature on congressional elections has shifted from a virtually exclusive focus on the incumbency advantage in congressional elections to an appreciation of the importance of the factors leading to strong challengers. An interest in challengers currently shapes much of the congressional elections literature, as researchers investigate the conditions under which quality challengers decide to run and are best able to conduct effective challenges. Scholars have developed increasingly sophisticated measures of challenger quality and have examined the importance of incumbents' resources and voting records in either inviting challenges or deterring them. Important measurement issues involve both halves of the equation—research on how to measure the incumbency effect is matched by studies of how to measure challenger quality.

The greater focus on challengers does not mean that the importance of incumbency should be dismissed. Indeed, a new avenue of research has opened as measures of *incumbent* quality have been developed by McCurley and Mondak (1995). In spite of the defeat of several Democratic incumbents in the 1994 midterm election, the advantages of incumbency remain powerful and the new congressional Republican majority continues to learn how to use their status to garner PAC funds for their campaigns. In fact, Mondak, McCurley, and Millman

(1999) show that incumbent competence and integrity were the important factors in determining reelection success in the 1994 and 1996 House elections.

In addition to the direct effects of the incumbency factor, incumbency has substantial side effects. Take, for example, its effect on the election of women to Congress. In a legislature without an incumbency advantage, quality female candidates should be elected as often, or nearly as often, as quality male candidates. In a legislature that has an incumbency advantage, though, quality female challengers will often lose to male incumbents. Since a large majority of members of Congress are male, the incumbency advantage serves as a barrier to the election of women. Thus a very slow growth in the proportion of members of Congress who are female should be expected (Andersen and Thorson 1984; Darcy, Welch, and Clark 1994), though term limits could drastically accelerate this process.

Running through current discussions of both incumbents and challengers is the notion of candidates as strategic actors. Incumbents purposely take actions in office to bolster their reelection chances, while rationally calculating whether they should instead try for higher offices. Potential challengers time their candidacies strategically, deciding when to run on the basis of their likelihood of winning. Viewing all candidacies through a strategic perspective clarifies not only how candidacies affect elections, but also the relative roles of incumbents and challengers.

The most damning assessment of the research on congressional elections has been given by Linda Fowler (1993), who concludes that we have not obtained a coherent body of knowledge about congressional candidacies. She claims that most scholars emphasize only the linkage between candidate member characteristics and institutional decisions, with the importance of candidacies being neglected. She attributes the weakness of the literature about candidacies to scholars' "preoccupation" with the careers of incumbents (vi). Even the focus on ambition theory has not sufficed, since in her view the focus on progressive ambition has led to a neglect of candidate emergence.

This suggests a refocusing of the elections literature to emphasize candidacies and thereby achieve a more integrated view of candidate behavior from their initial decisions to run to the end of their legislative careers. What Fowler sees as missing is theory that would permit researchers to identify a pool of prospective congressional candidates and differentiate that pool from those who do actually run.[3] According to Fowler, if this task were undertaken, scholars could address "the true influence of candidacy in framing the public's choice from among competing elites" (vi). In any case, understanding candidacies should be seen as the key to understanding congressional elections.

NOTES

1. Another ingredient of the solution to this puzzle (Kinder and Kiewiet 1981) is that citizens vote for Congress more on the basis of the national economy ("sociotropic voting") than on the basis of their own economic situation ("pocketbook voting"), but that story is not relevant to our discussion of strategic politicians.

2. The question of whether elections matter is usually taken to ask whether elections in fact indicate a general policy direction that the nation should take. That is, what is the meaning of election outcomes—a general indicator or an all too blunt instrument? For a collection of studies addressing this question, see Ginsberg and Stone (1996).
3. In 1996 Sandy Maisel and Walter Stone started a major study of candidacy decisions along the lines that Fowler describes, identifying potential candidates in districts and interviewing them. That study, however, became very controversial for unrelated reasons. It was funded by the National Science Foundation, which upset some incumbent members of Congress who felt that the researchers were trying to foster challenges to them. The results of the Maisel and Stone study may fill in some of the gaps that Fowler identifies, though unfortunately the political controversy over their study makes funding of similar candidate emergence studies in the future less likely.

CONTEMPORARY ISSUE:

Divided Government

Repeated election outcomes in the 1970s and 1980s resulted in a Republican White House and a Democratically controlled Congress and led to an interest in "divided government" among scholars and political observers. This interest has intensified since 1995, with a Democratic president forced to govern in an unwilling coalition with Republican congressional majorities. This type of U.S. "coalition" party government exposed the weaknesses of the theory of responsible party government and of many political scientists' belief in strong presidential leadership. Political parties cannot link the legislative and executive branches when the president's party is the congressional minority.

Political observers fiercely debated the normative consequences of divided partisan control of the executive and legislative branches. In the process of doing so, many called for structural reforms to avoid "legislative gridlock," but scholars soon began to debate whether political reform could prevent episodes of divided government. That debate prompted political scientists, particularly those interested in voting behavior and elections, to focus their research on the causes of divided government.

THE CAUSES OF DIVIDED GOVERNMENT

A wide variety of explanations have been given for divided government in the United States. Voting behavior specialists tend to see divided government in terms of an increase in ticket splitting among voters, with more people casting their votes for one party for president but the other party for Congress. As many as 40% of the congressional districts in some recent elections have experienced divergent election outcomes with one party's candidate getting a majority of the presidential vote while the other party won the House seat, though it is possible for this to happen with only a small minority of voters actually splitting their ballots (Sundquist 1992).

The increased occurrence of divided government suggests to many scholars that the bases of voting for president and members of Congress have diverged, with personal and local considerations exerting a larger influence on congressional voting than previously. One argument of this sort (by Ansolabehere, Brady, and Fiorina 1992) is that Mayhew's "vanishing marginals" thesis (reprinted here as chapter 10) contributed to the occurrence of divided government as members were able to increase their reelection margins quite apart from national political trends. For example, the diversity of the Democratic party nationally made the formation of winning coalitions of support difficult for the party's presidential candidate, but House Democrats could easily focus on local issues in their races. Doing so permitted them to construct bases of support independent of the national party. For example, Southern Democrats could portray themselves as socially conservative or anti-gun control and retain seats in districts that were voting Republican for president.

Divided government in the 1970s and 1980s occurred when Republican presidents governed with Democratic Congresses. That was seen by some observers as due to the

Democratic party's inability to unite behind strong presidential candidates (Petrocik 1991) and by others as due to the Republican party's weakness in fielding strong congressional candidates. On the latter point, Ehrenhalt (1991) argued that young Republicans have less incentive to run for office since they do not believe in government intervention, while Fiorina (1996) posits that legislative seats are more attractive as jobs to Democrats, who support government activism and whose membership is drawn from lower-income groups. The exceptions to these arguments are instructive. The successful candidacies of Jimmy Carter in 1976 and Bill Clinton in 1992 led to unified government precisely because the Democrats chose moderate presidential candidates. Meanwhile the Republicans were able to create divided government in the mid–1990s under a Democratic president by aggressively recruiting congressional candidates who might not otherwise have decided to run.

Yet governing during episodes of divided government alters presidents' ability to lead their parties in subsequent congressional elections. When Republican presidents Reagan and Bush had to compromise with the Democratic majority in Congress, they hampered congressional Republicans' ability to run against House and Senate Democrats on Republican issues. House Republicans found it difficult to advocate change during a Republican administration. After all, it was Republican presidents who agreed to tax increases and few domestic spending cuts. The reverse is true as well. When President Clinton portrayed himself as a moderating influence on Republican spending cuts, he improved his own reelection chances, not those of congressional Democrats. Divided government makes it difficult for voters to hold a single party accountable at election time. Both parties can legitimately claim credit for policy successes and each is able to avoid voters' blame for unpopular decisions.

An alternative perspective suggests that voters value different qualities when voting for president and Congress. Jacobson (1990) has argued that divided government in the 1980s represented public preferences for Republican positions on issues voters associate with presidential responsibilities (such as foreign policy) combined with a preference for Democratic positions on issues associated with congressional responsibilities (such as funding for local projects). This exact explanation cannot, of course, account for the pattern of divided government in the mid–1990s, though one could instead argue that the public preferred Democratic positions on social and domestic issues and Republican positions on balanced budgets.

Petrocik (1991) argues that voters rarely conceive of representatives and senators in terms of policy issues, yet they relate issues to their choice of a presidential candidate. His theory of "issue ownership" is similar to Jacobson's in that the public credits each party with handling some issues better than their opposition does. When these issues are salient in a campaign, the party credited with superior handling of those issues benefits. According to this theory, elections are decided by the relative salience of Democratic issues versus Republican ones. Voters choose candidates based on the issues. However, Jacobson assumes that almost all House elections concern distributive issues affecting that congressional district and almost all presidential elections focus on national collective goods (Petrocik and Doherty 1996). For Petrocik, the issue content of House elections varies and depends on context and the strategic actions of the candidates. Ticket splitting occurs when the issues dominating a congressional election differ from those of the presidential election. The voters most likely to split their ballot between the parties in this case are those who think that the most important problem facing the country is better handled by one party but that the most important problem in their congressional district is more ably addressed by the other party.

Some researchers have gone beyond the above explanations to argue that voters consciously prefer divided government. Erikson (1988) and Alesina and Rosenthal (1989) speculate that voters consciously put the parties in a position where each can check the other, adding a partisan dimension to the constitutional system of checks and balances for limiting government power. This idea appeals to voters when they are questioned, and clear pluralities accept the idea as a desirable consequence of divided government (Lacy 1998; Petrocik and Doherty 1996). However, this approach offers no evidence that voters consciously seek the outcomes of divided government and does not describe elections after which all branches of government were controlled by the Democratic party (1960, 1964, 1976, 1992). Fiorina (1996) further has developed a formal model in which moderate voters would prefer the policies that would pass under divided government to the policies that would be enacted under unified Democratic or Republican control, though empirical evidence of voters behaving in this manner is mixed at best (Lacy 1998). The results depend in part on what questions are asked— greater support for divided government is found when the questions asked of respondents specify which party controls the presidency.[1]

Polling data do offer evidence that little issue consensus exists and that the public holds contradictory preferences, however (Jacobson 1990). For example, most voters favor less government intervention and object to the cost of government, but a majority also opposes cuts in entitlements and other popular government programs. In the 1980s, voters were able to express all of these preferences at the polls because Republican candidates for president ran on platforms of low taxes and Democrats campaigning for Congress pledged to maximize benefits to their own constituents. There appeared to be two camps of opinion, but a majority of voters seemed to belong to both. The ticket splitting that resulted in episodes of divided government likely occurred without the conscious calculation of voters. Majorities simply picked the presidential candidate they expected to reduce spending and the member of Congress they believed would protect their own benefits.

CONCLUSION

Some might contend that research on divided government is itself divided into two camps: those who believe divided partisan control of Congress and the executive leads to government nonperformance and those who argue that divided government is of little substantive consequence. The latter assert that many factors contribute to interbranch conflict— institutional structure and weak political parties, for example—but that good public policy and decision making are not impossible in that setting when there is an elite and public consensus. Certainly we have provided only a sample of many conflicting views on the causes of divided government; the Contemporary Issue following chapter 24 deals with the consequences of divided government. Most of the research on divided government is based on a Democratic majority in Congress, so the presence of a Republican majority in the mid–1990s should permit more complete tests of both the causes and effects of divided government.

Scholars of congressional elections face a particular challenge in identifying and refining explanations of the origins of divided government. Additionally, many of the explanations recounted here may become less compelling as a new cohort of voters enters the electorate and the parties' ownership of issues or voters' conceptions of each governmental branch's responsibilities change. Ultimately, the identification of divided government's origins may be as fragmented as political power itself in American politics. More than one of the above explanations may be true and any single explanation might present only one of many contributing factors. That is, it is likely that many factors contribute to the existence of divided government; pinning the blame on only institutional structure, voters, office-holders, or political parties presents an incomplete explanation.

NOTES

1. Lacy (1998) found greater support for divided government using the following question items: "If the president is a Democrat, would you prefer that the Democrats or the Republicans control Congress? If the president is a Republican, would you prefer that the Democrats or the Republicans control Congress?" This question wording differs from that used in the National Election Study: "Do you think it is better when one party controls both the presidency and Congress; better when control is split between the Democrats and Republicans; or it doesn't matter?"

Chapter 9

Risk-Bearing and Progressive Ambition: The Case of Members of the U. S. House of Representatives

DAVID W. ROHDE

Ambition lies at the heart of politics. Politics thrive on the hope of preferment and the drive for office" (Schlesinger 1966, 1). Since Joseph Schlesinger wrote those introductory lines to his superb study of career patterns in the United States, a substantial amount of research has been conducted on ambition and office-seeking behavior.[1] Most of this research has, however, been primarily empirical in nature, and has not attempted to provide a more explicit theoretical framework for ambition analysis.[2] In addition, most of this research has followed Schlesinger's example in selecting for analysis persons who actually achieved or tried for an office, and examining their career patterns and characteristics.

The present study departs from both of these trends. The theoretical focus is progressive ambition; the focus of the empirical analysis is on members of the U.S. House of Representatives between 1954 and 1974 and their decisions on whether or not to seek either a U.S. Senate seat or the governorship of their state. We begin by formulating a theory of progressive ambition and deriving a set of testable hypotheses from that theory. We then proceed to test those hypotheses on data on the office-seeking behavior of [members of congress] in relation to Senate seats and governorships. Instead, however, of analyzing the backgrounds of members of the House who sought those offices (analysis which has already been done—see Frost 1972; Hain and Smith 1973), we will examine each member who had an opportunity to run for one of those offices and whether or not the opportunity was taken. Finally, we will return to the theoretical level and offer some hypotheses for future consideration.

Source: David W. Rohde, "Risk Bearing and Progressive Ambition." *American Journal of Political Science.* Volume 23, number 1. 1–26. Copyright © 1979. Reprinted by permission of The University of Wisconsin Press.

A THEORY OF PROGRESSIVE AMBITION

Schlesinger (1966, 9–10) discusses three "directions" or types of ambition: discrete, static, and progressive. Briefly, discrete ambition relates to the politician who seeks an office for one term and then seeks neither reelection nor another office. Static ambition relates to the politician who seeks an office with the intent of attempting to retain it for as long as possible. Progressive ambition relates to the politician who holds an office and attempts to gain another regarded as more attractive.

Since Schlesinger's analysis considered people who behaved ambitiously, (i.e., sought certain offices), rather than (as in the present study) examining a selected set of politicians and predicting whether or not they would seek a given office, he did not address a certain conceptual question regarding the distinction between static and progressive ambition that we must consider. In discussing static ambition, he states (1966, 10): "How widespread such ambitions are we cannot tell, for the possibilities of making a career of one office are varied. Nevertheless, it is certainly a marked goal of many American congressmen and senators." Thus a retrospective analysis categorizes direction of ambition on the basis of manifest behavior, and (to use members of the House as an example) representatives who serve one term and leave voluntarily have discrete ambition, those who attempt to remain in the House have static ambition, and those who run for higher office have progressive ambition. A prospective analysis such as ours, however, cannot retain such a categorization. We believe, and here explicitly assume, that progressive ambition is held by almost all members of the House.[3] That is, we assume that if a member of the House, on the first day of service, were offered a Senate seat or[4] a governorship *without cost or risk*, he would take it. Thus static ambition is not something chosen a priori, but is a behavior pattern manifested by a member because of the risks of the particular opportunity structure he finds himself in, and his unwillingness to bear those risks.

Now we turn to some additional assumptions about the actors who are to be described by our theory. First, we assume that they are *rational*, in the sense of being maximizers of expected utility.

> Put most simply, being rational in a decision situation consists in examining the alternatives with which one is confronted, estimating and evaluating the likely consequences of each, and selecting that alternative which yields the most attractive set of expectations (Goldberg 1969, 5).

Whatever one's position on the usefulness or the range of applicability of rational choice models of politics, such models should be most useful in such calculated political choice situations as the choice between alternative offices.

Next we assume a particular calculus of decision making for the actors. For this purpose we adopt the simple decision calculus outlined by Riker and Ordeshook (1973, chapter 3), a variant of which is employed by Black (1972, 146). The calculus we posit is as follows:

$$E(a_i) = P_1(O_1)U(O_1) + P_1(O_2)U(O_2) + P_1(O_3)U(O_3) - C(a_1) \tag{1}$$

$$E(a_2) = P_2(O_1)U(O_1) + P_2(O_2)U(O_2) + P_2(O_3)U(O_3) - C(a_2) \qquad (2)$$

where

$E(a_i)$ is the expected utility of choosing alternative i,

$P_i(O_j)$ is the probability that outcome j will occur if alternative i is chosen,

$U(O_j)$ is the utility the actor receives if outcome j occurs,

$C(a_i)$ is the direct utility cost incurred by choosing alternative i,

and where specifically:

O_1 = no office is occupied after the election,

O_2 = the presently held office is occupied after the election,

O_3 = the higher office being considered is occupied after the election,

a_1 = the actor runs for the presently held office (i.e., reelection),[5]

a_2 = the actor runs for the higher office.

An actor will not be able to occupy the present office if he runs for the higher one, nor occupy the higher one if he runs for reelection, therefore $P_1(O_3) = P_2(O_2) = 0$. Since we will eliminate from the empirical analysis those representatives who retire, we can theoretically ignore the case where O_1 is most preferred. In addition, we can further simplify our discussion by assuming that O_1 is the least preferred outcome. This eliminates from theoretical consideration the rare case of the representative who wants to leave the House and decides to run for higher office instead of retiring. This situation seems to occur so seldom that we can safely ignore it at this time.

. . . Since we assume that O_1 is the least preferred outcome, we can arbitrarily set $U(O_1) = 0$, and expressions (1) and (2) simplify to the following:

$$E(a_1) = P_1(O_2)U(O_2) - C(a_1) \qquad (3)$$

$$E(a_2) = P_2(O_3)U(O_3) - C(a_2) \qquad (4)$$

Thus, for each office the expected value of running for the office is a function of the probability of winning, the value of the office, and the costs of running; by our rationality assumption, an actor will run for higher office only if $E(a_2) > E(a_1)$.

From the above we see, in a more formal context, the relevance of the "opportunity structure" that Schlesinger found so important in his research, for the values of the elements on the right-hand side of expression (4) are in large measure set by the opportunity structure and determine the risks of running for higher office. The higher the risks, the less likely is an actor to run. We will now proceed to apply these predictions to the specific situation of House members and the prospect of running for senator or governor, and to offer a series of hypotheses about the situation. . . .

The Value of the Higher Office

We have assumed that (almost all) members of the House have progressive ambition. They would choose, if presented with a costless and riskless opportunity, to be senator or governor. . . .

While there is certainly individual variation in the evaluation of the two offices, making a Senate seat more attractive to some and the governorship more attractive to others, there are also certain salient features of the opportunity structure of members of the House that affect the relative value of the two offices and make running for the Senate generally more attractive than seeking the governorship.

First, and probably foremost, is the six-year Senate term. The maximum term for a governor in the United States is four years, and a number of states even have two-year gubernatorial terms.[6] A longer term permits an actor more time to enjoy the benefits of holding office instead of spending his time attempting to retain the office.

Second, there is the question of vulnerability. Recent research indicates that governors running for reelection are at least somewhat more vulnerable to defeat than are senators in the same situation. Data for the period 1950–70 show that 85.5% of Senate incumbents running for reelection were successful (Kostroski 1973, 1217). However, data on incumbent governors running for reelection in almost exactly the same period (1950–69) show that only 64.4% were successful.[7] Certainly the likelihood of reelection to a prospective office will affect the value of that office to an individual.

Closely related to the prospects for reelection, and probably even more relevant to our discussion, is a third consideration: the prospects for a career in an office. Beyond a Senate seat and the governor's chair, the only major elective offices are the presidency and vice-presidency—offices which few seek and even fewer attain. Thus, at this level, career considerations loom large. Nelson Rockefeller (R-NY) holds at least the modern record for service as governor: 15 years. Indeed, Schlesinger (1972b, 12) shows that of the 151 governors serving during the decade 1950–59, only 30.5% served more than four years. However, by the time of Rockefeller's resignation from the governorship in December 1973, 35 members of the Senate had equalled or surpassed his length of tenure, and 60% had served more than four years.[8]

A final consideration in this regard is one noted by Schlesinger (1966, 99–100).

> The second manifest tie between offices is the similarity of functions. The legislative function requires similar skills and talents whether in the city council or the federal Senate. Different demands are made upon judges or executives. . . . Manifestly, the functional resemblance of offices is a condition which affects the course of political careers.

On all of these grounds—greater length of term, lower electoral vulnerability, greater career prospects, and similarity of functions—we would expect, in general, members of the House to place a higher value on a Senate seat than a governorship, and we are thus led to our first hypothesis.

H_1:   Among House members, the proportion of opportunities to run for the Senate that is taken will be greater than the proportion of opportunities taken to run for governor.

While we argue that Senate seats are more attractive than governorships, it is clear that not all governorships are equally attractive. Governorships differ in the powers the occupant of the office has under the various state constituents (see Schlesinger 1972a). We would expect that a House member from a state with a powerful governorship would find that office more attractive than would a member from a state with a weak governorship. While we do not have data on governors' powers for the entire period under consideration, and therefore cannot test this expectation, there is one feature on which governorships differ and on which the data are readily available: length of term. We have already noted that an office with a longer term should be generally more attractive than an office with a shorter term, and that states vary in the length they set for their governor's term. A member of the House, who serves a two-year term, is going to find an altnerative office which also has a two-year term less attractive, ceteris paribus, than an alternative office with a four-year term. Therefore, our second hypothesis is:

H$_2$:   Among House members, the proportion of opportunities to run for governorships with a four-year term that is taken will be greater than the proportion of opportunities taken to run for governorships with a two-year term.

The Probability of Winning the Higher Office

We assumed above that a member of the House would accept a Senate seat or governorship if they could get it without cost or risk. However, such circumstances are seldom, if ever, present. Members seeking higher office often have to bear substantial costs and risks. For many members $P_2(O_3)$ (the probability of winning the higher office) will be relatively small, while for others it will be substantially larger.

One factor which will affect the probability of winning higher office is whether or not the office in question is held by an incumbent running for reelection. As we have seen incumbent senators and governors have a substantially better than even chance of being reelected. Thus the risk of running against an incumbent is a good deal greater than the risk of running if there is no incumbent in the race. Indeed, for an actor who has decided to make a try for another office, such considerations can determine the timing of such an attempt. . . .

Thus the third hypothesis is:

H$_3$:   Among House members, for both Senate and gubernatorial races, the proportion of opportunities to run for higher office that is taken in situations where no incumbent is seeking reelection will be greater than the proportion of opportunities taken in situations where an incumbent is seeking reelection.

In addition to incumbency, another factor that will affect the probability of winning is the partisan bias of the electoral situation. Although party identification is no longer the dependable predictor of voting that it once was (see, for example, DeVries and Tarrance 1972), there do remain some states (notably those in the deep South) which are relatively "safe" for one party or the other. If this is so, then obviously the likelihood of a candidate winning in a state which is "safe" for the other party is less than if the state is competitive or safe for his own party. Therefore:

H$_4$:   Among House members, for both Senate and gubernatorial races, the proportion of opportunities to run for higher office that is taken in states which are "safe" for the opposition party will be less than the proportion of opportunities taken in states which are competitive or "safe" for their own party.

A final consideration which will affect the probability of winning relates to the base from which a candidate runs. It is fairly well known that name recognition is an important consideration in electoral situations. Potential candidates often poll their prospective constituency to determine how well known they are, and the results of such polls affect their decision on whether or not to run. Whether a candidate is known to a voter affects that voter's decision (see Ferejohn 1977; Stokes and Miller 1962). One thing that will have a substantial impact on voter recognition is the degree of overlap between the constituency a prospective candidate presently represents and the constituency he would like to represent (see Schlesinger 1966, 99). For example, a randomly selected voter from Delaware is more likely to have heard of the single congressman from that state than is a randomly selected voter from California to have heard of any one of the state's 43 congressmen. . . .

Therefore, we argue that the greater the degree of overlap between a potential candidate's present constituency and his prospective constituency, the more likely he is to seek higher office.

Thus, in general, we would expect congressmen from small states to be more likely to run for higher office than congressmen from large states. There is, however, an additional factor affecting the value of the higher office which leads us to modify this expectation. While we would expect that there is little difference between the attractiveness of a Senate seat from a big state and one from a small state, such would not seem to be true in the case of governorships. First, and tautologically, a governor from a large state governs more people than one from a small state. He can have a substantial impact on the lives of a larger number of people, usually deals with a greater range of public policy matters, and is more likely to be observed by the national media.[9]

Second, there appears to be a relationship between the size of a state and the powers granted to its governor. Schlesinger (1972a) has constructed an index of the powers of governors in 1969.[10] If we divide the states by whether they are above or below the median state population and also divide them by whether they are above or below the median value of Schlesinger's index, it appears that in 1969 large states had relatively more powerful governors, and small states relatively weaker ones. Among the large states, 64% were above the median index value, while among the small states only 28% were above the median.

For governorships, then, something of an inverse relationship exists between the attractiveness of the office and the probability of winning. Thus there should be no clear effect from state size on House members seeking governorships, and so we restrict our next hypothesis to Senate candidacies:

H[5]: Among House members, for Senate races, the probability that a House member will run will be directly related to the proportion of the state's population the population of his House constituency comprises.[11]

The Value of the House Seat

It is commonplace to note that power in the House rests largely in its committees, and that the way to power in committees is through the seniority system. This is still largely true despite recent reforms designed to reduce the power of committee chairmen. Therefore, if we assume that a major motivation of members is to have power within the House (whether for its own sake, to increase their probability of winning reelection, or because they are concerned about policy outcomes), then the more senior a member is, the more power he will have, the higher will be the value of his seat to him, and the less likely he will be to seek higher office. Thus hypothesis six states:

> H_6:   For both Senate and gubernatorial races, the probability that a House member will run will be inversely related to his seniority.

Risk Acceptance and Progressive Ambition

To this point, our theory has outlined the impact of various situational factors (or the "opportunity structure") on the congressman's decision on whether to seek higher office. These situational factors determine the risks a potential candidate must face in trying to move up. The risks do not, however, tell the whole story. That is (returning to expressions 3 and 4 above), if two candidates are faced with the same levels of $P_i(O_j)$ and $C(a_i)$, and each has an identical preference ordering in which O_3 is preferred to O_2 which is preferred to O_1, it may still be the case that one will run and the other will not. This is because "some people are more likely to select risky alternatives than are others" (Riker and Ordeshook 1973, 75).[12] People with the same preference ordering will differ in the *intensity* of those preferences. . . . Indeed, we believe that it is differences in intensity of preference, and thus willingness to take electoral risks in seeking offices, that distinguishes the ambitious politician from the nonambitious.

These considerations lead us to our next hypothesis:

> H_7:   If two House members are presented with similar opportunities to seek higher office, and one is a "risk taker" and the other is not, then the "risk taker" will have a greater probability of running for higher office than the other.

This concludes the discussion of hypothesis on which we will bring data to bear. We will discuss further consequences of our theory after presenting some empirical results.

THE DATA

The data used to test the hypothesis relate to all members of the U.S. House of Representatives who were presented with an opportunity to run for either a Senate seat or the governorship in elections between 1954 and 1974 inclusive. To test the hypotheses we require information on the length of governors' terms, whether an incumbent is running for reelection to the prospective higher office, the degree of interparty competitiveness of the state, the size of the state, and the seniority of each congressional incumbent.

All election statistics, information on length of gubernatorial terms and information on whether an incumbent was seeking reelection to the higher office[13] are taken from appropriate volumes of *America Votes*. Seniority data were taken from *Members of Congress 1945–1970* (1971), supplemented by information in the 1973 *Congressional Directory*.

We consider a member to have an opportunity to run for higher office if he is a member of Congress (subject to the exceptions discussed below) in a year when an election is held in his state for a Senate seat or the governorship, and the office in question is either held by an incumbent of the other party or has no incumbent seeking reelection. Thus for the present study we do not consider the possibility of a congressman opposing an incumbent of his own party. While we expect the nature of the calculations to be basically the same in such a case, the situations are quite different and require separate analyses.

We have already stated that we would exclude members with discrete ambition from our theoretical discussion and from our empirical analysis. Therefore, members who resign from the House or who announce their retirement at the end of a term are not considered to have had an opportunity to run for higher office. Second, since our consideration of progressive ambition is limited to the Senate and governorships, any House member who ran for any other office is excluded from the analysis. Third, since we have limited our discussion to situations where a congressman must give up his House seat to run for higher office, five states[14] which elect their governors at times other than November of even-numbered years are omitted from the analysis of members seeking governorships, as are members from other states who run in special elections held at times other than November of even-numbered years.[15] Finally, we exclude from our analysis of any given election all members who were elected to the House in special elections since the previous November election. Because of the necessity of planning ahead for a statewide race, such congressmen are almost precluded from running and, in fact, no such member did run.[16]

Of course, to test hypothesis seven we need some indicator of which members of the House are risk takers. . . . [W]e assume that it is possible to employ previous behavior as an indicator of risk taking. Specifically, we examined the situation in which each member first sought election to the House.[17] We classified situations[18] in which (1) an incumbent was running for reelection, or (2) no incumbent was running, but the other party averaged 57% or more of the vote in the three previous elections[19] as high-risk situations and a member who first sought election in such a situation was classified as a risk taker. A race with no incumbent that did not fit (2) above was classified as low risk, and members who first sought election in such a situation are classified as "others."[20]

This compilation yields a data set of 3,040 opportunities to run, of which 111 (or 3.7%) were taken.

TESTING THE HYPOTHESES

In this first exploratory analysis, we will employ cross-tabulation to examine the impact of one or two independent variables at a time. Each table will present the proportion of opportunities taken and will control for whether or not the members in question are risk takers.

Table 9.1 presents the data on hypotheses one and two, relating to the relative value of the higher offices, controlling for whether or not the members are risk takers. Overall, House members are about three times more likely to run for senator than for a four-year governorship and about eleven times more than [for] a two-year governorship. This pattern is true for both risk takers and for others. Again overall, risk takers are about two and one-half times more likely to run for higher office than are nonrisk takers.

In order to make the compilation of data manageable, we combined the test of hypotheses three and four. Members who faced an opportunity to run were placed in one of two categories: low probability of winning or high probability of winning. The former category included members who would have to face an incumbent, or who were in a state in which the other party averaged 57% or more of the vote for senator and governor over the previous four years; the latter category includes other members. (Note that this classification implies no absolute meaning; these probabilities are high or low relative only to each other.) Thus our combined prediction is that the proportion of members who run for higher office when the probability of winning is high will be greater than the proportion who run when the probability is low. Table 9.2 presents the relevant data.

While the results are in the predicted direction, the impact of probability of winning appears to be minimal. The reason for this apparent lack of relationship becomes clear, however, when we control for type of office (see Table 9.3). When we compare each cell in part A (the upper half) of Table 9.3 to the corresponding cell in part B, we almost always find a fairly substantial difference between the two

Table 9.1

Proportion of members running for higher office, controlling for risk taking and type of office

Office:	Member is:		
	Risk taker	Other	Total
Two-year governorship	0.6 (180)*	0.4 (252)	0.5 (432)
Four-year governorship	3.6 (522)	0.8 (623)	2.1 (1145)
Senate seat	7.8 (715)	3.9 (748)	5.8 (1463)
Total	5.4 (1417)	2.2 (1623)	3.7 (3040)

*Number of opportunities

proportions. The difference between the results here and those in Table 9.2 is due to the fact that Senate races offered mostly low probability opportunities while gubernatorial races offered primarily high probability opportunities. (This is because incumbents are more likely to be involved in Senate races.)

The data in Table 9.3 offer a fairly strong test of the theory since the first four hypotheses plus hypothesis seven are all considered simultaneously. We can see that each of the elements that have been considered thus far have independent effects. If we look at the highest-probability case from the point of view of the theory (risk takers with Senate opportunities and a high probability of winning), the proportion who run is more than one in ten, while in a number of low-probability cases the proportion running is zero. The fact, however, that in the most attractive situation reflected in this table only one opportunity in ten is taken indicates how high the risks are even then. The situation is, again, only attractive relative to the others, not in absolute terms. . . .

One alternative available to test hypothesis five would be to ascertain . . . the amount of overlap between the district constituency and the statewide constituency by the number of congressional districts the state has: 1 or 2 districts, 3–6 districts, 7–10 districts, 11–19 districts, and 22 or more districts.[21] These data are presented in Table 9.4.[22]

We see that the prediction is supported by the data. For both risk takers and others combined, the proportion of opportunities taken decreases monotonically as the number of districts in a state increases. Moreover, the relationship is clearly not linear. The likelihood of a House member seeking a Senate seat in a state with only one or two districts, where the constituency overlap is great, is more than one in three. This drops sharply to about one in ten for the next category, drops sharply again for the third, with the proportion of opportunities taken in the last three categories being about the same. Furthermore, in four of the five district categories, a comparison of the proportions for risk takers and for others shows that the former is substantially larger than the latter. Indeed, in that theoretically most

Table 9.2

Proportion of members running for higher office, controlling for risk taking and probability of winning

Member is:	Percent of opportunities taken when probability of winning was:		
	High	Low	Total
Risk Taker	6.0	4.9	5.3
	(603)*	(814)	(1417)
Other	2.8	1.6	2.2
	(795)	(828)	(1623)
Total	4.1	3.2	3.7
	(1398)	(1642)	(3040)

*Number of opportunities

Table 9.3

Proportion of members running for higher office, controlling for risk taking, probability of winning, and type of office

A. Probability of winning is high

Office:	Member is:		
	Risk taker	Other	Total
Two-year governorship	1.1 (90)*	0.0 (124)	0.5 (214)
Four-year governorship	4.5 (309)	1.2 (410)	2.6 (719)
Senate seat	10.3 (204)	6.5 (261)	8.2 (465)
Total	6.0 (603)	2.8 (795)	4.1 (1398)

B. Probability of winning is low

Office:	Member is:		
	Risk taker	Other	Total
Two-year governorship	0.0 (90)	0.8 (128)	0.5 (218)
Four-year governorship	2.3 (213)	0.0 (213)	1.2 (426)
Senate seat	6.8 (511)	2.5 (487)	4.7 (998)
Total	4.9 (814)	1.6 (828)	3.2 (1642)

*Number of opportunities

attractive situation (risk takers, one or two districts) the proportion that runs approaches one in two, 40 times larger than the least attractive situation.

We now turn to the last of our initial hypotheses [—seniority]. . . . The average number of consecutive terms in office served by House members between 1953 and 1969 was 5.22;[23] the average number of terms served by the 111 members who ran for higher office was 3.52. Thus, House members seeking higher office served about one and one-half terms less than the average House member. Furthermore, we find that the amount of seniority possessed by candidates varies with risk-taking category, type of office, and probability of winning (see Table 9.5). Among members who sought Senate seats, the only large difference is between members with the least attractive opportunity (nonrisk taker, low probability of winning) and all those in other cells. However, most of the other possible comparisons (e.g., among gubernatorial candidates) show more substantial differences.

This is, of course, the least direct test of any of the hypotheses, and the results must be regarded as extremely tentative.

CONCLUSIONS

This study has differed from most other analyses of ambition in two ways; first, we have attempted to give a more concrete theoretical base to the study of progressive ambition, and second, our analysis has been prospective rather than retrospective. That is, we have attempted to predict which potential candidates would actually run for higher office, rather than analyze the career patterns of actors who ran. . . .

As we noted earlier, the results presented are preliminary. Any final conclusions must await a multivariate analysis in which all of the variables we have discussed are considered simultaneously. Furthermore, in addition to the hypotheses we presented above, others also follow from the theory and will have to be tested at a later date. Before concluding, it is appropriate to outline a number of these.

First, regarding the probability of winning the higher office, other features of the situation are obviously relevant in addition to whether or not there is an incumbent and the degree of party competition. Incumbents are not invulnerable; some *are* beaten. An incumbent's previous margin of election, particularly if he was an incumbent then, is an indicator of how vulnerable he is. The lower that margin, the greater should be the likelihood that a representative would accept the opportunity to run. Another consideration related to this point which should be important

Table 9.4

Proportion of members running for senator, controlling for risk taking and number of districts in state

Number of districts in state	Percent of opportunities taken when member is:		
	Risk taker	Other	Total
1 or 2	45.9	28.3	36.1
	(37)*	(46)	(83)
3–6	9.3	11.3	10.1
	(86)	(53)	(139)
7–10	4.9	2.4	3.9
	(182)	(124)	(306)
11–19	6.5	1.8	3.8
	(124)	(163)	(287)
22 or more	4.9	1.1	2.8
	(286)	(362)	(648)
Total	7.8	3.9	5.8
	(715)	(748)	(1463)

*Number of opportunities

Table 9.5

Seniority of House members seeking
higher office, controlling for risk taking,
type of office, and probability of winning

A. Senate seat		
Member is:	Probability of winning was:		
	High	Low	Total
Risk Taker	4.05	3.46	3.68
	(21)	(35)	(56)
Other	3.88	2.58	3.34
	(17)	(12)	(29)
Total	3.97	3.23	3.56
	(38)	(47)	(85)

B. Governorship		
Member is:	Probability of winning was:		
	High	Low	Total
Risk Taker	4.19	2.50	3.85
	(16)	(4)	(20)
Other	2.00	1.00	1.83
	(5)	(1)	(6)
Total	3.67	2.20	3.38
	(21)	(5)	(26)

Note: Cell entries give the mean consecutive terms served by members in the cell (number of members in cell in parentheses).

is the nature of competition for the nomination for the higher office in both parties. A representative would find a situation in which the only opponent he faced for his party's nomination was a local office holder or someone who had never held office to be a good deal more attractive than a situation in which his primary opponent would be the state's governor. A similar argument would hold relative to the competition for the nomination in the other party if no incumbent were running. Thus we would expect that the more formidable the prospective opposition is, the less likely it is a representative would take an opportunity to run for higher office.

With respect to the value of the member's present seat, we must consider more than seniority in the House. Party is one consideration; Republicans have less power in the House than Democrats, and their minority status is almost certain to continue; therefore they should be more likely to seek higher office than their majority party counterparts. Other related matters are: whether the member serves on a prestige committee; whether he is a committee or subcommittee chairman or ranking member; or whether he is a member of the party leadership. All of these are power positions in the House and thus members who occupy them should be less likely to seek higher office.

Finally, there is the matter of the probability of winning the present seat. While previous margin of victory is probably the best indicator available, there does not appear to be a simple relationship between it and the probability of seeking higher office. In general, a large margin in the previous election indicates that a member is relatively safe from a challenge. Thus, his probability of reelection is high and he should be less likely to seek higher office than another member who is less secure. However, in the case of members from small states, a large margin is not only insurance against a challenge but also potentially an advantage in seeking another office. If a representative from a state with a single congressional district received a much larger vote in his previous election than did an incumbent senator or governor the representative is considering opposing, then that incumbent's advantage may be largely wiped out. This would make a potential challenge more attractive. As the number of congressional districts increases, the potential benefit of a large previous margin of election in the statewide arena declines. Thus, while it is not clear from the theory what the precise relationship is between margin of election and probability of seeking higher office (since these two forces would push a representative in opposite directions), it *is* clear that there should be a stronger positive relationship (or weaker negative one) between previous margin and running for higher office among representatives from states with few districts than among those from states with many districts.

In addition, one other factor related to the probability of retaining the present office is the impact of redistricting. If a member is injured by redistricting, he should be more likely to seek higher office; conversely, if he is made safer he should be less likely to run.[24]

This concludes our discussion of the implication of our theory of progressive ambition. While a full test of the theory was not possible at this time, we believe that the evidence that has been adduced strongly indicates that the theory has a good deal of potential.

NOTES

1. Some examples are Fishel (1971), Mezey (1970), Black (1972), Hain and Smith (1973), Frost (1972), Swinerton (1968), and Prewitt and Nolan (1969). Ambition theory has even found application in nondemocratic situations; see Ciboski (1974).
2. One salient exception in Black (1972).
3. We say "almost all" because we believe that discrete ambition should be maintained as a separate category. There are some members of the House who begin service with the intent of simply filing out the present term. The most obvious case of this is the wife of a deceased member who agrees to run in a special election to fill the vacancy and serve only as a "caretaker" until the next regular election. Such cases are, we believe, few and uninteresting. In any event, we ignore them theoretically and will remove them from the empirical analysis below.
4. The use of the word "or" here is in the inclusive rather than the exclusive sense. That is, we do not assume that if only one of these offices were offered every member would take it, but that if both were offered, every member would be willing to accept at least one.

5. By adopting these descriptions of a_1 and a_2, we restrict our consideration to those situations where the actor must give up the presently held office to run for the higher office. We will elaborate on this point below.

6. In 1969, the number was ten. See Schlesinger (1972a, 143).

7. These data are derived from Turett (1971, 118). Turett only considers a subset of states. He eliminates those states which did not permit reelection at some time during the period of analysis, and states which were "not competitive" at some time during the period. Obviously, eliminating the latter group deflates the success rate of governors. It seems unlikely, however, that including these states would bring the governors' success rate up to that of the senators', especially since some of these states (e.g. AR, CA, KS, MA, MN, SD) have seen incumbent governors defeated during the period under discussion.

8. The tenure figures on Senators were compiled from *Congressional Quarterly Report*, January 6, 1973, 24.

9. Such media coverage can, potentially, be translated into a national candidacy. Governors of the largest states are often considered to be potential presidential candidates (e.g., Reagan of California and Rockefeller of New York). Presidential candidates from the Senate, on the other hand, seem to be as likely to come from small (McGovern, Muskie) or medium-sized states (Jackson, Humphrey) as from large ones. For further discussion of these points see Peabody, Ornstein, and Rohde (1976).

10. A summary of the index values appears on p. 149 [of Schlesinger 1966]. We have subtracted from the combined index the values derived from tenure potential since we have considered that aspect separately.

11. A third consideration, that we may mention in passing, is that governors from small states often have relatively small salaries. This may be of no small import if an officeholder is not independently wealthy.

12. See also Shepsle (1972a, 1972b).

13. A congressman seeking higher office is considered to be opposing an incumbent even if the incumbent was defeated for renomination and thus was not an opponent in the general election. We do, however, limit our definition of incumbents to officeholders elected to an office. Thus senators who were appointed to vacancies and governors who succeeded to the office because of the death or resignation of the previous occupant of the office are not considered to be incumbents.

14. Kentucky, Louisiana, Mississippi, New Jersey, and Virginia.

15. An exception is made in the case of members from states in which their party, at the time of the member's opportunity to run, made nominations for statewide office in party conventions rather than in primaries. All members in such situations (who otherwise fit our definition of opportunity) are considered to have had an opportunity to run, and any such member who announced his candidacy for senator or governor is counting as having run, even though he did not have to give up his House seat unless he actually achieved his party's nomination. (Information on such cases was obtained from appropriate issues of *Congressional Quarterly Weekly Reports.*) The rationale for this exception is that such members were in a situation similar to a member who could run unopposed in his party's primary.

16. All information on congressmen who ran for reelection, for higher office, or who followed anther course during the period 1954–74 was gathered from appropriate volumes of *Congressional Quarterly Almanac* and checked against information in the *Biographical Directory of the American Congress, 1774–1971* for accuracy.

17. The reader should note that we used the situation in which the member first sought election, rather than the one in which he was first elected. That is, if an actor ran for the

House at t_1, lost, and then ran again at t_2 and won, the situation at t_1 is used as the indictor of willingness to take risks.

18. Information on recruitment situations was gathered from various volumes of *Congressional Quarterly Almanac*, various volumes of Scammon's *America Votes*, and *The Biographical Directory of the American Congress, 1774–1971*. The data in *America Votes* only go back to 1946, and thus we do not have data on election margins of members before that date. If a state did not redistrict, whether a member defeated an incumbent could be ascertained by comparing rosters of congressmen in *The Biographical Directory*. If a member did not defeat an incumbent, then for the period before 1946 we classed a district which was represented for five or more consecutive years by one congressman as a high-risk situation for a candidate of the other party. A few members about whom we could not determine such information because of redistricting were omitted from the entire data set.

19. If, because of redistricting after 1946, election statistics were only available for one or two elections, those data were used to classify the situation. If a redistricting took place immediately before the relevant election, maps of the old and new lines were compared up to 1972. If the lines were little changed, statistics for the three previous elections were employed. If the lines were substantially changed, the situation was classified as low risk. For members who first sought election in 1972, we employed the data in *Congressional Districts in the 1970s* (1973) on previous party votes within new district lines.

20. Not as "risk averters" because we do not know that they would not have run if the previous incumbent had been running.

21. The omission of 20 and 21 districts from the groupings is due to the fact that no state had that many districts during the period.

22. Four opportunities of members from at-large seats in states with more than two districts are included in the 1 or 2 district category.

23. These data on House seniority were gathered as part of a study of House turnover from 1791 through 1968, reported in Fiorina, Rohde, and Wissel (1975).

24. The reader will note that no separate mention has been made of either of the cost factors—$C(a_1)$ or $C(a_2)$. This is because we have been unable to devise any variable indicators of costs which are not already taken into account elsewhere. For example, costs of running for higher office will be higher, ceteris paribus, in large states than in small ones. Thus a representative in a big state should be less likely to seek higher office.

Chapter 10

Congressional Elections: The Case of the Vanishing Marginals

DAVID R. MAYHEW

Of the electoral instruments voters have used to influence American national government few have been more important than the biennial "net partisan swing" in United States House membership. Since Jacksonian times ups and downs in party seat holdings in the House have supplied an important form of party linkage.

The seat swing is, in practice, a two-step phenomenon. For a party to register a net gain in House seats there must occur (*a*) a gain (over the last election) in the national proportion of popular votes cast for House candidates of the party in question. That is, the party must be the beneficiary of a national trend in popular voting for the House.[1] But there must also occur (*b*) a translation of popular vote gains into seat gains.[2] Having the former without the latter might be interesting but it would not be very important.

The causes of popular vote swings have only recently been traced with any precision. There is voter behavior that produces the familiar midterm sag for parties in control of the presidency (Campbell 1966). There is the long-run close relation between changes in economic indices and changes in the House popular vote (Kramer 1971). There are doubtless other matters that can give a national cast to House voting, including wars (Kramer 1971, 140).

The consequences of partisan seat swings (built on popular vote swings) have been more elusive but no less arresting. As in the case of the Great Society Congress (1965–66), House newcomers can supply the votes to pass bills that could not have been passed without them. Presidents with ambitious domestic programs (Woodrow Wilson, Franklin Roosevelt, Lyndon Johnson) have relied heavily on the votes of temporarily augmented Democratic House majorities. . . .

The foregoing is a preface to a discussion of some recent election data. The data, for the years 1956–72, suggest strongly that the House seat swing is a phenomenon of fast declining amplitude and therefore of fast declining significance. The first task here will be to lay out the data—in nearly raw form—in order to give

Source: David R. Mayhew. 1974. "Congressional Elections: The Case of the Vanishing Marginals." *Polity* 6:295–317.

a sense of their shape and flow. The second task will be to speculate about causes of the pattern in the data, the third to ponder the implications of this pattern.

The data are presented in Figure 10.1, an array of 22 bar graphs that runs on for three pages. If . . . read as if they were one long multipage display, the graphs appear in three columns of nine, nine, and four. It will be useful to begin with an examination of the four graphs in the right-hand column.

Each of the four right-hand graphs is a frequency distribution in which congressional districts are sorted according to percentages of the major-party presidential vote cast in them in one of the four presidential elections of the years 1956–68.[3] The districts are cumulated vertically in percentages of the total district set of 435 rather than in absolute numbers. The horizontal axis has column intervals of 5%, ranging from a far-left interval for districts where the Democratic presidential percentage was 0–4.9 to a far-right interval where the percentage was 95–100. Thus the 1956 graph shows that the Stevenson-Kefauver ticket won 50 to 54.9% of the major-party vote in about 7% of the districts (actual district N = 30) and a modal 40 to 44.9% of the vote in about 20% of the districts (actual N = 87).

In themselves these presidential graphs hold no surprises; they are presented for the purpose of visual comparison with the other data. The presidential mode travels well to the left of the 50% mark in 1956 and well to the right in 1964, but the four distributions are fundamentally alike in shape—highly peaked, unimodal, not far from normal.

The center and left columns give frequency distributions, organized on the same principles as the four presidential graphs, in which House districts are sorted

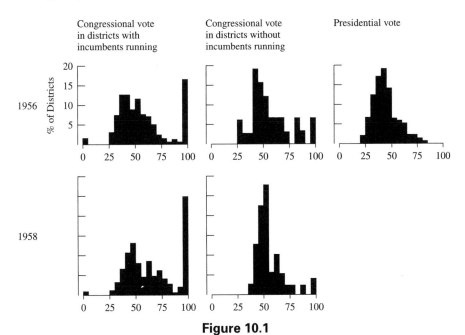

Figure 10.1

Frequency distributions of Democratic percentages of the two-party vote in House districts.

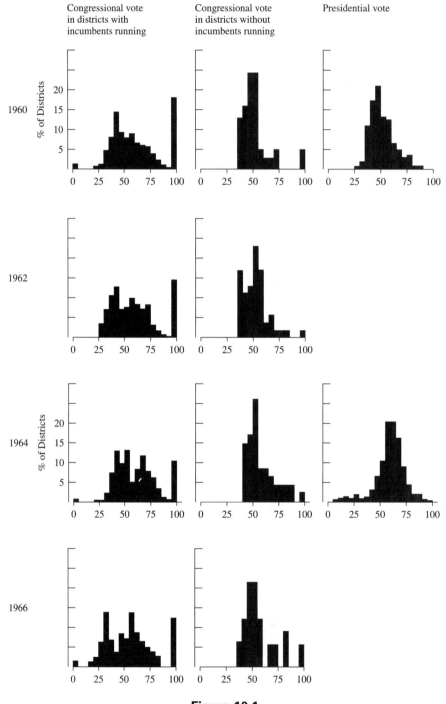

Figure 10.1
Continued

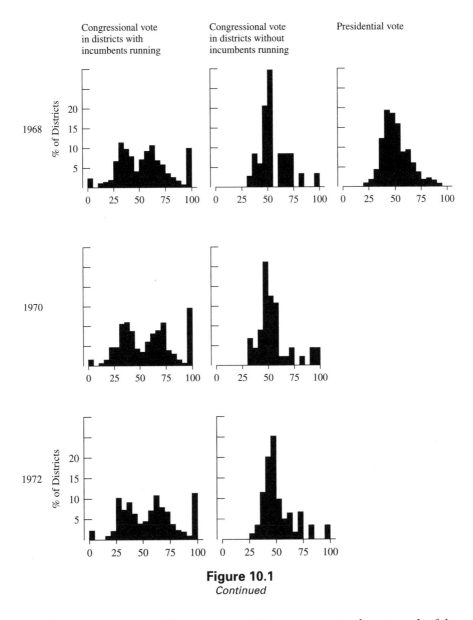

Figure 10.1
Continued

according to percentages of the major-party House vote cast in them in each of the nine congressional elections in the years 1956–72. But for each House election there are two graphs side by side. For each year the graph in the left column gives a distribution of returns for all districts in which an incumbent congressman was running, the center column a set of returns for districts with no incumbents running.[4]

The center graphs, the "open seat" distributions, are erratically shaped because the N's are small. The number of House districts without incumbents running averages 43 (about a tenth of the membership) and ranges from 31 (in 1956) to 59 (in 1972); there is no discernible upward or downward trend in the series. With allowances made for erratic shape these nine "open seat" distributions are much alike. All are highly peaked and centrally clustered. In 1958 and 1968 nearly 30% of the readings appear in the modal interval (in both cases the 50–54.9% Democratic interval). Over the set of nine elections the proportion of "open seat" outcomes falling in the 40–59.9% area ranges from 54.8% to 70.2%, the proportion in the 45–54.9% area from 29.0% to 50.1%. All of which imparts the simple and obvious message that House elections without incumbents running tend to be closely contested.

The nine graphs in the left-hand column give distributions for districts with incumbents running.[5] Thus in 1956 about 9% of districts with incumbents running yielded returns in the 45–49.9% Democratic interval. In some of these cases the incumbents were Democrats who thereby lost their seats; in any of these nine graphs the election reading for a losing incumbent will appear on what was, from his standpoint, the unfortunate side of the 50% line. In an appendix [of Mayhew 1974b] the nine data sets are disaggregated to show where in fact incumbents lost.

Immediately visible on each of these incumbency graphs is the isolated mode in the 95–100% interval, recording the familiar phenomenon of uncontested Democratic victories—mostly in the South. But, if these right-flush modes can be ignored for a moment, what has recently been happening in the contested range is far more interesting. In 1956 and 1960 the distributions in the contested range are skewed a little to the right, but still not far from normal in shape. In the 1958 and 1962 midterm years the distributions are somewhat flatter and more jagged.[6] In 1964 and 1966 they appear only tenuously normal. In 1968, 1970, and 1972 they have become emphatically bimodal in shape. Or, to bring in the uncontested Democratic seats again, the shape of incumbency distributions has now become strikingly trimodal. Thus in the 1972 election there was a range of reasonably safe Republican seats (with the 25–29.9% and 35–39.5% intervals most heavily populated), a range of reasonably safe Democratic seats (peaked in the 60–64.9% interval), and a set of 44 uncontested Democratic seats.

The title of this paper includes the phrase, "The Case of the Vanishing Marginals." The "vanishing marginals" are all those congressmen whose election percentages could, but now do not, earn them places in the central range of these incumbency distributions. In the graphs for the most recent elections the trough between the "reasonably safe" Republican and Democratic modes appears in the percentage range that we are accustomed to calling "marginal." Figure 10.2 captures the point, with time series showing how many incumbent congressmen have recorded percentages in the "marginal" range in each election from 1956 through 1972.[7] The lower series on the two Figure 10.2 graphs show, for comparative purposes, the number of "open seat" outcomes in the marginal range. In one graph marginality is defined narrowly (45–54.9 Democratic percentage of the major-party vote), in the other broadly (40–59.9%). By either definition the number of incumbents running in the marginal zone has roughly halved over the 16-year period.[8] For some reason, or reasons, it seems to be a lot easier now than it used to be for a sitting congressmen to win three-fifths of the November vote.

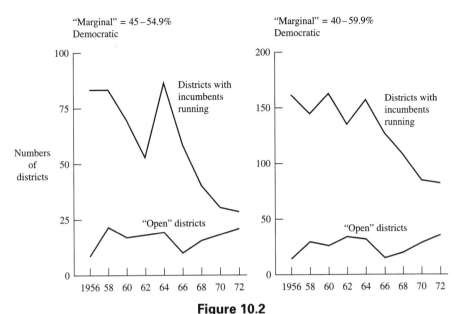

Figure 10.2

Numbers of House elections won in the "marginal" range, 1956–72, in districts with and without incumbents running.

Why the decline in incumbent marginality? No clear answer is available. Adding complexity to the problem is the fact that the proportion of House seats won in the marginal range has been slowly declining for over a century (Jones 1964). Whatever mix of causes underlies the long-run change could account for much of the rapid current change as well. On the assumption that the contemporary decline is not ephemeral, perhaps the most useful thing to do here is to set out some hypotheses which may singly or in combination account for it. Five hypotheses are offered below. . . .

(1) The line-drawing explanation is easy to reach for. In the last decade of chronic redistricting the possibility of building districts to profit incumbents has not been lost on House members or others acting in their interest. With county lines less sacred than they once were, ingenious districts can be and have been drawn. And there are good examples of cross-party districting deals among congressmen of large state delegations (Mayhew 1971). But the problem with the line-drawing hypothesis is that it seems not to explain very much. Manipulation of the aggregate national data does not yield an impressive relation between redistricting and electoral benefit (Erikson 1972, 1238). Moreover, if voters are being partitioned into safe House districts it can be argued that bimodal patterns ought to appear sooner or later in presidential and "open seat" distributions of the sort displayed in Figure 10.1. . . .

The next four hypotheses hinge on the assumption that House incumbency now carries with it greater electoral advantages than it has in the past. There is evidence that it does.[9] One way to try to find out is to look at what happens to party fortunes in districts where congressmen die, retire, or lose primaries—to compare the last November percentages of veteran incumbents with the percentages of their successor nominees. Table 10.1 does this for the six elections in the years 1962–72. Figures are given for transitions in which the retirees were at least two-term veterans and where the bracketing elections were both contested by both parties. It is hard to tease conclusions out of these data; the universes for the six elections are small, the districts in each interelection set vary widely in their change percentages, national trends affect Democrats and Republicans differently, and there is the redistricting problem throughout. But those are all of the data there are on the point. Most of the columns in the table include figures on districts with line changes. Including these raises the obvious problem that redistricting itself can affect party percentages. But there is some justification for the inclusion. For one thing, no systematic difference appears here between what happens electorally in redrawn and untouched districts. For another, it is impossible to

Table 10.1

Change in party percentage in House districts where incumbents have retired, died, or lost primaries

| | Transitions in districts without line changes | | | | | | Transitions in districts with line changes | |
| | Democratic districts | | Republican districts | | All districts | | All districts | |
	N	Mean	N	Mean	N	Mean	N	Mean
1962	(4)	−5.2	(4)	−0.2	(8)	−2.7	(9)	+1.3
1964	(12)	+5.5	(13)	−8.2	(25)	−1.6	*	
1966	(3)	−6.2	(3)	−2.5	(6)	−4.3	(7)	−7.7
1968	(4)	+1.1	(3)	−14.9	(7)	−5.8	(12)	−8.6
1970	(15)	−4.9	(17)	−7.9	(32)	−6.5	(4)	−5.7
1972	(2)	−26.7	*		(2)	−26.7	(25)	−9.5

Transitions in districts with and without line changes

| | Democratic districts | | Republican districts | | All districts | | All districts | | All districts | |
| | | | | | | | | Weighted | | |
	N	Mean	N	Mean	N	Mean	N	Mean	N	Median
1962	(5)	−6.0	(12)	+1.8	(17)	−0.5	(17)	−2.1	(17)	−3.1
1964	(12)	+5.5	(13)	−8.2	(25)	−1.6	(25)	−1.3	(25)	−3.1
1966	(8)	−8.9	(5)	−1.8	(13)	−6.2	(13)	−5.4	(13)	−8.2
1968	(10)	−1.4	(9)	−14.5	(19)	−7.6	(19)	−8.0	(19)	−4.7
1970	(19)	−5.1	(17)	−7.9	(36)	−6.4	(36)	−6.0	(36)	−5.6
1972	(12)	−13.1	(15)	−9.0	(27)	−10.8	(27)	−11.1	(27)	−10.2

get any reading at all on the 1972 election without inspecting the redrawn districts; 25 of the 27 "succession nominations" occurred in 1972 in districts with line changes. If handled carefully the altered districts can yield information. Redrawn districts are covered here if they were treated in the press as being more or less "the same" as districts preceding them. . . .

What to look for in Table 10.1 is whether switches in party nominees bring about drops in party percentages. The bigger the drop the higher the putative value of incumbency. Interelection changes in party percentage are calculated here by comparing party shares of the total congressional district vote in the bracketing elections.[10] The first three columns in the table give data only on districts without line changes. Thus in 1962 there were four Democratic retirements (or deaths, etc.) in districts with 1960 lines intact; the Democratic share of the total vote fell an average of 5.2% in these four districts between 1960 and 1962. In the four Republican retirement districts in 1962 the Republican share of the total vote fell an average of 0.2%. In 1964 there was an understandable party gain in the Democratic retirement districts, and an especially heavy mean loss in the Republican set. Fortuitously the numbers of retirement districts for the two parties are almost identical in each of the five elections in 1962 through 1970, so it makes sense to calculate mean change values for all retirement districts regardless of party in each year in order to try to cancel out the effects of election-specific national trends. This is done in the third column, a list of cross-party percentage change means for the six elections. (Thus in 1964 the average change in the 25 retirement seats was a –1.6% even though the average party values were far apart; Republicans generally lost more in their transitions than Democrats gained in theirs.) Here there emerges some fairly solid evidence. Mean drops in percentage were higher in 1966, 1968, and 1970 than in 1962 and 1964. (1972, with its N of 2, can be ignored.) The best evidence is for 1964 and 1970, with their large N's. Loss of incumbents cost the parties a mean of 1.6% in 1964, a mean of 6.5% in 1970.

In the fourth column figures on transitions in redrawn districts are introduced. The values are mean changes for redrawn retirement districts by year regardless of party. It will be seen that these values differ in no systematic way from the values for undisturbed districts in the third column. There is the same general trend toward bigger drops in percentage. Especially striking is the 1972 value of –9.5%, lower than any other reading in the list of values for redrawn districts. . . .

These readings, tenuous as they are, all point in the same direction. Incumbency does seem to have increased in electoral value, and it is reasonable to suppose that one effect of this increase has been to boost House members of both parties out of the marginal electoral range. If incumbency has risen in value, what accounts for the rise? The second, third, and fourth hypotheses below focus on electorally useful activities that House members may now be engaging in more effectively than their predecessors did ten or 20 years ago.

(2) House members may now be advertising themselves better. Simple name recognition counts for a lot in House elections, as the Survey Research Center data show (Stokes and Miller 1962). A name perceived with a halo of good will around it probably counts for more. If House members have not profited from accelerated advertising in the last decade, it is not from want of trying. The time

series in Figure 10.3 shows, in millions of pieces, how much mail was sent out
from the Capitol (by both House and Senate members) in each year from 1954
through 1970.[11] The mail includes letters, newsletters, questionnaires, childcare
pamphlets, etc., some of them mailed to all district boxholders. Peak mailing
months are the Octobers of even-numbered years. Mail flow more than sextupled
over the 16-year period, with an especially steep increase between 1965 and 1966.
In fact the mail-flow curve matches well any incumbency-advantage curve deriv-
able from the data in Table 10.1. There is no let-up in sight; one recent estimate
has it that House members will send out about 900,000 pieces of mail per member
in 1974, at a total public cost of $38.1 million.[12] So the answer to the incumbency

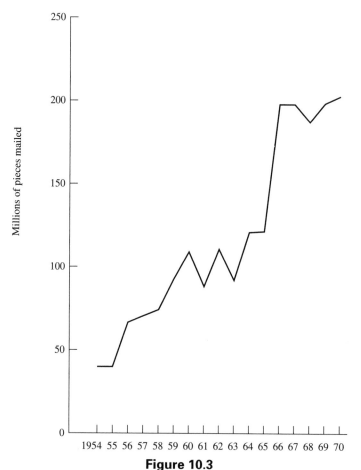

Figure 10.3

Franked mail sent out by House and Senate members, in millions of
pieces, 1954–70. (*Source*: U.S. Congress, House, Committee on
Appropriations. *Hearings Before a Subcommittee of the Committee
on Appropriations, Legislative Branch Appropriations for 1970,*
91st Cong., 1st sess., 1969, p. 501 has 1954–68 data. Subsequent
annual hearings update estimated franking use.)

advantage questions could be a remarkably simple one: The more hundreds of thousands of messages congressmen rain down on constituents the more votes they get. Whether all this activity has significantly raised the proportion of citizens who know their congressmen's names is uncertain. There are some Gallup readings showing that the share of adults who could name their congressmen rose from 46 to 53% between 1966 and 1970.[13]

(3) Another possibility is that House members may be getting more political mileage out of federal programs. The number of grant-in-aid programs has risen in the last decade at something like the rate of Capitol mail flow. The more programs there are, the more chances House members have to claim credit ostentatiously for the local manifestations of them—housing grants, education grants, anti-pollution grants, etc.

(4) Yet another possibility is that House members have become more skilled at public position taking on "issues." The point is a technological one. If more congressmen are commissioning and using scientific opinion polls to plumb district sentiment, then House members may have become, on balance, more practiced at attuning themselves to district opinion (Erikson 1971b). There is a possibility here, however hard it is to try to measure. . . .

(5) The fifth and last hypothesis has to do with changes in voter behavior not inspired by changes in incumbent activities. It is possible that incumbents have been profiting not from any exertions of their own but from changes in voter attitudes. A logic suggests itself. Voters dissatisfied with party cues could be reaching for any other cues that are available in deciding how to vote. The incumbency cue is readily at hand. This hypothesis assumes a current rise in discontent with parties; it assumes nothing about changes in the cues voters have been receiving from congressmen.

There is no point in speculating further here about causes. But it is important that the subject be given further treatment, if for no other reason than that some of the variables can be legally manipulated. The congressional franking privilege comes first to mind.

If fewer House members are winning elections narrowly, and if the proportion of "open seats" per election is not rising, it ought to follow that congressional seat swings are declining in amplitude. The argument requires no assumption that national swings in the House popular vote are changing in amplitude—and indeed there is no evidence in the contemporary data that they are. It does require the assumption that a congressman's percentage showing in one election supplies information on his strength as he goes into the next. That is, a House member running at the 60% level is less likely to be unseated by an adverse 5% party trend next time around than one running at the 54% level. It is easy to predict that a popular voting trend will cut less of a swath through a set of congressmen whose last-election percentages are arrayed like those in the 1968, 1970, and 1972 incumbency graphs of Figure 10.1 than through a set whose percentages are centrally and normally distributed.

There is evidence suggesting that the flight from marginality is having its posited effect. Edward Tufte has found that a "swing ratio"—a rate of translation of votes into seats—built on data from the 1966, 1968, and 1970 elections yields an exceptionally low value when compared with ratios for other election triplets over the last century (Tufte 1972, 549–50). The figures in Table 10.2 point in the same direction. Supplied here are data on popular vote swings, net partisan seat swings, and incumbency defeats for each and both parties in the election years from 1956 through 1972.[14] It is worth noting that the large seat swings of 1958, 1964, and 1966 were heavily dependent upon defeats of incumbents. Very few incumbents have lost since 1966. (Almost all of the 1972 losers were victims of line changes.) Especially interesting are the figures for 1970, a year in which the popular vote swing was a fairly sizable 3.3%. Yet only nine incumbents of the disfavored party lost and the net swing over 1968 was only 12—of which three changed over in 1969 by-elections. Part of the explanation here is doubtless that the disfavored party had relatively few incumbents in the vulnerable range to protect. Only 47 Republicans running in 1970 had won under the 60% mark in 1968, whereas there had been 82 comparably exposed Republicans running in 1958, 76 Republicans in 1964, and 79 Democrats in 1966.

What general conclusions can be drawn? If the trends hold we are witnesses to the blunting of a blunt instrument. It may be too soon to say that seat swings of the 1958 or 1964 variety can be consigned to the history books, but it is hard to see how they could be equaled in the newer electoral circumstances. There is probably another manifestation here of what Walter Dean Burnham calls "electoral disaggregation"—a weakening of the peculiar links that party has supplied between electorate and government (Burnham 1969). There is a concomitant triumph for the Madisonian vision; a Congress less affected by electoral tides is, on balance, one less susceptible to presidential wiles. But there is a long-run danger that a Congress that cannot supply quick electoral change is no match for a presidency that can.

Table 10.2
House vote swings and seat swings, 1956–1972

	Change in national popular vote over last election	Net partisan seat swing over last election	Incumbent losses to opposite party challengers		
			D	R	Total
1956	1.5% D	2 D	8	7	15
1958	5.1% D	49 D	1	34	35
1960	1.1% R	20 R	22	3	25
1962	2.2% R	2 R	9	5	14
1964	4.7% D	36 D	5	39	44
1966	6.2% R	47 R	39	1	40
1968	0.4% R	5 R	5	0	5
1970	3.3% D	12 D	2	9	11
1972	1.4% R	12 R	6	3	9

NOTES

1. To put it yet another way, voting for House candidates must have a "national component" to it. See Stokes (1967).
2. The best analysis of translation formulas is in Tufte (1973).
3. At the time of writing no comparable figures were yet available for the 1972 election. Dealing with the 1968 returns by calculating percentages of the major-party votes poses obvious problems—especially in the South—but so does any alternative way of dealing with them. Congressional district data used in Figure 10.1 and following tables and figures were taken from *Congressional Quarterly* compilations.
4. An incumbent is defined here as a congressman who held a seat at the time he was running in a November election, even if he had first taken the seat in a recent by-election.
5. The center graphs cover districts with no incumbents, the left-hand graphs districts with one incumbent. This leaves no place in the diagram for districts with two opposite-party incumbents running against each other. There were 16 of these throw-in cases over the period: seven in 1962, one in 1966, four in 1968, one in 1970, three in 1972. Republicans won in 10 of them.
6. On balance it can be expected that distributions will be more centrally clustered in presidential than in midterm years, for the reason that presidential elections enroll expanded electorates in which disproportionate numbers of voters violate district partisan habits in their congressional voting. See Kabaker (1969).
7. Again, the 16 throw-in cases are not included. It should be recalled here that some of these incumbents in the marginal range moved across the 50% mark and lost their seats. (See the appendix [of Mayhew 1974b].) Of the 198 incumbents who lost elections to opposite-party challengers in the 1956–1972 period, only four plummeted far enough to fall outside the broadly defined (40–59.9%) marginal range.
8. The decline has come in spite of Republican inroads in Southern House districts. One reason here is that, once they have gotten their seats, Southern Republican incumbents tend to win elections handily; 16 of 22 of them won with over 60% of the major-party vote in 1970, 18 of 22 in 1972.
9. Robert Erikson (1971a; 1972, 1240) estimates that incumbency status was worth about 2% of the vote in the 1950s and early 1960s, but about 5% in 1966 and thereafter.
10. Figures 10.1 and 10.2 are built on candidate percentage of the major-party vote, Table 10.1 on percentages of the total vote.
11. Data supplied by Albert D. Cover.
12. Norman C. Miller, "Yes, You Are Getting More Politico Mail; And It Will Get Worse" *Wall Street Journal*, 6 March 1973.
13. Gallup survey in *Washington Post*, 20 September 1970.
14. The incumbency defeat figures cover only losses to opposite-party challengers. Thus once again the 16 throw-in cases are disregarded. Also ignored are the November losses of two highly visible Democrats—Brooks Hays (1958) and Louise Day Hicks (1972)—to independents who thereupon enrolled as Democrats themselves in Washington. It might be added here that some incumbents do after all lose their primaries. The figures for losses to primary challengers are: six in 1956, four in 1958, five in 1960, eight in 1962, five in 1964, five in 1966, three in 1968, nine in 1970, eight in 1972. The figures for losses where redistricting has thrown incumbents into the same primary: five in 1962, three in 1964, three in 1966, one in 1968, one in 1970, six in 1972. Whatever their qualitative effects, primaries have not rivaled the larger November swings in turnover leverage.

Chapter 11

Strategic Politicians

GARY C. JACOBSON AND SAMUEL KERNELL

V. O. Key (1966, 2) felt it necessary to argue in his last book that "voters are not fools." Neither, we contend, are politicians. Their career plans and decisions are strategically adapted to the political environment. National political forces which politicians expect to have some impact on voters shape their election plans. As a result, the relative quality of a party's candidates and the vitality of their campaigns—the things which have the strongest impact on individual voters—are not at all independent of national events and conditions. Rather, they are a direct function of them. This has important implications for understanding how aggregate national phenomena affect aggregate election outcomes. The crucial links, we will show, are provided by strategic politicians.

THE OPPORTUNITY STRUCTURE

Electoral politics in America is a competitive business. The demand for political offices is greater than the supply. Yet this oversupply of ambitious politicians does not make an election a free-for-all. Instead, competition for public office tends to be structured and orderly; candidates sort themselves out among the many offices in a predictable fashion. In some political systems the coordination of politicians and offices is performed centrally through strong party organizations that recruit candidates and direct careers. In the United States this coordination is a product of individual politicians behaving strategically—that is, looking out for their own best interest—within a commonly perceived structure that offers advantages and incentives for political mobility.

The marketplace for political office is structured, but not overly so. The plethora of offices, peculiar to America, invites a large number of potential competitors, provides numerous opportunities for mobility, and raises some uncertainty

Source: Gary C. Jacobson and Samuel Kernell, *Strategy and Choice in Congressional Elections,* 2nd edition (New Haven: Yale University Press) pp. 19–34. Copyright © 1983 by Yale University Press.

about the prospects for success. Under these circumstances successful politicians must be acutely strategic in making career choices. How the structure of opportunities determines the targets and, more importantly, the timing of career moves has important implications for a theory that views the collective strategic behavior of politicians as an important determinant of election outcomes.

A central element of the structure of political opportunities is the stratification of offices. Only in the most poorly developed political system would one expect to find all institutional offices equally desirable (or, more accurately in such an instance, undesirable). Since the late nineteenth century, public offices in America have been ranked into a loose but widely acknowledged hierarchy with more attractive offices fewer in number and competition for them stiffer.[1] At the top of the heap is the presidency; next are seats in the Senate and governorships; below those are the somewhat more numerous seats in the House of Representatives; and at the bottom lie a multitude of state legislative and local offices. Some offices do not fit neatly into this sequence; consider the careers of recent New York City mayors. And from state to state the ranking of offices, especially at the lower rungs, will vary considerably, depending upon such factors as the size of the office's constituency, the number of offices available, and the office's value as a stepping-stone to higher offices. Nonetheless, the general pattern adequately describes the sequences of offices sought by most politicians across the nation.

In addition to stratifying offices, the opportunity structure guides the strategic behavior of politicians in a couple of other ways. First, it institutionalizes competition, making politicians cautious risk takers. The pyramidal distribution of office eases the entry of men and women into public life but, as they attempt to move up the hierarchy, the steady attrition of offices creates competition and uncertainty for all politicians, including the incumbents. Second, the opportunity structure differentially allocates resources among offices within levels such that transitions from one status level of offices to the next is nonrandom. Certain officeholders are favored by virtue of their current position in seeking some target office. Over time, these advantages define highly visible career paths. The linkage of offices across levels reflects, to use Joseph Schlesinger's term, their "manifest" similarities (Schlesinger 1966, chapter 6). For one thing, the structural isomorphism of national and state governments creates functionally similar offices throughout the hierarchy. From justice of the peace to the Supreme Court and from the state house to the U.S. Senate, offices at different levels are associated by similar tasks. This makes some officeholders at a lower level more plausible, hence advantaged, successors to a higher office than others.

The federal tiering of the office hierarchy also introduces a network of overlapping constituencies. Congressional districts, for example, generally subsume several state legislative districts and are in turn subsumed within the Senate's statewide constituency. With upward political mobility in America largely occurring through sequential capturing and expanding of constituencies, the politician's current office becomes an important vehicle for career advancement.

At first glance an opportunity structure that produces many more aspirants for Congress than there are seats available would appear to guarantee that there will always be well-qualified (politically experienced) candidates within each party trying to get the nomination (see also Kazee 1980). If so, this would support the conventional assumption . . . that the quality of candidates will be constant in the aggregate and therefore can be ignored in explaining the national congressional vote. Upon closer inspection, however, the opportunity structure yields two general conclusions which together deny the assumption of consistent candidate quality.

First, we note that because of dissimilar institutional resources even within ranks, some politicians make better candidates for a target office than others. This in itself is not a profound observation but it does lead to the second point. To the degree a politician's current office is a resource for advancement, it becomes a stake or risk in considering whether and when to attempt a move. Offices have investment value beyond whatever intrinsic rewards they provide their occupants. Even the politician who serves in an office solely to enhance his future mobility must plan carefully the timing of his move. The institutional advantages provided by the opportunity structure mean that running and losing, and in the process losing one's office base, not only interrupts a career, but well may end it.

THE STRATEGIC CALCULUS

A base office as a resource inspires ambition but as a stake it urges caution. To appreciate better how politicians resolve their dilemma and how the decision to seek some higher office relates to partisan electoral conditions, consider Gordon Black's formal statement of the upwardly mobile politician's decision calculus (Black 1972).

$$U_o = (PB) - R, \tag{1}$$

where

U_o = utility of target office O,

P = probability of winning election to office O,

B = value of office O,

R = risk (e.g., cost of campaign, intrinsic value of base office, opportunity cost of losing base office).

According to this formulation, if the value of target office O (B) discounted by the probability of victory (P) is greater than the cost of seeking the office (R), the utility of seeking the office (U_o) is positive and the politician becomes a candidate.

In explaining variations in the quality of congressional candidacies over a series of elections the main message of this equation is that the more the politician risks, the greater must be the probability of winning before he or she becomes a candidate. Stakes vary widely among potential candidates, reflecting their position in the opportunity structure, and therefore so too will the electoral conditions necessary to trigger their candidacy. The political neophyte wishing to go straight to Congress risks little more than the personal cost of the campaign; even a low likelihood of success may not deter the attempt. The seasoned state senator whose district represents a large chunk of the congressional district, however, will await optimal political conditions before cashing in his investment.

The collective result of these individual calculations can be viewed as an equilibrium process, diagrammed in Figure 11.1. Since the base office is both a stake and resource, the quality (Q) of a party's congressional challengers will be a function of its perceived probability (P) of winning the fall elections. And since Democratic and Republican electoral fortunes are inversely related to each other, short-term partisan forces will have opposite motivational impact on prospective Democratic and Republican candidates. The more extreme the electoral climate, the greater will be the divergence between the parties in the overall quality of their candidates.

The better a party's candidates, the better its performance in the election. Given the relationship described in Figure 11.1, the collective strategic choices of politicians to become candidates reinforce and augment the effects of the current political environment on the election. These decisions determine, in aggregate, the kinds of candidates and campaigns voters are offered in an election year. National events and conditions shape the expectations of potential candidates and their supporters about their party's electoral prospects. And this, in turn, structures the choices voters are offered in districts across the nation. The election outcome becomes in part the aggregate consequence of many politicians individually making strategic decisions about their political careers. In this way, macroelectoral behavior can be derived directly from straightforward features of the opportunity structure.

AN ALTERNATIVE COLLECTIVE STRATEGY

One need not look too hard at Figure 11.1 to discover an alternative strategy for political parties facing an unfavorable political environment. If they were somehow able to reverse the relationship so that unfavorable conditions were greeted with high quality candidacies, they would minimize the effects of adverse political conditions upon the vote. The party's collective goal of minimizing the loss of congressional seats serves the interest of every loyal congressman, especially when the threatened losses would reduce his party to minority status.[2] As attractive as this alternative strategy may be for promoting the party's collective

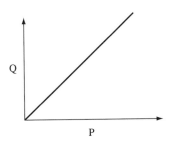

Figure 11.1
The quality of a party's congressional challengers as a function of its electoral prospects.

goals, it is nonetheless unavailable, for it requires individual politicians to behave in direct contradiction to their own self-interest. The provision of collective goods requires collective action. Strong political parties which centrally coordinate candidacies and campaigns by sanctioning reluctants and compensating victims of defeat may have such a strategy as an option. But the weak American party system and the evolved opportunity structure guarantee that politicians will be entrepreneurs and that only the individually calculated relationship described in Figure 11.1 will occur.

CONGRESSIONAL INCUMBENTS

Although the net result of the aggregated individual strategic decisions should be to accentuate the relationship between the partisan political climate and election results, it is not obvious that all strategic decisions relating to congressional candidacies and campaigns must have this effect. With the strategic calculus in equation 11.1 describing the choice to leave one office and seek another, the discussion thus far best applies to nonincumbent congressional candidates. How well can this equation be adapted to depict the calculus of the incumbent congressman content with his position and ambitious only to protect it? Moreover, do incumbents' strategic responses to political conditions have the same multiplier effect on elections? We think that they do.

Every two years the incumbent congressman must decide whether to seek reelection (most do), to run for higher office, or to retire. Although this last choice is more often subject to nonstrategic considerations, it can similarly be couched in strategic terms. A decision to stand for reelection rather than seek a Senate seat (PB) will generally reflect the unacceptable cost (R) involved in giving up the House seat to make the attempt. In considering whether to run for reelection or to retire, the risk term is greatly discounted since in both instances the "risk" involves losing the House seat. Understandably, most congressmen in any given year run for reelection. So many run so successfully that the incumbency effect has emerged in recent years as an overwhelming deterrent to quality challengers. After many years in Congress, however, each additional two-year term may grow marginally less attractive (B) and at some point when confronted with adverse political conditions (P) and a tough campaign (R) the senior congressman will "strategically" retire. Because incumbents have been winning reelection at an 85% clip or better since the late nineteenth century (Keefe 1976; Kernell 1977), retirement decisions should, of course, be relatively resistant to short-term partisan conditions. However, . . . partisan retirement rates are in fact marginally associated with election year political conditions (Jacobson and Kernell 1983, chapter 5).

Threatened with the prospect of defeat, most incumbent congressmen who are not near retirement will redouble their campaign effort in order to minimize the effects of unfavorable political conditions. Ostensibly, such behavior contradicts our theory. The quality of the candidacies appears to improve the more severe the threat. But the redoubled efforts of incumbents drain resources from party candidates running for open seats or those challenging vulnerable opposition incumbents. Because these resources are far more effective when used in the campaigns of nonincumbents, this collective "circle-the-wagons" strategy becomes self-defeating.

Suppliers of campaign resources also act strategically. Decisions about how much to give to whom are guided by perceptions of national conditions. Contributors' strategies, like those of politicians, accentuate the advantages of the favored party. . . .

STRATEGIC POLITICIANS: READING TEA LEAVES

This account of political strategies is, we believe, intuitively compelling, but of course its validity depends on how well it coincides with the actual behavior of politicians. A variety of data suggests that politicians do think and act strategically, with consequences that match those predicted by our theory.

If, to begin, congressional elections are largely the product of strategic politicians making choices in anticipation of the outcome, then we should expect to find current and prospective officeholders showing more than passing curiosity in signs about their party's electoral prospects. They do. Potential participants in congressional campaigns begin assessing the prevailing breezes well before the election—and before the final decisions about candidacy have to be made. There are plenty of possible indicators from which to choose. . . .

In [some] instances, a poor economy and the administration's inability to deal with it effectively were the sources of partisan joy or depression. In other years, however, the president emerged as the central issue either as an asset or liability for his party. . . .

[One] year in which the president's standing with the public was a central factor was of course 1974. The *Times* reported in February that "Republican leaders have begun to confront publicly a crucial question: how to win in 1974 and 1976 despite President Nixon's precipitous decline in popularity."[3] The Republicans' question for 1974 quickly became how not to lose so badly, and their answer was principally to separate themselves from Nixon and emphasize their own integrity.[4]

Politicians and journalists rely on more than bare economic indicators and presidential popularity ratings. Other signs are available. In some years, the Gallup poll spoke directly to the issue of congressional elections by soliciting voting preferences early in the election year. At each election the reported polls are regularly cited as significant straws in the wind. . . . In 1974, Republican depression deepened as the reported voting intentions showed their party once again in the worst shape since 1936.

A more concrete, and so perhaps more convincing, indicator of political tides is the occasional special election to fill vacant House seats. . . . A great deal of attention was given to the six special elections held early in 1974. All six seats had been won by Republicans in 1972 with between 52.1 and 73.9% of the vote; Democrats won five including Vice President Ford's seat. "Rep. Phillip Burton (D-CA) asserted that if the pattern of the Michigan election held, there would be more than 100 Republicans who would not return to the House in January, 1975. House Speaker Carl Albert (D-OK) said the results 'mean the Democrats are going to sweep the nation this year.'"[5]

Signs and portents are readily available, widely noted and generally believed, and so inform strategic choices. Speculation about the party's November prospects starts early. Polls, by-elections, economic news, and other, more intuitive, political soundings are combined to build expectations about the political future which serve to measure opportunity and risk and thus to guide career decisions and political strategies. Imperfect as any of these omens may be, they become, in the absence of better information, important to the strategies of candidates and their potential supporters.

STRATEGIC RESPONSES: GOING WITH THE FLOW

Republican and Democratic responses to the exceptionally strong and decisively unidirectional spring indicators in 1974 provide the clearest examples of strategic behavior. Republican leaders found it nearly impossible in many districts to recruit good candidates to challenge Democratic incumbents, while Democrats fielded an unusually formidable group of challengers. . . . The chairman of the Republican party in Georgia reported that the "biggest problem was candidate recruitment. We couldn't get the enthusiasm built up. Our county chairmen would just sit on their hands."[6] He argued that Watergate led people to expect a bad Republican year and they refused to extend themselves in a losing cause.[7]

Republican troubles were taken as Democratic opportunities. Linda Fowler (1980, 11) who interviewed all of the New York House candidates in 1974, reported that "more than one Democrat in 1974 believed he could capitalize on the Watergate scandal . . . and several echoed the sentiments expressed by this candidate: 'I chose this year because I thought I could win . . . With Watergate and the things ———— was saying, I thought this year would be a good time.'"

. . . Anecdotal evidence is entirely consistent with the idea that the relative quality of the parties' candidates is a function of spring electoral prospects; the relationship posited in Figure 11.1 seems to hold. Summary data on congressional candidates are even more persuasive. Our discussion of the opportunity structure suggests that the quality of candidates can be measured by their prior office-holding experience. The base office itself is an important resource. Intuitively, we assume that people who previously managed to get elected to public office at least once should be more effective campaigners than those who have not. They have some experience of (successful) campaigning and wider opportunities for developing skills, contacts, and insights. The evidence in Table 11.1, although crude, is quite consistent with this assumption. In every election from 1972 through 1978, challengers who had held elective office did distinctively better on election day than did those who had not.[8]

By the standard of prior officeholding, Democrats clearly fielded an unusually large and Republicans an unusually small proportion of strong challengers in 1974. In Table 11.2, the largest percentage of experienced Democratic challengers and the smallest percentage of experienced Republican challengers are found for the 1974 election. An additional figure, the percentage of experienced candidates divided by the percentage of seats held by their party in state legislatures at the time of the election, is also included. This adjusts the proportion of "good" candidates to the size of the available pool of such candidates (roughly measured by seats held in legislatures; no other clearly comparable data are published).[9] The need for this is apparent from the table. The proportion of experienced Republicans is relatively low in 1976 and 1978 even though no strong national tide seemed to be running against Republicans in these years. With this simple adjustment for the size of the pool of experienced Republicans, the difference between these two years and 1972 disappears.

Table 11.1
Average vote received by House challengers, by electoral office experience, 1972–78 (in percentages)

	Democrats		Republicans	
	Prior elective office			
Year	Yes	No	Yes	No
1972	39.6	33.7	39.7	32.4
1974	45.9	41.6	37.1	27.6
1976	39.3	35.0	40.1	31.5
1978	39.8	32.2	43.9	32.4

Table 11.2
Nonincumbent House candidates with experience in elective office, 1972–78 (in percentages)

	Democrats		Republicans	
	%	pool ratio*	%	pool ratio*
Challengers				
1972	21.5	.36	21.7	.55
1974	38.3	.64	12.6	.31
1976	29.5	.43	16.9	.53
1978	25.4	.37	16.2	.51
Candidates for open seats				
1972	41.4	.68	51.7	1.30
1974	54.7	.91	49.1	1.22
1976	60.0	.88	59.0	1.84
1978	50.0	.73	44.2	1.39

*Ratio of the percentage of candidates who have held elective office to the percentage of seats won by their party in state legislatures two years earlier.

More than 38% of the Democratic challengers but fewer than 13% of the Republican challengers in 1974 had ever held elective office. More than 30% of these Democrats, but only 7% of the Republicans, were in office at the time of the election. Clearly, assessments of the political climate had an important effect on career decisions at this level.

Notice that another strategic factor—one largely, but by no means entirely, local—also has a powerful influence on the quality of House candidates. Experienced candidates are much more likely to be found in races for open seats, regardless of the election year. This was true even of Republicans in 1974. The explanation is obvious. Incumbency has such a crucial effect on the opportunity to move up to a House seat that its absence inspires good candidates to enter the contest regardless of other, perhaps less hopeful, signs. This is not an entirely local phenomenon because decisions by incumbents to retire, opening up the "open seats," are . . . also influenced by national political conditions (Jacobson and Kernell 1983, chapter 5).

Additional evidence that career decisions were influenced by national factors in 1974 is apparent at the level of competition for nominations in the primaries. Fowler reports that among Republicans she interviewed "the feeling that there would be a substantial backlash made it much easier for several candidates to obtain the nomination. In the districts where the incumbent retired, several candidates stated that they had not had to compete in a primary because 'this is going to be a bad year for Republicans.' Others were asked to run because no one else would do it" (Fowler 1980, 16).

The pattern of competition for nominations in 1974, compared to 1972, 1976, and 1978, indicates that the phenomenon was general. Table 11.3 lists, according to incumbency status, the percentage of Republican and Democratic House candidates who ran in primary elections in these four election years. Notice that, among challengers, the highest percentage of Democrats but the lowest percentage

Table 11.3

House candidates with contested primary elections
1972–78 (in percentages)

Year and party	Incumbents	Challengers	Open seats
1972			
Democrats	39.0	46.1	78.5
Republicans	15.7	37.2	73.4
1974			
Democrats	42.1	66.7	91.1
Republicans	25.6	26.3	80.0
1976			
Democrats	40.8	57.0	95.7
Republicans	13.3	38.5	67.3
1978			
Democrats	39.4	44.3	98.1
Republicans	21.3	36.6	68.0

of Republicans had to win a primary to be nominated in 1974. Incumbents were affected less, though a larger percentage of Democrats than usual faced primary challenges in 1974.

As one would expect if politicians operate strategically, competition is much more common for nominations to contest open House seats, regardless of the election year. . . .

The principal conclusions reached in this chapter can be summarized briefly. Politicians do act strategically. Their career decisions are influenced by their assessment of a variable political environment. Their choices reflect, among other things, the conventional wisdom that national events and conditions affect individual voting behavior. National phenomena thought to be important are consistently monitored and noted; indicators abound. More and better candidates appear when signs are favorable; worse and fewer when they are unfavorable. Clearly, the choices presented to voters between a pair of particular candidates in the district are not at all independent of national conditions; indeed, they are a function of them. The implications of these facts for understanding the links between national events and individual voter behavior are unmistakable.

NOTES

1. For a discussion of the evolution of the modern opportunity structure during the nineteenth century see Kernell (1977, 1979).
2. We argue in chapter 5 [of Jacobson and Kernell 1983] that the probability of attaining the collective goal of minimizing the loss of congressional seats affects the value some politicians place on the office and hence their strategic decision about running.
3. R. W. Apple, Jr., "Election Problems of the G.O.P. Assayed." *New York Times*, 10 February 1974, part 4, 3.
4. See, for example, "Republicans: Running Hard in Watergate's Shadow." *Congressional Quarterly Weekly Report* 32(16 February 1974):352–58.
5. "Democratic Joy, Republican Gloom in Michigan's 5th." *Congressional Quarterly Weekly Report* 32(23 February 1974):493.
6. "Southern Republicans: Little Hope This Year." *Congressional Quarterly Weekly Report* 32 (26 October 1974):2959.
7. This effect was not confined to congressional candidates. A Republican official in Tennessee lamented that his party was only contesting 65 seats in the state legislature, "Good, attractive candidates just said this was not the year to run." "Southern Republicans: Little Hope This Year." *Congressional Quarterly Weekly Report* 32 (26 October 1974):2961.
8. Note that a difference remains when party is controlled for, although it tends to be greater for Republicans than for Democrats.
9. State legislatures are the most frequent source of elective office experience for nonincumbent congressional candidates. National Republican leaders have recognized this explicitly and have contributed to state legislative campaigns with the acknowledged purpose of building up their pool of congressional talent.

PART IV

LEGISLATIVE NORMS AND RULES

Chapter 12

How Do Legislatures Operate?

Legislatures are among the most formal of organizations. They have detailed rules that specify the procedures to be followed at every stage of passing legislation. However, formal rules are not all that is relevant to the operation of institutions. Every institution also develops more informal "rules of the game," and these "norms" can affect the operation of the institution as well.

While formal rules and informal norms influence the behavior of members of an institution, political science has placed different emphasis on these concepts at different times. Early descriptive studies of Congress focused great attention on the formal rules and structures of the institution, but gave little attention to how these rules were used strategically by individual members (cf. Gross 1953). Informal norms and roles were emphasized during the 1950s and 1960s when sociology had a large influence on political science. Norms and roles were prominent "imported" concepts. As economic theories and methods gained greater prominence in political science by the 1980s and 1990s, norms and roles were studied less, with more attention to goals and the formal constraints on legislative behavior as provided by rules and institutions. Despite the shift in study, informal norms are still important for understanding the behavior of legislators.

There are several concerns to keep in mind about informal rules of the game and formal rules in legislatures. Why do they exist? Are they enforced? Why do they change over time? And, most fundamentally, what do they tell us about the relationships between legislators and legislative institutions?

INFORMAL NORMS AND ROLES

The very early literature on legislatures generally and Congress in particular emphasized the formal rules under which they operate. An important change occurred when some of the first studies relying on empirical observation and interviewing discovered the importance of informal norms, folkways, and rules of the game.

Norms

A norm is an unwritten but mutually agreed upon expectation of how members "ought" to behave. Norms require clarity and opportunities for practice, as well as consequences when they are violated (Gertzog 1970, as cited in Parker 1985, 75). They are not absolute determinants of legislators' actions, but are considerations in deciding how to behave, especially if violating norms reduces members' ability to achieve goals. The extent to which norms exist in a legislature can be controversial. If members largely conform to these shared expectations, is it because they are mutually agreed upon and internalized by members, or is it because there are penalties for violating them? Or is legislators' behavior consistent with norms due to their rational allocation of their time, interests, and resources? As we will see, scholars have seriously debated these questions.

In a general sense, norms exist in order to help the institution function. They provide rewards to achieve necessary but unappealing tasks, such as hard work and specialization on a few issues, that allow Congress to legislate effectively. They provide a common basis of expectations regarding the behavior of others, which helps form the basis for cooperative action between members with different goals and priorities. For example, being civil to others despite disagreements (often termed the courtesy or "comity" norm) allows for a continued working relationship on other issues and preserves ability of the institution to operate without becoming bogged down in personal disputes.

Yet norms may have "negative" consequences when they protect the goals of a set of legislators who developed and enforce the norms but inhibit the goal achievement of legislators with different needs. For example, Senator Joseph Clark (1964) decried "the Senate Establishment." The liberal Clark saw the Senate inner club as ideologically based. He argued that the Senate of the 1950s was set up so as to give an advantage to conservatives, and that the norms were just excuses for ideological discrimination.

Norms exist in every legislature, but they have been studied most in the U.S. Senate. Senate rules empower the individual member more than is the case for most other legislatures, making informal constraints on behavior particularly important. Donald Matthews (1960) wrote about the norms that existed in the 1950s Senate, reprinted here as chapter 13. Journalist William S. White (1956) had earlier written a popular book about the Senate, entitled *The Citadel*, in which he described the existence of a Senate "Inner Club." Members of this inner club were more successful in getting their bills passed than were other members. Matthews examined the Senate more systematically. He described a series of norms, which he termed Senate folkways: apprenticeship, specialization, legislative work, courtesy, reciprocity, and institutional patriotism. Additionally, he took the important (and rare) step of trying to measure the effectiveness of senators so he could check whether senators who followed these norms were more effective as senators. Effectiveness could, of course, be measured in many ways. For example, a senator might feel that the test of effectiveness is visibility, or ability to bring home projects for the home state, or reelection. Matthews chose to measure effectiveness

effectiveness by the proportion of all bills and resolutions introduced by a senator that were passed by the Senate. He found an effect—senators who followed the folkways were more effective, though this could be due to his choice of operationalization. Matthews's study is considered a classic because many studies of norms in Congress since have accepted the norms he described and have attempted to elaborate on how these norms are maintained or how they have declined over time.

Norms have been studied in many other legislative bodies, including non–U.S. legislatures and U.S. state legislatures. An influential study in the 1950s by Wahlke, Eulau, Buchanan, and Ferguson (1962) asked legislators in four states about informal "rules of the game" and developed a lengthy list of such norms. For example, important rules of the game were performing obligations, respecting others' legislative rights, impersonality, and self-restraint in debate. The authors also asked about perceived sanctions and found that members listed bill obstruction, ostracism, mistrust, and fewer political rewards. However, the study did not determine how common such sanctions were. That is, there might be folklore that such sanctions could be used even if they were rarely used in practice, but the folklore itself might deter norm violation.

For norms to affect members' behavior, it was thought that there would have to be some way to pass the norms of the institution on to new members. Asher (1973b), reprinted here as chapter 14, studied freshmen legislators to see how fast they learned House norms. However, he found next to no change in norms between successive interviews with his sample of new legislators. Asher's work is considered a classic because it was the first to document the changes and decline of norms in Congress–a topic which will be discussed in detail later. The freshmen understood the congressional norms nearly immediately, so norm learning did not exist. This fast learning may be due to the nonpartisan orientation sessions nowadays given to newly elected legislators by nongovernmental groups (including Harvard University's Kennedy School and the conservative Heritage Foundation). Such sessions could help freshmen perceive the norm structure early. This fast learning could also be due to the high level of previous political experience of freshmen members that year, but also due to the fact that many legislative norms are just common sense guides to behavior that hold in most organizations.

Legislative norms were first studied in the 1950s, but they were reinterpreted in the 1970s and 1980s from a rational choice perspective. These norms are now seen as means for achieving legislators' goals. As Weingast (1979, 259) states, "The informal rules of the legislature further collective goals and individual members' goals." Particular attention has been given in this literature to the "universalism norm" that is evident when bills are passed unanimously because they include projects (such as constructing post offices in local districts) that benefit all members (Weingast 1979). This rational choice perspective permeates many recent studies of norms, such as Sinclair's (1989) discussion of the costs and benefits of norms for senators.

Roles

Norms imply conformity to a single set of standards. An alternative focus is on the roles of legislators, which suggests that there may be alternative modes of legislative behavior acceptable to the group. Some of these differences are based on the individual's position within the organization. For example, the Speaker of the House is not expected to behave in the same way as a freshman member representing a marginal district. At the same time, individuals may participate in defining their own roles, since not everyone views his or her job identically or performs the job in the same way. According to this perspective, roles can be studied empirically by asking legislators to describe their jobs or by studying variation in their behaviors.

The Wahlke–Eulau (Wahlke et al. 1962) study tried to measure differences in job perceptions. Among the many types of roles they discuss, some of the most important are four types of purposive roles: the ritualist who emphasizes the pomp and circumstance of legislation, the tribune who defends the public interest, the inventor who initiates policy ideas, and the broker who develops legislative compromises. This typology has been applied to other legislatures, including the U.S. House (Davidson 1969). The problem with this approach is that it is not obvious that role orientations matter for behavior either in a legislature or by a legislature. The fact that there are multiple role perceptions is important to learn, but does not take us far in understanding legislatures.

A special role in a legislature is that of the maverick. Ralph Huitt (1961b) wrote of the maverick role that William Proxmire played in the 1950s–1960s Senate. Huitt shows that Proxmire intentionally violated the usual Senate norms by blocking unanimous consent and filibustering when the Senate was ready to adjourn for the year. However, he was not punished by the Senate, at least not in ways that mattered to him. Indeed, Huitt claims that Proxmire was able to win policy conflicts by use of his outsider style. The Outsider is a tolerated alternative role, according to Huitt. The point here is that effectiveness measures (e.g., Matthews 1960) are usually not based on the goals of the legislator; sanctions do not matter unless the actual goals of the legislator are hindered. Matthews (1961) countered in a response that the toleration of a role did not make it legitimate, but presumably Proxmire and other mavericks do not care whether their fellow legislators view their behavior as legitimate.

The maverick role that Huitt described in the 1950s remains today. Senate procedures permit individual senators to place "holds" on bills or nominations that they are not ready to have go to the floor for a vote and to filibuster to stop bills they oppose from coming up to a vote. Most senators use these procedures on occasion, but mavericks carry them to extremes. These tactics are used by mavericks of the political right (as when Jesse Helms, R-NC, placed holds on ambassador appointments) and the political left (as when Howard Metzenbaum, D-OH, killed bills by just threatening to filibuster late in a session when Congress was getting ready to adjourn for the year). Fellow legislators may view such behavior as violating the norms, but the rules have not been changed to prevent these uses. Mavericks probably exist in most legislatures, using their positions and the rules to their advantage.

In contrast to most of the literature on legislative roles, Searing (1991) has argued that the role concept is appropriate only when used more narrowly. In particular, he emphasizes the importance of "positional roles," roles that exist because of the legislator's official position such as party and committee leaders. Searing demonstrates the importance of norms associated with such positional roles, such as the lower frequency of votes against one's party's position in the British House of Commons by party leaders (none by members of the government for the Conservatives when he interviewed members of parliament in the early 1970s and only 38 for the Labour party's front bench spokespersons at that time) as compared to party backbenchers (by 61% of Conservatives and 77% of Labourites). Searing distinguishes positional roles from what he terms "preference roles," roles which vary between legislators with different views of their jobs as legislators. In his British interviews, for example, he described three preference roles—constituency member for the backbenchers who spent a lot of time in their districts, a generalist role for members who sought to influence several different policy areas, and a specialist role for members who tried to influence a limited number of policy realms.

Norm Change

Norms and roles are not constant over time. Asher (1973b) first noted the disappearance of apprenticeship as a norm in the U.S. House. The norm had been that freshmen legislators were to be seen, but not heard. Asher instead found that senior members were no longer expecting adherence to that norm and that freshmen were expected to be active legislators.

Generally, the recent literature on norms picks up on this theme and focuses on evaluating which norms have changed since the 1950s and why. These studies clearly are influenced by the "classics" in that they accept the existence of informal consensual rules as guides to behavior. For the most part, they attempt to determine the current status of the norms described by Matthews in the 1950s, rather than discover what the current "norms" are (cf. Harris 1993). The important exception to this line of argument is Richard Hall (1996), who challenges whether norms ever existed. His perspective is summarized later in this chapter.

There is general agreement that the apprenticeship and specialization norms are dead in Congress. In interviews, members of Congress indicate that they no longer expect that members will wait several terms before becoming fully involved in the legislative process or that members will only become involved legislatively in matters where they serve on a committee that handles the issue (Harris 1993; Sinclair 1989). In both the House and Senate, members increasingly have been active on legislation outside the jurisdictions of their committee memberships (Sinclair 1989; Smith 1989). On apprenticeship, Hibbing (1991) shows that while junior members of the House are more active legislatively than they were in 1950s, senior members are more active as well. Thus, the gap between senior and junior members in legislative participation is wider than ever. Hibbing concludes that "apprenticeship" remains in the House, but no longer because of an apprenticeship norm (see also Hall 1996).

Several other norms, if not totally dead, have declined as well (Loomis 1981; Sinclair 1989; Uslaner 1993). Certainly the limits of what are considered acceptable behaviors have broadened and are more ambiguous (Sinclair 1989, 96). Harris

(1993) argues that the norms of the 1950s have evolved into the norms that exist in the contemporary U.S. Senate. He claims that the courtesy norm for the most part still is observed (cf. Loomis 1981 on the House), and that while clear violations occur today, such violations have occurred throughout the history of the Senate. The legislative work norm has been replaced by two norms: national advocacy and diligence. The national advocacy norm is the expectation that senators will be activists and spokespersons on behalf of national causes. The diligence norm demands that a senator work hard at the job. Moreover, the legislative work norm no longer makes the distinction between work horses and show horses discussed in the Matthews chapter; Harris claims that senators now are expected to be both. The reciprocity norm has been weakened, as evidenced by the greater use of floor amendments and filibusters. It is not dead, however, since senators who go too far with their obstructionism lose the respect of others. Last, senators may now run for president or make public appeals to build support for their causes, neither of which are precluded by the current norm of institutional patriotism. Likewise, members can offer constructive criticisms of the Senate, but still do not "run against" the Senate or criticize it as an institution, as members of the House often do.

It would also appear that a new norm of partisan and ideological loyalty developed in Congress in the period from the 1970s to the 1990s. Democratic majorities at the beginning of this period occasionally dealt with the question of whether to remove committee seniority from members who opposed their party's presidential candidate. In 1995 there was an attempt among Senate Republicans to remove Mark Hatfield (R-OR) as Appropriations Committee chair when he cast the decisive negative vote to defeat a Balanced Budget Amendment to the Constitution. The partisan and ideological purity norm is not fully accepted yet, but it has become more important as Congress has become more polarized (see chapter 20).

As norms change, formal rules based on those norms also change. An example is the case of the seniority rule, which was based on the apprenticeship and specialization norms. As these norms have declined, the seniority rule for distributing chairs and ranking positions on committees has also declined. Through most of the twentieth century the longest serving member of a committee was chosen to be its chair or ranking member, but congressional reforms of the early 1970s helped to undermine this seniority system by having the party caucus (all the members of a congressional party meeting together) elect the chairs through a secret ballot.

The 1970s seniority reforms mainly affected Democrats until the Republican takeover of Congress in 1995. That year, three ranking Republicans deemed too "lethargic" to implement the Contract with America aggressively were not nominated by Speaker Gingrich to become committee chairs. Robert Livingston (R-LA) was appointed chair of the Appropriations Committee over four others with greater seniority. Robert Bliley (R-VA) was chosen to chair the Commerce Committee and Henry Hyde (R-IL) was selected to chair the Judiciary Committee, though Carlos Moorhead (R-CA) ranked first in seniority on both committees. In addition, Republicans limited the terms of committee chairs to six years and limited the Speaker's term to eight years. Under this rule change, after a chair's six years are over, the most senior member must surrender the chair. Thus, the seniority system, while not fully dead, has certainly been modified.

Explaining Norm Change

Norms change when the costs of adhering to the norms are greater than the costs of the sanctions imposed for violating them for a substantial number of members (Sinclair 1989). This is particularly true when no one has the willingness or ability to impose sanctions when norms are violated. When more and more members see the norms as a barrier to their goal achievement and violate the norms, the shared expectation that members will conform declines. The consensus that supports the norm breaks down and norms change.

Several explanations for breakdown of the congressional consensus supporting traditional norms have been offered. One explanation centers on the entrance of new members with different goals and values from the old members (Smith 1989). For example, the classes of Democratic senators in 1958 and the election cycles thereafter were more liberal ideologically and were from more electorally marginal states. These new members needed to participate actively in the Senate in order to achieve their policy goals and to be visible in order to appeal to constituents in their home states. The norms changed to meet goals of the new members, for whom the costs of conformity were higher than the penalty for breaking the norm. The large influx of new Republicans in the House of Representatives in 1994 similarly led to changes since the new members wanted to achieve their conservative policy goals and wanted to show their constituents that a Republican House would produce real changes. Similarly, the election of women to both houses of Congress has slowly changed the male-club atmosphere that pervades Matthews' description of the Senate in chapter 13.

As another example, a small band of Republican conservatives first elected in 1978 and 1980 decided that their party's adherence to the House norm structure benefited the majority Democrats. The Conservative Opportunity Society, led by Newt Gingrich (R-GA) became more confrontational with the Democratic leadership on ethical issues and policy disagreements, in the hope that would lead to a Republican House. Gingrich's strategy helped force Democratic House Speaker Jim Wright to resign in 1989 and helped lead the Republicans to win control of the House in the 1994 election.

Cox and McCubbins (1993) make a similar argument for the breakdown of the seniority system in the House. Throughout the 1950s and 1960s, the distribution of committee chairs reflected the distribution of membership in the majority party. But by the 1970s, new members with new values changed the balance of power within the Democratic party, allowing the liberal Northern wing to undermine the seniority system, the base of power for Southern conservatives.

A second factor that contributed to the change in congressional norms was a changing external political environment (Sinclair 1989). The 1960s and 1970s saw an expansion of the issues on government's agenda, a rise in the number and diversity of interest groups, and broader political coverage by the media. In reaction, members use legislative activism to appeal to constituents and to lay claims to national leadership on policy issues. The apprenticeship and specialization norms that were a barrier to these new goals fell.

A third explanation for the change in congressional norms is that norms have changed outside of Congress as well. Eric Uslaner (1993) argues that people as a whole are more distrustful and less civil towards one another. Congress is a reflection of this society. Uslaner provides evidence that measures of trust, such as levels of "trust in people" found in public opinion surveys and levels of charitable contributions, are potent predictors of behavioral indicators of congressional norms (amending activity) and reciprocity-based legislation (e.g., agricultural price supports and nonincremental programs). Similarly, one might argue that increased partisan and ideological polarization in society (as in radio and television talk shows) is leading to the development of the new partisan and ideological purity norms in Congress.

A related point is that Congressional rules changes can have implications for changing congressional norms. For example, the decision to televise House and Senate decisions led to members of Congress being able to address the nation directly from the floor. The debate became more polarized and more shrill, with the comity norm being one of the first casualties. As another example, the adoption of electronic voting in the House permitted many more votes to be taken during a short period of time. House floor activity increased, with a resultant decline in deference to committees and the reciprocity norm.

Richard Hall (1996) takes exception to the argument that norms have declined, or indeed, were ever influential. Hall develops a theory of participation in Congress. He argues that participation can be explained by the goal-oriented choices of individual legislators within the constraints of their interests and resources for participation. Behaviors consistent with norms, such as freshmen participating less than senior members, are due to these choices and constraints rather than norms. Freshmen participate less because they have not yet become expert on policy or congressional procedures nor have they established networks of colleagues, interest groups, and executive branch officials that would facilitate policy development. Members specialize or defer to other committees because their lack of interest and expertise puts them at a disadvantage when more informed members are involved. Furthermore, Hall argues that norms did not significantly influence behavior in prereform congresses either. His analysis of participation in the Education and Labor Committee shows few differences between the 1960s, when norms supposedly existed, and the 1980s. Therefore, according to Hall, norms have not necessarily declined because they never were important constraints on members' legislative involvement.

The study of norms is an excellent example of how the study of Congress has evolved over time in concert with both changes on Capitol Hill and in the science of politics. In the committee-dominated prereform Congress and sociological era of political science, research focused on group norms. As new members entered Congress and the institution reformed, giving more leeway for individual policy entrepreneurialism, political scientists documented the "decline" of norms. More recently, economic theories have led to the questioning of whether norms ever were important influences on legislatures' behavior. Likewise, as the study of norms has declined, the New Institutionalist school of economic-oriented analysis has led to increased emphasis on the ways in which rules and institutional structures influence legislative behavior.

FORMAL RULES AND THEIR EFFECTS

Whereas legislative scholars were discovering the importance of legislative norms and folkways in the 1950s and 1960s, formal legislative rules and their effects were rediscovered in the 1980s and 1990s. In part, this reflected the apparent decline of some longstanding House norms along with senators beginning to act more as individuals than on the basis of Senate norms. Also, the numbers of floor amendments and votes increased sharply in the House in this period, as did the number of Senate filibusters, calling attention to the importance of rules. Norms and roles emphasize the informal ways in which legislatures operate, but formal rules are of great consequence for legislative action as well. In the discussion that follows, we will review several themes in the research of formal legislative rules and how the two chambers differ in this regard. The common element in all such research is that formal rules are no more neutral than norms or roles. Rules frequently serve to structure outcomes.

Rules in Each Chamber

Every legislative chamber develops its own procedures for bill consideration, amendment, and passage (Oleszek 1996). These rules can get very complicated, so complicated that only skilled parliamentarians can follow them. Indeed, most legislatures employ parliamentarians, who often give the presiding officer word-by-word instructions as to what to say in presiding over the consideration of legislation. However, knowledge of formal rules can be used by individual legislators as well. For example, Robert Byrd (D-WV) is considered to be one of the most skilled parliamentarians in the Senate, and he often employs this skill to his advantage. Whether such parliamentary maneuverings are a blessing or a curse seems to depend on whether one supports or opposes the legislation under consideration.

The United States Senate and House provide two opposite cases of the formality of conducting business. The Senate operates as a body of equals, as if each senator were an ambassador from his or her sovereign state. One corollary of this equality is that each senator should be able to exercise considerable control over the flow of legislation. Legislation and voting on the floor are scheduled as much as possible to accommodate the calendars of the individual senators. Bills are usually considered by the Senate under a unanimous consent agreement in which members agree when the Senate will vote on the bill. When a bill is so important to senators that some are willing to try to kill it by filibustering, the attempt to talk the bill to death can only be ended by a three-fifths vote of the members to invoke "cloture." Even when there is no filibuster, a large number of amendments may be offered to bills, debated on the floor, and voted upon.

While a 100-member Senate may be able to function with wide discretion for individual members, that would be impossible for a body as large as the House. In fact, new House members upon taking office receive 11 large, bound volumes detailing the formal rules of the chamber. These rules describe such specific points as the order of votes on amendments to bills, substitutes for bills, and amendments to those substitutes.

Additionally, the large size of the House makes it necessary to determine in advance how many and which amendments will be considered for each bill. The House Rules Committee has the role of recommending the "rule" for the consideration of a bill on the House floor, a rule which specifies the extent to which the bill will be open to amendment. "Open rules" permit a wide variety of amendments to be offered, but the House is too large to use open rules often. By contrast, "closed rules" preclude amendments—members must either accept or reject the standing committee's text. Closed rules are usually reserved for complicated issues, such as taxes, that members feel should not be subject to logrolling on the floor. The most common approach is to employ "restrictive rules," which allow some, yet not unlimited, challenges to a bill. Such a rule typically indicates how many amendments would be permitted, identifies the permissible amendments, or bars all amendments to certain portions of the bill or on certain subjects (Bach and Smith 1988). The majority party leadership often favors closed rules which give them fairly complete control (see also chapter 20), whereas minority party members tend to prefer open rules which make it easier to change bills. The use of closed and restrictive rules by the majority party as a means of controlling the legislative process increased during the 1980s and 1990s (Bach and Smith 1988) over considerable protest by the minority. After chafing for years under the restrictive rules used by majority Democrats, the Republicans vowed to rely on such rules less when they won control of the House in 1994 election. However, they too have frequently found the use of restrictive rules helpful for controlling the flow of legislation. In any case, the reliance of the House on closed and restricted rules is in sharp contrast to the more freewheeling Senate style.

Yet the contemporary legislative process, as conducted in both chambers, is itself more freewheeling today than it once was. Textbooks depict the passing of a bill as a fixed and linear path, starting with its introduction and referral to a committee which considers the bill and sends it to the floor with recommended amendments. This is followed by passage of the bill by the chamber, negotiation of compromises between the House and Senate in conference committee, and then transmittal of the bill to the president for his signature. Sinclair (1997) has found that the process of passing bills in Congress rarely follows this textbook version nowadays. She terms the procedures and practices that are commonly employed in the legislative process nowadays as "unorthodox lawmaking." In chapter 15 of this volume, we reprint her account of new and more frequently applied legislative procedures in the House as a Contemporary Perspective and an example of the renewed interest in scholarship concerning formal legislative rules and procedures. Sinclair's research also offers an excellent account of the discretion that the majority party may exercise in the application of procedural rules.

While the majority party is able to establish the rules, it is also important to examine how legislative minorities function under parliamentary constraints. Charles O. Jones's (1970) *The Minority Party in Congress* is the early classic on this topic. More recently, Connelly and Pitney (1994) wrote about *The Permanent Minority*. They point out how reforms of the rules affect the minority party. For example, in the mid–1970s when House committees were required to hold open formal meetings, it became more difficult for the Democratic committee chair to compromise with Republican minority members. As a result, Republicans channeled their efforts into floor speeches and voting. Because reforms also brought about recorded votes on floor amendments, Republicans were able to force Democrats to cast public votes on controversial issues. Connelly and Pitney observe that under such conditions, it is not surprising that the House was soon characterized by procedural warfare and the decline of comity.

The Paradox of Voting

Rules of legislative bodies can be very arcane as well as detailed. The traditional treatment of rules was to treat them as facts (Smith 1989). A newer approach in the literature is to analyze their functions and emphasize how rules, particularly those rules governing voting procedure, structure outcomes. This literature recognizes that institutional rules constrain actions, so legislators behaving rationally can produce different outcomes depending on the rules.

Consider the "paradox of voting" [also known as Arrow's paradox, for Nobel-laureate Kenneth Arrow (1951)]. This famous problem illustrates that different institutional settings (as defined by formal rules) lead to different outcomes, even when voters' preferences are stable, or unchanging. In the following diagram, there are three individuals (1, 2, and 3) using the simple majority decision method to select a winner from three alternatives (a, b, and c). Each voter ranks the alternatives from best to worst, but when there are three alternatives to consider, there might not be a single position which commands majority support. Suppose the preferences of the voters are as follows:

		Ranked Outcomes		
		1st	2nd	3rd
Voters:	1:	a	b	c
	2:	b	c	a
	3:	c	a	b

In a vote between a (say an amendment to a bill) and b (the unamended bill), a wins, supported by voters 1 and 3, so the amendment is adopted. Between a and c (the status quo), c wins a majority, supported by voters 2 and 3, so the amended bill is defeated. We might think that since c wins over a and a wins over b, that c would be able to win over b, and that the unamended bill would also be defeated. This would be true if majority rule guaranteed transitive outcomes, but here we see that voters 1 and 2 prefer b to c, so the unamended bill could pass if a vote were taken on it. Therefore, a defeats b, c defeats a, but b defeats c,—a cycle, or "intransitivity." Although individual legislators have ranked preferences, they cannot rank alternatives from best to worst *as a group*. The paradox is that the group preferences can be intransitive even when individual preferences are all transitive. Ultimately with these preferences, for any of the three possible outcomes there is a winning coalition of voters interested in overturning it. There is no equilibrium, and, without one, predictions of outcomes cannot be made. Voting rules, such as the order of votes, instead determine which alternative is chosen.

Legislators may not be familiar with the literature on the voting paradox, but they do recognize that they can sometimes manipulate the outcome of the legislative process by voting against their preferences. Thus, "sophisticated voting" can lead to the paradox. For example, some legislators might help adopt a "killer amendment" that they would otherwise oppose in the hope that adopting that amendment would cause defeat of the bill.

The classic example of the paradox of voting is the "Powell amendment" of the late 1950s and early 1960s. This was a period of time in which Democrats were trying to extend the role of the federal government into new areas, such as helping to finance hospitals and provide aid to education, while Republicans opposed such extensions of federal authority. Southern Democrats were sometimes willing to support these new programs, so long as Congress did not use this social legislation as a means of forcing racial integration. Adam Clayton Powell, an African-American Democrat who represented the Harlem area of New York City, sponsored amendments to many of these bills to forbid the use of federal funds on segregated facilities. Let us call b the unamended bill, a the amended bill, and c the status quo which would be maintained if the bill were defeated. Northern Democrats favored integration and the bills, and so had the preference order in the first row of the above chart. Southern Democrats were willing to pass the unamended bill but opposed the amended bill, and so had the preferences represented in the second row. Republicans opposed these bills, but voted for the Powell amendments as if they had the preferences shown in the chart's third row. As a result, the Powell amendment was added to several of these bills, leading to their defeat even though they might have been passed otherwise. Many analysts felt that the Republicans were engaging in sophisticated voting and that the Powell amendment, regardless of the intentions of its sponsor, was essentially a killer amendment (Fenno 1963; Riker 1965; cf. Krehbiel and Rivers 1990). By introducing a measure almost certain to fail, Powell brought about a continuation of the status quo.

Powell's killer amendments illustrate only the simplest "paradox" in voting. Leaders can utilize legislative rules to control the agenda and shape voting outcomes. For example, a committee chair can determine the order of pairwise voting on policy alternatives. Say that the preferences are again as in the above table. Committee members might first be asked to decide between measure a and measure b with the winner then placed against measure c. By this agenda, the outcome of these two votes would be measure c—a defeats b, but c defeats a. Yet if the chair schedules the first vote between measures c and a with the winner then placed against measure b, the outcome will be measure b. That is, c beats a but cannot gain sufficient support to defeat b. A third possible agenda—c versus b, then the winner of that vote, b, versus a,—yields measure a.

Like the paradox of voting and the Powell amendment, the preceding example illustrates that when there are cyclical preferences, even simple majority rule can be subject to the strategic actions of congressional leaders. Typical events in

Congress are even more complicated—perhaps six motions on the floor with formal rules determining which measures are paired for votes and the order of those votes. In this situation, there are many opportunities for members to manipulate the legislative outcome by strategically introducing additional alternatives to the existing agenda. Furthermore, in the House of Representatives, the Speaker and the Rules Committee determine the rules of debate, whether amendments can be offered from the floor, and whether roll-call votes will be taken, all to the advantage of the chamber's majority party. By contrast, Senate rules permit members to offer an unlimited number of amendments, bestowing advantages on individual senators and giving more power to minority factions.

Formal Theory Approach to Voting

There has been considerable formal theory work relating to the paradox of voting. To give a quick view, a voting cycle cannot occur when voting on a unidimensional issue continuum (as when politics is dominated by a single liberal–conservative debate). The position of the median voter on the dimension is an equilibrium position, meaning that a majority cannot be created to support another alternative once the voting has moved to the equilibrium. Yet voting is not always unidimensional. Plott (1967) showed that equilibria exist in the general multidimensional case only under the rare circumstance where individual preferences are distributed in a perfectly symmetric circular fashion around the equilibrium position. Furthermore, McKelvey (1976) showed that there are no bounds to cycles when they occur in multidimensional spaces, so any point in the space can defeat some other point in that space by a majority. These results seem to suggest that legislative bodies should be characterized by fluidity and disequilibrium, but that does not accord with most observers' understanding of legislatures.

In a landmark work, Shepsle and Weingast (1981) addressed this inconsistency by suggesting a distinction between a "preference-induced equilibrium" (based on the issue positions of the legislators) and a "structure-induced equilibrium" (based on rules and voting order). The median voter result, along with the work by Plott and McKelvey, all involve preference-induced equilibria and show that preference-induced equilibria are unlikely in multidimensional spaces. Shepsle and Weingast argue that legislative rules help create an equilibrium position even when preference-induced equilibria would not exist. That is, the rules that control which amendments are considered and in what order can create an equilibrium when one would not otherwise exist.

The result has been a new focus on rules. Several formal theory pieces have analyzed detailed legislative rules to understand their operation and their implications for congressional outcomes. For example, Weingast (1989) has demonstrated that open rules in the House can protect the wishes of the committee through permitting counteramendments. Huber's (1992) analysis of procedures in the French National Assembly has shown that a package vote procedure (where the government chooses which amendments to include) is used by the government against its own majority, while their "guillotine rule" (by which a bill is considered passed unless the government is censured) is used to protect its majority from undesirable votes.

This new work focusing on legislative rules is part of what is termed the "new institutionalism" (see chapter 1). Studies of Congress in the nineteenth century often focused on formal legislative rules. These studies lost favor as later generations of scholars found new methods of study and began observing Congress in session, studying legislative votes, and examining the members' relationships with their districts. The new institutionalism returns to the early interest in rules, studying their nature and effects. The goals of this work are to describe and understand the institutional structures and procedures of Congress in greater detail, viewing legislative activity as strategic interaction within the context of fixed institutional arrangements.

An intriguing example of the new institutionalism perspective is Riker's (1983) notion of "heresthetics"—using strategies to win. Riker argues that politicians employ a variety of techniques to get the results they want. For example, they may strategically propose or support an alternative they oppose in order to get the alternative they sincerely support to pass, as illustrated in the above discussion of the voters' paradox. They may raise new facets of issues when they would lose on the older facets of those issues (see also the discussion of "framing" in chapter 24). They may try to manipulate the order of voting on alternatives if that would increase the chance of their favored alternative winning. The heresthetical actions that Riker discussed are not limited to the legislative arena, but they certainly can be seen often in legislative consideration of bills (Arnold 1990, reprinted here as chapter 27). None of this would be very surprising to a skilled politician. Wily legislative leaders have long known how to make the rules work to their advantage.

CONCLUSION

Norms exist in any institution because of the needs of its members. Yet, it is important to consider the policy implications of these norms. On the one hand, some would argue that norms help the legislature function effectively. On the other hand, the norms may make it harder for some members to represent their districts. The norms can bias the legislative process in a particular direction, as when Senate norms of the 1950s bolstered the conservative Senate Establishment.

Institutions also require formal rules in order to function effectively. These formal rules are not neutral—they structure outcomes and establish the institutional setting within which legislators must operate. Rules influence not only how things are done, but what is done. This is why legislators often are unwilling to change the rules, even when mavericks exploit the rules to their advantage. Individual members use the rules as leverage to achieve their goals. Although rules provide order, they also can lead to fragmentation and decentralization. Thus, for a bill to become a law in the U.S. Congress it must pass many veto points established by formal rules, passing through substantive committees, the House Rules Committee, and both chambers. This also emphasizes how rules generally favor the status quo. Rules, however, are more than procedure. They ensure that bargaining must take place.

The renewed scholarly interest in rules can be attributed to the recognition that the choice of rules can decide the outcome of a policy dispute. As Sinclair (1997) notes, capturing how legislatures currently operate is a difficult endeavor. As scholars interested in the legislative process, political scientists emphasize that although legislative rules are detailed and precise, they are also open to the interpretation of party leadership. Moreover, existing norms affect this interpretation. Legislatures have detailed rules, but they are applied at the discretion of members. Member goals affect adherence to norms, and norms, in turn, affect legislative procedures (which rules are employed), not simply the content of formal rules.

The real issue for a legislator is how to maximize her or his influence over legislative outcomes. Norms and rules can help members exert their influence, but they also can act as limitations on this influence. Norms are informally changed and rules are formally changed when too many members find themselves constrained by the existing structure of norms and rules.

Are norms or rules more important to the functioning of a legislature? This question is less reasonable than it may seem to be. Legislatures require rules to enact legislation, while norms for behavior develop in all human institutions. The congressional literature has swung back and forth, from its original concentration on formal rules, to the discovery of norms, folkways, and rules of the game in the 1950s, and back to the new institutionalism's refocusing on formal rules since the 1980s. However, it is probably fairer to conclude that rules have always been important and that norms have always existed. There are still norms in Congress today, just not the same ones as in the 1950s.

What is more interesting is to examine the factors which lead to change in norms and rules. Changes in the composition of a legislature, in the external political environment, and in society itself can lead to changes in legislative norms. Changes in the distribution of power in the legislature make it possible to change its rule structure. It might appear at any single point of time that the norms and rules are in a stable equilibrium, as was the case during the period of the so-called "textbook Congress" of the 1950s, but over a longer time frame it becomes clear that neither norms nor rules are immutable. Legislatures, in both their informal and formal operation, are affected by individual goals and the quest for power, and these will always necessitate minor and major adjustments in legislative norms and rules. Changing conditions will inevitably provide further opportunities to research the conditions which lead to norm and rule change.

Chapter 13

The Folkways of the Senate

Donald R. Matthews

The Senate of the United States, just as any other group of human beings, has its unwritten rules of the game, its norms of conduct, its approved manner of behavior. Some things are just not done; others are met with widespread approval. "There is great pressure for conformity in the Senate," one of its influential members said. "It's just like living in a small town."

What are the standards to which the senators are expected to conform? What, specifically, do these unwritten rules of behavior say? Why do they exist? In what ways do they influence the senators? How, concretely, are they enforced? What kinds of senators obey the folkways? Which ones do not, and why?

These are difficult questions for an outsider to analyze. Only those who have served in the Senate, and perhaps not even all of them, are likely to grasp its folkways in all their complexity.[1] Yet, if we are to understand why senators behave as they do, we must try to understand them.

APPRENTICESHIP

The first rule of Senate behavior, and the one most widely recognized off the Hill, is that new members are expected to serve a proper apprenticeship.

The freshman senator's subordinate status is impressed upon him in many ways. He receives the committee assignments the other senators do not want. The same is true of his office suite and his seat in the chamber. In committee rooms he is assigned to the end of the table. He is expected to do more than his share of the thankless and boring tasks of the Senate, such as presiding over the floor debate or serving on his party's Calendar Committee. According to the folkways of the Senate, the freshman is expected to accept such treatment as a matter of course.

Moreover, the new senator is expected to keep his mouth shut, not to take the lead in floor fights, to listen and to learn. "Like children," one freshman said, "we

Source: From U. S. SENATORS AND THEIR WORLD by Donald R. Matthews. Copyright © 1973 by the University of North Carolina Press. Used by permission of the publisher.

should be seen and not heard." Just how long this often painful silence must be maintained is not clear, but it is certainly wiser for a freshman to postpone his maiden efforts on the floor too long than to appear overly aggressive. Perhaps, ideally, he should wait until pushed reluctantly to the fore. . . .

Freshmen are also expected to show respect for their elders ("You may think you are smarter than the older fellows, but after a time you find that this is not true") and to seek their advice ("'Keep on asking for advice, boy,' the committee chairman told me. 'That's the way to get ahead around here'"). They are encouraged to concentrate on developing an acquaintanceship in the Senate. ("Young senators should make a point of getting to know the other senators. This isn't very hard: There are only ninety-nine of them. And if the other senators know and like you, it increases your effectiveness.") . . .

Even so, the veterans in the Senate remark, rather wistfully, that the practice of serving an apprenticeship is on the way out, and, to some extent, they are undoubtedly correct. The practice seems to have begun well before the popular election of senators and the exigencies of the popularly elected official have placed it under considerable strain. As one very senior senator, whose service extends back almost to the days before popular election, ruefully explained: "A new senator today represents millions of people. He feels that he has to *do* something to make a record from the start."

This judgment is also colored by the tendency in any group for the oldtimers to feel that the younger generation is going to hell in a handbasket. To the present-day freshmen in the Senate, the period of apprenticeship is very real and very confining. As one of them put it, "It reminds me of a little of Hell Week in college." Indeed, the nostalgic talk of the older senators regarding the unhappy lot of the freshman in the good old days is one way the senior senators keep the younger men in their place. One freshman Democrat, for example, after completing a floor speech found himself sitting next to Senator George, then the dean of the Senate. Thinking that he should make polite conversation, the freshman asked the Georgia patriarch what major change had taken place in the Senate during his long service. Senator George replied, "Freshmen didn't use to talk so much."

LEGISLATIVE WORK

"There are two kinds of Congressmen—show horses and work horses. If you want to get your name in the papers, be a show horse. If you want to gain the respect of your colleagues, keep quiet and be a work horse."[2] Senator Carl Hayden of Arizona remembers being told this when he first came to the Congress many years ago. It is still true.

The great bulk of the Senate's work is highly detailed, dull, and politically unrewarding. According to the folkways of the Senate, it is to those tasks that a senator *ought* to devote a major share of his time, energy, and thought. Those who follow this rule are the senators most respected by their colleagues. Those who do not carry their share of the legislative burden or who appear to subordinate this responsibility to a quest for publicity and personal advancement are held in disdain.

This results, at first, in a puzzling disparity between the prestige of senators inside and outside the Senate. Some of the men most highly respected by their colleagues are quite unknown except on the Hill and in their own states; others whose names are household words are thought to be second-raters and slackers.[3]. . .

But this does not mean that all publicity is undesirable. It takes publicity to get, and stay, elected. This publicity, as long as it does not interfere with the performance of legislative duties, is considered necessary and desirable. Nor is there any objection to publicity calculated to further the cause of a program or policy or to publicity which flows from a senator's position or performance. But the Senate folkways do prescribe that a senator give first priority to being a legislator. Everything else, including his understandable desire for personal and political publicity, must be secondary to this aspect of his job.

SPECIALIZATION

According to the folkways of the Senate, a senator should not try to know something about every bill that comes before the chamber nor try to be active on a wide variety of measures. Rather, he ought to specialize, to focus his energy and attention on the relatively few matters that come before his committees or that directly and immediately affect his state. "When you come to the Senate," one administrative assistant said, "you have to decide which street corner you are going to fight on."

In part, at least, senators ought to specialize because they must: "Thousands of bills come before the Senate each Congress. If some senator knows the fine details of more than half a dozen of them, I've never heard of him." Even when a senator restricts his attention to his committee work, the job is more than one man can do. "I belong to twelve or thirteen committees and subcommittees," a leading senator says. "It's physically impossible to give them all the attention I should. So I have picked out two or three subcommittees in which I am especially interested and have concentrated on them. I believe that this is the usual practice around here."

. . . The limit of human endurance is not, however, the only reason for a senator to specialize. By restricting his attention to matters concerning his committee work and his home state, the senator is concentrating on the two things he should know best. Only through specialization can he know more about a subject than his colleagues and thus make a positive contribution to the operation of the chamber. . . .

Almost all the senators are agreed that: "The really effective senators are those who speak only on the subjects they have been dealing with at close quarters, not those who are on their feet on almost every subject all the time."[4] Why this pressure for specialization? Why does this folkway exist? There would seem to be a number of reasons.

The formal rules of the Senate provide for what amounts to unlimited debate. Even with the folkways limiting the activity of freshmen, discouraging "playing to the galleries," and encouraging specialization, the Senate moves with glacial speed. If many more senators took full advantage of their opportunities for debate and discussion, the tempo of action would be further slowed. The specialization folkway helps make it possible for the Senate to devote less time to talking and more to action.

Moreover, modern legislation is complex and technical, and it comes before the Senate in a crushing quantity. The committee system and specialization—in a word, a division of labor within the chamber—increase skill and decrease the average senator's work load to something approaching manageable proportions. When a senator refuses to "go along" with specialization, he not only challenges the existing power structure but also decreases the expert attention which legislative measures receive.

COURTESY

The Senate of the United State exists to solve problems, to grapple with conflicts. Sooner or later, the hot, emotion-laden issues of our time come before it. Senators as a group are ambitious and egocentric men, chosen through an electoral battle in which a talent for invective, righteous indignation, "mud-slinging," and "engaging in personalities" are often assets. Under these circumstances, one might reasonably expect a great deal of manifest conflict and competition in the Senate. Such conflict does exist, but its sharp edges are blunted by the felt need—expressed in the Senate folkways—for courtesy.

A cardinal rule of Senate behavior is that political disagreements should not influence personal feelings. This is not an easy task; for, as one senator said, "It's hard not to call a man a liar when you know that he is one."

Fortunately, a number of the chamber's formal rules and conventions make it possible for him to approximate this ideal—at least so far as overt behavior is concerned. The selection of committee members and chairmen on the basis of their seniority neatly bypasses a potential cause of grave dissention in the Senate. The rules prohibit the questioning of a colleague's motives or the criticism of another state. All remarks made on the floor are, technically, addressed to the presiding officer, and this formality serves as a psychological barrier between antagonists. Senators are expected to address each other not by name but by title—Earle C. Clements does not disagree with Irving M. Ives, but rather the Senior Senator from Kentucky disagrees with the Senior Senator from New York. . . .

This kind of behavior—avoiding personal attacks on colleagues, striving for impersonality by divorcing the self from the office, "buttering up" the opposition by extending unsolicited compliments—is thought by the senators to pay off in legislative results. Personal attacks, unnecessary unpleasantness, and pursuing a line of thought or action that might embarrass a colleague needlessly are all though to be self-defeating—"After all, your enemies on one issue may be your friends on the next." Similar considerations also suggest the undesirability of excessive partisanship. . . . "The fellows who go around the country demagoguing and calling their fellow senators names are likely to be ineffective senators. It's just human nature that the other senators will not cooperate with them unless they have to." . . .

In private, senators are frequently cynical regarding this courtesy. They say that "it doesn't mean a thing," that it is "every man for himself in the Senate," that some of their colleagues "no more should be senators than I should be Pope," that it is "just custom." Senator Barkley's advice to the freshman senator—if you think a colleague stupid, refer to him as "the able, learned and distinguished senator," but if you *know* he is stupid, refer to him as "the *very* able, learned and distinguished senator"—is often quoted (Barkley 1954, 255). Despite its blatant hypocrisy, the practice persists, and after serving in the Senate for a period of years most senators grow to appreciate it. . . .

Courtesy, far from being a meaningless custom as some senators seem to think it is, permits competitors to cooperate. The chaos which ensues when this folkway is ignored testifies to its vital function.

RECIPROCITY

Every senator, at one time or another, is in a position to help out a colleague. The folkways of the Senate hold that a senator should provide this assistance and that he be repaid in kind. The most important aspect of this pattern of reciprocity is, no doubt, the trading of votes. . . .

. . . Senator Douglas of Illinois, who tried unsuccessfully to combat this system, has analyzed the way in which a public works appropriation bill is passed.

> . . . This bill is built up out of a whole system of mutual accommodations in which the favors are widely distributed, with the implicit promise that no one will kick over the applecart; that if senators do not object to the bill as a whole, they will "get theirs." It is a process, if I may use an inelegant expression, of mutual backscratching and mutual logrolling.
>
> Any member who tries to buck the system is only confronted with an impossible amount of work in trying to ascertain the relative merits of a given project; and any member who does ascertain them, and who feels convinced that he is correct, is unable to get an individual project turned down because the senators from the state in which the project is located, and thus is benefiting, naturally will oppose any objection to the project; and the other members of the Senate will feel that they must support the senators in question, because if they do not do so, similar appropriations for their own states at some time likely will be called into question.[5]

Of course, *all* bills are not passed as the result of such implicit or explicit "deals."

On the other hand, this kind of bargaining (or "logrolling" or "backscratching" or "trading off," phrases whose invidious connotations indicate the public's attitude toward these practices) is not confined just to the trading of votes. Indeed, it is not an exaggeration to say that reciprocity is a way of life in the Senate. "My boss," one highly experienced administrative assistant says, "will—if it doesn't mean anything to him—do a favor for any other senator. It doesn't matter *who* he is. It's not a matter of friendship, it's just a matter of I won't be an S.O.B. if you won't be one."

It is this implicit bargaining that explains much of the behavior of senators. Each of them has vast power under the chamber's rules. A single senator, for example, can slow the Senate almost to a halt by systematically objecting to all unanimous consent requests. A few, by exercising their right to filibuster, can block the passage of all bills. Or a single senator could sneak almost any piece of legislation through the chamber by acting when floor attendance is sparse and by taking advantage of the looseness of the chamber rules. While these and other similar powers always exist as a potential threat, the amazing thing is that they are rarely utilized. The spirit of reciprocity results in much, if not most, of the senators' actual power not being exercised. If a senator *does* push his formal powers to the limit, he has broken the implicit bargain and can expect, not cooperation from his colleagues, but only retaliation in kind. "A man in the Senate," one senator says, "has just as much power as he has the sense to use. For this very reason he has to be careful to use it properly or else he will incur the wrath of his colleagues."

To play this game properly and effectively requires tolerance and an understanding of the often unique problems and divergent views of the other senators. "No man," one highly placed staff assistant says, "can really be successful in the Senate until he has adopted a *national* point of view. Learning what the other senators' problems are and working within this framework to pass legislation gives him this outlook. If he assumes that everyone thinks and feels the same way he and his constituents do, he will be an ineffective legislator." It demands, too, an ability to calculate how much "credit" a senator builds up with a colleague by doing him a favor or "going along." If a senator expects too little in return, he has sold himself and his constituents short. If he expects too much, he will soon find that to ask the impossible is fruitless and that "there are some things a senator just can't do in return for help from you." Finally, this mode of procedure requires that a senator live up to his end of the bargain, no matter how implicit the bargain may have been. "You don't *have* to make these commitments," one senator said, "and if you keep your mouth shut you are often better off, but if you *do* make them, you had better live up to them."

These are subtle skills. Some men do not have them in sufficient quantity to be successful at this sort of bargaining. A few take the view that these practices are immoral and refuse, with some display of righteous indignation, to play the game that way. But these men are the exceptions, the nonconformists to the Senate folkways.

INSTITUTIONAL PATRIOTISM

Most institutions demand an emotional investment from their members. The Senate of the United States is no exception. Senators are expected to believe that they belong to the greatest legislative and deliberative body in the world. They are expected to be a bit suspicious of the president and the bureaucrats and just a little disdainful of the House. They are expected to revere the Senate's personnel, organization, and folkways and to champion them to the outside world. . . .

A senator whose emotional commitment to Senate ways appears to be less than total is suspect. One who brings the Senate as an institution or senators as a class into public disrepute invites his own destruction as an effective legislator.

One who seems to be using the Senate for the purposes of self-advertisement and advancement obviously does not belong. Senators are, as a group, fiercely protective of, and highly patriotic in regard to, the Senate.

This, after all, is not a great deal different from the school spirit of P.S. 34, or the morale of a military outfit, or the "fight" of a football team. But, as we shall see, its political consequences are substantial, for some senators are in a better position than others to develop this emotional attachment.

INFLUENCES ON CONFORMITY

We have seen that normative rules of conduct—called here folkways—exist in the Senate. Moreover, we have seen that they perform important functions.[6] They provide motivation for the performance of legislative duties that, perhaps, would not otherwise be performed. They discourage longwindedness in a chamber of 100 highly verbal men who are dependent upon publicity and unrestrained by any formal limitations on debate. They encourage the development of expertism and division of labor and discourage those who would challenge it. They soften the inevitable personal conflict of a legislative body so that adversaries and competitors can meet (at the very least) in an atmosphere of antagonistic cooperation or (at best) in an atmosphere of friendship and mutual respect. They encourage senators to become "compromisers" and "bargainers" and to use their substantial powers with caution and restraint. Without these folkways the Senate could hardly operate in anything like its present form.

Yet the folkways are not universally accepted or adhered to; indeed, there is some covert hostility toward them in certain circles. If most senators do observe them, why not all?

Previous Training and Experience

Senators often express pride in the fact that their chamber is "democratic." "No matter," one senior senator says, "what you were before—a rich man or a poor man, a man with a good reputation or an unknown—you've got to prove yourself in the Senate. It's what you do when you arrive and not what you've done before that determines the amount of respect you get from your colleagues." Or as another has expressed it, everyone "must begin at the foot of the class and spell up" (Connally 1954, 88). This point of view overlooks the fact that it is a great deal harder for some men than others to start at the foot of the class.

A former governor who becomes a senator is often accustomed to a higher salary, more power and perquisites, a grander office, a larger staff, and more publicity than the freshman senator enjoys. He is likely to find the pace of legislative life slow and to be frustrated by the necessity of cooperating with 99 equals. To move from the governorship of one of the larger states to the role of apprentice senator is, in the short run, a demotion. The result for the one-time governors is a frequent feeling of disillusionment, depression, and discouragement. . . . At the same time, the other senators complain that the former governors "are the hardest group to handle; they come down here expecting to be big shots" and that they often are unwilling to realize that "they are just one of the boys." Some governors, they feel, never make the adjustment; a larger number make it slowly and painfully.

It is possible to subject this hypothesis to a rough empirical test. Crude indices of conformity can be obtained by counting the number of speeches senators make and by determining the extent to which the bills they introduce are on similar or disparate subjects.[7]

These measures of the former governors' floor activity and legislative specialization were calculated and are compared to those of men elected from other offices in Tables 13.1 and 13.2.

In giving floor speeches during the Eighty-third and Eighty-fourth Congresses, the former governors were more vocal than the former congressmen, state legisla-

Table 13.1

Last public office and frequency of floor speaking (83rd and 84th Congresses)

Last public office	Frequency of floor speaking			
	High	Medium	Low	Total
Governor	10%	35%	55%	100% (20)
U.S. representative	0%	52%	48%	100% (23)
State legislator	0%	33%	67%	100% (6)
State executive	17%	17%	67%	100% (6)
Local official	50%	50%	0%	100% (6)
Judge	0%	60%	40%	100% (5)
Federal executive	33%	22%	45%	100% (9)
None	0%	50%	50%	100% (4)

Note: The two floor leaders, Johnson (D-TX) and Knowland (R-CA) have been omitted from this and all subsequent tables on frequency of floor speaking. A high level of floor activity is an inevitable consequence of their positions and is not considered a breach of the folkways.

Table 13.2

Last public office and index of specialization (83rd and 84th Congresses)

Last public office	Index of specialization			
	High	Medium	Low	Total
Governor	35%	15%	50%	100% (20)
U.S. representative	8%	46%	46%	100% (24)
State legislator	28%	43%	28%	100% (7)
State executive	0%	33%	67%	100% (6)
Local executive	0%	50%	50%	100% (6)
Judge	40%	40%	20%	100% (5)
Federal executive	0%	44%	56%	100% (9)
None	0%	25%	75%	100% (4)

tors, judges, and men with no officeholding experience. The former local government officials and federal executives, on the other hand, gave even more floor speeches than the onetime governors. In legislative specialization, only the former judges appear to have had a narrower range of legislative interests than the governors. Indeed, of the other senators, only the former congressmen and state legislators came even close to matching them in this respect. If our indices of conformity are of any value, the governors as a whole seem to "go along" with the Senate folkways fairly well.

But it is the governors from the larger states, coming to the Senate with national reputations, who seem to find their initial experiences in the chamber especially trying. Moreover, their record for conformity to the folkways is bad. While they do tend to specialize quite highly, they are extremely active on the floor, even when compared to other senators from similar states (Table 13.3).

There is another peculiar feature of the former governors in the Senate: those with low seniority conform to the folkways more closely than those with high seniority. In Table 13.4, we can see that the higher the seniority of the former governors, the more active they were in floor debate, while just the opposite is true among the former representatives. . . .

Among the present crop of senators at any rate, prolonged exposure to the folkways seems to have resulted in a high degree of conformity among the former congressmen, state legislators, and judges but *not* among former governors, federal executives, and local government officials.[8]

The Amateur Politicians, distinguished business and professional men who entered politics relatively late in life and became senators with little political experience, face many of the same problems that the former governors do, compounded by their relative ignorance of political ways. One must learn to be a senator and the Amateurs have a great deal to learn. As can be seen in Table 13.5, they are more likely to ignore the folkways regarding floor activity and legislative specialization than are the Professionals. Moreover, the Amateurs usually must learn how to be legislators in less time than those who follow other career lines to the Senate; they are the oldest group of freshmen. A relatively young man can afford to be patient, to devote two or four or six years to learning the ropes and climbing the seniority ladder. A 60-year-old man, with sufficient vigor to win election to the Senate and a

Table 13.3

Frequency of floor speaking of big-state senators, by last public office (83rd and 84th Congresses)

Last public office	Frequency of floor speaking		
	High + Medium	Low	
Governor	50%	50%	100% (6)
U.S. representative	20%	80%	100% (6)
All Other	38%	62%	100% (8)

Note: "Big state" is defined as one with more than 4,000,000 population in 1950. See note to Table 13.1.

Table 13.4

Last public office, frequency of floor speaking, and index of specialization by seniority level (84th Congress)

Last public office	seniority	Percentage low, floor speaking	Percentage high, index of specialization	
Governor	High	78%	45%	(9)
	Medium	88%	25%	(8)
	Low	100%	20%	(5)
U.S. representative	High	100%	67%	(6)
	Medium	88%	22%	(9)
	Low	94%	0%	(17)
State legislator	High	66%	100%	(3)
	Medium	50%	0%	(2)
	Low	50%	0%	(2)
State executive	High	100%	0%	(1)
	Medium	50%	0%	(2)
	Low	100%	0%	(4)
Local official	High	0%	0%	(1)
	Medium	0%	0%	(2)
	Low	25%	0%	(4)
Judge	High	100%	50%	(2)
	Medium	0%	33%	(3)
	Low	100%	0%	(1)
Federal executive	High	25%	0%	(4)
	Medium	0%	0%	(2)
	Low	100%	33%	(3)
None	High	0%	0%	(1)
	Medium	0%	0%	(1)
	Low	100%	0%	(2)

distinguished career behind him, is not so likely to take the long view. At any rate, a larger proportion of the men elected to the Senate relatively late in life tend to "talk too much" than is the case with the others (Table 13.6).

We find a curious situation in the Senate. The greater a man's pre-Senate accomplishments (either in or out of politics) and the greater his age at election, the less likely he is to conform. For those reasons, a sort of reverse snobbism is quite widespread in the Senate. As one oldtimer said, "We are skeptical of men who come to the Senate with big reputations." From the standpoint of protecting the Senate folkways, this skepticism is justified.

POLITICAL AMBITIONS

Higher political ambitions—and for senators this means a desire to become either president or vice-president—can also lead to nonconformity.

Table 13.5

Percentage of pre-senate adult life in public office, frequency of floor speaking, and index of specialization (83rd and 84th Congresses)

Percentage of pre-Senate adult years in public office	Frequency of floor speaking			
	High	Medium	Low	Total
Under 40%	21%	37%	42%	100% (36)
40–60%	0%	48%	52%	100% (21)
60% plus	5%	35%	60%	100% (20)

	Index of Specialization			
	High	Medium	Low	
Under 40%	10%	31%	59%	100% (39)
40–60%	10%	43%	48%	100% (21)
60% plus	33%	38%	29%	100% (21)

Note: See note to Table 13.1.

Table 13.6

Age at first election/appointment to the Senate and frequency of floor speaking (83rd and 84th Congresses)

Age at first election/ appointment	Frequency of floor speaking			
	High	Medium	Low	Total
30–39	8%	54%	38%	100% (13)
40–49	4%	46%	50%	100% (28)
50–59	17%	33%	50%	100% (30)
60 plus	25%	25%	50%	100% (8)

Note: See note to Table 13.1.

First of all, strong and exalted ambitions are likely to lead to restiveness during the period of apprenticeship. A national following is seldom acquired by "being seen and not heard" or through faithful service on the District of Columbia Committee. In order to overcome this initial handicap, the highly ambitious freshman may resort to extreme and unsettling tactics, as, for example, Senator Kefauver is thought by his colleagues to have done in his crime investigation and Senator McCarthy certainly did in his "crusade" against communism. His legislative duties are likely to be neglected in the ceaseless quest for publicity and personal advancement. His ears are likely to be "attuned to noises outside the workaday drone of the Senate chamber."[9] Since the senator with higher ambitions is almost invariably shooting for the presidency, he is likely to be attuned to the voices of somewhat different groups than are most senators. Close presidential elections are won and lost in the doubtful states containing large metropolitan populations.

Popularity in these areas is generally a prerequisite for nomination and election to the presidency. Yet these very groups are the ones underrepresented in the Senate, the ones most often at odds with its present power structure. To the extent that ambitious senators anticipate the wants of possible future constituents, they find themselves challenging the Senate *status quo.*

. . . As a general rule, it seems that a man who entirely adheres to the Senate folkways has little chance of ever becoming president of the United States.

Constituency Problems

A third factor which encourages nonconformity to Senate folkways is a competitive two-party, or a large and complex, constituency.

The political insecurity of a senator from this kind of state is likely to result in a shortened time perspective, an eagerness to build a record quickly, an impatience with the slowness of the seniority system. The approved attitude for the new senator was voiced by a freshman: "I want to be a *Senator.* I want to gain the respect of my colleagues so that I can represent my state better. I want to establish a reputation as a hard-working committee member who does his homework, who has integrity and good judgment rather than to get my name in the paper every morning. This is taking the long view. It takes time to establish this kind of a reputation in the Senate. It's rather like starting a law practice in a new and small town, as I did in ———, ———. You can't rush it." A senator whose seat is in grave danger is much more likely to try to "rush it" than one who can count on reelection unless he makes a major blunder.

Table 13.7 seems to support this line of reasoning. The senators from two-party states are a little more likely to be frequent floor speakers than those from

Table 13.7

Type of party system in home state, frequency of floor speaking, and index of specialization (83rd and 84th Congresses)

Type of party system	Frequency of floor speaking			
	High	Medium	Low	Total
Two-party	16%	35%	49%	100% (43)
Modified one-party	11%	39%	50%	100% (18)
One-party	0%	50%	50%	100% (18)

	Index of specialization			
	High	Medium	Low	Total
Two-party	16%	41%	43%	100% (44)
Modified one-party	6%	33%	61%	100% (18)
One-Party	26%	26%	47%	100% (19)

Note: See note to Table 13.1.

modified one-party constituencies. Both are considerably more vocal than those from pure one-party states. The picture is a little different so far as legislative specialization is concerned. One-party state senators seem to be the most specialized; those from modified one-party states, least specialized; while the senators from two-party areas fall between.

The size and complexity of a senator's state also influences the likelihood of his conforming to Senate norms. A senator from a large state has a far greater burden of "case work" to process and errands to run, mail to answer, and speeches to give back home than the man from a small state; and he has to do this without a proportionately larger staff. He is just not likely to have as much time for legislating as a senator from Nevada, Wyoming, or Delaware. The large states also tend to be the politically complex states, shot through with sectional, religious, economic, and ethnic conflicts. As a result, a senator from one of these states is subject to greater cross pressures than is a man representing a homogeneous state with only one or two real issues, as, for example, has been the case for the Southern states. He is also expected by his constituents to be active on more issues than the man from the smaller and simpler states, and so he will be tempted to challenge the specialization folkway. Generally he is forced to grapple with these problems without the benefit of substantial seniority, which men from closely contested, large, and complex states seldom achieve.

Table 13.8 appears to reinforce this speculation; the larger in size and the more urban a senator's state, the more likely he is to be hyperactive on the Senate floor. Table 13.9 presents the relationships between the same two variables and legislative specialization. Urban state senators definitely specialize less than ones from rural states. The size of a senator's state, however, does not seem to have any effect on the range of his legislative interests.

Table 13.8

Size and complexity of home state and frequency of floor speaking (83rd and 84th Congresses)

	Frequency of floor speaking			
	High	Medium	Low	Total
Percentage urban, state population (1950)				
80% plus	38%	12%	50%	100% (8)
60–79%	13%	33%	54%	100% (24)
40–59%	6%	48%	46%	100% (33)
Under 40%	7%	43%	50%	100% (14)
Size of state population (1950)				
4,000,000 plus	40%	13%	47%	100% (15)
2,000,000–4,000,000	6%	54%	40%	100% (35)
Less than 2,000,000	10%	35%	55%	100% (31)

Note: See note to Table 13.1.

Table 13.9

**Size and complexity of home state and index of specialization
(83rd and 84th Congresses)**

	Index of specialization			
	High	Medium	Low	Total
Percentage urban, state population (1950)				
80% plus	11%	33%	55%	100% (9)
60–79%	8%	32%	60%	100% (25)
40–59%	15%	42%	42%	100% (33)
Under 40%	36%	29%	36%	100% (14)
Size of state population				
4,000,000 plus	13%	33%	53%	100% (15)
2,000,000–4,000,000	17%	40%	43%	100% (35)
Less than 2,000,000	16%	32%	52%	100% (31)

Political Ideology

Senators are, of necessity, tolerant of differences of opinion. A senator's political views make less difference to his acceptance or nonacceptance by his colleagues than is generally realized. Yet a senator's stance on political issues *does* make it easier (or harder) for him to conform to the folkways and thus, indirectly, influences his prestige and effectiveness in the chamber.

The folkways of the Senate, as we have already seen, buttress the *status quo* in the chamber, and the distribution of power within the chamber results in moderate to conservative policies. The liberals are more likely to challenge Senate norms than the conservatives. "A reformer's life is perhaps not easy anywhere," one close observer of the Senate has remarked. "In the Senate it can be both bitter and fruitless. . . ."[10]

A man elected to the Senate as a "liberal" or "progressive" or "reformer" is under considerable pressure to produce legislative results in a hurry. The people who voted for him are not likely to be happy with small favors—dams built, rivers dredged, roads financed—but want major national legislative policy changed. Yet as a freshman or a junior senator, and many never become anything else, the liberal is in no position to do this alone. If he gives in to the pressure for conformity coming from the folkways, he most postpone the achievement of his liberal objectives. If he presses for these objectives regardless of his junior position, he will become tabbed as a nonconformist, lose popularity with his colleagues and, in most cases, his legislative effectiveness as well.

The conservative does not face this problem. He has committed himself to fewer changes in basic policies; he finds the strategic positions in the Senate occupied by like-minded senators regardless of which party organized them. He is able to identify more strongly with the folkways of the chamber and side more easily

Table 13.10

Political ideology, frequency of floor speaking,
and index of specialization

Political ideology	Frequency of floor speaking			
	High	Medium	Low	Total
Liberal	12%	23%	65%	100% (34)
Moderate	0%	0%	100%	100% (19)
Conservative	0%	8%	92%	100% (37)
	Index of specialization			
	High	Medium	Low	Total
Liberal	20%	31%	49%	100% (35)
Moderate	21%	37%	42%	100% (19)
Conservative	24%	42%	34%	100% (38)

Note: See note to Table 13.1 and Appendix.

with Congress in its running feud with a generally more liberal president. Nor is he, as is the liberal, so dependent on the support of broad, often unorganized groups which can be reached only through the mass media. At any rate, the liberals seem to talk considerably more and to specialize somewhat less than do senators of different political persuasion (Table 13.10).[11] Conservatives can afford to be quiet and patient. Reformers, by definition, find it difficult to be either.

CONFORMITY AND "EFFECTIVENESS"

All this would be very "interesting" but not particularly important to serious students of politics if the Senate folkways did not influence the distribution of power within the chamber.

The senators believe, either rightly or wrongly, that without the respect and confidence of their colleagues they can have little influence in the Senate. "You can't be effective," they said over and over again, "unless you are respected—on both sides of the aisle." The safest way to obtain this respect is to conform to the folkways, to become a "real Senate man." Those who do not run a serious risk. "In the Senate, if you don't conform, you don't get many favors for your state. You are never told that, but you soon learn."

In order to test this hypothesis, a crude index of "Legislative Effectiveness" was constructed for the Eighty-third and Eighty-fourth Congresses by calculating the proportion of all public bills and resolutions introduced by each senator that were passed by the Senate.[12] While such an index does not pretend to measure the overall power or influence of a senator, it does seem to reflect his efficiency as a legislator, narrowly defined. To the extent that the concept as used on Capitol Hill has any distinct meaning, "effectiveness" seems to mean the ability to get one's bills passed.

The "effectiveness" of the conforming and nonconforming senators is presented in Table 13.11. The less a senator talks on the Senate floor, and the narrower a senator's area of legislative interest and activity, the greater is his "effectiveness." Conformity to the Senate folkways does, therefore, seem to "pay off" in concrete legislative results.[13]

There are unwritten rules of behavior, which we have called folkways, in the Senate. These rules are normative, that is, they define how a senator ought to behave. Nonconformity is met with moral condemnation, while senators who conform to the folkways are rewarded with high esteem by their colleagues. Partly because of this fact, they tend to be the most influential and effective members of the Senate.

These folkways, we have suggested, are highly functional to the Senate social system since they provide motivation for the performance of vital duties and essential modes of behavior which, otherwise, would go unrewarded. They discourage frequent and lengthy speechmaking in a chamber without any other effective limitation on debate, encourage the development of expertness and a division of labor in a group of overworked laymen facing unbelievably complex problems, soften the inevitable personal conflicts of a problem-solving body, and encourage bargaining and the cautious use of awesome formal powers. Without these folkways, the Senate could hardly operate with its present organization and rules.

Nonetheless, the folkways are no more perfectly obeyed than the nation's traffic laws. Men who come to the Senate relatively late in life, toward the close of a distinguished career either in or out of politics, have a more difficult time fitting in than the others. So do those elected to the Senate with little prior political experience. The senators who aspire to the presidency find it hard to reconcile the expectations of their Senate colleagues with their desire to build a national following. Finally, all senators belong to, or identify with, many other groups beside

Table 13.11

**Floor speaking, index of specialization, and legislative effectiveness
(83rd and 84th Congresses)**

Level of floor speaking	Index of legislative effectiveness			
	High	Medium	Low	Total
High	0%	33%	67%	100% (9)
Medium	3%	68%	29%	100% (31)
Low	15%	59%	26%	100% (39)
	Index of Specialization			
High	23%	69%	8%	100% (13)
Medium	10%	62%	28%	100% (29)
Low	8%	51%	41%	100% (39)

Note: See note to Table 13.1.

the Senate, and the expectations and demands of these groups sometimes conflict with the folkways. This seems to happen most often with the liberals from large, urban two-party states. When confronted with such a conflict situation, a senator must choose between conforming to the folkways, and thus appearing to "sell out," or gaining popularity back home at the expense of goodwill, esteem, and effectiveness in the Senate, a course which diminishes his long-run ability to achieve what his followers demand. For this reason, conflicts between the demands of constituents and legislative peers are by no means automatically resolved in favor of constituents.

It would be a mistake to assume that the folkways of the Senate are unchangeable. Their origins are obscure, but sparse evidence scattered throughout senatorial memoirs suggests that they have changed very little since the nineteenth century. Certainly the chamber's small membership and gradual turnover is conducive to the transmission of such rules virtually unchanged from one generation to the next. Yet the trend in American politics seems to be toward more competitive two-party politics; a greater political role for the mass media of communications and those skilled in their political use; larger, more urban constituencies. All these are factors which presently encourage departure from the norms of Senate behavior. In all likelihood, therefore, nonconformity to the folkways will increase in the future if the folkways remain as they are today. Moreover, the major forces which presently push senators toward nonconformity tend to converge upon a relatively small group of senators. Certainly, this is a more unstable situation than the random distribution of such influences—and, hence, of nonconforming behavior— among the entire membership of the Senate.

APPENDIX

The Index of Floor Speaking

The index of floor speaking was obtained simply by counting the number of speeches made by each senator during the Eighty-third and Eighty-fourth Congresses. . . . All senators who gave more than 500 speeches were ranking as high in floor speaking, those who gave from 250 to 499 speeches were ranked as medium, those giving fewer than 250 speeches were ranked as low. (Cutting points of 200 and 400 were used to distinguish between the low, medium, and high floor speakers in individual Congresses.). . .

The Index of Specialization

The index of specialization was computed from data in the *Congressional Quarterly Almanac* by determining the proportion of all public bills and resolutions introduced by each senator that were referred to the two committees receiving the largest number of the bills and resolutions he sponsored. . . . Senators with scores below .50 were considered to have low; those from .50 to .69, medium; and those about .70, high indices of specialization. . . .

Index of Conservatism-Liberalism

The *New Republic* magazine publishes voting charts for each Congress in which it indicates approval or disapproval of every senator's and congressman's votes on selected roll calls. The index of conservatism-liberalism was constructed simply by dividing the total number of "liberal" votes (according to the editors of this magazine) a senator had cast by the number of the selected votes on which he took a position. . . . Roll-call votes on foreign policy issues were excluded from this analysis. . . . [S]enators with scores of .67 and above are considered liberals; those with scores between .34 and .66, moderates; and those with scores below .34, conservatives. . . .

The Index of Legislative Effectiveness

. . . [T]he data for the index of legislative effectiveness was obtained from the *Congressional Quarterly Almanac*. The index was obtained by dividing the number of bills and resolutions that a senator sponsored which passed in the Senate by the total number he introduced. . . . All senators with scores below .15 were considered low in effectiveness; those with scores from .15 to .34, medium; and those with scores of .35 and above were rated as high.

This measure is, of course, based on the assumption that a senator's bill-sponsoring "batting average" is a fair index of his over-all "effectiveness" in the Senate. This assumption might be disputed on a number of grounds. First, a man might be highly "effective" in, say, his committee work but not be highly successful in shepherding his own bills through the legislative machinery. It is the author's impression that this is a rare occurrence. Second, by weighting all bills equally, the measure gives disproportionate weight to minor pieces of legislation. It is precisely on this kind of measure that a senator's standing with his colleagues is important in getting legislative results. Third, the measure ignores the fact that many bills and resolutions are not expected to pass by the sponsors who take little if any action in their behalf. But senators who habitually introduce bills with no intention of their passing differ from those who introduce bills only when they intend to see them through. The first type of senator is concerned with the propaganda consequences of his actions outside the chamber. The latter's actions are directed toward direct legislative payoffs. Legislative "effectiveness" as used in the study should not, therefore, be confused with overall political influence. Some men with considerable influence on public opinion were quite ineffective as legislators, narrowly defined.

The Index of Party Unity

. . . Party unity scores for individual senators have been figured by the *Congressional Quarterly Almanac*. . . They show the proportion of the time, when he took a stand, that a senator voted with a majority of his party on roll calls in which a majority of the Republican voted against a majority of the Democrats. . . .

NOTES

1. Significantly, the only major work on the Senate which gives much attention to these questions is White (1956). At the time he wrote this book, Mr. White was chief Congressional correspondent for the *New York Times* and very much an "insider." White's book both gains and suffers from the intimate position from which he viewed the Senate. On this point see Chapter IX [of Matthews (1960)].

2. *Washington Post and Times Herald*, 19 February 1956.
3. Cf. Harry S Truman's comments. "I learned [upon entering the Senate] ... that the estimates of the various members which I formed in advance were not always accurate. I soon found that, among my 95 colleagues the real business of the Senate was carried on by unassuming and conscientious men, not by those who managed to get the most publicity." *New York Times*, 3 October 1955.
4. *Providence* (R.I.) *Evening Journal*, 8 February 1956.
5. *Congressional Record* (Daily Edition), 13 June 1956, 9153.
6. That is, the folkways contribute to the survival of the system without change. For a brilliant analysis of the promise and pitfalls of functional analysis see Merton (1949, chapter 1).
7. These indices are described in the detail in the Appendix.
8. This conclusion must be treated with more than the usual scholarly caution. Only a longitudinal study or one using far more elaborate cross tabulation than is possible here can adequately isolate the effects of seniority on conformity to the folkways.
9. Douglass Cater, "Estes Kefauver, Most Willing of the Most Willing." *The Reporter*, 3 November 1955, 16.
10. William S. White, "Realistic Reformer from Tennessee," *The New York Times Magazine*, 4 March 1956, 32. On the same point, cf. Voorhis (1947), especially at page 62.
11. For a detailed discussion of the construction of the Index of Conservatism-Liberalism see the Appendix.
12. See the Appendix for a description and discussion of the Index of Legislative Effectiveness.
13. It should be pointed out, as one friendly critic remarked after reading a draft of this analysis, that it is possible that "concentration and silence may be a product of legislative effectiveness, rather than the other way around." Statistical analysis is unable to tell us which came first. However, our Capitol Hill informants *overwhelmingly* argued that conformity leads to effectiveness and not the other way around. Until such time as a more refined analysis is possible, this seems to be the best evidence we have upon which to determine which is cause and which is effect.

    See Appendix E, Table 7 [of Matthews (1960)] for evidence that the types of senators which tend not to conform to the folkways also tend to be relatively "ineffective" senators.

Chapter 14

The Learning of Legislative Norms

HERBERT B. ASHER

Studies of legislatures have uncovered the existence of informal norms or folkways or rules of the game that are presumed to be important for the maintenance of the legislative system. It is often argued that the institution, be it the House or the Senate or a state legislature, must transmit its norms to legislative newcomers in order to insure the continued, unaltered operation of the institution, and that the member himself must learn these norms if he is to be an effective legislator. Whether or not this be necessary, it certainly is plausible to view freshman members of the legislative body as undergoing a socialization process which involves the learning of legislative norms. Yet previous studies have largely concentrated on the identification of legislative norms and have devoted little attention to their transmission to the newcomer. Is the freshman legislator aware of the expected types of behavior prior to taking his seat or does he learn them while in office? If he learns them in office, who actually are the agents of transmission? Or is the socialization process so informal that we cannot even speak of well-defined agents?

These questions and others have not been fully addressed, and thus the focus of this paper is on the learning of norms by freshman members of the United States House of Representatives.[1] My interest is in individual learning of legislative norms, regardless of whether the content learned is in conformity or opposition to the norms. Too often the emphasis in socialization research has been on system maintenance rather than individual adaptation, leading one to dismiss findings of deviance too readily. The data come from a broader panel study of the learning that freshman members elected to the House of Representatives in November, 1968, underwent with respect to perceptions of their jobs, legislative norms, and sources of voting cues (Asher 1970). Since a research interest in learning is a longitudinal concern, a two-wave panel design was employed, the first set of interviews conducted in late January and February of 1969, and the second set the following May. The purpose of the panel was to capture the changes that the Ninety-first class members underwent in the first few months of their legislative service, a period that seemed a priori to be crucial in

Source: *American Political Science Review* (1973) 67:499–513. Reprinted by permission of the publisher.

talking about learning. Of the 37 freshmen in the Ninety-first Congress, 30 were interviewed at t_1 (late January and February) and of these 30, 24 were interviewed at t_2.[2]

A norm has been defined herein as a rule or standard of conduct appropriate to be a person in a specified situation within a group. The norm describes the type of behavior expected by almost all of the other members of the group and often, though not necessarily, has associated with it sanctions for deviance. Since concepts such as role and norm are useful because of their normative or mutual expectations component, and since a definitional attribute of a norm is that it be shared to a high degree by the members of the group, a sample of nonfreshman members of the House was also interviewed. Certainly if incumbent representatives agreed to the norms there would be an environment more supportive of freshmen learning them. Conversely, if there were marked disagreement about the norms on the part of nonfreshmen, we might then wish to reformulate or even reject these "norms."[3]

A variety of approaches can be used to ascertain information and attitudes about legislative norms. Wahlke and his colleagues (1962) employed an open-ended question that asked the respondents to identify the rules of the game in their respective state legislatures. Such an approach is particularly valuable for identifying those norms most salient to the representative, but it may fail to elicit the nascent attitudes that freshmen early in their careers are likely to possess. Hence, freshmen and nonfreshmen were queried about specific norms, the determination of which was based upon a survey of the existing literature. The main norms investigated were specialization, reciprocity, legislative work, courtesy, and aspects of apprenticeship including learning the House rules, restrained participation, and attendance on the floor and in committee.[4] A focused interview approach was selected to collect information about these norms, although this procedure raises certain problems. For example, one cannot simply ask the representative whether a norm of reciprocity exists in the House, for such a label may be without meaning to the legislator. We must attach some behavioral tag to reciprocity, and in so doing we have a wide leeway. Thus, we might ask the representative whether he thought members should do favors for one another, but unless the representative was particularly misanthropic, we would expect unanimously affirmative responses to such an item, thereby reducing the discriminatory capacity of the question to zero. Therefore, reciprocity was operationalized in this study by placing it in the context of a voting situation, with all the attendant ambiguities and pressures. The actual question was: "Would you vote a certain way on a bill that you cared little about in order to gain the vote of a fellow representative on a bill that you did care about?" The general point to be made here is that questions seeking to uncover information about norms are best framed within a fairly specific behavioral situation. If we cannot observe behavior directly (and most often we cannot), then our questions should be as behaviorally oriented as possible. . . .

FRESHMAN ATTITUDES TOWARD THE NORMS AT t_1

[Table 14.1 presents the attitudes to the norms by freshmen and incumbents. Note the marked disagreement on apprenticeship by incumbents, which calls into question the very existence of this norm.]

The responses of the newcomers are quite similar to those of their more senior colleagues, suggesting a generally shared set of expectations.[5] Both groups agree most strongly with the importance of friendly relationships; perhaps this implies that this norm, rather than being specific to the House, is carried over from general life experience. The freshmen also unanimously believed the rules to be important. The major difference between the newcomers' and incumbents' responses concerned the norm of apprenticeship; an additional 20% of the freshmen agreed that it is necessary. This may reflect a caution on the part of freshmen early in their incumbency.

Since the concept of norms involves shared expectations, the freshmen were queried about their perceptions of nonfreshman attitudes. They were asked whether they thought that more senior representatives favored the specialist or the generalist. All the newcomers who could answer said that senior members favored the specialist, which in effect confirmed their own earlier endorsement of specialization and committee work, but 29% (8 of 28) said that they did not know the preferences of senior members. And while the newcomers generally cited committee work over floor work, fully 73% thought it worthwhile, especially for freshmen, to spend time on the House floor. Attendance on the House floor was deemed important because it enabled the freshman representative to learn the procedures and thereby complete his apprenticeship much sooner.

Deviant Responses of the Freshmen

One can conclude from this brief outline that freshmen shared to a similar degree the norms of nonfreshmen, a situation certainly conducive to the learning of norms, but not one that automatically implies that norms were formally transmitted from senior to freshman members. It is interesting to examine some of the deviant responses given by freshmen. Numerous hypotheses were entertained

Table 14.1

Attitudes to the norms at t_1

	% Freshmen agreeing	N	% Nonfreshmen agreeing	N
Friendly relationships important	100	30	97	40
House rules important	100	30	82	40
Important work of House done in committee	90	30	95	40
Congressman should be a specialist	73	30	80	40
Worthwhile to spend time on House floor	73	30		
Would be likely to trade votes	72	29	81	21
Senior members favor the specialist	71	28		
Would not personally criticize a fellow representative	71	28	82	40
Freshman should serve apprenticeship	57	30	38	65

about the causes of noncompliance to the norms. For example, it was thought that freshmen with prior political experience, especially in the state legislature, would be apt to give "correct" responses. It was also thought that freshmen with a strong dedication to a career in the House would be more sensitive to the norms. These hypotheses and others were neither confirmed nor refuted because of the very small number of cases involved. The most fruitful approach to the problem is a norm-by-norm analysis of the deviant responses.

Specialization

Eight of the 30 freshmen interviewed at t_1, did not unqualifiedly opt to be specialists. Two freshmen asserted that congressmen should be generalists, five said that it depended on the individual or that a member must be both, and one did not know. One representative who chose to be a generalist cited the heterogeneous nature of his district as the determining factor in his decision. This representative had the most extensive state legislative experience of any freshman in the Ninety-first Congress, thereby leading one to reject the too facile linkage of state legislative service with specialization. The other generalist appeared to be motivated by two forces: a suspicion of accepting others' advice and a recognition that congressmen had to vote on a wide range of issues and should therefore be broadly informed. The theme of distrust occurred throughout this interview; the representative was very much an ideologue with little confidence in the judgment and motives of his colleagues and with a very rigid view of his job. This suspiciousness was reflected in his responses to questions on voting cues: He was very wary of members giving him wrong information and was generally expecting his votes to be uninfluenced by his colleagues. Newcomers who said that a member had to be both a specialist and a generalist argued that assignment to a committee forced one to specialize, while floor voting on a wide variety of issues compelled one to be a generalist. . . .

An analysis of such background variables as prior political experience uncovered no systematic differences between specialists and nonspecialists.

Committee Work

Only three of 30 freshmen did not assert that most of the important work of the House was done in committee. One member, a Southern Democrat with state legislative experience and highly directed toward a career in the House, said that he did not know where the work was done since the committees had only just organized. Another freshman, our distrustful ideologue mentioned above, said without qualification that most of the important work was done on the floor, since that was where the actual passage or defeat of a piece of legislation occurred. For him, voting was the crucial aspect of the job with the events preceding any vote being of only minor importance. The third freshman who failed to assert the primacy of committee work thought, in fact, that neither the committees nor the floor was the most significant arena:

The important work is not done in either. It is too early to say where the important work is done, if, in fact, important work is done. The important work is to stir up public opinion about the important issues.

This representative more than any other freshman had an active national constituency. His energies were constantly spread thin over a number of liberal causes that were outside the immediate context of House legislative activity. He was one of the most active and reformist freshmen, yet his behavior very much followed the traditional, accepted patterns even though he denied the importance of committee and floor work. For example, in the interview, he coupled a stinging attack on the proceedings on the House floor with a statement and explanation as to why it is important to spend time there.

> Yes, it is worthwhile to spend time on the House floor. This is where the member lobbies, where he talks to others about bills, trades information, does logrolling. People will think you are arrogant if you don't spend much time there. Debate on the floor is a sham; it's dishonest. People get things in the *Record* without saying them in debate as happened in the HUAC controversy.

And his response to the item about the importance of friendly relationships probably best typifies the difference between the activist who is careful to observe the amenities and the would-be reformer who allows personal relationships to deteriorate.

> It's very important to maintain friendly relationships. I think a big mistake is made when people who come up here hoping to change things, are frustrated and allow their frustrations to create personal animosities. I get along with everyone here: I like everyone. I even get along well with Mendel Rivers; I tease him a lot. . . .

Personal Criticism

There were eight freshmen out of 28 who said they would personally criticize a fellow representative. For three of these representatives, this willingness to criticize their colleagues seemed to be rooted in a certain outspokenness of personality and intensity of belief that they realized would surface at some point in their congressional careers, although they did not consciously intend to make personal criticism a regular occurrence. Included among these three is our distrustful ideologue; he said that it was possible he would criticize a fellow representative "if he needed it." None of the five other freshmen had served in the state legislature, so perhaps their earlier experiences had not taught them that personal attacks were normally out of bounds. For one of these five, the lack of state legislative experience was probably less influential than the member's own weak attachment to the House. Two factors that lessened his commitment to the House were his age and his relative financial independence: He perceived himself to be too old to have any lengthy career in the House, and therefore far removed from the worries of career advancement; furthermore, as he mentioned more than once, he had a lucrative business to return to if House service ever became too compromising. Even if he were to criticize, he said that he would do it "with velvet gloves."

Reciprocity/Trading Votes

A striking similarity emerges among the freshman representatives who were not likely to trade votes: All six were Republicans. And the three members of the non-freshman sample who unqualifiedly refused to trade votes were also Republicans. Four of the freshman responses were resounding "No's," while another was "I hope not," which seemed to imply that vote trading was wrong, but that somehow the representative might be tempted to participate in it. The only respondent who tried to explain the negative opinion toward vote trading stated that ten years earlier in the state legislature he had been "burned" because he did not anticipate the consequences of the bill to which he had given his vote. Perhaps what we have here is a tendency by Republicans to view politics more moralistically or ideologically so that trading votes becomes tantamount to catering to unworthy special interests and to abdicating one's own sense of right and wrong.

The Usefulness of Time Spent on the House Floor

The final two forms to be investigated for deviant responses were the ones asked only of freshmen. One inquired whether they thought that senior representatives favored the specialist or the generalist. As mentioned earlier, while eight freshmen did not know the answer to this at t_1, none answered "generalist." The second item was concerned with the value of spending time on the House floor. At t_1, five representatives (four Democrats and one Republican) said that it was not worthwhile because so little was going on. Since we are interested in behavior as well as in attitude, a crude measure of time spent on the House floor was constructed; it is simply the percentage of the quorum call votes that the member answered in the first session of the Ninety-first Congress. This measure has severe limitations, including our expectation that members from districts relatively close to the Capitol would score low because of the extensive amount of time they would spend in their easily reached constituencies. And, obviously, members who do answer quorum calls regularly may spend very little time on the floor. Be that as it may, there was a weak, yet consistent relationship between attitudes and behavior. The 22 freshmen who felt floor time was worthwhile missed 13% of the quorum calls; the 3 who were neutral missed 19%; and the 5 who felt floor experience was not worthwhile missed 28%.

Forces Contributing to Deviant Responses to the Norms

From this discussion of deviant responses, we can winnow out a number of influences that promote compliance and noncompliance to the norms, but we cannot weight these influences in any quantitative fashion because of the very small N involved. Career orientation to the House appeared to be important in furthering adherence to the norms, while aspirations to other office encouraged nonadherence. Also reducing the salience of the House for the newcomer were financial security and age; older freshmen realized that they would be less likely to advance to any great degree up the House hierarchy. Finally, the extremism of the member's ideological views was related to norm compliance: The more ideological members, whether of the left or right, were somewhat more willing to violate the norms, especially those on speaking out in proper fashion. It was significant that only one representative—the distrustful ideologue—gave responses that repeatedly departed from the norms. Personality traits in combination with his view of politics seemed to account quite well for his beliefs. But for most other freshmen, deviant responses were very infrequent, so that it was impossible to talk of types of freshmen who generally did not abide by the norms. In other words, noncompliance to one norm did not predict very well attitudes toward other norms. Probably the most important finding overall is that noncompliance was minimal, implying that by one means or another, freshmen had learned the norms well, the topic to which we now turn.

FRESHMEN AND THE LEARNING OF NORMS

As already mentioned, and in contradiction to initial expectations, most of the freshmen at t_1 were giving "correct" responses to the norms items. This observation has implications for the amount of learning that the panel can uncover. If learning be defined in terms of attitude change, then we would expect little learning from t_1 to t_2 because of the correctness of the t_1 responses. While learning might come in the form of strengthening initial attitudes, the inappropriateness of Likert items for elite populations such as legislators makes it difficult to get a handle on changes in attitudinal intensity. As it was, the responses to the unstructured norms questions were coded to incorporate direction and intensity of attitudes, and changes in both are reflected in the coefficients presented in Table 14.2.

The low incidence of later norm learning may mean that the freshmen knew the norms before entering Congress. If this be true, it is an interesting datum in and of itself. Or perhaps freshmen learned the norms in the short interval between taking office and being interviewed by this investigator, although this possibility appears unlikely (see note 2). One way of demonstrating the minimal learning of norms from t_1 to t_2 is to cross-tabulate the t_1 and t_2 responses to each item and examine the intra-item correlations. This is done in Table 14.2 for those norms questions that were coded in an ordinal fashion with at least four valid codes; the measure of association is tau-b.

Table 14.2
Intra-item correlations on the norms question (t_1 and t_2)

	Tau-B	N
Friendly relationships important	1.000	24
Would be likely to trade votes	.721	20
Freshman should serve apprenticeship	.696	24
House rules important	.693	24
Would not personally criticize a fellow representative	.310	22
Worthwhile to spend time on House floor	.169	24

As one can observe, all of the items except two—personal criticism and spending time on the House floor—were very stable. Of the 22 representatives who responded to the personal criticism question at t_1 and t_2, 13 did not give identical answers at the two time points. Eight of the 13 gave answers at t_2 that made it less likely that they would engage in personal criticism, but the other five indicated a greater willingness to criticize which runs counter to the learning or reinforcement of "proper" behavior. There were no background variables that explained the changes on this item, nor did the freshmen volunteer any information that was helpful in accounting for the shifts. What we may have here is response unreliability elicited by a question whose wording left in doubt just what was meant by personal criticism.

The situation was very different on the other unstable item; here half of the 24 responses were identical from t_1 to t_2. Four of the six Republicans who changed thought it more worthwhile at t_2 to spend time on the House floor, while five of the six Democrats felt just the opposite, and each group was able to justify its own position. The Democrats were all active liberals dismayed by what they considered the scarcity of significant floor work. Republicans, however, generally cited the instructional value of being on the House floor. Thus, a part of the reason for the low intracorrelation on this item was the growing dissatisfaction on the part of some Democrats. As this discontent was basically programmatic, it did not affect the less issue-oriented Republicans, whose changes on this item in the opposite direction were less easily explained.[6]

Subdividing the freshmen according to characteristics such as party and district competitiveness does not change the tau-b's very much. There is, however, some tendency for freshmen with state legislative experience to exhibit greater stability than those without such experience, and this is especially pronounced on vote trading. While the correlation for this item for all freshmen was .721, it rose to .792 for newcomers who had had state legislative service and plummeted to −.200 for those who had not had such service. Attitudes on vote trading, therefore, appear to be more stable if one has already had the opportunity to confront the situation in reality (as in a state legislature) and not just hypothetically. That is, members who had experienced vote trading firsthand were more consistent in their attitudes toward it, an intuitively appealing result.

Finally, let us examine the percentage agreement with each of the norms at t_1 and t_2, looking only at freshmen interviewed at both t_1 and t_2. This will indicate whether support for the norms increases or decreases (erodes) over time. The appropriate figures are presented in Table 14.3.[7]

The striking point about Table 14.3 is that support for the norms more commonly decreased than increased, although most of the percentage changes were small and probably mean little. The norm that suffered the greatest and most real erosion was apprenticeship; this finding will be analyzed in depth in the next section. Also suffering erosion of more than 10% were the items on specialization and the importance of the rules. What may be happening here is that at t_1 freshmen knew the "right" responses and uttered them automatically but that subsequent legislative experience enabled them to take a more sophisticated, knowledgeable, and qualified view of the norms. The norm showing the greatest gain in support was restraint in personal criticism, but no ready explanation comes to mind except that attendance on the House floor would indicate to the freshman, if he did not already know, that personal attacks were very rare, indeed.

The other interesting result in Table 14.3 is that the t_2 freshman responses are somewhat closer to the nonfreshman replies than are the t_1 answers. This does not hold for specialization, committee work, and friendly relationships; here the t_1 answers come closer to the incumbent responses, but the differences involved are small. But for the other norms, the t_2 freshman responses are substantially closer than the t_1 responses to the nonfreshman replies. For apprenticeship, the difference between the t_1 and nonfreshman responses was 20%, but only 4% when the t_2 replies are used. Eight and 13% differences between the t_1 and nonfreshman replies on House rules and personal criticism drop to 6% and zero when the t_2 responses are substituted. Thus, the freshmen were basically similar to their more senior colleagues at t_1, and by t_2 the coincidence of views toward the norms was even closer, suggesting that informal socialization to the norms was still occurring at t_2.

THE NORM OF APPRENTICESHIP

It is the norm of apprenticeship that is most relevant to freshmen. If the traditional description of the freshman representative as unsure in his actions and ignorant of House rules and procedures is correct, then apprenticeship is obviously the crucial norm for newcomers to follow. The natural expectation is that apprenticeship would be a very commonly accepted norm given the widespread familiarity of the

Table 14.3
Level of agreement to the norms at t_1 and t_2

	Freshmen				Nonfreshmen	
	% agreeing t_1	% agreeing t_2	Change	N	% agreeing	N
Freshman should serve apprenticeship	58	42	−16	24	38	65
Congressman should be a specialist	83	70	−13	23	80	40
House rules important	100	88	−12	24	82	40
Important work done in committee	96	87	−9	23	95	40
Friendly relationships important	100	92	−8	24	97	40
Would be likely to trade votes	68	68	0	22	81	21
Worthwhile to spend time on House floor	71	75	4	24		
Senior members favor specialist	70	78	8	23		
Would not personally criticize a fellow representative	69	82	13	22	82	40

adage about freshmen being seen and not heard. But as Table 14.4 indicates, the very existence of a norm of apprenticeship as defined herein must be called into question.[8] Almost half of the nonfreshman sample flatly denied the necessity of serving an apprenticeship, and if the qualified disagreements are added to this figure, almost two-thirds of the incumbents rejected apprenticeship. And while there was majority agreement to the norm at t_1 on the part of freshmen, a sizable minority of 43% deemed it unnecessary. Those freshmen who saw the need for serving an apprenticeship were asked how long they felt it would take in their own particular cases. Four newcomers said that they could not set a specific time limit, two said a year, and only one said the full two years of his first term in office. The remaining ten all indicated that apprenticeships between two and six months would be desirable. Thus, even for freshmen who agreed to apprenticeship, the learning period was usually seen as relatively short, most often under six months. The range of freshman responses to the apprenticeship item is illustrated by the following replies:

> Yes, I'll serve an apprenticeship. Its length depends upon the individual; it will prob-ably take me less time because of my previous legislative experience. A newcomer needs to be informed to be effective.
>
> Yes. The length depends, probably a few months. You can't lead the army the first day. But you do represent a district that elected you for two years and you can't just sit and do nothing.
>
> There is no reason for an apprenticeship. You learn best by jumping right in.
>
> No, you don't have to serve an apprenticeship. But one should not just jump into things. A freshman Congressman is not like a freshman in college; he is a man of some special competence. Senior people will listen to you if you have something to say.

An examination of the apprenticeship replies by party indicates some party differences, as shown in Table 14.5. Seven of the nine freshman Democrats who rejected apprenticeship were urban liberals from districts with heavy constituent demands. These men were generally active and concerned with programs, and, for them, apprenticeship implied a severe restriction on the activities that they deemed most important, particularly speaking up on the floor on such issues as Vietnam, national priorities, and school desegregation. The intention to engage in specific

Table 14.4

The norm of apprenticeship

	t_1 Freshman responses	Nonfreshman responses
	%	%
Agreement	40	24
Qualified agreement	17	12
Qualified disagreement	17	20
Disagreement	26	44
Total %	100	100
N	(30)	(66)

legislative activity, shared by a number of Democratic freshmen, itself runs counter to the image of the bewildered newcomer. For most Republicans, the idea of an apprenticeship or limited participation was not as restrictive, mainly because they were not as concerned with programs and problems. Thus, one's view of the job of the representative appears to influence one's opinions about apprenticeship.

It is reasonable therefore that freshmen who agreed to the importance of apprenticeship would be less active. Table 14.6 presents some evidence on this point using as measures of activity three simple indices constructed from the *Congressional Record*.[9] As expected, Democratic nonapprentices were substantially more active than their apprentice colleagues across all three measures. But this pattern does not hold for Republicans; here the differences between apprentices and nonapprentices are small and inconsistent. Interestingly, Republican and Democratic apprentices had comparable levels of activity, but Democratic nonapprentices were far more active than their GOP counterparts. Thus, Democratic freshmen are less likely to welcome serving an apprenticeship than Republican newcomers, and only for Democrats is the decision to choose or reject an apprenticeship reflected in varying levels of activity.

To help explain this finding one must recall that the Democratic party is the entrenched majority party in the House. The decision to serve an apprenticeship may be more salient for majority party members in general, since it is the majority party that sets the legislative pace, controls the committee, and the like. But more consequential for the freshman Democrat is the domination of his party by senior members, many of them Southerners, who comprise a much larger proportion of

Table 14.5

Freshman apprenticeship responses by party

	Republicans	Democrats
"Apprenticeship necessary"	73	40
"No apprenticeship necessary"	27	60
Total %	100	100
N	(15)	(15)

Table 14.6

Levels of activity vs. apprenticeship by party

	Republicans		Democrats	
	App.	No app.	App.	No app.
Mean number of House remarks	22	17	22	39
Mean number of extension remarks	15	19	21	40
Mean number of nonprivate bills and resolutions introduced	54	53	56	81
N	11	4	6	9

his party than senior Republicans do of the GOP. . . . The question of an apprenticeship is not nearly as salient for Republican freshmen—members of a relatively junior, minority party, who early in their House careers had the vaguest legislative plans, a condition that would make serving an apprenticeship less onerous.

In addition to one's programmatic intentions, the other variable that was often cited by freshmen as influential in their apprenticeship decision was their perception of their own legislative competence. Three members specifically stated that because of their previous experience in the state legislature, their period of apprenticeship could either be shortened or be totally unnecessary. The relationship between state legislative service and attitudes toward apprenticeship is presented in Table 14.7. For all freshmen, service in the state legislature does not materially affect opinions about apprenticeship. Table 14.7 further indicates that party differences with respect to apprenticeship remain even when previous state legislative experience is considered, thereby suggesting that previous experience is less important than one's own legislative goals in the decision whether or not to serve an apprenticeship. Again, Democratic freshmen were more oriented to legislation than their GOP colleagues.

The nonfreshman responses to apprenticeship are truly surprising in the extent of their disagreement with the norm. The common political lore has it that nonfreshmen, particularly the more senior among them, would be the strongest advocates of an apprenticeship norm. The nonfreshmen responses to the apprenticeship item was usually brief and to the point, indicating little difficulty in replying to the item. A few of the more detailed, qualified responses are given below:

> Apprenticeship is necessary for a period of time, but I have encouraged them [freshmen] to participate as soon as possible. I suggest that they choose as their area of expertise an area that they've had experience in previously which will let them participate earlier.
>
> I don't think freshmen congressmen should serve a period of apprenticeship. As a matter of fact, I don't think that term can apply in Congress. Any member has an equal right with any other member. The very nature of the legislative process does require that new members take more time to become acquainted with committee activities than those who have served for many years.

Table 14.7
Apprenticeship vs. state legislative service and party

	State service			No state service		
	R	D	All	R	D	All
"Apprenticeship necessary"	70	43	59	80	38	54
"No apprenticeship necessary"	30	57	41	20	62	46
Total %	100	100	100	100	100	100
N	(10)	(7)	(17)	(5)	(8)	(13)

This is a difficult question to answer because of the varying backgrounds of the new members of Congress . . . Hence, it seems to me that it would be difficult to establish any rule of thumb . . . I am frank to say that I have observed instances of over-enthusiastic freshman congressmen who would have done well to have been a bit more observant of the processes and legislative procedure before offering the panacea to a particular problem.

Table 14.8 presents the nonfreshman replies to the apprenticeship item by seniority and party. The results in this table are somewhat unexpected. Overall, the more senior one is, the less likely he will say that apprenticeship is necessary. For all groups except Republicans with less than six years of service, a sizable majority of respondents were against apprenticeship, and even for this group of Republicans the division was almost even. The reader should have greater confidence in the Republican figures than in the Democratic ones which do not include sufficient senior representation, especially from the South and border states.

Table 14.8 seems surprising because we have been led to believe that it is senior members who keep junior men in their place. But perhaps only a subset of senior members performs this function. The probable candidates would be the senior Southern and border (Democratic) members and others who also dominate the committees. After all, it was Texan Sam Rayburn who was credited with the terse description of apprenticeship as "being seen and not heard" and who advised members to go along in order to get along. There are only four Southern and border Democrats in the sample with more than ten years of service in the House (in a representative sample, there would be about twice that number), and three of the four said that no apprenticeship was necessary. These figures are too small to be conclusive, especially since it is almost impossible to interview the real patriarchs of the House. We can, however, divide the sample into gross regional categories to see whether apprenticeship is more common in the South, the likely home of a disproportionate number of carriers of the creed. The results of such a division reveal no substantial regional differences; 4 of 12 Southern members said that apprenticeship was necessary as compared to 38% of the non-Southern members ($N = 54$). This conclusion must be hedged a bit because of shortcomings in the Southern subsample.

Table 14.8
Nonfreshman apprenticeship responses by party and seniority.

	6 or fewer years of service			7 to 10 years of service			More than 10 years of service		
	R	D	All	R	D	All	R	D	All
Apprenticeship	53	27	41	43	13	27	36	25	32
No apprenticeship	47	73	59	57	87	73	64	75	68
Total %	100	100	100	100	100	100	100	100	100
N	(17)	(15)	(32)	(7)	(8)	(15)	(11)	(8)	(19)

Thus, apprenticeship is far from being a universally accepted norm. Indeed, one wonders why a majority of the freshmen at t_1 still subscribed to the norm, unless it represents a false anticipation. As one newcomer observed, "It may be that freshman classes have been browbeaten before they ever got here by the establishment." The browbeating may very well take place through the widespread circulation of such political lore as Speaker Rayburn's advice cited earlier. Such information about their status may be the only kind available to freshmen at first. Thus, in a sense, freshmen may have to be socialized *out of* the norm of apprenticeship. Two freshmen at t_1 said that Speaker McCormack himself had urged them to participate fully right from the outset of their service. Yet because of their prior conditioning, they were leery of such advice; they thought the Speaker was "just being nice." As noted earlier, there was erosion in support for apprenticeship from t_1 to t_2 by the Ninety-first class; perhaps this is indicative of learning that is really unlearning. Freshmen may have seen some of their colleagues participate early, observed that no sanctions were levied, and therefore altered their views about apprenticeship. Of course, it is possible that senior members who deny the importance of apprenticeship are saying one thing and believing another. A sophomore Republican argued:

> . . . [M]any senior congressmen might say that a freshman should not serve an apprenticeship, but when it came to actual practice, the situation was quite different. I know of numerous instances of senior members grumbling when a freshman member spoke on a subject. Typical comments were: "What's he doing talking, he's a freshman." "What does he know about it, he's only a freshman."

But it seems unreasonable to consider the senior members' responses against apprenticeship as largely misstatements of the members' underlying beliefs.

This argument does not mean that apprenticeship is unnecessary or unexpected. There will be many topics about which the freshman will be uninformed because of his inexperience, and in such areas, his more senior colleagues will expect him to proceed cautiously and to learn gradually. But this type of apprenticeship is a far cry from one in which the newcomer is expected to remain silent in all situations, even when he has a contribution to make. . . .

Finally, it is clear that the House is not alone in its skepticism about apprenticeship; the norm of apprenticeship has fallen into bad times in the United States Senate as well, especially since 1964. The "Inner Club" has declined in recent years and a new type of senator, less concerned with internal Senate operations, has become more prominent (Polsby 1971, 105–10; Ripley 1969b, 185).

CONCLUSION

The main finding of this chapter is that the amount of norm learning between January and May by the freshman members of the Ninety-first Congress was unexpectedly low. As the concept of norms incorporates the notion of shared expectations, the attitudes of a sample of nonfreshmen were first analyzed to insure that we were studying genuine norms. Apprenticeship was found to be less restrictive on freshmen than originally thought, while other norms were largely adhered to. It appeared that freshmen largely knew the general House norms prior to entering Congress, which made it impossible to talk about the formal agents of socialization involved in transmitting the norms to newcomers. And the extent of change once in office was minimal.

Now this finding may be an artifact of the particular freshman class under investigation, in the sense that the Ninety-first class was unusually well-prepared by prior political experience for House service. Of the six most recent freshman classes, the 91st class had the largest proportion of members with state legislative experience— 51%. But an alternative explanation seems more satisfactory, that is that freshman representatives would generally know many of the norms simply because they are rules of behavior appropriate to many institutional settings. Thus, one does not have to be a member of Congress to know that personal criticism and unfriendly relationships may be dysfunctional to one's institution or group or one's own career. This argument asserts that almost any type of prior experience would make the freshman sensitive to the basic rules of behavior. Overall, it was difficult to link compliance and noncompliance to the norms to any particular characteristics because of the small number of deviant responses, but a number of plausible influences were suggested.

These data do not address the learning of committee-specific norms. These norms may not be as salient or as transferable from other contexts as the ones discussed above, and hence they may actually have to be learned anew by freshmen.[10] Unfortunately, the data in this article span only January to May, 1969, a time of very little legislative action, both in committee and on the floor. The Ninety-first Congress in its early months was sharply criticized for the slowness of its legislative pace, a slowness that was due in part to the change in partisan complexion of the national administration. And this slowness of legislative pace may have retarded the learning of committee-specific norms. In their California study, Price and Bell found that the norms cited at their later interviews were most often those that concerned committee work and the handling of legislation (Price and Bell 1970, 355).

In summary, then, it seems as if the traditional image of the freshman congressman as ignorant and bewildered had mistakenly led us to expect substantial learning of norms on the part of supposedly ill-informed newcomers. This expectation was unwarranted on two counts: The general House norms were not so abstruse as to require formal learning, and the traditional image of the freshman Congressman was found to be out of date.

NOTES

1. Recently, there has been a greater emphasis on the legislative newcomer and his adaptation to the institution, with one article specifically concerned with the rules of the game, although from a different perspective than employed herein. See Bell and Price (1969), Gertzog (1970), and Price and Bell (1970).
2. The selection of the times of the two waves, particularly the first, was no easy matter. Since a prime concern of my research was freshman attitudes to legislative norms, I wished to interview sufficiently early so as to ascertain these attitudes while uninfluenced

by House service. But seminars for freshman representatives were held early in the session (January 8 through January 13) and at these meetings a large amount of material, some of it relevant to legislative norms, was presented to the freshmen. Thus, it would have been advantageous to talk to the newcomers before these seminars were held. But in terms of my interest in internal House voting cues, interviewing in early January would have made little sense as almost no legislative business was under way. In retrospect, the problem was not very serious as evidenced by a question included in the interview schedule designed to measure the impact of the freshman seminars. Freshmen generally indicated that the seminars were interesting and highly informative with respect to parliamentary procedures and the services available to congressmen, but generally attributed little influence to the seminars vis-à-vis House norms. Similar opinions were expressed by freshman participants in the 1959 seminars. My thanks go to Representative Morris Udall for allowing me to rummage through his files on previous freshman seminars.

3. The nonfreshman members of the House were stratified according to party, region, and seniority, and proportionate samples were selected randomly within these strata. The interviews obtained were very representative of Republican House membership, while they underrepresented Democrats in general and senior Southern Democrats in particular. . . . Despite the underrepresentation of senior Democrats, there were no significant ideological differences between the samples selected from each stratum and the corresponding parent stratum as measured by CQ conservative coalition support scores and ADA and ACA ratings.

4. The norm of institutional patriotism was also investigated, but its operationalization was so narrow that the responses obtained were not very interesting. Members were asked whether they would ever criticize the House, and, not unexpectedly, most said that they would which presumably implies that institutional patriotism is far more complex than merely refraining from criticism so that nothing more will be said about the norm in the remainder of this chapter.

5. . . . The actual questions for each of the norms were: Do you think congressmen should specialize in a field or should try to be generalists? Do you think most of the important work of the House is done on the floor or in committees? How important do you think it is to maintain friendly relationships with your fellow congressmen? Do you think that freshman congressmen should serve a period of apprenticeship, that is, be more an observer than an active participant in the legislative process? How important do you think learning the House procedural rules is? Would you ever personally criticize a fellow representative on the floor of the House? Would you vote a certain way on a bill that you cared little about in order to gain the vote of a fellow congressman on a bill that you did care about?

6. The issue orientation of the freshmen was determined by impressionistically content-analyzing their responses to a series of questions dealing with their legislative goals, the specific pieces of legislation, if any, that they planned to introduce or work for, and the kinds of legislative matters about which their districts were most concerned.

7. The percentages of Table 14.3 are for freshmen in the aggregate. Thus, zero percent change does not necessarily mean that all the freshmen interviewed at t_1 and t_2 remained perfectly stable; shifts in one direction may have balanced out those in the other. As it was, there was general stability in the replies except for the two items discussed in the text (personal criticism and spending time on the House floor) so that the percentage differences in Table 14.4 do not mask much additional shifting.

8. As a reminder to the reader, the actual apprenticeship question was: Do you think that freshman congressmen should serve a period of apprenticeship, that is, be more an observer than an active participant in the legislative process? In the subsequent discussion,

apprenticeship will be treated as a dichotomous variable by collapsing the agreement and qualified agreement categories and by combining the disagreement and qualified disagreement categories.

9. These measures are merely counts of the total number of entries in the *Record* and the total number of nonrelief bills and resolutions introduced. . . . A better indicator might be the number of amendments introduced. But since amendments from freshmen are relatively rare (only about one-fourth sponsored any), they cannot provide us with sufficient information.

10. A good example of such research is Fenno's treatment of apprenticeship in the context of the House Appropriations Committee. See Fenno (1966, 166–67).

Chapter 15

Multiple Paths: The Legislative Process in the House of Representatives

BARBARA SINCLAIR

The legislative process in the contemporary Congress is varied and complex. The old "textbook" process was predictable and linear with one stage following another in an inevitable sequence. At many stages now there is no single, normal route but rather a number of different paths that legislation may follow. The best way to understand the contemporary legislative process is to begin with the introduction of a bill and proceed step-by-step through the process in each chamber, examining frequently used options at each stage.

. . . Procedures that are obscure and seldom employed are of no interest here. Rather, my aim is to make understandable the procedures and practices that occur on the major legislation considered during any contemporary Congress.[1] . . .

SPECIAL RULES

In the House the majority party leadership schedules legislation for floor debate. When a committee reports a bill, it is placed at the bottom of one of the House calendars, the Union Calendar if major legislation. Considering legislation in the order it is listed on the calendar would make little sense, since optimal floor scheduling dictates attention to a host of policy and political factors. The House has developed ways of getting legislation to the floor that provides the needed flexibility. The primary ways of bringing legislation to the floor are through suspension of the rules and through special rules from the Rules Committee, both procedures that the majority party leadership controls.

Noncontroversial legislation is usually considered under suspension of the rules. In 1991–92, for example, 52% of all bills that passed the House did so by way of the suspension procedure. Most legislation considered under suspension is narrow in impact or minor in importance. Examples include H.Con. Res. 146, a concurrent resolution authorizing the 1996 Special Olympics Torch Relay to be

Source: *Unorthodox Lawmaking: New Legislative Processes in the U.S. Congress,* Barbara Sinclair, (Washington, DC: CQ Press, 1997), pp. 9, 20–31. Reprinted by permission of the publisher.

run through the Capitol Grounds, or S1341, a bill to provide for the transfer of certain lands to the Salt River Pima-Maricopa Indian community and the city of Scottsdale, Arizona. Legislation of more far-reaching significance also may be considered under suspension of the rules. This happens if the bill is so broadly supported that using much floor time is unwarranted. One example is HR2778, a 1995 bill affecting members of the armed forces performing services for the peace-keeping effort in the Republic of Bosnia and Herzegovina. The bill entitled them to certain tax benefits in the same manner as if their services were performed in a combat zone.

The motion to suspend the rules is in order on Mondays and Tuesdays. Legislation brought up under this procedure is debated for a maximum of 40 minutes. No amendments are allowed, and a two-thirds vote is required for passage.

The Speaker has complete discretion over what legislation is considered under suspension. When a committee reports a bill that the committee chair considers appropriate for suspension, the chair writes the Speaker requesting that procedure. The Speaker is guided by party rules restricting the use of the procedure. The Democratic Caucus and the Republican Conference both have rules specifying that, to be considered under suspension of the rules, bills should be bipartisan, have strong committee support, and cost less than $100 million.

Most major legislation is brought to the House floor by a special rule that allows the measure to be taken up out of order. The Rules Committee reports such rules, which take the form of House resolutions, but a majority of the full membership must approve each one.

The rule sets the terms for a measure's floor consideration. A rule always specifies the amount of time allowed for general debate and who is to control that time. One or two hours of general debate are typical, though major measures are sometimes granted considerably more time. The time is always equally split between the chairman and the ranking minority member of the committee that reported the legislation; if several committees worked on the bill, each will control some of the general debate time.

A rule may restrict amendments, waive points of order (against what would otherwise be violations of House rules in the legislation or in how it is brought up), and include other special provisions to govern floor consideration. The extent to which a rule restricts amendments and the manner in which it does so also may vary. An *open rule* allows all germane amendments, while a *closed rule* prohibits all amendments other than these offered by the reporting committee. Between the two extremes are rules that allow some but not all germane amendments to be offered; the Rules Committee labels them a *modified open rule* or a *modified closed rule*, depending on just how restrictive the rule is. Some rules of this kind allow only specific amendments enumerated in the Rules Committee report to be offered. Others allow only amendments that have been submitted to the Rules Committee or printed in the *Congressional Record* by a specific time. Still other rules set a time limit on the amending process and allow all germane amendments that can be offered during that time period.

In the contemporary House most rules are somewhat restrictive; in the Congresses of the early 1990s, two-thirds or more of all rules were modified open or modified closed or, occasionally, closed. In recent Congresses three-fourths of all major bills were considered under a restrictive rule.

When major legislation is ready for floor consideration, a decision on what type of rule to use must be made. Given the variety in contemporary rules, the choices are many. The Rules Committee is officially charged with making the decision, and the leaders of the reporting committee make their preferences known, but since the majority party members of Rules are selected by the Speaker, the party leadership strongly influences what is decided. On major legislation the decision on the character of the rule is considered crucial to the bill's success; not surprisingly, the leadership decides.

Because there are many options in the design of a rule, special rules can increasingly be tailored to the problem at hand. Thus, when a bill is referred to several committees, setting the ground rules for floor consideration can present a host of complicated and delicate problems (Bach and Smith 1988, 18–23). Debate time must be divided. When two or more committees have reported different provisions on a given matter, a decision also must be made about which committee's language will constitute the base text and how the other committees' versions will be considered. The first rule for the consideration of the 1992 energy bill, which had been referred to nine committees, split five hours of general debate among the committees. The Energy and Commerce Committee received one hour; the other eight were allotted a half-hour each. The committees worked out as many of the conflicts among themselves as they could. In the remaining cases, the Rules Committee decided which committee's version would go into the base bill that would serve as the original bill for the purpose of amendment on the floor. Other committees could offer their language as amendments on the floor. The rule limited the amendments to those listed in the Rules Committee's report, set debate time for each amendment—ranging from five to 20 minutes per side—and specified that those amendments "shall not be subject to amendment except as specified in the report".[2] And this rule governed consideration of only the first seven titles of the bill. The remaining titles were considered under a second rule that again limited the amendments that could be offered and permitted the chairman of the Energy and Commerce Committee "to offer amendments en bloc consisting of the text of amendments printed in the report and germane modifications".[3]

The Uses of Special Rules

Special rules can be used to focus attention and debate on the critical choices, to save time and prevent obstruction and delay, and sometimes to structure the choices members confront on the floor in a way that promotes a particular outcome. When the rule gives members a choice among comprehensive substitutes but bars votes on narrow amendments, it is focusing the debate on alternative approaches, on the big choices rather than the picky details. In recent years rules allowing a choice among comprehensive substitutes have been used to bring to the floor tax bills, budget resolutions, civil rights bills, and social welfare legislation on issues such as parental leave, minimum wage, and child care.

Rules that restrict amendments and waive points of order save time and prevent obstructionism. Before Republicans gained a House majority in the 1994 elections, they had promised, if they took control of the chamber, to use less restrictive rules than had the Democrats when in power. Yet House Republicans also promised to pass the Contract with America during the first 100 days of the 104th Congress. When they brought one of the early contract items to the floor under an open rule, Democrats naturally enough offered multitudes of amendments. Thereafter, the Republican-controlled Rules Committee usually included in its otherwise unrestrictive rules a time limit on total amending activity.

Any restrictions on amendments, even simply the requirement that amendments be submitted to the Rules Committee several days before being offered on the floor, help the bill's proponents by reducing uncertainty. Proponents can focus their efforts and plan strategy more efficiently; opponents lose the element of surprise.

In addition to reducing uncertainty, carefully crafted rules can structure choices to advantage a particular outcome. . . . In 1995 Republicans . . . used a cleverly constructed restrictive rule to protect their rescission bill. The rule specified that anyone wishing to restore spending that had been cut in the bill had to offset the cost by cutting something else in the same section of the bill. Thus, no money could be transferred to social programs from defense spending or from disaster relief for California, for example, since these programs were in different sections of the bill. The rule for the Republicans' omnibus tax-cut bill disallowed an amendment on one of its most controversial provisions. The bill gave families earning up to $200,000 a year a $500 per child tax credit; moderate Republicans wanted to reduce the eligibility to families making less than $100,000; conservative Republicans were adamantly opposed. Since Democrats agreed with moderate Republicans, had the amendment been made in order it would have passed and then conservative Republicans might have opposed the bill. The Republican leadership gambled that moderate Republicans would not desert their party and simply refused them a vote on their amendment.

New Parliamentary Devices

New parliamentary devices developed in recent years have made special rules even more flexible and potent tools for structuring choices. A "king-of-the-hill" provision in a rule specifies that a series of amendments or entire substitutes are to be voted on *ad seriatim* and the last one that receives a majority prevails. This device makes possible a direct vote on each of several alternatives; in ordinary parliamentary procedure, if an amendment or substitute receives a majority, no further alternative amendments to that part of the bill already amended can be offered. Clearly, when this procedure is employed, the amendment or substitute voted on last is advantaged. The procedure also makes it possible for members to vote for more than one version, which is sometimes politically advantageous. When Democrats were in the majority, budget resolutions were often considered under "king-of-the-hill" rules. Members were thus guaranteed a vote on each of the substitute versions of the resolution made in order by the rule. The House Budget Committee version was always placed in the advantageous last position.[4]

The rule for the 1991 civil rights bill illustrates how the procedure can be used strategically. The rule stipulated that the three substitutes made in order were to be offered in a specific order under the king-of-the-hill procedure. The rule gave liberals a vote on their much stronger version but put that substitute first in line. Having cast a vote in favor of the tough bill favored by civil rights activists, these members then could support the leadership's more moderate compromise. The rule next gave House Republicans and the Bush administration a vote on their preferred version. It put the Democratic compromise last—that is, in the advantaged position.

In the 104th Congress Republicans began using a "queen-of-the-hill" variant, which allows a vote on all the versions but specifies that whichever version gets the most votes, so long as it receives a majority, wins. The rules for the welfare reform bill and the term-limits constitutional amendment took this form; in the former case, a liberal Democratic substitute, a more conservative Democratic substitute, and the Republican version were considered under the queen-of-the-hill procedure. On term limits, votes on four versions were made in order. In both cases the option the Republican leadership supported was placed last, which is still the preferred position. Supporters of the last option, unlike those of earlier ones, know how many votes they need in order to win.

Another new device—a self-executing rule—provides that when a rule is adopted by the House, the accompanying bill is automatically amended to incorporate the text of an amendment either set forth or referenced in the rule. The procedure provides a simple way of inserting last-minute corrections or compromises into a bill and prevents a direct and separate vote on the language in question. Thus, in 1993 after the reconciliation bill implementing President Clinton's economic program was reported from committee, the leadership, in order to amass the votes needed to pass the bill, worked out a compromise on entitlements with conservative Democrats. The language was incorporated into the legislation by a self-executing provision in the rule. The Republican leadership used the device frequently in 1995.

ON THE FLOOR

Floor consideration of a bill begins with a debate on the rule. One hour is allotted, half controlled by a majority member of Rules and half by a minority member. The majority member explains and justifies the rule, the minority member gives his party's position, and then both yield time to other members who wish to speak. If neither the rule nor the legislation is controversial, much less than the full hour may be used. If the legislation is controversial but the rule is not, members frequently will use the time to discuss the legislation substantively. Since rules today are often restrictive and complex, they are often highly controversial, and debate may well revolve around the character of the rule itself and consume the entire hour. During this period, no amendments to the rule are in order.

The House must approve the rule before consideration of the legislation can begin. The Rules Committee member managing the debate on the rule for the majority party will *move the previous question.* If successful, the motion cuts off debate, and the House then proceeds to vote on the rule itself. The only way to amend the rule is to defeat the previous question motion. If opponents defeat the previous question motion, they control the floor and may propose the special rule they would like to see. Losing on the motion to order the previous question is devastating for the majority party and seldom happens; a member who votes against his or her party on this crucial procedural motion is not quickly forgiven.

One memorable vote on the previous question occurred in 1981 on the reconciliation bill that implemented President Reagan's economic program. The key battle on that legislation was over the rule. Reagan and House Republicans wanted a single vote on Reagan's package of spending cuts; they could then make the vote a test of whether members supported or opposed the popular president's program to rescue the economy. Democrats, who controlled the House, proposed a rule that forced a series of votes on cutting specific popular programs. Knowing they were likely to lose at least some of those votes and thereby major chunks of Reagan's economic plan, Republicans decided to try to defeat the previous question on the rule. With the help of some conservative Democrats, they were successful and so were able to substitute their own rule that called for a single vote on the package as a whole.

Votes on the previous question are usually far less visible, and disgruntled majority party members can be persuaded by their leadership to vote "yes" on that motion and show their displeasure, if they must, by voting against the rule. Fearing they lacked the votes to pass their rule for the consideration of the Department of Interior appropriations bill in the summer of 1995, Republicans nevertheless made an attempt to do so—but only after forcefully explaining to their freshmen members that they had better not join the minority in voting against the previous question.[5] The rule was, in fact, defeated. The leadership then worked out a compromise among House Republicans, got the Rules Committee to incorporate it in a new rule, brought that to the floor, and passed it. When the majority party lost the rule, it did not lose control of the floor as it would have had it lost the previous question vote.

Once the previous question has been approved, the House votes on the rule itself. When the rule is not controversial, these votes may be by voice; on controversial rules the votes will be recorded. They are called roll-call votes, although the House seldom calls the roll as it once did in the days before electronic voting. Because rules are frequently contentious, recorded votes are likely. In the One hundredth and 101st Congresses (1987–90), 71 major measures were brought to the floor under special rules, and 52 (73%) of the rule votes were decided by roll call; in 1995, 58% of all the rules provoked roll calls.

The majority party sometimes loses votes on rules but not often. The vote on the Interior appropriations rule was the first that Republicans lost during 1995; from 1981 to 1992, Democrats lost on average just over one rule per year. During the highly charged 103rd Congress (1993–94), Democrats lost five rules. Increasingly, majority party members are expected to support their party on such procedural votes. Over the period 1987 to 1991, the mean Democratic vote in favor on passage or on ordering the previous question (whichever was closer) was 93%. Votes on rules as well as votes on ordering the previous question tend to fall along party lines, especially when the rule is restrictive. Of rules for major legislation in the One hundredth and 101st Congresses, 48% saw a majority of Democrats supporting the rule and a majority of Republicans opposing it; 72% of modified closed rules were decided by such party votes.

If the House approves the rule, it thereby resolves itself into the Committee of the Whole, where the debate and amending of the legislation takes place. A sort of parliamentary fiction, the Committee of the Whole has the same membership as the House but somewhat more streamlined rules. The quorum for doing business in the Committee of the Whole is 100 members rather than 218 members (half the full membership, which constitutes a quorum in the House). In the Committee of the Whole when a member is recognized to offer or speak on an amendment, it is for only five minutes. The Speaker does not preside over the Committee of the Whole, but since he chooses the presiding officer and always picks a majority party member, the majority party remains in control of the chair.

General debate begins the consideration of the bill in the Committee of the Whole. The rule has specified who controls the time. The chair of the committee or of the subcommittee that reported the bill serves as floor manager for the majority and actually controls the time allotted to the committee majority; his or her minority counterpart controls the minority's time. The majority floor manager begins with a prepared statement explaining what the legislation does and why it deserves to pass.

The minority floor manager then makes a statement, which may range from wholehearted agreement with his or her opposite number to an all-out attack on the bill. When the committee has come to a broad bipartisan agreement, general debate may be a lovefest, with committee members congratulating each other on the wonderful job they did and on the admirably cooperative way in which they did it. When the committee reporting the legislation is split, especially if it is split along party lines, the tone of floor debate will be contentious and sometimes bitter. If the legislation is the product of several committees, each will have floor managers, who will each make an opening statement.

After opening statements the floor managers yield time—usually in small amounts—to other members who wish to speak. By and large, the majority floor manager yields time to supporters of the legislation and to majority party members, while the minority floor manager yields time to minority party members and, assuming the bill is controversial, to bill opponents. Often not all majority party members support the bill and not all minority party members oppose it. Therefore, both managers may yield time to opponents of their position. An opponent today, especially if a fellow party member, may be a supporter tomorrow and should not be alienated.

When general debate time has expired, the amending process begins. What happens now depends on the rule. If all germane amendments are allowed, members are recognized to offer amendments. House rules give the chair of the Committee of the Whole discretion to determine the order of recognition, but by custom members of the reporting committee are given preference in gaining recognition, and they are recognized in order of seniority (Tiefer 1989, 231). Once a member is recognized to offer his or her amendment, the member has five minutes to explain it. The floor manager has five minutes to reply, then other members may speak. They gain time by offering pro forma amendments "to strike the last word" or "to strike the requisite number of words." The member who offers a pro forma amendment does not actually want it to pass, but by offering it he or she gets five minutes to speak on the amendment that is really at issue.

A House member may offer an amendment to the amendment being considered. Such a second degree amendment may be intended sincerely to improve the amendment to which it is offered. Alternatively, the purpose behind a second degree amendment may be to lessen the impact or even negate altogether the effect of the original amendment. If a bill's supporters believe they cannot defeat a popular but, in their view, harmful amendment, they may try to come up with a second degree amendment to at least weaken its effect.

Debate on an amendment under the five-minute rule may go on for a considerable period of time, but eventually when everyone who wants to has spoken, a vote on the amendment occurs.

Sometimes a floor manager has no objections to an amendment or actually supports it and will simply "accept" the amendment without asking for a recorded vote. In that case the amendment is usually approved by voice vote. If the floor manager—or another member—opposes the amendment, a vote will be demanded. The first vote may be by voice, but if the amendment is at all controversial, the losing side in a voice vote will demand a recorded vote. Only 25 members are needed to force a recorded vote.

The House's electronic voting system works in this way. Members have individualized cards that look rather like a credit card; they insert their card into one of the ten voting stations attached to the backs of seats on the House floor and punch the "yea," "nay," or "present" button. The vote is recorded by a computer, and it also shows up as a green, red, or amber light next to the member's name on a huge lighted display behind the Speaker's dais.

After the amendment has been disposed of, another member is recognized to offer another amendment. Under an open rule the amending process continues as long as there are members wishing to offer amendments and on the floor prepared to do so. The House can by majority vote cut off debate, though amendments that have been "preprinted" in the *Congressional Record* at least one day before floor consideration are guaranteed ten minutes of debate (Tiefer 1989, 401–03). Unlike senators, House members have limited patience for protracted floor debate. In January 1995 Republicans brought the unfunded mandates bill to the floor under an open rule; after six days of debate and with 170 amendments still pending, they voted to cut off debate.

A more frequently used way of controlling the length of the amending process is through the rule. Under many rules the amending process proceeds pretty much as described above except that the amendments allowed are limited, perhaps to those preprinted in the *Congressional Record*. In other cases the rule specifies the amendments that are in order and the member who may offer them. In these cases the rule frequently specifies a time limit on debate on a specific amendment—perhaps 20 minutes or one hour if a major amendment. The rule also is likely to prohibit amendments to the amendments made in order.

What happens in the Committee of the Whole thus varies depending on the number of committees involved and the character of the rule. Clearly, a structured rule makes floor proceedings more orderly and predictable.

After general debate and whatever amending is allowed have been completed, the Committee of the Whole rises and reports back to the House. The Speaker again presides and the rules of the House again are in effect. Amendments adopted in the Committee of the Whole must be approved by the House, which gives opponents of an amendment a second chance to defeat it. Usually, however, the House votes on all the amendments adopted as a package and approval is certain. Occasionally, if a vote was very close and the amendment makes major and unacceptable changes in the legislation, an effort to change the outcome will be made. In 1995 Democrats, with some help from moderate Republicans, successfully passed in the Committee of the Whole an amendment to an appropriations bill deleting controversial language barring the Environmental Protection Agency from enforcing various environmental laws. The amendment won a close 211–206 vote and the provision was important to many staunchly antiregulatory Republicans, so the leadership called for a second vote in the House and defeated the amendment on an even closer 210–210 vote. (Motions die on a tie vote.) In that case the leadership got lucky; although no Republicans switched their votes, several Democrats who had supported the amendment the first time were absent for the second vote. Usually, however, amendments that win in the Committee of the Whole win again in the House. After all, the membership of the two bodies is identical.

The minority may now offer a motion to recommit the legislation to committee with or without instructions. A motion to recommit without instructions is essentially a motion to kill the bill and seldom prevails. By this point too many members have a stake in the legislation's enactment; if it lacked majority support, it would probably not have gotten so far. A motion to recommit with instructions— that is, instructions to report the bill back with specified changes—is, in effect, a motion to amend the bill. It is the minority's last chance to change the legislation. The motion may propose substituting the minority's version of the bill for the majority's, or it may propose much more modest changes. Again, because it is the minority's motion, it seldom wins—though more frequently than the motion to recommit without instructions. Assuming the legislation survives, a vote on final passage is taken, usually by recorded vote. At this point the legislation will almost certainly pass. Constitutional amendments requiring a two-thirds vote have been defeated on a floor vote in the House, but they are an exception from the norm; in the One hundredth, 101st, and 103rd Congresses, the only major measures to be defeated at this stage were two competing proposals to aid the Nicaraguan contras, one President Reagan's and the other sponsored by the Democratic leadership in 1988, and the first 1990 budget summit agreement (though that technically was the defeat of a conference report).

If the legislation does pass, a motion to reconsider is made and laid upon the table. This ensures the issue cannot be reopened. The legislation is then sent to the Senate.

UNORTHODOX LAWMAKING IN THE HOUSE

If the textbook legislative process can be likened to climbing a ladder, the contemporary process is more like climbing a big old tree with many branches. The route to enactment used to be linear and predictable; now it is flexible and varied. To be sure, the textbook model was never a complete description of how bills became laws. There have always been alternative routes. In the past, however, the alternatives were infrequently used on major legislation. Now variation is the norm. . . . [N]o two major bills are likely to follow exactly the same process.

Although the new practices and procedures arose in response to different problems and opportunities, their consequences are similar. The new practices and procedures in the House facilitate lawmaking. Most make it easier for the majority party leadership to advance its members' legislative goals. The leadership now has more flexibility to shape the legislative process to suit the particular legislation at issue. When climbing a ladder there isn't much one can do if a rung is broken; when climbing a tree with many branches, if one route is blocked there is always another one can try.

NOTES

1. I have relied heavily on Tiefer (1989) and Gold et al. (1992) for the fine points of procedure. The interested reader should also consult Oleszek (1996). The people at the Congressional Research Service, especially Stanley Bach, Richard Beth, and Walter Oleszek, were invaluable sources of information. Peter Robinson was also extremely helpful.
2. *Congressional Record*, 20 May 1992, H3462.
3. *Congressional Record*, 21 May 1992, H3705.
4. When the leadership was confident that it could defeat all the alternatives and no post-committee adjustments in the budget resolution were needed, the Budget Committee version was not offered as an amendment at all but constituted the base bill.
5. Timothy J. Burger. 1995. "After Defeat House Leaders Must Regroup." *Roll Call*, 17 July, 1, 22.

PART V

LEGISLATIVE COMMITTEES

Chapter 16

What Affects Committee Power and Success?

Congressional government is committee government. That was the conclusion of Woodrow Wilson, writing as a political scientist several years before he sought elective office. In his landmark study of *Congressional Government,* Wilson ([1885] 1956, 69) was the first scholar to point out that "Congress in its committee-rooms is Congress at work."

More than a century later, scholars still see committees as crucial components of Congress. Accordingly, many aspects of committees have been the subjects of scholarly research, though with less explicit attention to a single controversy than is the case for most of the other topics considered in this book. We would contend, however, that there is a main theme underlying much of the research on committees: what factors lead to committee power and success. This should be one of the most important concerns about committees in the U. S. Congress, a legislature in which committees affect the content of legislation. Not all of the literature on committees explicitly recognizes this debate, but most of that literature ends up speaking to it. This debate is especially useful as it orients the committee literature to a clear "dependent variable." If it is still true that "congressional government is committee government," then understanding the determinants of committee success is very close to understanding the policy output of Congress.

Committee success is an important topic only to the extent to which committees are powerful. Before turning to the determinants of committee success, we will therefore examine the power of congressional committees as well as the foundations of this power.

COMMITTEE POWER

Not all legislative committees play as central a role in policy making as those in the U.S. Congress. In the classical English system, for example, committees had very little power. They did not even have fixed jurisdictions or the ability to make major substantive changes to government proposals. The U.S. system has been very different. Standing committees have been set up with fixed jurisdictions, such as an agriculture committee or a commerce committee. These committees hold public hearings on bills and then consider amendments to each bill during the "markup stage." Few bills emerge from committee without substantive amendments.

There are several sources of the influence congressional committees have over policy content.[1] First, committees have the power of "gatekeeping." After bills are introduced and referred to a committee, the committee decides whether these bills will be debated by the full chamber or die in committee. Although committees can serve a useful screening function—helping to manage the time of the chamber by forwarding only the most workable proposals—a negative implication of this gatekeeping power is that opponents in the committee may block legislation favored by a majority of the chamber.

Second, committees have the power of proposal. Those who participate in writing the legislation will have a larger influence over policy than those who do not (Hall 1987). The content of legislation can be rewritten in committee during markup sessions so committee members have an advantage in writing bills in ways that favor their own and their constituents' preferences.

Committees also have an information advantage in the consideration of legislation. The committee system is an efficient process in which experts on a subject can share information with generalists (Krehbiel 1991). Since committees specialize in issues within their jurisdiction, committee members gain expertise on those policies. Legislators outside a particular committee generally defer to committee members, either because they respect committee members' expertise or because they expect the same deferential treatment in the consideration of their own committee's bills (the reciprocity norm discussed in chapter 12).

Shepsle and Weingast (1987) instead contend that the power of committees depends on their role in conference committees. Differences between House and Senate versions of bills are negotiated by ad hoc conference committees whose members are drawn from the relevant committees of the two chambers. Not only does this add to the committee's power in shaping legislation, but it means that committee members can kill a bill by refusing to agree to a conference settlement if the bill has been amended on the floor in a way that conferees find unacceptable. Shepsle and Weingast argue that the potential for exercising this "ex post veto" gives additional power to committees when their legislation first reaches the floor.

The considerable power of committees should not be viewed as totally positive. With deference and specialization, the risk exists for the development of policies that benefit individual committee members to the detriment of other legislators and public policy more generally. Committees can develop policies that meet committee members' preferences but not necessarily those of the whole chamber or even those of the majority party. Also, members often get very close to the executive agencies and interest groups that they are supposed to be regulating, so that the committee, agency, and interest group sometimes virtually become a subgovernment (Ripley and Franklin 1991) which controls public policy on a topic.

Other institutions could perform the functions associated with committees. Indeed, the Speaker of the House of Representatives has experimented with task forces as an alternative mechanism. Task forces differ from committees in three main respects: They are ad hoc, established for particular bills rather than standing bodies; they consist of members of the majority party rather than both parties; and they are unofficial bodies without their own official staff. They have been used by both Democratic and Republican leaders as a way of developing policy proposals and mobilizing votes for important issues that cross committee jurisdictions. During the 104th Congress, Speaker Gingrich also used task forces as a method to circumvent the interests entrenched in the standing committees. However, the lack of the usual vetting of bills and compromises in committees may have made it more difficult to pass those bills on the House floor. As a result, the House committees regained their traditional power by the 105th Congress.[2]

Committees have been very powerful in the U.S. Congress, but it would be a considerable oversimplification to view all committees in Congress as equal. Some committees are more important than others, some are more powerful than others, and some are more successful than others. These differences lead to several questions: What explains the differential success rates of congressional committees? Why are some committees very successful in getting their bills passed by their parent chambers, while others are not? Why are some committees able to get bills passed that are closer to their preferences than are other committees?[3] More fundamentally, what is committee success, and how should it be measured? There are several possible perspectives on what leads to committee success. The first we will discuss concerns factors internal to each committee, such as its leadership; the second focuses on external factors, the characteristics of the political environment in which each committee must operate. Whether internal or external factors have greater influence on committee success is the main focus of this chapter.

COMMITTEE SUCCESS DETERMINED BY INTERNAL FACTORS

One view is that the success of a committee in passing its legislation is primarily a function of its internal characteristics. Two internal aspects have been emphasized in the literature. One is the committee leadership—some committee chairs are more effective in getting their committees' bills passed. The other is the committee's cohesion—committees that are more integrated in terms of goals are more successful in getting bills passed than are divided committees.

Committee Leadership

The best exposition of the leadership argument comes from Manley's (1965, 1970) study of the House Ways and Means Committee when it was chaired by Wilbur Mills (D-AR). This committee processes revenue legislation and, over the years, that jurisdiction has been defined broadly to include income taxes, tariffs, Social Security, and Medicare. It is considered one of the most prestigious committees in the House. Manley documents the considerable success Ways and Means had under Mills in getting its bills passed by the House, generally without changes. In explaining this success, Manley focuses on Mills's leadership. Apparently, one of the first bills he brought to the floor was returned by the House to committee, hence defeated. Mills vowed not to have that happen again. He became an astute committee leader, learning how to put together a coalition that would win on the floor, making sure to count votes in advance so he would not lose, and trying to get "closed rules" from the House Rules Committee which would bar amendments on the House floor.

Manley's book (1970) shows the many tactics Mills used to establish a reputation for success and then to maintain that success. He traces Mills's influence in his committee to a combination of expertise in the subject matter of the committee, his formal leadership power, the rewards he could offer members, the identification of most committee members with him, and the sanctions Mills could use against committee members who opposed him. Manley also attributes Mills's success to his listening to others on the committee (especially its ranking minority member) and his pivotal position as a swing vote on the committee.

The limits to the role of committee leadership are also manifest in the case of Mills. Mills hit personal scandal in 1974, resigning as committee chair after being hospitalized following his jump into the Washington Tidal Basin with a strip-tease dancer. The Democratic caucus quickly enacted a series of reforms, which diminished the power of Ways and Means (Rieselbach 1994; Rudder 1977). Mills's leadership style might have been highly successful, but it was not universally appreciated and did not save his position as chair or his committee's power. House Democrats did not want his accumulation of power to be passed on to his successor.

The role of committee leadership has also been limited by the House reforms. Strahan (1993) focuses directly on the leadership style of a later House Ways and Means chair, Dan Rostenkowski, showing how he adapted his leadership style to the new reform context of the House. His leadership power had limits and he had failures as well as successes, but his success shows that leadership remains an important factor influencing committee success. Similarly, Andree Reeves (1993, 232), in a study of House Education and Labor committee[4] chair Carl Perkins, argues that because chairs in the postreform era were more restricted in their institutional powers than previous chairs, they had to rely more on personal resources and had to use their limited institutional resources more strategically in order to be successful.

Obviously the role of leadership in committee success extends beyond the case of any one committee or chair. Unekis and Rieselbach (1984) take a comparative approach and attempt to understand committee leadership by examining the place of the chair within the committee's voting factions. They find three patterns of committee leadership: extreme, partisan middleman, and bipartisan consensual. The extreme pattern occurs when the chair attempts to mobilize the dominant majority party faction, as with Democratic chairs and the liberal wing. The partisan middleman pattern occurs when the chair adopts a centrist position within his or her own party in an attempt to generate party cohesion, as when Democratic chairs vote with moderate Democrats. The bipartisan consensual pattern occurs when the chair works with any voting bloc, in which case the chair is part of a nonideological bipartisan voting bloc and behaves in a manner similar to that of the ranking minority member. They find that committees with chairs who exhibit the bipartisan consensual pattern have the greatest success on the floor (98). It is an open question, however, whether the chair's voting record is a good measure of leadership style. For example, a chair may vote with the liberals because he or she is in fact liberal, but still may be receptive to working with Republicans and to allowing wide participation by all members.

A broader model of committee leadership has been provided by Evans (1991). He portrays Senate committee leadership as affected by contextual characteristics (such as the homogeneity of policy preferences on the committee, subcommittee power, and allocation of committee staff) and individual characteristics (the leader's policy preferences, leadership experience, and career plans). Evans uses these factors to compare leadership on four committees during the Ninety-ninth Congress. His book is the most extensive treatment to date of the role of the leadership factor in affecting committee success, as based on the leaders' control of the legislative agenda, their interactions with subcommittee leaders and with the opposite party leader on the committee, and especially their success in modifying bills to anticipate reactions on the Senate floor. This model reflects an increasing favor in the discipline for more contextual models of leadership (see chapter 20) as well as the realities of modern committee chairs' power. There are few recent committee chairs who exercise the power that a Wilbur Mills once did. Chairs must now share leadership with subcommittees and negotiate with committee members who expect that each of their chairs will act only as a first among equals.

Committee Integration

Another variant of the argument that factors internal to committees affect their success rates arose out of Richard Fenno's (1962) influential application of systems theory to congressional committees. Fenno argues that some congressional committees are more "integrated" than others. His first study, reprinted here as chapter 17, was of the House Appropriations committee, which became the prototype in the literature of an integrated committee.

Earlier empirical research on committees focused on their internal characteristics. In particular, Huitt (1954) examines the roles of senators within the Senate Committee on Banking and Currency, and Jones (1961) considers the representational roles of members on the House Agriculture Committee. These studies treat the committee as an interesting decision-making body in its own right, but Fenno's analysis of Appropriations provides the crucial link between the internal operation of a committee and its subsequent success.

Fenno describes the Appropriations Committee as having a consensus in terms of goals. The committee at that time wanted to protect the federal Treasury as well as to cut budget estimates that were submitted, and the members wanted to serve their own constituencies. The committee accepted such norms as specialization on subcommittees, reciprocity between subcommittees, and subcommittee unity. New members were socialized into these expectations. These factors led to high integration of the committee and, in turn, according to Fenno, to high levels of committee success in passing legislation unamended. For example, he cites statistics that of 443 separate bureau appropriations he examined, the House accepted committee recommendations on 387 (87%) and their exact dollar recommendations became law on 159 (34%). While Fenno describes Appropriations as a highly successful committee, his data also show the limits of that argument—the committee often lost on the floor, and there are important differences in success rates between its subcommittees that do not fit the integration story that Fenno tells.

The Fenno piece is a classic not only because it represents the impetus for further research but also in that it shows that each congressional committee is a distinct body. Committees share important features, but each retains distinctive features that offer important insights for understanding legislative activity.

Of course, one case cannot establish a generalization. Establishing this line of argument requires comparisons across committees. Fenno (1963) provided an important comparison in a subsequent study of the House Education and Labor Committee that traces House action on federal aid to education bills from 1945 through 1962.[5] The federal government had not been involved in giving money to education prior to this time, and the Fenno study indicates, in part, why. The committee was not cohesive, and it did not build a consensus. Committee members were generally chosen on the basis of their position on labor issues, and that led to sharp ideological and partisan division on the committee which carried over to the education area. Furthermore, the committee chairs did not produce internal unity, especially Southern conservative Democrat Graham Barden (NC), who sought to create internal conflicts so as to defeat programs he opposed (as in 1956 when he resigned as floor manager of a bill during its consideration on the House floor). Note that this point shows how the committee leadership discussed above can be directly relevant to the committee's integration.

At a more normative level, the integration argument can be considered to have a status quo bias because integration is generally easiest to achieve when there is consensus to maintain current policy. Describing committee integration as desirable for maximizing committee success is therefore nearly an argument for accepting status quo solutions. If social change is to occur, it might be necessary to have a fractionalized committee, as typified by the Education and Labor Committee.

A fuller test of Fenno's integration hypothesis required study of a fuller range of committees. The first such test was devised by Dyson and Soule (1970). They rank House committees according to their attractiveness (as measured by having few freshmen members, high average seniority, and few voluntary retirements) and integration (the proportion of times each committee member votes with every other committee member on committee proposals). The more integrated committees are more successful in getting their bills passed on the floor, but partisanship plays the key role: Committees are more successful when party disagreement is low. They find minimal partisanship to be more important than integration, and they even challenge Fenno's results on the Appropriations Committee, finding that it is only middling in integration, high in partisanship, and one of the least successful committees on the House floor.

In a similar study of Senate committees, Dodd (1972) operationalizes committee integration in terms of the mean cohesion on roll-call votes on the floor from that committee and other committees. Post Office and Public Works are found to be the most integrated committees, whereas Appropriations and Finance are least integrated by this measure. There is only a modest correlation between committee integration and success.[6]

These two sets of results provide minimal support for Fenno's integration theory and even for his interpretation of the Appropriations Committee. However, there are major limitations to the overly mechanical operationalizations in these studies. Both use only floor passage votes, whereas Fenno is more directed to internal decisions prior to reporting to the floor. Their measurement of integration in terms of members' voting agreement is also fairly distant from Fenno's discussion of that topic. An alternative explanation of these results would be that prestigious committees are more prone to floor challenge and defeat because they handle conflictual and highly salient issues, as will be discussed in the second half of this chapter.

A more proper test of the committee integration argument would require comparisons between committees but without the awkward operationalizations of integration. Fenno (1973) himself provided the most important work of this type in his monumental comparative committees study: *Congressmen in Committees.* In this book, Fenno studies six House committees, comparing their success and explaining the differences that emerge. His model is much more sophisticated than are those of the earlier studies. He does not rely directly on the integration concept, but instead works from the goals of members. He begins by positing three possible goals of members of Congress: reelection, power, and policy. His interviews show that members of different committees tend to have different goals. Members of Appropriations, for example, tend to have power goals, since service on this all-important committee gives them power in the House. By contrast, members of Education and Labor tend to have policy goals while members of Interior tend to have reelection/constituency goals.

The full Fenno model is depicted in Figure 16.1. Member goals and environmental constraints (such as the parent chamber, the executive branch, clientele groups, and party leaders) affect each other. Each also affects the strategic premises of the committees—such as the Appropriations Committee's focus on reducing budget requests and providing adequate funding for programs, or Education and Labor's focus on prosecuting policy partisanship with individual policy goals being pursued when policy and party conflict. These strategic premises affect the decision-making process—such as the participation-specialization approach to subcommittees for Appropriations, or the policy partisanship of Education and Labor. The strategic premises and the decision-making process both affect the actual decisions, as when Appropriations has greater success on the House floor than does Education and Labor. Overall, Fenno provides a very rich model of committee success, with a depth of understanding of committee differences.

The arguments reviewed in this section suggest that committee success on the floor is determined by internal factors—their leadership and their integration, either taken separately or together. These are factors that are seemingly in the committee's control, as if a chair and a committee that want to be successful should be able to develop the leadership style and cohesion necessary to achieve success. This theme in the literature, however, is counterbalanced by the view that

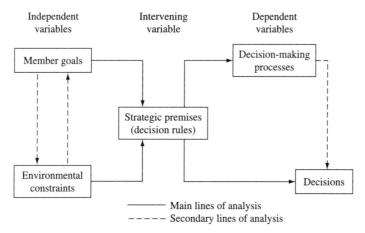

| Independent variables | Intervening variable | Dependent variables |

Figure 16.1

From CONGRESSMEN IN COMMITTEES by Richard F. Fenno, Jr.
Copyright © 1973 by Harper & Row, Publishers, Inc. Reprinted by
permission of Addison-Wesley Educational Publishers Inc.

committee success is instead determined by external factors that are beyond the control of either the chair or the committee as a whole.

COMMITTEE SUCCESS DETERMINED BY EXTERNAL CONSTRAINTS

While committee success may be affected by its internal features, some would argue that other matters affect it more. The committee's jurisdiction—the subject matter it considers—can affect its success since it is easier to be successful in some policy domains than others. Also, the committee whose composition mirrors that of the parent chamber should be more successful in getting its bills passed than a committee that is more ideologically extreme than the parent chamber. These are factors that are not easily controlled by the committee members or chair, and thus can be regarded as environmental constraints on the committee.

Subject Matter

The simplest version of this argument is that the committee's subject matter is what affects its success. Some committees deal with topics on which it is difficult to achieve consensus, so those committees are going to have low success rates. For example, battles on the abortion issue are so conflictual that it is difficult for any committee to be successful on the floor if antiabortion amendments are added to its bills. By contrast, other committees deal with topics on which it is easy to reach compromises, so those committees are going to have high success rates. Government appropriations are usually such a topic, since the relative ease in splitting differences on dollar amounts for programs facilitates compromise. Even more fundamentally, appropriations bills will have a very high passage rate because the government must be funded.

While the committee's subject matter is an obvious alternative explanation of its success, it is too easy for this to be used as an ad hoc explanation with more successful committees categorized as having noncontroversial jurisdictions. It is therefore important to develop prior hypotheses as to which types of subject matters would be expected to be less controversial.

Policy type

One way to consider the effect of subject matter on committee politics and success would be to examine differences across different types of policy. The best known policy typology, developed by Lowi (1964) and refined by Ripley and Franklin (1991), distinguishes three main types of domestic public policy areas (see also chapter 24). There is least conflict among policy actors on distributive policy in which the government allocates goodies across the nation, such as pork-barrel projects. There is more conflict on regulatory policy, including both measures in which the government protects the public (such as protecting worker health and safety) and in which the government regulates an industry (such as setting up rules for broadcast media). The greatest conflict is over redistributive policy, which involves "zero-sum" issues such as taxes in which winners win what the losers lose. Different patterns of committee success could be related to these different policy types, such as expecting greater success for committees dealing with distributive topics than for those dealing with redistributive policy.

The first systematic analysis of subject matter differences affecting committee success was provided by Hinckley (1975), reprinted here as chapter 18. Her research is significant in that she challenges Fenno's study of committee success for its focus on committee integration without consideration of each committee's subject matter and in that she is able to develop some systematic measures of subject matter. She posits two dimensions for differences between committees—whether their subject domain is zero-sum, and whether their range of topics is broad or narrow. Committees tackling zero-sum topics are expected to be less successful than those dealing with positive-sum areas such as Public Works, which can buy success by tossing in an extra government project for every congressional district. Hinckley also argues that policy agreement will be higher for committees with a narrow scope of policy concerns than those with a broad scope. Note that she is not directly studying committee success on the floor, but committee cohesion in recommendations is likely to correlate highly with floor success. Smith (1989, 176–80) provides additional evidence to support Hinckley's position: Bills from committees with the largest, most highly visible, and most controversial agendas are most subject to floor amendment.

An alternative policy classification was proposed by Price (1978), who looks at the salience and conflict of committee agenda items. Salience is affected by the number of people who care about an issue. Conflict involves the degree to which interests are seen as competing or compatible. Although Price applies these policy categories to explain why a single committee (Commerce) handles the several issues within its jurisdiction differently, Smith and Deering (1990, 84) classify all congressional committees on these dimensions. Their measure of salience is based on television news coverage of topics within the committee's domain, and their measure of conflict is based on interviews with committee members and staff. Smith and Deering find considerable differences between committees—for example, Education and Labor is high on both, Appropriations moderate on both, and Agriculture low on both. Again, these features of the committee's jurisdiction can affect its ability to achieve legislative success.

Issue salience and conflict depend, in part, on how an issue fits within existing partisan and ideological cleavages. Issues that are congruent with party or ideological divisions will be more conflictual and more salient because they are the basis on which party "success" is claimed, whereas issues that cut across partisan boundaries cannot be used for partisan credit claiming. On issues where parties cannot attract a substantial number of votes by position taking and credit claiming, interest groups rather than parties have an advantage in providing information and cues (Hansen 1991). Salience makes committees come closer to majority party or floor position (Maltzman 1995). Members are more careful about how they vote on high-profile issues—they must anticipate constituent reaction. Committees may be closer to the floor position on high salience issues due to either party control of the appointment process or committee anticipation of floor reaction. At the same time, variation in conflict and salience on different issues allow individual committees to handle different issues differently, allow for different politics and success rates across committees, and allow for committee change over time.

Issue change
The salience and conflict of committee agenda items also can vary across time. In their case studies, both Strahan (1990) and Reeves (1993) note the central importance of change in the issues dealt with by committees and how that influenced committee politics. For example, Reeves shows how the Education and Labor Committee had minimal output in the 1950s when there was little consensus on social welfare issues, was more successful in the 1960s when its agenda became highly salient and a national consensus for federal activism led to the passage of landmark legislation, and then spent most of the next few decades fighting over budget cuts to those programs during an era in which the committee's issues were less salient.

The effect of the change in the salience of committee issues can also be seen by examining attempts at amending committee bills on the floor (Smith 1989, 178–81). For example, the House Labor Committee's high ranking in attempted floor amendments fell in the 1970s as the salience of the issues it handled declined. In contrast, there were more attempts on the floor to amend bills from the House Energy and Commerce Committee as its jurisdiction expanded and its issues (consumer protection, environmental protection, health care, energy) became more salient.

In addition, change in the salience of issues can be a spur for jurisdictional change among congressional committees. Jones, Baumgartner, and Talbert (1993) find that when an issue becomes salient, other committees will hold hearings on the issue in an attempt to redefine the issue so that they can claim jurisdiction over it. For example, tobacco issues were once handled solely by the Agriculture Committee, but the Energy and Commerce Committee used its jurisdiction over health issues to hold hearings on the health effects of tobacco and then claimed jurisdiction over bills dealing with tobacco regulation. This jurisdictional change may affect the level of committee success over time. Committees that gain jurisdiction over highly salient and increasingly conflictual issues might expect a decline in their success rates because it would be difficult to resolve the issues. Floor challenges would also be more likely, especially from members of the committee that is losing jurisdiction over the issue, and these intercommittee fights would again serve to decrease the probability of legislative success on the floor.

Member goals

A final perspective on how committee success can be affected by the committee's subject matter is based on Fenno's (1973) focus on member goals. Fenno argues that members seek out the type of committee that best allows them to achieve their highest priority political goals: power within the chamber, reelection or constituency service, or influence of policy on subjects of intense interest. Committees, then, can be classified based on the products that attract the members who serve on them: reelection, policy, or power committees. This classification is echoed and restated by Smith and Deering (1990) who differentiate among constituency, policy, and prestige committees.

Reelection/constituency committees present opportunities to deliver concentrated benefits to one's constituents with diffuse costs to everyone else so as not to attract intense opposition, and these committees are likely to be highly successful in getting their bills passed. These committees' issues have low national salience, high local salience, low conflict, narrow jurisdictions, and a clear set of beneficiaries of committee products (Smith and Deering 1990, 86–110). By contrast, policy committees attract members who seek to shape important national policies. Finally, power/prestige committees, particularly the "exclusive" committees in the House (Appropriations, Ways and Means, and Rules), are attractive to members because of their leverage over other committees which are dependent on them for funding, adequate revenues, or access to the floor under favorable conditions.

Smith (1989, 188–91) argues that floor-amending activity supports this goal-oriented interpretation of committee behavior: The power and policy committees are most likely to attract floor amendments because they deal with issues that draw attention and controversy. On the other hand, constituency committees have narrow, parochial agendas, bring few bills to the floor, and receive little attention on the floor. Prestige committees and, to a lesser extent, policy committees are more likely to receive special restrictive rules (rules that limit the number of floor amendments that can be offered on a bill and limit time for debate) because of the controversies surrounding their bills and the importance of those bills to the majority party and its leadership.

Committee Representatives

Certainly the power and independence exercised by congressional committees lead to concern over their representativeness of the congressional membership as a whole. An unrepresentative committee is composed of members with policy views that greatly differ from those of the median member of Congress. The concern with unrepresentative committees has been longstanding in the literature on "iron triangles" and subgovernments, but recent debate has emerged from formal analyses of committee power that are based on the benefits of committees for individual committee members rather than for Congress as a whole.

The representativeness of a committee might be a function of the type of members appointed to the committee, such as when mainly members from farm districts are appointed to Agriculture and mainly Westerners are appointed to Interior, and also a matter of ideology, as when a committee is more liberal (or conservative) than the rest of the chamber. Representativeness is thought to be related to committee success: A committee that is representative of the parent chamber should be more likely to gets its legislation passed than a committee whose membership is not representative.

Committee assignments

At the center of the representativeness controversy is the process by which members are assigned to committees. Legislators attempt to gain seats on committees that they believe will enhance their careers. Because their own preferences are taken into account, members can be thought of as at least partially self-selecting their committees (limited, of course, by the availability of seats).[7] As a result, committees may be composed largely of members with a special interest in a policy area and with a policy outlook not shared widely by other legislators.

The assignment process was first studied in a systematic manner by Masters (1961). The Speaker of the House made committee assignments prior to the 1910–11 revolt against the Speaker. Since then, the parties have had separate committees-on-committees which make the assignments. Masters documents several considerations in assignments, from the member's "legislative responsibility" (which is a key consideration for assigning members to the most important House committees) to whether the assignment would help the member get reelected. Assignments can also be influenced by many actors, including the Speaker, state delegations, committee chairs, and interest groups, who want committee membership to reflect their desires. Later studies of the assignment process have analyzed member requests for committee assignments and committee changes that were maintained by House Democrats (Rohde and Shepsle 1973; Shepsle 1978).

It might be possible to assign members in such a way that would make committees more "representative" of the chamber, but that would challenge the very incentives that members have to serve on committees as well as how committees can serve members' goals. Hall (1987) concludes that the way in which committee assignments are made guarantees that committees are deep in "interesteds," but also makes them unrepresentative of regional, ideological, and seniority patterns in the parent chamber.

Committee outliers

The scholarly literature is, however, divided as to how representative congressional committees are of their total chambers. The work of Shepsle and Weingast (1987) is most associated with the unrepresentative committees argument. They argue that committees are composed of members with homogeneous goals and policy preferences. Furthermore, Shepsle and Weingast conclude that the legislative process is biased toward unrepresentative committees getting their way at the expense of the chamber majority. The technical literature terms committees that are extremely unrepresentative of the chamber as "outliers." According to this view, outlier committees can get their way against chamber majorities by presenting a bill that the chamber prefers to the status quo but that is closer to the committee's preference than to the chamber's preference and then using the ex post veto of the conference process (discussed earlier in this chapter) to keep the bill from being amended on the floor. Further support for the outlier position is obtained by Adler and Lipinski (1997) who measure the demand of constituents for the policy and distributive benefits of committees and find evidence of committee outliers among both service and policy-oriented committees.

Such outlier committees could be expected to be less successful. They would be less likely to find acceptable compromises in advance of floor consideration of proposals, so their bills would be more likely to be amended by the full chamber and to lose on final passage votes. Yet these outliers can be successful when they block legislation by refusing to act on bills referred to them, since the chamber rarely considers bills that have not been reported by their committees.

However, some scholars do not accept the view that committees are unrepresentative. Krehbiel (1990) finds little to support the notion that the views of committee members are more extreme or more homogeneous than those of the entire legislature. With his measure, only the House Armed Services Committee was a homogeneous committee whose median position differed considerably from that of the chamber. He treats legislatures as rational organizations that distribute committee assignments so as to gain "informational efficiency" in the sense that committee members have expertise and interest in the issues under the committee's jurisdiction. Self-selection of committee slots enhances informational efficiency, without leading necessarily to policy bias. Additionally, the chamber can undermine committee outliers by refusing to give their bills restrictive rules, by not sending their bills to conference committee, or by appointing a conference committee that represents the preferences of the chamber.

A second line of dissent challenges the assumption that committees are independent from the party leadership. Cox and McCubbins (1993) provide the strongest argument. They reason that if committees are both self-selected and immune from external discipline, then many of them should produce unrepresentative policy outcomes. In addition to determining that they typically do not, Cox and McCubbins find fewer geographically or ideologically unrepresentative committees than the previous literature had suggested. They also argue that the majority party controls committees through its establishment of favorable party ratios, its use of the appointment power to advance those loyal to the party, and its partisan use of the scheduling power. Since their study, the balance of power between committees and the party leadership shifted further when House Republican leaders took a strong role on bills central to their party's agenda in the 104th Congress.

Cox and McCubbins's account of how the majority party controls the legislative agenda and uses committees as vehicles of party government is reprinted in chapter 19 as a Contemporary Perspective on legislative committees. It rejects the committee government perspective of previous research, but at the same time, it incorporates many questions traditionally addressed in the committees literature, including power, leadership, cohesion, the assignment process, and policy subject matter. Like Fenno and Hinckley, Cox and McCubbins examine factors influencing committee success, but Cox and McCubbins investigate how the majority party gains advantages by structuring the committee system. That is, the work of Congress is done in committees, so the majority party is successful to the extent that committees work as its agents.

Other scholars have attempted to document the conditions under which committee bias is likely to be influential versus when it can be controlled. Maltzman's (1995) modeling of committee-specific votes finds that the more important committees, such as Appropriations, are more loyal agents of the chamber and of the majority party and are more likely to represent the preferences of their noncommittee colleagues. This is especially true when the issues the committee addresses are highly salient to the chamber's members and to the committee members' constituents. Hall and Grofman (1990) argue that bias is more likely to occur in informal activities (e.g., agenda setting and issue framing) than in voting and is more likely within subcommittees than full committees. Bias is less likely when the committee considers a heterogeneous set of issues or issues tangential to the committee's primary mission. A study of committee testimony (Jones, Baumgartner, and Talbert 1993) concludes that committee bias is common since committees hear testimony from selected sources only. However, the authors contend that bias is mitigated when committee jurisdictions overlap so that no committee enjoys an "issue monopoly." They also give several examples of how flagrant committee bias can generate controversy and jurisdictional conflict that reduces the initial bias.

The effect of biased committees depends on what we assume the primary goals of legislators are. If members of Congress are primarily interested in reelection, they are likely to use their committee assignment to provide their constituents with a maximum quantity of benefits, but through a logroll with members of other committees so that all legislators benefit from the gravy train. If members of Congress are interested in getting good public policy passed by the chamber, they may anticipate the policy that the chamber or the majority party is likely to prefer and incorporate these preferences into their proposals. In either case, the committee can "succeed"—by trading favors to maximize local benefits and by writing legislation acceptable to a majority in order to ease passage. Also, if committees provide information to legislators that allows them to be more certain of policy effects, committees succeed by satisfying the chamber's informational needs and by persuading the chamber that what the committee wants is in the chamber's best interest (Krehbiel 1991).

It is important to recognize that the effects of outlier committees depend on the chamber's procedures. Important bills are now often referred to multiple committees in the U.S. House (Davidson, Oleszek, and Kephart 1988; Young and Cooper 1995). Sequential referral of a bill to a more representative committee might compensate for the unrepresentativeness of the original committee. Indeed, the House leadership can use multiple referral or a task force when assigning to an outlier committee would impede its chances for passage.

As seen in this section, external factors can influence committee success. A representative committee can be more likely to get its program passed through the chamber. Committees dealing with certain types of issues also may have a higher chance of success. Neither of these factors is within the control of the committee itself, since the committee is constrained by the membership assigned to it and its jurisdiction. In a real sense, these external factors limit the potential for internal factors to affect committee success. Even the strongest committee chair might not be able to lead an unrepresentative committee dealing with a divisive subject matter to success. Nor could a committee dealing with a highly salient, divisive subject matter be expected to adopt the integrative style that Fenno found led to the success of the Appropriations Committee during the period of his study. Committees are not the sole masters of their success.

CONCLUSION

The work reviewed in this chapter opened up the important area of congressional committees to systematic empirical inquiry. In addition to studying the determinants of committee success, it helped to increase our understanding of the functions of committees, the sources of their power, and the various forms of committee success.

Committees provide benefits both to the individual legislator and to the legislative chamber. These benefits can reinforce each other, but they also contain elements of tension, since logrolling to pass bills by giving more electoral benefits to individual legislators can detract from the legislative agenda of the majority party. Committees can exercise power only as long as they are perceived to be successful, but committee success varies. Success not only varies between committees but over time, as reforms alter the resources of committee chairs and change the balance of power between committee and party leadership.

Formal theorists view committees as part of a division-of-labor system in which expertise is rewarded through a reciprocity norm. Committees provide an opportunity for members to achieve their goals, including activities that can aid members in reelection. However, by providing another means for individual members to achieve their goals, they simultaneously provide another way in which the collective interest is subordinated to individual interests in legislatures.

The power of committees relies on their ability to control which bills get to the floor, to propose the content of legislation, to use their informational advantage (as Krehbiel argues), and to serve on conference committees (as Shepsle and Weingast maintain). However, their power also depends on their role vis-à-vis the legislative parties (see, especially, Cox and McCubbins 1993). The parties usually allow committees to have great policy latitude, but sometimes the majority party tries to enforce policy obedience.

Committee success can be measured as the proportion of bills from a committee that are passed by the chamber, but such a measure is too mechanical. Committee success also depends on its ability to forestall amendments on the floor, as well as its ability to prevail during the conference stage. Furthermore, a committee can be more successful in some of its policy areas than in others, so it is important to look at its success in a differentiated manner.

Committee success, however defined, inevitably depends on both internal and external factors. Leadership counts, as does committee cohesion, but these factors cannot be viewed in isolation from the subject matter of the committee and its own representativeness. Figure 16.2 shows one possible composite model of committee success. Goals are one factor that affects recruitment; recruitment affects the representativeness of the committee; and representativeness, in turn, is among the factors that contribute to committee cohesion and integration. Subject matter affects committee recruitment, but also, we would argue, directly affects the committee's cohesion and integration. Looked at this way, committee cohesion and integration are not independent of other causes of committee success. Ultimately, committee success is affected by the committee's subject matter, its representativeness, its leadership, and its integration.

It is important to emphasize that the topics discussed in this chapter vary over time. The functions of committees, their power, and their success are not constants. There can be an equilibrium position for power in a legislature, but there are inevitably pressures for changes in the distribution of power. As this happens, informal changes occur in the system and formal changes soon follow. The committees were very powerful in the "textbook Congress" of the 1950s and 1960s, but subcommittees attained independent power in the "reform Congress" of the 1970s and 1980s. Meanwhile, the party leadership of the House gained in its formal powers, which further served to tame committee powers. This helped legitimate the moves of the House Republican leadership in the 104th Congress to reduce subcommittee power, to choose some committee chairs without regard to seniority, and to move some bills through task forces rather than through standing committees. It also would be useful to reexamine some of the committees that

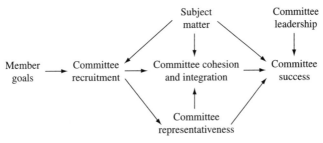

Figure 16.2
Composite model of committee success.

were studied extensively in previous decades to see, for example, if the strategic premises of particular committees changed as the nation entered an era of less government. Many of our understandings of particular committees thus might be found to have been timebound.

The study of committees developed in many ways over the years. For example, the availability of committee records following the 1970s reforms led to analysis of cleavages on committee votes (see especially Parker and Parker 1985; Unekis and Rieselbach 1984; Ward 1993). Similarly, subcommittee reforms led to some greater scholarly attention to subcommittees, particularly Hall's (1996) study of participation at that level. The extensive debate in the literature over committee representativeness strikes many readers as a case of academic overkill, but this debate led to innovations in the conceptualization of the relationship between committees and parties as well as in the study of committee assignment.

In the end, though, the continuities of committee research are greater than the changes. A committee must be successful if it is to maintain an image of being powerful. While there are alternatives to committees, the need for an efficient legislative system ensures that congressional government will always be committee government.

NOTES

1. This listing of committee powers is based on Shepsle and Weingast (1987), though they emphasize that the committee role in conference committees is what makes the other powers effective.
2. Another alternative to the usual committee process involves special negotiating summits between congressional leaders and the White House, as has been used on Social Security reforms (Light 1985) and some budget negotiations. This approach is usually successful, but has occasionally been torpedoed by congressional leaders or committee chairs who felt excluded from this process.
3. Technically, the most successful committees are those that minimize the spatial distance between those committees' median preference points and the positions of legislation on the same continuum.
4. Committee names used in this chapter are those of the committees at the time they were studied, even if their names were later changed. For example, several studies are mentioned of the House Education and Labor Committee during the period of Democratic control of the House, though majority Republicans renamed it "Economic Opportunity" in the 104th Congress and " Education and the Workforce" in the 105th Congress.
5. Later studies of single committees conducted by researchers influenced by Fenno's work include Murphy's (1974) study of Public Works and Perkins' (1980) study of Judiciary.
6. The correlation becomes nearly perfect when Dodd excludes three committees that deal with pork-barrel legislation, but that exclusion seems too ad hoc.
7. Parties traditionally have exercised more control over assignments to "prestige" committees. Cox and McCubbins (1993) offer evidence that the parties exercise greater control over committee assignments and transfers than the self-selection argument suggests.

Chapter 17

The House Appropriations Committee as a Political System: The Problem of Integration

RICHARD F. FENNO, JR.

Studies of Congress by political scientists have produced a time-tested consensus on the very considerable power and autonomy of congressional committees. Because of these two related characteristics, it makes empirical and analytical sense to treat the congressional committee as a discrete unit for analysis. This paper conceives of the committee as a political system (or, more accurately as a political subsystem) faced with a number of basic problems which it must solve in order to achieve its goals and maintain itself. Generally speaking these functional problems pertain to the environmental and the internal relations of the committee. This study is concerned almost exclusively with the internal problems of the committee and particularly with the problem of self-integration.[1] It describes how one congressional committee—the Committee on Appropriations of the House of Representatives—has dealt with this problem in the period 1947–61. Its purpose is to add to our understanding of appropriations politics in Congress and to suggest the usefulness of this type of analysis for studying the activities of any congressional committee.

The necessity for integration in any social system arises from the differentiation among its various elements. Most importantly there is a differentiation among subgroups and among individual positions, together with the roles that flow therefrom.[2] A committee faces the problem, how shall these diverse elements be made to mesh together or function in support of one another? No political system (or subsystem) is perfectly integrated; yet no political system can survive without some minimum degree of integration among its differentiated parts. Committee integration is defined as the degree to which there is a working together or a meshing together or mutual support among its roles and subgroups. Conversely, it is also defined as the degree to which a committee is able to minimize conflict among its roles and its subgroups, by heading off or resolving the conflicts that arise.[3] A concomitant of integration is the existence of a fairly consistent set of norms, widely agreed upon and widely followed by the members. Another concomitant of

Source: *American Political Science Review* (1962) 56:310–24. Reprinted by permission of the publisher.

integration is the existence of control mechanisms (i.e., socialization and sanctioning mechanisms) capable of maintaining reasonable conformity to norms. In other words, the more highly integrated a committee, the smaller will be the gap between expected and actual behavior. . . .

COMMITTEE CHARACTERISTICS

Five important characteristics of the Appropriations Committee which help explain committee integration are (1) the existence of a well-articulated and deeply rooted consensus on committee goals or tasks; (2) the nature of the committee's subject matter; (3) the legislative orientation of its members; (4) the attractiveness of the committee for its members; and (5) the stability of committee membership.

Consensus

The Appropriations Committee sees its tasks as taking form within the broad guidelines set by its parent body, the House of Representatives. For it is the primary condition of the committee's existence that it was created by the House for the purpose of assisting the House in the performance of House legislative tasks dealing with appropriations. Committee members agree that their fundamental duty is to serve the House in the manner and with the substantive results that the House prescribes. Given, however, the imprecision of House expectations and the permissiveness of House surveillance, the committee must elaborate for itself a definition of tasks plus a supporting set of perceptions (of itself and of others) explicit enough to furnish day-to-day guidance.

The committee's view begins with the preeminence of the House—often mistakenly attributed to the Constitution ("all bills for raising revenue," Art. I, sec. 7) but nevertheless firmly sanctioned by custom—in appropriations affairs.

It moves easily to the conviction that, as the efficient part of the House in this matter, the Constitution has endowed it with special obligations and special prerogatives. It ends in the view that the Committee on Appropriations, far from being merely one among many units in a complicated legislative-executive system, is *the* most important, most responsible unit in the whole appropriations process.[4] Hand in hand with the consensus on their primacy goes a consensus that all of their House-prescribed tasks can be fulfilled by superimposing upon them one, single, paramount task—*to guard the Federal Treasury*. Committee members state their goals in the essentially negative terms of guardianship—screening requests for money, checking against ill-advised expenditures, and protecting the taxpayer's dollar. . . . To the consensus on the main task of protecting the Treasury is added a consensus on the instrumental task of *cutting whatever budget estimates are submitted.*

As an immediate goal, Committee members agree that they must strike a highly critical, aggressive posture toward budget requests, and that they should, on principle, reduce them. In the words of the Committee's veterans: "There has never been a budget submitted to the Congress that couldn't be cut." "There isn't a budget that can't be cut 10 percent immediately." "I've been on the Committee for 17 years. No subcommittee of which I have been a member has ever reported out a bill without a cut in the budget. I'm proud of that record." The aim of budget cutting is strongly internalized for the Committee member. "It's a tradition in the Appropriations Committee to cut." "You're grounded in it. . . . It's ingrained in you from the time you get on the Committee." For the purposes of a larger study, the appropriations case histories of 37 executive bureaus have been examined for a 12-year period, 1947–59.[5] Of 443 separate bureau estimates, the Committee reduced 77.2% (342) of them.

    . . . To the major task of protecting the Treasury and the instrumental task of cutting budget estimates, each Committee member adds, usually by way of exception, a third task—*serving the constituency to which he owes his election.* This creates no problem for him when, as is sometimes the case, he can serve his district best by cutting the budget requests of a federal agency whose program is in conflict with the demands of his constituency. Normally, however, members find that their most common role-conflict is between a Committee-oriented budget-reducing role and a constituency-oriented budget-increasing role. Committee ideology resolves the conflict by assigning top, long-run priority to the budget-cutting task and making of the constituency service a permissible, short-run exception. No member is expected to commit electoral suicide; but no member is expected to allow his district's desire for federal funds to dominate his Committee behavior.

Subject Matter

Appropriations Committee integration is facilitated by the subject matter with which the group deals. The committee makes decisions on the same controversial issues as do the committees handling substantive legislation. But a money decision—however vitally it affects national policy—is, or at least seems to be, less directly a policy decision. Since they deal immediately with dollars and cents, it is easy for the members to hold to the idea that they are not dealing with programmatic questions, that theirs is a "business" rather than a "policy" committee. The subject matter, furthermore, keeps committee members relatively free agents, which promotes intracommittee maneuvering and, hence, conflict avoidance. Members do not commit themselves to their constituents in terms of precise money amounts, and no dollar sum is sacred—it can always be adjusted without conceding that a principle has been breached. By contrast, members of committees dealing directly with controversial issues are often pressured into taking concrete stands on these issues; consequently, they may come to their committee work with fixed and hardened attitudes. This leads to unavoidable, head-on intracommittee conflict and renders integrative mechanisms relatively ineffective.

    The fact of an annual appropriations process means the Committee members repeat the same operations with respect to the same subject matters year after year—and frequently more than once in a given year. Substantive and procedural repetition promotes familiarity with key problems and provides ample opportunity to test and confirm the most satisfactory methods of dealing with them. And the absolute necessity that appropriations bills do ultimately pass gives urgency to the search for such methods. Furthermore, the House rule that no member of the committee can serve on another standing committee is a deterrent against a fragmentation of committee member activity which could be a source of difficulty in holding the group together. If a committee has developed (as this one has) a number of norms designed to foster integration, repeated and concentrated exposure to them increases the likelihood that they will be understood, accepted and followed.

Legislative Orientation

The recruitment of members for the Appropriations Committee produces a group of individuals with an orientation especially conducive to committee integration. Those who make the selection pay special attention to the characteristics which Masters has described as those of the "responsible legislator"—approval of and conformity to the norms of the legislative process and of the House of Representatives (Masters 1961). . . . A key criterion in [members' selection] was a demonstrable record of, or an assumed predisposition toward, legislative give and take.

The 106 Appropriations Committee members serving between 1947 and 1961 spent an average of 3.6 years on other House committees before coming to the committee. Only 17 of the 106 were selected as first-term congressmen. A House apprenticeship (which Appropriations maintains more successfully than all committees save Ways and Means and Rules)[6] provides the time in which legislative reputations can be established by the member and an assessment of that reputation in terms of Appropriations Committee requirements can be made. Moreover, the mere fact that a member survives for a couple of terms is some indication of an electoral situation conducive to his "responsible" legislative behavior. The optimum bet for the committee is a member from a sufficiently safe district to permit him freedom of maneuver inside the House without fear of reprisal at the polls.[7] The degree of responsiveness to House norms which the committee selectors value may be the product of a safe district as well as an individual temperament.

Attractiveness

A fourth factor is the extraordinarily high degree of attractiveness which the committee holds for its members—as measured by the low rate of departure from it. Committee members do not leave it for service on other committees. To the contrary, they are attracted to it from nearly every other committee.[8] Of the 106 members in the 1947–61 period, only two men left the committee voluntarily; and neither of them initiated the move.[9] Committee attractiveness is a measure of its capacity to satisfy individual member needs—for power, prestige, recognition, respect, self-esteem, friendship, etc. Such satisfaction in turn increases the likelihood that members will behave in such a way as to hold the group together.

The most frequently mentioned source of committee attractiveness is its power—based on its control of financial resources. . . . They prize their ability to reward or punish so many other participants in the political process . . . The second important ingredient in member satisfaction is the governmentwide scope of committee activity. The ordinary congressman may feel that he has too little knowledge of and too little control over his environment. Membership on this committee compensates for this feeling of helplessness by the wider contacts, the greater amount of information, and the sense of being "in the middle of things" which are consequent, if not to subcommittee activity, at least to the full committee's overview of the federal government.

Thirdly, committee attractiveness is heightened by the group's recognizable and distinctive political style—one that is, moreover, highly valued in American political culture. The style is that of *hard work;* and the committee's self-image is that of "the hardest working committee in Congress." His willingness to work is the committee member's badge of identification, and it is proudly worn. It colors his perceptions of others and their perceptions of him.[10] . . .

The mere existence of some identifiable and valued style or "way of life" is a cohesive force for a group. But the particular style of hard work is one which increases group morale and group identification twice over. Hard work means a long, dull and tedious application to detail, via the technique of "dig, dig, dig, day after day behind closed doors"—in an estimated 460 subcommittee and full committee meetings a year. And virtually all of these meetings are in executive session. By adopting the style of hard work, the committee discourages highly individualized forms of legislative behavior, which could be disruptive within the committee. It rewards its members with power, but it is power based rather on work inside the committee than on the political glamour of activities carried on in the limelight of the mass media. Prolonged daily work together encourages sentiments of mutual regard, sympathy and solidarity. This *esprit* is, in turn, functional for integration on the committee. . . .

The strong attraction which members have for the committee increases the influence which the committee and its norms exercise on all of them. It increases the susceptibility of the newcomer to committee socialization and of the veteran to committee sanctions applicable against deviant behavior (Thibaut and Kelley 1959, 247; Cartwright and Zander 1953, 420).

Membership Stability

Members of the Appropriations Committee are strongly attracted to it; they also have, which bears out their selection as "responsible legislators," a strong attraction for a career in the House of Representatives. The 50 members on the committee in 1961 had served an average of 13.1 years in the House. These twin attractions produce a noteworthy stability of committee membership. . . . This extraordinary stability of personnel extends into the staff as well. . . .

The opportunity exists, therefore, for the development of a stable leadership group, a set of traditional norms for the regulation of internal committee behavior, and informal techniques of personal accommodation. Time is provided in which new members can learn and internalize committee norms before they attain high seniority rankings. The committee does not suffer from the potentially disruptive consequences of rapid changeovers in its leadership group, nor of sudden impositions of new sets of norms governing internal committee behavior.

COMMITTEE INTEGRATION

If one considers the main activity of a political system to be decision making, the acid test of its internal integration is its capacity to make collective decisions without flying apart in the process. Analysis of committee integration should focus directly, therefore, upon its subgroups and the roles of its members. Two kinds of subgroups are of central importance—subcommittees and majority or minority party groups. The roles which are most relevant derive from: (1) positions which each member holds by virtue of his subgroup attachments, e.g., as subcommittee member, majority (or minority) party member; (2) positions which relate to full committee membership, e.g., committee member, and the seniority rankings of veteran, man of moderate experience, and newcomer;[11] (3) positions which relate to both subgroup and full committee membership, e.g., chairman of the committee, ranking minority member of the committee, subcommittee chairman, ranking subcommittee member. Clusters of norms state the expectations about subgroup and role behavior. The description which follows treats the ways in which these norms and their associated behaviors mesh and clash. It treats, also, the internal control mechanisms by which behavior is brought into reasonable conformity with expectations.

Subgroup Integration

The day-to-day work of the committee is carried on in its subcommittees each of which is given jurisdiction over a number of related governmental units. The number of subcommittees is determined by the committee chairman, and has varied recently from a low of nine in 1949 to a high of 15 in 1959. The present total of 14 reflects, as always, a set of strategic and personal judgments by the chairman balanced against the limitations placed on him by committee tradition and member wishes. . . .

Each subcommittee holds hearings on the budget estimates of the agencies assigned to it, meets in executive session to decide what figures and what language to recommend to the full committee (to "mark up" the bill), defends its recommendations before the full committee, writes the committee's report to the House, dominates the debate on the floor, and bargains for the House in conference committee. Within its jurisdiction, each subcommittee functions independently of the others and guards its autonomy jealously. The chairman and ranking minority member of the full committee have, as we shall see, certain opportunities to oversee and dip into the operations of all subcommittees. But their intervention is expected to be minimal. Moreover, they themselves operate importantly within the subcommittee framework by sitting as chairman or ranking minority member of the subcommittee in which they are most interested. Each subcommittee, under the guidance of its chairman, transacts its business in considerable isolation from every other one. One subcommittee chairman exclaimed,

> Why, you'd be branded an impostor if you went into one of those other subcommittee meetings. The only time I go is by appointment, by arrangement with the chairman at a special time. I'm as much a stranger in another subcommittee as I would be in the legislative Committee on Post Office and Civil Service. Each one does its work apart from all others.

All members of all subcommittees are expected to behave in similar fashion in the role of subcommittee member. Three main norms define this role; to the extent that they are observed, they promote harmony and reduce conflict among subcommittees.[12] Subcommittee autonomy gives to the House norm of *specialization* an intensified application on the Appropriations Committee. Each member is expected to play the role of specialist in the activities of one subcommittee. He will sit on from one to four subcommittees, but normally will specialize in the work, or a portion of the work, of only one. Except for the chairman, ranking minority member and their confidants, a committee member's time, energy, contacts and experience are devoted to his subcommittees. Specialization is, therefore, among the earliest and most compelling of the committee norms to which a newcomer is exposed. Within the committee, respect, deference and power are earned through subcommittee activity and, hence to a degree, through specialization. Specialization is valued further because it is well suited to the task of guarding the Treasury. Only by specializing, committee members believe, can they unearth the volume of factual information necessary for the intelligent screening of budget requests. Since "the facts" are acquired only through industry an effective specialist will, perforce, adopt and promote the committee's style of hard work.

Committeewide acceptance of specialization is an integrative force in decision making because it helps support a second norm—*reciprocity*. The stage at which a subcommittee makes its recommendations is a potential point of internal friction. Conflict among subcommittees (or between one subcommittee and the rest of the committee) is minimized by the deference traditionally accorded to the recommendation of the subcommittee which has specialized in the area, has worked hard, and has "the facts." "It's a matter of 'You respect my work and I'll respect yours.'" "It's frowned upon if you offer an amendment in the full committee if you aren't on the subcommittee. It's considered presumptuous to pose as an expert if you aren't on the subcommittee." Though records of full committee decisions are not available, members agree that subcommittee recommendations are "very rarely changed," "almost always approved," "changed one time in fifty," "very seldom changed," etc.

No subcommittee is likely to keep the deference of the full committee for long unless its recommendations have widespread support among its own members. To this end, a third norm—*subcommittee unity*—is expected to be observed by subcommittee members. Unity means a willingness to support (or not to oppose) the recommendations of one's own subcommittee. Reciprocity and unity are closely dependent upon one another. Reciprocity is difficult to maintain when subcommittees themselves are badly divided; and unity has little appeal unless reciprocity will subsequently be observed. The norm of reciprocity functions to minimize intersubcommittee conflict. The norm of unity functions to minimize intrasubcommittee conflict. Both are deemed essential to subcommittee influence.

One payoff for the original selection of "responsible legislators" is their special willingness to compromise in pursuit of subcommittee unity. The impulse to this end is registered most strongly at the time when the subcommittee meets in executive session to mark up the bill. Two ranking minority members explained this aspect of markup procedure in their subcommittees:

> If there's agreement, we go right along. If there's a lot of controversy we put the item aside and go on. Then, after a day or two, we may have a list of ten controversial items. We give and take and pound them down till we get agreement.

> We have a unanimous agreement on everything. If a fellow enters an objection and we can't talk him out of it—and sometimes we can get him to go along—that's it. We put it in there.

Once the bargain is struck, the subcommittee is expected to "stick together."

It is, of course, easier to achieve unity among the five, seven, or nine members of a subcommittee than among the 50 members of the full committee. But members are expected wherever possible to observe the norm of unity in the full committee as well. That is, they should not only defer to the recommendations of the subcommittee involved, but they should support (or not oppose) that recommendation when it reaches the floor in the form of a committee decision. On the floor, committee members believe, their power and prestige depend largely on the degree to which the norms of reciprocity and unity continue to be observed. Members warn each other that if they go to the floor in disarray they will be "rolled," "jumped," or "run over" by the membership. It is a cardinal maxim among committee members that "You can't turn an appropriations bill loose on the floor." . . .

One of the most functional committee practices supporting the norm of unity is the tradition against minority reports in the subcommittee and in the full committee. It is symptomatic of committee integration that custom should proscribe the use of the most formal and irrevocable symbol of congressional committee disunity—the minority report. A few have been written—but only nine out of a possible 141 during the 11 years, 1947–57. That is to say, 95% of all original appropriations bills in this period were reported out without dissent. The technique of "reserving" is the committee member's equivalent for the registering of dissent. In subcommittee or committee, when a member reserves, he goes on record informally by informing his colleagues that he reserves the right to disagree on a specified item later on in the proceedings. He may seek a change or support a change in that particular item in full committee or on the floor. But he does not publicize his dissent. The subcommittee or the full committee can then make an unopposed recommendation. The individual retains some freedom of maneuver without firm commitment. Often a member reserves on an appropriations item but takes no further action. A member explained how the procedure operates in subcommittee,

> If there's something I feel too strongly about, and just can't go along, I'll say, "Mr. Chairman, we can have a unanimous report, but I reserve the right to bring this up in

full committee. I feel duty bound to make a play for it and see if I can't sell it to the other members." But if I don't say anything, or don't reserve this right, and then I bring it up in full Committee, they'll say, "Who are you trying to embarrass? You're a member of the team, aren't you? That's not the way to get along."

Disagreement cannot, of course, be eliminated from the committee. But the committee has accepted a method of ventilating it which produces a minimum of internal disruption. And members believe that the greater their internal unity, the greater the likelihood that their recommendations will pass the House.

The degree to which the role of the subcommittee member can be so played and subcommittee conflict thereby minimized depends upon the minimization of conflict between the majority and minority party subgroups. Nothing would be more disruptive to the committee's work than bitter and extended partisan controversy. It is, therefore, important to Appropriations Committee integration that a fourth norm—*minimal partisanship*—should be observed by members of both party contingents. Nearly every respondent emphasized, with approval, that "very little" or "not much" partisanship prevailed on the committee. One subcommittee chairman stated flatly, "My job is to keep down partisanship." A ranking minority member said, "You might think that we Republicans would defend the administration and the budget, but we don't." Majority and minority party ratios are constant and do not change (i.e., in 1958) to reflect changes in the strength of the controlling party. The committee operates with a completely nonpartisan professional staff, which does not change in tune with shifts in party control. Requests for studies by the committee's investigating staff must be made by the chairman and ranking minority member of the full committee and by the chairman and ranking minority member of the subcommittee involved. Subcommittees can produce recommendations without dissent and the full committee can adopt reports without dissent precisely because party conflict is (during the period 1947–61) the exception rather than the rule.

The committee is in no sense immune from the temperature of party conflict, but it does have a relatively high specific heat. Intense party strife or a strongly taken presidential position will get reflected in subcommittee and in committee recommendations. . . . Partisanship is normally generated from the environment and not from within the committee's party groups. Partisanship is, therefore, likely to be least evident in subcommittee activity, stronger in the full committee, and most potent at the floor stage. Studies which have focused on roll-call analysis have stressed the influence of party in legislative decision making (Truman 1959; Turner 1951a). In the appropriations process, at any rate, the floor stage probably represents party influence at its maximum. Our examination, by interview, of decision making at the subcommittee and full committee level would stress the influence of committee-oriented norms—the strength of which tends to vary inversely with that of party bonds. In the secrecy and intimacy of the subcommittee and full committee hearing rooms, the member finds it easy to compromise on questions of more or less, to take money from one program and give it to another and, in general, to avoid yes-or-no type party stands. These decisions, taken in response to the integrative norms of the committee, are the most important ones in the entire appropriations process.

Role Integration

The roles of subcommittee member and party member are common to all.

Other more specific decision-making positions are allocated among the members. Different positions produce different roles, and in an integrated system, these too must fit together. . . . Two crucial instances of role reciprocity on the committee involve the seniority positions of oldtimer and newcomer and the leadership positions of chairman and ranking minority member, on both the full committee and on each subcommittee.

The differentiation between senior and junior members is the broadest definition of who shall and who shall not actively participate in committee decisions. Of a junior member, it will be said, "Oh, he doesn't count—what I mean is, he hasn't been on the committee long enough." He is not expected to and ordinarily does not have much influence. His role is that of apprentice. . . .

Among the committee's veterans, the key roles are those of committee chairman and ranking minority member, and their counterparts in every subcommittee. It is a measure of committee integration and the low degree of partisanship that considerable reciprocity obtains between these roles. Their partisan status nevertheless sets limits to the degree of possible integration. The chairman is given certain authority which he and only he can exercise. But save in times of extreme party controversy, the expectation is that consultation and cooperation between the chairman-ranking minority member shall lubricate the committee's entire work. For example, by committee tradition, its chairman and ranking minority member are both ex officio voting members of each subcommittee and of every conference committee. The two of them thus have joint access at every stage of the internal process. A subcommittee chairman, too, is expected to discuss matters of scheduling and agenda with his opposite minority number. He is expected to work with him during the markup session and to give him (and, normally, only him) an opportunity to read and comment on the subcommittee report.[13] A ranking minority member described his subcommittee markup procedure approvingly:

> Frequently the chairman has a figure which he states. Sometimes he will have no figure, and he'll turn to me and say, "———, what do you think?" Maybe I'll have a figure. It's very flexible. Everyone has a chance to say what he thinks, and we'll move it around. Sometimes it takes a long time. . . . He's a rabid partisan on the floor, but he is a very fair man in the subcommittee.

Where influence is shared, an important exchange of rewards occurs. The chairman gains support for his leadership and the ranking minority member gains intracommittee power. The committee as a whole insures against the possibility of drastic change in its internal structure by giving to its key minority members a stake in its operation. Chairmen and ranking minority members will, in the course of time, exchange positions; and it is expected that such a switch will produce no form of retribution nor any drastic change in the functioning of the committee. Reciprocity of roles, in this case, promotes continued integration. . . .

Reciprocity between chairmen and ranking minority members on the Appropriations Committee is to some incalculable degree a function of the stability of membership which allows a pair of particular individuals to work out the kind of personal accommodation described above. The close working relationship of Clarence Cannon and John Taber, whose service on the committee totals 68 years and who have been changing places as chairman and ranking minority member for 19 years, highlights and sustains a pattern of majority-minority reciprocity throughout the group.

Internal Control Mechanisms

. . . From what can be gathered, however, from piecing together a study of the public record on appropriations from 1947 to 1961 with interview materials, the committee has been markedly successful in maintaining a stable internal structure over time. As might be expected, therefore, changes and threats of change have been generated more from the environment—when outsiders consider the committee as unresponsive—than from inside the subsystem itself. One source of internal stability, and an added reason for assuming a correlation between expected and actual behavior, is the existence of what appear to be reasonably effective internal control mechanisms. Two of these are the socialization processes applied to newcomers and the sanctioning mechanisms applicable to all committee members.

Socialization is in part a training in perception. Before members of a group can be expected to behave in accordance with its norms, they must learn to see and interpret the world around them with reasonable similarity. The socialization of the committee newcomer during his term or two of apprenticeship serves to bring his perceptions and his attitudes sufficiently into line with those of the other members to serve as a basis for committee integration. The committee, as we have seen, is chosen from congressmen whose political flexibility connotes an aptitude for learning new lessons of power. Furthermore, the high degree of satisfaction of its members with the group increases their susceptibility to its processes of learning and training.

For example, one half of the committee's Democrats are Northerners and Westerners from urban constituencies, whose voting records are just as "liberal" on behalf of domestic social welfare programs as noncommittee Democrats from like constituencies. They come to the committee favorably disposed toward the high level of federal spending necessary to support such programs, and with no sense of urgency about the committee's tasks of guarding the Treasury or reducing budget estimates. Given the criteria governing their selection, however, they come without rigid preconceptions and with a built-in responsiveness to the socialization processes of any legislative group of which they are members. It is crucial to committee integration that they learn to temper their potentially disruptive welfare-state ideology with a conservative's concern for saving money. They must change their perceptions and attitudes sufficiently to view the committee's tasks in nearly the same terms as their more conservative Southern Democratic and Republican colleagues. . . .

The younger men, in this case the younger liberals, do learn from their committee experience. . . . Repeated exposure to committee work and to fellow members has altered their perceptions and their attitudes in money matters. . . . These men will remain more inclined toward spending than their committee colleagues, but their perceptions and hence their attitudes have been brought close enough to the others to support a consensus on tasks. They are responsive to appeals on budget-cutting grounds that would not have registered earlier and which remain meaningless to liberals outside the committee. In cases, therefore, where committee selection does not and cannot initially produce individuals with a predisposition toward protecting the Treasury, the same result is achieved by socialization.

Socialization is a training in behavior as well as in perception. For the newcomer, conformity to norms in specific situations is insured through the appropriate application, by the committee veterans, of rewards and punishments. For the committee member who serves his apprenticeship creditably, the passage of time holds the promise that he will inherit a position of influence. He may, as an incentive, be given some small reward early in his committee career. One man, in his second year, had been assigned the task of specializing in one particular program. . . . At some later date, provided he continues to observe committee norms, he will be granted additional influence, perhaps through a prominent floor role. . . .

The important function of apprenticeship is that it provides the necessary time during which socialization can go forward. And teaching proceeds with the aid of punishments as well as rewards. Should a new member inadvertently or deliberately run afoul of committee norms during his apprenticeship, he will find himself confronted with negative sanctions ranging in subtlety from "jaundiced eyes" to a changed subcommittee assignment. . . .

One internal threat to committee integration comes from new members who from untutored perceptions, from ignorance of norms, or from dissatisfaction with the apprentice role may not act in accordance with committee expectations. The seriousness of this threat is minimized, however, by the fact that the deviant newcomer does not possess sufficient resources to affect adversely the operation of the system. Even if he does not respond immediately to the application of sanctions, he can be held in check and subjected to an extended and (given the frequency of interaction among members) intensive period of socialization. The success of committee socialization is indicated by the fact that whereas wholesale criticism of committee operations was frequently voiced among junior members, it had disappeared among the men of moderate experience. And what these middle seniority members now accept as the facts of committee life, the veterans vigorously assert and defend as the essentials of a smoothly functioning system. Satisfaction with the committee's internal structure increases with length of committee service.

An important reason for changing member attitudes is that those who have attained leadership positions have learned, as newcomers characteristically have not, that their conformity to committee norms is the ultimate source of their influence inside the group. Freshman members do not as readily perceive the degree to which interpersonal influence is rooted in obedience to group norms. They seem to convert their own sense of powerlessness into the view that the committee's leaders possess, by virtue of their position, arbitrary, absolute, and awesome power. Typically, they say: "If you're a subcommittee chairman, it's your committee." "The chairman runs the show. He gets what he wants. He decides what he wants and gets it through." Older members of the committee, however, view the power of the leaders as a highly contingent and revocable grant, tendered by the committee for so long and only as long as their leaders abide by committee expectations. In commenting on internal influence, their typical reaction is: "Of course, the committee wouldn't follow him if it didn't want to. He has a great deal of respect. He's an able man, a hardworking man." "He knows the bill backwards and forwards. He works hard, awfully hard and the members know it." Committee leaders have an imposing set of formal prerogatives. But they can capitalize on them only if they command the respect, confidence and deference of their colleagues.

It is basic to committee integration that members who have the greatest power to change the system evidence the least disposition to do so. Despite their institutional conservatism, however, committee elders do occasionally violate the norms applicable to them and hence represent a potential threat to successful integration. Excessive deviation from committee expectations by some leaders will bring countermeasures by other leaders. Thus, for example, the chairman and his subcommittee chairmen exercise reciprocal controls over one another's behavior. The chairman has the authority to appoint the chairman and members of each subcommittee and fix its jurisdiction. "He runs the committee. He has a lot of power," agrees one subcommittee chairman. "But it's all done on the basis of personal friendship. If he tries to get too big, the members can whack him down by majority vote."

In the Eighty-fourth Congress, Chairman Cannon attempted an unusually broad reorganization of subcommittee jurisdictions. The subcommittee chairman most adversely affected rallied his senior colleagues against the chairman's action—on the ground that it was an excessive violation of role expectations and threatening to subcommittee autonomy. Faced with the prospect of a negative committee vote, the chairman was forced to act in closer conformity to the expectations of the other leaders. . . . On the subcommittees, too, it is the veterans of both parties who will levy sanctions against an offending chairman. . . . Committee integration is underwritten by the fact that no member high or low is permanently immune from the operation of its sanctioning mechanisms.

IMPLICATIONS

Data concerning internal committee activity can be organized and presented in various ways. One way is to use key functional problems like integration as the focal points for descriptive analysis. On the basis of our analysis (and without, for the time being, having devised any precise measure of integration), we are led to the summary observation that the House Appropriations Committee appears to be a well-integrated, if not an extremely well-integrated, committee. The question arises as to whether anything can be gained from this study other than a description of one property of one political subsystem. If it is reasonable to assume that the internal life of a congressional committee affects all legislative activity involving that committee, and if it is reasonable to assume that the analysis of a committee's internal relationships will produce useful knowledge about legislative behavior, some broader implications for this study are indicated.

In the first place, the success of the House Appropriations Committee in solving the problem of integration probably does have important consequences for the appropriations process. Some of the possible relationships can be stated as hypotheses and tested; others can be suggested as possible guides to understanding. All of them require further research. Of primary interest is the relationship between integration and the power of the committee. There is little doubt about the fact of committee power. Of the 443 separate case histories of bureau appropriations examined, the House accepted committee recommendations in 387, or 87.4% of them; and in 159, or 33.6% of the cases, the House Committee's original recommendations on money amounts were the exact ones enacted into law. The hypothesis that the greater the degree of committee unity the greater the probability that its recommendations will be accepted is being tested as part of a larger study (cf. Marvick 1952). House committee integration may be a key factor in producing House victories in conference committee. This relationship too, might be tested. Integration appears to help provide the House conferees with a feeling of confidence and superiority which is one of their important advantages in the mix of psychological factors affecting conference deliberations.

Another suggested consequence of high integration is that party groups have a relatively small influence upon appropriations decisions. It suggests, too, that committee-oriented behavior should be duly emphasized in any analysis of congressional oversight of administrative activity by this committee. Successful integration promotes the achievement of the committee's goals, and doubtless helps account for the fairly consistent production of budget-cutting decisions. Another consequence will be found in the strategies adopted by people seeking favorable committee decisions. For example, the characteristic lines of contact from executive officials to the committee will run to the chairman and the ranking minority member (and to the professional staff man) of the single subcommittee handling their agency's appropriations. The ways in which the committee achieves integration may even affect the success or failure of a bureau in getting its appropriations. Committee members, for instance, will react more favorably toward an administrator who conforms to their self-image of the hard-working master-of-detail than to one who does not—and committee response to individual administrators bulks large in their determinations.

Finally, the internal integration of this committee helps to explain the extraordinary stability, since 1920, of appropriations procedures—in the face of repeated proposals to change them through omnibus appropriations, legislative budgets, new budgetary forms, item veto, Treasury borrowing, etc. Integration is a stabilizing force, and the stability of the House Appropriations Committee has been a force for stabilization throughout the entire process. It was, for example, the disagreement between Cannon and Taber which led to the indecisiveness reflected in the short-lived experiment with a single appropriations bill (Nelson 1953). One need only examine the conditions most likely to decrease committee integration to ascertain some of the critical factors for producing changes in the appropriations process. A description of integration is also an excellent baseline from which to analyze changes in internal structure.

All of these are speculative propositions which call for further research. But they suggest, as a second implication, that committee integration does have important consequences for legislative activity and, hence, that it is a key variable in the study of legislative politics. It would seem, therefore, to be a fruitful focal point for the study of other congressional committees.[14] Comparative committee analysis could usefully be devoted to (1) the factors which tend to increase or decrease integration; (2) the degree to which integration is achieved; and (3) the consequences of varying degrees of integration for committee behavior and influence. If analyses of committee integration are of any value, they should encourage the analysis and the classification of congressional committees along functional lines. And they should lead to the discussion of interrelated problems of committee survival. Functional classifications of committees (i.e., well or poorly integrated) derived from a large number of descriptive analyses of several functional problems, may prove helpful in constructing more general propositions about the legislative process.

NOTES

1. On social systems, see: Homans (1950); Merton (1957); Parsons and Shils (1951, 190–234). Most helpful with reference to the political system has been Easton (1957).
2. On the idea of subgroups as used here, see Johnson (1960, chapter 3). On role, see specifically Newcomb (1951, 280); see generally Gross, Mason, and McEachern (1958). On differentiation and its relation to integration, see Greer (1955).
3. The usage here follows most closely that of Merton (1957, 26–29).
4. This and all other generalizations about member attitudes and perceptions depend heavily on extensive interviews with committee members. Semistructured interviews, averaging 45 minutes in length were held with 45 of the 50 Committee members during the 86th Congress. Certain key questions, all open-ended, were asked of all respondents. The schedule was kept very flexible, however, in order to permit particular topics to be explored with those individuals best equipped to discuss them. In a few cases, where respondents encouraged it, notes [were] taken during the interviews. In most cases notes were not taken, but were transcribed immediately after the interview. When unattributed quotations occur in the text, therefore, they are as nearly verbatim as the author's power of immediate recall could make them. These techniques were all used so as to improve rapport between interviewer and respondent.
5. The bureaus being studied are all concerned with domestic policy and are situated in the Agriculture, Interior, Labor, Commerce, Treasury, Justice and Health, Education and Welfare departments. For a similar pattern of committee decisions in foreign affairs, see Carroll (1958, chapter 9).
6. In the period from 1947 through 1959 (80th to 86th Congress), 79 separate appointments were made to the Appropriations Committee, with 14 going to freshmen. The committee filled, in other words, 17.7% of its vacancies with freshmen. The Rules Committee had 26 vacancies and selected no freshmen at all. The Ways and Means Committee had 36 vacancies and selected two freshmen (5.6%). All other committees had a higher percentage of freshmen appointments. Armed Services ranked fourth, with 45 vacancies and 12 freshmen appointed, for a percentage of 26.7. Foreign affairs

figures were 46 and 14, or 30.4%; Un-American Activities figures were 22 and 7, or 31.8%; cf. Masters (1961).

7. In the 1960 elections, 41 out of the current 50 members received more than 55.1% of the vote in their districts. By a common definition, that is, only 9 of the 50 came from marginal districts.

8. The 106 members came to Appropriations from every committee except Ways and Means.

9. One was personally requested by the Speaker to move to Ways and Means. The other was chosen by a caucus of regional congressmen to be his party's representative on the Rules Committee. Of the 21 members who were forced off the committee for lack of seniority during a change in party control, or who were defeated for reelection and later returned, 20 sought to regain committee membership at the earliest opportunity.

10. A sidelight on this attitude is displayed in a . . . feud between the House and Senate Appropriations Committees over the meeting place for their conference committees. The House committee is trying to break the century-old custom that conferences to resolve differences on money bills are always held on the Senate side of the Capitol. . . . The House Appropriations Committee feels that it does all the hard work listening to witnesses for months on each bill, only to have the Senate Committee sit as a court of appeals and, with little more than a cursory glance, restore most of the funds cut." *Washington Post*, 24 April 1962, 1.

11. "Newcomers" are defined as men who have served no more than two terms on the committee. "Men of moderate experience" are those with three to five terms of service. "Veterans" are those who have six or more terms of committee service.

12. A statement of expected behavior was taken to be a committee norm when it was expressed by a substantial number of respondents (a dozen or so) who represented both parties, and varying degrees of experience. In nearly every case, moreover, no refutation of them was encountered, and ample confirmation of their existence can be found in the public record. Their articulation came most frequently from the veterans of the group.

13. See the exchange in 101 *Congressional Record*, 3832, 3844–3847.

14. This view has been confirmed by the results of interviews conducted by the author with members of the House Committee on Education and Labor, together with an examination of that committee's activity in one policy area. They indicate very significant contrasts between the internal structure of that committee and the Appropriations Committee—contrasts which center around their comparative success in meeting the problem of integration. The House Committee on Education and Labor appears to be a poorly integrated committee. Its internal structure is characterized by a great deal of subgroup conflict, relatively little role reciprocity, and minimally effective internal control mechanisms. External concerns, like those of party, constituency, and clientele groups, are probably more effective in determining its decisions than is likely to be the case in a well-integrated committee. An analysis of the internal life of the Committee on Education and Labor, drawn partly from interviews with 19 members of that group appears in *National Politics and Federal Aid to Education*, by Frank Munger and the author, Syracuse University Press, 1962. See also Masters (1961, 354–55) and Scher (1960).

Chapter 18

Policy Content, Committee Membership, and Behavior

BARBARA HINCKLEY

After more than ten years of endeavor, congressional committee research can show considerable accomplishment. Single-committee studies offer richly detailed understanding of the Appropriations, Ways and Means, Labor, and Banking committees, among others (Bibby 1967; Fenno 1962; Manley 1965). Macrocomparative studies can rank order all committees and test propositions concerning their prestige, cohesiveness, and success (Dodd 1972; Dyson and Soule 1970). A major work comparing six House committees has been published (Fenno 1973). . . . So we can rank them and interrank them, recognize them in operation, appreciate their differences, interview their members, analyze their chairmen, and make informed judgments as to their reform (Fenno 1973; Manley 1973). And there's a lot left to do. There are a half dozen House committees, a chance at their Senate counterparts, and the possibility of redoing the earlier studies as members and chairmen change and time goes by.

Nevertheless, little of this cumulates or comes together into more than a set of disparate, and at times contradictory, findings—employing widely different conceptualizations and kinds of data. Having found that "committees vary," we need now the kind of analysis that can order and explain this variation and that can begin to bring some of these very diverse results together.

One such integrative effort may be to organize committees by subject matter or "policy content" of the legislation they consider. It might be expected that policy content profoundly affects the committee assignment process—as to who wants what, who asks for what, and who gets what—and thus shapes the attractiveness of committees, the stability of their membership, and the kind of members selected and self-selected by the process. But it might also be expected that policy content would affect behavior on committees, independently of attractiveness or membership. Thus some subject areas permit more cohesiveness among members than others. In other words, attractiveness, membership, and behavioral attributes may all be arrayed and explained within a subject matter classification,

Source: Hinckley, Barbara. "Policy Content, Committee Membership, and Behavior." AMERICAN JOURNAL OF POLITICAL SCIENCE, Vol. 19 (1975) pp. 543–557. Reprinted by permission of The University of Wisconsin Press.

and any attempt to interrelate these attributes would first need to isolate the subject matter effect.

For a very well-known case in point, Appropriations' "integrated" behavior (defined in part as agreement among members on committee business) is explained by the following variables: the committee's subject matter, its attractiveness as an assignment, the stability of members, the proportion of "responsible" (senior, accommodating, compromising) members, and consensus on goals of members (Fenno 1962). This has led some to infer, perhaps beyond the author's intention, that committee attributes such as attractiveness and stability should be more generally related to agreement among members: that is, to infer a proposition holding for all committees and not only for Appropriations. Testing the inference has produced results at odds with the Appropriations study (Dodd 1972; Dyson and Soule 1970). But at least three of the variables appear closely interrelated. The more attractive a committee, the more its members should wish to stay and the more likely that senior, accommodating congressmen will be accommodated in turn by being assigned to it. And if subject matter shapes (1) attractiveness, (2) membership, and (3) behavior, then most of the variables, including the dependent variable, may be explained by subject matter effects.

This study, then, offers a first exploration of subject matter effects on committee membership and behavior. It selects as its focus those disparities in the literature relating attractiveness and stability of membership to cohesive behavior, and attempts to reconcile and explain them by two selected subject matter effects. . . .

TWO POLICY CONTENT DIMENSIONS

As part of the exploratory nature of the inquiry, two policy content dimensions have been selected, of general applicability in that they could be used to classify any political subject matter (e.g., see Froman 1968a; Lowi 1964), and of particular relevance for their effects on membership and behavior. These dimensions are subject matter *stakes* and *scope:* stakes defined as subject matter permitting positive-sum versus zero-sum solutions; scope defined as subject matter attracting a broad versus restricted number of "interested" actors, in proportion to the total number in whatever political unit is under analysis. If mixed-motive political actors seek influence among their peers, as well as other goods, they may find participation in broad as opposed to restricted subject matter more widely and generally valued by these peers, and esteemed as prestigious. Such participation is more difficult to achieve, and is therefore won by those with more influence to start with. Furthermore, legislators may find it easier to compromise and to exhibit cohesive behavior on subject matter permitting positive-sum as opposed to zero-sum solutions. In other words, we may take Froman's general proposition that "political processes vary in accord with the issues and the stakes of the game" and make it more specific: Political processes of membership selection and conflict management may vary across these two subject matter dimensions. Scope and stakes may affect both personnel and procedure—both who does what and how they do it.

More particularly, committees vary in scope, since some raise issues of concern to virtually all congressmen while some raise issues of concern to a more limited number of "interested" congressmen. Committees vary in stakes, since they raise issues that are perceived as tending toward zero-sum (win or lose) versus positive-sum (more or less) congressional allocations. These dimensions are defined by their relevance to congressmen, not in terms of interests outside the Congress or some abstract definition of "intrinsic" scope or stakes, since it is the congressman's attraction to and behavior on the committee that is to be explained. And needless to say, we are talking of tendencies and not absolute, rigid categories. Most committees' subject matter includes both broadly relevant and narrowly restricted congressional interests and both zero-sum and positive-sum allocations. But the assumption is that they may be classified—by congressional researchers and congressmen—in terms of a predominant character.

If subject matter shapes membership, we would expect that broad-scope committees would be more attractive to members, therefore more stable in membership and possessing more senior members than restricted committees (whether competitive or noncompetitive). The extent of intercorrelation among attractiveness, seniority, and stability variables also needs investigation. If subject matter shapes behavior, we would obviously expect that competitive committees should be less cohesive than noncompetitive committees (whether broad or restricted). Moreover and most critically, if subject matter is important, we would expect strong intercorrelations in the ranking of these attributes for House and Senate committees handling essentially the same jurisdiction. . . .

DESIGN OF THE STUDY

These propositions can be examined for 16 House and Senate committees, matched for subject matter jurisdiction and selected from committees previously studied in some detail. A panel device was employed for the classification, by asking six other congressional scholars to classify the committees for a specific point in time (the Eighty-seventh through the Ninetieth Congresses) on the two policy content dimensions.[1] Committees as placed in Table 18.1 have received either five or six out of six agreements from the panel on subject matter stakes, and four, five, or six out of six agreements on subject matter scope. Clearly some placements need to be treated more tentatively than others. Nevertheless, the possibility of some agreement among researchers is worth attention. Moreover, the placement accords well with earlier descriptive classifications (Goodwin 1970; Matthews 1960). Two additional committees originally offered—Armed Services and Foreign Affairs—received no consensus and were dropped from the analysis. . . .

The sixteen committees, then, can be classified by subject matter stakes and scope as in Table 18.1.

Very briefly, policy content for the 16 committees in the Eighty-seventh through Ninetieth Congresses can be summarized as follows, corroborated by the research from earlier committee studies. Ways and Means and Finance handle issues of great controversy and concern to a large number of congressmen: tax policy, Social

Table 18.1

Classification of committees by subject matter stakes and scope

	Stakes	
Scope	Zero-sum (competitive)	Positive-sum (noncompetitive)
Broad	Ways & Means/Finance (6,5)* Judiciary/Judiciary (4,6)	Appropriations/Appropriations (6,5)
Restricted	Education & Labor/Labor (4,5) Banking & Currency/Banking & Currency (5,6)	Interior/Interior (6,5) Public Works/Public Works (4,6) Post Office/Post Office (5,6)

*Numbers in parentheses refer to the number of six panelists agreeing to the placement by scope and stakes, respectively.

Security, Medicare, and so forth. The Judiciary committees are charged with consideration of constitutional questions, controversial "law and order" issues, and others of considerable ideological controversy, visibility, and congressional concern. The Appropriations committees, whose distribution of federal funds may be life or death to the individual congressman, can deal with questions of more or less, with controversy depressed by the nature of money amounts that can be compromised. By contrast, the Labor and Banking committees have dealt with a more restricted set of congressional interests, but one of considerable partisan and ideological controversy: labor legislation, aid to education, housing, big versus small business interests, larger versus smaller federal role. Public Works and Interior committees, while also dealing with a restricted set of congressional interests, were at that point in time perceiving their committees' business as the distribution of federal funding for local and regional purposes. Perception of a restricted, regional set of interests is attested to by the peculiar nature of the committees' membership: overwhelmingly Western for Interior, and border-Southern and west-of-the-Mississippi for Public Works. Post Office committee members may have less to distribute than Interior members, but have been found similarly concerned with patronage, helping constituents, and serving reelection goals (Fenno 1973).

We have, then, a tentative classification on two subject matter dimensions that can receive some agreement from other congressional scholars. It is limited in that it falls short of unanimity, deals with slightly less than half of the congressional committees, and is restricted to one particular time period. . . .

SUBJECT MATTER, COMMITTEE ATTRACTIVENESS, AND MEMBERSHIP

To what extent do the scope and stakes of subject matter shape such committee attributes as attractiveness, stability of membership, and proportion of senior members? We expect that broad-scope committees will be more attractive, stable, and senior than restricted committees, and expect no difference for zero-sum versus positive-sum stakes.

Table 18.2 reports results employing the traditional index of attractiveness based on transfers to and from the committee from the Eighty-first through Ninetieth Congresses (Goodwin 1970; Miller and Stokes, unpub. ms.). Stability is measured by mean years' consecutive service of members on the committee, and seniority by mean years' congressional service. (Similar results are obtained if seniority is measured by percent freshman members or percent members with ten or more years' service). While stability and seniority have only been calculated for the Ninetieth Congress, both measures reflect the formation of committee membership over time, and could easily be shown to hold over a number of congresses.

A number of observations can immediately be made from the table. First, broad-scope committees are consistently ranked higher in attractiveness, are more stable and composed of more senior members than restricted committees. Second, there is no observable difference between competitive and noncompetitive committees for these attributes within the broad-scope category and only slight differences between them within the restricted category, with the competitive committees on the average slightly more stable and more senior. In stability, competitive committees average 5.5 years and noncompetitive committees 4.4 in the House, and 6.3 and 5.8, respectively, in the Senate. In seniority, competitive committees average 6.4 and noncompetitive committees 6.0 years in the House, and 8.3 and 7.5 years, respectively, in the Senate. Third, there is strikingly strong intercorrelation between the *rankings* of House and Senate committees dealing with the same subject matter. Matching House and Senate committees produced the following rank order coefficients (Kendall's tau), two of which are significant beyond the .05 level:

House and Senate Intercorrelations

Committee attractiveness	tau = .61($p < $ .05)
Committee stability	tau = .25(ns)
Committee seniority	tau = .64($p < $ 0.5)

This House-Senate similarity suggests that subject matter alone is a powerful shaper of committee attractiveness and senior membership. Beyond the ranking, however, the scope distinction alone arrays committees almost perfectly into two categories—of greater or less attractiveness, stability, and seniority.[2] Of the 16 committees thus arrayed on three dimensions, for a total of 48 placements, there would be only two errors made: Senate Interior and Senate Judiciary would be misplaced for committee stability.

SUBJECT MATTER AND COMMITTEE BEHAVIOR

We can now address the other major possibility concerning the effects of subject matter—that is, its effect on cohesive or noncohesive committee behavior. Cohesive behavior was observed by Fenno in the committee context, and tested by Dodd and by Dyson and Soule using members' roll-call voting on the floor. While roll calls permit a convenient and justifiable measure of one important kind of

Table 18.2
Policy content, committee attractiveness, and membership

Committees	Attractiveness (rank)		Stability (mean years consecutive committee service)				Seniority of members (mean years congressional service)			
	House	Senate	House	(Rank)	Senate	(Rank)	House	(Rank)	Senate	(Rank)
Broad-Competitive										
Ways and Means/Finance	2	2	6.9	2	9.3	2	12.6	1	12.8	2
Judiciary	3	3	7.0	1	6.5	5	9.0	3	10.6	3
Broad-Noncompetitive										
Appropriations	1	1	6.6	3	10.5	1	10.6	2	17.3	1
Restricted-Competitive										
Banking and Currency	6 1/2	6	5.0	6	5.6	7	6.7	4	8.5	5
Education and Labor/Labor	5	5	6.0	4	6.9	4	6.0	7	8.0	6
Restricted-Noncompetitive										
Interior	6 1/2	4	4.4	7	7.2	3	6.5	6	9.5	4
Public Works	4	8	5.2	5	4.4	8	6.6	5	5.2	8
Post Office	8	7	3.6	8	5.8	6	5.0	8	7.7	7

Committees are ranked from high to low attractiveness, stability, and seniority. The preference ranking for attractiveness is based on transfers to and from the committees in the Eighty-first–Ninetieth Congresses. See Goodwin 1970, 114, 115. Stability and seniority are calculated for the Ninetieth Congress, but similarly reflect membership changes over behavior, it is the behavior of individuals outside the committee habitat and not the behavior of the committee-as-group. Moreover, behavior may change as congressmen move from committee to floor. Thus, a member of a cohesive committee may vote with the group in committee, warning members he will have to dissent on the floor. So a closer testing of the proposition inferred from the Appropriations study may be gained from the committee recommendation stage.

One measure of members' cohesive behavior is the percent of nonunanimous recommendations the committee reports. *Congressional Quarterly* (1967, 1968) records for each bill recommended to the floor whether there was a unanimous recommendation, a minority (party) dissent, or dissent by some individuals, either mentioned by name or by number dissenting. . . .

If subject matter affects the cohesiveness of committee behavior, then what we have called the zero-sum committees will be less cohesive than the positive-sum committees, and there will be no relationship of attractiveness of membership with cohesive behavior.

The results, reported in Table 18.3, show strong support for these expectations. Zero-sum committees, of whichever scope, exhibit less cohesive behavior than positive-sum committees for both the Senate and the House. Of the 16 committees, at most three would be misplaced by a classification based on subject matter stakes: the two Labor committees and House Public Works. For the House and Senate, the most attractive, stable, and senior committees are found at the most cohesive and least cohesive extremes. If we were to correlate committees ranked from high to low attractiveness and from high to low cohesion, results would show a slight inverse relationship for the House, with tau $= -.18$, and an inverse, still statistically nonsignificant relationship for the Senate of tau $= -.39$ (coefficients based on Kendall's tau). In this case, subject matter stakes, not scope, is the important organizing dimension.[3]

We can note again the strong correlation between House and Senate committees dealing with the same subject matter. The House overall uses more nonunamious recommendations than the Senate, but correlating the committees' ranked positions within each chamber, a fairly strong correlation coefficient is produced: tau $= .46$, p $= .07$. . . . What we are saying, then, for behavior as for the earlier results reported for membership, is that House and Senate committees dealing with the same subject matter exhibit quite similar attributes.

Controlling for subject matter controversy, within the classification as presented in Table 18.3, one can then ask if attractiveness or membership has any independent effect on behavior. For the House, no relationship is observable. Within the competitive category, broad-scope committees (of high attractiveness, seniority, and stability) are on the average less cohesive than clientele committees (of lower attractiveness, stability, and seniority). Within the noncompetitive category, Appropriations is more cohesive. For the Senate, no relationship can be inferred from the noncompetitive category, while for the competitive category, broad-scope committees exhibit less cohesive behavior than restricted committees.

These results may help reconcile some of the very disparate and apparently contradictory findings of the earlier studies. Using interview data, Fenno documented

Table 18.3

Policy content and committee cohesion in recommendations (percent nonunanimous recommendations[a])

House:	Stakes	
	Competitive	Noncompetitive
Scope		
Broad	Ways and Means 67%	Appropriations 6%
	Judiciary 56%	
Restricted	Banking and Currency 58%	Interior 36%
	Education and Labor 33%	Public Works (43%)
		Post Office (29%)
Senate:	Stakes	
	Competitive	Noncompetitive
Scope		
Broad	Finance 33%	Appropriations 6%
	Judiciary 47%	
Restricted	Banking and Currency 29%	Interior 18%
	Labor 13%	Public Works 0%
		Post Office (0%)

[a]Percentages based on less than 10 recommendations are reported in parentheses.

the exceptionally cohesive behavior of the stable, senior, and attractive Appropriations Committee. Using roll-call data, Dyson and Soule found no relationship between attractiveness and cohesion in the House. Neither study controlled for subject matter controversy. Also using roll-call data, but controlling for subject matter controversy, Dodd found an inverse relationship between attractiveness and cohesion in the Senate. The present study based on committee recommendations indicates, supporting Fenno, that Appropriations is indeed exceptionally cohesive, and supporting Dyson and Soule, that House committees overall show no relationship between attractiveness and cohesion. And controlling for subject matter controversy, the study indicates some support for the inverse relationship for Senate committees that Dodd reported, and no relationship for House committees. The picture that begins to emerge, then, from these very different investigations is that attractiveness and membership attributes appear to be only coincidentally linked with cohesive behavior.

One final summarizing point is necessary. The classification based simply on subject matter stakes and scope can explain a considerable amount of committee variety. In other words, if we arrayed committees by high and low attractiveness (also seniority and stability) and by high and low cohesion, dichotomizing at clear breakpoints in the data, we would produce *almost the same results as if we arrayed them by subject matter scope and stakes* (see Table 18.4). With the exception of placement of the two Labor committees, this is identical to the organization of

Table 18.4

Committee rankings by attractiveness and cohesion

	Cohesion	
Attractiveness	Low (ranks 6–8)	High (ranks 1–5)
High (ranks 1–3)	Ways & Means/Finance Judiciary/Judiciary	Appropriations/Appropriations
Low (ranks 4–8)	Banking & Currency/Banking & Currency	Interior/Interior Post Office/Post Office Public Works/Public Works Labor/Education & Labor

committees by stakes and scope, presented earlier. In other words, the two subject matter dimensions could place 14 committees and miss two.

CONCLUSIONS

In this exploratory study, two findings are of particular importance. First, strong House-Senate intercorrelations of committees dealing with the same jurisdictions argue for some subject matter effect: At least, they suggest an influence beyond the single committee, its group interaction, its chairman, or particular institutional constraints. And second, the two illustrative subject matter dimensions selected for the study are indeed capable of organizing varieties of attractiveness, membership, and cohesive behavior. Perhaps they can help reconcile and explain apparent contradictions between the single committee studies and the macrocomparative studies on the relationship between the attractiveness complex and cohesive behavior. And they indicate that at least some of the bewildering diversity of committees so frequently recorded may be explained by the permutations of attractiveness, membership, and behavior as shaped by subject matter. A provision summary matrix may then be suggested as in Table 18.5. By identifying major patterns within this diversity, it should be possible to highlight deviant cases requiring more detailed attention. The differences between the two Public Works committees and the curiously cohesive behavior of the Labor committees are cases that would be worth further study for this reason.

Note, further, that the scheme accords with Fenno's classification of committees by the predominant goals of members (1973). As committee subject matter varies by scope and stakes, it would be more suited to some members' goals than others. Members seeking congressional influence would desire committees dealing with subject matter of widespread congressional interest: i.e., committees of broad scope, whatever the stakes. Those seeking the making of good public policy may be drawn to those committees handling the most relevant, controversial legislation, which would tend to be the zero-sum committees, whether broad

Table 18.5
Provisional summary matrix

Stakes	Scope	Goals (Fenno)	Attractiveness	Membership	Behavior
Zero-sum	Broad	Prestige	High	More senior, stable	Less cohesive
	Restricted	Policy	Lower	Less senior, stable	Less cohesive
Positive-sum	Broad	Prestige	High	More senior, stable	More cohesive
	Restricted	Reelection	Lower	Less senior, stable	More cohesive

or restricted. And those looking toward a reelection fight may seek the positive-sum, distributive committees, whether broad or restricted.

One final comment may be in order. There are three widely reported ways of "accounting for" congressional behavior—each with its own considerable popular following and academic application. One emphasizes the desire to be reelected, and cites the distribution of pork, as well as congressional avoidance of controversial issues. A second emphasizes internal social processes: norms and sanctions, socialization, affective leadership, and a Senate Club. A third emphasizes ideology, cites a "Conservative Establishment," and explains assignments or a Rules Committee decision from that point of view. These three, of course, point toward the three separate congressional goals suggested by Fenno's comparative committee study. And the above analysis suggests, corroborating Fenno, that no *one* of these is sufficient for congressional explanation. With congressmen seeking satisfaction for different goals with different kinds of subject matter, some committees will more appropriately fit one explanatory mode than another. Thus Public Works may fit a reelection accounting; Appropriations a sociological accounting, and Judiciary an ideology accounting. So by classifying committees by subject matter, we may not only reduce some of the variety of past committee accounts, but may also point out some of the more fundamental variety that remains.

NOTES

1. Six of eight scholars responded to the questionnaire and five gave permission for their names to be used: John Bibby, Charles Bullock, Richard Fenno, David Mayhew, Robert Peabody. The panel was asked to classify the committees according to the dimensions set forth in Table 18.1.
2. It should also be noted that the attractiveness, seniority, and stability variables are highly intercorrelated in the House and strikingly so in the Senate—so much so that they may more usefully be treated in future committee analysis as a complex, rather than a number of separate attributes:

	House Intercorrelations	Senate Intercorrelations
Attractiveness & Seniority	tau = .68, p < .05	tau = .93, p < .001
Attractiveness & Stability	tau = .68, p < .05	tau = .79, p < .01
Seniority & Stability	tau = .57, p < .05	tau = .71, p < .01

3. Seven committees filed some minority party dissents: both Labor committees, both Banking committees, Ways and Means and Finance, House Public Works. These are all what we have called zero-sum committees. Committees highest in nonpartisan dissent (dissent by three or more individuals) include House Interior, House and Senate Judiciary, House Banking and Currency, and House Post Office. So the measure of nonunanimous roll calls is heavily, though not exclusively, reflecting partisan dissent.

Chapter 19

Controlling the Legislative Agenda

GARY W. COX AND MATHEW D. MCCUBBINS

Are committees agents of the House, of the majority party, or of no one but themselves? It is uncontroversial to say that committees are *in principle* agents of the House. It is, after all, the House that decides whether there will be any committees at all and, if so, determines their jurisdictions, staff allowances, party ratios, and everything else of consequence. The very word *committee* originally denoted a person (later, a group) to whom some charge, trust, or function had been committed.[1]

The argument arises over who exercises the power that the House undoubtedly possesses. The committee government model essentially argues that no one group or coalition is able to use this power effectively; it is so little exercised that committees might just as well be taken as autonomous. We argue, by contrast, that the most important function of the majority party is precisely to usurp the House's power to structure the committee system.

The rest of this chapter deals with three questions that naturally arise regarding our claims. First, how does the majority party use the structuring power of the House to influence the committee system? Second, what are the consequences of this structural power? Third, how does our view inform one's reading of the postwar history of the House?

THE MAJORITY PARTY AND THE COMMITTEE SYSTEM

Asking how the majority party structures the committee system entails two subsidiary questions: one about the instruments of control it uses and one about how its members can agree to their use. We consider both these questions in turn.

The Instruments of Control

In principle, the majority party might seek to control committees in the same way that management in other large organizations attempts to control subunits: by cre-

Source: *Legislative Leviathan: Party Government in the House* (Berkeley: University of California Press) pp. 253–73. Copyright © 1993 The Regents of the University of California.

ating and destroying them, by assigning them tasks and giving them the resources to accomplish those tasks, by regulating their personnel, and by providing for the review and revision of their decisions. Broadly speaking, each of these techniques is used by the majority party in the House. . . .

Creating and Destroying Subunits

The fundamental power of creating and destroying committees has, since the Legislative Reorganization Act of 1946, been used only sparingly in the House. In the . . . most important instances where this power has been used, however, it has been used to promote the interests of the majority party. . . .

Assigning Tasks and Resources

The majority party affects the tasks undertaken by committees by (re)defining their jurisdictions, by giving substantial agenda-setting power to committee chairs, by using the referral power, and by allocating staff and other resources among and within committees. . . .

[One] source of influence that the majority party has over the tasks that a committee takes up arises simply because the chairs of House committees and subcommittees have been endowed with substantial agenda-setting powers and are always members of the majority party. This condition means that most of the key decisions about what each committee will and will not consider are made by senior members of the majority party. To a first-order approximation, we can model events as if chairs had vetoes over what their panels considered.[2] The literature has focused on politically controversial uses of this veto power—that is, on cases where a chair vetoes a bill that a substantial portion of the majority party wishes to see reported to the floor. But for every such use of the veto, there are many more in which the bill vetoed is a proposal of some member of the minority party. Indeed, the attention drawn to "improper" use of the veto suggests the typical use: to weed out proposals from the minority party, along with unimportant or quack proposals, leaving only those which are innocuous or for which there is substantial support in the majority party or in the House as a whole.

In addition to setting committee jurisdictions and endowing their chairs with scheduling power, the majority party can also influence the tasks that committees take up through the referral power of the Speaker. A classic example is the 1963 Civil Rights Bill, "which was drafted somewhat differently for each chamber so that it could be referred to the Judiciary Committee in the House and the Commerce Committee in the Senate" (Oleszek 1989, 87). More recently, the majority party has made increasing use of multiple referrals, in tandem with complex rules, in order to control legislative outcomes (Bach and Smith 1988; Collie and Cooper 1989; Davidson, Oleszek, and Kephart 1988).

A final example of how the majority party influences committee agendas is the allocation of staff resources within committees. . . . By the early 1960s the Republicans were complaining loudly about their measly share of staff, which, by one account, was about one in ten.[3] But Republican complaints had only a limited impact: Minority staff never constituted more than 16.9% of all committee staff over the next decade and a half.[4] By the 1980s continued Republican complaints had resulted in a more substantial improvement: One-third of partisan committee staff were allocated to the minority party.[5]

Regulating Subunit Personnel

The majority party decides both how many total members each committee will have and what share of this total each party will get. It has used these powers throughout the postwar era to enhance its control of key committees. The power to set the size of committees was used to "pack" the Rules Committee in 1961, for example, thereby making it more representative of the party as a whole.[6] The power to set party ratios on committees has been used to give the majority party at least 60% of the seats on the control committees (Appropriations, Rules, Ways and Means, and Budget) in every postwar Congress.

The majority party has also influenced committee personnel through the appointment process. This includes both a general influence exerted through the promotion of those more loyal to the leadership . . . and more specific kinds of influence, as when the Democrats . . . attempted to coopt Boll Weevil [conservative Southern] Democrats by giving them positions on the Budget Committee (Rohde 1991, 47), and so forth.

Reviewing and Revising Subunit Decisions

Committee proposals must pass muster with several other bodies after they are reported. If they authorize the expenditure of money, they must be approved by the Appropriations Committee, which has extra seats for the majority party. If they need a special rule, they must be approved by the Rules Committee, which also has extra seats for the majority party (and, since the 1970s, a particularly close relationship with the majority leadership). If they are to be scheduled advantageously, they must please the majority leadership. Finally, if they are to be sent to the Senate or president, they must be approved on the floor of the House itself—under terms and conditions that are largely set by the majority party leadership and (sometimes) the Rules Committee.

Can the Majority Party Act?

Even with all the instruments that the majority party has at its disposal to control committees, the question remains whether the members of the party can agree on their use often enough to establish any real control. In answering this question, it helps to recognize that the majority party exerts two different kinds of control. One is a kind of "automatic pilot" control: Give members of the majority party significant advantages at every stage of the legislative process, and then let that process go, confident that the result will be substantially biased to the majority side of the aisle. Because this kind of control entails giving individual members of the majority party increased power and resources—more seats on powerful committees, a bigger say in setting the legislative agenda in committee or on the floor, more staff, and so forth—there is an automatic constituency for much of the structure that the party sets up (namely, the beneficiaries of that structure).

A second kind of control is active: disciplining those members or committees who have failed to produce the kind of legislative proposals of which the majority party can consistently approve. There is certainly some of this kind of control—committees are purged (e.g., HUAC [House Un-American Activities Committee] in 1949), packed (e.g., Rules in 1961), stripped of jurisdiction (e.g., Ways and Means in 1975), discharged (e.g., Ways and Means in 1954), and so forth—but the primary idea is to bias the committee system enough in the majority party's favor so that real difficulties seldom arise. Thus, active control does not appear, and does not *need* to appear, very often.

Active control in the form of sanctions may appear infrequently for a variety of reasons. Of course, the typical story in the literature is that sanctions such as violating a member's seniority or discharging a committee's bill are rare because parties are weak and committees strong. This is one possible explanation for the paucity of sanctions, but there are many others.

We have already considered the case of seniority violations at length in chapter 2 [of Cox and McCubbins 1993], so we focus here on discharge petitions. The main point is that, from the infrequency of successful discharge petitions alone, one cannot validly infer that committees are strong or protected by norms of reciprocity. It is just as possible that the committee, once the discharge petition was filed, took whatever actions were necessary to forestall the petition's passage—commencing hearings, say, or incorporating certain provisions in a related bill. These possibilities have not been systematically investigated in the literature, so we do not know for sure what the impact of discharge petitions has been; all we know is that few of them have actually acquired enough signatures to discharge.

The more general point is that active sanctions in any system are applied most when there is uncertainty about their application. If the balance of power between leaders and followers is well understood, then the difference between what is possible and what is not is well understood, and sanctions are incurred rarely and meted out rarely. If, by contrast, there is uncertainty about what can be got away with, then probings of the boundaries of acceptable behavior can be expected, with consequent sanctions. So the frequency of sanction may depend more on uncertainty than on centralization of power.

When the necessity for active control does appear, the majority party often seeks to lessen the potential that the party will split by putting changes in the sessional rules or other omnibus devices. Thus, for example, the 21-day rule for discharging the Rules Committee was adopted in the Eighty-first Congress by incorporating it in the sessional rules, the Democratic Caucus having previously voted to bind its members to support said rules (Robinson 1963, 64). . . .

THE CONSEQUENCES OF STRUCTURAL POWER: THE LEGISLATIVE AGENDA

In the previous section we sketched out some of the primary tools with which the majority party might seek to influence committees and made a distinction between automatic pilot control and active control. Much of the literature concentrates on the paucity of active control by the majority party as evidence that, to borrow a phrase from Gertrude Stein, there is no there there. But this inference ignores automatic pilot control. If all of the most important agenda-setting positions are staffed by members of the majority party, then the legislative agenda will certainly be affected. It will, at the very least, be dominated by the interests of those members of the majority party endowed with scheduling power. It may even reflect some sort of collective agenda of the majority party, to the extent that the majority party leadership is influential.

Is the legislative agenda in fact dominated by the majority party? Is the set of bills making it out of committee something like a majority party agenda? How could one tell if it was? . . .

Sponsorship and Committee Reports

In this section we consider evidence bearing on two questions: Who sponsors the bills that are reported from committee? And who dissents from the majority opinion in committee reports?

To answer the first of these questions, we have randomly sampled about one hundred reported bills from four Congresses—the Eighty-second, Eighty-third, Ninety-second, and Ninety-seventh—and ascertained for each such bill the party of the member(s) who introduced it. Prior to the Ninetieth Congress no more than one member could sponsor a given bill, so the difference between the majority and minority party can be given simply by the percentage of bills in the sample that were sponsored by members of the minority party. As it turns out, this figure is 26% for the Eighty-second Congress (controlled by the Democrats 234–199) and 13% for the Eighty-third Congress (controlled by the Republicans 221–213). A loss of only 13 seats thus reduced the Democratic sponsorship rate from 74% of all sample bills reported from committee to 13%.

After the rules change allowing more than one member to sponsor the same bill, one can no longer divide bills into just those sponsored by Democrats and those sponsored by Republicans; many bills have mixed sponsorship. In the Ninety-second Congress, for example, 22% of all sampled bills were sponsored solely by Republicans, 24% solely by Democrats, and 54% by both Republicans and Democrats. The analogous figures for the Ninety-seventh Congress were 12.4%, 40.1%, and 46.7%.

These figures are, of course, ambiguous. Because the bills were chosen at random, they include bills important and unimportant, partisan and nonpartisan, controversial and uncontroversial. The mere fact of sponsorship, moreover, does not tell us much about the political content of the bills involved. Nonetheless, the figures for the Eighty-second, Eighty-third, and Ninety-seventh Congresses all suggest the predominance of the majority party in the setting of the legislative agenda. This predominance was well recognized by members of Congress in the 1950s, especially concerning important legislation. As Clapp (1963, 157) put it: "In the House . . . few members succeed in getting their names on important legislation. Junior members of the House have little chance for such fame, and members of the minority party virtually none."

Another clue to the partisan coloration of committee bills is the lodging of dissenting or minority opinions with the committee report. We have investigated each of the 5,789 reports issued from committee in the Eighty-fourth, Eighty-sixth, Eighty-eighth, Ninetieth, Ninety-second, Ninety-fourth, Ninety-sixth, and Ninety-eighth Congresses, identifying all members who dissented from the majority report.[7] The percentage of reports from which at least one Democrat dissented is small: 4.4% on average. Not surprisingly, in view of how few reports are dissented from by any Democrat, the average percentage of committee Democrats endorsing committee reports exceeds 99%.

The percentage of bills on which Democrats dissent is smaller in each of the Congresses examined than the corresponding percentage for Republicans. Over all eight Congresses, Republicans dissented more than twice as frequently as Democrats (10.2 versus 4.4%). The contrast between the parties is even greater if the number of dissidents is taken into account: when committee Republicans dissented, on average 36% joined the dissent; when committee Democrats dissented, on average only about 5% participated.

A final indication of the dominance of the majority party in committee is simply members' allocation of time. Davidson (1981b, 127) notes: "It is no accident that, according to the [1977] Obey Commission, Democrats tend to spend more time in subcommittee and committee sessions, while Republicans tend to devote more time on the floor. In other words, those not in control at the committee stage find in floor debate a chance to appeal to the court of public opinion."[8]

Deference to Committee Proposals

In the previous section we showed that most bills reported from committee are sponsored by members of the majority party and come to the floor with the support of almost all of the majority party's committee contingent. In this section we investigate how committee bills are received on the floor. Our general expectation is that the set of bills making it to the floor, having already run a gauntlet of veto points guarded by important majority-party interests, will appeal to a substantial segment of the majority party.[9] The minority party, by contrast, having had less of a say in what committees consider to begin with and less of a say in what they actually report to the floor, will be less pleased. Members of the minority party will be more likely to push amendments, call for roll calls, and in other ways show their displeasure with committee decisions.

The evidence of displeasure on which we focus here is simply voting against the position taken by a majority of committee members.[10] We have computed a series of committee support scores for each MC in each of the Eighty-fourth, Eighty-sixth, Eighty-eighth, Ninetieth, Ninety-second, Ninety-fourth, Ninety-sixth, Ninety-eighth, and Hundredth Congresses. For example, the Agriculture support scores for the Ninety-sixth Congress were calculated as follows: for all 31 roll-call votes pertinent to bills reported out by the Agriculture Committee, the position (aye or no) adopted by the majority of the committee was identified; each member's score was then computed as the percentage of times that the member's vote agreed with the committee's position.[11] These scores tap the "deference" that each member accords to the Agriculture Committee, in that members who more frequently defer to the committee's judgment (as expressed by the majority of its members) will have higher scores. They may also tap constituency similarities, ideological similarities, and other bases of agreement between the member and the committee.

We have computed the average committee support score among two classes of member—noncommittee Democrats and noncommittee Republicans—for each committee in each of the nine Congresses in our purview. The results for all exclusive and semiexclusive committees (except Budget and Rules) are displayed graphically in Figures 19.1–19.12. . . .

The data displayed in Figures 19.1–19.12 and Table 19.1 show that the typical committee receives a fairly high level of support from noncommittee Democrats and substantially more support from them than from noncommittee Republicans. Moreover, Democratic support also varies less from Congress to Congress than does Republican support.[12]

The primary exceptions to this characterization are Small Business, Veterans' Affairs, Armed Services, and HUAC. The first two of these are service committees with client groups (small business owners and veterans) that give the Republicans considerable electoral support. Thus, the average level of support among noncommittee Republicans is very high—86.5% for Small Business and 91.0% for Veterans' Affairs. Nonetheless, the level of support among noncommittee Democrats is even higher—96.3% and 96.7%, respectively. Thus, although the difference in support levels between the two parties is not very large, it can hardly be maintained that these committees are doing anything that seriously displeases the majority party.

Armed Services and HUAC are a different story, however. They are the only two committees whose decisions were consistently supported more by Republicans than by Democrats. . . . We do not think that there is any denying that these two committees have been somewhat "out of control" from the majority party's viewpoint. But the party has certainly *tried* to rein these committees in. Indeed, along with the control committees, Armed Services and HUAC have come in for some of the most obvious attempts at restructuring and realignment. . . .

THE CONSEQUENCES OF STRUCTURAL POWER: PUBLIC POLICY

If the majority party does control the legislative agenda, as suggested in the previous section, then what passes will also tend to have a partisan cast. . . . [Cox and McCubbins go on to argue that there have been substantial and clear cut policy consequences from partisan control of the House in the post—World War II era, especially in the realms of fiscal, spending, and welfare policy.]

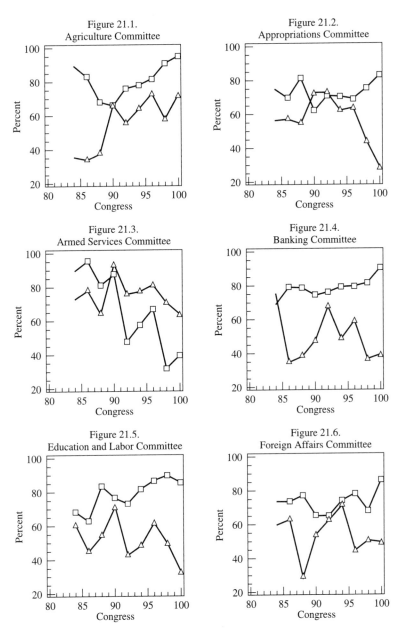

Figure 21.1.
Agriculture Committee

Figure 21.2.
Appropriations Committee

Figure 21.3.
Armed Services Committee

Figure 21.4.
Banking Committee

Figure 21.5.
Education and Labor Committee

Figure 21.6.
Foreign Affairs Committee

□ Average committee support score among noncommittee Democrats
△ Average committee support score among noncommittee Republicans

Figures 19.1–6
Committee leadership support scores, by committee.

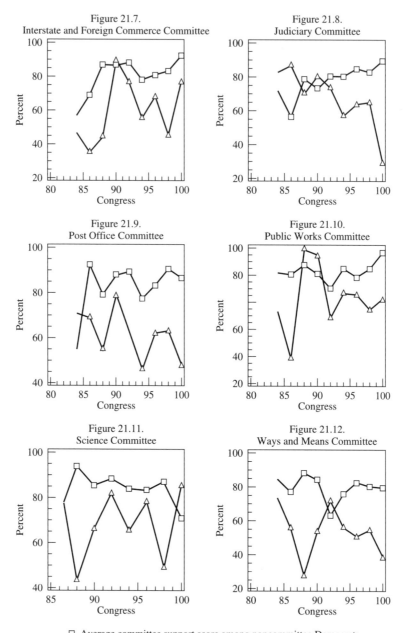

Figure 21.7.
Interstate and Foreign Commerce Committee

Figure 21.8.
Judiciary Committee

Figure 21.9.
Post Office Committee

Figure 21.10.
Public Works Committee

Figure 21.11.
Science Committee

Figure 21.12.
Ways and Means Committee

□ Average committee support score among noncommittee Democrats
△ Average committee support score among noncommittee Republicans

Figure 19.7–12
Committee leadership support scores, by committee.

Table 19.1

Average committee support scores, by party

Committee	Democrats		Republicans			Difference in overall averages
	Overall average	Std. dev.	Overall average	Std. dev.	N	
Banking	79.3	.06	50.3	.15	9	29.0
Education and Labor	79.1	.09	51.9	.12	9	27.2
Foreign Affairs	73.4	.07	53.2	.12	9	20.2
Ways and Means	79.8	.07	53.8	.14	9	26.0
Agriculture	81.5	.10	55.5	.16	9	26.0
Appropriations	74.6	.07	58.4	.14	9	16.2
Commerce	80.8	.12	60.5	.19	9	20.3
Post Office	82.4	.12	61.3	.11	9	21.1
Dist. of Columbia	77.3	.11	62.3	.20	8	15.0
Public Works	83.9	.08	63.0	.24	9	20.9
Gov. Operations	84.2	.10	66.0	.21	9	18.2
Interior	84.6	.08	66.6	.15	9	18.0
Merchant Marine	86.6	.07	67.6	.17	9	18.9
Judiciary	77.7	.10	67.9	.18	9	9.8
Science	84.1	.07	68.8	.16	8	15.3
House Admin.	81.7	.20	72.2	.27	7	9.5
Armed Services	75.6	.18	82.3	.07	9	−6.7
Small Business	96.3	.06	86.5	.11	4	9.8
Veterans	96.7	.05	91.0	.13	9	5.7
HUAC	72.2	.23	91.2	.08	4	−19.0

Note: The analysis pertains to nine Congresses: the Eighty-fourth, Eighty-sixth, Eighty-eighth, Ninetieth, Ninety-second, Ninety-fourth, Ninety-sixth, Ninety-eighth, and Hundredth. For each of these Congresses we have computed a series of committee support scores for each member and then averaged these scores among noncommittee Democrats and noncommittee Republicans, as described in the text. The "overall averages" given in the table are (simple) averages of the Congress-by-Congress averages. The standard deviations give an indication of the extent to which average levels of support for a committee vary from Congress to Congress. Column 5 gives the number of Congresses for which average committee support scores were calculated (in some Congresses some committees did not exist, or no roll calls were taken on the committee's bills). The committees are presented in ascending order of their overall average Republican support.

COMMENTS ON THE POSTWAR HOUSE

The picture of the postwar House . . . is one in which the majority party acts as a structuring coalition, stacking the deck in its own favor—both on the floor and in committee—to create a kind of "legislative cartel" that dominates the legislative agenda. The majority party promotes its agenda-setting advantage in two basic ways: by giving its members greater power to veto legislative initiatives; and by giving its members greater power to push legislative initiatives onto the floor.

Although these powers might be thought of as two sides of the same agenda-setting coin, they also inherently in tension: One person's power to push proposals to the floor may run up against another's power to prevent them from getting there. Such conflicts could be resolved on a case-by-case basis, of course, but it is also possible to give a general advantage either to those wishing to enact legislation or to those wishing to prevent legislation. For example, the requirement that expenditures be authorized *and* appropriated separately; the necessity for many major bills to be both reported from committee *and* given a rule by the Rules Committee; and the requirement that two-thirds vote for suspension of the rules—all these conditions improve the chances of those seeking to stop legislation relative to the chances of those seeking to pass legislation. Depending on what structural choices are made, rather different systems of agenda control can result with different consequences for internal party politics.

NOTES

1. In the American colonies the term *committee* was often used as a synonym for "representative" (McConachie 1898).
2. Of course, the strength of this veto varies by position (full committee chair or subcommittee chair) and time (pre- or postreform).
3. *Congressional Quarterly Almanac* 1963, 80; *Congressional Quarterly Weekly Report*, 8 February 1963, 151.
4. See Fox and Hammond (1977, 171); U.S. Congress, Joint Committee on the Organization of Congress (1965, 354); U.S. Congress, House Rept. 93–916, part 2, (1974, 358). Note that some staff were "nonpartisan"; the minority proportion of "partisan" staff would be higher.
5. Committee activity can also be influenced by the allocation of other resources. In 1947, for example, the Republican majority conferred subpoena powers on several committees in order to facilitate investigations into labor racketeering and—in the words of Adolph Sabath (D-IL)—"to scare our administrative agencies into impotence" (*Congressional Quarterly Almanac* 1947, 68).
6. Many other committees have also been expanded when the majority leadership saw fit to do so, although the link to party control has rarely been as clear as it was in the case of Rules (cf. Westefield 1974).
7. Members use many adjectives to describe the additional reports that they write or endorse, including *separate, additional, individual, minority,* and *dissenting.* Only the last two were counted as really "dissenting" from the majority report (and even then a small but noticeable percentage of "minority" reports do not so much dissent as provide a different perspective or different reasons for supporting the bill).
8. The dominance of the majority party over the committee stages of legislation is also reflected in data on recorded votes in committee. Parker and Parker (1985, 40–41), who study votes over the 1973–80 period for most committees, note that "nonunanimous procedural and final-passage votes tend to be partisan in nature." Indeed, they exclude these votes from their analysis because "to include these votes ... might strengthen the effect of partisan forces to the point that they obscure other salient influences in a committee's environment." Even after excluding these votes, Parker and Parker still find that *every* committee had a salient partisan cleavage in the period under study (249).
9. These is an important distinction to make between bills that form part of what might be called the majority party's agenda, defined here as bills that the party's leadership favors, and bills that do not form part of the party agenda. The expectation of

widespread support in the majority party is even stronger for bills in the party agenda. But even bills that are not in the party agenda were typically promoted by some Democrat and mustered enough support to get through committee, so that substantial majority party support is likely.

10. The evidence on amendment sponsorship (Smith 1988, 148) does not show a sustained impact of reform on Republican activity. Sponsorship may not be a good measure of who is really behind an amendment, however, since Republicans can get Democrats to "shill" for them. In the postreform era, it is mostly Republicans who vote for amendments (Rohde 1990). Statistics compiled by David Rohde show that Republicans called for 60% of all roll calls in 1969, 68% of all roll calls in 1979, and 74% of all roll calls in 1987 (personal communication).

11. By *majority of the committee* we mean the majority of committee members, not the majority party members of the committee. If the committee was evenly split on a roll call, as has happened on rare occasions, that roll call was deleted from the analysis. A member who paired in support of a committee's position was counted as supporting it. . . .

12. Nearly all of the differences in average levels of support pictured in Figures 19.1–19.2 and reported in Table 19.1 are significant at conventional levels of significance.

PARTY LEADERSHIP

Chapter 20

Is Party Leadership Personal or Contextual?

How important are political parties and party leadership in Congress? News stories on Congress focus attention on the congressional parties and their leaders. Newt Gingrich certainly received a lot of press as Speaker of the House, as did Trent Lott and Bob Dole as Senate Majority Leaders. But is this just sound and fury, signifying nothing? How important are these political actors?

The research literature is more divided on that topic than on nearly any other topic regarding Congress. Party is consistently found to be the best single predictor of roll-call voting in Congress, but party leaders are often portrayed as lacking power and the desire to exercise power. In part, this reluctance to emphasize the role of party leadership is because the U.S. Congress is far removed from the "responsible party model" underlying some conceptions of how strong parties and party leaders could operate in a legislature. Even more, the role of party leadership is dismissed in much of the literature because it is hard to study congressional leadership in a systematic manner. Indeed, studies often treat particular cases (a particular leader or a particular election to the leadership) without focusing on a larger issue or analytical question.

Political parties are the organizing mechanisms of legislatures. Legislative parties consist of officeholders who share common values and policy orientations, though parties differ in how cohesive they are. Parties seek to secure majority status in government, to identify national problems to put on the agenda, and to work towards the accomplishment of that agenda. Yet the legislative parties in the United States are able to operate with remarkable autonomy from their national party organizations and even from the president when he or she is from their party. The majority party tries to pass its legislative program in order to fulfill campaign pledges to the public and remain in office. It can pass its program fairly easily in a political system operating under the "responsible party model" in which all members automatically vote with their parties on issues central to the party's agenda, as in the textbook portrayal of Great Britain's parliamentary system. However, party discipline in the United States is generally weaker than in parliamentary systems, so the enactment of policy requires the effective exercise of legislative leadership.

The two basic functions of majority party leadership in Congress are coalition building and party maintenance (Sinclair 1983, 1). Coalition building is required to pass legislation when legislators vote on the basis of their reelection interests rather than just voting with the parties. Party maintenance is important because it is necessary to keep the peace among party members who have conflicting power and policy goals. The party maintenance goal serves as a reminder that there is more to effective legislative leadership than enacting the party's legislative agenda. Although the importance of party to individual members of Congress has varied over time, we can study congressional politics by starting with the belief that the party is driven in its pursuit of goals and agendas by its leadership.

What makes a legislative leader powerful? What role does the personal style of the leader play? Can the importance of personal style be eclipsed by institutional context? That is, does the exercise of legislative strategy depend more on the individual leader or on the legislative context? While some congressional leaders are considered to have been very strong, others have been characterized as quite weak. Are these differences attributable to personality factors or institutional arrangements? Or in the words of the old cliché, "Do the times make the leader, or does the leader make the times?" This platitude, however, begs another relevant question: Is leadership most effective when a resourceful leader acts wisely or when the context permits the leader's efforts to make a difference?

The early literature on party leadership assumed the "great leader" perspective and approached the question of congressional party leadership through the study of particular leaders and leadership succession battles. Leadership was viewed as personal, and leadership style and effectiveness were seen as the results of personality and political skill. That focus made leadership appear too individualistic to permit generalizations to be drawn, which might explain why later political science research has instead emphasized the contextual view of congressional leadership. The contextual approach has provided many insights, but largely neglects the possibility of leaders varying in style and efficacy within a given context. This suggests that leadership is best viewed not as the result of personality or context separately but as based on the conjunction of the two, as we argue below. Before explaining these different approaches to understanding the sources of leadership power, it is useful to consider changes in the congressional party itself.

PARTY LEADERSHIP WITHIN THE PARTY SYSTEM

Studies of congressional leadership inevitably have implications for the broader political parties literature. Thus the early literature focused on the general weaknesses of congressional party leadership along with the occasional exception created by a powerful personality. The U.S. system of weak party leadership was portrayed in this literature as a vivid contrast to the strong leaders under parliamentary systems of government and to the responsible party model. Now, however, congressional parties have become more cohesive and therefore better able to act as centralizing forces that exercise discretion in making and using institutional rules, and this has allowed for more assertive party leadership. As a result, the later literature focuses on the increase in the strength of congressional party leaders and congressional parties more generally.

Changes in Congressional Parties

David Rohde (1991), as reprinted in chapter 23, argues that parties inside and outside of Congress have become more ideologically cohesive, which has allowed for more assertive party leadership. Starting in the 1960s, the ideological bases of the parties began to polarize, resulting in more homogeneous congressional parties. As the Democrats took the lead in passing and enforcing civil rights laws and other liberal legislation, traditionally Democratic white Southerners began to vote for the Republican party, while newly enfranchised African Americans became voting constituents in districts represented by Southern Democrats. As Southern Democrats had to appeal to African-American voters to win reelection, their voting records became more like those of their northern colleagues. As a result of greater party unity, members delegated increased powers to the party leadership to advance a party program. Thus, the 1970s reforms put in place by Democrats strengthened the party caucus and party leadership (see also Rieselbach 1994). Republicans in Congress were affected by these changes in the party system as well (Connelly and Pitney 1994). The Republican caucus shifted geographically from the Northeast and Midwest to the West and South, becoming more ideologically conservative. In the early 1990s, Republicans frustrated by being members of the "permanent minority" turned to the more aggressive and policy-oriented leadership style of Newt Gingrich.

Upon attaining majority status after the 1994 elections, Republicans instituted reforms that continued the trend of increasing party leadership's resources. In order to facilitate rapid consideration of the provisions of the Contract with America, the leadership pushed reforms to centralize the normally fragmented policy formulation process by making committees more responsible to the party. The number of committees and committee staff were cut, a new steering committee to make committee assignments was created with increased leadership influence, seniority was violated in three instances to allow party loyalists to chair committees (see chapter 12), and the powers of committee leaders were curtailed by imposing six-year term limits on chairs and removing their power to cast proxy votes on behalf of absent members. A small Speaker's Advisory Group (SAG) even supplanted some of the powers of committees in the 104th Congress, but the resultant failure to include Democrats in the negotiation process made it harder to develop compromises with the Democratic president. One key to strengthening the party leadership was the support of the large freshman class, who believed that strong leadership would lead to the policy changes they desired. However, the Republicans stepped back from some of these changes in the 105th Congress. With the narrower Republican majority, committees regained many of their powers. The Speaker's Advisory Group was disbanded and replaced with a larger, more representative leadership group, including people from wings of the party which felt excluded from the SAG.

The Congressional Party Reconceptualized

These institutional changes have led to a reconsideration of the committee government view of congressional politics that dominated studies of the "textbook Congress" of the 1950s and 1960s. A literature based on theories of New Institutionalism (see chapter 1) emphasizes the importance of party leadership. For example, based on their study of the House Appropriations Committee, Kiewiet and McCubbins (1991) argue that committees are actually agents of party leadership and that committee memberships and the actions of committees have become increasingly responsive to the views of party caucuses.

An especially important book along this line is Cox and McCubbins's (1993) *The Legislative Leviathan*. It reevaluates the role of parties and party leadership, arguing that parties in the House are actually "legislative cartels" that govern the legislative process. The majority party creates the rules, controls the procedures, makes committee appointments, permits committee transfers, and sets the legislative agenda. As a result, the House of Representatives and its committee system are stacked in favor of majority party interests (see chapter 19). Members of the majority party are the key players in most legislative deals, and the majority party's agreements are facilitated and enforced by cartel rules and leadership. This advantages party members in advancing legislation they favor and in blocking legislation they oppose. The preferences of the majority party are integrated into public policy without pressure from party leaders because the party's preferences are incorporated into legislation at every stage of the process. During the years the Democrats were divided between Southern conservative and northern liberal wings, each faction could block the legislation it disliked most. Once the preferences of the Southern and northern wings of the party became more similar, the party could use its advantage in the legislative process to pass policies it favored.

The Cox and McCubbins argument is based on rational choice theories of organizations. They ask "why and how might a group of legally equal and often contentious legislators nonetheless create and maintain parties?" and answer that parties are "invented, structured, and restructured in order to solve a variety of collective dilemmas that legislators face" (83). Legislators can solve some of these dilemmas by creating "central agents" in the form of leadership positions, which is to say that party leaders are supposed to act on behalf of the legislators. These leaders are "political entrepreneurs" who: (1) bear the personal costs involved in supervising the House; (2) have individually targetable rewards they can give to legislators who cooperate with them along with punishments they can use on defectors; and (3) are themselves rewarded in some way for serving as leaders.

This new emphasis on the strong congressional party fits well with Republican party control of the House in the 104th Congress. The Republican party tried to dominate House proceedings, with committees often relegated to a lesser position. Yet the Republicans failed to pass many features of their legislative agenda because they did not work out compromises in committee that would have helped their proposals get through the Senate and be signed by President Clinton. As a result, and because the Republican majority in the 105th Congress was so slim that the majority party had less discretion, committees became more important again.

It is premature to say how this will affect the new scholarly view of stronger parties in Congress.

The Exceptional Senate

The emphasis in the literature on explaining the increasing strength and assertiveness of party leadership has focused almost exclusively on leadership in the House of Representatives. Senate leaders traditionally have been thought to be even weaker than their House counterparts. Senate rules protect the independence of all 100 members and leaders have few institutional resources to encourage senators to cooperate.

Levels of party voting also have increased in the Senate, and some retiring senators have cited partisan acrimony as one reason for leaving Capitol Hill. However, increased partisanship has not resulted in changed expectations of party leadership as in the House, nor in the delegation of greater powers to the leadership. The Senate continues to protect the prerogatives of individual senators (Sinclair 1989). Senate leaders are still regarded as "janitors in an untidy chamber" (Davidson 1985), relying on their personal skills to mediate among individual activists. For example, while provisions of the Contract with America quickly and easily passed the House in the 104th Congress, many provisions languished or died in the Senate, despite the effort of Majority Leader Dole to mediate between House conservatives and a number of moderate Republican Senators. Yet the shift in the scholarly perspective on the House leadership suggests that a reconsideration of the nature of Senate leadership may eventually occur.

PERSONAL LEADERSHIP

Political leadership is generally treated in the press as a function of the leader's personality. A great president is seen as possessing the personality necessary to be a strong leader. This popular view of the nature of leadership carried over to the early literature on congressional leadership.

Leadership Strength

The "great leader" perspective is best represented in the congressional literature by several studies on the Speaker of the House. In her early study *The Speaker of the House of Representatives*, Follett engaged in an historical analysis of the office and concluded that "the Speakership is not only an institution, it is an opportunity, in which men of strong character have shown their leadership" (1896, 64). Subsequent studies also took this view in documenting the evolution of the speaker's powers (Galloway 1961; Jones 1968; Peabody 1976). The emphasis on personal factors in leadership has also affected the study of congressional committees, as was detailed in chapter 16.

The personality interpretation of legislative leadership is particularly prominent in studies of Senate leadership. Huitt's (1961a) study of Lyndon Johnson's style as Senate majority leader took the view that leadership is highly personal

Table 20.1

Congressional leaders, 1953–97

Speakers of the House of Representatives

Joseph Martin (R–MA)	1953–54	(83rd Congress)	party lost House in 1954
Sam Rayburn (D–TX)	1955–61	(84th–87th)	died in 1961
John McCormack (D–MA)	1962–70	(87th–91st)	did not run for House in 1970
Carl Albert (D–OK)	1971–76	(92nd–94th)	did not run for House in 1976
Thomas "Tip" O'Neill, Jr. (D–MA)	1977–86	(95th–99th)	did not run for House in 1986
Jim Wright (D–TX)	1987–89	(100th–101st)	resigned in 1989
Tom Foley (D–WA)	1989–94	(101st–103rd)	lost House seat in 1994
Newt Gingrich (R–GA)	1995–98	(104th–105th)	resigned after 1998 election

Senate Majority Leaders

Robert Taft (R–OH)	1953	(83rd Congress)	died in 1953
William Knowland (R–CA)	1953–54	(83rd)	party lost Senate in 1954
Lyndon Johnson (D–TX)	1955–60	(84th–86th)	elected vice president in 1960
Mike Mansfield (D–MT)	1961–76	(87th–94th)	did not run for Senate in 1976
Robert Byrd (D–WV)	1977–80	(95th–96th)	party lost Senate in 1980
Howard Baker, Jr. (R–TN)	1981–84	(97th–98th)	did not run for Senate in 1984
Robert Dole (R-KS)	1985–86	(99th)	party lost Senate in 1986
Robert Byrd (D–WV)	1987–88	(100th)	became Appropriations chair
George Mitchell (D–ME)	1989–94	(101st–103rd)	did not run for Senate in 1994
Robert Dole (R–KS)	1995–96	(104th)	resigned to run for President
Trent Lott (R-MS)	1996–	(104th–)	

(Because of the large number of past congressional leaders referred to in this chapter, Table 20.1 provides a listing of Senate and House leaders). Johnson was the rare exception—the strong Senate leader. Although Huitt acknowledged constraints on leadership, he concluded that Johnson's leadership was largely based on his own personality and his approach to the position. As Johnson commented, "[t]he only real power available to the leader is the power of persuasion. There is no patronage; no power to discipline; no authority to fire senators like a president can fire his members of cabinet" (Huitt 1961a, 337).

In chapter 21, we reprint Stewart's (1971) comparison of Johnson with his successor Mike Mansfield to provide a strong example of studies that focus on personal differences in leadership. While many studies are biographical in their focus on an individual leader, Stewart explicitly contrasts the leadership styles of Johnson and Mansfield and explores the "effectiveness" of each. Like Huitt, Stewart emphasizes Johnson's skill in using his limited institutional resources to maximum effect as well as his aggressive use of informal powers to exercise a highly personalized, centralized leadership style. Mansfield, on the other hand, operated as a "coequal" with other senators. He allowed widespread participation and did not use many of the formal powers and party institutions on which Johnson relied. While Stewart concludes that environmental factors, such as the demands of the senators themselves and presidential leadership, are important in explaining the "effectiveness" of Senate leadership, the differences between Johnson's and Mansfield's use of resources to achieve party goals are quite stark and it is not a coincidence that these differences correspond to differences in their personalities.

Scholars of party leadership in the Senate have generally continued to emphasize its personalized nature (Patterson 1989), as evidenced by large style differences between later leaders. On the Republican side, Howard Baker's conciliatory leadership was followed by Bob Dole's more assertive partisanship (Baumer 1992). On the Democratic side, Robert Byrd relied on his mastery of parliamentary rules, while his successor George Mitchell exercised a more inclusive leadership style (Baumer 1992). Leadership is more individualized in the Senate than the House because Senate leaders lack the institutional resources available to House leaders.

Although the House leaders may have greater institutional resources and formal powers than those of the Senate leadership, House leadership patterns also vary. In his research on House leadership, Ripley (1967) classified Speakers of the House based on their "style of leadership." He identified three styles: the figurehead style, evident when the Speaker does not participate in major legislative decisions but defers to the president or to other House leaders; the collective style, apparent when the Speaker and other major figures in the party make decisions together; and the personal style, characterized by the Speaker making legislative decisions alone or in concert with the president. The personal style remains possible even in the contemporary House, as witnessed recently by Speaker Newt Gingrich in the Republican 104th Congress.

Strong leadership is even less frequent among the minority party in Congress. Jones (1970) offers the explanation that the minority leader has no incentive to innovate in policies, since the public is unlikely to credit the minority for innovation. The exception may be the situation of unified government where the minority power is able to act as the opposition party to both the president and the congressional majority (Connelly and Pitney 1994).

The most aggressive personal style for a congressional leader is when the leader goes beyond the usual coalition building and party maintenance functions and pursues an independent policy agenda. Congressional leaders do not generally have their own agendas, but the exceptions are fascinating. Lyndon Johnson had his own program in the 1950s, partly to build a base for his run for the Democratic presidential nomination in 1960. Democratic Speaker Jim Wright tried to use his position to oppose the Reagan administration policy on aiding Contra forces in Nicaragua. These actions went far enough beyond the usual functions of party leaders that they were viewed as excessive by many members and resulted in the selection of successors who would not pursue a separate policy agenda, as will be further discussed shortly.

Leadership Selection

If leadership depends primarily on personality, then the next natural question is how leaders are chosen. The early studies of leadership selection were of two main types. One portrayed leadership selection as routine with little competition, with leaders moving up a succession ladder when vacancies occur at the top—for example, party whips moving up to party leaders and party leaders becoming Speakers. The other treated the occasional leadership contest as an isolated political struggle between two individuals, relying on descriptions of the personal psychology of those involved and their strategic behavior during the selection contest. While enjoyable to read, most of this work is specific to particular leadership fights. The most important finding of this early work is that legislative parties have a high degree of autonomy, choosing leaders regardless of external pressures from national party leaders (Peabody 1976; Polsby 1963).

Leadership selection and succession can be based on personality and style. Leaders can be predisposed to particular leadership styles. Some are strident partisans and ideologues who excel at pushing a partisan agenda, while others are compromisers, expert at arbitrating differences to produce solutions. Still others are good at ameliorating conflict. Party caucuses are aware of these different styles and choose leaders with their stylistic differences in mind, except to the extent that Congress defers to a leadership succession ladder.

One intriguing generalization emerged from early systematic research on party leadership. David Truman (1959) developed the middleman hypothesis, arguing that an effective floor leader must be a moderate in the party voting coalition. The party leader not only should be an intraparty negotiator, but also should avoid being at one of the party's extremes. This prescription implies certain personal characteristics of the leader: nonideological, compromise-oriented, and adept at sensing the needs of different party factions in order to maintain party unity.

Truman's linkage of leadership selection and behavior is an important one that has generated further research testing its applicability. Thus Hinckley (1970) found that high party support in voting behavior is a prerequisite to leadership selection, although Sullivan (1975) concluded that the middleman hypothesis is correct only in regard to the House where the selection process precludes ideologically extreme mavericks. Yet there is no proof that leaders were moderate and/or were strong party supporters before becoming leaders, rather than becoming more moderate and voting more with their parties as a result of being selected as leaders.

If leadership is fundamentally personal, then an important question is what happens to the powers that a strong leader accumulates once that leader is no longer on the scene. To the extent that leadership power depends on the personality of the leader, the next leader may prove to be a weaker leader. Indeed, the successor will inevitably have a different personality, and therefore use the leadership resources differently. As examples, Johnson's accession to the vice presidency was followed by Mike Mansfield's milder style of Senate majority leadership (Stewart 1971) just as Wright's resignation from the speakership led to Thomas Foley's milder form of House leadership. These changes partly reflect idiosyncratic personality differences between successive leaders, but they often also have a more intentional aspect. Bader (1996) argues that successors learn from the successes and mistakes of their immediate predecessors. Furthermore, "excessive leadership" (a phrase coined by Charles Jones 1968) may create pent-up demands from followers for weaker central leadership along with greater power for fol-lowers, demands that can be met only if the new leader adopts a different form of leadership. This is not to argue that the next leader need be ineffective, just that a more conciliatory and collegial form of leadership may be required after a period of excessive leadership.[1]

Leadership is, of course, also examined in many nonlegislative settings—including studies of presidential leadership (Barber 1972), the personality of leaders of various countries (Hermann 1984; Winter et al. 1991), and the nature of leadership in the Supreme Court, besides the popular literature on how to achieve success in management situations. Some of these approaches may have implica-tions for the study of legislative leadership, but they have not yet been applied to the legislative arena.

CONTEXTUAL LEADERSHIP

The emphasis on personality in legislative leadership generally treats leadership as idiosyncratic. The interest in moving to broader generalizations has led to greater emphasis in the political science literature on how legislative leadership depends on the political and institutional context.

Elements of the Leadership Context

Context is variously defined in this literature, with different studies focusing on different aspects of the legislative context. These can be roughly categorized as the institutional context, the partisan context, and the agenda-related context of Congress (Strahan 1992, 201).

Institutional context
Institutional context is defined by constitutional forms, legislative rules and orga-nization, and norms governing members' behavior. Together these define the rewards leaders can offer to members for their cooperation, and these differ between legislatures.

United States legislative leaders are typically less powerful than those in par-liamentary systems where the leader of the majority party is the prime minister who is expected to enact the party platform. By contrast, the relatively equal status of members in Congress makes individual leadership more difficult, especially in the case of the Senate. The rules in Congress even permit individual members to offer amendments on the floor, with comparatively limited institutional resources available to leaders to influence members of their party. Outside of Congress, Jewell and Whicker (1994) have studied the effects of variations in institutional structure and leadership resources on state legislative leadership.

Although the institutional characteristics of Congress typically allow for little impact of individual leadership, this varies over time as the majority decides to give the leadership more power (Cooper and Brady 1981a; Rohde 1991). For example, the Democratic majority in the House moved to centralize power during the Reagan administration in order to act more effectively, as the Republican majority did in the 104th Congress (1995–96).

Partisan context

The partisan context includes factors related to the party system, electoral politics, the role of party organization in candidate recruitment, and most critically, the degree of unity or factionalism in the congressional party. The occurrence of divided government defines the partisan context of party leadership as well.

For party leaders, the number of fellow partisans in the chamber and their ideological cohesiveness are the strongest determinants of effective, or successful, legislative leadership (Brady, Cooper and Hurley 1977; Collie and Brady 1985; Ripley 1969a; Rohde 1991; Sinclair 1983). As we note earlier in this chapter, party cohesion is the result of the relationships between members of Congress and their constituents and of district homogeneity. Strong parties exist when each party's mass base is homogeneous, yet the bases of each party differ (Cooper and Brady 1981a). Under these electoral conditions, the legislators in a party are likely to be ideologically like-minded, the party can play a strong organizational role in the chamber, and legislators would be most likely to grant more power to their leaders.

This argument has an important corollary: A necessary condition for leadership power is the demand of "followers" for action. A critical feature of the context for leadership powers is the desire of the majority for an activist legislative agenda, which in turn derives from the nature of the party coalition. Strong party leadership is required to enact major new legislative initiatives, especially if there is a high level of conflict between the parties or if the majority party does not enjoy a wide margin of control. Under these conditions, the party caucus may vest unusual power in its leadership and/or might elevate to the leadership members who are known activists. Thus, the new Republican majority in the 104th House was willing to cede wide powers to its leadership in order to get its agenda through a highly partisan Congress.

The context may impact the minority party leadership even more than it does the majority party leadership. Jones (1970) finds that the minority party leadership is strongest when the president has been aggressive and strong since the minority party must rise to respond to the presidential initiatives (except in national crises when the country unifies behind the president).

Agenda-related context

The legislative agenda is also part of the context that affects leadership power. In their study of House Democrats, Froman and Ripley (1965) emphasized the importance of issues as part of the contextual setting and suggested the types of votes on which the party leadership is likely to be more effective. They concluded that leadership victories are more likely to occur when leadership activity is high, the issue is more procedural than substantive, the visibility of the issue and action is low, counterpressure from members' constituencies is lower, and state delegations do not join to make demands. That is, Froman and Ripley found that congressional party leadership activity serves as a counterbalance to other contextual factors. When all other contextual factors are operating against the likelihood of a leadership victory (especially on a substantive issue with high visibility), party leadership activity is most necessary to coordinate members.

Context and Style

The contextual view is well exemplified by Cooper and Brady (1981a) in their study of the speakerships of Joseph Cannon and Sam Rayburn, reprinted here in chapter 22. They generate four broad hypotheses to account for the different, yet equally successful, leadership styles of these Speakers. First, the institutional context is the primary determinant of leadership power. Second, no direct relationship exists between leadership style and effectiveness; both effectiveness and style are situational. Third, party strength is the primary factor determining the impact of institutional context on leadership behavior. Fourth, institutional context, rather than personal traits, primarily determines a Speaker's leadership style.

Cooper and Brady argue that the nature of the party system is most important for understanding the styles and effectiveness of congressional leadership. Under Speaker Cannon, the parties inside and outside Congress were homogeneous. Members of Congress were relatively like-minded with other members of their party and with their constituents. Thus, the demands of constituency and party were not in conflict and members would allow aggressive party leadership in order to fulfill the party agenda that they and their constituents desired.

By the time of Speaker Rayburn, the partisan context was quite different. The majority Democrats were split into liberal northern and conservative Southern factions both inside and outside Congress. Aggressive party leadership would threaten the policy preferences and electoral fortunes of either party faction. In this context, party maintenance was the main function of leadership. For example, Cooper and Brady observe that in the House at the time they were writing, party leaders "function less as the commanders of a stable party majority and more as brokers trying to assemble particular majorities behind particular bills" (1981a, 417).

Cooper and Brady's hypotheses have greatly influenced the subsequent study of parties and leadership in Congress. Rather than understanding leadership from the perspective of the leader's individual characteristics, many subsequent studies understand congressional leadership through the perspective of the members and their electoral situations. Leaders are seen as delegates of their membership (Fiorina and Shepsle 1989; Sinclair 1995) and only can act in ways members permit.

Taking that point further, Rohde (1991) argues that Congress is best understood as a "conditional party government." Unlike "responsible" parties in Europe, we are likely to see strong party leadership activity in Congress only when there is broad agreement on a party agenda. When such agreement exists, party leaders are expected to use their institutional powers to facilitate passage of the agenda. Members of the party who disagree with parts of the agenda would be expected to let the party majority work its will, lest they risk their committee chairmanships or choice committee assignments. But without the "condition" of a unified party, leaders will not assert a strong party agenda and instead will act to coordinate and facilitate members' achievement of their own goals.

In contrast to Cooper and Brady's hypothesis that institutional context is the primary cause of leadership style, Rohde argues that a homogeneous party permits an assertive leadership style, but does not automatically produce it (38). In the end, the leader must choose to exercise the powers granted by party members.

PERSONAL LEADERSHIP VIEWED IN CONTEXT

Although the usual debate is between whether legislative leadership should be seen as personal or contextual, a third possible position is that leadership depends on the interplay between personal and contextual factors. Actually two such arguments have been developed. One view is that a leader can temporarily exercise personal power beyond what the context suggests, which leads to a condition termed "excessive leadership." The other position is that personality cannot lead to strong leadership unless the context permits such leadership, although context by itself cannot create strong leadership unless the incumbent has the requisite personality. These two positions are somewhat contradictory, but both yield insights about the sources of leadership power.

Excessive Leadership

Some legislative leaders have developed power sources that made them independent of their majorities. Charles Jones (1968) describes this as "excessive leadership." This is personal leadership in the sense that the leaders used their positions to grab more power than their members actually support. If leaders abuse power in the eyes of followers, members can depose them or restrict their powers. Excessive leadership sometimes results in revolts and reforms, such as the 1910 revolt against the "czar rule" of Speaker Cannon (Galloway 1961; Jones 1968) and the 1961 floor vote enlarging the House Rules Committee in order to diminish the powers of its chair "Judge" Howard Smith (Cummings and Peabody 1963). The possibility of such revolts usually restrains leaders from exercising stronger leadership than the context permits. When the excessive leader has so much power that followers are reluctant to mount a direct revolt, at the next leader transition the followers can subtract leadership resources in reaction to the abuses of the previous leader. For example, Strahan (1990) and Reeves (1993) document how committees have limited the prerogatives of incoming chairs in response to perceived abuses by the departing chair.

Thus, past events or contexts influence the present context in what can be viewed as a cyclical fashion. The implications of this argument are fascinating. On one hand, it points to the fact that legislative rules often permit leaders to accumulate great powers, more powers than the membership would want one person to have. On the other hand, this makes legislative reform cycles inevitable, since there will always be the need to reduce leadership powers after periods of excessive leadership. For example, after conservative chairs during the 1960s used their positions to stifle junior members' policy preferences and desires to participate, the 1970s reforms restricted their powers by increasing the independence of subcommittees and making chairs into positions elected by the party caucus. Since then, elected chairs have had to be solicitous of member and party needs in order to be reelected (see the discussion of seniority reforms in chapter 2).

Similarly, after centralizing power to pass the Contract with America, Speaker Gingrich found such leadership hard to sustain in the Republican 105th Congress. At the beginning of the Congress, he accepted a House reprimand on ethical charges and paid a $300,000 fine. This, his very low levels of popularity in public opinion polls, his penchant for making decisions unilaterally, and some conservatives' frustration with his insufficient energy in pushing their agenda and his budget compromises with President Clinton created discontent in various factions of the leadership team and Republican caucus. In July 1997, a group of mostly young, conservative legislators, with the perhaps unintentional encouragement of other members of the leadership (particularly Whip Tom DeLay), discussed calling for a House vote to remove Gingrich as Speaker. For a lack of consensus on another candidate for Speaker, the "coup" fizzled. Allies urged Gingrich to spend more time on day-to-day management. In short, the post-coup Gingrich had to act as a more traditional Speaker. Dissatisfaction resurfaced in October 1998 after his capitulation to Clinton's budget priorities. He resigned when this was followed by unexpected Republican losses in the midterm elections. Gingrich successfully led Republicans to majority status, but could not demonstrate the leadership skills necessary to govern with a small majority and a Democratic president.

Innovative Leadership

Most of the time, the institutional structures and rules of Congress are quite stable, and members, including the leadership, make their strategic choices within the limits provided by these structures. But there are times when, due to internal or external pressures (see chapter 2), institutional structures and rules are changed. The pressure for changes upsets the previously stable institutional equilibrium. In his study of the role of personality and politics, Greenstein (1987) claims that the influence of individual leaders matters most under conditions of a "precarious equilibrium"—when the old institutional equilibrium has been upset, yet before a new equilibrium has been established. Leaders can define the situation most in an unstructured environment by redefining the situation, manipulating the agenda, framing the debate, and persuading others to implement the changes they desire. Greenstein's focus on a precarious equilibrium also serves as a reminder that there can be critical moments when strong leaders can provide innovative leadership.

Following Greenstein, Strahan (1992) argues that leadership matters under conditions where the situation is complex or ambiguous and allows the leader to define the situation. Under equilibrium conditions, leadership is constrained by the institutional environment and the demands of the followers. The "maintaining" leader facilitates the followers' achievement of their goals by helping them navigate political and institutional minefields, using the resources and techniques that are allowed by the followers.

Strahan contends that change occurs only when innovative leadership acts at a critical moment in which the contextual constraints on leadership are ambiguous or the developing conflicts require new or reformed institutions. At such critical moments innovative leaders can initiate changes in institutional structure or leadership style (see Table 20.2). Thus, context creates and limits opportunities for innovative leadership. For leadership to "make a difference," powers must be there for a leader to use, and the leader must be willing to use them. In "critical moments," innovative leaders can take advantage of changes in the usual operating mode of the institution (and perhaps help instigate those changes) so as to gain more influence.

The rejected leaders would be those who continued an old style of leadership despite the opportunity to produce real change. Speaker Cannon and Rules Committee Chair "Judge" Howard Smith became rejected leaders because they continued in their old patterns of leadership once it was no longer contextually appropriate. Similarly, House Speaker John McCormack (D-MA) was eased out in favor of Carl Albert (D-OK) partially because McCormack continued the old style of leadership, including deference to conservative committee chairs and resistance to reformers, despite the "critical moment" of the reform era of the early 1970s.

Without a "critical moment," leaders with an innovative style have little ability to change the institution as they desire and are, in Strahan's words, "frustrated visionaries." The frustrated visionary pushes for change, but does not have the opportunity created by disequilibrium to put those changes into effect. Newt Gingrich might have been described as a frustrated visionary had the Republicans remained the minority party in the House.

The difference the presence of an innovator makes in taking advantage of a critical moment can be seen by comparing the actions of Speaker Gingrich to those of the Democratic leadership during the 1970s reform period. Gingrich was active and influential before becoming Speaker. He sought ways to make the Republicans the majority party in Congress by crusading against the ethical lapses and perceived abuses of power by the Democratic leadership, by establishing

Table 20.2

Strahan's four leadership types

Contextual conditions	Leader type	
	Traditionalist	Innovator
Institutional equilibrium	Maintaining leader	Frustrated "visionary"
Critical moment	Rejected leader	Innovative leader

Source: Randall Strahan, "Reed and Rostenkowski: Congressional Leadership in Institutional Time." In *The Atomistic Congress: An Interpretation of Congressional Change*, ed. Allen D. Hertzke and Ronald M. Peters, Jr., (Armonk, NY: M.E. Sharpe, Inc., 1992), p. 207. Reprinted by permission of the publisher.

GOPAC to develop a "farm team" of Republican candidates to run for Congress, and by developing the Contract with America as a policy agenda on which Republicans ran for Congress. Once the Republicans took control of the House, Gingrich was able to institute reforms that centralized power in the party leadership at the expense of committees. In contrast, the Democratic leadership was not at the forefront of the 1970s reforms. Indeed it was liberals in the Democratic Study Group who pushed to increase the power of the leadership in hopes that a future Speaker would be able to take advantage of them and help to pass policies they desired (Davidson 1981a; Rohde 1991).

Strahan's argument is an attack both on the contextual view of congressional party leadership and on the assertion that leaders can influence leadership styles and institutional arrangements only at the margins. This perspective grants the importance of the legislative context but also recognizes that leadership success varies according to the style of leaders, a contention underlying so many case studies of congressional leadership.

CONCLUSION

Leadership is never easy to achieve, as is made clear by the endless stream of popular books for business executives on how to lead their organizations effectively. Leadership is even more difficult to achieve in a body of elites, where all the members consider themselves to have attained a top position because of their own abilities and feel they have been invested by others (here those who voted for them in their district) with the power to make their own decisions. Yet an organization as complex as a legislature cannot function without effective leadership. This might indeed be considered to be the "paradox of leadership in Congress": Leadership is essential in a setting where no one wishes to defer to the leadership of others.

Leadership is often seen as personal, due to the personality and style of the "great leader," and there is clearly support for this position in the congressional literature. More often, leadership in Congress has been seen as contextual, constrained by the institutional, partisan, and issue contexts. Yet studies that consider leadership to be primarily contextual are still prone to characterize particular leaders as strong or weak in a manner that is reminiscent of the personalized way in which media treats legislative leadership. After all, even if the ability of an individual leader is unlikely to be the primary cause of political outcomes, it is intuitively appealing that who individual leaders are and how they behave still matter in explaining party activity in Congress. In the end, the problem lies in the inability to address counterfactuals—we do not know how other individuals would have behaved in the same situation, nor how the specific leader would have behaved under different circumstances.

Our own reading is that congressional leadership is best understood as due to the interaction of personal and contextual factors, an interaction that is most evident when leaders' personalities make them go beyond what the context permits and allow them to take advantage of the context to increase their powers. The result can be cycles in leadership selection and behavior, as when the excesses of one leader result in less aggressive behavior by the next leader and when prolonged leadership lethargy results in the opportunity for more assertive leadership. Members contribute to this cycle too by selecting leaders whom they believe will be more or less aggressive, often in response to perceptions of whether they need a leader who is more or less partisan than their previous leader.

Another problem underlying the literature on congressional party leadership is the difficulty in measuring the success of leaders. Often a particular leader develops a reputation of being strong or weak, effectual or ineffectual, and the scholarly literature echoes this theme in describing that person. Yet there is no agreement as to how to measure the strength or success of legislative leaders. An occasional piece develops an operational measure, but the deficiencies of the existing measures are all too obvious. In part this is because leadership is multidimensional. In part it is because successful leadership may involve behind-the-scenes action and strategizing which cannot be directly observed. In any case, this is an area where systematic analysis would be useful.

An important theme of this chapter is the need for inequality in an organization of equals. In order for a legislative body to function effectively, it is necessary to have leaders who are able to use the rules to push an agenda. One important matter is the nature of this agenda—if it is the party's agenda or only the leader's agenda. The instances of leaders using their power to push their own agendas often result in rejected leaders. This returns us to the main functions of majority party leadership discussed in the beginning of this chapter—coalition building and party maintenance. Coalition building is important if bills are to be enacted through a legislative process, but party maintenance is equally important. Leaders who pursue their own agenda are ignoring that party maintenance function, often at the risk of maintaining their leadership positions.

As is often the case, a further permutation involves the differences between the U.S. House and Senate. It is obvious to all members that the large size of the House requires effective leadership if the body is to be able to function. It is less obvious to Senators that leadership is required for that smaller chamber to function effectively, so it has been common to have Senate leaders who predominately serve as coordinators. Leadership becomes even more difficult when Senators act as if they are ambassadors from semisovereign states, as media hounds, or as presidential contenders. The Senate can process legislation without assertive leadership, but assertive leadership is more necessary in defending Senate positions and prerogatives when dealing with the House and the president. Furthermore, assertive leadership may be becoming necessary even in the Senate, now that individual senators are becoming more aggressive in using their stalling tactics (such as filibustering and placing holds).

The differences between the majority party and minority party leadership are considerable, particularly in the House. The majority leadership in the House can generally work through the Rules Committee to control the rules of debate on individual bills, allowing the minority leadership little ability to modify legislation or to obstruct. By contrast, Senate rules allow for substantial influence and obstruction by a cohesive minority, as when Senate Democrats stalled all legislation in 1996 until the majority Republican leadership permitted a vote on raising the minimum wage. While these differences are fairly apparent, much more study of the minority party leadership in Congress is appropriate. The Republicans were the minority party in the House for such a long time (1955–94) that it became difficult to differentiate features of the minority party leadership from features of the House Republican leadership. With the Democrats becoming the minority party in 1995, we can compare the Republicans as the minority party prior to 1995 with the Democrats as the minority party to develop more generalizations about the contemporary minority party.

In the end, leadership in a legislature is centrally related to the role of parties in that legislature. When the parties defer to committees for agenda setting and policy formulation, party leadership takes on a minimal, coordinating role mainly facilitating the consideration of bills proposed by the committees. However, when parties are the central actors in developing policy, the leaders must accept a more assertive role in agenda setting, policy formulation, and interactions with the president and the public. The strong party government model requires strong party leaders. Thus, not only does leadership depend on the conjunction of personality and context, but we would argue that party government does too.

NOTE

1. This followership argument fits well with the more general match theory in political psychology where leader traits must match the needs of followers. Thus, different leadership styles are necessary depending on the needs of followers at different times.

Chapter 21

Two Strategies of Leadership: Johnson and Mansfield

JOHN G. STEWART

The consecutive incumbencies of Lyndon B. Johnson and Mike Mansfield as leaders of the Democratic majority in the Senate illustrate two strikingly different approaches to the same job.[1] A product partially of their individual notions as to the proper role of the party leadership, as well as their respective techniques for executing that role, these differences also reflected the pressures of the political environment on Johnson and Mansfield in their development of a strategy of party leadership. This analysis will attempt to describe the opportunities for control of the senatorial party which are available to the majority leader, as well as the limited effectiveness of this position.

THE LEADERSHIP OF LYNDON B. JOHNSON

Expressed in baldest terms, Lyndon Johnson's tenure as majority leader of the Senate (1955–60) is likely to stand for some time as the classic example of an elected party leader who with unusual zeal, dedication, and skill sought to control the realistic choices open to senators in such a way that a sufficient majority saw their immediate political interests better served by supporting the senatorial party program than by opposing it. Johnson will be remembered not only for his efforts to wring the last ounce of effectiveness from his meager store of institutionalized power but also as a leader who set about diligently augmenting these fragments of power in a number of informal and highly personal ways. He set for himself no less an objective than *running* the Senate, in fact as well as in theory, by wielding decisive influence in generating majority support for the issues he permitted to come before the Senate for decision.

His election as leader of the senatorial Democrats coincided with the party's loss of the presidency to the Republicans. But the presence of Dwight D. Eisenhower in the White House provided Johnson with a crucial measure of independence and

Source: *Congressional Behavior,* ed. Nelson W. Polsby (New York: Random House, 1971) pp. 61–76, 87–88. Reprinted by permission of the author.

flexibility usually denied a majority leader of the president's party. Operating without the constant pressure and the inevitable restraints imposed by the obligation to push forward the legislative program of his party's president, Johnson was in a position to exercise greater personal discretion in picking his battles, choosing his tactics, and defining for the Democrats what would comprise an acceptable outcome. And he made full use of this relative independence and flexibility. Although Johnson was also denied the political leverage which a Democratic president might have provided from time to time in support of presidential legislative initiatives, the assets of flexibility and independence more than compensated for this deficiency (whereas Mansfield would have probably discovered the absence of presidential leverage to have been a serious handicap).

As Democratic leader, Johnson's most pressing challenge was to identify areas of agreement between the northern and Southern factions of the party. He recognized that unless a minimum of approximately 40 Democratic votes, necessarily drawn from the ranks of both North and South, could be delivered on most roll calls, his ability to control the outcome of issues would be seriously impaired. Grounds for common action had to be established. Johnson attacked this problem with the conviction that the interests of reasonable men, even northern and Southern Democrats, could be served simultaneously if an affirmative effort was made to structure each legislative encounter in a way which recognized in some manner the legitimate interests of those senators most interested in the pending issue and which offered those senators a basis for justifying and defending their vote.

"Party loyalty" in itself was seldom sufficient, especially for Southern Democrats who often acted as though their political survival depended upon a posture of opposition to the national party. There was, moreover, no Democratic president to dramatize more forcefully the need for party unity and support. Johnson knew he would have to produce additional reasons in order to convince a senator to follow his party's leadership, reasons which spoke primarily to a senator's political interests and standing in his state or his position within the Senate. He therefore sought to develop for any given legislative issue: (1) the methods to identify the vital interests of a majority of the senators, (2) sufficient political leverage to take account of these interests through bargaining and accommodation among the contending parties, and (3) the ability to control the parliamentary situation, especially on the Senate floor, so that these accommodations would not be undone by pressures from other sources. The effect of this strategy of leadership went beyond closing the traditional breach between North and South within the Democratic party; its use in lining up any senator's vote was equally feasible.

In accumulating the resources to render this strategy operational, Johnson drew from two basic sources: (1) the institutionalized powers at his disposal as majority leader and (2) the influence developed through his personal involvement in almost every aspect of senatorial life. Looking first at Johnson's institutional powers, his election as Democratic floor leader also brought with it the chairmanship of the Democratic Conference, the Policy Committee, and the Steering Committee. From each of these formal assignments he sought to extract a maximum contribution to the total bundle of resources he needed to sustain his three-pronged strategy of leadership.

Floor Leader

Although Johnson's techniques for controlling events on the Senate floor will be discussed below in greater detail, it should be noted at this point that his only recognized prerogative as floor leader was the traditional right of recognition by the chair over the competing claims of other senators. This permitted Johnson to seize the parliamentary initiative whenever he desired, but it did nothing to ensure the outcome of the issue at hand.

Party Conference

The Democratic Party Conference is composed of every Democrat senator. . . . Johnson viewed the conference as a place ill suited to execute his highly personalized strategy of leadership. During Johnson's years as leader the conference met primarily to ratify his selections for party officers, party committees, and standing committees and to provide an appropriate platform for dissemination of his "state-of-the-union" message presented at the opening of a congressional session. Given his strong distaste for any device which could exacerbate and highlight differences within the Democratic senatorial party, these meetings were infrequent: From 1953 through 1958 a total of only five Party Conferences were held. . . .

Policy Committee

Traditionally charged with drawing up the schedule of legislation on the Senate floor rather than formulating specifics of party policy, the Policy Committee during Johnson's regime served several additional functions. Its regular membership of seven Democrats appointed by the majority leader included a hard core of independently powerful senators whose cooperation, or at least whose acquiescence, was required for the successful execution of the majority leader's major strategems and tactics. The members generally carried over from one Congress to the next. In this sense the Policy Committee served as a council of major power holders of the Democratic senatorial party. . . .

Johnson also saw the Policy Committee as capable of providing the party's major geographical and ideological factions with a recognized position in his leadership system. Although distribution on the Policy Committee did not necessarily correspond with a faction's numerical strength in the party, the imbalance on the committee against the more liberally disposed Democrats in comparison to their numbers in the party became severe after the Democratic landslide in the 1958 elections. Johnson responded by inviting the three freshmen members of the Legislative Review Committee to sit ex officio with the Policy Committee in its deliberations (the whip and the secretary of the Party Conference already met with the committee as ex officio members). . . .

In practice the Policy Committee did little more than formally ratify scheduling decisions which in most cases Johnson had already made on the basis of more informal consultations with the minority leader, chairmen of standing committees, and other senators involved with the legislation under discussion. But the comments of Policy Committee members on the bills Johnson proposed to call from the calendar helped him refine his tactics and avoid pitfalls during the floor debate. The major factions within the party represented on the committee were also afforded a final opportunity to voice their feelings in a confidential setting. In the event of unforeseen difficulties, the majority leader could use this safety-valve procedure to delay legislation until the problems had been worked out to Johnson's satisfaction.

In summary, the operations of the Policy Committee, together with the work of its staff, contributed primarily to two components of Johnson's three-pronged leadership strategy—the identification of the interests of major senatorial factions and the control of the parliamentary situation on the Senate floor.

Steering Committee

Composed of 15 members selected by the majority leader, the Democratic Steering Committee met principally during the opening days of a new Congress to assign Democratic senators to the various Senate committees. Although the Steering Committee made the formal assignments, the committee members seldom ignored Johnson's recommendations.

The standing committees provide more than an arrangement to handle the Senate's work load. Given their recognized authority in determining substantive policy, they also represent important allocations of power within the senatorial party and the Senate. The process of assigning senators to the committees distributes this power in a way which can affect how the party leadership is able to function. For example, a Committee on Appropriations controlled by Johnson's allies was a distinct asset; one controlled by his critics would have been a major handicap. It was, therefore, not surprising that Johnson sought to exercise tight control over the assignment process.

Johnson also viewed each committee assignment as an opportunity for augmenting his personal resources for bargaining and negotiation on other issues. A desirable assignment could reward a senator for past support and assistance, or, more likely, establish a fund of credit to be drawn upon in the future. In addition, the distribution of cooperative senators among the committees expanded Johnson's communication and intelligence system: A strategically placed ally could help guide a bill still in committee or suggest the elements of subsequent negotiation which would ensure its passage on the Senate floor. Finally, assignments to the major standing committees provided one important measure of the party leadership's responsiveness to the interests and concerns of individual senators. Johnson's decision in 1953 to guarantee every senator, regardless of seniority, at least one major committee assignment reflected, among other things, a conviction that the choice spots should be available to all members of the party and not remain solely the province of the senior senators. This decision also served to advance Johnson's standing among the more recent members of the Senate. . . .

In summary, the activities of the Steering Committee, although limited to the early days of any Congress, supported all aspects of the Johnson strategy of leadership. The work of the committee was especially valuable in helping Johnson accumulate political resources and other leverage to expend in bargaining and negotiation and in controlling the parliamentary environment by placing reliable senators on the crucial committees.

Finally, Johnson appointed the chairman and members of the Democratic Senatorial Campaign Committee. Charged principally with raising and disbursing funds to assist in the reelection of incumbent Democrats, the committee's duties were less related to the activities of the senatorial party and the party leadership than either the Policy Committee or the Steering Committee.[2] But by his appointments Johnson made sure the Campaign Committee was run by senators who were responsive to his judgments on channeling funds to senatorial races where the contributions would be appreciated by the recipients and would expand the majority leader's fund of personal credit. In short, the committee provided an informal source of influence which, in a given situation, could help Johnson achieve a particular tactical objective.

Johnson relied little on his whip, or, as he is also called, the assistant majority leader. . . . Johnson had no intention of handing these duties to anyone, not even a good friend . . .

The Extension of Influence

Despite Johnson's vigorous exercise of these formal prerogatives of leadership, he recognized clearly that such fragments of power could never provide the information, leverage, or access he needed to meet his expectations of control. He therefore developed a variety of more informal and personal techniques to build the influence that could compensate for the institutional deficiencies of the majority leadership.

Johnson believed that simply knowing more than anyone else about all facets of a legislative situation would generally prove to be decisive, first, in identifying the various interests of those senators who held the balance of power on a given bill, and, second, in designing the precise set of tactics which could capitalize on these interests. As noted above, the deliberations of the Policy Committee and the distribution of allies among the standing committees helped Johnson achieve his objective of knowing more than anyone else about the activities of the Senate. But his intelligence and communications system reached far beyond these bounds. Johnson himself ceaselessly roamed the Senate floor and the cloakrooms talking to senators and staff, listening, questioning, probing, and persuading. His principal assistants, particularly Majority Secretary Bobby Baker, scoured the terrain for useful reports, tidbits of information, or speculation. Various members of the Washington political community—executive branch officials, lawyers, newsmen, party officials—kept him abreast of developments beyond the immediate confines of the institution. Little escaped his notice. . . .

Other miscellaneous activities became part of Johnson's efforts to compensate for the lack of institutionalized power in the majority leadership. He apportioned office space in the Senate office building with an eye toward the level of cooperation a senator had displayed in the past or might be encouraged to display in the future. He willingly helped cooperative colleagues secure banquet speakers, locate additional staff assistance, or attend overseas conferences. Scarcely any aspect of senatorial life, however routine and seemingly removed from the formulation of national policy, escaped Johnson's watchful eye or his uncanny talent for translating these activities into resources which could be used in running the Senate according to the Johnson formula.

Floor Business

Johnson's maximum use of the prerogatives of the majority leadership and his diligent efforts to develop additional sources of persuasion and influence ultimately had a single objective—to control the senatorial party program when it reached the Senate floor. His extensive preparation and diligent attention to the minutiae of Senate life had little rationale unless Johnson could produce a sufficient majority when the crucial roll-call votes were taken.

Johnson viewed each difficult legislative encounter as a puzzle: Once one had identified all the pieces and knew their precise location, the rest was easy. By the time a bill reached the floor under Johnson's strategy of leadership, the solution to the puzzle should have been in hand. He did not view the Senate floor as a place for identifying or locating the various pieces; rather, the floor debate was the point in the legislative process for unveiling the previously determined solution and passing the legislation. It was, in short, on the Senate floor where the full impact of Johnson's strategy of leadership could be experienced and appreciated.

Working from estimates of voting strength provided by Majority Secretary Baker and consulting with committee chairmen and other key senators, Johnson would strive to identify as early as possible those senators who held the balance of power on the given legislation. His subsequent efforts could be focused on devising and executing the tactics which would capture these crucial votes. This would sometimes require substantive change to the bill itself and the adjustment of certain features of the legislation which the senators wanted passed. Some situations might call for commitments from the majority leader for his assistance on other legislation in which the crucial senators were interested. The prearranged absence of a senator or two or a well-timed parliamentary maneuver might be sufficient to secure the margin of victory.

In collecting the margin of votes necessary for victory, Johnson might concentrate his prefloor efforts in winning the support of an influential senator considered to be a likely opponent of the bill in question. . . . In these negotiations and consultations prior to the crucial roll calls, Johnson would not hesitate to approach Republicans for the winning votes if that was necessary. But while he consulted regularly with the minority leadership, he never relinquished his initiative or control of the legislative situation simply to encourage a more cordial bipartisan climate (a charge later directed against Mansfield). And once a sufficient majority had been counted, Johnson would seldom attempt to enlarge it: Why expend limited bargaining resources which might be needed to win future battles?

In each specific legislative situation Johnson followed the same guiding principle: Control the choices of senators in such a way that a sufficient majority would conceive their interests better served by supporting the majority leader than by opposing him. Seldom did a senator achieve all he wanted, but seldom did he go home empty-handed.

Due to his control of the legislative schedule through the Policy Committee and his ability to influence the shape of legislation through his allies on the various standing committees, Johnson could usually delay those bills deemed likely to run into serious difficulties on the floor until the necessary adjustments were made and a sufficient majority of the votes clearly identified. Johnson also regulated carefully the timing and pace of the floor debate, stalling for time when additional votes were needed and driving the issue to a conclusion when victory was assured. He became especially proficient in reducing the Senate's natural proclivity for lengthy discussion by limiting debate under the terms of a unanimous consent agreement specifying the precise time that a vote would occur. . . .

Ultimately this strategy of leadership depended on Johnson's ability to persuade other senators that their interests were irretrievably bound up in his objectives. This, in turn, called for a prodigious expenditure of energy in identifying relevant interests, in accumulating the currency of bargaining and compromise, and in man-to-man negotiation. . . .

But the Johnson strategy was not without its deficiencies, and these became more evident during the Eighty-sixth Congress, the last two years of his incumbency as majority leader. His willingness to accommodate a broad spectrum of interests in rounding up votes for a particular bill tended to blur the differences between the positions of the Democratic majority in the Senate and the positions advocated by the Eisenhower administration. Following the congressional elections of 1958 which increased Johnson's majority from two to 30 Democratic seats, the larger contingent of activist northern and Western Democrats grew increasingly dissatisfied with his reliance on tightly structured accommodations and his preference for avoiding sharply partisan attacks on the Republican administration.[3] Moreover, in these latter years Eisenhower became more emboldened to veto even the more moderate Johnson bills, leaving the Democrats with neither programs-in-being nor sharply defined issues to take to the electorate in the presidential election of 1960. . . .

The deep involvement of the majority leader in a broad spectrum of senatorial activities and his efforts to establish centralized control of the senatorial party program also tended to restrict the opportunities of other senators for personal participation or responsibility in legislative decision making. They came to see themselves increasingly as minor functionaries on the execution of the majority leader's elaborate stratagems and maneuvers. Moreover, Johnson's constant attention to detail and the effectiveness of his intelligence and communications system often left them with a feeling that someone was constantly peering over their shoulders. Gradually the Johnson strategy exacted a toll in terms of their patience, good humor, and willingness to submit indefinitely to this style of hard-driving and intense leadership. Although few persons have ever questioned Johnson's strong personal attachment and loyalty to the Senate as an institution, it is ironic that his ability to structure the total legislative situation and generally dominate the actions of the senatorial party tended to detract from the Senate's traditional aura as a place which highly regarded and protected the prerogatives of individual senators to order and control their activities and decisions. This became a matter of increasing irritation to many senators in the final two years of Johnson's incumbency.

Finally, it is worth noting again the importance of the Eisenhower presidency in creating a political environment hospitable to Johnson's style of leadership. It seems clear that this added measure of personal discretion and independence which Johnson acquired by not having to bear responsibility for a presidential legislative program was an essential condition for his method of operations. His efforts could be less consciously directed toward rationalizing the separated powers of the executive and legislative branches and the disparities of interests between the national and senatorial parties and more toward producing legislative decisions which were viable in the senatorial arena alone. It is, however, also true that his efforts to produce *some* action by the Senate in a period of divided government helped avoid total stagnation and deadlock between a Republican administration and a Democratic Congress. In working to achieve this more limited objective, Johnson demonstrated that party leaders could exercise significant control over the activities and decisions of the Senate; in the process, he developed an impressive collection of techniques and procedures for maximum utilization of the leadership's formal powers and for augmenting these powers through personal and informal actions. Operating in a political environment with the potential for Democratic party leaders to exercise unusual initiative in managing the Senate, Johnson used his great talents and energy precisely to this end.

THE LEADERSHIP OF MIKE MANSFIELD

In nominating his senior colleague from Montana for his fourth term as majority leader, Lee Metcalf said of Mike Mansfield: "We have a majority leader who regards every senator as an equal in a peerage he respects. He enjoys the profound respect and deep affection of all who have served—not under him, the majority leader—but with him as a coequal."[4] This word, "coequal," sums up Mike Mansfield's view of his role as leader of the majority Democrats in the Senate: His principal duty was to maintain a system which permitted individual, coequal senators the opportunity to conduct their affairs in whatever ways they deemed appropriate. A more distinct departure from the approach of his immediate predecessor, Lyndon Johnson, would be difficult to conceive.

Having served as Democratic whip during the first four years of Johnson's tenure, a position of little responsibility in that highly centralized system of leadership, Mansfield nevertheless was the logical and undisputed choice to assume the party leadership in 1961. Reserved, almost austere in bearing, unobtrusive, considered a liberal but respected by the conservatives, and possessing immense pride and affection for the Senate as an institution, Mansfield's selection as party leader satisfied all major elements of the Democratic senatorial party. Moreover, after eight years of Johnson's hard-driving, take-charge leadership, many Democrats seemed eager for the reins to be loosened and for the leadership to encourage broader and less structured participation in the affairs of the senatorial party. "After eight years of Lyndon Johnson," one observer noted, "a lot of senators were just worn out."

During the Eisenhower years Johnson had provided the senatorial Democrats with a rallying point and an identifiable spokesman . . . But the election of John F. Kennedy as president and the continuation of the Democrats' 30-seat majority in the Senate (65 to 35 in the Eighty-seventh Congress) placed upon the majority leader, regardless of his identity, the primary task of moving the president's program and sharply reduced the need, and the latitude, for him to function as an independent and identifiable personality.

In addition, there existed a substantial backlog of Democratic legislative proposals which had never passed or which had been vetoed during the Eisenhower presidency. These proposals, principally in the areas of housing, education, minimum wage, depressed areas, and Social Security, seemed destined to occupy the Senate for most of the Eighty-seventh Congress. . . . Mansfield seemed ideally suited to perform this task effectively.

An enthusiastic admirer of John F. Kennedy, both the man and the president, Mansfield conscientiously sought to bring his legislative program before the Senate for prompt and favorable action. . . . In fulfilling what he considered to be both a personal desire and party obligation to move Kennedy's program, Mansfield did not attempt to retain Johnson's centralized system of party leadership or to employ his techniques for controlling the choices facing the senatorial party.

Indeed, in striking contrast to his predecessor's constant efforts to expand the power and influence of the majority leadership, Mansfield, free of the burden of implementing Johnson's high-powered strategy, refrained from using even the fragments of institutionalized power at his disposal, much less did he attempt the more difficult task of augmenting these limited resources. One could even say Mansfield deliberately abandoned recognized powers of the majority leadership. He encouraged a decentralization of leadership responsibilities and a reassertion of the Senate as an independent institution of government which, at least in the short run, appeared to run certain risks as far as the president's legislative program was concerned.

Operationally the Mansfield strategy produced almost a mirror image of Johnson's methods. Where Johnson saw the process of controlling the choices of senators as necessarily involving a rather direct appeal to their individual political or legislative interests, Mansfield believed he could achieve sufficient leadership control by relying on each senator's ability to act responsibly in most legislative situations and to participate more actively in the life of the institution, in addition to each senator balancing his obligations to party and constituency with a proper respect for the Senate's reputation and integrity. Temperamentally unsuited to operate in the style of Lyndon Johnson, Mansfield based his leadership strategy on an appeal to the senatorial interests of institutional pride and personal participation, interests seemingly far removed from Johnson's harsh world of political reality. As one observer remarked, "Mansfield seemed to believe that belovedness would become the guiding force in the Senate."

Despite the striking differences in conception and execution from Johnson's strategy, Mansfield believed that his approach, if applied consistently across the range of his responsibilities, would deliver adequate levels of support for the senatorial party program in the political environment created by the Kennedy administration.

Moreover, his strategy would help achieve another objective which Mansfield valued highly—the strengthening of the Senate as an effective and independent institution of government. In the process of working for passage of the president's legislative program, Mansfield had no desire for the Senate or its members simply to become functionaries of the New Frontier. He considered it feasible to operate in a manner which testified to his loyalty both to the president and to the Senate.

How, then, did he execute this strategy? How did his methods differ from the ones employed by Johnson?

Party Conference

Under Mansfield's chairmanship, the Party Conference became a more genuine forum for reaching decisions affecting the senatorial party and the legislative program. Johnson had zealously used the recognized prerogative of the majority leader to choose the senators he personally wanted to fill other positions of party leadership and the party committees. Approval by the conference of Johnson's choices was strictly pro forma. But after Mansfield's formal election as leader, the conference, on January 4, 1961, adopted a resolution sponsored by Senator Proxmire directing that membership on all party committees should reflect more accurately geographical and philosophical distribution within the senatorial party and that the majority leader should consult with the president pro tempore and the other party officers before recommending the members of party committees to the conference. It is likely that this resolution, motivated at least in part by the liberal Democrats' growing disaffection for Johnson's methods, set forth a general procedure which Mansfield would have followed even if the resolution had not been passed. . . .

Mansfield remained totally uncommitted in two subsequent contests for party office . . . and genuine contests developed in both instances. The elections were conducted by secret ballot, a procedure which further masked the majority leader's preferences and protected each senator against any manner of retribution for his vote. It has been suggested that the results of these two contests, the election of Russell Long (LA) as whip and Robert C. Byrd (WV) as conference secretary, elevated to the party hierarchy men opposed to crucial aspects of the president's legislative program, particularly in the area of civil rights, and men who were little help to Mansfield personally in the exercise of his leadership duties.[5] As in the other areas of leadership activity where Mansfield actually abandoned power, it was a question whether the majority leader could afford this commitment to neutrality and noninvolvement, given the expectations of accomplishment which normally attend his position.

Although Mansfield recommended senators to fill vacancies on the other party committees, he did so after explicit consultation with the president pro tempore and other party leaders, as spelled out in the Proxmire resolution adopted by the conference in January 1961. The conference was then asked to concur in these recommendations after an opportunity for additional nominations from the floor. Johnson simply announced his selections after informal checking among the influential Democratic senators.

The Party Conference was convened more frequently during Mansfield's tenure as chairman. He considered it to be an appropriate forum for deciding routine housekeeping matters facing the Senate or, less frequently, for proposing procedures to follow in more difficult and controversial matters. He encouraged full discussion and debate of these questions within the conference. The interchange among individuals and factions was useful to Mansfield in evaluating the tenor of opinion within the senatorial party and in determining the course of action to follow. Everyone had the chance to go on record in the presence of his party colleagues. Johnson had gathered this information through more informal and private consultations and from his intelligence and communications system. But though the conference became more active under Mansfield and even served as an instrumentality for choosing party officers in contested elections, it remained a body of secondary importance in senatorial party affairs, still eclipsed by other party committees and the far more significant standing committees of the Senate.

Policy Committee

Although members of the Democratic Policy Committee are normally carried over from one Congress to the next, the composition of the committee under Mansfield became somewhat more representative of the total party membership than was the case during Johnson's chairmanship. The Legislative Review Committee members continued to attend as ex officio members and provided additional representation for the more liberal Democratic forces.

The Policy Committee met more frequently during Mansfield's tenure. The deliberations within the committee were less concerned with ratifying the majority leader's predetermined objectives, the approach followed under Johnson, and more concerned with discovering the course generally acceptable to committee members. Mansfield usually listened to the members discuss the prospects of bills and resolutions currently on the Senate calendar; he would formulate a schedule of bills ready for floor debate on the basis of these opinions. For the legislation that needed additional consultation or attention, Mansfield would usually delegate to the principal proponents and opponents the task of working out as many of the snags and disagreements as possible before it was cleared for action by the full Senate. . . .

. . . Mansfield also kept in close touch with Everett Dirksen, the minority leader, and afforded the Republican viewpoint full consideration in determining the Senate's work schedule.

From time to time during a congressional session, the Policy Committee staff would request from each committee chairman a general estimate of the legislation likely to be approved in the coming weeks, but rarely would the majority leader or his staff attempt to interfere with or disrupt the chairman's plan for processing the business before his committee. Mansfield believed that the party leadership's responsibility for any bill must await its final approval by the standing committee when the bill would then go to the Senate calendar and be considered by the Policy Committee.

Steering Committee

In a manner fully consistent with his general strategy of nondirective and decentralized leadership, Mansfield radically changed the procedures for appointing Democrats to standing committees. Johnson had exercised close personal scrutiny and control over all committee assignments, and he considered this function to be a crucial aspect of his leadership system. On the other hand, Mansfield relinquished almost all personal control and influence over the Steering Committee's decisions. It was estimated that under Mansfield about 90% of the decisions were based on careful, preliminary decisions reached by the majority leader's staff, i.e., matching up requests with vacancies, applying the Johnson rule of one major committee assignment for every Democrat, and using the factor of seniority to help resolve competing claims for a committee seat. Of the remaining 10% of the cases where the staff failed to provide a recommendation which the Steering Committee considered acceptable, about half were settled by the Steering Committee through further discussion until a consensus was reached and about half were decided by secret ballot. Once again, this procedure deliberately curtailed Mansfield's opportunities for personally guiding the Steering Committee to a particular outcome; he concentrated instead on facilitating the discussion and stating the consensus of the committee members when it developed. This also provided an opportunity for factions within the Steering Committee to reach certain decisions which some segments of the party found to be inimical to the legislative agenda proposed by the president.[6]

Mansfield continued to follow the recognized procedure of the majority leader selecting the chairman and members of the Democratic Senatorial Campaign Committee, although he did not participate or attempt to control the committee's decisions on allocating funds among senators up for reelection. The majority leader simply gave the chairman a free hand in running and staffing the committee in whatever fashion he deemed appropriate.

Regardless of the forum, Mansfield displayed a remarkably consistent approach to his formal duties as Democratic leader: (1) He sought to decentralize and broaden the base of participation in the decision-making process; (2) he encouraged full and unstructured discussion of the matter in question; and (3) he limited his own participation primarily to that of neutral chairman and executor of the decisions finally reached. This strategy of leadership rested fundamentally on Mansfield's view of the coequal status of the majority leader with all members of the senatorial party and his rejection of the notion that the party leadership assumed special responsibility for leading the senatorial party in certain directions or affecting decisively the outcome of legislative decisions.

Floor Business

Just as the conduct of business on the Senate floor reflected Johnson's strategy of leadership in various ways, Mansfield's style had its impact on the procedures and techniques used to handle bills during floor debate. As discussed above, the pace established by the individual committee chairmen determined in large measure the flow of bills to the calendar. The movement of bills from the calendar to the

Senate floor was largely determined, in turn, by consultations between the majority and minority leaders and unstructured deliberations within the Policy Committee. Mansfield maintained this pattern of minimum control and intervention by the party leadership once legislation reached the Senate floor.

He instituted the practice of clearing the Senate calendar regularly of all noncontroversial items. The large majority of bills passed by the Senate, not requiring extensive floor debate, were approved immediately with the consent of both parties upon being called from the calendar. It was, however, within the province of the majority leader to hold certain of these bills on the calendar for extended periods of time, a practice which had been known to strengthen his bargaining position with senators whose help was being sought on other issues; i.e., cooperation with the majority leader's request increased the probability of the senator's legislation moving off the calendar. But in line with his established hands-off policy, Mansfield seldom used his position to delay action on these more minor bills otherwise ready for final passage. Mansfield would generally clear the Senate calendar of all noncontroversial "consent" items at least once every week of the session.

Once the floor debate on a bill was under way, the floor manager, usually the chairman of the committee or subcommittee reporting the legislation, assumed major responsibility for bringing it through in acceptable shape. Mansfield remained in the background, following the debate and standing ready to offer his assistance to the floor manager should it be requested. . . . This aid was limited generally to the logistical tasks of locating absent senators, maintaining a quorum, working out with Dirksen agreements on the time to vote, arranging pairs for absent senators, and moving the Senate along to the next item of floor business. Only on rare occasions did Mansfield assume command of the specific tactics for passing a particular bill or attempt to use his influence as majority leader to round up crucial votes.

The application of Mansfield's strategy of decentralized and nondirective leadership fostered conditions on the Senate floor where unforeseen crises occasionally erupted in the midst of debate, and it placed a premium upon a senator's capacity for fast footwork and parliamentary improvisation. Compared to the precise estimates of voting strength on every bill prepared under Johnson, the nose counts conducted by Mansfield and his staff were less frequent and sometimes inaccurate. In the later years of Mansfield's incumbency, the problem of accurate nose counts became less severe, primarily because the majority leader's staff had become better able to estimate quickly the doubtful senators on any bill. But Mansfield still remained opposed to the open nose counting that went on continually by Johnson and Baker.

Since Johnson's intelligence and communications system no longer functioned, it was more difficult to receive advance warnings of potential trouble, and less information existed about ways to resolve these difficulties once they were known. In these circumstances the business of floor leadership became more of a collective enterprise and drew upon the talents of lesser party officers, committee chairmen, legislative specialists from the White House, and other executive agencies as a means of executing certain essential leadership activities.

During his tenure as whip (1961–64), Humphrey performed a number of tasks which Johnson had reserved to himself. He would, for example, often draw up nose counts on legislation in consultation with the Policy Committee and White House staff, the bill's floor manager, as well as lobbyists and other groups backing the legislation. Humphrey's departure in 1965, and the failure of his successor, Russell Long, to assume these duties, tended to bring executive branch officials and members of the standing committees more directly into the process of estimating voting strength and working out parliamentary obstacles prior to floor debate. Mansfield, moreover, appointed four assistant whips in 1966 to perform various routine functions on the floor and to increase the leadership's resources for controlling the debate more effectively. . . . In short, these minimum tasks of floor leadership were not so much abandoned under Mansfield as they were taken over by persons other than the majority leader himself. But this necessarily resulted in a much less centralized system of floor management than existed under Johnson, one less able to predict and control the Senate's response to the president's legislative agenda.

On the other hand, Mansfield's great restraint in using the prerogative of the majority leadership also produced certain advantages that contributed to the impressive record of achievement compiled during his tenure, senators of both parties, for example, genuinely respected Mansfield's willingness to let the legislative process proceed with minimum interference from the party leadership. There developed among many senators a sense of obligation to live up to Mansfield's assumption that a senator would conduct himself responsibly and honorably; those senators who abused the majority leader's permissiveness for personal advantage found themselves the object of their colleagues' opprobrium.

The Mansfield strategy encouraged greater individualism in the Senate and a broader participation of senators in important aspects of senatorial party life. Although he shunned the center stage himself, Mansfield could help others function in a more visible and self-satisfying way than was generally possible under Johnson. Since most senators valued this sense of greater importance and the attendant opportunities for personal recognition, they generally responded favorably to these policies despite their disappointment or frustration over a particular parliamentary crisis which might have been avoided through more forceful leadership. . . .

In his relations with the Republicans, Mansfield established an unusual degree of trust and mutual respect. In recognition of his efforts to take their views into account and of his unfailing habit of consulting frequently with Minority Leader Dirksen, the Republicans seldom took any action which might have embarrassed Mansfield personally in the course of achieving some short-term partisan advantage. Moreover, blind obstructionism and partisan sniping were largely forsaken in the expression of the normal differences and disagreements between the parties over the major portions of the president's legislative program. . . .

Some of the more active northern Democrats, however, expressed the view that Mansfield's strategy of leadership permitted, in effect, the organized factions within the Senate, principally the Southern Democrats and conservative Republicans, to exercise more than their share of influence and control over the activities of the body.[7] They alleged that a lack of coordinated, positive initiative by the leadership allowed the Senate to entangle itself unnecessarily in parliamentary snarls and needlessly sacrificed elements of the presidential and senatorial party programs. . . .

In evaluating the effectiveness of Mansfield's strategy, one must always remember that he served during the administrations of two active Democratic presidents. Following passage of the initial legislative program of President Kennedy, essentially holdovers from the Eisenhower years, the pace of legislative achievement slackened in both House and Senate. By the fall of 1963, party leaders were faced with a growing logjam of priority measures. Whether this logjam would have been broken in 1964 under Kennedy's leadership can never by known. But it is a fact that the shock over Kennedy's assassination and President Johnson's vigorous assumption of the Kennedy legislative program propelled the Congress into a period of great legislative accomplishment, one which was extended through the Eighty-ninth Congress by Johnson's landslide victory over Senator Goldwater and the election of large Democratic majorities in both houses of Congress. In sum, with the exception of the first nine months in 1963, Mansfield served during periods when a two to one Democratic margin in the Senate, combined with substantial momentum for action flowing from the White House, provided an environment ripe for legislative achievement. In these circumstances Mansfield did not face for any sustained period the burden of rationalizing substantial disparities of interest between a Democratic president and a Democratic senatorial party.

His posture of restraint also contributed to an environment within the Senate conducive to building a viable relationship between the legislative and executive branches. . . . The Senate's performance record might have been less impressive if other persons, such as Humphrey and the White House legislative operatives, had not moved in to assume certain more routine tasks of party leadership which the majority leader tended to avoid, e.g., nose counts and other prefloor planning and preparation.

Whether Mansfield's strategy of leadership would prove adequate in periods of greater partisanship, or if the size of the Democratic majority in the Senate was significantly reduced, is another question. Given the normal disparities between the interests of the president and the senatorial party, compounded by the impact of the separation of powers, the need for more forceful and self-conscious leadership would likely become evident. This situation would increase the desirability of the majority leader's greater use of the institutionalized powers at his disposal and of his attempts to augment these resources. But this judgment, even if true, cannot detract from the considerable record of accomplishment compiled by the senatorial party under Mansfield or dispel the affection and support which he received from other senatorial party members during his tenure as majority leader. . . .

THE ROLE OF SENATORIAL PARTY LEADERS: SOME PROPOSITIONS

Despite the differences between Johnson and Mansfield in the conception and execution of the majority leadership, there are nevertheless certain propositions about the role of party leadership per se which appear justified by the foregoing analysis:

1. The prevailing political environment will be a major factor in determining the content and success of a majority leader's strategy of leadership. Indeed, pressures within the senatorial party as well as the party affiliation and expected conduct of the president may even influence the choice of majority leader. The composition and expectations of the majority Democrats in 1961 made it difficult to conceive of their selecting a replacement for Johnson who would have continued his highly aggressive and centralized leadership. Johnson's conduct after the 1958 congressional elections, moreover, suggested that he would have made significant adjustments in his strategy if he had remained as majority leader in the Kennedy administration. As suggested by the marked differences between two leaders, however, there also exists latitude for the majority leader to devise a leadership strategy which takes into account his personal objectives and particular skills.

2. Regardless of the political environment or the personal objectives and skills of the majority leader, he will be faced with a deficit of institutionalized power which must be compensated for in some fashion if he is to establish adequate control over the Senate's response to the president's legislative agenda. This deficit of leadership power can be traced fundamentally to the nature of the two-party system and the effect of the separation of powers on the standing of the Senate among the institutions of government.

3. In establishing adequate control over the Senate's response to the president's programs, the majority leader will likely give priority to methods which permit individual senators to serve their interests by the outcome. In his efforts to control the choices available to senators in a given legislative situation, Johnson gave priority to relatively short-term political or legislative objectives held by individual senators. Mansfield, on the other hand, was more concerned with appealing to the interests of senators in preserving the reputation of the Senate as a responsible and effective participant in the governmental process and in senators performing identifiable and self-satisfying roles in the legislative process.

4. Granting the impact which procedure can have on substantive decisions, the majority leader's position within the senatorial party makes him better equipped to control the *way* a decision is reached than to affect its substance. His use of his limited institutionalized powers and his methods for augmenting these powers will affect primarily his control over such matters as the scheduling and management of legislation on the Senate floor and the opportunity for other senators to participate in these procedural decisions.

5. If the majority leader is better equipped to affect the procedures of senatorial decision making, the president and the chairmen and members of the standing committees are more dominant in deciding matters of substance. For example, the president's legislative agenda, more than any other single factor, will define the issues likely to occupy the Senate and will establish a range of responses which the Senate is likely to make. Whether or not the committee chairmen choose to cooperate with the president on policy matters will be a major factor in determining the nature of this response, in

addition to affecting the problems likely to be confronted by the majority leader.

6. Despite the president's dominance on questions of substance and the majority leader's influence on procedure, both are likely to consider activities on the Senate floor, the parliamentary dimension of Senate life, as more relevant and congenial to their respective objectives than the operations of the committee system, the working dimension of Senate life. Even for Johnson, the Senate floor was the place where his dominance could become visible and his capacity for control fully demonstrated. There exists an affinity of interest between the majority leader and the president to preserve the legitimacy of the floor as a place for reaching meaningful decisions. Moreover, the majority leader and the president will usually find it mutually profitable to bolster their respective abilities to influence procedure and substance, i.e., the majority leader can help the president by devising procedures which foster certain substantive results; the president can work for these ends in a way which makes the procedure possible to execute. There are, however, definite limits to which one can productively assist the other: The majority leader, in particular, cannot appear simply in the guise of presidential operative or apologist.

NOTES

1. The descriptions of the leadership strategy of Lyndon Johnson and Mike Mansfield are compiled from various published sources, interviews, and, in the case of Mansfield, the personal observations of the author. The most useful published works include: Evans and Novak (1966); White (1956); Huitt (1961a).

2. For a more detailed discussion of the Senatorial Campaign Committees see Bone (1956).

3. See the excellent chapter, "Too Many Democrats," in Evans and Novak (1966, 193–224).

4. As quoted to the author by a participant at the Democratic Conference, January 10, 1967.

5. This point was made frequently to the author in his interviews concerning Mansfield's leadership strategy.

6. This view was expressed by Senator Clark of Pennsylvania in his well-publicized speeches on "the Senate Establishment" delivered on the Senate floor in February, 1963, following the Steering Committee's assignments for the Eighty-eighth Congress. He charged that "when the Democratic steering committee met, it became obvious that in filling committee membership vacancies, the establishment would ignore seniority when to ignore it would strengthen the establishment's control, but would follow it when to do so would have the same result." *Congressional Record*, 88th Cong., 1st Sess., 1963, 109, 22, 559. [See Clark (1964).]

7. The most publicized outburst was delivered spontaneously on the Senate floor by Thomas Dodd (D-CT), on November 6, 1963. He said (*Congressional Record*, 88th Cong., 1st Sess., 1963, 109, 22, 247): "Mike Mansfield is a gentleman, Senators, we are of one mind about that . . . But I worry about his leadership. He must assume it . . . he must behave like a leader. Because a leader is one who leads . . ." He apologized the next day, noting (*Congressional Record*, 88th Cong., 1st Sess., 1963, 109, 21, 372): "I felt this morning somewhat like a skunk at a lawn party . . . I fear I was harder than I meant to be last night toward him . . ."

Chapter 22

Institutional Context and Leadership Style: The House from Cannon to Rayburn

Joseph Cooper and David W. Brady

Leadership is an aspect of social life which has been extensively studied in a variety of institutional or organizational settings (Miner 1980). Yet it remains a topic in which our intellectual grasp falls far short of our pragmatic sense of the impacts leaders have on organizational operations and performance.

This is as true, if not more true, of Congress than of other organizations. Here too analysts are perplexed by the difficulties of conceptualizing key variables, treating highly transient and idiosyncratic personal factors, and identifying relationships amidst a maze of interactive effects. Moreover, the task is rendered even more complex by the highly politicized character of the Congress as compared with most of the organizational contexts in which leadership has been studied.

This is not to say that knowledge and understanding of congressional leadership have remained static. Peabody (1976), Jones (1968), Ripley (1967), Polsby (1963), Manley (1969), Hinckley (1970), and Nelson (1977) have all done instructive and insightful work. Nonetheless, our grip on the topic is as yet not firm; we continue to lack a developed sense of what we should be looking at and how to proceed.

The purpose of this article is to aid in remedying this deficiency. It is premised on two key assumptions. First, the study of leadership requires comparative evidence regarding both behavior and contexts. Hence our use of history as a laboratory and our choice of Cannon and Rayburn as focal points of analysis. Second, the study of leadership requires abstract or analytical concepts to aid in formulating and testing important relationships. Hence our historical analysis relies on several broad concepts and relationships, drawn both from organization theory and from recent work on the operation of the Congress.

In sum, though this article deals with the transition from Cannon to Rayburn, its main objective is not to fill in the historical record. Its primary goals are rather to bring evidence and analysis to bear to improve our understanding of the key determinants and underlying dynamics of congressional leadership, and to suggest

Source: *American Political Science Review* (1981) 75:411–25. Reprinted by permission of the publisher.

a set of propositions or hypotheses that can serve as a basis for more focused and elaborate forms of investigation and theory building.

THE HOUSE UNDER CZAR RULE

The legacy the House of the nineteenth century left to that of the twentieth was a set of rules which placed the majority firmly in control of the House and centralized power in the hands of the Speaker as the agent of this majority. It was this legacy the House rejected when it revolted against the Speaker in 1910. In so doing it not only stripped the Speaker of many of his important powers, but also paved the way for a metamorphosis in the nature of the House as a political institution.

The Speaker and the House

It was with good reason that Speakers of the House in the years between 1890 and 1910 were often referred to as czars (Galloway 1961, 134–36). The Speaker appointed the committees. He served as the chairman of and had unchallengeable control over the Rules Committee (Brown 1922, 87–90). He had great, though not unlimited, discretion over the recognition of members desiring to call business off the calendars, to make motions, or to address the House, and absolute discretion over the recognition of motions for unanimous consent and suspension of the rules (Chiu 1928, 175–97).

These prerogatives gave the Speaker great power to control outcomes in the House. At the committee stage, those who had received prized assignments from the Speaker naturally felt a sense of gratitude and obligation to him. Those who desired a change in assignment knew full well that their chances of advancement depended on the good graces of the Speaker. Conversely, since in this age seniority was far from as sacrosanct as it is today, members were also aware that to alienate the Speaker was to risk loss of a chairmanship, an assignment, or rank on a committee (Abram and Cooper 1968; Polsby et al. 1969).

Nor was the appointment power the Speaker's only source of leverage in controlling outcomes at the committee stage. Members of any particular committee were also disposed to cooperate with the Speaker because of the vast array of rewards and sanctions his position in the House bestowed on him. For example, the Speaker could provide access to the floor by granting a rule or recognizing a motion to suspend the rules; he could lend invaluable assistance in getting a project included in a bill or in getting a bill out of committee. Moreover, if all the rewards and sanctions at the disposal of the Speaker still proved to be insufficient, there was yet another factor that discouraged opposition at the committee stage. The plain fact was that to oppose the Speaker would in all probability be fruitless. If a committee refused to report a bill the Speaker wanted reported, the Speaker could pry the bill out of committee either through use of the Rules Committee or suspension of the rules. Similarly, if a committee reported a bill the Speaker opposed, the bill had little chance of reaching the floor. The power of the Speaker was such that he could obstruct the consideration of any bill he did not want considered.

Given the various and potent types of leverage the Speaker possessed, it is not surprising that in this period committee chairmen took their cue from the Speaker regarding which bills they would report and that Speakers referred to the committee chairmen as their "cabinet" (Busby 1927, 219).

As for action on the floor, here too the Speaker's prerogatives under the rules gave him great power. A number of factors combined to give him control over the agenda of the House. Through use of the Rules Committee and other privileged committees, he could interrupt the regular order of business either to give priority to a bill he wanted considered or to block a bill he opposed.[1] He could use unanimous consent and suspension of the rules to give access to the floor to bills he favored and could deny the use of these procedures to bills he opposed. In addition, his discretion in the recognition of motions calling bills up for consideration was a source of leverage.

The Speaker's ability to control the agenda, however, stemmed not merely from his powers of repression, but also from the necessity of relying upon him if the House was to reach the bills it wanted to consider. The volume of legislation before the House made it exceedingly cumbersome to follow the involved order of business set forth in the rules. As a result, the House did not insist on following its regular order. Indeed, the points in the order where committee members could call business off the calendars were usually not reached. Instead, the House relied on the Speaker to bring bills up for its consideration and to determine the time of consideration through the use of privileged reports and special procedures, such as unanimous consent. In short, then, both because of the powers of the Speaker over the agenda and the unwieldiness of proceeding according to the regular order, the House gave the Speaker even more power over the agenda than his power under the rules bestowed on him.[2]

A second aspect of the Speaker's power over floor decisions concerned his ability to control considerations on the floor. Here again, his command of the Rules Committee and his power as presiding officer gave him considerable leverage over floor debate and dilatory tactics. In addition, many of the same rewards and sanctions at the Speaker's disposal for controlling committee decisions could also be used to control floor decisions. Especially for members of the majority party, to oppose the Speaker was to risk the loss of his assistance in matters of vital importance to one's constituency and therefore also to impair one's chances of reelection. Moreover, through bestowing favors over a number of years, the Speaker could build up a substantial fund of credits, credits which could then be expended as needed to secure the cooperation of members in his debt. Thus, the ability of the Speaker to control decisions on the floor and in committee stemmed not only from the immediate impacts the exercise of his formal powers involved, but also from their long-run dividends.

The Speaker as Party Chief

To complement his prerogatives under the rules, the Speaker possessed another source of power that was equally significant. In placing a potent array of rewards and sanctions at his disposal, the rules did of course provide him with considerable leverage. However, the Speaker's ability to command majority support in committee and on the floor was materially aided by another factor: party discipline.

In an age when party regularity is far from an overriding consideration, it is difficult to appreciate how important party was in the House at the turn of the century. In this period the great majority of members in both parties subscribed to the doctrines of party government. Representative government was seen to depend on the existence of a responsible majority which had the power to rule and which, as a result, could be held accountable for performance (Jones 1968). Only under such conditions, it was believed, could the people effect their wishes. The individual representative was thought to be elected on the basis of a party's platform and was therefore regarded to have an obligation to support party positions, even against personal convictions or desires.

The fact that members in this age thought and spoke in terms of the doctrines of party government had more than rhetorical importance. Party government served as the main justification for vesting great power in the Speaker and permitting him to play the role of czar. Though the Democrats never fully accepted the proposition and ended by rejecting it, a cardinal tenet of Republican faith was that rule by a responsible majority party required centralizing organizational power in the Speaker.

The Speaker's position as head of his party thus also provided him with an important source of leverage. It is true, of course, that even in this period many issues were not treated as party issues. Nonetheless, most important issues were regarded as matters on which the party as a whole should stand together. In such a context the Speaker derived considerable power from his position as party chief. Initiative in the definition of party policies belonged to him. Moreover, if he could not win the support of all elements in the party, he had at his disposal a powerful mechanism for enforcing adherence to his wishes—the caucus. Through a binding vote in the caucus, he could oblige the opposition to support his policy positions out of party loyalty (Brown 1922, 92–93, 100, 161–62; Wilson 1961, 96). In short, the Speaker could rule the House through the force of party discipline. As long as the bonds of party held taut, he had only to command the support of a majority of his party to command a majority in the House.

We may conclude, then, that the House of Reed and Cannon contained a highly centralized power structure with control resting essentially in the hands of the Speaker. The key to the Speaker's power lay not simply in his prerogatives under rules, nor in his position as party chief, but rather in the manner in which these two sources of leverage reinforced each other (Cooper 1970). The existence of a stable party majority insured the Speaker's ability to implement his formal powers and gave him a degree of maneuverability and control that the rules alone could not give him. Similarly, the rewards and sanctions the rules placed in the Speaker's hands gave party regularity a degree of priority it would not have possessed if it had rested merely on the extent of agreement among party members or their devotion to the doctrines of party government. Speakers could therefore quite appropriately refer to committee chairmen as their "cabinet." During this period the committee and party systems were blended to an extremely high degree. The Speaker was both the party leader and the chairman of the Rules

Committee. The majority leader was the chairman of the Ways and Means or Appropriations Committee and, with the start of the whip system in 1897, the whip was chairman of Judiciary or a top member of Ways and Means. Unlike the contemporary House where party leaders and committee chairs are separate, committee and party leaders were one and the same. Tensions between the two systems were accordingly greatly reduced. . . . It was thus not a mere figure of speech to refer to committee chairs as a "cabinet." Both structurally and behaviorally, committee and party leaders were a cabinet (Brady 1973).

The Bases of Czar Rule

We have argued that the interaction of the Speaker's formal powers and the strength of party resulted in a centralized form of leadership—czar rule. This can be shown empirically. Data exist which strongly buttress the argument we have made deductively on the basis of the historical record.

First, if party strength functioned as a key ingredient of czar rule, then levels of party voting should be markedly higher in Congresses with centralized leadership. Table 22.1 presents data on party votes (90% of one party versus 90% of the other) for congresses from 1881 to 1921. It thus includes "czar rule" Congresses in

Table 22.1
Czar rule and levels of party voting in the House (1881–1921)

Congress	Year	Percentage party votes	Majority party	Centralized leadership	Differential
47	1881	16.6	Republican	No	36
48	1883	7.0	Democratic	No	15
49	1885	15.5	Democratic	No	25
50	1887	8.7	Democratic	No	24
51	1889	42.5	Republican	Yes	41
52	1891	4.2	Democratic	No	19
53	1893	6.1	Democratic	No	22
54	1895	24.8	Republican	Yes	36
55	1897	50.2	Republican	Yes	43
56	1899	49.8	Republican	Yes	33
57	1901	38.9	Republican	Yes	35
58	1903	64.4	Republican	Yes	39
59	1905	34.6	Republican	Yes	41
60	1907	26.3	Republican	Yes	36
61	1909	29.4	Republican	Yes/No	31
62	1911	23.0	Democratic	No	24
63	1913	19.9	Democratic	No	12
64	1915	21.7	Democratic	No	11
65	1917	9.4	Democratic	No	14
66	1919	14.9	Republican	No	18

Source: David Brady and Phillip Althoff. 1974. "Party Voting in the U.S. House of Representatives, 1890–1910: Elements of a Responsible Party System." *Journal of Politics* 36: 753–75.

which the Speaker possessed the formal powers described above and a ready ability to use the caucus, and Congresses in which one or more of these sources of leverage was absent.

Table 22.1 shows a strong connection between centralized leadership power and levels of party voting. In the period from 1881 to 1899 party voting scores attained levels of 25% or more only in the three Congresses in which centralized leadership power existed. In the period from 1899 to 1921 party voting did not drop below 25% until after the 1910 revolt against the Speaker, and then fell to below 10% in 1917 for the first time in a quarter-century. To further substantiate our argument, we ran a point biserial analysis of the data. This statistic is used when the data are dichotomous and is appropriate for Table 22.1, given a distinction between centralized and noncentralized leadership power. The point biserial for this data set was a striking .89, demonstrating the degree to which levels of party voting can be seen as associated with concentrated leadership power.

Second, if an interactive relationship exists between concentrated formal power and party strength, then party strength must have its own sources of determination and impact. Indeed, in our view the causal impact of party strength on the distribution of power in the House is of primary importance. For the Speaker to have the power involved in czar rule, a majority of the House members had to agree to bestow such power. Since the House is organized on the basis of party and since during this period the Republicans were usually in the majority, it was their potential for group cohesion and loyalty that established the conditions for centralized leadership. In short, the vehicle through which centralized leadership developed was the congressional Republican party (Brown 1922, 71–126). The rationale underlying this development was that without party government the industrial gains of the late nineteenth century would have been negated by congressional Democrats.

However, to sustain the role and significance we have accorded party strength, we must be able to identify and demonstrate independent sources of determination. In this respect it may be noted that the development of strong party systems in Europe and Britain is associated with the rise of leftist-socialist parties and that in the United States those states where the parties represent polarized constituencies have high levels of party voting. Our argument is therefore that the fundamental bases of party strength at the turn of the century, as in all periods of our history, are largely external, that party strength is rooted in polarized constituency configurations.

In order to ascertain the constituency bases of the congressional parties as well as the differences between them, we calculated the degree to which each congressional party represented agricultural as opposed to industrial districts. For example, in the Fifty-fifth House (1897–99), 69% of the Democrats and 26% of the Republicans represented agricultural districts, that is, districts where the ratio of farms to industrial workers was at least three to one. Thus the difference between the parties was 43 percentage points. This differential was computed for the Forty-seventh through the Sixty-sixth Houses (1881–1921) and serves as a measure of electoral polarization. The specific hypothesis is that there should be a strong relationship between polarization and party voting. Table 22.1 confirms the hypothesis. When polarization was high, so too was party voting. Conversely, in Houses where the differential was less than 20, that is, where the parties were less polarized, the proportion of party votes did not rise above 20% and dropped to as low as 4.2%. However, perhaps the best overall statistic is Pearson's r, which is .81 for the two variables presented in Table 22.1.

The data also show that during the period from the realignment of 1894–96 to approximately the election of Woodrow Wilson (the Fifty-fourth through the Sixty-first House), the parties remained polarized and levels of party voting remained high. On the other hand, during the "period of no decision" (Forty-seventh through the Fifty-third Houses), the degree of polarization fluctuated, and levels of party voting varied accordingly. Similarly, after 1908 the congressional parties became less polarized as the Democratic party became more competitive in industrial districts, and party voting in the House again declined.

In sum, then, it is critical to note the correspondence between a polarized electoral system and a highly centralized leadership structure. Though the Speaker's formal powers reinforced party strength, the polarized electoral bases of the party system provided an indispensable platform for czar rule. Thus, when electoral polarization began to decline, the centralized internal structure also began to come apart (Brady et al. 1979).

THE HOUSE FROM CANNON TO RAYBURN

Despite its power, the system of czar rule could not maintain itself. It proved to be too rigid a system to accommodate the factional tendencies in the party system. During the early years of the twentieth century, economic and social ferment in the Midwest and West brought to Congress a group of young Republicans passionately devoted to enacting a whole series of reform measures. Cannon used his power as Speaker and party chief to contain and frustrate the desires of these members. In so doing, he soon aroused their enmity not merely for his policies but also for the whole system of power then prevalent in the House (Jones 1968).

The Revolt Against the Speaker

Though the number of Insurgent Republicans in the House was never large, by 1909 their strength in combination with the Democrats was sufficient to bring the revolt to a successful conclusion. The first step came in 1909 with the establishment of a Consent Calendar and a call of the committees every Wednesday to take up business on the House or Union Calendars. At this time more sweeping change was prevented by the defection of a group of conservative Democrats (Hechler 1940, 42–63). The next year, however, the Insurgent Republican-Democratic coalition gained a decisive victory. On March 19, 1910, after a dramatic two-day fight, the House passed a resolution removing the Speaker from the Rules Committee, enlarging its membership, and providing for election of the committee by the House. This victory was followed two months later by the passage of a resolution which established a procedure through which individual members could initiate the discharge of bills from committees (Brown 1922, 143–88). Finally, in 1911 the last major objective of the opponents of czar rule was achieved.

The House, now under Democratic control, amended its rules to provide for the election of all standing committees and their chairmen (Hasbrouck 1927, 11).

The immediate results of the revolt against the Speaker did not greatly impair the ability of the party leadership to lead the House on behalf of the party majority. In acting to weaken the Speaker, the Democrats had no intention of weakening the ability of the party majority to pass its program. Most Democrats believed as strongly in party government as most Republicans. Their objection was not to party government and party responsibility but to domination of the majority party and the House by the Speaker. Thus, when the Democrats gained control of the House in 1911, they set up an effective system of rule through the majority party. On the one hand, they made extensive use of the caucus and binding votes in caucus (Haines 1915, 53–110). On the other hand, they centralized power in the party by making the chairman of the Committee on Ways and Means, Oscar Underwood, both floor leader and chairman of the Committee on Committees.[3] Under Underwood's leadership, the Democrats controlled the House as tightly as the Republicans had under Cannon. Indeed, it is fair to say that the Insurgent Republicans were no happier in the new "reformed" Democratic House than they had been in the old "tyrannical" Republican one. They had no greater liking for "King Caucus" than for "czar rule."

The long-run results of the revolt, however, were quite different. If czar rule was unable to maintain itself in the face of centrifugal pressures in the party system, caucus rule was even less fitted to do so. In the absence of the buttress the formal powers of the Speaker provided for party cohesion, increases in factional discord within the party alignments easily asserted themselves and led both to a disintegration of party control mechanisms and to a dispersion of power within the House (Cooper 1961, 1970).

The disintegration of party control mechanisms was gradual but extensive. The caucus was the first to go. Once the Democrats achieved the major items in their domestic programs, the power of the caucus began to wane. From 1916 on, the divisions within the parties made it difficult to rely on the caucus and usage quickly declined (Luce 1922, 513). This is consistent with the data presented in Table 24.1 that shows party voting at less than 15% in the 1917–21 period—a 22–year low. There were small upsurges in activity in the early 1920s and early 1930s during the initial years of party turnover in the presidency. However, its use for policy purposes soon became rare in the 1920s and simply disappeared in the late 1930s. Thus by the end of the 1930s the caucus was virtually moribund as a mechanism for determining party policy (Kefauver 1947, 102–3).

When the Republicans regained control of the House in 1919, they set up a Steering Committee and began to rely on it rather than the caucus (Brown 1922, 195–224; Chiu 1928, 329–34). Though this committee from the first was less of a control device than the caucus and more of a coordinating and planning mechanism, during the early 1920s it did serve to augment the leadership's power to direct its partisans. However, the same tendencies toward factionalism and bloc voting that reduced the caucus to marginal significance had a similar effect on the Steering Committee. By the late 1920s the party leadership had come to see the Steering Committee as a hindrance to their maneuverability and effectiveness. As a result, they abandoned the mechanism and began to rely instead on informal meetings among themselves, i.e., on an informal board of strategy composed of the Speaker, the floor leader, and a few trusted lieutenants (Chiu 1928, 334–36). The situation did not change when the Democrats took control of the House in 1931. Though they too established a Steering Committee, their leadership operated in much the same fashion as the Republican leadership had in the late 1920s (Galloway 1961, 145). In short, then, by the late 1920s reliance on party control mechanisms to coordinate action and enforce cohesion had largely passed from the scene. Instead, the majority party was reduced to operating primarily through a small coterie of men, gathered around the Speaker, who met to plan strategy and whose power of direction was much less than that of the caucus or even the Steering Committee in their heyday.

Nor were the caucus and the Steering Committee the only party control mechanisms to lose power and effectiveness in the period after 1916. The power of party mechanisms to control committee personnel also declined. Republican Speakers from 1890 to 1910 respected seniority, but they were quite prepared to violate it in the interests of party policy. The same is true of Underwood. By the 1920s the situation was substantially different. The decline of the caucus and, to a lesser extent, of the Steering Committee enhanced the power and independence of party factions. Their sheer willingness to stand together and cooperate with the leadership became more important than ever before. In addition, as the power and independence of party factions increased, the appointment mechanisms became more decentralized. Thus, by 1919 the Republicans had taken the power of appointment from the leader of the party and had vested it in a Committee on Committees, composed of nearly 40 members. Similarly, after 1923 the Democrats no longer combined the posts of floor leader and chairman of the Committee on Committees. In such a context seniority was transformed from an important consideration to a sovereign principle. It alone provided a standard in terms of which decentralized appointment mechanisms could distribute key committee positions among party factions without provoking disputes that would weaken the party. As a result, in contrast to earlier eras, departures from seniority were rare in the 1920s and even rarer thereafter (Abram and Cooper 1968; Polsby et al. 1969).

From Hierarchy to Bargaining

Given the reductions in the formal powers of the Speaker between 1909 and 1911, the disintegration of party control mechanisms after 1916 produced a dispersion of power in the House. If in Cannon's day the Speaker's prerogatives as Speaker and as party chief combined to centralize power in the House, now the reduction in the formal powers of the Speaker and the disintegration of party control mechanisms combined to decentralize power in the House.

On the one hand, the rewards and sanctions which the rules placed in the hands of party leaders were reduced. The party leadership no longer had absolute control over committee appointment, the Rules Committee, or the consideration of minor business. On the other hand, the ability of party leaders to consolidate and maintain support in their own ranks was also reduced. If it is true that factionalism in the party system led to the decline of party control mechanisms, it is also true that the decline of these mechanisms had the further effect of allowing party factionalism greater expression. The result of these developments was to heighten the power and independence of the individual member and of key organizational units in the House. Denied the power they possessed over the individual member under czar rule or caucus rule, party leaders began to function less as the commanders of a stable party majority and more as brokers trying to assemble particular majorities behind particular bills. Denied the power they possessed over the organizational structure under czar rule or caucus rule, party leaders began to function less as directors of the organizational units and more as bargainers for their support.

These tendencies intensified as time passed. During the 1920s the breakdown of the Steering Committee and the rise of seniority to predominance cast party leaders more firmly in the roles of brokers and bargainers than had been the case at the start of the decade (Chiu 1928, 315–35; Hasbrouck 1927, 48–50). Similarly, events during the 1930s confirmed and strengthened these roles. If the level of party cohesion during the 1920s was not high enough to permit reliance on party control mechanisms, it was still of such proportions that in general the holders of key organizational positions were loyal to the leadership and willing to cooperate with it. Nor, despite the increases in factionalism and bloc voting, did party leaders during the 1920s confront any stable and comprehensive basis of division among their fellow partisans, any extensive and consistent split across a whole range of issues. By the late 1930s, however, the situation had changed in both these regards.

After a brief increase in party voting during the initial years of the New Deal, party strength again began to decline in a steady and substantial fashion (Sinclair 1978). Moreover, this decline gave birth to a new and distinctive feature, the Conservative Coalition (Brady and Bullock 1980; Manley 1977). Table 22.2 provides supportive data on both trends.

Thus, as the 1930s came to an end, party politics in the House began to display characteristics and configurations that were to become entrenched in the 1940s and to endure for several decades. These changes, however, made the task of the majority party leadership more, not less arduous. First, party divisions in the majority party now assumed a pronounced bifurcated form. In seeking to build majorities from issue to issue, the leadership accordingly was frequently threatened with the loss of support of a substantial portion of the Southern wing of the party, a wing that from the late 1930s to late 1950s was roughly equal in size to the northern wing of the party (Cooper and Bombardier 1968). Second, the divisions within the majority party now began to be translated into the organizational structure in a manner that far exceeded previous experience. The party leadership's ability to use the machinery of the House to suit its own purposes accordingly declined. It began to encounter difficulty securing the support of particular committees and committee chairmen much more frequently. This was especially true of the one committee in the House on which the leadership was most dependent and which historically had always been regarded as falling within the province of the leadership—the Rules Committee. For the first time in history the leadership found itself confronted with a Rules Committee that regarded itself and acted as an independent agent, rather than as an arm of the leadership (Galloway 1961, 145–48; Jones 1968).

Table 22.2

The decline of party voting in the House and the rise of the Conservative Coalition (1909–53)

Congress	Year	Percent party votes	Percent coalition activity	Percent coalition victories
61	1909	29.4	—	—
62	1911	23.0	—	—
63	1913	19.9	—	—
64	1915	21.7	—	—
65	1917	9.4	—	—
66	1919	14.9	—	—
67	1921	35.2	—	—
68	1923	13.4	—	—
69	1925	5.3	3.5	63.5
70	1927	5.6	1.4	100.0
71	1929	13.6	5.8	80.0
72	1931	13.8	4.9	62.0
73	1933	18.9	2.1	48.0
74	1935	14.2	4.3	56.0
75	1937	11.8	7.6	67.0
76	1939	17.6	9.3	95.0
77	1941	10.5	12.5	92.0
78	1943	9.6	21.8	96.0
79	1945	12.1	22.1	88.0
80	1947	12.7	19.6	100.0
81	1949	6.5	16.4	83.0
82	1951	4.9	24.9	86.0

Sources: David Brady, Joseph Cooper and Patricia Hurley. 1979. "The Decline of Party Voting in the U.S. House of Representatives." *Legislative Studies Quarterly* 4: 381–407; David Brady and Charles Bullock. 1980. "Is There a Conservative Coalition in the House?" *Journal of Politics* 42: 549–59.

These developments further weakened the power and position of the leadership and in so doing further enhanced the independence of individual members and organizational units. Moreover, the impact was long-lasting, not transitory. A divided majority party was less amenable to leadership direction and control than an incohesive one. From the late 1930s on, the leadership was forced to place even more reliance on brokerage and bargaining than had been necessary in the early 1930s or 1920s (Herring 1940, 21–45).

THE RAYBURN HOUSE

The period from 1910 to 1940 may therefore be seen as a period of transition in the character of the House as a political institution. By 1940, the year Sam Rayburn assumed the speakership, a new and distinctive type of House had emerged. It was a House that was destined to endure in most of its essential features until the reform of the Rules Committee in the early 1960s and in many of its essential features until the reemergence of the caucus in the late 1960s (Cooper 1970; Brady et al. 1979).

The House Under Decentralized Rule

The Rayburn House was a far different body from the House of Cannon or Reed. Centralization of power and hierarchical control had given way to a diffusion of power and bargaining.

On the one hand, the majority party leadership could no longer command the organizational units due to the breakdown of party control mechanisms and the elimination of the Speaker's prerogatives over appointment and the Rules Committee. Rather, it had to seek to win their support and do so in a context in which divisions in the majority party had become so pronounced that they had begun to appear at key vantage points in the organizational structure. On the other hand, the majority party leadership could no longer command overwhelming support from the ranks of its partisans on the floor due both to the decline in party strength and the decline in the fund of rewards and sanctions at its disposal. Rather, it had to seek to build majorities from issue to issue and do so in a context in which a deep split existed in the ranks of the majority party and distaste for party discipline was intense and pervasive. Political scientists writing about the House in the 1940s and 1950s accordingly emphasized themes quite different from those emphasized in the initial decades of this century: the primacy and amount of catering to constituency, not party loyalty or discipline; the dispersed and kaleidoscopic character of power in the House, not the authority and responsibilities of party leaders; the role of committee chairmen as autonomous and autocratic chieftains, not their operation as loyal party lieutenants (Young 1943; Gross 1953).

However, the fact that power became decentralized in the House does not mean that significant centers of power did not continue to exist. What occurred was a wider dispersal of power, not its fractionalization.

First, the party leadership retained substantial ability to influence and even control outcomes in the House. If party voting decreased, the party bond remained important both because of the degree of agreement still present and because of the interest most members had in establishing some kind of party record. Thus, though the leadership could no longer rule the House on the basis of votes drawn from its own party, it could still usually count on a large and stable reservoir of support from its fellow partisans (Mayhew 1966). In addition, party leaders continued to derive leverage from other sources. The formal powers remaining to the Speaker aided their ability to control access to the floor and proceedings on the floor. The influence party leaders maintained over the party Committee on Committees enabled them to alter the political complexion of particular committees through the screening of new appointments. The power party leaders retained, due to their positions in the House and in the party, to dispense favors and build up credits augmented their capacity to secure the cooperation of ordinary members and holders of organizational positions (Ripley 1967). Finally, the leadership could rely on the president's influence to win the support of reluctant partisans both in committee and on the floor.

Second, committees and committee chairmen emerged as rival power centers of great importance. In a context in which House rules gave the committees immense power over the handling of legislation within their jurisdictions and committee rules and practice gave their chairmen immense power within their committees, the decline in leadership authority and power redounded to the advantage of the committees and their chairmen. Typically, committee opposition to legislation sealed its fate, even when favored by the leadership. Conversely, committees that operated in a unified fashion were accorded great deference on the floor and had high levels of success (Fenno 1962). Party leaders thus could not treat committees merely as instruments of their will nor chairmen simply as loyal lieutenants. Rather, they had to function largely as petitioners of committee support and floor managers of committee legislations.

In the Rayburn House the committees accordingly reemerged as the feudal baronies they had been in the decades immediately preceding czar rule. And, indeed, to a significant degree the story of the Rayburn House is a story of conflict among northern majorities in the Democratic party, the majority party leadership, and Southern-dominated committees in which northern pressure for action was continuing, leadership efforts sporadic, and committee obstruction very difficult to overcome. Ironically enough, then, the ultimate result of the revolt of 1910 was to redefine the problem of majority rule in the House, not to solve it. A new and equally serious difficulty, i.e., minority obstruction, simply replaced the difficulty that had aroused passions in the preceding era, i.e., autocratic leadership power.

Leadership Style in the Rayburn House

In sum, by 1940 the role and power of the party leadership in the House had been substantially altered. Though the leadership retained responsibility for and continued to provide overall guidance and direction in the conduct of the House's business, it now had to operate within a far harsher set of constraints than in 1910. At the floor stage, the leadership usually had no choice but to engage in the painful process of assembling shifting majorities behind particular bills through bargaining and maneuver. At the committee stage, the leadership was often forced to engage in intricate and prolonged negotiation with committees and committee chairmen. Indeed, the leadership was now placed in a position where inability to accommodate an organizational unit would mean failure to pass party legislation, unless it was able to organize a majority of such strength and intensity that it could force a vote on the floor through the pressure of opinion in the House or the use of a mechanism such as discharge. The result was that by 1940 the personal, political skills of the leadership, rather than its sources of institutional power, had become the critical determinant of the fate of party programs.

All this, in turn, led to the emergence of a leadership style that contrasted markedly with that of Cannon and Reed. The components of this new style emerged gradually in the 1920s and 1930s as power in the House decentralized. It crystallized under Rayburn and was fully applied by him. It represented his experienced and finely tuned sense of what made for effective leadership in a House in which the Speaker lacked the formal powers of a czar, had to mobilize a majority party fairly evenly balanced between discordant northern and Southern elements, confronted a set of committees and committee chairmen with great power and autonomy, and had to deal with individual members who rejected party discipline and prized their independence.

The main facets of the Rayburn style can be analyzed in terms of the following categories: personal friendship and loyalty, permissiveness, restrained partisanship and conflict reduction, informality, and risk avoidance.

Whereas Cannon and Reed relied on their authority and power as Speakers and party chiefs, Rayburn relied on personal friendship and loyalty. If the Speaker could no longer command the House, his vantage points in the formal and party systems as well as his personal prestige provided a variety of opportunities to do favors for members. Rayburn exploited these opportunities in a skillful and imaginative manner. He sought continually to bind members to him as a person on the basis of favors rendered to them as persons, favors which eased their lives in Washington, enhanced their sense of personal worth, and/or advanced their political careers. In contrast to Cannon and Reed, who emphasized policy goals over personal relationships, Rayburn sought to attain policy goals through personal relationships, through nurturing friendships and creating obligations (Bolling 1965, 65–68; Daniels 1946, 56–58).

Whereas Cannon and Reed were quite intolerant of party defection and quite amenable to employing punishments as well as rewards as means of inducement, Rayburn was very permissive. He explicitly legitimized party irregularity on the basis of policy disagreement or constituency pressure and was reluctant ever to punish or coerce a member. To be sure, he did withhold rewards or favors from those he felt failed to cooperate with him for light or insubstantial reasons. Nonetheless, his prevailing inclination was not to alienate members whose vote or help he might need on future occasions (Steinberg 1975, 178).

Whereas Cannon and Reed were highly partisan and accepted both intraparty and interparty conflict as necessary aspects of majority party leadership, Rayburn sought to temper partisanship in personal relationships and to restrain conflict generally. He saw party mechanisms, such as the caucus and Steering Committee, as mechanisms for exacerbating party divisions and studiously ignored them. He established friendly relations with minority party leaders receptive to his overtures and extended advice and favors to rank-and-file minority members. He emphasized reciprocity and compromise as the prime behavioral rules for all members. Thus the guiding motif of his regime was not "serve party policy goals," but rather "to get along, go along," i.e., trade favors (MacNeil 1963, 84–85).

Whereas Cannon and Reed sought to achieve party programs by mobilizing partisan majorities and working through a stable set of partisan lieutenants, Rayburn's approach was more informal and ad hoc. Bargaining needs and opportunities determined his legislative strategies and personal contact served as his main means of implementing these strategies. Thus, on the whole, he worked through varying sets of trusted friends who were loyal Democrats and whom he had placed in key positions in the committee system. However, he was not averse when pressed at the committee stage to appealing to powerful opponents, who were nonetheless close friends, for help . . . [including] the Republican leader, Joe Martin. Similarly, at the floor stage he customarily asked varying sets of members, who were close friends and/or owed him favors, to insure his majority by standing ready to vote for him if needed, even against their policy preferences and/or constituency interests (Clapp 1963, 286–87).

Finally, whereas Cannon and Reed were aggressive in the pursuit of party policy goals, Rayburn was cautious. His inclination was to avoid battles when the outcome was uncertain. To be sure, in instances when a Democratic president and/or large number of his fellow partisans pressed him, he would usually wage some sort of fight. But both because he felt that defeat undermined his influence and because he did not like to expend his credits in losing causes, his clear and decided preference was to refuse battle, to wait until prospects for victory were favorable. Similarly, he shied away from challenging any of the key facets of decentralized power in the House, despite their restrictive impact on his ability to lead. His inclination was to work with what existed and endure, rather than to seek basic change. Only when extremely provoked did he contest the power of senior chairmen or the prerogatives of the Rules Committee and even then only indirectly. Thus he did not discipline Graham Barden but rather took over the Education and Labor Committee by filling vacancies with liberal Democrats. Thus he did not discipline Howard Smith or Bill Colmer or limit the power of the Rules Committee. He rather chose to expand its membership. In short, then, Rayburn was far more inclined to accept the defeat of party programs than to risk his influence and prestige in battles to attain them (Clapp 1963, 66–69; Wicker 1968, 43–54).

The Bases of Personalized Leadership

Earlier we argued that czar rule derived from the interaction of the Speaker's formal powers and his leverage as party chief. We further argued that party strength was the determining factor in this interaction and that it was rooted primarily in the polarized constituency bases of the two parties. The emergence by 1940 of a new type of House and a new leadership style, both of which we may identify with Sam Rayburn, can be explained in terms of the altered character and impact of these same variables.

Confining ourselves simply to events in the House, the interaction between formal power and party strength again played a critical, though quite different, role. As we have already suggested, the interaction of these variables now worked to reduce leadership power. Party strength could no longer support or justify high concentrations of formal power in the leadership. Limited formal power, however, allowed party divisions fuller expression and increases in these divisions undermined party control mechanisms. The atrophy of these mechanisms, in turn, augmented the power and independence of party factions and transformed the leadership into bargainers and brokers, into middlemen rather than commanders (Truman 1959, 202–27).

Evidence of the continuing decline in party strength, which we interpret as both cause and effect of the decentralization of power in the House, has already been presented in Table 22.2. To reinforce our tabular evidence we regressed party voting against time for the whole period from 1894 to 1952. The results are presented in Figure 22.1. The slope of the line is negative (B = −1.3) and the correlation between time and party voting −.74. Clearly, changes in party strength and changes in institutional structure covary in a manner that is consistent with our argument.

Nonetheless, if we again would acknowledge the impact of the internal, interactive effect between formal power and party strength and accord party strength the determining role in this interaction, we again would also argue that levels of party strength are subject primarily to external determination. In short, though restricted formal power provided a context in which party divisions could be expressed and extended, the primary engine of increased divisiveness was increased disharmony in the constituency bases underlying the majority party coalition. Thus, as in the case of leadership power and style during the period of czar rule, the key to the Rayburn House and the Rayburn style lies in electoral alignment patterns.

Table 22.1 shows that from 1881 to 1921 party strength was high when the constituency bases of the parties were highly polarized and that it declined when these bases became less polarized. We have argued that increased factionalization in the party system was the primary source of the increased divisiveness that undermined the use of party control mechanisms in the 1920s. In order to show how constituency alignments are related to the further decline of party and the emergence of the Rayburn House, it is necessary to analyze the New Deal realignment and its aftermath.

The political revolution known as the New Deal was the product of the Great Depression. The votes providing the Democrats their majority came primarily from those groups most affected by the Depression, farmers and low-income city dwellers, including blue-collar workers, ethnic groups, and blacks. Thus, the New Deal resulted in an increase in Democratic party allegiance across all constituent characteristics. Rather than recreating polarized congressional parties as in the period of czar rule, the New Deal created a monolithic majority party which encompassed all types of constituencies. To the Democratic party's traditional base of support, the rural South, it added the urban Northeast and the urban and rural Midwest (Sundquist 1973, 183–218; Ladd and Hadley 1975, 31–88).

Table 22.3 illustrates and supports this point. It includes the following data, collected from the 1930 census and mapped onto congressional districts: the number of blue-collar workers, value added by manufactures, and population density. Constituencies are ranked as high or low in relation to these characteristics in terms of the national mean and the percentage increase as well as the absolute ratio increase calculated for Democratic congressmen.

The monolithic majority party coalition created by the New Deal was formed around the basic issue of government aid to combat the effects of the Depression. Hoover and the Republican party favored voluntarism and nonintervention, whereas the Democrats favored active government involvement. As long as the issue of the

Table 22.3

Increases in congressional majority party composition during
1932 realignment

District characteristic	Percent Democratic Congressmen			
	70th House (1927–29)	73rd House (1933–35)	Percentage increase	Absolute ratio increase
Blue-collar				
Low (farm)	57	82	25	1.37
High (labor)	32	64	32	1.97
Value added				
Low (nonindustrial)	54	81	27	1.40
High (industrial)	34	67	33	1.89
Density				
Low (rural)	53	77	24	1.38
High (urban)	30	67	37	1.96

Source: Compiled from U.S. Bureau of Census. 1930. *Fifteenth Census of the United States. Agriculture*, Vol. 2, parts 1, 2 and 3; *Manufactures*, Vol. 3; *Population*, Vol. 3, parts 1 and 2 (Washington, D.C.: U.S. Government Printing Office).

role of government in combating the Depression remained the central and defining one, congressional Democrats had a broad basis for unity, despite their increased disparateness. And, indeed, in the 1930s there was a break in the long-term trend toward declining party voting (see Figure 22.1). However, as is now evident, the Roosevelt coalition could not maintain its cohesion across changing issue dimensions (Sinclair 1978). As a monolithic rather than polarized coalition, it was particularly vulnerable to the emergence of issues that would divide its various components rather than unite them as the Depression had done.

In the late 1930s and early 1940s two factors combined to redefine the political climate and render it far less hospitable to majority party unity. The first was the alteration in the character and thrust of the New Deal, which focused attention and controversy on the federal government's general role as an agent of social welfare rather than its narrower role as an agent of economic recovery. The divisive potential of this development was signaled by the battle over New Deal legislation in the Seventy-fifth Congress (1937–39), a battle that in the eyes of many analysts marks the true emergence of the Conservative Coalition (Brady and Bullock 1980). The second was the worsening international situation, which finally led to World War II. This development focused attention and controversy not only on defense and foreign policy, but on the management of a war economy as well. In so doing, it also bypassed or submerged old bases of Democratic unity and reinforced divisions along liberal-conservative lines (Young 1956).

The emergence and growth of the Conservative Coalition in the late 1930s and early 1940s, documented in Table 22.2, testifies to the impact of these factors in producing a new and enduring split in the congressional Democratic party that

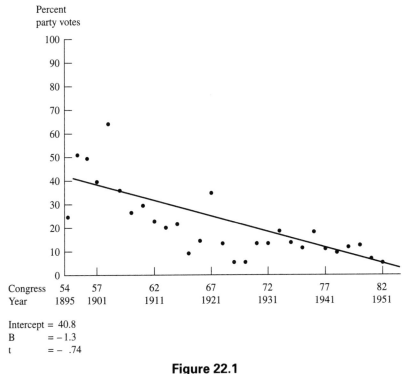

Percent
party votes

Figure 22.1

Party voting in the House of Representatives (1895–1953). *Source:* Compiled
from U.S. Bureau of Census, *Fifteenth Census of the United States* (1930):
Agriculture, Vol. 2, parts 1, 2 and 3; *Manufactures,* Vol. 3; *Population,* Vol. 3,
parts 1 and 2 (Washington, D.C.: U.S. Government Printing Office).

was rooted in differences between rural conservative Southern constituencies and
urban liberal northern ones. Nor is it surprising that as the dimensions of the split
increased and finally stabilized, party voting declined. A comparison of the data in
Table 22.2 broadly demonstrates the point; but to pin it down we calculated the
correlation (Pearson's r) between Conservative Coalition activity and party voting
for the period 1931–53. The result is an impressive −.67.

In short, then, external factors are of primary importance in accounting for
personalized rule as well as czar rule. In a context in which the interaction of
restricted formal power and declining party strength had already combined to disperse power, the emergence of a basic split in the majority party, rooted in constituency differences, further substantially undermined leadership power. Rayburn's
highly personalized style was thus a reaction to his party situation, to the corps of
independent and divided partisans he had to work with and lead. Indeed, his style
is not only distinguishable in kind from that of Cannon and Reed, but even in
degree from that of preceding Democratic Speakers, such as Garner and Rainey,
who did not have to worry continually about Southern support on key committees
and the floor (MacNeil 1963, 34).

CONCLUSION

Our historical analysis of the transition from Cannon to Rayburn suggests several broad propositions or hypotheses that explain House leadership roles and behavior and have general import or significance for the analysis of legislative leadership. They are as follows.

First, institutional context rather than personal skill is the primary determinant of leadership power in the House. To be sure, leadership power, like other forms of power, is a combination of the fund of inducements available and the skill with which they are used. Nonetheless, skill cannot fully compensate for deficiencies in the quality or quantity of inducements. Indeed, the very skills required of leaders themselves vary in terms of the parameters and needs imposed by the character of the House as a political institution at particular points in its history. Thus, Rayburn was not and could not be as powerful a Speaker as Cannon or Reed. His sources of leverage in the formal and party systems were simply not comparable. Nor did Reed or Cannon require the same level of skill in building credits or bargaining as Rayburn to maximize their power. Similarly, it is doubtful that O'Neill can be as strong a Speaker as Rayburn whatever the level of skill he possesses, given the increased fractionalization in both the formal and party systems that has occurred in the past two decades.

Second, institutional context rather than personal traits primarily determines leadership style in the House. To be sure, style is affected by personal traits. Nonetheless, style is and must be responsive to and congruent with both the inducements available to leaders and member expectations regarding proper behavior. Indeed, the personal traits of leaders are themselves shaped by the character of the House as a political institution at particular points in time through the impact of socialization and selection processes that enforce prevailing norms. Thus, if Rayburn was a more permissive and consensual leader than Cannon or Reed, this is not because he was inherently a less tough or more affective person, but rather because of his weaker sources of leverage and the heightened individualism of members. . . . Similarly, though leaders remain distinct personalities . . . range of tolerance for personal traits or predispositions that conflict with prevailing norms is restricted. . . . In contrast, members who cannot eliminate or temper traits that run counter to prevailing norms are disadvantaged in the pursuit of leadership office. . . . In a basic sense, then, the impact of context on leadership style has something of the character of a self-fulfilling hypothesis.

Third, there is no direct relationship between leadership style and effectiveness in the House. This is true whether effectiveness is interpreted relatively or absolutely. Interpreted relatively, effectiveness is a matter of the skill with which resources are used, not actual results. However, whereas style is primarily determined by the parameters and needs imposed by the political character of the House as an institution at certain points in his history, particular styles can be applied with varying degrees of skill. . . . Similarly, if effectiveness is interpreted absolutely, i.e., in terms of actual results of achievements, there is still no direct or simple relationship between style and effectiveness. On the one hand, there is no one best "style"; the relationship between style and effectiveness is rather a highly contingent or situational variable. On the other hand, even when contexts dictate roughly similar styles, they do not necessarily accord them roughly equal chances of success. . . .

Fourth, and last, the impact of institutional context on leadership power and style is determined primarily by party strength. To be sure, the degree of organizational elaboration substantially affects the intensity of the demands imposed on integrative capacity and is largely a produce of factors other than party strength, e.g., size and work load. Nonetheless, integrative capacity derives or flows primarily from party strength (Cooper 1975). The higher the degree of party unity or cohesion the more power in both the formal and party systems can be concentrated in the hands of party leaders and the more leadership style will be oriented to command and task or goal attainment. The lower the degree of party unity or cohesion the more power in both the formal and party system will be dispersed and the more leadership style will be oriented to bargaining and the maintenance of good relations. The infrequency of eras of centralized power in the House is thus explicable in terms of the very high levels of party strength required to support it, requirements which have increased as the organization itself has become more elaborate. Similarly, the degree of power dispersion now present is explicable in terms of present weaknesses in party unity or coherence both in absolute terms and relative to an organizational structure that has grown far more complex in the past two decades. Given the dependence of internal party strength on appropriate constituency alignments, all this, in turn, means that leadership power and style are ultimately tied to the state of the party system in the electorate, that external or environmental factors have a decisive bearing on the parameters and needs that institutional context imposes on leadership power and style. In short, then, to be understood Cannon and Reed must be seen in the context of an entire party system, and the same applies to Rayburn in the 1940s and 1950s. . . .

NOTES

1. Aside from the Rules Committee, nine other committees were privileged to report at any time on certain matters. In addition, the eight committees charged with general appropriation bills also were privileged to report at any time on such bills. *Hinds' Precedents* (1907), Vol. 4, Sec. 4621. It should also be remembered that the unanimous consent procedure at this time consisted simply of motions on the floor to that effect. The rule providing for a Consent Calendar was not adopted until 1909 (Chiu 1928, 179–88).
2. The total control the Speaker exercised over the consideration of minor legislation thus resulted from the combined impact of the lack of a regular order of business and the need to secure recognition by the Speaker to use either unanimous consent or suspension to bring constituency bills to the floor (Chiu 1928, 228–30).
3. In changing the rules to provide for election of the standing committees by the House, the Democrats took care to maintain centralized party control. Thus, they blocked the alternative preferred by the Insurgent Republicans, which would have provided for party committees on committees elected by geographic regions. Instead, the Democrats adopted a rule that only provided for election by the House and then made the Democratic members of Ways and Means, led by Underwood, their Committee on Committees (Brown 1922, 172–77).

Chapter 23

The Changing Role and Impact of Parties and Leaders

DAVID W. ROHDE

THEORY AND EVIDENCE

... The main driving force behind the resurgence of partisanship in the [postreform] House is the exogenous influence of electoral change. The elections of the late 1950s and the 1960s brought to the House many new liberal Democrats. These members found institutional arrangements (especially the disproportionate powers of committee chairmen) to be biased against their interests and in favor of those of the "Conservative Coalition." They sought to redress the institutional imbalance through the reforms of the 1970s, which weakened chairmen and strengthened the majority party. After the reform era, electoral forces again had an impact through national and district-level changes that resulted in electoral coalitions of representatives that were more similar within parties and more different between them. These changes resulted in party caucuses in the House that were more homogeneous with regard to policy preferences, and which therefore found it easier to find common ground on previously divisive issues. This increased homogeneity also provided the basis for more aggressive use of reform-granted powers by the Democratic party leadership. Finally, partisanship was enhanced in the 1980s by the impact of individual personalities: Democratic leaders, who were progressively more willing to use their powers to advance partisan interests, and President Reagan, whose inclination to press his relatively extreme policy views made it easier for Democrats to arrive at satisfactory compromise positions within their party. As a result of all these factors, outcomes in the House—in committee and on the floor—more frequently reflected the preferences of House Democrats. We will now review more fully these aspects of the theory and their interrelationships.

Source: *Parties and Leaders in the Postreform House* (Chicago: University of Chicago Press, 1991) pp. 162–72, 177–79. Reprinted by permission of the publisher.

Electoral Forces, Member Goals, and the Rise of Reform

In 1958 and the early 1960s, many Democrats with liberal policy preferences were first elected to the House. . . . [T]he assertion that these junior Democrats were concerned about policy outcomes does not imply that this was the exclusive, or even the paramount, goal for all of them. Many of these representatives were primarily concerned with getting reelected, some had higher office in mind, and others wanted power in the House. However, it is also true that for many Democrats there was little or no conflict between policy goals and others. . . . [Although we can distinguish] between personal preference (the policy outcome actually preferred by a member) and operative preference (the outcome the member supports when all relevant political influences are taken into account), for many northern Democrats the two types of preferences were the same. Both they and their supportive (i.e., reelection and primary) constituencies favored expanded government services, efforts to influence the economy, new civil rights laws, etc. Thus for them the pursuit of policy interests was an electoral advantage. Moreover, even when there was goal conflict, members often found it possible to balance reelection and policy interests by taking some electoral risks and compromising some policy positions.

When these new Democrats got to the House, they found that although their party was in the majority and theoretically could control outcomes, in reality the Conservative Coalition of Southern Democrats and Republicans stood as an effective roadblock to the achievement of their policy goals. This was possible for four related reasons: (1) committees dominated the policy-making process, (2) committee chairmen and other senior members had disproportionate power within committees, (3) conservative Southern Democrats held power positions on committees out of proportion to their numbers in the party (especially on the most important committees), and (4) these conservatives were able to ally with the Republicans against the majority of their own party because the seniority system automatically granted and protected their positions of influence on committees. As Richard Bolling said (1965, 36), these circumstances resulted in a situation in which "the majority of House Democrats has not had effective control of the House."

Liberal House Democrats began searching for ways to improve their situation. The Democratic Study Group was formed to provide like-minded members with useful legislative information and to rally them behind liberal initiatives. It became clear, however, that this wasn't going to be sufficient, and (when their situation worsened with Richard Nixon's election in 1968) the DSG leadership tried to devise changes in the institutional arrangements in the House that would given them greater influence over policy outcomes.

Diverse Goals and the Patterns of Reform

. . . [T]he effort to alter the rules operated on three distinct tracks. These reforms were intended to alter the conditions that permitted the Conservative Coalition to prevail against the majority of Democrats. The DSG leaders who devised the series of reform packages saw them as means to advance liberal policy goals. More important, this was the main reason that they publicly articulated in trying to rally support for reform among House Democrats. They argued that senior committee conservatives didn't support party positions, that the unrestricted use of the seniority system made this possible, and that the proposed reforms would change things. However, the DSG leaders also recognized that members were not solely motivated by policy concerns. Other interests had to be protected in the reform process, and those interests sometimes provided additional incentives for supporting reform.

The first, and most essential (from the liberals' point of view), reform track was the set of measures that undermined the powers of committee chairmen. The Subcommittee Bill of Rights protected the operating independence of subcommittees, providing guaranteed staff and explicitly establishing jurisdictions. In addition it removed the appointment of subcommittee chairmen and members from the control of committee chairmen. Some limits were also placed on the dominant and independent influence of committees on policy outcomes within their jurisdictions. One aspect of this was the adoption of the recorded teller vote, which altered the relationship between the committees and the floor. Members chose to put their decisions regarding proposed changes in committee bills on the public record. They thereby pitted the pressures of their interest in reelection and policy against the influences that committee leaders could bring to bear, another recognition of the mixed goals pursued by congressmen.

Committee independence and influence was also counterbalanced by the measures that strengthened Democratic party leaders, the second reform track. The transfer of Democratic committee-assignment powers to the Steering and Policy Committee, coupled with direct Speaker control over Rules Committee appointments, expanded leadership influence over members' access to the most desirable spots in the committee system. Other changes (multiple referral, influence over special rules, expanded ability to use suspensions) increased the leaders' ability to shape the floor agenda to enhance the prospects of committee products they endorsed, or to undermine those they did not.

Finally, the third track of reform was designed to ensure that the new distribution of power that resulted from the first two tracks did not result in new independent and autocratic practices. It put in place mechanisms of collective control for each of the significant repositories of power granted through the Democratic party. Top party leaders could, as had always been true, theoretically be replaced at the beginning of any Congress, but this power was never used (or needed). However, the leadership's accountability to the members was enhanced through regular and special meetings of the Democratic caucus, and through weekly meetings of an expanded whip system, which provided avenues for members to communicate their concerns and complaints. Committee chairmen (and subcommittee chairs on Appropriations) were made responsible to the caucus through regular secret-ballot votes at the beginning of each Congress, whereby House Democrats could approve or reject their occupancy of those positions. Employing these procedures, the caucus rejected chairmen five times between 1974 and 1988. Similarly, other subcommittee chairmen were made responsible to party caucuses on their respective committees, and this power was also exercised a number of times. These new rules were all designed to accomplish the goal that Rep. Don Fraser set up at the beginning of the reform effort: "to make the people who held positions of power . . . responsible to rank-and-file Democrats" (Sheppard 1985, 40).

Thus the reform movement was a multifaceted effort intended to revise the balance of power within the House and to increase rank-and-file influence over party and committee leaders. . . . [T]he reforms were primarily concerned with the top committees that made national policy on matters that frequently provoked partisan division, committees like Appropriations, Budget, Ways and Means, Energy and Commerce, and Armed Services.

The obligation to support party positions, moreover, was not intended to apply equally to all members. There was no intention to create a system of party responsibility like those that operate in parliamentary democracies, imposing on every member the requirement to support every party position. Instead, obligation was to be imposed on members "who held positions of power"—party leaders, committee chairmen, members of prestige committees. In effect, seeking and accepting positions of influence within the committee or party leadership meant accepting an implied contract: Such leaders were obliged to support—or at least not to block—policy initiatives on which there was a party consensus. If these expectations were violated, members risked the loss of their influential positions. Party support was also expected from representatives who aspired to these positions. Taken together, these elements define the system that we have termed conditional party government. Committee and party leaders were to be responsible to the members, not vice versa. Members were to be free to pursue their own goals within a generally decentralized system. The exceptions were to be limited to those areas that were of concern to the party collectively, and, among those, to issues on which there was a reasonably wide consensus among party members. Moreover, the degree of responsibility was roughly proportional to the amount of power the members had been granted by the party. Party and top committee leaders had the greatest obligations.

Electoral Forces Again: The Increase in Party Homogeneity

. . . [R]egional differences among Democratic voters played a prominent role in producing the deep divisions that were apparent within the House Democratic party in the 1960s and 1970s. As new issues (like civil rights, the Vietnam War, and expansion of government service) rose to prominence—issues that found different preferences among northern and Southern Democratic voters—sharply different patterns of positions were taken by northern and southern Democratic congressmen. Then, gradually, the composition of each party's electorate began to change. Most profoundly, the Voting Rights Act added large numbers of black voters to the electorate, most of whom identified with the Democratic party and had relatively liberal policy preferences. At the same time, many conservative white voters joined the Republican party in the South. Some of these were northern migrants; others were disaffected Democrats who were choosing a new and more hospitable home for their conservative preferences. As a consequence of

these changes, and some concurrent shifting among northerners, the policy positions of the coalitions of voters supporting congressional candidates became more
similar within the parties across regions, and more different between the parties.

... [I]n the wake of these shifting patterns of preferences among voters, the
positions supported by members of Congress also changed, especially among
Southerners. Some Southern conservatives were replaced by (usually even more
conservative) Republicans; others were succeeded by moderate to liberal Democrats.
In still other instances, the same representative continued serving, but supported
Democratic party positions more frequently in response to the liberalization of
their supportive constituencies. In the north there were changes too, with the
number of Democrats (most of whom were party loyalists) increasing, and the
number of moderate Republicans declining.

This trend toward increased party homogeneity was reinforced by the operation of those reform provisions that were intended to enhance collective control of
those in power positions. Senior Democrats, and more junior members who
wanted leadership or prestige committee positions, were encouraged to support
party positions and discouraged from allying with the Republicans. The combined
effect of these electoral and institutional forces was similar to the new pattern
among voters; the responses of members within the parties to many issues became
more similar, and collectively the responses of the two parties became more divergent. Even on issues that we examined which were previously very divisive for
Democrats—civil rights, defense, and budget policy—more common ground was
found in the 1980s, frequently resulting in partisan victories over the Republicans.

Increased Use of Leadership Power

The growth of preference homogeneity among Democrats (at least in terms of
operative preference, but probably also with regard to personal preferences)
increased the scope of conditional party government. Within that set of issues that
were of partisan interest, there were more and more instances in which there was
sufficient consensus to support employment of the expanded powers that were
granted to the leadership by the reforms. There were more issues on which the
Steering and Policy Committee could declare important floor votes to be party
policy, to be taken into account when committee assignments were made. There
were more bills on which Democratic members were willing to support the use of
restrictive rules to limit amendments, and votes to approve these rules increasingly provoked sharp partisan opposition from Republicans. Important bills often
required action by multiple committees, and the Speaker increasingly played the
role of arbiter in instances of intercommittee conflict. While the scope of the party
leadership's activities had been expanding under Speaker O'Neill, the aggressive
use of these powers was sharply increased when James Wright succeeded to the
position. He articulated an agenda that he believed reflected party views, and then
pressed that agenda to passage despite facing opposition from the president and
House Republicans in almost every instance.

As Democratic homogeneity grew and the leadership increasingly employed
its powers, the party's whip system was expanded to serve the interests of both

leaders and rank-and-file Democrats. Members wanted an effective means to communicate their preferences and complaints to the leaders. The leaders, in turn, needed this communication to assess the degree of party consensus, and also wanted the resources it provided to persuade reluctant or undecided colleagues on important votes. The perceived effectiveness of the strengthened Democratic leadership in advancing party interests was well reflected in Republican moves to grant similar increased powers to their leaders.

Presidential Influences on Partisanship

. . . [M]any analysts had argued that divided government would tend to reduce partisanship, while united government would enhance it. However, we [contend] that this generalization [is] not theoretically valid in all cases. Rather, the degree of partisanship would depend not only on whether partisan control was divided or united, but also on the nature of a president's preferences vis-à-vis those of members of Congress, and on the inclination of each side to compromise.

These hypotheses were supported by evidence from the Carter and Reagan administrations. Carter pressed a wide-ranging agenda that divided rather than rallied his party, reducing instead of increasing partisanship. Reagan initially proposed policy shifts in a conservative direction that found substantial support among Southern Democrats as well as Republicans. However, he attempted to build on his early successes with further conservative initiatives. These revealed the different preferences of Republicans on the one hand and Southern conservatives and moderates on the other, and made it easier for Democrats to arrive at a consensus on alternatives to presidential proposals. The result was an increasing proportion of bills on which the combination of committee and floor action produced results that found the two parties on opposite sides and President Reagan opposing passage.

Partisanship and Legislative Outcomes

. . . [T]he pattern of legislative outcomes in the House . . . changed as a result of the resurgence of partisanship. The proportion of amendments that were Democrat-favored declined, and the Republicans' ability to get amendments they favored passed also decreased. This indicates that committee bills were better reflecting the preferences of House Democrats. Taking the combination of committee and floor action into account, the proportion of bills that were more favored by Democrats also increased. Finally, Democratic victories on floor votes on which party majorities opposed one another grew to levels that were generally higher than previous Congresses in which the presidency was in Democratic hands.

The combination of greater homogeneity in both parties based on changing electoral conditions, and the employment of institutional powers to buttress that homogeneity and advance party-favored initiatives, created the context for the operation of conditional party government. It didn't function on all issues, because members didn't intend it to. And it didn't function in some instances because there wasn't sufficient consensus to offer a chance of party victory. But during the 1980s, the Democratic majority was more and more frequently able to arrive at party positions on a wide range of nationally important issues in the face of determined opposition from House Republicans and a popular Republican president. This is not the American equivalent of parliamentary party responsibility, but it is a remarkable change from the way the House used to operate, and to a situation that involves a much stronger role for parties than most analysts thought was possible.

CHANGING PERSPECTIVES ON POLITICS IN THE HOUSE

Kenneth Shepsle (1989, 238) said that when scholars talk about Congress, they have in mind "a textbook Congress characterized by a few main tendencies and described in broad terms." Probably none of the aspects of this textbook Congress characterization would find unanimous support among analysts, but they would secure widespread agreement. We would argue that in light of the cumulative research described here—both the original findings and the reported results of others—certain aspects of the shared picture of politics in the House need revision, at least as a matter of emphasis.

The Role and Impact of Parties and Leaders

The most significant change relates to the perceived importance of parties and their leaders. Collie (1986) found few examples of research in journals in 1985–86 that dealt with congressional parties, and those that did mostly indicated that they were unimportant. These views are more recent ratifications of the shared view, dominant over the last quarter-century, that parties and leaders in the House are weak and relatively inconsequential. That perspective was succinctly articulated by David Mayhew in his *Congress: The Electoral Connection* (1974a, 27): "The fact is that no theoretical treatment of the United States Congress that posits parties as analytic units will go very far. So we are left with individual congressmen, with 535 men and women rather than two parties, as units to be examined. . . ." Mayhew was writing in the midst of the reform era, when both legislative parties were experiencing deep divisions. Levels of party loyalty were low, the incentives for party support were weak, and party leaders were usually disinclined to try to influence outcomes. Thus the textbook picture was fairly accurate for that time.

However, inherent in Mayhew's characterization is the view that members are connected either to parties *or* to electoral incentives. He indicated that if legislators' interests are not linked to their parties through organizational arrangements as they are in parliamentary systems, then they will respond to their constituencies and not be supportive of their party.[1] What this characterization does not recognize is that members may be linked to their parties *through* their constituencies. We can imagine a hypothetical election system in which all politicians are motivated only by the desire to win elections, all voters decide whom to support based solely on a common set of issues, and all voters who support the more liberal position belong to the Democratic party while all conservatives are Republicans. In this system the party primaries in each district would naturally choose Democratic candidates who espouse more liberal positions than do the chosen Republican candidates. Then the general-election outcome would depend on the partisan balance among voters in each district. Once in office these members would tend to support the conflicting positions of their respective parties, solely on the basis of their own electoral incentives.

Of course the real-world context of congressmen that we have been discussing is not nearly so neat and simple as this hypothetical world, but the evidence indicates that in the wake of changes in the electorate over the last 25 years or so it is closer to that situation than it used to be. Both the earlier literature on party voting and more recent analyses have indicated that northern and Southern Democrats, for example, disagreed on many issues largely because the positions of their constituents were different on those issues. In contrast, even when party voting was at its nadir, there was a relatively high level of agreement on issues (and of party loyalty) among northeastern Democrats and among Midwestern Republicans. This was because the views of their respective constituencies were fairly similar.

As the cumulative effects of electoral changes began to be felt during the 1970s and 1980s, the supportive constituencies of party candidates became more similar in their policy views across regions. This does not mean that northern Democrats' constituencies and Southern Democrats' constituencies became identical. It just means that they tended to become noticeably more similar than they had been, and in particular that northern and Southern Democratic constituencies tended to become more like one another than the latter were like Republican constituencies. As a consequence, the positions taken by northern and Southern Democratic representatives became more similar—in their election contests, in their committees, and on the House floor. Thus there is no *necessary* conflict between evidence of high party loyalty and the view that members are motivated solely by electoral interests, although we have argued that other motivations are at work as well. Parties in the House have become more cohesive, and in turn more active and influential, and this has happened partly as a *consequence* of congressmen's individual electoral interests. It is perhaps useful to refer to the level of partisanship that is the result of exogenous, electorate-based forces as the "natural level of partisanship." Then we can talk of the actual level of partisanship as higher or lower than this natural level due to other factors, like organizational and personal influences.

Our textbook picture must change not only to encompass stronger parties in the House, but also to include stronger and more influential party leaders. Much of the literature on party leadership . . . emphasized the restrictions context exerted on leaders, and that literature generally expected that leaders would remain weak because their context wouldn't permit anything else. Cooper and Brady (1981a, 423), for example, expressed doubt that Speaker O'Neill (and by inference his successors) could even be as strong a party leader as Rayburn, whom they had described as very much at the mercy of strong committee chairmen and a divided party. Yet . . . we have seen that perhaps O'Neill, and certainly Wright, headed a stronger leadership. This is not a demonstration that Cooper and Brady and their contemporaries were incorrect in their theoretical arguments, but rather that the context of the leaders has changed in ways that were not foreseen.

The interaction of increased Democratic homogeneity with enhanced leadership powers has created conditions under which there is substantial membership support for (and even demand for) strong leadership action on behalf of a range of party-supported initiatives. And recently, parallel conditions have increasingly developed within the Republican party. It is important to emphasize that these developments provide general support for, not refutation of, the contextual theory of leadership. This newly strengthened leadership is not analogous to the powerful party heads of parliamentary systems or to the House speakerships of Cannon and Reed—leaders who commanded their memberships. Instead, these are leaders who are strong because (and when) they are agents of their memberships, who want them to be strong. When the legislative situation involves an issue that party members care about and on which their preferences are homogeneous, the stages is set for maximal use of the leadership's powers. If, however, the party is deeply divided, then leaders will be reluctant to use the tools at their disposal, and they can appear as weak as the leadership looked immediately after the reform era.

Despite this general support for the contextual theory, we must recall the argument for a qualification to that view: that there is an asymmetry between the circumstances which constrain leaders and those which are permissive. When conditions won't support strong leadership activity, then leaders who want to exercise power and those who do not will probably yield roughly the same results. When the membership is permissive or demanding of strong leadership, however, leaders who are aggressive and enthusiastic will likely exhibit substantially more activist behavior than will leaders who are reluctant about the exercise of their powers. Yet even reluctant leaders must, in these situations, be responsive to demands for action by the membership. . . .

Some Thoughts Regarding the Senate

This analysis has focused on the House, but it would seem useful and necessary to say something about how the different elements of the theoretical argument might apply to the Senate. Such a comparison is interesting because the pattern of readily available evidence indicates that the resurgence of partisanship in the Senate, while present, has not been nearly so pronounced as in the House. One would hope that we could find plausible hypotheses regarding differences between the houses on theoretically relevant variables to help to explain these contrasting patterns.

The contrast between the two bodies is most apparent in data on floor voting. In the two decades from 1969 to 1988, the frequency of party-unity voting (i.e., party majorities opposing one another) in the House went from a low point of 27% (1970) to a high of 64% (1987), a range of 37 points.[2] In the Senate, the variation was between 35% (1970) and 52% (1986), only 17 points. Data on average party-unity scores also indicate higher levels of loyalty in the House during the 1980s among Democrats in general and Southern Democrats in particular.

One possible source for explanations of these differences is electoral forces, which have been the principal explanatory factor for the changes in the House. It would seem that the effects of district versus statewide elections would be very potent. The constituencies of senators will, on average, be considerably more het-erogeneous than those of House members. No state can be as dominated by urban interests as a district in Manhattan, and no state can be as focused on automobile manufacturing as the Seventh District of Michigan, centered on Flint. The diver-sity of Senate constituencies increases the variety of winning electoral coalitions that candidates can put together. This may lead to greater preference conflict within the parties in the Senate, and less difference between them.

Also the liberalizing impact of black enfranchisement in the South was unequally distributed across districts within states. Thus while in some districts the effect would be strong and in others negligible, the statewide effect would be the diluted average of these two. For example, 58% of the population in the Second District of Mississippi is black (leading to the election of black Democrat Mike Espy in 1986), while only 19% of the Fifth District (served by conservative Republican Trent Lott for 16 years, until 1988) is black. The black population of the state is in between at 35%, and both senators are Republican. Thus the natural level of partisanship produced by electoral forces may be lower in the Senate than in the House.

Another possible explanation lies in differences in institutional arrangements and leadership powers. First, the distribution of power across individuals is much more equal in the Senate. The potential for extended debates (commonly known as filibusters) has no parallel in the House, and it vests considerable power in minori-ties. This has become even more true as time pressure has increased due to the Senate's growing workload (Oppenheimer, 1985). Individual senators also have greater access to desirable committee positions. In 1988, 86% of the senators were members of one of the four most desirable committees, while the same was true of only 30% of representatives.[3] Senators also serve on more committees and subcom-mittees than do representatives, which gives them more vantage points from which to influence legislation. In the Senate, moreover, committees have long been less important, and the floor more important, than in the House (Fenno 1973). Senators have been less inclined to specialize in their committees' jurisdictions, even though those obligations covered a broader range of legislation. For example, Smith (1989, 143) shows that from the 1950s through the 1980s, a higher proportion of floor amendments was offered in the Senate compared to the House by members not on the committee with jurisdiction over the legislation. Thus a wider range of mem-bers tends to participate in legislating on any given issue in the Senate.

Growing out of the more equal distribution of power across individuals is the fact that power is also more evenly divided between the two parties. Because of the potential for filibusters and the related need to employ frequently unanimous consent agreements to deal with bills on the floor (Smith 1989, chapter 4), the minority party has a much greater potential to block action in the Senate. Thus the Senate majority party has usually had to make accommodations with the minority, whereas the House majority party (if it can hold its votes) can usually work its will.

Third, the Senate majority-party leadership simply doesn't have the kinds of tools at its disposal that the House leaders do. Senate leaders can offer few incen-tives to encourage loyalty; assignments to top committees come almost automati-cally to senators. Similarly, Senate leaders don't have powers over the agenda analogous to those possessed by the House majority leadership. There is no Rules Committee to shape floor action with the assent of only a bare majority of the body. Instead, the need to use unanimous consent agreements puts the ultimate control over the agenda in the hands of the broad spectrum of the Senate membership.

Finally, the Senate parties haven't employed mechanisms like those in the House directed toward the collective control of power. It is not that such mechanisms don't exist. Party leaders in both parties in the Senate can be voted out at the beginning of any Congress, and both parties adopted rules in the early 1970s that would permit the party caucuses to remove top committee leaders (Ornstein and Rohde 1978, 290–91). These procedures have not, however, been used to encourage party loyalty. No Senate committee chairman has been successfully challenged because of too-frequent support for the other party's positions, or for any other reason. Due to these and other factors, parties (and especially the majority party) in the Senate have less influence over outcomes than in the House, and they can do less for (and to) members.

A third area for explanations of the difference in partisanship between the institutions, at least regarding floor voting, is a difference in the respective agendas. To be sure, since both houses must act on bills for them to become law, the issues dealt with will tend to be generally the same. That does not mean, however, that the mix of votes on these issues will be the same. That could be one source of variation. Also, the proportion of types of votes may be different. For example, the Senate may vote on more amendments than the House. That also could make a difference.

These are some of the reasons that may account for the greater resurgence of partisanship in the House over the past two decades. There are surely others we could discuss. It is important to note, however, that we are talking about differences in rates and levels of change. The direction of change has been similar in both institutions; partisanship has increased. . . .

NOTES

1. These arrangements include party control of nominations and of the electoral power base, and the need to sustain a cabinet; see Mayhew (1974a, 25–27).
2. All data cited here through 1988 are taken from Ornstein, Mann, and Malbin (1990, 198–99). Recall that these data employ all votes, and do not remove the effect of protest votes in the House.
3. The four Senate committees are Appropriations, Armed Services, Finance, and Foreign Relations. The four House Committees are Appropriations, Budget, Rules, and Ways and Means. The committee assignment data are taken from *Congressional Quarterly Weekly Report*, 6 May 1989.

PART VII

LEGISLATIVE VOTING DECISIONS

Chapter 24

How do Legislators Decide How to Vote?

"Party continues to be more closely associated with congressional voting behavior than any other discernible factor" (Turner 1951b). Julius Turner wrote those words in 1951 in a public dissent against the American Political Science Association's report "Toward a More Responsible Two-Party System." That prestigious report had taken as its starting point the untested assertion that in the U.S. system "alternatives between the parties are so badly defined that it is often difficult to determine what the election has decided in even the broadest terms" (APSA 1950, v). Turner challenged that claim by looking at roll-call voting in Congress. He found that party was a more consistent correlate of votes than the other factors he could measure—particularly constituency factors such as the metropolitan-rural dimension, ethnic and racial pressures, or sectionalism—a result that held up when Schneier updated Turner's book in 1970 (Turner 1970).

By contrast with Turner's simple result, more complex, multifaceted models of roll-call voting in Congress have been developed in recent years. Just as models of how the mass public votes have become complex, some models of how members of Congress vote are now equally complex. These models differ in their detail, but they are in fundamental accord that legislators take into account many different cues in deciding how to cast their votes, including such diverse factors as ideology, constituency, the White House, and interest groups in addition to party.

Additionally, there has been considerable attention to *how* legislators decide how to vote on legislation. The starting point in considering this question is recognition that legislative decision making inevitably occurs in a context of limited information. Legislators may have to cast floor votes on hundreds of motions per year (plus a large number of motions in committees). Given the many time demands on legislators, they do not have enough time to study each motion before voting on it. Thus voting by legislators can be seen as a special case of decision making under conditions of limited information, a topic that has received considerable attention in the psychology literature.

A special issue that arises in the legislative context is how to interpret these votes. The early legislative roll-call literature treated votes as indicators of the true attitudes of members. However, it was soon realized that many other factors affect votes. In particular, it is now recognized that several audiences pay attention to roll-call votes, including interest groups and constituents. Votes are thus a way of signaling the members' stands on the issues to interest groups and constituents, and this can be different from the legislators' own attitudes.

This problem of how to interpret legislative votes does not suggest that they are meaningless. The votes have potential consequences to the members themselves. Their opponents go through the large number of votes that members cast to find a few votes that can be used against them at the next election. As a result, legislators have an incentive to generate a voting record that will not interfere with their reelection efforts.

Legislative voting occurs with limited information in another sense: Not every member knows in advance how every other member will vote. Sequence is important in some strategic situations, when decision makers can examine the previous moves by other players before making their next moves. However, sequence is generally of minimal importance in legislative voting, with most members announcing their positions virtually simultaneously. Occasionally the press reports which members waited to the last minute to see if one side needed their votes or changed their votes when they saw which way the vote was going. Yet even when there is some order in legislative voting, analysts generally do not know the full sequence information, so analysis of vote sequence is rare (cf. Box-Steffensmeier, Arnold, and Zorn 1997).

While the research literature generally accepts the view that legislative voting is a case of decision making under conditions of limited information, there are different arguments as to which information strategies are adopted by members. The prime distinction is between a long-term voting strategy in which members maintain a consistent voting pattern over time and a short-term voting approach in which members take cues on how to vote. This is not only a dialogue as to what matters in voting, but it is also a debate as to what is necessary in order to influence the votes of legislators.

LEGISLATIVE VOTING AS BASED ON LONG-TERM POLICY POSITIONS

One way to think about legislative voting is to presume that members adopt long-term strategies for deciding how to vote. By taking a long-term position, the members are presumably saved from carefully thinking through every separate voting decision. This idea may seem simple, but it actually is not. One complication is that members must still decide when to deviate from their long-term voting position, so they still must evaluate each vote. The other major issue is the choice of long-term position. The literature actually suggests several possible long-term strategies—party, policy domain, ideology, and program-specific voting history—each of which we review below.

Political Party

In a responsible party system, the political parties stand for specific programs that are stated in their platforms. The party that is elected to office is then expected to enact its program. Legislators from the majority party vote for its program, while opposition party members vote against. The parties are each internally cohesive, but they vote against one another. This description fits the British party system fairly well, but fits the U.S. Congress much less well.

Much of the early roll-call analysis literature involved developing measures of partisan roll-call voting that would allow a quantitative assessment of fit to this model. A. Lawrence Lowell (1902) developed an early measure of party voting, defined as the proportion of times in a session that at least 90% of one party voted in opposition to at least 90% of the other party, though current party voting measures usually just examine the proportion of votes in a legislative session in which the majorities of the two parties vote in opposite directions. Stuart Rice (1925) developed two additional measures. His index of party cohesion was the average proportion of members of a party voting with its majority minus the proportion voting with its minority, so that higher scores represent greater party cohesion. His index of party likeness was one minus the absolute difference between the proportions of the two parties voting affirmative on a motion, so that higher scores represent a lack of party difference. These measures have been used extensively in the study of party voting in Congress. David Truman (1959) used bloc analysis to analyze the structure of voting in *The Congressional Party*, to find which groups of party members vote together versus which other groups and to show the types of issues that lead to unity or disunity for each party.

There is a research literature that traces party voting across U.S. history, including studies of its correlates. For example, Brady, Cooper, and Hurley (1979) showed how party voting in the House declined from a high in 1890–1910 to a low in 1941–68.[1] Clubb and Traugott (1977) found there is an additional cyclical effect, with party voting in the House from 1861 through 1974 declining with the time since the last party realignment (see also Brady 1978 for a demonstration of how party voting increased around the 1896 and 1932 realignments as party/constituency crosspressures diminished). Patterson and Caldeira (1988) used regression analysis to examine the causes of the decline in party voting in the 1949–84 period. They found that electoral change and the large influx of new members in particular years did not increase party voting. Rather, the existence of sharp differences between the parties over major issues ("external political conflict") was a significant factor, as was control of the presidency and the House by the same political party. Also, large partisan majorities, regional homogeneity, and weak support for the president all led to higher party voting. Patterson and Caldeira were less successful in explaining changes in party voting in the Senate, but they found it largely driven by presidential factors—party voting is higher when the same party controls the presidency and the Senate and when senators' bipartisan support for the president's legislative program is weak. However, Hurley and Wilson (1989) showed over a longer time frame that patterns of party voting over time in the Senate and House are very similar.

The difficulty with these measures is that they do not assess causation. Does party voting mean that party leaders have pressured their members to follow the party line? Or is it just the inevitable consequence of members of the same party sharing similar attitudes? Or, for that matter, is it due to members of the same party representing constituencies that have similar characteristics? It is obvious that party is not as important in the United States as in many other countries, but that does not help us understand when party is more important in the U.S. and when it is less important. As a result, the roll-call voting literature gradually moved away from studying party as a long-term cue and shifted to a focus on ideology.

Multiple Policy Domains

Another view of legislative voting as long-term focuses on continuing policy dimensions in roll-call voting. The journalistic approach is that legislators are liberals, moderates, or conservatives and vote accordingly on legislation. This idea is also incorporated in analyses which use liberal or conservative interest group ratings, such as using Americans for Democratic Action (ADA) ratings of how liberal members of Congress are, or Americans for Conservative Action (ACA) ratings of how conservative members are. However, these ratings are often criticized in that they use a small number of votes which may not be representative of the full range of the legislative agenda. Furthermore, many researchers would argue that legislators have different positions in different policy domains, which a single composite rating would miss.

MacRae's (1958) study of *Dimensions of Congressional Voting* provided a major shift from just using ADA or ACA ratings. MacRae analyzed each party separately and obtained several unidimensional scales that differed in their policy content. The statistical model underlying his analysis was Guttman scaling. Guttman scaling seeks "cumulative" dimensions that order the legislative motions from the least liberal to the most liberal. Each legislator can be thought of as having a "threshold" as to the extent of liberal content in legislation he or she will vote for. The most conservative members would vote against all liberal proposals. Moderate members vote for some weak motions. More liberal members vote for those motions plus some more liberal proposals. The most liberal members vote for all the motions.[2] Given the logic of the situation, the Guttman scale not only orders the motions but also orders the members from the most conservative to the most liberal.

Scaling models are judged by their fit to the data. Scale "error" occurs when a member votes for a very liberal proposal but against a less liberal one, such as favoring extreme reforms of the welfare system but opposing more moderate reforms. There are guidelines as to how much error is acceptable in a scale. Excessive error rates can mean that a particular motion does not fit with the rest of the scale, that the votes are multidimensional rather than fitting a single dimension, or that the votes simply do not fit a cumulative dimension. The actual scaling can be performed by a variety of different but fairly equivalent algorithms, as when MacRae (1970) and Clausen (1973) look for the large clusters of motions whose correlations with one another (as measured by particular coefficients such as Yule's Q) are very high.

The Guttman scaling approach is very common, but some work has suggested alternatives. Weisberg (1972) shows how a "proximity scale" can explain legislative voting in which moderates vote against both motions that are too conservative and motions that are too liberal. MacRae (1970), Weisberg (1968), Anderson, Watts, and Wilcox (1966), and more recently Poole and Rosenthal (1997) review these various methodological techniques as applied to legislative roll calls.

The Guttman approach was used in the Miller and Stokes analysis of representation, reprinted as chapter 6. It is also the basis of Clausen's (1973) systematic study of policy domains underlying congressional voting. Whereas Miller and Stokes looked at three issue domains in one Congress, Clausen examined five issue domains—social welfare, government management (which typically involves the government's economic policies), civil liberties, agricultural assistance, and foreign policy—for the entire 1953–64 period. He classified roll calls into these domains and then found that one major Guttman scale accounted for most of the voting in each issue domain. The scales in each issue domain correlated strongly across Congresses, demonstrating that members had fairly stable positions in these five issue domains. Clausen then correlated these scales with other variables to analyze how such factors as party, constituency, and the presidency affect each issue domain differently. Clausen and Van Horn (1977) subsequently extended this work into the 1970s, finding fairly similar results except that new dimensions appeared in some areas—such as a national security dimension in foreign policy voting during the Vietnam War era. Sinclair (1978, 1982) has extended the Clausen typology and methodology back in time, showing that these dimensions can be traced at least to New Deal days, but with changes around party realignment periods (see especially Sinclair 1977 and Brady 1988) and with voting becoming less partisan and more regional in some policy areas. Collie (1988a) looked at these policy areas in selected Congresses from the 1930s through the 1970s, finding that a small number of major clusters included a high proportion of the votes in each policy domain when partisanship was at its peak after the New Deal realignment. There were more clusters of votes with a lower proportion of votes in those clusters by the less partisan 1970s, however. All in all, this body of literature treats voting in policy domains as reflecting long-term decisions by legislators, but this approach has been counterbalanced by the view that ideology should be treated as singular.

Single Ideology Factor

While the early use of ADA or ACA ratings as measures of ideology was seen as crude, later studies have shown that it is possible to adopt a more systematic approach to viewing ideology as singular. This was evident in the early literature's focus on the Conservative Coalition of Republicans and Southern Democrats. *Congressional Quarterly* even keeps track of the extent to which each member votes with the Conservative Coalition, operationalized as votes where the majority of Republicans and the majority of Southern Democrats vote together in opposition to the majority of northern Democrats. This coalition was so strong in the middle of the twentieth century that Shelley (1983) wrote a book calling it *The Permanent Majority*. The coalition, however, proved not to be permanent. In particular, by the 1990s the Southern Democrats in Congress were considerably less conservative than at midcentury, with many winning their seats because of their strength among black voters (Rohde 1991, reprinted as Chapter 23). As a result, there has been a precipitous decline in Conservative Coalition votes in Congress. However, one can still make a strong argument that voting in Congress is ideological (see, for example, Schneider 1979).

Whereas Clausen's work depended on dividing the legislative motions a priori into different policy areas, an alternative is to analyze all the motions in a particular Congress together. The landmark work of this type is Poole and Rosenthal's, culminating in their 1997 book *Congress: A Political-Economic History of Roll-Call Voting*. Using a measure that they call D-NOMINATE scores, they find that a single liberal-conservative ideological dimension accounts for more than 80% of the roll-call voting in Congress. They have traced this over a very lengthy time period, showing how the voting dimension and the parties have evolved in Congress since the beginning of the Republic.[3] The only periods of instability they obtained were when the Federalist party collapsed in the 1815–25 period and when conflict over slavery led to the demise of the Whig party in the early 1850s.

The controversy remains between viewing congressional voting as a series of separate policy domains per Clausen and as a single ideological dimension à la Poole and Rosenthal. However, the many-dimension result and the few-dimension result can both hold simultaneously. As one explanation (Wilcox and Clausen 1991), Clausen's theory is based on members having separate positions on the different policy domains, but these policy domains can be highly correlated, so that a Poole-and-Rosenthal-like "super" liberal-conservative dimension can underlie them. (See also Koford 1989 for a mathematical demonstration of how both results can occur at once.)

Voting Histories

Rather than see roll-call voting as multidimensional or unidimensional, several analysts emphasize the long-term voting patterns of legislators on very specific issues. Legislators develop their own voting histories on specific recurrent bills and they maintain this position for the sake of consistency.

As Fenno (1978) and Kingdon (1973) argue, members believe they will have an easier time explaining their votes to their constituents if they maintain a consistent voting pattern over time. The local newspapers will rarely notice if members keep voting as they always have on foreign aid, for example, whereas newspaper stories are more likely to appear if the members begin to flip-flop on the issue.

The Asher and Weisberg (1978) selection (chapter 26) is an analysis of the importance of legislators' "voting histories" on a series of issues. It finds considerable stability in voting, but with changes over lengthy time spans as issues evolve and as membership replacement changes the composition of Congress. This piece is important because it gives a strong argument for one theory of congressional voting—that members tend to follow their previous voting history—and for one interpretation of voting change—that voting change is most often a case of slow conversion in voting. They clearly view congressional voting as long-term, though within the context of the specific recurrent bill.

In contrast to the Asher and Weisberg stress on evolutionary change, Brady (1978) emphasizes membership replacement in realigning elections as a cause of policy change in Congress. Brady and Sinclair (1984) have further analyzed this topic in the civil rights and social welfare issue areas. While they find examples of partisan membership replacement and of conversion being critical in transforming a minority on a bill into a majority at a later point in time, they found the two usually operate together. For example, they suggest that the 1964 landslide election was a signal to continuing members who converted their positions, adding to the replacement effect of the election. Brady and Sinclair argue that a gradualism model is not an accurate depiction of coalition building for nonincremental legislation. They instead find discontinuities due to the disruptions of a severe crisis or a social movement. Their results still fit with the view that legislators take long-term positions on issues, albeit positions that can change under extreme circumstances. The real contrast is between these views and the approach to legislative voting as based on more short-term considerations.

Policy Types

The above discussion of legislative voting was at a micro level, focusing on the votes of individual legislators. There has also been attention to voting at a more macro level, examining how voting patterns in Congress vary by policy type. As introduced in chapter 16, Lowi (1964) provided an initial demarcation of policy types, but a more complete set was developed by Ripley and Franklin (1991). Rather than focus on the subject matter (such as agricultural policy in Clausen's study), these classifications emphasize the type of conflict involved in the policy type. There are three sets of relevant actors in these conflicts—the president along with the government bureaus or agencies that deal with the policy, Congress along with the relevant committee and subcommittees, and the private sector, including interest groups—and the power relationships among these three actors differ across policy types.

   Thus one category of domestic policy is distributive, where benefits are being given out by the government. A second category is redistributive, where benefits are shifted from one set of actors to another. A third category is protective regulatory policy, which establishes a general rule and requires that covered individuals obey in order to protect the general public. Pork-barrel legislation is an example of distributive policy, whereas pesticide regulation is an example of protective regulatory policy, and tax legislation is redistributive. The basic argument is that the nature of the policy-making process differs according to the policy type. Distributive policy is often set by near unanimous coalitions in Congress, as when every district gets some public buildings in a pork-barrel bill. Protective regulatory policy is more visible and conflictual, with the participants varying depending on the policy. The power relationships get particularly complicated when regulated agencies are captured by the interests they regulate. Redistributive policy is more partisan, often passing by a minimum winning coalition, since there are losers as well as winners (recall the discussion of zero-sum issues in chapter 18).

   Ripley and Franklin also distinguish three policy types in the foreign and defense areas. One is structural policy, such as giving out army or navy posts, which can be viewed as similar to domestic distributive policy. The second is strategic policy, such as the stationing of U.S. troops abroad or foreign economic policy. Ripley and Franklin find this area to be fairly similar to protective regulatory policy, except that Congress usually ends up deferring to the president even if it has misgivings about the policy. Finally, crisis policy deals with emergency situations in which Congress generally accepts presidential actions.

The general points here are that there are different constellations of conflict in different types of policy, and the nature of legislative decision making will vary accordingly. Members will vote differently on redistributive policy than on crisis policy, to take two extremes, because of the vast differences in the array of considerations. Unanimous votes, or near-unanimous votes, are most likely in distributive, structural, and crisis policies, though for very different reasons, whereas partisan votes are most likely in redistributive policy and bargaining and compromise prevail in protective regulatory and strategic policies.

LEGISLATIVE VOTING AS BASED ON SHORT-TERM CUES

While the research just reviewed considers legislative voting primarily long-term, an equally distinguished line of research emphasizes instead its short-term aspects. Some of this work emphasizes voting on the basis of short-term cues, while other pieces look at the framing of issues in Congress.

A Cue Theory Approach

According to this viewpoint, members consider how each vote impacts their constituents, their party, and so on, and then decide how to vote on that basis. Short-term approaches generally discuss voting "cues"—that members look to others for information and advice on how to vote. Voting cues are particularly important when decisions must be made with limited information, so that just seeing how another member from a similar constituency has voted can help a legislator determine how he or she should vote.

The best single piece of research along this line is Kingdon's (1973) analysis of roll-call voting. Kingdon interviewed members of the U.S. House about what was important in making their voting decisions on a particular motion within the week prior to his interview (using different motions for each week). He asked specifically about the importance of constituency, party, presidential, interest group, staff, media, and other influences on their votes. His original analysis tallied up the extent to which each voting "cue" was considered important by the members. He found, for example, that fellow members of Congress were the most important of these sources of voting cues, followed closely by constituency. Interest groups and the administration were next in importance, while party leadership and staffs were least important.

Kingdon's open-ended interviews gave him considerable information to flesh out what these cues meant in practice and how they operated. For example, most mentions of constituency influence focused on the district as a whole rather than elites, but members viewed constituent opinion as more important in their decision making when they were referring to elites.

Kingdon's (1977) later analysis, reported in chapter 25, puts the several cues together into a single model of the voting decision. Members see whether a relevant "field of forces" is in consensus on the motion, or whether some of their career goals are invoked by the vote, and they decide accordingly how to vote. Kingdon is able to model the great preponderance of the votes accurately on this basis. This work also illustrates the importance that the literature on Congress places on member goals (see chapter 2). It effectively argues that legislators decide how to vote on the basis of cues associated with the roll call. Long-term factors are accommodated in Kingdon's model as part of the process by which consensus is produced.

The difficulty in assessing the importance of particular cues in voting is exemplified by the role of legislative staff. The literature on congressional staff itself is quite meager, but the work on their influence is of particularly questionable validity. Studies using interviews with legislators, including Kingdon's study, tend to dismiss staff influence as minor, while staff usually consider their role to be greater. The problem, of course, is that each side tends to overstate their own independent role. Members do not want to seem overly dependent on mere staff, while the staff may naturally exaggerate their own importance. The best judgment (DeGregorio 1996; Salisbury and Shepsle 1981) is that staff have wide discretion but within parameters set by the members.

The same argument can be made about the low level of importance that Kingdon finds for the party leadership—legislators are unlikely to admit that they pay attention to party influence. They are more likely to claim that they are good legislators who follow the wishes of the people back home, which may be why Kingdon finds constituency so much more important than party.

Voting cues were also studied by Matthews and Stimson (1975). They developed a simulation model of voting in Congress, which they supplemented with personal interviews about cue taking. The cues they examined included the party majority, the president, party leaders, committee chairs and ranking minority members, ideological caucuses (Conservative Coalition on the right and the Democratic Study Group on the left), the House majority, and state party delegation. Matthews and Stimson developed a model of cue diffusion, with lobbyists giving information to leaders ("initial cue givers") who give cues to specialists on the committee that considers the bill ("intermediate cue givers") who provide cues to rank-and-file members ("cue takers"). They found that the most important initial cue givers are members of the committee that considered the bill, especially the committee chairs and secondarily the ranking minority members. The intermediate cue givers who are most trusted are members of the same state party delegation. Party leaders also frequently serve as initial or intermediate cue-givers. The Matthews and Stimson simulation based on members voting with cues from the above listed sources had high predictive success (89%), though Weisberg (1978) shows that one could predict nearly as well by just predicting that members vote with the majority of their party (82%, and

85% if Southern Democrats are treated as a separate party from northern Democrats). A later study of voting cues by Sullivan, Shaw, McAvoy, and Barnum (1993) shows that the parties differ as to sources of cues and their importance across policy areas.

Issue Framing

Another approach that emphasizes the short-term aspect of legislative voting is one that views influence attempts as a matter of giving legislators "frames" for issues. There are usually multiple ways to interpret a particular roll-call vote, and each side attempts to influence which way members view that vote. In doing this, they offer the members ways they can justify their votes to their constituents. Members can listen to these different frames and then choose which they feel will work with their constituency. The "framing" concept is popular in social and political psychology, as a way of understanding how people make decisions. The framing perspective is based on the contention that individuals are often ambivalent about political matters. They have values that would lead them to support either side of many controversial issues. For example, many individuals support spending government money to address specific societal problems, but also believe that government is too big and should spend less overall. How they make a decision on which policies to support, then, is based on which value is made more salient by the "frame" of the debate.

There have been explicit references to framing in the legislative literature. It clearly underlies some important work in the interest group (Smith 1984), presidential influence (Fenno 1986), agenda getting (Baumgartner and Jones 1993; B. Jones 1994), and coalition leadership (Arnold 1990) areas. We reprint a chapter of Arnold's work on this topic as a Contemporary Perspective in this area to give a flavor of why this concern is important, even though Arnold does not explicitly use the "framing" terminology.

Interest groups

The framing notion has arisen in several legislative areas, but it is particularly relevant in the area of interest group influence. Interest groups can be especially important as a short-term influence since they clearly mobilize to affect particular bills. Interest groups are thought to be particularly influential because they can reduce legislators' uncertainty about legislation. Specifically, interest groups can provide information about the potential reactions of interested constituents, on the technicalities of the legislative process, and on the potential effects of the legislation—especially whether the policy will work as planned (Wright 1996).

The influence of interest groups has been studied for a long time. Several times in U.S. history there has been a major uproar about particular groups trying to buy influence in Congress, so scholars have often tried to document the real role of interest groups. For example, lobbyists were thought to be particularly influential in passing the Smoot-Hawley tariff bill in the 1920s (Schattschneider 1935). David Truman, in his influential book *The Governmental Process* (1951), portrayed members of Congress as mere representatives of group interests. Others argued that interest groups were able to dominate policy making through subgovernments—tight, interdependent relationships between congressional committees, bureaucratic agencies, and interest groups on a particular policy (see Ripley and Franklin 1991).

However, the influence of lobbyists was called into question by Bauer, Pool, and Dexter's study (1963) of reciprocal trade legislation in the early 1950s. They found that lobbies acted as "service bureaus" to members of Congress, providing technical information to legislators who already agree with them rather than per-suading undecided legislators to vote their way. Thus, they argued lobbyists were more dominated by members of Congress than the other way around. Even today, the studies that account for legislators' personal beliefs and the preferences of their constituencies find little systematic relationship between political action commit-tees' campaign contributions and the votes of members of Congress in committee (Wright 1990) or on the floor (Grenzke 1989; see Smith 1995 for a review of the mixed evidence of this literature). Yet there is evidence that receiving PAC contri-butions makes a member of Congress more active in promoting a group's interests on legislation by participating in committee mark-ups, offering amendments, and participating in behind-the-scenes negotiations (Hall and Wayman 1990).

The importance of interest groups as providers of information is best docu-mented by Richard Smith (1984). He argues that groups provide interpretations of legislation to members of Congress that can be used to explain their votes to con-stituents. Lobbyists meet with undecided legislators in order to provide interpre-tations of the legislation that will persuade them to support the group's position. Interest groups also lobby their traditional supporters in order to explain how the current legislation is consistent with their previous voting history—how this bill will allow them to meet their policy goals. Other studies also have found significant effects of lobbying contacts on the votes of members of Congress (Langbein 1993; Rothenberg 1992; Wright 1990).

Though Smith argues lobbyists are most likely to meet with undecided legisla-tors and traditional supporters, there currently is substantial debate over whom lobbyists choose to lobby (see Austen-Smith and Wright 1996; Baumgartner and Leech 1996). The traditional view is that lobbyists focus on contacting their friends in the legislature (Bauer, Pool, and Dexter 1963; Milbrath 1963). Indeed, Kingdon's study of congressional voting (1989) finds that interest groups lobby leg-islators from districts where the group has a strong membership base. Austen-Smith and Wright (1994) show that groups only lobby their supporters in order to "counteract" the lobbying by opposition groups. Otherwise, groups would be wasting scarce organizational resources by lobbying those who are likely to support them regardless. They argue that groups will lobby opponents in order to persuade them of the group's position. Still others find that undecided, "swing" votes are most likely to be lobbied. Rothenberg (1992) provides evidence that "fence strad-dlers" were most likely to receive lobbying contacts on MX missile legislation, and Langbein (1993) found that ideological moderates were the targets of lobbyists during gun control debates. In essence, the debate surrounds which type of legis-lator is most efficient for the group to lobby—who can most help the group's cause at the least cost of time and persuasive effort—and who they do lobby.

Presidential influence and party leadership

There have been many studies of presidential influence on Congress (see this section's Contemporary Issue for a review of these studies). Some simply correlate statements of presidential positions with congressional actions in order to tally presidential success rates. Some of the most interesting studies, though, are those that take the framing perspective. Take, for example, Fenno's (1986) discussion of the Senate 1981 vote on permitting U.S. sales of AWACS advanced military technology to Saudi Arabia. Fenno studied this vote by observation, with a special focus on the sequence of vote decisions by senators. Fenno shows how administration lobbyists turned a potential defeat to victory by reframing the issue, so that many Republican senators saw it as a matter of support for their new president on his first foreign affairs vote in Congress rather than as taking a position on the many rivalries in the Middle East.

Not only can the president try to reframe a debate, but party leaders, committee leaders, and legislative entrepreneurs can try to structure the legislative situation so that their side will win. Arnold (1990, reprinted here as chapter 27) provides a discussion of how such leaders frame debates so as to win, as does DeGregorio (1996) in a more general discussion of policy advocacy in Congress. Arnold, for example, argues that coalition leaders seek to frame the debate over a new program in terms of its consistency with existing programs or its relation to widely shared goals such as economic growth. Or coalition leaders frame the debate by forcing public votes on items that are very popular with the public (and thus hard to oppose) while hiding legislators' involvement with and support of more unpopular provisions by never taking a direct vote on those items. B. Jones (1994) suggests that member preferences need not be changed by such leaders—all they need do is make one element of a decision more salient than others.

This emphasis on how a vote is framed fits in well also with some more theoretical work. In particular, Riker (1986) developed the notion of "heresthetics" to convey that political actors often use strategic devices in their attempts to win (see also Chapter 12). One strategic device is shifting the focus of debate. If one side knows that it will lose if an issue is framed in the manner that it has been framed in the past, then that side will attempt to reframe the issue. This is fully equivalent to the concern in this section with how legislative votes are framed.

Attempts at framing qualify as short-term influences on congressional voting decisions because each frame depends on the particular issue under discussion. Though a situational cue, the frame may be effective in persuading particular members of Congress because it links the current vote to their longstanding policy goals and voting histories (Smith 1984); the frame convinces them that the desired position on this particular vote is consistent with their beliefs and record.

CONCLUSION

Voting in the mass electorate and voting in legislatures are both best conceived of as combinations of long-term and short-term factors. In the mass electorate, party and ideology are relevant long-term factors whereas issues and candidates are treated as more short-term influences. Legislative voting can be considered somewhat similar, with members being predisposed to vote in particular directions on the basis of long-term policy dimensions, but with voting cues alerting members to short-term considerations that should lead them to vote otherwise. This two-stage theory has been implemented in a legislative voting simulation (Cherryholmes and Shapiro 1969) that was quite successful in predicting votes in a pair of issue areas. The first phase of the model was a predisposition stage, using a set of variables to apply long-term predispositions to the specific motion, while their second phase was a "communications" stage, simulating conversations between members of Congress in which a preponderance of influence from members with one position on a motion can sway the member's initial intention to vote in the opposite direction. The specifics of this model are unusual, but recognition of the relevance of both long-term and short-term factors is highly appropriate.

One caution to give on all the work cited in this chapter is that legislative votes may be fairly easy to predict on a chance basis. Weisberg (1978) has shown that predictions on the basis of party alone or party taken together with region can explain statistically a large proportion of congressional voting. As a result, usual statistical considerations should be modified, making sure that the prediction level in a model is higher than chance alone would suggest.

The later literature on this topic has developed in many different ways at once. One of the most interesting (e.g., Krehbiel and Rivers 1988) is an attempt to separate out a legislator's "personal ideology" by predicting voting in Congress from constituency characteristics and then examining the residuals to see whether the member is voting more liberally or more conservatively than would be predicted given the nature of the constituency. This approach is also controversial. Jackson and Kingdon (1992) have attacked it as flawed because ideology itself is measured through interest-group ratings rather than independently of roll calls.

A final direction in the research literature on legislative decision making is broadening the focus from roll-call analysis to other aspects of the congressional system. Studies of voting in congressional committees have already been mentioned in chapter 16. Additionally, Box-Steffensmeier, Arnold, and Zorn (1997) argue that another important aspect is the timing of vote decisions, as when some legislators announce early for strategic reasons (see also Fenno 1986). Kessler and Krehbiel (1996) have analyzed the timing of decisions to cosponsor legislation as a means of signaling fellow legislators. Hall (1996) also calls attention to the importance of studying the decisions of members to participate in the development of legislation. Thus, there is increased recognition that the most important decisions that members make on bills may be at stages prior to the final floor votes (cf. Van Doren 1990).

The congressional voting literature has become very sophisticated methodologically, much more than in the early days when A. Lawrence Lowell, Stuart Rice, and Julius Turner were trying to assess the impact of party. The methodological entry price into these debates has certainly increased, which may be appropriate given the greater theoretical understanding of forces affecting voting in Congress.

Arguably the most important change in this subfield over the years has been in our understanding of the role of party in congressional decision making.

Understanding voting in Congress is much more complicated than the emphasis on party that Turner gave in the quotation that began this chapter. Party is certainly a central factor in voting in the U.S. Congress, but that only begs the question of why members vote along party lines. As discussed in this chapter, do members of a party vote together because of shared attitudes or because they represent constituencies with similar characteristics? And when members vote against their party, is it because of their perception of their constituency, or because they do not want to provide an electoral opponent with ammunition in the next election? It is difficult to pull apart these different motivations on the basis of roll-call data. Yet at least it is very clear that over the past 30 years the constituencies of the parties have become more similar, the parties in the electorate have become more differentiated, congressional parties have become more ideologically homogeneous, and the increased polarization of the parties has led to more party voting in Congress (see also chapters 20 and 23).

A major difficulty in modeling the voting decision is that party is an inherent part of other factors affecting legislators' votes. When taking voting cues from colleagues, members most often look to others from their party (Kingdon 1989, 81). Similarly, members might be persuaded by a president of their own party to take risks on votes that they would not otherwise take. Many interest groups tend to be aligned predominantly with one party, so that interest-groups' mobilization indirectly leads to partisan voting.

Julius Turner was correct in pointing out that party provides an important voting division in the U.S. Congress, but party is neither the be-all nor the end-all of understanding how members decide how to vote. As reviewed in this chapter, policy voting is also important, whether that is interpreted in terms of separate policy areas, a single underlying ideological factor, members maintaining consistent voting histories on specific recurrent bills, or different voting patterns across different types of policies. Furthermore, members must decide how to vote on each specific motion, which brings into consideration the cues that members receive as to how to vote along with how the vote is framed by interest groups, the president, and the party leadership. Thus, party voting must be understood within the context of the many factors that affect the voting decisions of members of Congress. There is consensus on that result, despite the many different theories and methods of the studies discussed in this chapter, which serves to emphasize that this is one subfield of research in which the similarity of findings is more impressive than the differences.

NOTES

1. Collie (1988b) shows that universalistic votes—where at least 90% of the voting members vote in the same direction—increased across this time span.
2. This logic requires each motion to have the same direction. Voting yes on some legislative motions has, however, the same meaning as voting no on others, such as voting for passage of a bill and against a recommital motion designed to kill the same bill. This problem can be handled by "reflecting" some motions so that each is turned in the same direction.

3. Poole and Rosenthal do find that a second dimension could be added, but it would explain only an additional 3% of the voting. As a result, they term their findings a "1.5" dimensional fit. Their second issue has to do mainly with North-South regional conflict. Allowing for a linear trend in legislator positions (such as a member becoming more conservative over time) adds another 1% in explanatory power.

CONTEMPORARY ISSUE:

Presidential Leadership and Its Limits

Citizens, or at least political commentators, have high expectations of presidents as legislative activists. Presidents are expected to identify public problems, develop effective solutions, and aggressively persuade the public and the Congress to support their ideas. Presidents' activities as the legislator-in-chief have become one of the major foci of scholarly attention. In short, presidents' legislative activities and successes have become an important means by which presidents are judged.

Many recent presidents have been criticized for their lack of legislative production. For example, President Clinton was elected in 1992 promising to end the legislative "gridlock" between previous Republican presidents and Democratic congresses. Although Clinton was highly successful in terms of Congress's support for his positions in his first two years in office, he was unable to pass health care, welfare or campaign finance reforms through a Democratically controlled Congress (see the contributions to Campbell and Rockman 1996). A frustrated public responded by electing a Republican majority to Congress in 1994 for the first time in 40 years. Clinton's difficulties in working with Congress only increased with Republicans in charge, as exemplified by vetoes of several provisions of the Republicans' Contract with America and the 1995–96 government shutdowns due to a failure to agree on a budget.

This concern regarding presidential-congressional relations is not a new one. In fact, the framers established a governmental structure that separated powers among three branches to assure that power would not become centralized. The president would be the chief executive—not the prime minister who leads his party in the legislature. They also gave each branch the incentive to exercise checks and balances in order to prevent the branches from encroaching on one another's responsibilities. Thus, they provided only limited incentives for Congress to follow the lead of the president.

The opposing view, that the proper role of the president is as a legislative leader, is articulated by Woodrow Wilson ([1908] 1961). The president, Wilson argues, is elected by and is the representative of the entire nation. Congress represents narrow, parochial district interests. In order to achieve the national interest, presidential leadership, particularly as exercised through a political party, is necessary to coordinate across the system of separated powers. Since Wilson, presidents and other commentators have argued that elections give the president a mandate from the people to implement campaign promises. The people have chosen one candidate and his agenda, so Congress should follow the will of the people.

With high expectations but limited powers for presidential legislative involvement, the actual relationship between the president and Congress is thus uncertain. The key questions are: How much can the president influence Congress? Under what circumstances is presidential influence most successful? Finally, to what extent should members of Congress follow the president's lead? We will explore several facets of congressional-presidential relations in order to assess the conditions under which presidential leadership is more or less likely to be successful. In particular, we will focus on presidential agenda setting, influence over congressional voting decisions, the impact of divided partisan control of government, and potential presidential advantages in making foreign policy and appointments.

AGENDA SETTING

Many argue that presidents are most successful in their relations with Congress in terms of their ability to set the agenda—to influence what issues Congress considers seriously at any point in time. Discussions of presidential honeymoons and "first 100 days," the traditional window of opportunity for new presidents to push their most important policy programs, are based on the fact that the media and the public expect the president to set a legislative agenda for Congress.

Congress at times seeks presidential leadership because its decentralized structure makes it difficult to develop or pass comprehensive programs (including the budget) when left on its own. Presidents are better suited to developing comprehensive programs, articulating a conception of the national interest, and educating the public as to the dimensions of national problems. Presidential proposals give Congress something to react to and modify, or more cynically, make the president take political risks first while Congress can appease affected interests.

Presidential agenda setting is important less because the president is the source of new ideas, than because he helps a fragmented Congress prioritize (C. Jones 1994; Kingdon 1995; Light 1991). Thousands of bills are introduced each Congress, and with institutional bottlenecks in committees and on the floor, there is no time to consider them all. By drawing attention to certain issues and proposed solutions, the president helps Congress decide on which issues to work. In addition, when it becomes associated with the president, a specific proposal achieves greater prestige and is more likely to be considered seriously (Peterson 1990).

Still, presidents cannot control the outcome of the legislative process, even for their own proposals. In fact, presidents cannot introduce legislation; they must rely on a member of Congress to introduce bills on their behalf. Presidents, then, are dependent on Congress to consider their legislation and preserve its content.

PRESIDENTIAL INFLUENCE ON VOTING DECISIONS

Certainly there are moments when individual presidents are crucial in determining congressional outcomes, but Edwards (1989) argues that presidents are, more often than not, just marginal actors (also see Bond and Fleisher 1990; Peterson 1990). In studying the circumstances under which the president's personal involvement can make a difference, Edwards concludes that the importance of the president as an individual actor depends on the degree of conflict that exists on the issue. For legislative matters, if there is an opposing majority for a given proposal, it does not matter what the president wants. The president can have discretion only when real and important conflict exists and even then the president can act only at the margins—tilting a few votes through persuasion, promises of favors, or deal making. Presidential lobbying efforts are not irrelevant, but these actions alter any situation only slightly. As a result, only when close conflict exists can actions "at the margins" affect congressional outcomes.[1]

Ultimately, voting in Congress is due more to stable factors such as party, ideology, and constituency interests than to presidential leadership. Most members of Congress have determined how they will vote on a given issue according to these factors before the president even attempts to exercise skill or leadership. When scholars control methodologically for the president's party and public standing, presidents considered to be skillful legislatively are no more successful in winning support in Congress than are other presidents.[2]

Presidents usually expect the members of their party in Congress to support their positions, but even that is not always the case. Members of Congress from the president's party do not always think that supporting the president will help them get reelected. Indeed, there are notable cases when supporting the president leads to defeat in the next election—as when Democratic Representative Marjorie Margolies-Mezvinsky (PA) cast the key vote in passing the Clinton tax increase in 1993 and this was used to defeat her in the 1994 midterm election. Leaders of the president's party in Congress do not always support presidential programs. The House vote on NAFTA in the 103rd Congress is an extreme case in point. President Clinton asked Congress to ratify the North American Free Trade Agreement with Canada and Mexico that had been negotiated under President Bush. House Democratic leaders (including majority leader Richard Gephardt and majority whip David Bonior) opposed the agreement, though Republican leaders (principally minority whip Newt Gingrich) supported it.

Still, the legislative success of a president is largely constrained by the makeup of Congress. The larger the delegation of members of the president's party in Congress, the more likely Congress will support the president's positions on legislation. In his first two years in office (1993–94) with a Democratically controlled Congress, Clinton had one of the highest success rates ever, 86%. In 1995, with a Republican-controlled Congress, his success rate plunged to 36%. To the extent that political parties in Congress are more polarized politically (Rohde 1991) and Congress reacts to presidential positions in a partisan fashion (Shull 1997), presidents are more dependent on their party in Congress and have less ability to fashion bipartisan coalitions.

THE EFFECTS OF DIVIDED GOVERNMENT

The dependence of presidents on their congressional partisans has led many to argue about the consequences of divided party government—whether government operates differently when partisan control of the federal executive and legislature is split. Most observers assume that divided government leads to gridlock, with the branches unable to agree on policy initiatives. Cox and Kernell (1991) argue that negative effects of divided government are seen especially in fights over budget priorities and competition to control the bureaucracy. Budgeting under divided government becomes a game of delay and brinksmanship as each branch tries to get the other to back down rather than facing the risk of no agreement. The 1995–96 government shutdowns would be prominent examples. Even worse, divided partisan control of Congress (a Republican Senate and Democratic House, for example) has been blamed for the budget deficits of the 1980s, with the parties compromising their different spending priorities by increasing spending on both military and domestic programs (McCubbins 1991).

An important study by David Mayhew (1991) found, however, very little effect of divided government on the legislative output of Congress or on investigations of the executive branch. Mayhew's results are controversial in the field. For example, he focused on "important" legislation that was considered "both innovative and consequential" when it was passed, but he did not consider whether divided government yielded more "watered-down" bills or whether it also resulted in more legislative failures. Mayhew challenges the usual view that divided government leads to gridlock by showing that gridlock can occur even under unified government.

Krehbiel (1998) concurs with Mayhew's conclusion. He emphasizes that the rules of Congress often require supermajorities to pass legislation. Although a simple majority passes legislation, a three-fifths majority in the Senate is necessary to impose cloture to end a fili-buster; a two-thirds vote in each chamber is necessary to overcome a presidential veto. Krehbiel argues that legislation passes when it meets the preferences of the "pivotal" legislator who casts the vote that overcomes the filibuster or veto threat. It is the difficulty of attracting the vote of the pivotal legislator, not unified or divided government, that causes gridlock.

The instances of divided government in the mid–1990s will certainly lead to more studies of its effects as scholars seek to challenge Mayhew's conclusions. Minimally there were serious fights over budget priorities, fights that led to two shutdowns of the federal government in late 1995. Additionally, heightened partisanship was evident in Congress's reactions to Independent Prosecutor Kenneth Starr's September 1998 report to the House on impeachment of President Clinton. Looking at important bills that failed, Edwards, Barrett, and Peake (1997) show that divided government matters in preventing important legislation from passing in the 1947–92 period. Rohde and Simon (1985) find greater presi-dential use of the veto under divided government.

Yet President Clinton was able to compromise enough with the Republican Congress to enact landmark welfare reform legislation in 1996, a balanced budget and tax cut plan in 1997, and greater education funding in 1998, all after failing to get his health care reform legislation through the Democratic Congress in 1994. This suggests that divided govern-ment is more conducive to the passage of moderate legislation rather than ideologically pure proposals—which may be why the U.S. public chose divided government in the first place (Fiorina 1996).

ADDITIONAL CONDITIONS OF PRESIDENTIAL SUCCESS

Presidential success may depend on other conditions as well. Some claim that Congress should defer to the president on foreign policy because of the executive branch's greater expertise in this area. This argument has led to a claim in the research literature (Wildavsky 1966) that there are "two presidencies"—a foreign and a domestic presidency—because presidents seem to be more successful in getting Congress to go along with them on foreign policy than on domestic policy. More recent work, however, finds little support for the two presidencies hypothesis (Hinckley 1994)—or at least that it depends on the situation (Ripley and Lindsay 1993; Shull 1991), with Congress being more supportive of the presi-dent in crisis management situations than in foreign policy more generally.

Another claim is that Congress should defer to the president in making appointments. Though the Constitution is unclear on whether the president or Congress should predomi-nate in appointments (e.g., the meaning of Congress's power of "Advise and Consent"), the research literature shows that Congress generally defers to the president, but will exercise independent judgment when a nomination reaches a high level of controversy. For example, Segal and Spaeth (1993) find that Senate confirmation votes on Supreme Court nominations are shaped by partisanship, presidential strength, and ideology. Conflict with the president is more likely to occur when the Senate majority party is not of the president's party or when the president is considered to be politically weak. The president's political strength might vary with presidential popularity or the point the president has reached in the four-year term (i.e., presidents in their fourth year are more likely to face difficulties in the confirmation process).

Thus, the ability of presidents to overcome the separation of powers depends largely on the political context: on the number of the president's partisans in Congress, on the president's popularity or perceived electoral mandate, or on whether the issue is one on which many members of Congress believe it is appropriate to defer judgment to the president. In addition, while Congress may give presidential proposals serious attention, they often change the content according to their own preferences (Peterson 1990).

CONCLUSION

The relationship between the president and Congress is not a simple one. Congress often asks for presidential leadership, but it does not always consider itself obligated to follow. Members of the president's party are more likely to look to the president, but in the end they can go their own way if constituent pressure runs in the opposite direction. Thus, perhaps not surprisingly as congressional scholars, we concur with the recommendations of Peterson (1990) and C. Jones (1994) that political scientists cannot study government with a presidency-centered model. Instead, scholars of both institutions must account for the effects of the branches (including the judiciary) on one another.

In addition, we must be aware that just as congressional-presidential relations have evolved in the past, so this evolution will continue. The increased partisanship of Congress will affect how presidents attempt to build legislative coalitions. The increased assertiveness of Congress in foreign affairs (Ripley and Lindsay 1993) affects the president's interaction with foreign leaders as well as relations with Congress. The current balanced budget may result in less "summitry" between the president and congressional leaders in order to negotiate yearly budget agreements. The adoption of the line-item veto would add a new weapon to the president's arsenal. This is a common power of state governors, but the Supreme Court has ruled that a constitutional amendment would be required at the federal level.[3]

The topic of presidential leadership thus brings us back to some of the core legislative concerns: What should the role of the representative be in a presidential system of government with checks and balances? When should the national interest that is supposedly embodied in the president trump the more constituency-oriented interests of representatives? When is the political party an effective means of bridging the separated branches of government, and when does it just exacerbate the natural tensions between the branches?

NOTES

1. Edwards stands in opposition to the work of Bowles (1987). Bowles's thesis is that the quality of presidents' political judgments, or how effectively they lobby or influence Congress, affects their chances of legislative success. In studying the White House Office of Congressional Relations, however, Bowles focuses on unique situations that are neither decisive nor definitive. Although he maintains that his thesis is confirmed, he ultimately concludes that a president with a clear program, partisan and ideological backing in Congress, public opinion and interest group support, and well-organized legislative White House staff stands a greater chance of success (Bowles 1987, 241). In the end, Bowles makes a case for the importance of context just as Edwards does.
2. See Bond and Fleisher (1990) for an excellent discussion of the merits and disadvantages of these measures.
3. In *Clinton* v. *City of New York* the Supreme Court ruled in 1998 that Congress cannot give the President the power to cancel provisions of bills he has signed into law.

Chapter 25

Models of Legislative Voting

JOHN W. KINGDON

In recent years various specialists in legislative behavior have found themselves troubled by what they have considered to be a deficiency in theory building in the field. After an extended review of the literature on Congress for instance, Robert Peabody argues, "The critical need is for *theory* at several levels for, quite clearly, in congressional research the generation of data has proceeded much more rapidly than the accumulation of theory" (Huitt and Peabody 1969, 70).

While it is not clear that "the" theory of legislative behavior is on the horizon, scholars have recently developed a number of models of legislative voting which promise substantial theoretical payoff. . . . If we were to be able somehow to arrive at a way to fit important aspects of these models together, our theoretical thinking about behavior might be advanced considerably. . . .

[The] approach . . . I take in this chapter, is to treat each of these models as having a grasp on an important part of reality. In this view, then, we do not have a case of incompatible, competing models. Instead, there are several compatible models which are in need of a persuasive means of integrating them.

CONSTRUCTING AN INTEGRATIVE MODEL

. . . [W]e start the task of developing an integrative model by noticing that most of the previous work on legislative voting begins with similar assumptions about information processing, search behavior, and decision-making capacity. These assumptions, entirely familiar to readers of Herbert Simon and other students of decision making (Barnard 1966, 189–91; Bauer, Pool, and Dexter 1963, chapter 29; Cyert and March 1963, 120–22; March and Simon 1958, chapter 6), posit that legislators, like other decision makers but perhaps even more than most, must make a large volume of complex decisions, while constrained by limits on

---

Source: "Models of Legislative Voting" by John W. Kingdon from *Journal of Politics* 39, pp. 563–95; by permission of the author and University of Texas Press. All rights retained by University of Texas Press.

time and cognitive capacity to do so without extensive study of each issue. Taking account of this decisional overload, the previous models and our integrative model all largely agree on the need for decision-making procedures that cut legislators' information costs and simplify their choices. They also agree that legislative voting is a repetitive problem-solving situation which calls for standard ways of making voting decisions which can be applied vote after vote. . . .

In building an integrative model, we also begin with an assumption that is not particularly emphasized in many previous models of legislative voting (cf. Ferejohn and Fiorina 1975), namely, that legislators are goal seekers. Their behavior is purposive, and is not simply reaction to external forces. A natural preliminary step in dealing with that behavior is to identify the goals which seem to affect most legislators most of the time. For the purposes of this paper, I find it useful to work with adaptations of the goals which Fenno specifies. His formulations—the goals of reelection, influence within the House, and good public policy—are restated here so as to make them somewhat more comprehensive. Thus the primary goals of legislators are as follows:

(1) *Satisfying constituents.* It could be that constituency considerations come back ultimately to an interest in reelection. But one observes congressmen taking account of constituency reaction long before and much more frequently than they worry explicitly about gain or loss of votes in the next election.[1] Hence, the more comprehensive formulation here.

(2) *Intra-Washington influence.* Another set of considerations in voting has to do with satisfying a set of actors within Washington, who are not necessarily closely connected to the constituency. These include going along with one's party leadership, favor trading among fellow legislators, and following the lead of the administration, particularly if the president is of the deciding legislator's party. One takes these into account, presumably, in order to build influence within the government, a set wider than the House itself. The same concept, retitled, could be used for state or foreign capitals.

(3) *Good public policy.* Most legislators have their conception of good public policy, and act partly to carry that conception into being. Their policy attitudes, their ideology (if it can be called that) decidedly affect their behavior. Their previous pattern of behavior, their voting history, enters here as well, since that pattern represents their traditional policy position on the issue currently confronting them.

These appear to be the goals which most legislators seek most of the time. I will shortly present ways of introducing them into an integrative model of legislative voting and of operationalizing and using them empirically.

The Place of Various Previous Models

Building on these assumptions about information processing and goal orientations, we are now in a position to discuss how various previous models of legislative voting might inform the development of a more integrative model.

I have found it useful to portray congressmen's decision making as a sequential process, for which a version of modelling familiar in this and other contexts seems quite suitable. Such a process model pictures the legislator as beginning with a very simple decision rule. If that rule can be applied, he does so, and is done with that decision on that particular vote or bill. If he cannot apply that rule, he proceeds to one which is somewhat more complex, which is applied if it can be. Previous steps are seen as controlling subsequent steps in the model, in the sense that if the early decision rule suffices, the congressman uses it and need not proceed further. This feature is both plausible as applied to congressmen and congruent with a good bit of more general literature on decision making (Cyert and March 1963; Simon 1969).

. . . [T]he essential driving logic of an integrative model—the legislator's search for some sort of agreement among a set of possible influences on the vote which predisposes him in a certain direction, and some further decisional process in the absence of that agreement—is a thread common to a number of the models of legislative voting previously developed (Cherryholmes and Shapiro 1969; Kingdon 1973; Matthews and Stimson 1970).

As I see it, cue taking enters the decisional process in two critical ways. First, it is a means to an end. If legislators are goal-oriented, as we have portrayed them as being, then, as Matthews and Stimson rightly argue, taking cues from fellow legislators is a prominent way to translate their goals into votes. If a congressman wants to vote so as to satisfy his goal of bringing about good public policy, for instance, one easy and frequently used way to accomplish this aim is by picking fellow congressmen as cue sources who agree with his own general philosophy. I have developed some evidence elsewhere (Kingdon 1973, 72–79) that this choice of colleagues according to agreement with one's own policy attitude on the issue is in fact what is happening. As Clausen persuasively argues (1973, 33–35), recognition of this phenomenon implies that a cue-taking model and a policy dimension interpretation of legislative voting, far from being incompatible, are actually quite complementary. The same general line of thinking applies to goals other than the policy goal. For example, a deciding congressman may follow the guidance of colleagues whom he considers to have "good political judgment," particularly from the same state delegation, in order to vote in a way most likely to satisfy constituents.

The second occasion on which cue taking enters the decisional process is when such other possible influences on the vote as goals, predispositions, ideology, or constituency considerations do not provide sufficient guidance to make a decision. This situation is particularly exemplified by the many low-visibility, minor issues which come to the floor, about which very few people apart from a few involved colleagues care. Yet these votes must be cast, since a poor attendance record is a considerable liability with constituents in the next campaign. In such a case, the congressman's own policy attitude does not provide guidance, since he does not care about the issue; his constituency may be utterly indifferent; and there may be no intra-Washington consideration which would prompt him to vote one way or the other. This is not the same case as the cue being a means to an end, since here, there appears to be no goal-oriented consideration which would point the legislator in a given direction. Both the literature and practical experience are replete with examples of such votes, in which a deciding congressman is bereft of other guidance and simply follows a trusted colleague, sometimes quite blindly.

. . . [T]here may be ways in which a policy dimension theory can be seen as part of the decisional processes themselves, as Clausen [1973] argues. As I see it, these ways fall generally into two categories. First, policy demensions enter the process through some attitudinal mechanism. The congressman has a set of attitudes about matters of public policy, obviously closely connected to policy goals, discussed above, which affect his voting quite directly. Thus, a congressman sorts a given issue into a policy dimension, matches his own position on that dimension to the proposal under consideration, and picks the alternative which has the best match to his own position. His policy attitudes also very prominently affect his choice of cues, as stated above. Second, as Clausen argues, policy positions taken by the congressman are affected not only by his attitudes but also by such political actors as his constituency and party which he feels are important to him. Thus constituency considerations figure prominently in voting on civil liberties matters, while party affects voting on Clausen's government management dimension. As I have treated these actors above, their importance derives from their clear connection with a congressman's goals: constituency and interest groups with reelection, party and administration with intra-Washington influence, and so forth.

Finally, a legislator's previous voting history is closely aligned with his policy position. If he has a well-established voting history, it is quite likely that he will also have a rather firm policy attitude on the issue, and vice versa. It would be possible, of course, to have a voting history without a very firm attitude, particularly in the case of rather minor issues to which a congressman has not paid a great deal of attention over the years and has simply taken to voting on by habit. Even in that probably infrequent case, however, the voting history defines the congressman's policy position on the issue, and hence, his position on the policy dimension of which the issue is a part. Thus voting according to voting history and according to policy position [are] seen in this paper to be closely connected.

An Integrative Model

We are now in a position to present a model which attempts to integrate the various models in a fashion which incorporates the features just discussed. That model is displayed in Figure 25.1.

The first two steps are the same as the first two in the consensus mode of decision, which I have presented elsewhere (1973, chapter 10). If there is no controversy in the environment at all, the congressman's choice is simple: He votes with that environment and is done with it. On many bills, for instance, a unified committee reports the bill and nobody opposes the committee position in any particular. If there is some controversy, he subsets the environment, considering only the actors which are most critical to him—his own constituency, his party leadership, his trusted associates in the House, his own policy attitude, etc.—which I call the "field of forces" which bear on his decision. If there is no conflict among those actors, he votes with his field. I assume, as a legislator does, that if there appears to be no consideration which would prompt him to vote in a way different from that toward which he is impelled by every factor in his field of vision, then there is no reason to think twice. . . .

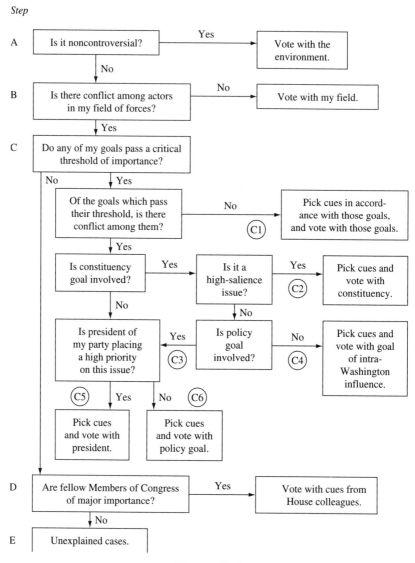

Figure 25.1
An integrative model of legislative voting decisions.

If there is some conflict among the congressman's relevant actors, he then proceeds to consider his goals, which I conceive for the purposes of this paper as being the three discussed above—constituency, intra-Washington influence, and public policy. But a goal is not brought to bear on the decision if it seems unimportant to him on this issue. It must pass what I have labelled a critical threshold of importance in order to be evoked and relevant to the decision. For example, a congressman's constituency may have a vague and largely unarticulated opposition to foreign aid. In that case, he would say that there was a constituency opinion on the issue, but that it was not intense enough to bother taking account of. The same could apply to the other goals. . . .

If none of the goals is important enough to the congressman in the given decision to be relevant, he then proceeds to follow trusted colleagues within the House. He chooses colleagues who are on the committee that considered the bill and who agree with him in general philosophical, policy terms (Kingdon 1973, chapter 3). If one or more goals are important enough, he asks if there is conflict among the goals which have been evoked. If there is none, the choice is then clear: to vote with the evoked goal or goals (Step C1). It could be in this case that only one of them is relevant to the decision, or that two or even all three are, but that they all point him in the same direction. For example, it could be that the policy goal on a given issue is the only one which passes its critical threshold, and the other two, while either opposed to, favorable to, or neutral concerning his conception of good public policy, are not in any event important enough to him on that issue to be potentially controlling. He votes in that case according to his conception of good public policy. As the model specifies, part of this decision may well be picking cues within the House to reinforce his policy goal, as a means to that end, in the fashion discussed above. Other examples of no conflict among evoked goals could be given, but this one will perhaps suffice.

If there is some conflict among the goals which the legislator considers relevant to his decision, he proceeds implicitly to some decision rules which help him sort out the conflicts and make a satisfactory choice. It might be helpful at this point in the argument to present all the logically possible combinations of conflict among the three goals, which is done in Table 25.1. In the first column, the possible combinations are listed, and the second and third columns contain the outcomes which the model would predict for each of the combinations. The numbers are relevant to the operationalization, which is explained in the next section of the chapter.

There is a variety of ways in which the decision rules could be stated in this part of the model. I hypothesize that the congressman considers the constituency interest first. He may not end up voting with the constituency, but he always considers it when it is above the minimal level of importance. Placing this goal first is in keeping with the fact that the congressman owes his tenure in office to his constituency, and as Fiorina (1974) and Mayhew (1974a) argue, reelection is of critical importance to him.

If the constituency is not involved, the only logically possible conflict among the three goals left is between policy and intra-Washington influence. In that case, I hypothesize that the congressman has a disposition to vote with his policy goals, unless he is of the same party as the president and the president places a high priority on the issue. Intra-Washington considerations other than that one, such as party leadership requests or favor trading, would not, I would argue, be enough to overcome a really strong policy predisposition. But a high-priority request from a president of his party would (Kingdon 1973, chapters 4 and 6). The results in Steps C5 and C6 of the model reflect this reasoning.

If the constituency goal is involved, the congressman weighs that consideration against policy and/or intra-Washington influence. I have set forth elsewhere

Table 25.1
All possible combinations of conflicts among goals, and the resultant outcomes

Combinations	Outcomes;[a] expected and actual		Totals
	High-salience issues[b]	Low- or medium-salience issues[b]	
Policy and constituencies vs. intra-Washington	Constituency (C2) 1/2[a]	Policy or president[c] (C3) 2/2	3/4
Policy and intra-Washington vs. constituency	Constituency (C2) 0/0	Policy (C3) 3/3	3/3
Constituency and intra-Wash. vs. policy	Constituency (C2) 0/0	Policy or president[c] (C3) 0/0	0/0
Policy vs.constituency	Constituency (C2) 1/2	Policy (C3) 6/6	7/8
Constituency vs. intra-Washington	Constituency (C2) 0/0	Intra-Washington (C4) 3/4	3/4
Policy vs. intra-Washington	President[b] (C5) 3/5	Policy[b] (C6) 3/3	6/8
Totals	5/9	17/18	22/27

[a]The goal stated in each cell is the expected outcome, the goal which the model would predict would dominate the decision. The notation in parentheses refers to the appropriate step in Figure 25.1. The actual performance is captured in the numbers in each cell. The first is the number of cases in which the outcome is as predicted by the model, the second is the total number for that cell. For instance, in the case of a conflict between the constituency and intra-Washington influence goals, on low- or medium-salience issues, the model would predict that the representative would vote according to the intra-Washington consideration. Of the four cases in which there was such a conflict on such an issue, the congressman voted as the model expects in three.

[b]In the case of the conflict between policy and intra-Washington, "high-salience" refers to the presidential involvement specified in Figure 25.1, Step C5, low-salience to noninvolvement (Step C6). In the others, the salience of the issue refers to the general visibility of the issue in the press, in the public, and among participants. See Kingdon (1973, 292–93) for the coding particulars.

[c]In these cases, since the congressman cycles through Steps C5 and C6, there is a chance that the president's requests may overturn the policy consideration, and it did in fact happen in one case. Thus that case is coded as accounted for by the model, even though policy did not control, because the model predicted the outcome correctly. In the other case, the president's priority is not involved, so the congressman votes according to his policy position. See the text for further explanation.

an account of that sort of balancing[2] (Kingdon 1973, 35–44). The key here is that there is a filter for the salience of the issue—the general visibility of the issue in the press, in the attentive public, and among the participants in the legislative process. If the issue is of high salience, and if constituency is a relevant consideration, the model postulates that in view of the likelihood that important constituents will notice and disapprove of a vote out of keeping with their interests, the constituency consideration will dominate the others (Step C2). If the issue is of lower salience, however, the congressman has more freedom to allow his policy views or intra-Washington considerations to control the choice.

In the case of low- or medium-salience issues, if the policy goal is relevant to the issue, the congressman is disposed once again to favor it. He must check the possibility, however, that the intra-Washington goal would be involved and would center on a priority request from a president of his party which conflicts with his policy goal. He therefore (at Step C3) cycles through the presidential step described above, but in most cases ends up voting in accordance with his policy views (Step C6). If the policy goal is not relevant, the only logically possible conflict (Step C4) is between constituency and intra-Washington influence. Since it involves a low- or medium-salience issue at that point, I hypothesize that the congressman decides in favor of the intra-Washington consideration, in line with the argument presented above.

I have now discussed a framework . . . which is at once comprehensive, parsimonious, and plausible. I have detailed, both verbally and through the integrative model, the ways in which a set of decision processes may be tied together. It remains now to present ways of operationalizing the key concepts and applying them to a set of data on congressmen's voting decisions.

ANOTHER LOOK AT THE DATA

In this section, I apply the concepts discussed above to my interview data, which are described at length in *Congressmen's Voting Decisions*.[3] Briefly, I repeatedly interviewed a sample of members of the U.S. House of Representatives in 1969, concerning their sources of information and voting cues, their decision rules, and the importance of various political actors in their decisions. Each of the interviews, in contrast to a survey type of instrument, concentrated on one decision which they had recently made. Generalizations are thus based on my cumulation of these decision histories over the course of the entire session, and the unit of analysis is the decision ($n = 222$).

I should make clear at the outset that, strictly speaking, the theory which I have presented above is not to be completely tested in the pages to follow. The model was generated from the previous literature and from the data set used in my own previous study. Hence, a complete validation would have to rest on a testing against new, independently generated data sets. . . .

As far as the first two steps in the integrative model are concerned (Figure 25.1), the operationalization is the same as that presented in my earlier model. Since the votes were chosen partly to maximize conflict, there are no cases in these data of noncontroversial votes. As far as the second step is concerned, the congressman's field of forces includes his own specific policy attitude toward the issue under consideration, his constituency, fellow congressmen to whom he paid attention, interest groups, his staff, his party leadership, and the administration. There is no conflict among the actors in this field 47% of the time, and respondents voted with their fields in all these cases.[4] Given that the votes selected were relatively high-conflict votes, the fact that the first two steps account for nearly half of these cases argues that these steps must have quite a high predictive power for legislative votes in general, since the general case is surely less conflict-ridden than these votes.

Starting with Step C, a major question of operationalization is the critical threshold of importance for each of the three important goals. What indicators would tell that a constituency interest, for instance, is sufficiently important that the congressman considers that constituency goal at Step C, rather than noticing but largely neglecting the constituency position in his decision? There is such an indicator in my data, the "importance" coding for each actor. With this coding, the congressman's comments relative to each actor were coded into four categories: (1) the actor was of no importance in the decision; (2) the actor was of minor importance; that is, the congressman noticed the actor's position, checked it, or the like, but the actor was of no greater importance; (3) the actor was of major importance; that is, whether or not the congressman ended up voting with the actor, he weighed the actor's position carefully and the actor had a major impact on his thinking; (4) the actor determined the decision, to the exclusion of other influences. The intercoder reliability for this variable was very good (see Kingdon 1973, 16–23, 288–89).

Building on this coding, the critical thresholds of importance for the goals are operationalized as follows: for the constituency goal, the congressman passes that threshold on the decision at hand if his constituency for that decision is coded as being of major or determinative importance. If it is coded as being of minor or no importance, we consider that the threshold has not been passed, and that the constituency goal is not sufficiently important to the congressman on that decision to be involved in Step C of the model. Substantively, passing this threshold could be due to one or both of two reasons: Either the constituency feeling is quite intense on the issue and any congressman would want to take account of it, or the congressman considers catering to constituency interest an important goal regardless of constituency intensity. For present purposes it is not so critical which or what combination of these two reasons is responsible for the constituency being of major importance in the decision. Whatever the reason, the congressman's goal of satisfying constituents is evoked.

The constituency position, it should be noted, may not be the whole constituency, the mass public, or even a majority of the constituency. It could be these, but it could as easily be the position of a fairly narrow subset of the constituency, such as school administrators on education funding. In this connection, interest groups do not appear as a separate force in the model, since, as I have maintained elsewhere, they appear to have little impact on congressmen's voting decisions apart from their constituency connections (Kingdon 1973, 143–46). Thus interest groups are subsumed under constituency for present purposes, and ignored as being important in their own right.

It might be possible that a coding of "major" or "determinative" importance would be closely associated with the congressman's vote in accordance with the constituency position. If such were the case, the test of the model would not be as good as could be hoped, since passing the critical threshold would by itself imply a constituency-oriented vote, lending an artificial predictive power to the model. It turns out, however, that these apprehensions can be alleviated somewhat. Of the cases in which there is some conflict in the congressman's field, constituency is coded as being of major or determinative importance in 42. Of these 42 cases, the congressman votes with the constituency position 62% of the time, a performance somewhat better than chance (which is 50%), but not dramatically better. By contrast, the model correctly predicts 93% of those cases. Thus, while there is naturally some association between the importance coding and the vote, it is not so strong as to negate the value of defining the critical threshold in the fashion described. The coding does not by itself produce the predictive performance.

The intra-Washington goal is treated in a similar fashion. If either the congressman's party leadership or the administration is coded as being of major or determinative importance, the congressman is considered to have passed the threshold on this decision and the goal is evoked. In addition, fellow congressmen could define the passing of the threshold on this goal, if they are coded as being of major or determinative importance, *and* if some consideration of vote trading or intra-House power is involved. In other words, fellow congressmen do not trigger this goal, even if coded major or determinative, if the deciding legislator uses his colleagues simply to reinforce ideology, constituency, or party, or if colleagues are used in the absence of other guidance. These uses of fellow congressmen are provided for elsewhere in the model. To be relevant to the goal of intra-Washington influence, colleagues must be important for their own sakes, not because they are convenient surrogates for something else or because they are the only cues left. This supplementary coding was made by a rereading of the interview protocols in the cases involved, to see how colleagues were being used.

The goal of good public policy presents something of a problem in these data. Because the interviewing was done at the time of decision, respondents nearly always held some articulated policy attitude toward the bill or vote at hand, and voted consistent with it. But it would be very difficult, given these data, to determine the intensity or background of that attitude earlier in the process of decision. Therefore, some measure of the importance of the policy goal other than the intensity of the congressman's policy attitude toward the vote at hand is needed. Instead of trying to tap that intensity, I use here two measures of the congressman's policy position. The policy goal is considered to pass the critical threshold of importance if *either* his voting history on similar issues is coded as being of major or determinative importance in his decision, *or* his ideology as measured by Americans for Democratic Action (ADA) and Americans for Constitutional Action (ACA) scores is sufficiently extreme as to be a good guide to his decision. Some congressmen are simply considered extreme "liberals" or "conservatives," by themselves and by everyone associated with the process. If they are, I assume that their ideology is sufficiently strong to give them considerable guidance, and to cause the congressman to pass the threshold on the policy goal. Because of a well-established voting history or a relatively extreme ideological position, in other words, he has a pretty fair notion of what constitutes "good public policy" for him in the current instance. Operationally, the ADA and ACA scores are used to form an index, in which a congressman is considered to be sufficiently extreme if either the ADA or ACA score is 90–100 or 0–10, and if the opposite score is in the opposite three deciles among my respondents. If the ADA score is zero, for instance, and the ACA score is in the upper three deciles, the congressman is considered to be a conservative; if the ADA score is 100 and the ACA score is in the bottom three deciles, for another example, the congressman is defined as liberal. Congressmen who do not meet the criteria described are considered to have a sufficiently "moderate" record that ADA-ACA position is not a guide to votes, and thus do not evoke the policy goal.

An impressionistic scanning of the members so classified confirms that those labelled the most liberal and conservative by the ADA-ACA criterion would be clearly regarded by most observers of the House as being correctly labelled. The index fails to identify some members for whom certain policy goals are clearly relevant, as, for instance, some very public doves on ABM deployment. In that sense, it may underestimate the importance of policy goals, since it discards some members for whom policy goals may be highly important. That underestimation also lowers the overall predictive performance of the model a bit. But the index does not make the other error: Those who are identified as liberal or conservative are not mislabelled. As far as triggering the policy goal is concerned, the ADA-ACA index and the coding for the importance of voting history make a roughly equal contribution. Of the cases which exhibit some conflict in the field of forces in which the policy goal is evoked, the ADA-ACA index alone is responsible for that triggering in 30 cases, voting history alone in 27, and the two together in 25.

Other operationalizations of the model are fairly straightforward. (1) Salience of the issue is a trichotomy (low, medium, high), as defined by the attention the issue appears to be receiving in the press, among congressmen, and among other participants in the legislative system (Kingdon 1973, 292–93). The model's specification of the cutting point being between high and medium salience is consistent with evidence presented elsewhere (Kingdon 1973, 42–44), that high-salience issues are distinctively constituency-oriented, whereas low or medium-salience issues are less so. (2) The priority which the president places on the issue is determined from my knowledge of the administration's position and lobbying activities. . . . (3) At Step D, fellow congressman importance is once again the importance coding, major or determinative constituting the criterion of entrance into that step.

The quantitative fruits of the model generation and data analysis are presented in Table 25.2, with a subset for Steps C2 through C6 more fully elaborated in Table 25.1. Overall, the model correctly predicts 92% of the voting decisions. Of those, only 10% are accounted for by Steps C2–C6, the most elaborate part of the model, which itself is not very elaborate. It seems clear that legislators' voting decisions can be understood as the workings of extremely simple decision rules, rules which are not generated in some arbitrary fashion, but in a way which is consistent with quite a rich body of previous literature on legislative voting. It must be remembered also that this particular sample of votes contains those decisions which should be the hardest to predict. I deliberately selected votes which were among the most conflict-ridden of the session, which makes the high degrees of consensus (at Steps B and C1) really quite striking. One would not have expected these results, given the votes selected. Thus the model should do even better for run-of-the-mill votes. If there is as little conflict among actors and goals with these relatively "big," high-visibility votes, then there should be even less with more routine votes. I would expect, however, that for those votes, the simpler Steps A, B, C1, and D (stressing no conflict and House colleagues) would account for more of

Table 25.2

Quantitative performance of the integrative model

Step (see Figure 27.1)		Accuracy[a]	Percentage of cases[b]	Cumulative percentages[c]
A	Noncontroversial votes	—	0%	0%
B	No conflict in field	104/104 = 100%	47	47
C1	No conflict among goals	74/79 = 94%	33	80
C2–C6	Conflict among goals (from Table 25.1)	22/27 = 81%	10	90
D	Fellow congressmen	5/5 = 100%	2	92
E	Unexplained cases	n = 7		

[a]Accuracy equals the percentage of the cases in which the congressman votes as the model specifies. For example, at Step C1, there are 79 cases in which there is no conflict among the goals, and the congressman votes in accordance with the evoked goals in 74 of those cases. Thus accuracy = 74/79 = 94%. The number of "mistakes" made by the model at this step is five.

[b]Percentage of cases equals the percentage of the total ($n = 222$) accounted for by that decision step. For example, in Step C1, it is 74/222 = 33%.

[c]The cumulative percentage equals percentage of 222 accounted for by that step plus all previous steps. For example at Step C1, it is (74 + 104)/222 = 80%.

the total than these data indicate, and the more elaborate Steps C2–C6 would be resorted to even less frequently than these data indicate.

The model does specify that the congressman *picks cues and votes* in accordance with the specified goal. Thus far, we have only considered the percentage of *votes* predicted, without reference to whether or not the congressman also picked cues to reinforce those votes. I take it that "picking cues" here refers to choosing fellow congressmen on whom to rely according to their agreement with the goal specified in the model. Thus fellow congressmen at Step C2 should not be opposed to the constituency position, if the model is right; or at Step C6, they should not be opposed to the deciding legislator's policy position. If this factor is taken into account, we lose five cases which would otherwise be correctly predicted. That is to say, there are five cases in which the actor "fellow congressman" is opposed to a decision which was governed by the specified goal. Building this loss into the overall figures, therefore, the overall performance of the model, defined as the congressman's *both* voting as the model specified *and* avoiding colleagues who are opposed to that vote, is 90%. The predictive performance, in other words, remains high.

Alternative Formulations

[Kingdon next tests alternative formulations of the model and finds that his integrative model predicts the votes of members of Congress most accurately.]

A Caution about Quantitative Performance

It is appropriate to close with a caution that models of legislative voting should not be accepted solely because of their good ability to account for cases in quantitative terms (Simon 1968). In some situations in the social sciences, a good fit to the data is regarded as a sufficient condition to accept a model, since it is difficult to predict outcomes. In other situations, such as the case of legislative voting models, a good quantitative performance is a necessary but not sufficient condition to accept a model, since outcomes are quite easy to predict. The null hypothesis in the legislative case predicts 50% of the cases by itself, since if a congressman were flipping coins between "yes" and "no" in order to decide, and a random model were also flipping coins, the random model and the congressman's behavior would agree half the time. Beyond this "impressive" chance performance, quite a simple model constructed from commonplaces in the literature—e.g., some combination of party, region, constituency, and president position—would probably do quite nicely in a statistical sense. Indeed, a model which simply postulated that all congressmen vote "yea," while not theoretically interesting, would yield a fairly good prediction.[5] As a matter of fact, most of the previous models discussed in this chapter do quite nicely on their data sets, and we have become accustomed to models which predict about 85% of the cases. This is not to say that all possible models do well in terms of a criterion of ability to predict, as we have seen. Some models can be falsified, but that still leaves a number of models which do well.

In evaluating those remaining models of legislative voting, then, one should add to conventional criteria of statistical fit and quantitative performance, and use more conceptual and theoretical considerations. I outlined above some of these considerations, including plausibility, simplicity, political realism, and comprehensiveness. The advantages of the model presented in this paper have to do with those considerations. Our discussion attempts to use the virtues of various previous models to construct a more integrated view of legislative voting. The resulting model is quite comprehensive, and yet does not achieve this comprehensiveness at the expense of simplicity, plausibility, and realism. There is also a compelling logic to the progression portrayed, as congressmen are seen as moving from the simple to the complex, from a simple judgment about the whole environment, to a subsetting of that environment, to a further subsetting which concentrates explicitly on goals. These sorts of considerations, rather than simply an impressive ability to account for cases quantitatively, commend the model. . . .

One advantage of the new model rests not in negating previous models but in providing a more comprehensive framework within which they can all be better understood.

CONCLUSION

. . . There may be a wider applicability of the key concepts presented here beyond the case of legislative voting, in the sense that wide varieties of decision makers may use versions of a similar general approach to their decisions. Legislators, bureaucrats, judges, and others may all be thought to search for consensus in their environment, to subset that environment in the event that agreement is lacking and to search for consensus within the most critical subset, to identify their most important goals and ask if there is agreement among them, and to get into more complex decisions if these simpler rules fail them. The well-known use of standard operating procedures in bureaucracies, for example, may be due to consensus among the relevant actors in the bureaucrat's environment—his superiors, the agency clientele, his coworkers, his professional associates outside the agency—that given SOPs are appropriate for a given class of cases. Or judges deciding on sentencing of convicted defendants, for another example, have been found to impose the sentence recommended by policy, prosecutor, and probation departments if the three agree; if they do not agree, the judge must enter a more complex set of decision rules. Mass public voting behavior exhibits similar characteristics: when various important influences agree, the voting decision is made; when they do not, the voter is said to be under "crosspressure," and the decision becomes more complicated. Space does not permit an extended discussion of the possible applications, but it is worth noting that the model presented here may represent a general decision strategy, an approach to decision making which is widely used. Thus this work hopefully contributes not only to further understanding of legislative behavior, but also to the general building of theory about decision processes.

NOTES

1. Subsets of constituents, such as constituency elites interested in the content of certain public policy outcomes, are also influential without necessarily being directly relevant to reelection chances. On these points, see Kingdon (1973, chapter 2).
2. The same balancing logic applies to Step C1. If constituency is not sufficiently intense to pass the critical threshold and policy position is sufficiently extreme, for example, policy dominates the constituency.
3. For readers who are not familiar with the earlier study, it may be useful to present some details of the research design beyond what is presented in the text. The core of this study, which provides the database for the quantitative analysis presented in this article, was a set of interviews with congressmen. In contrast to relying on roll-call analysis or on standard survey interviewing, each of these interviews concentrated on some specific vote or votes that were currently or very recently under consideration. It sought to develop a kind of life history of that decision, including the steps through which the congressman went, the considerations which he weighed, and the political actors who influenced him.

   There are two sampling questions involved: choosing the respondents, and choosing the votes about which to ask. As to the first, the sample of respondents is a probability sample of members of the U.S. House of Representatives in 1969, stratified by party, seniority, and region. I interviewed fifteen congressmen for each vote chosen. Once four draws of 15 congressmen ($n = 60$) had been made, I started to return to the first 15-member sample, and went through the sample in that fashion for the rest of the congressional session, 15 per vote, returning to a given congressman every fourth vote. It should be emphasized that the *decision*, not the congressman, is the unit of analysis. Since each congressman was interviewed about several voting decisions, the resultant number of cases is approximately the number of congressmen interviewed times the number of decisions each was asked about, or precisely, 222 decisions.

   As to the selection of votes, given the issue-by-issue design, I had to choose votes weekly, as the issues came up for floor consideration. I therefore could not rely on conventional sampling procedures, which require a final population list of votes as a sampling frame. I thus chose votes which were receiving some attention by congressmen, press, lobbyists, and others; votes in which several political actors (e.g., constituency, party, administration, etc.) might have the potential for being involved in decisions; and votes about which there was fairly extensive and intense conflict, upon which people appeared to be expending energy and political resources. The result was a sample of "big" votes of the session: ABM deployment, surtax extension, tax reform, HEW appropriation, state control over the poverty program, cigarette advertising, agriculture payment limitations, electoral college reform, water pollution abatement, foreign aid, campus unrest, elementary and secondary education, the debt limit, HUAC, and the seating of Adam Clayton Powell, 15 issues in all. While these were all important votes, they were clearly not uniform in importance or in public salience, with some being considerably more salient than others.

    The interview was conducted in a conversational fashion, with no notes taken. After I cited the vote which I wanted to discuss, I asked a general open-ended question: "How did you go about making up your mind? What steps did you go through?" After the questions was answered completely and appropriate probes were exhausted, I asked a series of question about each of several hypothesized influences on the vote, which were designed to pick up any other influence which was not spontaneously mentioned in response to the first question. I asked about the possible involvement of fellow congressmen, party leadership and informal groups within the party, staff, constituents, administration or executive branch, interest groups and reading. Answers to these questions were then coded according to the direction in which each influence would point the congressman and the importance which he appeared to attach to each influence. For more detail on these procedures and the rationales for them, please consult Kingdon (1973, chapter 1, Appendixes A and B).

4. Some intra-actor conflict (e.g., among constituents, among colleagues) is ignored here, and properly so. The key question is whether a given *consideration* (constituency, party, etc.) points in one or another direction, and what is the state of conflict among these considerations.

5. For a discussion which makes the same point, see Matthews and Stimson (1975, 115). Weisberg (1978) has calculated various null models in addition to the 50% model, and has concluded that some of them can account for well into the 80% range. That fact places all the more importance on such considerations as plausibility, simplicity, and comprehensiveness.

Chapter 26

Voting Change in Congress: Some Dynamic Perspectives on an Evolutionary Process

HERBERT B. ASHER AND
HERBERT F. WEISBERG

The policy decisions of the U.S. Congress as reflected in voting outcomes exhibit substantial continuity over time. When change does occur, it tends to be evolutionary and incremental as opposed to revolutionary and dramatic. Change is evolutionary because the congressional agenda is largely recurrent, members most often follow their previous votes on an issue, and congressional personnel and procedures are characterized by a high degree of stability. At times dramatic change does occur in Congress; certainly the famous Eighty-ninth Congress (1965–66) was characterized by substantial membership replacement as well as congressional approval of an impressive array of new social welfare programs. Yet even here the amount of change can be too easily overstated. Despite the sizable influx of freshman Democrats elected in the 1964 Johnson landslide, total membership turnover in the House was still only about 20%. And the numerous social programs finally receiving approval in 1965 had in many cases lengthy legislative histories going back years and even decades. Moreover, while the passage of these measures in 1965 after years of defeat certainly represented a dramatic reversal of past congressional decisions, the predominant voting pattern of members who served in the Eighty-ninth and previous congresses was one of stability, not change. The point is that voting change in the Congress can best be characterized as an evolutionary process. This assertion need not imply increasing complexity as does the Darwinian usage of evolution, although the changes observed in congressional voting patterns do often entail a shift from relatively simple to more complex patterns.

Hence, the aim of this chapter is to present and test an evolutionary model of congressional voting change. The claim that change is gradual implies the existence of some forces that limit the amount of change. At the level of the individual legislative decision maker, the major force promoting stability to be discussed is

Source: Herbert B. Asher and Herbert F. Weisberg, "Voting Change in Congress: Some Dynamic Perspectives on an Evolutionary Process." *American Journal of Political Science.* Volume 22, Number 2. Pp. 391–425. Copyright © 1978. Reprinted by permission of University of Wisconsin Press.

the legislator's previous voting history on an issue. The presence of individual voting histories in conjunction with low membership turnover guarantees that the collective decisions of Congress will normally not change much over the short run.

Yet change does occur and is due to a variety of sources. One is membership replacement, particularly when large numbers of seats change partisan hands. But if this were the only source of change, even evolutionary would be too strong an adjective to describe the process. There is, however, one other major source of change, member conversion, in which the legislator switches his stance on an issue for any of a variety of reasons. One such reason is a change in the policy debate surrounding an issue. For example, if an increase in the public debt ceiling is perceived as needed in order to support domestic welfare programs, the liberal Democrat might favor such an increase. But if raising the debt limit is viewed as providing funds for an unpopular war in Southeast Asia, the liberal Democrat may move to oppose debt increases. In short, policy redefinition may result in vote change. Another source of conversion is a change in the external forces impinging on the legislator; foremost among these is a switch in partisan control of the national administration. On many issues, the desire to support the president of one's own party may be sufficient to override previous voting patterns. What makes partisan control of the presidency so important is that it affects entire groupings of legislators simultaneously. Other changes in the external environment are more specific, affecting only a limited number of congressmen. For example, a change in district boundaries or a transfer to a new committee may result in altered voting patterns, but these changes will be idiosyncratic to the specific legislators involved.

The previous paragraphs have laid out in very general and cursory terms some of the key concepts to be used in the chapter. The next task is to provide a more systematic justification for positing an evolutionary model and to delineate further the significance of such concepts as *voting history, conversion, policy redefinition,* and others. After that is accomplished, a general model of congressional voting change will be presented followed by a series of case studies that will test the model.

THE EVOLUTIONARY HYPOTHESIS

Vote History

An evolutionary model assumes that the legislator's votes on recurrent issues exhibit more constancy than change. The congressman's voting history on an issue is, in effect, his "standing decision" on that issue. Once he has decided how to vote on an issue, he can continue to vote that way unless there is a relevant change in the decisional context.

There are numerous reasons to argue that a voting history on an issue would be likely to produce constant behavior on that issue. In interviews with congressmen, Kingdon (1973, 254–57) found that a voting history on an issue simplified the representative's decision-making task; voting on an issue as one has done in the past is an economizing device, particularly when previous votes have not hurt the legislator. Legislators may be forced to fall back on previous votes given the magnitude of their decision-making task. They must cast many votes, often on complex issues, with little opportunity to devote substantial attention to each issue. In such situations, representatives must resort to simplifying strategies. One such strategy may be to rely on cues from various sources; another is to repeat previous votes on an issue unless the situation has changed dramatically since the earlier votes. As one of Kingdon's respondents stated:

> I was precommited in a way. I had fought that out with myself some time ago—a year or longer—and had decided at that time to support funding for Viet Nam. I'd already been through that, and nothing in my circle of relevant factors had changed since (Kingdon 1973, 257).

This quote conveys well that the forces impinging upon the legislator are best considered relative to his previous voting history. Departure from previous voting history depends on change in that field of forces.

In addition congressmen do not want to call undue attention to themselves. Explaining one's vote to the constituency is simpler if the member continues to vote as he has always done rather than having to explain a shift in his position. If the electorate has accepted the previous votes, then a continuation of that voting position is deemed a simple and safe decision rule.

Finally, the sources of voting history seem likely to result in constant behavior on an issue over time. Often, voting history is based on party-constituency cues as when a northern, urban, Democratic representative supports certain social welfare programs or when a rural Republican legislator favors certain farm programs. In these cases, voting history is so based in party and constituency interests that a replacement from the same party would undoubtedly continue to vote as his or her predecessor.

How is a voting history formed and how is it maintained? It initially is likely to be a function of certain "background" factors such as party, ideology, and constituency. The stability of these elements over time facilitates continuity in the legislator's vote decisions. Voting history, however, also simultaneously causes and reflects learned behavior. As the representative learns that previous votes have not worked to his disadvantage, he realizes that he can safely keep voting that way. Given the uncertainty as to what issues a potential challenger may raise at the next election, the incumbent may decide to stick with positions that have worked well in the past rather than give his opponent more ammunition—particularly the ammunition that the representative is wishy-washy in his voting on an issue.

New congressmen establish a voting history very quickly; Kingdon (1973, 255) found voting history to be of major importance about half the time for votes cast by second-term congressmen. A special problem occurs when a "new issue" arises. However, most new issues are actually related to some previous issue, often several. Thus the foreign aid program was not a totally new program when the Mutual Defense Assistance Act of 1949 was passed. It had clear antecedents in terms of aid to European countries after World War II and even aid to the allies prior to the war. The "newer" an issue, the less settled the voting patterns will be initially, though we would expect vote decisions to settle eventually into a fairly steady pattern in accord with the voting history logic.

The Congressional Agenda

The concept of voting history makes sense only if the congressional agenda is largely recurrent. This point is essential to our argument because an analysis of voting change is possible only if Congress confronts the same issues repeatedly. This does not require that bills be identical over time, only that the general content of legislation be sufficiently similar so as to bring the legislator's previous voting history into play on the current decision. . . .

The best way of arguing for the recurrence of the legislative agenda is to consider what the business of Congress is in a typical session. First, Congress must fund a large number of governmental programs and departments by passing a set of appropriations and authorization bills. This is explicitly a recurrent agenda, having to provide funding for the same departments and programs year after year. The specific dollar amounts and statutory limitations may certainly change from year to year, but the general content of the legislation exhibits substantial continuity.

Second, many bills have lengthy legislative histories as representatives remain dissatisfied with the existing state of legislation in an area. For example, the initial attempts to introduce new programs often fail so that proponents must introduce them repeatedly before they become public policy. Legislation involving the federal government in aid to education and health care falls into this category. Other areas such as abortion, school prayer, reform of legislative procedures such as cloture, and the like are so controversial that they come up repeatedly for consideration as the losing side tries to reverse the previous outcomes.

Another category of recurrent legislation is that of bills which expire (or effectively expire) and so must be renewed if they are to remain effective. Much legislation such as the Voting Rights Act requires periodic renewal. Other legislation must of necessity be reconsidered due to changing circumstances. For example, the national debt ceiling is fixed "permanently" by legislation at a level sufficiently low so that it must be increased after a few years if the government is to expend money lawfully. Minimum wage and Social Security legislation falls in a similar situation, having to be increased every few years in response to inflationary trends.

Certainly not all legislation is recurrent; many bills involve topical problems that are inherently nonrepetitive, such as ratification of a particular treaty, confirmation of a particular appointment, admission of a particular territory to statehood, or the authorization of a particular investigation. Such motions are certainly important and often controversial. Nevertheless we would argue that the vast majority of significant congressional business falls in the recurrent category.

Note that our argument pertains more to votes on the passage of bills than to amendments and procedural votes. Some amendments are recurrent (e.g., the Powell amendment and the amendments to end the war in Southeast Asia), but most are not. Moreover, voting history is more likely to be relevant for more visible passage votes than less visible procedural votes. The lesser visibility of the latter to constituents enables party and other pressures to have a greater impact, thereby reducing the impact of voting history on the member's decisions. Our emphasis in this chapter will be on passage votes, though some extension to other votes is possible.

Once the congressional agenda is viewed as largely recurrent, this enables us to switch our research focus from the typical enterprise of studying the correlates of legislative voting cross-sectionally (Cherryholmes and Shapiro 1969; Jackson 1971; Truman 1959) to analyzing the patterns of congressional voting change (as in Asher 1973a; Clausen 1973; Kesselman 1961, 1965). One reason to switch to a change perspective is to construct a more powerful theory of legislative voting; certainly any theory will be more powerful to the extent that it can account for voting change *as well as* cross-sectional voting outcomes. A focus on change obviously requires a longitudinal design extending over a number of congresses as well as a change in the explanatory model employed. The explanatory variables used in most legislative voting studies—party and constituency characteristics—vary little over time for most congressmen and hence cannot be very helpful in accounting for change. Political and policy variables outside of Congress must be examined in order to account for change; these will be discussed shortly.

In addition, an investigation of voting change departs from the usual emphasis in voting studies of describing or predicting the *collective* decisions of legislators on a *collection* of issues. Such a focus has tended to mask the voting patterns of individual legislators, has usually treated all votes as if similar decisional processes characterized them, and has often ignored the fact that many of the specific issues analyzed are ones that the congressman has made a decision on in previous years. A focus on *individual* decisions of legislators on *specific* and *recurrent* issues overcomes these limitations. Thus we would argue that many interesting substantive questions central to a theory of legislative voting can best be studied with a longitudinal design.

Sources of Change

Although continuity best characterizes legislative voting, change does occur and is due to three sources which themselves can be subdivided into systematic and idiosyncratic (see Table 26.1). The greater payoff for theory development is in initially concentrating on the systematic as opposed to the idiosyncratic sources of change.

The first type of change occurs when the meaning of an issue changes over time in response to new conditions in the external environment. For example, foreign aid programs may initially be viewed in terms of thwarting Soviet aims and hence receive widespread, uncritical congressional support. As the perceived Soviet threat decreases, however, congressmen may bring a different perspective to their decision making about ostensibly similar foreign aid programs. The changes in meaning of an issue are usually gradual, even if a particular external event sometimes accelerates the pace of change. We label this process "issue evolution" to underline its substantial continuity.

. . . [O]ur second source of systematic change—membership replacement—provides an opportunity for policy shifts and policy reversals by the Congress at large even when continuing members never change their votes. Yet the limits on change resulting from the election of new representatives are severe. For one thing, membership replacement in Congress is limited with the overwhelming

Table 26.1
Sources of voting change

Sources of vote change	Systematic	Idiosyncratic
Policy influence	Long-term issue evolution or policy redefinition	Short-term developments (crisis, scandal, etc.)
Membership effects	Membership evolution	Change in the status or district of an individual legislator
Presidential influence	Change in partisan control of the White House	Change in presidency without partisan change

majority of members reelected at each election. Moreover, newly elected legislators often replace predecessors of the same party, thereby resulting in substantial continuity in policy views. Only those infrequent elections which result in a sharp change in party strength in the legislature provide a large potential for change, and that more so on partisan issues than on issues related to the district. . . . Membership change is a continual process, but the most frequent types of change have such minor effects on voting in Congress that we speak of the process as "membership evolution."

The gradual nature of issue and membership effects is in marked contrast to the sudden and substantial shock that the legislature receives when the voting cue from the White House is altered. Instances in which a president changes his mind on a program are infrequent. But the significance of the White House cue on many issues can change when partisan control of the administration changes, even if the Democratic and Republican presidents take the same stance on an issue. For example, both Republican and Democratic presidents have requested increases in the public debt ceiling so that a switch in partisan control of the executive branch did not result in a change in presidential stance on the issue. However, the meaning of the presidential cue changed markedly for congressmen. Congressional Republicans who opposed debt ceiling increases under a Democratic president suddenly find themselves subjected to strong partisan White House lobbying when their Republican president deems a debt increase needed to carry out the functions of government.

A diagrammatic representation of the forces affecting legislative voting is given in Figure 26.1. Vote history is viewed as the long-term component of the legislator's vote decision and changes in the decisional setting as the short-term component. A vote on a specific bill reflects both long-term and short-term elements. The origins of vote history are found in the explanatory variables commonly cited in legislative voting research, namely party affiliation, ideology, and constituency characteristics. A dynamic enters this model because of changing conditions in the real world; vote history is the element of constancy, but it is confronted by continual change in the external environment. Some of these environmental changes may result in substantial departures from past vote history whereas others may have little impact at all. Our aim is to identify departures from vote history and

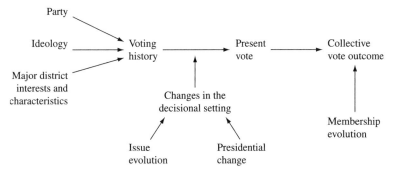

Figure 26.1
An overall model of congressional voting.

relate these shifts to changes in the decisional setting, particularly policy-related changes and shifts in partisan control of the executive. Overlaid upon these changes are those congressional membership changes which can alter the outcome on a recurrent bill even when continuing members maintain a constant voting pattern.

A further complication is that different sources of change may be prominent in different policy arenas. A massive infusion of freshman Democrats might have tremendous implications for policy in areas noted for partisan battles, such as Clausen's social welfare dimension. But in areas such as international involvement—where Clausen finds very weak party and constituency effects on voting—it may be the case that a change in partisan control of the presidency will be required to alter congressional voting patterns. Likewise, in areas where constituency effects are supreme (such as Clausen's civil liberties dimension), only long-term issue evolution is likely to result in voting change. . . .

In summary, our evolutionary model asserts that stability rather than change characterizes congressional voting and that when change does occur, it tends to be gradual rather than abrupt. Both issue evolution and membership replacement are likely to result in modest voting changes, whereas a switch in partisan control of the presidency can lead to more substantial voting shifts. In the next section . . . we devote considerable attention to delineating the types of vote changes associated with a change in the presidential occupant as well as presenting a model of the individual legislator's decision making.

AN INDIVIDUAL LEVEL MODEL OF CONGRESSIONAL DECISION MAKING

Our general model of legislative decision making is presented in Figure 26.2. According to the model, the key elements that the legislator considers in coming to a vote decision are his voting history on the issue, whether his party controls the White House, the position of the president if his party controls the White House (and in special circumstances the position of an opposition president), and

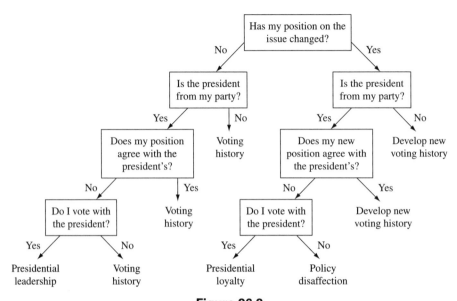

Figure 26.2

A flow chart depicting legislative decision making for representatives with a voting history on an issue.

whether his own position on the issue has changed. According to Figure 26.2, the member first asks whether his position on the issue has changed. Such change might arise because of policy redefinition or issue evolution as the issue assumes a new meaning, or because of more idiosyncratic factors, such as alteration in district boundaries or switch in committee assignments. If the member's position has not changed, he can routinely continue voting his voting history unless his old position disagrees with that of the president of his own party, in which case he must decide whether to go along with the president ("presidential leadership") or follow his voting history. If the member's position has changed, we would expect him to change his vote and develop a new voting history unless his new position disagrees with that of the president of his own party, in which case he must decide whether to switch his vote ("policy disaffection") or follow his voting history so as not to embarrass his party's president ("presidential loyalty"). In the case of presidential loyalty, we expect that the member would change his vote as soon as his party loses the White House, adopting a new voting history more in accord with his changed issue position.

While an evolutionary model guides our inquiry, we argued earlier that the most dramatic exception to gradual voting change would occur when partisan control of the White House shifted. An examination of the model presented in Figure 26.2 under a change in control in the national executive helps clarify the different outcomes depicted in Table 26.2, particularly the difference between presidential leadership and presidential loyalty. To simplify the following discussion, we are assuming that the issues under consideration are ones in which the presidential stance remains constant despite the shift in partisan control of the

Table 26.2

Types of individual voting change in Congress

	Congressman shifts to support president	Congressman shifts to oppose president
Administration changes from opposition party to congressman's party	Presidential leadership	Policy disaffection
Administration changes from congressman's party to opposition party	Idiosyncratic behavior	Presidential loyalty

executive.[1] Studying such issues allows us in effect to control for the president's position while allowing partisanship to vary. Foreign aid, the public debt ceiling, and executive reorganization are examples of issues on which the president's position is likely to be constant regardless of his party affiliation.

In comparing the presidential leadership and loyalty outcomes, the greater vote change would occur under the former as each partisan switch in control of the administration would result in substantial vote shifts. Under the leadership model, the presidential cue on certain issues is viewed as partisan rather than policy-based, resulting in Democrats supporting their own party's president on an issue, moving into opposition on the issue when Republicans win the White House, and moving back to support when Democrats recapture the presidency. However, the loyalty outcome suggests that once vote shifts have occurred, members will likely retain their new voting histories in spite of subsequent changes in the partisan complexion of the White House. This is because the voting change associated with the loyalty outcome is policy-based, even if originally timed so as not to embarrass one's own party's president. These differences will be illustrated in the analysis of foreign aid and public debt votes in the case studies in the next section.

THE CASE STUDIES

Introduction

Having developed the evolutionary hypothesis and our general model at some length, we now turn to a series of case studies designed to illuminate the advantages of our evolutionary perspective and to illustrate the methodology of analyzing vote changes in Congress. While a series of case studies cannot conclusively demonstrate the merits of our approach, a careful selection of issues emerging from past research efforts and theoretical perspectives can assure the reader that the deck has not been overly stacked by the choice of specific issues. Clausen (1973) has found five issue domains in postwar Congresses that are marked by continuity and stability: government management, agricultural assistance, social welfare, civil liberties, and international involvement. His analysis of party and

constituency effects on voting (see his Figures 6 and 11 [Clausen 1973, 93, 168])
indicates the following patterns:

Government management	High party effects
Agricultural assistance	High party effects plus some constituency effects
Social welfare	Moderate constituency and party effects
Civil liberties	High constituency effects
International involvement	Moderate constituency effects with much variance unexplained by party or constituency

We would expect that policy areas affected by party would be most susceptible to voting change induced by shifts in White House control and by membership replacement, whereas those areas most affected by constituency would show
the greatest vote stability unless long-term policy evolution or redefinition has
occurred. We use these expectations to select issues for analysis which minimize or
maximize the likelihood of different types of voting change. While Clausen talks of
issue domains, our evolutionary approach requires specific issues from broader
policy domains. Thus, we will talk about the Mutual Security Program rather than
international involvement and the public debt ceiling as opposed to government
management.

In general, our database involves voting in the House of Representatives from
1949 to 1972. This time frame was chosen in order to have three switches in partisan control of the White House—a Democratic administration from 1949 to
1952, Republican control from 1953 to 1960, Democratic control from 1961 to
1968, and a Republican administration from 1969 to 1972. We must occasionally
depart from this time frame when the number of votes taken exceeds computer
program capacities, when votes were not taken in all years, when there was a long
break in the years in which votes were taken, or when new issues arose in the latter
part of the time period. We restrict our attention to the House of Representatives
to obtain a large number of cases for generalization and to gain comparability with
previous studies on one of the issues we will investigate. The analyses we have performed on the Senate, however, do not suggest any contrary conclusions.

Our first two case studies focus on voting change associated with a partisan
shift on control of the presidency. We wish to see how much change in individual
voting *can* result from a change in partisan control of the executive. Hence we are
selecting issues in which we expect voting change to be maximal, implying that if
presidential effects are low here then they would be even lower on most other
issues. We anticipate maximal presidential effects in policy area where party
effects are greatest—Clausen's government management area—and in areas
where much of the variance in voting cannot be explained by either constituency
or party and hence the presidential cue might fill the void—Clausen's international
involvement domain. We shall test this by examining votes on public debt limit (a
government management issue) and foreign aid (the core of international involvement). Both of these issues are characterized by the absence of widespread, effective domestic constituencies for the programs involved, so that presidential appeals
for support from his party's congressional contingent could be very important.

The Debt Ceiling: Presidential Leadership Effects

The ceiling on the public debt is set by statute. Whenever the actual debt approaches that ceiling, the government must either decrease its spending or raise the ceiling with the latter being the choice invariably adopted. Fiscal conservatives, primarily Republicans, are most concerned about minimizing or preventing debt ceiling increases, yet Republican presidents have found it necessary to request debt ceiling hikes. Democratic legislators have been somewhat willing to assist Republican presidents with debt ceiling increases, particularly if a reasonable number of Republican representatives join in supporting the bill, while Republican representatives have been much less willing to support a Democratic president's request for a debt ceiling hike. The result is the classic situation leading to presidential leadership effects: members of each party more willing to support debt ceiling bills when their party controls the White House and moving to opposition when they lose the White House. This pattern is more pronounced for Republicans since Democratic liberals tend to support spending programs more than Republicans, and Democratic votes have been necessary to pass debt limit bills in recent Democratic-controlled Congresses, even under a Republican president.

Figure 26.3 shows the partisan support patterns on debt legislation in the House between 1949 and 1972. A majority of Democrats opposed the bill only in 1953, the one case in this period when the Republicans controlled Congress and

Percent supporting
debt ceiling increase

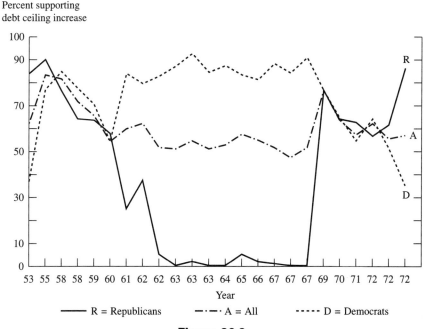

Figure 26.3
Support for debt ceiling increases by party, House 1953–72.

Table 26.3

House voting patterns on public debt bills for members with continuous service from 1964 to 1971, by party

| Party | Debt voting patterns | | | | | |
	Opposition under Democrats, support under Republicans	Support under Democrats, opposition under Republicans	Constant support	Constant opposition	Residual patterns	Total
Republicans	58%	0%	0%	19%	23%	100%
	(45)	(0)	(0)	(15)	(18)	(78)
Democrats	0%	2%	54%	6%	39%	100%
	(0)	(3)	(79)	(8)	(57)	(147)

the White House could be forced to pass a debt bill with minimal Democratic support, and in 1972 when an authorization for the Republican president to impose a spending limit was a part of the debt ceiling bill. Republican support clearly reflected changes in partisan control of the White House, with majority support forthcoming during Republican administrations only and no Republican votes whatsoever cast in favor of debt increases during many years when the Presidency was controlled by the Democrats.

A stronger test of presidential leadership effects is provided by examining the voting patterns of the same representatives over a change in administration. Table 26.3 summarizes the debt voting patterns of those 225 representatives who were in the House from 1964 through 1971, a period of four Democratic years of presidential control followed by three Republican years. Members are classified according to whether they *always* supported or opposed the debt ceiling during each administration; otherwise members are placed in the residual category. Note the strong presidential leadership effects for Republicans: 45 of 78 Republicans always opposed a debt increase between 1964 and 1968 and then moved to constant support for it between 1969 and 1971 when their own party held the presidency. For the Democrats, movement in the opposite direction is substantially less with only three Democrats actually changing from consistent support to opposition when their party lost the White House. Hence, presidential leadership effects are evident in debt ceiling voting, although they are still smaller than the degree of constancy, especially for Democrats of whom more than half maintained a constant position in support of debt increases throughout 1964–71.[2] . . .

Foreign Aid: Presidential Loyalty Effects

Some of the literature on foreign aid voting in Congress would lead one to expect presidential leadership effects similar to those found for debt votes. Particularly relevant here are Mark Kesselman's (1961, 1965) studies of the impact of presidential leadership on foreign aid votes in which he found that members of the president's party move to more internationalist voting records after a change in administration while the new opposition party becomes more isolationist. Kesselman's underlying model is one of presidential leadership; he would predict that not only do proponents of a program continue to support it when their party wins the presidency, but former opponents will shift to support the program. Furthermore, since the issue involves presidential support, the other party will move to opposition. And since presidential support is the basic element, the changes will occur in opposite directions when the next change in national administration takes place.

Another possibility is that foreign aid directly measures the internationalist-isolationist position of the representative or perhaps his fiscal conservatism stance (Jewell 1962). The representative may take a position on foreign aid and vote accordingly in line with his voting history until changing conditions (such as a change in the economic-military division of the program, a change in the nature of our foreign commitments due to such events as war, or a change in the nation's fiscal situation) result in departures from past voting history. This suggests that presidential leadership in our terms would prevail less than policy dissatisfaction and presidential loyalty considerations.

The regional voting trends on foreign aid shown in Figure 26.4 are quite different from those for debt bills. Northern Democratic support of foreign aid was relatively stable with only the most modest decline in the Eisenhower years and less support (albeit still majority support greater than any other regional party grouping) during the Nixon administration. Southern Democratic support for foreign aid decreased during the Eisenhower years and enjoyed a resurgence during the Kennedy-Johnson years although only back to the support levels of the early Eisenhower years rather than of the Truman era. Republican support increased slightly under Eisenhower, decreased under Kennedy and Johnson, and increased under Nixon, but except for one roll call Republican support levels on foreign aid were always less than that of northern Democrats. Hence, Figure 26.4 does not indicate sharply increased support for foreign aid when one's party wins the White House; instead, it shows that decline in support for the program occurs mainly when the opposition party controls the presidency. This illustrates very nicely the distinction between presidential leadership and loyalty effects. Loyalty effects dominate with policy disaffection causing decreased support for foreign aid over the years, but that disaffection is reflected in voting only when it would not embarrass the president of one's own party. Increased support of foreign aid when one's party wins the presidency is minimal; decline in support when one's party loses the White House is much more substantial. These initial findings already suggest a tempering of Kesselman's discussion of presidential leadership in foreign policy.

To further explore foreign aid voting change at the individual level, we have checked whether each representative voted for or against foreign aid on a majority of the final passage votes during each period of partisan control of the Presidency—the elected Truman term, the Eisenhower years, the Kennedy-Johnson administrations, and the first Nixon term.[3] The basic unit of analysis is the voting under successive administrations by a given representative. There are 1,071 such comparisons possible in this period, some involving the same representative

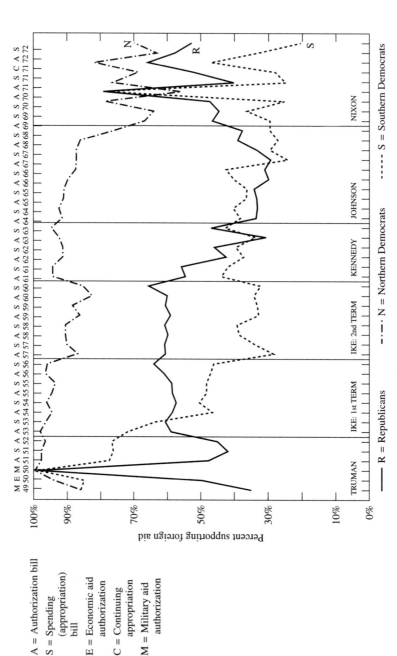

Figure 26.4
Support for foreign aid by party and region, House 1949–72.

A = Authorization bill

S = Spending (appropriation) bill

E = Economic aid authorization

C = Continuing appropriation

M = Military aid authorization

——— R = Republicans   —·—·— N = Northern Democrats   - - - - S = Southern Democrats more than once—as when a legislator serves during a change to a Republican administration and then through a subsequent change to a Democratic one. Table 26.4 shows the patterns of constancy and change associated with change in party control of the presidency.

A constant voting pattern occurred in fully 911 of these 1,071 cases—592 instances in which the representative voted for the program in two successive administrations and 319 cases in which he opposed it—for an overall stability rate of approximately 85%. This latter statistic emphasizes that House voting on foreign aid is not simply a matter of presidential support, that a change in partisan control of the executive does not result in many shifts in final passage voting.[4] Of the change that did occur, the greatest amount involved 85 representatives who stopped supporting the program when their party lost the presidency, mainly Southern Democrats during the Eisenhower years, Republicans during the Kennedy-Johnson administrations, and northern Democrats during the Nixon presidency. There are 54 cases which fit the presidential leadership model in moving to support foreign aid when their party wins the presidency, but these involve only 21% of the 254 representatives who were opposed to foreign aid at the time their party won the White House. The largest number of these shifts was 28 Republicans who moved to support foreign aid under Nixon, though some 82 Republicans still remained in opposition.

One of the best tests between the presidential leadership and loyalty models involves extending the time frame to two successive changes in partisan control of the White House. Presidential leadership would imply that a representative would change back and forth in his voting as his party gains and loses the White House, while the loyalty model would suggest continued opposition once opposition began. There are only eleven cases of complete voting partisanship across two successive partisan changes in control of the executive: five Republicans who moved from opposition under Truman to support under Eisenhower and back to opposition under the ensuing Democratic administrations, three Democrats with the

Table 26.4

House voting patterns on foreign aid bills for members serving in at least two successive administrations, 1949–72

Administration control	Foreign aid voting patterns				
	Opposition to support[a]	Support to opposition	Constant support	Constant opposition	Total
Own party takes control of the presidency	10% (54)	3% (17)	51% (287)	36% (200)	100% (558)
Opposition party takes control of the presidency	1% (4)	17% (85)	59% (305)	23% (119)	100% (513)

[a]Opposition and support are defined by how the representative voted a *majority* of the time in an administration.

reverse pattern, and three Republicans who switched from support under Eisenhower to opposition under the Democratic presidents and back to support in Nixon's first term. The three Democrats were the only ones in a group of 32 Democrats who favored foreign aid under Truman and opposed it under Eisenhower to move back to support under Kennedy and Johnson. Likewise, the three Republicans were the only ones among 27 GOP members who supported foreign aid under Eisenhower and opposed it under Kennedy-Johnson to move back to support under Nixon. Hence, the great bulk of the cases of change involved a change in voting history which was not reversed when the White House next changed hands.

These results contradict the substantial presidential influence found by previous investigators (Clausen 1973; Kesselman 1961, 1965; Tidmarch and Sabatt 1972). One critical difference seems to be the unit being analyzed. Previous studies have employed Guttman scales of roll calls within Congresses and then measured differences in scale positions between Congresses; we have instead considered only votes on final passage motions. The contrasting results suggest an important difference between final passage votes and the other roll calls which previous studies have included in their scales. Final passage votes are more visible to constituents so that representatives are more likely to follow their established voting history unless external conditions dictate a rethinking of that position. Other votes are less visible, so the member may be more vulnerable to the argument that going along with the White House on them would not be noticed by constituents. The member can explain to his party leader that his district would not accept a change in his vote on foreign aid passage, but finds it harder to justify a vote against his party's president on preliminary motions.

A dimensional analysis of foreign aid votes reinforces our conclusions about weak presidential (especially leadership) effects and also reveals long-term issue evolution in House foreign aid voting. Guttman scales were constructed of the votes taken within each four-year presidential term, omitting only two virtually unanimous votes and a roll call in the Nixon period on which the regional parties were in voting agreement and which was found by factor analysis to tap an independent dimension. The obtained scales all had high reproducibilities, .948 for the Nixon term and between .976 and .987 for the other administrations. A regional shift in support for foreign aid is evident over time, with greater support for the program among Southerners during the Truman years and among northerners thereafter. But the most notable trend is seen in the correlations among the scales presented in Table 26.5: higher correlations between adjacent terms and decreasing correlations as the time between terms increases, with the correlation between the Nixon and Truman scales (based on only 73 congressmen) falling to .35.

A similar evolutionary theme is seen in the issue space resulting from factor analysis of the tetrachoric r coefficients. An examination of the space presented in Figure 26.5 shows the Truman years at one point, the Nixon administration about 70 degrees away, and the intervening years along an arc between the two. American relations with the Soviet Union and the nature of the foreign aid program evolved considerably over the years and this evolution is mirrored in the dimensional change. To sum up, we find some evidence of presidential loyalty effects, but little

Table 26.5

Pearson r Correlations between Guttman scales of foreign aid passage votes by administration

Administration		Truman 1949–52	Eisenhower 1953–56	Eisenhower 1957–60	Kennedy-Johnson 1961–64	Johnson 1965–68	Nixon 1969–72
Truman	49–52						
Ike	53–56	.67					
Ike	57–60	.53	.81				
Dems	61–64	.62	.70	.80			
Johnson	65–68	.51	.66	.73	.86		
Nixon	69–72	.35	.53	.62	.66	.73	
Region[a]		.16	−.18	−.33	−.28	−.33	−.35
Party[b]		.52	.19	.04	.32	.35	.10

[a]Positive correlations indicate greater support among Southerners.

[b]Positive correlations indicate greater support among Democrats.

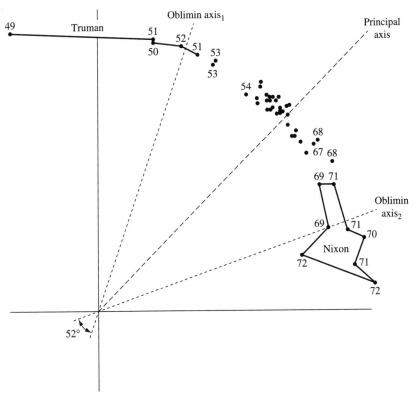

Key: Numbers show year of vote;
unmarked points are 1954–67.

Figure 26.5
Factor analysis of foreign aid passage votes, House 1949–72.

support for leadership effects as uncovered for the debt ceiling votes. And we find issue evolution in the dimension characterizing foreign aid voting.

School Construction: Membership Replacement Effects

The issue of federal aid to education is a good vehicle for demonstrating the effects of membership replacement on vote outcomes. Some of the early efforts to involve the federal government in education revolved around the question of aid for school construction. A school construction bill was defeated in the House in both 1956 (194–224) and 1957 (203–208) and gained ultimate passage in 1960 (206–189). To simplify our discussion we will focus on the first and last of these votes and identify the factors that changed a 194–224 defeat in 1956 into a 206–189 victory in 1960.

Table 26.6 presents the votes cast on school construction for only those representatives who were in the House in both 1956 and 1960. Note that the amount of individual vote change or conversion by the continuing members was minimal, with over 90% of the representatives who voted at both time points voting identically, a result in accord with our emphasis on voting history. In fact, among members who took a yea or nay position on school construction in both years, there was a net conversion of ten votes (18–8) or a 20-vote *loss* over time, even though the bill passed at the latter time. This 20-vote loss was partially offset by differential abstention rates from 1956 to 1960; eight fewer 1956 supporters than 1956 opponents abstained in 1960. Hence, individual vote changes and abstention patterns made a negative contribution to the ultimate passage of school construction in 1960.

We must turn to other factors facilitating the 1960 passage, focusing in particular on those districts experiencing membership replacement between 1956 and 1960. Table 26.7 presents the frequency of various vote patterns on the 1956 and 1960 school construction bills for those congressional seats which changed hands between 1956 and 1960.

Note that while 78 of the 107 seat changes did not result in vote changes, among the 29 seat changes that did lead to vote changes, there was a net switch in districts supporting school construction of 27 votes—which translates into a 54-vote gain. And most of this 54-vote gain came from the replacement of Republican incumbents with Democratic newcomers elected in the Democratic landslide of 1958. Thus, we have a situation where membership replacement provided the

Table 26.6

1956 and 1960 school construction votes for representatives in office at both time points

	1960 Vote			
1956 Vote	Yes	No	Did not vote	Total
Yes	109	18	11	138
No	8	130	19	157
Did not vote	1	4	1	6
Total	118	152	31	301

votes needed for a change in the aggregate vote outcome. Individual-level change was not very consequential, since school construction was one of those domestic welfare programs that was a genuine point of contention between the two parties in the late 1950s. As such, one would expect strong party pressures to keep members in line which would account for the high level of stability observed. The influx of new members was required to bring about a change in the basic vote outcome (Fenno 1963). Table 26.8 summarizes the components of school construction success; it shows clearly that membership replacement was the most important factor in the passage of school construction in 1960.

We can gain further insight into the nature of the outcome change on school construction by dividing the congressional districts into three groups: those represented by the same person in 1956 and 1960, those represented by different representatives from the same party, and those represented by different parties in the two years. The regression equations for predicting the votes of the member in 1960 from the vote of the member from that district in 1956 are as follows for the three groups:

$$V_{60} = 0.058 + 0.800V_{56} \quad R^2 = .65 \quad N = 265 \quad \text{Same person}$$
$$V_{60} = 0.182 + 0.818V_{56} \quad R^2 = .66 \quad N = 58 \quad \text{Same party, different person}$$
$$V_{60} = 0.880 + 0.078V_{56} \quad R^2 = .02 \quad N = 49 \quad \text{Different party}$$

The high regression coefficients for the first two groups reveal considerable stability in voting for the groups with the difference between the constant terms indicating that new members were slightly (.124) more likely to support aid to education than were continuing members.

Clearly we can do a very good job in predicting later votes from earlier votes when the party controlling a district has remained constant, even if the specific occupant of the seat has changed—but not when the district switched parties. This suggests that the observed stability in voting may to a large extent reside in party. But this in no way negates the importance of voting history; instead, it suggests an

Table 26.7

Frequency of school construction vote patterns for districts which changed hands between 1956 and 1960[a]

1956 vote	1960 vote	Always Republican	Always Democratic	Democratic to Republican	Republican to Democratic	Democratic to Republican to Democratic	Total
No	No	16	11	0	3	0	30
Yes	Yes	6	14	3	20	5	48
No	Yes	4	2	0	22	0	28
Yes	No	0	0	1	0	0	1
Total		26	27	4	45	5	107

[a]To keep this table manageable, only those districts in which the occupant changed and in which the occupants took yea or nay positions in both 1956 and 1960 are included. This excludes 33 districts in which the representative did not vote at least once, but this exclusion does not influence the direction of our results.

Table 26.8

Components of school construction success

−30	1956 defeat margin

−20	Net vote loss due to conversion
+8	Net gain due to 1956 voters who failed to vote in 1960
−3	Net loss due to 1956 nonvoters who voted in 1960
+54	Net gain due to replacement
	+12 Net gain due to same-party replacement
	+42 Net gain due to partisan replacement
+8	Additional net gain due to replacement, where abstention occurs in either 1956 or 1960

+17	1960 passage margin

explanation of the mechanism underlying the importance of voting history. On divisive, partisan issues such as school construction, the development of a voting history is very much rooted in party stances so that the vote outcome could only change if there was considerable partisan replacement.[5]

Civil Rights: Issue Evolution or Policy Redefinition Effects?

In this final case study, we will examine the effects of our third source of voting changes—issue evolution—by focusing on civil rights legislation between 1956 and 1972. This time span was chosen because it encompasses the major legislative developments in the civil rights movement and because the number of votes taken in this period (100) does not exceed computer program capacity.[6] It is not possible to trace a single civil rights bill through time so we instead have considered all bills directly relating to civil rights. Yet the difficulty in delimiting the area means that some votes have been included in our universe which do not scale with the others.

The analysis yielded two major dimensions in the civil rights area—a traditional and a partisan dimension. Traditionally, civil rights legislation has pitted the South against the north. The civil rights votes through the first half of 1966 exhibit strong cumulation because they all involve a virtually united South against the north. For example, the 1956–60 scale (with a reproducibility of .99) polarized the regions with 384 of 414 northerners on the liberal third of the scale and 105 of 122 Southerners on the conservative third. Within regions, party differences were negligible. This same dimension is visible in some later votes on traditional civil rights issues protecting blacks: votes on the Civil Rights Commission, a 1967 bill to protect civil rights workers, and a 1968 bill prohibiting discrimination in jury selection. A scale based on these votes has a reproducibility of .99 and has very high correlations with the pre–1966 scales (see Table 26.9).

A new set of civil rights concerns arose as the battle for black rights moved from the South to the north and as issues of busing and open housing became prominent. The changed concerns were related to the occurrence of urban riots

Table 26.9

Correlations (Pearson r's) among scales on civil rights issues

	Scale				
	1956–60	1961–65	1966–70 Traditional	1966–70 Partisan	1971–72 Partisan
1956–60	—				
1961–65	.88	—			
1966–70 Traditional	.85	.91	—		
1966–70 Partisan	.59	.73	.62	—	
1971–72 Partisan	.34	.48	.41	.73	—
Party[a]	.36	−.01	.15	−.32	−.29
North/South[b]	+.89	+.80	+.80	+.53	+.35
Reproducibility	.986	.984	.990	.964	.943
Number of motions	15	15	5	15	15

[a]Positive correlations show greater support among Republicans.

[b]Positive correlations show greater support among northerners.

beginning in Watts in August, 1965, and culminating in the major 1967 riots in Newark and Detroit, to the "white backlash" movement in the late 1960s, and to the Southern strategy of the Nixon administration as reflected in its attempt in 1969 to weaken some provisions in the Voting Rights Act extension. Northern support for the black position had decreased, particularly on the part of Republicans; new legislation aimed at blacks (e.g., antiriot bills) came to the fore.

The second dimension from our analysis corresponds to these changes. Loading high on the dimension are antiriot amendments and bills, the civil rights bills of 1966 and 1968 which involved open housing, and the Voting Rights Act extension votes of 1969 and 1970. In addition, the 1972 votes on Equal Employment Opportunities and the Civil Rights Commission load on this dimension though they are also related to the traditional dimension. It is the busing-related votes from 1968 to 1972, however, that form the core of this dimension.

This new civil rights dimension is characterized by party polarization in the north. On the scale comprised of 1966–70 votes, 164 of 197 northern Democrats are on the liberal third while 94 of 176 northern Republicans are on the conservative third. The 1971–72 results are similar except that a general conservative trend is evident. Where the traditional civil rights dimension splits the regions, the new civil rights dimension instead splits the central tendencies of the northern parties. The greatest shift is among northern Republicans, but there is a more general change in position from the traditional civil rights dimension to the new partisan one which stops the two sets from cumulating with one another, even though the constant Southern opposition on both dimensions and the substantial northern Democratic support on both results in a sizeable correlation between the dimensions—.51 between the factors and .34 to .73 between pairs of Guttman scales.

Civil rights is an issue area where constituency considerations would be expected to predominate. Under such circumstances, voting change would be expected to be slow. Yet the issue has evolved over a long enough time frame so that the original single dimension has split into two: one a clear continuation of traditional civil rights battles and the other a correlated but distinct dimension. The presence of a new dimension was very consequential for the extent of individual vote change on civil rights matters. Staunch opposition characterized the Southern stance on both dimensions so that the new dimension did not result in vote change. But for Republicans the new dimension resulted in substantially more opposition to civil rights than is visible on the traditional dimension. And even for northern liberal Democrats with a general record of support for a variety of civil rights measures, the level of support for civil rights measures loading on the second dimension, especially busing-related bills, was lower than their support for more traditional measures. Thus, the voting of individual legislators can and does change in response to evolution of an issue.

CONCLUSION

There are a number of lessons to be drawn from the preceding analyses. First, the forces of continuity predominate in congressional voting. Stability in individual voting was much more common than change even when the partisan control of the White House was altered and even in issue areas—such as foreign aid and the debt ceiling—where presidential impact was considered substantial. On the school construction votes, where membership replacement best accounted for the ultimate passage of the bill, it nevertheless was the case that the most frequent vote pattern on the issue was one of constancy. And while the dimensional structure of civil rights did change over time, there remained a substantial correlation between the old and new dimension. The point is that the tremendous continuity in congressional voting should be explicitly recognized in attempts to build a theory of legislative voting. Any static theory that ignores this impressive stability is failing to incorporate a central characteristic of legislative decision making.

Second, there are differences in the nature of change between different policy areas. The most substantial changes occurred in the areas with partisan effects (but only after a major election upheaval) and the areas with presidential-partisan effects (but only after the presidency switched partisan control). Change seems to be much slower in areas with constituency influence dominant and in areas with little party or constituency influence (in which case longer-term issue evolution is required if change is to result). Our analysis in this chapter does not fully test all these expectations, as a complete test would require a more exhaustive study of a large number of issues than could be reported here. However, the results are sufficient to disprove some prior expectations (the presidential leadership model in foreign aid voting as an example) and to demonstrate that different policy areas will be affected by different types of change.

Third, congressional voting change seems to be primarily evolutionary. There is stability in the process and the change that occurs is slow. More research will be required to determine the extent to which congressional voting fits the evolutionary hypothesis, but the current effort already demonstrates that a focus on patterns of voting change is appropriate. . . . Additional testing of the evolutionary hypothesis will further increase our understanding of Congress as an ongoing institution influenced by political and societal changes.

NOTES

1. Most instances in which the presidential stance changes when a new president takes office involve partisan issues on which most party members will just maintain their partisan vote. For example, conservative Republicans who oppose a social program under a liberal Democratic administration generally continue to do so when a more conservative Republican president also opposes it, and the opposite for liberal northern Democrats. Conservative Southern Democrats may pose an exception: They may support a social program to please a Johnson but would oppose it under a Nixon. In such instances changing their voting history is an instance of presidential support.

2. The residual cases in Table 26.3 generally support this theme with minimal modification, such as the "fair play" Democrats who supported the opposition president in his first years in office before moving to opposition, or the Republicans who supported Johnson's requests for debt increases in his honeymoon period but then moved to opposition until Nixon won office. The major residual pattern which suggests a different theme involves six GOP members who opposed debt increases constantly except for Nixon's first year in office, accepting the 1969 argument that the new Republican administration merited support in a fiscal situation over which it had no control (see also Kingdon 1973, 247).

3. By using how the representative voted on the *majority* of roll calls during each period, we maximize the possibility of obtaining change in voting associated with the presidential leadership model. Had we examined only those cases where the representative voted constantly for or against the program throughout an administration, we would have much less change than reported here.

4. The Republicans regained control of the White House twice during the time period being studied while the Democrats did so only once, so the top half of Table 26.3 tends to emphasize Republican congressmen while the bottom half tends to emphasize Democrats.

5. We could have formally included party in the regression equation for continuing members, and we would have found that much of the effect originally attributed to vote history (V56) would now be due to party, although the two predictor variables would have been so highly correlated that it would be impossible to talk about their separate effects. However, if we view party as a cause of voting history, then it makes sense to determine the effect of voting history in summary form while not caring about the extent to which it is itself determined by party.

6. There are three series of civil rights related votes since 1949. The House considered 29 civil rights votes 1949–51 but none 1952–55, then had 68 votes 1956–72 plus 32 votes on

busing 1968–72. The total of 129 votes is more than our available computer capacity permits, so we have had to drop some votes. Given the absence of votes 1952–55, the 1949–51 votes are those which can most obviously be dropped. Those votes actually cumulate very well with the votes taken in 1956–60, so that dropping them introduces no bias. The busing area is virtually unidimensional, but it will be of interest to see whether the busing votes fit in with the other civil rights votes. Therefore the civil rights votes to be analyzed are the civil rights and busing votes 1956–72. This analysis owes much to the work of Jeannette Frazer, Anita Pritchard, James Gearhart, and Lyn Halverson.

Chapter 27

Strategies for Coalition Leaders

R. DOUGLAS ARNOLD

How do leaders assemble winning coalitions for the proposals that they put before Congress? How do they anticipate legislators' electoral needs when they design policies, fashion arguments, and choose procedures? How do leaders harness legislators' electoral ambitions to advance their own goals? This chapter examines the strategies available for building coalitions and shows how leaders choose among them. Such strategies are general plans for attracting support, both within Congress and among attentive and inattentive publics.

Building winning coalitions is hard work. Legislators who merely drop bills in the hopper and wait for something to happen are invariably disappointed. Nothing happens in Congress unless someone plans for it and works for it. Someone must define the problems, shape the alternatives, initiate action, mobilize support, arrange compromises, and work to see that Congress passes specific bills. Those who perform these duties I refer to as coalition leaders.

Coalition leaders may be drawn from both inside and outside Congress. They include rank-and-file legislators, committee and subcommittee leaders, party leaders, congressional staff members, the president, presidential staff members, executive branch officials, bureaucrats, and interest group leaders. In this chapter I seek to explain the behavior of the generic leader; I do not try to isolate the differences in the strategies and tactics of various types of coalition leaders. Of course, there are enormous differences between the resources and talents of a president like Lyndon Johnson, the average chairman of a House committee, and a freshman legislator from the minority party. Most of these differences are well known. What are not well known are the ways in which successful leaders of every variety go about anticipating and responding to legislators' electoral needs as they build winning coalitions.

My analysis begins at the point that someone decides to build a coalition for a specific proposal. I do not examine why individuals choose to become coalition leaders in the first place, why they choose to attack specific problems or advance

Source: R. Douglas Arnold, *The Logic of Congressional Action* (New Haven: Yale University Press) pp. 88–118. Copyright © 1990 by Yale University Press.

specific remedies, or why they invest their scarce time and resources in mobilizing support. These are all interesting and important questions, but they are peripheral to my central argument. As far as my theory is concerned, individuals volunteer, for reasons of their own, to champion or oppose certain causes. Once they have volunteered, the problem for theory is to explain why they adopt specific strategies to advance or retard those causes (this chapter) and why one side wins and the other side loses (Arnold 1990, chapter 6).

The supply of coalition leaders is not uniformly distributed across the range of policy problems and policy solutions. Some policy proposals attract coalition leaders in droves, while others offer few incentives to leaders of any sort (see Kingdon 1984, 23–47; Price 1978). Most coalition leaders have an intense interest in at least one aspect of a policy proposal—perhaps its general costs or benefits, its geographic effects, or its group effects. Proposals with concentrated geographic effects tend to acquire legislators from the affected areas as leaders. Those with concentrated group effects tend to attract bureaucrats, interest group leaders, and some legislators.[1] Proposals that are heavily laden with general costs or benefits offer mixed incentives. Those with general effects that are highly salient tend to attract coalition leaders quite easily, whereas proposals with general effects that are either less visible or long delayed often have few champions. Finally, some individuals become coalition leaders because their current positions demand it. The president, the director of the Office of Management and Budget, and the chairmen of the House and Senate budget committees, for example, are natural candidates for building coalitions on budgetary matters.

Policies that promise large, early-order benefits tend to attract coalition leaders far more easily than those that promise only later-order benefits. When a policy offers both early-order and later-order benefits, it is generally the former that stimulates activism. The push for new educational programs invariably comes from teachers or school administrators, not students or their parents. The impetus for mass transit, mental health, or welfare programs comes from the professionals who deliver such services, rather than from those who receive the services.[2] Similarly, early-order costs are a greater stimulus to activism than are later-order costs. When the Senate battled over how strong automobile bumpers must be, the coalition leaders had nothing to do with automobiles, safety, or insurance. Senator Robert Byrd (D-WV) promoted standards that were met more easily by steel bumpers (produced in the great state of West Virginia), while Senator Warren Magnuson (D-WA) held out for a standard that favored aluminum bumpers (produced in the great state of Washington).[3] . . .

Coalition leaders are free to champion whatever policy proposals they choose.[4] Presumably most leaders select proposals that advance their own central interests. Once they have chosen a specific proposal, however, they face but a small set of potentially winning strategies. Success requires them to anticipate legislators' electoral needs, which itself requires them to anticipate the possible reactions of attentive and inattentive publics. These electoral needs place severe constraints on leaders' choices among strategies.

There are no universal strategies, appropriate for any proposal under any conditions. Leaders must tailor general strategies to fit the idiosyncrasies of specific policy proposals. Leaders can choose from three strategic approaches, each of which anticipates legislators' electoral needs in a different way. *Strategies of persuasion* create, activate, or change the policy preferences of legislators, attentive publics, and inattentive publics. The intent is to shape policy preferences, both inside Congress and among relevant publics, to fit the original proposal. *Procedural strategies* attempt to influence legislators' political calculations by adroit use of legislative rules and procedures. The aim is to structure the legislative situation in a way that decreases the ability of an instigator to rouse inattentive publics or of a challenger to make a campaign issue out of a specific roll-call vote. *Strategies of modification* involve altering the various components of a policy, ranging from the policy instrument to the incidence of costs and benefits. The aim is to mold a policy so that it conforms better with legislators' and citizens' preferences and potential preferences.[5] Each of these general strategies can also be used by opposition leaders who are attempting to block a particular proposal, and both sides can combine strategies in various ways.

STRATEGIES OF PERSUASION

Persuasion involves creating, activating, or changing the policy preferences of legislators, attentive publics, and (if necessary) inattentive publics. At times coalition leaders mount large-scale campaigns to shift elite and mass opinion toward a major programmatic initiative, such as national health insurance, energy policy, or the Equal Rights Amendment. Or leaders may confine their efforts to Washington and focus on legislators and the most attentive publics, as they shepherd a proposal through the various stages of the legislative process. Frequently coalition leaders and opposition leaders have but a few minutes to offer alternative interpretations of a surprise floor amendment that would change policy in some field.[6] No matter what the stage in coalition building, leaders seek to persuade legislators that a policy proposal is simultaneously a good idea *and* that it is unlikely to generate electoral problems for them. This deed can be accomplished either by generating favorable opinions among attentive and inattentive publics or by showing legislators that the program is unlikely to generate unfavorable opinions if people happen to hear about it.

An initial task for coalition leaders is to persuade people that a problem is one that government should tackle, and that the federal government should handle it. The easiest way to accomplish this goal is to link the new ends to some already well-established ends, making a new departure look like a logical extension of current policy rather than a dramatic shift in the role of government. Linkage strategies also make persuasion more economical because they build on established opinions rather than creating new opinion from scratch. . . .

The current favorite for linkage strategies is economic growth, productivity, and competitiveness. In fact, coalition leaders use economic productivity to justify some of the same policies that were once tied to national defense, such as education, basic scientific research, and various transportation and other infrastructure programs. The shift reflects both the increased political conflict associated with national security policy and the rise to prominence of macroeconomic policy. Today anyone who wants to create a tax loophole, change a regulation affecting industry, or establish a new program should first develop an argument about how those changes will lead to economic growth, for nothing sells better in the current political climate. . . .

Linkage strategies become easier to use as the government grows in size and scope. In the beginning, when government performed only a few functions, each new proposal seemed like a major departure from current policy and, thus, required extensive debate. As governmental functions multiplied, it became increasingly easy to find well-established precedents for new proposals. The battles in the 1960s to enact federal aid to education, medical care, and civil rights were long and intense. Once enacted, they became excellent precedents for many more federal initiatives in these and neighboring fields.

The logic of linkage strategies rests, in part, on the tendency of legislators to establish consistent voting histories on recurrent issues (Kingdon 1981, 274–78). When urban issues emerge legislators vote one way, when civil rights issues are on the agenda they divide along different lines, and so on for social welfare, education, agriculture, and dozens of other issues (Clausen 1973). Coalition leaders for new issues attempt to exploit voting histories by attaching the proper labels to their proposals so that legislators will vote in predictable ways. Although voting histories can be taken as evidence that legislators vote ideologically, they also reflect an explicit calculation that voting in favor of (or against) a given type of policy has been good politics in the past and provides a safe course for the future (Kingdon 1981, 277).

Proponents are not the only ones who use linkage strategies. Opponents attempt to derail proposals by linking them with undesirable ends. When public opinion polls revealed that the original Medicare proposal was popular, opponents claimed that it was merely the first step toward socialized medicine; they warned of bureaucrats telling patients whom to see and doctors how to practice medicine (Harris 1966; Kelley 1956; Marmor 1973). Proponents of federal funding for day care centers stressed the needs of single mothers and the problem of persuading welfare mothers to work, while opponents raised the specter of the disintegration of the American family (Steiner 1976, 108). . . . Each side of a controversy attempts to link the proposal in question to some other issue for which the distribution of opinion is both known and favorable to its position.

Linking new policy goals to established goals is not the only way to market proposals. Leaders also marshall arguments to justify the federal government's tackling a new problem. They typically offer arguments showing the extent of the problem, why neither the private sector nor state and local governments can solve it, and how the federal government might ameliorate it. The original advocates of clean air legislation, for example, attempted to show how air pollution adversely affected health, why industry would never, on its own, control it, and why the problem was beyond the capacity of state governments, given the ease with which pollutants cross state boundaries (Jones 1975).

These arguments are most effective if coalition leaders can connect them to recent public events or tragedies that can attract media coverage, dramatize the need for governmental action, and focus attention on anyone with a proposed solution. Advocates used the Soviet Union's launch of *Sputnik* to dramatize the need for NASA and the National Defense Education Act (Sundquist 1968, 173–80). . . .

Fortuitous events like these do not by themselves produce action. They merely create opportunities for coalition leaders to exploit. Their impact is greatest when proponents have already drafted legislation, held hearings, and prepared the way. A well-timed tragedy then forces an issue to the top of the agenda and creates the proper climate for rapid action. Leaders may even shape some events or affect their timing. . . .

Coalition leaders also seek to persuade legislators that the proposed policy instruments will actually produce the intended effects. This task is easiest for single-stage policies whose causal logic is simple and readily understandable. No one doubts, for example, that federal programs for the construction of roads, bridges, and sewers will actually increase the supply of each. The problems emerge when leaders attempt to market policies involving long, complex causal chains. Consider, for example, how difficult it was for proponents of deregulation to sell their proposals in Congress. Economists, even though united, could not reduce their arguments about the benefits of deregulation to a few simple sentences. . . . Coalition leaders can either conduct long educational campaigns in an attempt to persuade people that complicated programs would work, or they can substitute other policy instruments that are easier to market.

Coalition leaders can also seek to persuade legislators of a policy's merits by altering legislators' perceptions of the incidence of costs and benefits. This strategy is most obvious for geographic benefits. Proponents carefully calculate where the benefits will be concentrated and then inform those who will receive disproportionate shares of their good fortune. The Pentagon, for example, routinely assembles a list of subcontractors for each major weapons system so that each legislator can know exactly how his district will profit if it goes into production. . . .

Opponents employ complementary strategies. One approach is to identify inequities in the distribution of benefits and then sow seeds of dissension among groups and localities receiving "unjust" shares. If they choose their criteria carefully, opponents can always demonstrate injustices. If tax rates are cut by a fixed percentage, they point out that wealthy taxpayers reap greater dollar savings. . . .

An alternative approach is to identify those who will bear substantial group costs and then attempt to mobilize either those groups or their usual legislative champions. Opponents of the telephone access fee, for example, argued that residential and small business users would pay more so that large corporations could pay less.[7]. . .

Coalition leaders target their appeals to those most likely to support them while trying not to arouse potential opponents. If only a small minority will benefit from a program, proponents may seek to mobilize that minority as quietly as possible so that they do not alarm the even greater numbers who might oppose their efforts. They may attempt to resolve all conflict within a friendly subcommittee or committee so that others do not notice what is happening (Kingdon 1981, 262–65). They may add a small, seemingly innocuous section to a large and popular bill, or they may propose a floor amendment at the last minute, leaving little time for opponents to mobilize their troops.

Opponents of a change may attempt to broaden the scope of conflict in order to mobilize others who have contrary interests at stake (Schattschneider 1960, 1–19). They may attempt to open committee decision making to other points of view. If these interests are already organized, they activate those organizations. If not, opponents appeal to broader inattentive publics by holding hearings or staging other public events for the news media to cover. They may encourage journalists to write about specific proposals by providing them with easy access and free information. These moves may, in turn, encourage proponents to think about yet other groups of beneficiaries that they can mobilize to counteract the efforts of opponents.

In their arguments, proponents tend to magnify benefits and minimize costs. They market proposals as if the resulting programs were not only certain to achieve their intended ends but would also yield many pleasant byproducts, such as stimulating investment, revitalizing cities, decreasing unemployment, increasing tax revenues, curbing crime, and balancing the budget. At the same time, they tend to underestimate the budgetary costs required to implement their proposals. Proponents project tiny short-term costs so that their proposals do not threaten other people's favorite programs. They also tend to underestimate the less tangible costs, ranging from compliance costs for firms to the general losses of liberty associated with an increasingly bureaucratic society. Opponents suffer from the opposite disease. They tend to minimize a program's benefits and magnify its costs.

PROCEDURAL STRATEGIES

Procedural strategies involve attempts to influence legislators' political calculations by adroit use of legislative rules and procedures. Coalition leaders may erect procedural barriers to protect legislators from strong political winds that otherwise might drive them into the opposition camp. Alternatively, they might structure the legislative situation so that the prevailing winds blow legislators into the very coalitions they are endeavoring to build. Opposition leaders use similar strategies to force legislators to support their views. Frequently, the principal battle is over whose rules shall prevail—those of the proponents or those of the opponents—because each side believes that it can win its substantive points under the proper procedures.

Procedural strategies are used to manipulate the circumstances under which legislators are forced to take public positions.[8] From legislators' point of view, there is a big difference between voting in favor of an amendment that would increase by 5% the salaries of all federal workers and voting in favor of two separate amendments, one of which would increase legislators' own salaries and the other of which would increase the salaries of all other federal workers. The policy effects are identical, but the political effects are not. Legislators know that challengers delight in using votes on legislative salaries against them, whereas an across-the-board increase makes a poor political issue. The aim of all procedural strategies is to structure the legislative situation in a way that either increases or decreases the ability of an instigator to rouse inattentive publics or of a challenger to make a good campaign issue out of a specific roll-call vote.

Coalition leaders may adopt procedural strategies that either strengthen or break the traceability chain for policy effects. Those who seek to impose large, direct, or early-order costs usually search for procedural strategies that break the traceability chain, knowing that legislators' greatest concern is that citizens might trace those costs back to their own individual actions. Those who seek to block the imposition of such costs prefer procedural strategies that strengthen the traceability chain. When the issue is delivering large, early-order benefits, the preferred strategies are reversed; proponents seek to strengthen the traceability chain while opponents seek to break it. Even when effects are not potentially traceable, both coalition and opposition leaders can employ procedures that emphasize (or camouflage) legislators' connections with popular (or unpopular) policy positions.

Weakening the traceability chain is a superb method for protecting legislators from their constituents' wrath for imposing costs on them. According to the incumbent performance rule, citizens punish legislators for undesirable effects only if there are both identifiable governmental actions and visible individual contributions (see chapter 3 of [Arnold 1990]). It follows, then, that coalition leaders who seek to impose large, perceptible costs should either eliminate all identifiable governmental actions that produce those costs or make legislators' individual contributions as nearly invisible as possible.

One method of masking legislators' individual contributions is to delegate responsibility for making unpleasant decisions to the president, bureaucrats, regulatory commissioners, judges, or state and local officials. Congress may pass across-the-board budgetary cuts but leave it to the president or agency administrators to allocate the cuts among specific programs. Legislators thereby appear frugal while avoiding any association with specific reductions. Sometimes legislators know precisely what the executive will decide, but the process of delegation insulates them from political retribution. . . .

A second method of masking legislators' individual responsibility is secrecy. Committees frequently work behind closed doors so that outsiders are uncertain about how to apportion responsibility. Although closed committee meetings went out of style after the reforms of 1970 and 1973, they are coming back again. They are particularly useful when committees are drafting tax bills or other controversial measures.[9] Several years ago, the Senate Finance Committee, besieged by lobbyists, fled to a small, private chamber to write a $50 billion tax increase.[10]. . .

Eliminating identifiable governmental actions—those essential elements of retrospective voting—is also a relatively easy task. One method is to combine various proposals into a single omnibus bill so that legislators vote on an entire package rather than on each of the individual pieces. Such bills allow representatives to hide from their constituents. Legislators establish a series of nebulous positions on amorphous-sounding bills like the Clean Air Amendments of 1970, the Education Amendments of 1980, or the Omnibus Reconciliation Act of 1980, but they need never answer for the costs that specific provisions impose on particular groups or localities. Citizens affected by these provisions have a difficult time punishing their representatives, especially when legislators profess sympathy for their causes. Congress has relied increasingly on omnibus bills in the last few years, including budget resolutions, reconciliation bills, and continuing resolutions.[11] These omnibus bills are especially valuable in the fields of taxation, spending, budgetary policy, and Social Security. . . .

The principal tactical devices in the House for protecting omnibus bills from being split into their component parts are closed rules, which prohibit amendments, and restrictive rules, which allow only certain limited amendments.[12] The closed rule was once used routinely for tax bills and only occasionally for other bills. After the reforms of the early 1970s, the closed rule became less popular (Rudder 1977, 119). It has now largely been replaced by the restrictive rule, which limits the number, type, and content of amendments. Restrictive rules grew from 12% of all rules in 1977 to 45% in 1987.[13] They are essential for keeping large and complicated omnibus bills from unraveling.

These various methods—delegation to the executive, secrecy, and the creation of a single omnibus bill—can also be used in combination, in which case they become even more powerful. . . .

Legislators have been most creative in avoiding identifiable governmental actions when they endeavor to increase their own compensation (actually to restore what inflation has eroded).[14] Most legislators are reluctant to vote for a bill that would straightforwardly increase their salaries because they fear electoral retribution. So there is an endless search for a mechanism that avoids an identifiable action. In 1975 legislators appeared to have found a politically safe method when they voted to link their own salaries with those of other federal workers, who already received automatic cost-of-living adjustments. Unfortunately, their pay raises still required an annual appropriation, which legislators could no more support than they could support the pay raises themselves. In four of the next five years, Congress voted to block the increased appropriations. Legislators then devised a scheme that provided for automatic appropriations to match their automatic cost-of-living raises.[15] This mechanism has now delivered several automatic raises (Weaver 1988, 129–30).

While coalition leaders work to weaken or break the traceability chain, opposition leaders do everything in their power to strengthen it. This counterstrategy is obvious in the case of legislators' compensation. Whenever proponents of salary increases thought they had found a safe mechanism, opponents responded by creating a new identifiable governmental action for which legislators had to stand up and be counted. Under the scheme currently in force, salary increases are automatic unless they are blocked within 30 days; so proponents and opponents now scramble to control the agenda during that period. In 1987 opponents did manage to obtain a vote on a motion disapproving the salary increase, but proponents delayed the vote for a day beyond the statutory limit (by adjourning the House just when opponents were about to pounce). When the House reconvened legislators voted enthusiastically against their own salary increases, knowing that it was too late to stop them.[16] . . .

Conflict over substance can quickly evolve into conflict over procedures. When the House was battling over the contents of the Omnibus Budget Reconciliation Act of 1981, which eliminated $35 billion in domestic spending, the key vote was on which rule should govern floor consideration. Conservatives wanted a single up-or-down vote on the entire package so that legislators would have to stand up and be counted as either for or against the president's economic program. Liberals wanted separate votes in six programmatic areas so that legislators would have to go on record as either for or against cuts in Social Security, school lunches, energy programs, and the like. Both sides agreed that a majority of legislators would not agree to programmatic cuts if specific reductions could be traced back to their own individual actions. Several months of conflict over what programs to reduce and how much to reduce them boiled down to a single procedural vote (Sinclair 1983, 190–213). Once the conservatives prevailed on the procedural point (by four votes), the substantive battle was over (for complete details see chapter 7 [of Arnold 1990]).

Even when the policy effects are minimal, leaders can advance or retard their causes by the way they frame issues and design amendments. Positions matter, even when they are not directly connected to perceptible effects. One of the easiest ways to scuttle a bill is to devise several embarrassing amendments. Many proposals that might slip by if there were no recorded votes falter when legislators must stand up and be counted. Congress once rejected by voice vote an amendment that would have prohibited the Legal Services Corporation from using any funds to defend or protect homosexuality. Moments later, when Representative Larry McDonald (D-GA) demanded a recorded vote, legislators adopted the same amendment, 290 to 113.[17]. . .

When coalition leaders are dealing with group and geographic benefits, they employ an opposite approach. Rather than attempting to break the traceability chain, they do everything they can to accentuate the benefits and to strengthen the traceability chain. They allow other legislators to cosponsor legislation so that everyone can claim authorship. They arrange frequent roll-call votes so that legislators can go firmly on record in favor of these benefactions. They welcome "clarifying" or other friendly amendments. Coalition leaders arrange for legislators to have a marvelous time building records that they can proudly display to their constituents and contributors to show the strength of their connection to these positive effects.

Whether dealing with costs or benefits, legislators must agree to be bound by coalition leaders' procedural strategies. Legislators are not victims, they are coconspirators. Coalition leaders cannot force House members to be bound by a closed rule or a restrictive rule; they must first persuade a majority of them to accept such a rule.[18] Coalition leaders cannot force legislators to delegate authority to the president or bureaucrats; they must agree to do so. Opposition leaders cannot force House members to face lots of embarrassing amendments, for a simple majority could demand a closed rule. When coalition leaders propose restrictive rules, and when legislators accept those rules, it must be because the rules serve their joint purposes.[19]

STRATEGIES OF MODIFICATION

Strategies of modification involve altering the various components of a policy, ranging from the policy instrument to the incidence of costs and benefits. The aim is to mold a policy so that it conforms better to legislators' and citizens' preferences and potential preferences. Although coalition leaders can modify their proposals in dozens of ways, they can accept only a limited number of changes and still have a bill that serves their own central interests. They have every incentive to choose their modifications carefully so that they manage to strengthen a program's supporting coalition without sacrificing whatever it was that persuaded them to build a coalition in the first place.

One of the most productive approaches is to modify a proposal in ways designed to attract additional coalition leaders, who can then work to persuade others to join the cause. Whenever a program's initial coalition leaders come from outside Congress, they have no choice but to convince several legislators to join the team. Building coalitions is too complex for outsiders alone. They particularly need to acquire members of the appropriate House and Senate committees and make them enthusiastic about a program—enthusiastic enough to invest their scarce resources in its future. . . .

Proponents may also modify their proposals to dissuade potential opposition leaders from actively working against them. It is far cheaper to buy off a few lieutenants before they start their work than it is to ward off the legions that they would otherwise mobilize. Committee chairmen often accommodate the needs of their ranking minority members so that they can present a united front both in committee and on the floor. Bureaucrats sometimes allocate disproportionate geographic benefits to opposition leaders, intending either to convert them or at least to mute their opposition. Those who awarded model cities grants, for example, were especially generous with those committee and party leaders who had previously opposed the program's funding (Arnold 1979, 179–92). Coalition leaders may also sow seeds of disunity among interest group leaders. Robert Strauss helped to enact the Trade Act of 1979 by including substantial rewards for steel and textile workers; these rewards helped to split the AFL-CIO and thereby forced it to remain neutral.[20]

Coalition leaders often begin with plans to enact comprehensive programs or to institute fundamental reforms in some policy area. Wouldn't it be nice, they ask, to enact national health insurance, to reform the welfare system, to dismantle some regulatory commission, to redesign the tax system, or to expand assistance to college students so that everyone could afford college? Ordinarily coalition leaders must scale back such ambitious plans. Large new expenditure programs are particularly troublesome, for they quickly bump against the perpetual shortage of governmental funds. It makes little difference whether the budget is in surplus or deficit, because new claims on the federal treasury are potential threats to current claimants, to those who wish to expand current programs, and to those who wish to enact their own grandiose schemes.

Legislators are often willing to take a few small steps toward some distant goal, but they are usually reluctant to attempt the whole distance in a single leap. Small steps are less risky than grand leaps. The strategic response to their fears is to scale back policy proposals so that they appear cautious, limited, and experimental. Proponents of complete deregulation of financial institutions decide to push for modest reforms, to be phased in gradually. Advocates of national health insurance settle for less ambitious programs—first Medicare and Medicaid, then some form of catastrophic insurance, and so on. Even during the heyday of the Great Society, the Johnson administration sent Congress a lot of small, limited programs that individually appeared to cost little.[21] Coalition leaders hope that modifications to their proposals are temporary and that Congress will later expand limited programs into the comprehensive ones they originally wanted.[22]

Although it often makes sense to push for incremental rather than comprehensive reforms, "thinking small" is not always appropriate. One risk is that by solving the most egregious problem, one removes the political pressure for solving the broader problem. Establishing Medicare may have addressed the most serious problem in the financing of health care, but it also eliminated the most potent argument for national health insurance. Over the past two decades senior citizens have pushed hard to improve Medicare benefits for themselves, but they have had little interest in pushing for a broadened program that would include other classes of citizens. A second risk is that incremental reforms, especially of tax and regulatory systems, cannot deliver enough benefits to make them worth the trouble. For two decades proponents of tax reform attempted to cleanse the tax system one loophole at a time. They failed miserably. Eliminating a single provision could neither make the system noticeably more equitable nor generate much revenue, yet each loophole had its passionate defenders. It took comprehensive reform to make the benefits of tax reform worth the pain (see chapter 8 [of Arnold 1990]). It may well be that one can create small programs and watch them grow incrementally, but one cannot reduce or reform these programs with anything less than a comprehensive attack.[23]

Coalition leaders must somehow deal with the problem of costs. Costs are what inspire people to oppose changes in policy, and coalition leaders need to allocate costs carefully in order to minimize opposition. Concentrating all costs on a small minority of groups or localities, and thus leaving the majority unburdened, may seem like a winning strategy. Unfortunately, concentration inspires the victims to work actively against the policies, and determined minorities can frequently overpower majorities in a legislative arena noted for its many choke points (including the senatorial filibuster). Dispersing costs widely is often the safer strategy, for it minimizes the intensity of opposition. . . .

A second solution to the problem of costs is to compensate some of the victims for the group or geographic costs they would otherwise incur. . .

A third solution to the problem of costs is to make them as nearly invisible as possible. Most expenditure programs are financed through general taxation so that a decision to establish a new expenditure program does not directly increase anyone's taxes. The financial costs of these expenditure programs are essentially general costs. The two large programs that have dedicated taxes—Social Security and Medicare—have more visible costs, but these programs were cleverly designed so that only half of their costs are apparent to most voters. Workers see the portion of the payroll tax that is deducted from their own wages, but not the half paid on their behalf by their employers. The politics of Social Security would undoubtedly be much more contentious if the entire payroll tax (currently 15%) were deducted from each worker's paycheck. Conflict would be especially high if workers paid these taxes directly (in quarterly payments, say, like property taxes) rather than through automatic withholding.

Perhaps the most common way to keep the costs of a program relatively invisible is to use the tax code rather than the budget for delivering benefits. Most changes in the tax code are written in technical language and are relatively obscure to all except those who will use them, whereas all direct subsidies are listed prominently in the federal budget. Perhaps that is why tax deductions and tax credits have been the favorite devices for delivering benefits to corporations and wealthy groups in society. . . .

Finally, coalition leaders may modify the incidence of group or geographic benefits in order to attract additional supporters. When allocating benefits leaders face a dilemma similar to the one they face when allocating costs. Concentrating benefits by group or geographic areas may produce some very intense supporters, but too much concentration yields too few supporters to constitute a majority. Dispersing benefits more widely helps to attract additional supporters, but excessive dispersion may make the individual shares so small that both legislators and the affected publics become indifferent to a program's continued existence. Coalition leaders need to find an acceptable middle position between placing all their chips on one small group or locality and spreading their chips uniformly across all members of society.

Modifying the incidence of geographic benefits is one of the most direct methods for enticing reluctant legislators to support an expenditure program.[24] It gives legislators a pleasing answer to the age-old question, "What's in it for me?" When promoting proposed programs, coalition leaders have only a few geographic strategies available, since they do not yet have any specific benefits to promise individual legislators. All they can do is try to affect legislators' general expectations by modifying a program's character. First, they can enlarge a program's geographic scope so that more localities will be eligible for benefits and, as a consequence, more legislators will see opportunities for acquiring shares for their districts. Eligibility requirements for an urban program can be redefined so that even the most rural district will have at least one large town that qualifies for benefits. Second, they can multiply the number of shares to be allocated so that the probability of an individual legislator obtaining a share will increase. Legislators can better afford to remain indifferent when only a few shares will be distributed than when there are several hundred. The principal limitation on these two strategies is the size of a program's budget. Unless proponents can increase a program's proposed budget at the same rate they increase the number of shares to be allocated, the value of each share will decline and so too will each legislator's willingness to support the proposal.

Once a program is passed, the problem shifts from shaping legislators' expectations to satisfying those expectations. Most geographic benefits are allocated by bureaucrats, and the evidence shows that they are extraordinarily attentive to legislators' needs (Arnold 1979, 46–47). Bureaucrats are careful to disperse geographic benefits widely across all eligible areas so that most legislators have a stake in a program's continuance. Bureaucrats may also concentrate extra benefits on those who are especially crucial to a program's supporting coalition, including coalition leaders, opposition leaders, and members of the appropriate committees. If a program's supporting coalition continues to appear weak, they may further expand a program's geographic scope. This is essentially the story behind the expansion of urban renewal and the Economic Development Administration until each provided benefits to nearly all congressional districts.

Excessive expansion of a program's geographic scope can undermine its entire supporting coalition. Eventually legislators come to realize that their individual shares are too tiny to give them a real interest in its continuance. . . .

BUILDING COALITIONS

How do coalition leaders choose among these various strategies? On what do their choices depend? In ordinary circumstances strategies of persuasion are best, both because they are more effective at building long-term support and because they do not require coalition leaders to modify their most preferred policies. Coalition leaders usually seek to enact policies that can survive future battles over budgetary priorities, appropriations, and reauthorizations, and the best insurance of clear sailing ahead is to convince both legislators and citizens of a program's basic merits.

Although strategies of persuasion may be best in the long term, they are often very costly in the short term. Convincing legislators and citizens that the federal government should provide federal aid to education, or that it should regulate the sources of air and water pollution, or that it should regulate the design of automobiles for safety and energy efficiency (and creating opinions that were strong enough to overpower the many groups opposed to such policies)—all this took many years of effort and the combined talents of legislators, presidents, and the leaders of various public and private interest groups. Moreover, strategies of persuasion may be inappropriate for some policies. It is generally very difficult to convince people that they should favor policies that would impose large and direct costs on them in the short term, even for things that will in the longer term greatly benefit them. Perhaps during war or some other major crisis it can be done, but it is far easier to adopt procedural strategies or strategies of modification when large, early-order costs are involved. It is also very difficult to convince people that scarce governmental resources should be lavished on the rich and powerful. Apparently coalition leaders never even considered appropriating $5 to $7 billion to protect the stockholders of savings banks in 1981, for it would have been difficult to defend direct subsidies to this group just weeks after Congress had decimated several social welfare programs. It was far easier to provide the benefits as inconspicuously as possible through a complicated change in the tax code.

Procedural strategies are most attractive when legislators decide to impose costs on either attentive or inattentive publics. Delegating such tasks to the executive, or fashioning policies in secret that are then packaged in omnibus bills and protected by restrictive rules, helps to break the traceability chain and protect legislators from the wrath of their constituents and contributors. . . .

Strategies of modification allow leaders to target the publics that will benefit or suffer as a result of a policy, so they are especially useful for acquiring the support of particular legislators or groups. They are unsurpassed early in the coalition-building process, either for acquiring additional coalition leaders or for silencing potential opposition leaders. They are also excellent general strategies for dealing with programs that provide bundles of group or geographic benefits. Most tax bills are passed by carefully modifying the group benefits until the bill appeals to a majority of legislators. Most grant programs are passed by carefully manipulating the geographic benefits.

Coalition leaders need not choose a single strategy to advance their cause. These three general strategies (and all their variants) complement one another nicely. Leaders may begin by holding hearings to dramatize the need for a new program and to shape elite and mass opinion on the subject, they may then make small modifications to meet the objections of several groups who see their interests threatened, and they may eventually structure the legislative situation in a way designed to protect legislators from either attentive or inattentive publics who might be displeased with the final outcome. A typical bill may have to be modified several times as it passes through all the stages in the legislative process, each time moving further away from coalition leaders' original proposal.[25]

Coalition leaders differ widely in their abilities to employ the various strategies. Committee chairmen are often in a good position to influence the opinions of attentive publics by carefully orchestrating congressional hearings on a new subject. Presidents enjoy an advantage both for influencing inattentive publics and for mobilizing public opinion for comprehensive reforms. Procedural strategies, largely beyond the control of presidents, require the cooperation of both committee and party leaders. Presidents and interest group leaders may be able to modify proposals before they start their travels through Congress, but once they are launched on their way the legislative committees are in charge.

How large a coalition do leaders seek to build? Do they aim for a minimum winning coalition, or do they seek to build a grand coalition that includes all legislators (Arnold 1979, 43–44, 52; Mayhew 1974a, 111–14; Riker 1962)? All else equal, leaders prefer large coalitions because they provide the best insurance for the future. Each proposal must survive a long series of majoritarian tests—in committees and subcommittees, in House and Senate, and in authorization, appropriations, and budget bills. Large majorities help to insure that a bill clears these hurdles with ease. Moreover, large majorities are often required to overcome filibusters, presidential vetoes, and other obstructions that determined minorities may erect. Finally, once programs are passed and implemented, they need annual appropriations and occasional reauthorizations. Again, oversized majorities protect programs in the long run against defections, the retirement or defeat of habitual supporters, or changes in the mood of Congress.

But all else may not be equal. The real question is how much coalition leaders must sacrifice to gain solid majorities. When the marginal costs of attracting members are small, leaders can easily afford to build large coalitions. As these marginal costs increase, however, they tend to become content with more modest majorities. Marginal costs are easiest to calculate when strategies of modification are employed. Although coalition leaders are reluctant to make major modifications in their proposals once their majorities achieve minimum size, they are often eager to accommodate legislators who request only modest changes (Drew 1979, 158).

NOTES

1. Price notes that legislators shun policies with concentrated group effects when conflict is high and public salience is low. See Price (1978).
2. The issue is not merely one of concentrated effects, for surely students, welfare recipients, and mental patients have a great deal at stake. Nor is the issue simply one of organization, though it is true that groups organize more easily around early-order effects. The best explanation is that the incidence of early-order effects is far more certain than that of later-order effects. Those who deliver services can be fairly certain how they will profit from new infusions of money, and that knowledge encourages activism. Those who will eventually receive these services cannot know in advance exactly how they will profit, particularly as individuals. Even if students, welfare recipients, or mental patients as a class are certain to profit, today's individuals may well be replaced by others by the time a program begins delivering services.
3. Judy Sarasohn, "Titans Tangle in Senate Bumper Standards Dispute," *Congressional Quarterly Weekly Report* 37 (14 July 1979):1409–10.
4. Of course, there are constraints. Elected politicians do not champion proposals that they could not otherwise support, staff members cannot advance proposals without the approval of their superiors, and leaders of interest groups need to retain the support of their own members. My point is simply that most coalition leaders begin with a blank slate, rather than having to choose among paired or otherwise restricted alternatives.
5. These three approaches do not exhaust all the strategies available to coalition leaders, although they do exhaust the ones that rely most directly on the electoral connection. *Exchange strategies*, a fourth approach, involve the trading of support across different policy areas. The aim is to persuade legislators to vote against their true interests (incurring, if necessary, modest electoral costs) in exchange for leaders' or other legislators' assistance on matters of greater importance to these legislators (including matters that pay handsome electoral dividends). *Replacement strategies* involve replacing current legislators with those holding more congenial views. This is a long-term strategy adopted only when others have failed. Opponents of abortion and proponents of the Equal Rights Amendment are currently pursuing such strategies. On exchange strategies, see Arnold (1979, 47–50, 210–14).
6. For an excellent analysis of how leaders go about shaping legislators' interpretations of policy proposals, see Smith (1984).
7. Steven Pressman, "Panel Approves Phone Bill Despite AT&T Lobby Drive," *Congressional Quarterly Weekly Report* 41 (29 October 1983):2241.
8. There is a growing literature that uses formal theory to understand the consequences of various congressional procedures. This literature explores, among other things, the ways in which rules contribute to stable legislative outcomes, the effects of closed and restrictive rules on the power of agenda setters, and the consequences of restrictive procedures for considering conference reports. For a superb review of this literature, see Krehbiel (1988). I am more interested in explaining the *content* of legislation, and for that task I have focused on a different class of procedural strategies—those that adjust the context of congressional decision making in anticipation of the ways in which legislators will be held accountable by their constituents.

9. The House Ways and Means Committee and many of the subcommittees of the House Appropriations Committee now routinely close their markup sessions to reporters, lobbyists, and the public. See Jacqueline Calmes, "Few Complaints Are Voiced as Doors Close on Capitol Hill," *Congressional Quarterly Weekly Report* 45 (23 May 1987):1059–60.

10. Pamela Fessler, "Senate Panel Votes Tax Boosts," *Congressional Quarterly Weekly Report* 42 (17 March 1984):599.

11. Dale Tate, "Use of Omnibus Bills Burgeons Despite Members' Misgivings," *Congressional Quarterly Weekly Report* 40 (25 September 1982):2379–83; and Martin Tolchin, "In the Face of Controversy, Packaging," *New York Times* (21 February 1983):B6.

12. On the strategic use of congressional procedures, see Oleszek (1989); Bach (1981a, 1981b); and Bach and Smith (1988).

13. Janet Hook, "GOP Chafes under Restrictive House Rules," *Congressional Quarterly Weekly Report* 45 (10 October 1987):2449–52; and Oleszek (1989, 128).

14. On the politics of congressional pay, see Weaver (1988, 118–45).

15. Irwin B. Arieff, "Congress Votes Itself New Pay, Benefits," *Congressional Quarterly Weekly Report* 39 (3 October 1981):1892.

16. Jacqueline Calmes, "Pay Hike for Members of Congress Takes Effect," *Congressional Quarterly Weekly Report* 45 (7 February 1987):219–20.

17. Nadine Cohodas, "House Passes State, Justice Appropriations Bill," *Congressional Quarterly Weekly Report* 38 (26 July 1980):2139.

18. Although the Senate does not allow closed rules, and senators can therefore introduce as many amendments as they like, it does operate on the basis of unanimous consent agreements. Once adopted, these agreements can constrain both the number and content of floor amendments. See Oleszek (1989, 177–238); Krehbiel (1986); and Smith and Flathman (1989).

19. House members do defeat some restrictive rules, but the occasions are rare. Between January 1981 and August 1985 the House rejected exactly six rules. See Andy Plattner, "Rules under Chairman Pepper Looks Out for the Democrats," *Congressional Quarterly Weekly Report* 43 (24 August 1985):1674.

20. Bob Livernash, "Congress Faces Hard Choices on Trade Liberalization Pact," *Congressional Quarterly Weekly Report* 37 (14 April 1979):678–83.

21. Even Medicare, the most expensive of the Great Society programs, was projected to be relatively affordable. See Sundquist (1968, 320) and Marmor (1973, 67). The projections were a bit optimistic. Whereas in 1967 Medicare cost only $2.7 billion, which was less than 2% of federal spending, two decades later it totaled $72 billion, or more than 7% of federal spending. See U.S., Office of Management and Budget (1987, Table 3.3).

22. Sometimes Congress does expand programs to fit the original design. Social Security is a sterling example. After a long series of incremental additions spread over four decades, the original designers achieved almost everything they intended. See Derthick (1979, 295–377). These incremental changes transformed Social Security from a $781 million program in 1950, which consumed less than 2% of the federal budget and less than 0.3% of GNP, to a $199 billion program in 1986, which consumed 20% of the federal budget and nearly 5% of GNP. See Office of Management and Budget (1987, Tables 1.2 and 3.1).

23. On the difference between creating new policies and rationalizing old policies, see Brown (1983).

24. For further analysis of how leaders modify the incidence of geographic benefits, see Arnold (1979, 46–47).

25. Most bills still reflect coalition leaders' preferences far more than they do the preferences of other participants. See Rundquist and Strom (1987).

References

Abram, Michael, and Joseph Cooper. 1968. "The Rise of Seniority in the House of Representatives." *Polity* 1:52–85.

Adams, Henry. 1886. *John Randolph*. Boston: Houghton-Mifflin.

———1930. *History of the United States of America During the Administrations of Thomas Jefferson and James Madison*. New York: Boni.

Adler, E. Scott, and John S. Lipinski. 1997. "Demand-Side Theory and Congressional Committee Composition: A Constituency Characteristics Approach." *American Journal of Political Science* 41:895–918.

Alesina, Alberto, and Howard Rosenthal. 1989. "Partisan Cycles in Congressional Elections and the Macroeconomy." *American Political Science Review* 83:373–98.

Alexander, DeAlva Stanwood. 1916. *History and Procedures of the House of Representatives*. Boston: Houghton-Mifflin.

Alexander, Thomas. 1967. *Sectional Stress and Party Strength*. Nashville, TN: Vanderbilt University Press.

Alford, John R., and John R. Hibbing. 1981. "Increased Incumbency Advantage in the House." *Journal of Politics* 43:1042–61.

Alker, Hayward R., and Bruce M. Russett. 1965. *World Politics in the General Assembly*. New Haven: Yale University Press.

American Political Science Association Committee on Political Parties. 1950. "Toward a More Responsible Two-Party System." *American Political Science Review* 44: supplement.

Andersen, Kristi, and Stuart Thorson. 1984. "Congressional Turnover and the Election of Women." *Western Political Quarterly* 37:143–56.

Anderson, Lee F., Meredith W. Watts, Jr., and Allen R. Wilcox. 1966. *Legislative Roll-Call Analysis*. Evanston: Northwestern University Press.

Ansolabehere, Stephen, David W. Brady, and Morris P. Fiorina. 1992. "The Vanishing Marginals and Electoral Responsiveness." *British Journal of Political Science* 22:21–38.

Arnett, Alex M. 1937. *Claude Kitchin and the Wilson War Policies*. Boston: Little, Brown.

Arnold, R. Douglas. 1979. *Congress and the Bureaucracy: A Theory of Influence*. New Haven: Yale University Press.

———1990. *The Logic of Congressional Action*. New Haven: Yale University Press.

Arrow, Kenneth J. 1951. *Social Choice and Individual Values*. New York: Wiley.

Asher, Herbert B. 1970. "The Freshman Congressman: A Developmental Analysis." Ph.D. diss. University of Michigan.

———1973a. *Freshmen Representatives and the Learning of Voting Cues*. Beverly Hills: Sage Professional Papers in American Politics 04–003.

———1973b. "The Learning of Legislative Norms." *American Political Science Review* 67:499–513.

Asher, Herbert B., and Herbert F. Weisberg. 1978. "Voting Change in Congress: Some Dynamic Perspectives on an Evolutionary Process." *American Journal of Political Science* 22:391–425.

Austen-Smith, David, and John R. Wright. 1994. "Counteractive Lobbying." *American Journal of Political Science* 38:25–44.

———1996. "Theory and Evidence for Counteractive Lobbying." *American Journal of Political Science* 40:543–64.

Aydelotte, William O. 1971. *Quantification in History*. Reading, MA: Addison-Wesley.

———, ed. 1977. *The History of Parliamentary Behavior*. Princeton: Princeton University Press.

Bach, Stanley. 1981a. "The Structure of Choice in the House of Representatives: The Impact of Complex Special Rules." *Harvard Journal on Legislation* 18:553–602.

———1981b. "Special Rules in the House of Representatives: Themes and Contemporary Variations." *Congressional Studies* 8:37–58.

Bach, Stanley, and Steven S. Smith. 1988. *Managing Uncertainty in the House of Representatives: Adaptation and Innovation in Special Rules*. Washington: Brookings Institution.

Bader, John. 1996. *Taking the Initiative*. Washington: Georgetown University Press.

Barber, James David. 1972. *The Presidential Character*. Englewood Cliffs, NJ: Prentice-Hall.

Barkley, Alben W. 1954. *That Reminds Me*. Garden City: Doubleday and Company.

Barnard, Chester. [1938] 1966. *The Functions of the Executive*. Reprint. Cambridge, MA: Harvard University Press.

Bauer, Raymond A., Ithiel de Sola Pool, and Lewis Anthony Dexter. 1963. *American Business and Public Policy*. New York: Atherton.

Baumer, Donald C. 1992. "Senate Democratic Leadership in the 101st Congress." In *The Atomistic Congress: An Interpretation of Congressional Change*, ed. Allen D. Hertzke and Ronald M. Peters, Jr. Armonk, NY: M. E. Sharpe.

Baumgartner, Frank R., and Bryan D. Jones. 1993. *Agendas and Instability in American Politics*. Chicago: University of Chicago Press.

Baumgartner, Frank R., and Beth L. Leech. 1996. "The Multiple Ambiguities of 'Counteractive Lobbying.'" *American Journal of Political Science* 40:521–42.

Beard, Charles A., and John D. Lewis. 1932. "Representative Government in Evolution." *American Political Science Review*, 26:223–40.

Bell, Charles G., and Charles M. Price. 1969. "Pre-Legislative Sources of Representational Roles." *Midwest Journal of Political Science* 13:254–70.

Bendiner, Robert. 1964. *Obstacle Course on Capitol Hill*. New York: McGraw-Hill.

Beyle, Herman C. 1931. *Identification and Analysis of Attribute-Cluster-Blocs*. Chicago: University of Chicago Press.

Bibby, John. 1967. "The Politics of the Senate Committee on Banking and Currency." In *On Capitol Hill*, ed. John Bibby and Roger Davidson. New York: Rinehart and Winston.

Binder, Sarah A. 1995. "Partisanship and Procedural Choice: Institutional Change in the Early Congress, 1789–1823." *Journal of Politics* 57:1093–1117.

———1996. "The Partisan Basis of Procedural Choice: Allocating Parliamentary Rights in the House, 1789–1990." *American Political Science Review* 90:8–20.

Binder, Sarah A., and Steven S. Smith. 1997. *Politics or Principle? Filibustering in the United States Senate*. Washington: Brookings Institution Press.

Binkley, Wilfred E. 1949. "The President and Congress." *Journal of Politics* 11:65–79.

———1962. *President and Congress*. New York: Vintage.

Biographical Directory of the American Congress, 1774–1961. 1961. Washington: U.S. Government Printing Office.

———*1774–1971*. 1971. Washington: U.S. Government Printing Office.

Black, Duncan. 1958. *The Theory of Committees and Elections*. Cambridge: Cambridge University Press.

Black, Gordon S. 1972. "A Theory of Political Ambition: Career Choices and the Role of Structural Incentives." *American Political Science Review* 66:144–59.

Blalock, Hubert M. 1961. "The Relative Importance of Variables." *American Sociological Review* 26:866–74.

Blau, Peter M. 1964. *The Dynamics of Bureaucracy*. Chicago: University of Chicago Press.

Bolling, Richard. 1965. *House Out of Order*. New York: E. P. Dutton.

Bond, Jon R. 1983. "Constituent Diversity and Competition and Voting for Congress." *Legislative Studies Quarterly* 8:201–11.

Bond, Jon R., and Richard Fleisher. 1990. *The President in the Legislative Arena*. Chicago: University of Chicago Press.

Bone, Hugh A. 1956. "Some Notes on the Congressional Campaign Committees." *Western Political Science Quarterly* 9:134.

Bowles, Nigel. 1987. *The White House and Capitol Hill: The Politics of Presidential Persuasion*. New York: Oxford University Press.

Box-Steffensmeier, Janet M. 1996. "A Dynamic Analysis of the Role of War Chests in Campaign Strategy." *American Journal of Political Science* 40:352–71.

Box-Steffensmeier, Janet M., Laura W. Arnold, and Christopher Zorn. 1997. "The Strategic Timing of Position Taking in Congress: A Study of the North American Free Trade Agreement." *American Political Science Review* 91:324–38.

Brady, David W. 1973. *Congressional Voting in a Partisan Era*. Lawrence: University of Kansas Press.

———1978. "Critical Elections, Congressional Parties and Clusters of Policy Change," *British Journal of Political Science* 8:79–100.

———1988. *Critical Elections and Congressional Policy Making*. Stanford: Stanford University Press.

Brady, David W., and Phillip Althoff. 1974. "Party Voting in the U.S. House of Representatives, 1890–1910: Elements of a Responsible Party System." *Journal of Politics* 36:753–75.

Brady, David W., and Charles Bullock. 1980. "Is There a Conservative Coalition in the House?" *Journal of Politics* 42:549–59.

Brady, David W., Joseph Cooper, and Patricia A. Hurley. 1977. "Legislative Potential for Policy Changes: The House of Representatives." *Legislative Studies Quarterly* 2:385–98.

———1979. "The Decline of Party in the U.S. House of Representatives." *Legislative Studies Quarterly* 4:381–407.

Brady, David W., and Barbara Sinclair. 1984. "Building Majorities for Policy Changes in the House of Representatives." *Journal of Politics* 46:1033–60.

Brown, George R. 1922. *The Leadership of Congress*. Indianapolis: Bobbs-Merrill.

Brown, Lawrence D. 1983. *New Policies, New Politics*. Washington: Brookings Institution.

Browne, William P. 1995. *Cultivating Congress: Constituents, Issues, and Interests in Agricultural Policymaking*. Lawrence: University of Kansas Press.

Burke, Edmund. 1948. *Selected Prose*, ed. Sir Philip Magnus. London: Falcon Press.

Burnham, Walter Dean. 1969. "The End of American Party Politics." *Transaction* 7: 18–20.

Burns, James MacGregor. 1949. *Congress on Trial*. New York: Harper & Row.

———1963. *The Deadlock of Democracy*. Englewood Cliffs, NJ: Prentice-Hall.

Busby, L. White. 1927. *Uncle Joe Cannon*. New York: Henry Holt.

Butler, David, and Bruce E. Cain. 1992. *Congressional Redistricting*. New York: Macmillan.

Cain, Bruce E. 1996. "The Varying Impact of Legislative Term Limits." In *Legislative Term Limits: Public Choice Perspectives*, ed. Bernard Grofman. Boston: Kluwer Academic Publishers.

Cain, Bruce E., John Ferejohn, and Morris P. Fiorina. 1987. *The Personal Vote: Constituency Service and Electoral Independence*. Cambridge: Harvard University Press.

Cameron, Charles, David Epstein, and Sharyn O'Halloran. 1996. "Do Majority-Minority Districts Maximize Black Substantive Representation in Congress?" *American Political Science Review* 90:794–823.

Campbell, Angus. 1966. "Surge and Decline: A Study in Electoral Change." In *Elections and the Political Order*, ed. Angus Campbell, Philip E. Converse, Warren E. Miller, and Donald E. Stokes. New York: Wiley.

Campbell, Colin, and Bert A. Rockman. 1996. *The Clinton Presidency: First Appraisals*. Chatham, NJ: Chatham House.

Canon, David T. 1990. *Actors, Athletes, and Astronauts: Political Amateurs in the United States Congress*. Chicago: University of Chicago Press.

Canon, David T., Matthew M. Schousen, and Patrick J. Sellers. 1994. "A Formula for Uncertainty: Creating a Black Majority District in North Carolina." In *Who Runs for Congress?: Ambition, Context, and Candidate Emergence*, ed. Thomas A. Kazee. Washington: Congressional Quarterly Press.

Carey, John M. 1996. *Term Limits and Legislative Representation*. New York: Cambridge University Press.

Carey, John M., Richard G. Niemi, and Lynda W. Powell. 1998. "The Effects of Term Limits on State Legislatures." *Legislative Studies Quarterly* 23: 271–300.

Carroll, Holbert. 1958. *The House of Representatives and Foreign Affairs*. Pittsburgh: University of Pittsburgh Press.

Cartwright, Dorwin. 1959. "A Field Theoretical Conception of Power." *Studies in Social Power*. Ann Arbor: Research Center for Group Dynamics, Institute for Social Research, The University of Michigan.

Cartwright, Dorwin, and Alvin Zander. 1953. *Group Dynamics: Research and Theory*. Evanston, IL: Row, Peterson.

Chambers, William Nisbet. 1963. *Political Parties in a New Nation*. New York: Oxford.

———1967. "Party Development and the American Mainstream." In *The American Party Systems: Stages of Political Development*, ed. William Nisbet Chambers and Walter Dean Burnham. New York: Oxford.

Cherryholmes, Cleo H., and Michael J. Shapiro. 1969. *Representatives and Roll Calls: A Computer Simulation of Voting in the Eighty-Eighth Congress*. Indianapolis: Bobbs-Merrill.

Chiu, Chang-Wei. 1928. *The Speaker of the House of Representatives Since 1896*. New York: Columbia University Press.

Ciboski, Kenneth. 1974. "Ambition Theory and Candidate Members of the Soviet Politburo." *Journal of Politics* 36:172–83.

Clapp, Charles. 1963. *The Congressman: His Work as He Sees It*. Washington: Brookings.

Clark, Joseph S. 1964. *Congress: The Sapless Branch*. New York: Harper & Row.

Clausen, Aage R. 1964. "Policy Dimensions in Congressional Roll Calls: A Longitudinal Analysis." Ph.D. diss. University of Michigan.

———1973. "How Congressmen Decide: A Policy Focus." New York: St. Martin's Press.

Clausen, Aage R., and Carl E. Van Horn. 1977. "The Congressional Response to a Decade of Change: 1963–1972," *Journal of Politics* 39:625–66.

Clinton v. City of New York, 985 F. Supp. 168 (1998).

Clubb, Jerome M., and Santa A. Traugott. 1977. "Partisan Cleavage and Cohesion in the House of Representatives, 1861–1974," *Journal of Interdisciplinary History* 7:375–401.

Cohen, Linda, and Matthew Spitzer. 1992. "Term Limits and Representation." *Georgetown Law Journal* 80:477–522.

Collie, Melissa P. 1986. "New Directions in Congressional Research." *Legislative Studies Section Newsletter* 10 (November–December):90–92.

———1988a. "The Rise of Coalition Politics: Voting in the U.S. House, 1933–1980." *Legislative Studies Quarterly* 13:321–42.

———1988b. "Universalism and the Parties in the U.S. House of Representatives, 1921–1980," *American Journal of Political Science* 32:865–83.

Collie, Melissa P., and David W. Brady. 1985. "The Decline of Partisan Voting Coalitions in the House of Representatives." In *Congress Reconsidered*, 3rd ed., ed. Lawrence C. Dodd and Bruce I. Oppenheimer. Washington: Congressional Quarterly Press.

Collie, Melissa P., and Joseph Cooper. 1989. "Multiple Referral and the 'New' Committee System in the House of Representatives." In *Congress Reconsidered*, 4th ed., ed. Lawrence C. Dodd and Bruce I. Oppenheimer. Washington: Congressional Quarterly Press.

Congressional Directory. 1973. Washington: Government Printing Office.

Congressional Districts in the 1970s. 1973. Washington: Congressional Quarterly, Inc.

Congressional Quarterly Almanac. Various Years. Washington: Congressional Quarterly, Inc.

Connally, Tom. 1954. *My Name is Tom Connally*. New York: Thomas Y. Crowell Company.

Connelly, William F., and John J. Pitney, Jr. 1994. *Congress's Permanent Minority? Republicans in the U.S. House.* Lanham, MD: Rowman & Littlefield.

Cooper, Joseph. 1961. "Congress and Its Committees." Ph.D. diss. Harvard University.

———1970. *The Origins of Standing Committees and the Development of the Modern House.* Houston: Rice University Publications.

——— 1975. "Strengthening the Congress: An Organizational Analysis." *Harvard Journal of Legislation* 12:307–68.

———1977. "Congress in Organizational Perspective." In *Congress Reconsidered*, ed. Lawrence C. Dodd and Bruce I. Oppenheimer. New York: Praeger.

Cooper, Joseph, and Gary Bombardier. 1968. "Presidential Leadership and Party Success." *Journal of Politics* 30:1012–27.

Cooper, Joseph, and David W. Brady. 1981a. "Institutional Context and Leadership Style: The House from Cannon to Rayburn." *American Political Science Review* 75:411–25.

———1981b. "Toward a Diachronic Analysis of Congress." *American Political Science Review* 75:988–1006.

Cover, Albert D., and David Mayhew. 1977. "Congressional Dynamics and the Decline of Competitive Congressional Election." In *Congress Reconsidered*, ed. Lawrence C. Dodd and Bruce I. Oppenheimer. New York: Praeger.

Cox, Gary W., and Samuel Kernell, eds. 1991. *Politics of Divided Government.* Boulder, CO: Westview.

Cox, Gary W., and Mathew D. McCubbins. 1991. "On the Decline of Party Voting in Congress." *Legislative Studies Quarterly* 16:547–70.

———1993. *Legislative Leviathan: Party Government in the House.* Berkeley, CA: University of California Press.

Crick, Bernard. 1965a. "The Prospects of Parlimentary Reform." *The Political Quarterly.* 36: 333–46.

——— 1965b. *The Reform of Parliament.* Garden City: Doubleday Anchor.

Cummings, Milton C. Jr., and Robert L. Peabody. 1963. "The Decision to Enlarge the Committee on Rules." In *New Perspectives on the House of Representatives*, ed. Robert L. Peabody and Nelson W. Polsby. Chicago: Rand McNally.

Cunningham, Noble. 1963. *Jeffersonian Republicans in Power.* Chapel Hill: University of North Carolina Press.

Cutler, William Parkes, and Julia Perkins Cutler, eds. 1888. *Life, Journals and Correspondence of the Reverend Manasseh Cutler.* Cincinnati: Robert Clark and Company.

Cyert, Richard, and James March. 1963. *A Behavioral Theory of the Firm.* Englewood Cliffs, NJ: Prentice-Hall.

Dahl, Robert A. 1957. "The Concept of Power." *Behavioral Science* 2:201–15.

———1966. *Political Oppositions in Western Democracies.* New Haven: Yale University Press.

Daniels, Jonathan. 1946. *Frontier on the Potomac.* New York: Macmillan.

Darcy, R., Susan Welch, and Janet Clark. 1994. *Women, Elections, and Representation*, 2nd ed. Lincoln: University of Nebraska Press.

Davidson, Roger H. 1969. *The Role of the Congressman.* New York: Pegasus.

———1981a. "Congressional Leaders as Agents of Change." In *Understanding Congressional Leadership*, ed. Frank H. Mackaman. Washington: Congressional Quarterly Press.

———1981b. "Subcommittee Government: New Channels for Policy Making." In *The New Congress*, ed. Thomas E. Mann and Norman J. Ornstein. Washington: American Enterprise Institute.

———1985. "Senate Leaders: Janitors for an Untidy Chamber?" In *Congress Reconsidered.* 3rd ed., ed. Lawrence C. Dodd and Bruce I. Oppenheimer. Washington: Congressional Quarterly Press.

———1992. *The Postreform Congress.* New York: St. Martin's Press.

Davidson, Roger H., and Walter J. Oleszek. 1998. *Congress and Its Members.* 6th ed. Washington: Congressional Quarterly Press.

Davidson, Roger H., Walter J. Oleszek, and Thomas Kephart. 1988. "One Bill, Many Committees: Multiple Referrals in the U.S. House of Representatives." *Legislative Studies Quarterly* 13:3–28.

Davis, Oscar King. 1911. "Where Underwood Stands." *The Outlook,* 23 December 1911, 197–201.

Davis v. Bandemer. 478 U.S. 109 (1986).

de Grazia, Alfred. 1951. *Public and Republic.* New York: Alfred A. Knopf.

DeGregorio, Christine A. 1996. *Networks of Champions: Leadership, Access and Advocacy in the U.S. House of Representatives.* Ann Arbor: University of Michigan Press.

Dempsey, John Thomas. 1956. "Control by Congress over the Seating and Disciplining of Members." Ph.D. diss. University of Michigan.

Derthick, Martha. 1979. *Policymaking for Social Security.* Washington: Brookings Institution.

DeVries, Walter, and V. Lance Tarrance. 1972. *The Ticket-Splitter.* Grand Rapids, MI: William B. Eerdmans.

Dexter, Lewis. 1957. "The Representative and His District." *Human Organization* 16:2–14.

———1969. *The Sociology and Politics of Congress.* Chicago: Rand McNally.

Dodd, Lawrence C. 1972. "Committee Integration in the Senate: A Comparative Analysis." *Journal of Politics* 34:1135–71.

———1977. "Congress and the Quest for Power." In *Congress Reconsidered,* ed. Lawrence C. Dodd and Bruce I. Oppenheimer. New York: Praeger.

Drew, Elizabeth. 1979. *Senator.* New York: Simon and Schuster.

Durkheim, Emile. 1947. *The Division of Labor in Society.* Glencoe: The Free Press.

Dyson, James W., and John W. Soule. 1970. "Congressional Committee Behavior on Roll Calls: The U.S. House of Representatives." *Midwest Journal of Political Science* 14:626–47.

Easton, David. 1957. "An Approach to the Analysis of Political Systems." *World Politics* 9:383–400.

Edwards, George C., III. 1976. "Presidential Influence in the House: Presidential Prestige as a Source of Presidential Power." *American Political Science Review* 70:101–13.

———1980. *Presidential Influence in Congress.* San Francisco: W. H. Freeman.

———1989. *At the Margins: Presidential Leadership of Congress.* New Haven: Yale University Press.

Edwards, George C., III, Andrew Barrett, and Jeffrey Peake. 1997. "The Legislative Impact of Divided Government." *American Journal of Political Science* 41:545–63.

Ehrenhalt, Alan. 1991. *The United States of Ambition: Politicians, Power, and the Pursuit of Office.* New York: Times Books.

Eisenstadt, Shumel N. 1964. "Institutionalization and Change." *American Sociological Review* 29:235–47.

Erikson, Robert S. 1971a. "The Advantage of Incumbency in Congressional Elections." *Polity* 3:395–405.

———1971b. "The Electoral Impact of Congressional Roll Call Voting." *American Political Science Review* 65:1018–32.

———1972. "Malapportionment, Gerrymandering, and Party Fortunes in Congressional Elections." *American Political Science Review* 66:1238.

———1988. "The Puzzle of Midterm Losses." *Journal of Politics* 50:1012–29.

Eulau, Heinz. 1985. "Introduction: Legislative Research in Historical Perspective." In *Handbook of Legislative Research,* ed. Gerhard Loewenberg, Samuel C. Patterson, and Malcolm E. Jewell. Cambridge: Harvard University Press.

Eulau, Heinz, and Paul Karps. 1977. "The Puzzle of Representation: Specifying Components of Responsiveness." *Legislative Studies Quarterly* 2:233–54.

Eulau, Heinz, and Kenneth Prewitt. 1973. *Labyrinths of Power.* Indianapolis: Bobbs-Merrill.

Eulau, Heinz, John C. Wahlke, William Buchanan, and Leroy C. Ferguson. 1959. "The Role of the Representative: Some Empirical Observations on the Theory of Edmund Burke." *American Political Science Review* 53:742–56.

Evans, C. Lawrence. 1991. *Leadership in Committee: A Comparative Analysis of Leadership Behavior in the U.S. Senate.* Ann Arbor: University of Michigan Press.

Evans, Rowland, and Robert Novak. 1966. *Lyndon Johnson: The Exercise of Power.* New York: The New American Library.

Fairlie, John A. 1940. "The Nature of Political Representation." *American Political Science Review* 34:236–48, 456–66.

Farquharson, Robin. 1969. *Theory of Voting*. New Haven: Yale University Press.

The Federalist Papers: Alexander Hamilton, James Madison, and John Jay. [1787–8] 1961. New York: New American Library.

Fenno, Richard F., Jr. 1962. "The House Appropriations Committee as a Political System: The Problem of Integration." *American Political Science Review* 56:310–24.

———1963. "The House of Representatives and Federal Aid to Education." In *New Perspectives on the House of Representatives*, ed. Robert L. Peabody and Nelson W. Polsby. Chicago: Rand McNally.

———1966. *The Power of the Purse: Appropriations Politics in Congress*. Boston: Little, Brown, and Company.

———1973. *Congressmen in Committees*. Boston: Little, Brown.

———1975. "If, As Ralph Nader Says, 'Congress is the Broken Branch,' How Come We Love Our Congressmen So Much." In *Congress in Change*, ed. Norman Ornstein. New York: Praeger.

———1977a. "Strengthening a Congressional Strength." In *Congress Reconsidered*, ed. Lawrence C. Dodd and Bruce I. Oppenheimer. New York: Praeger.

———1977b. "U.S. House Members in Their Constituencies: An Exploration." *American Political Science Review* 71: 883–917.

———1978. *Home Style: House Members in Their Districts*. New York: HarperCollins.

———1986. "Observation, Context, and Sequence in the Study of Politics." *American Political Science Review* 80:3–15.

———1996. *Senators on the Campaign Trail: The Politics of Representation*. Norman, OK: University of Oklahoma Press.

Ferejohn, John A. 1977. "On the Decline of Competition in Congressional Elections." *American Political Science Review* 71:166–76.

Ferejohn, John A., and Morris P. Fiorina. 1975. "Purposive Models of Legislative Behavior." *American Economic Review* 65:407–14.

Fiorina, Morris P. 1973. "Electoral Margins, Constituency Influence, and Policy Moderation: A Critical Assessment." *American Politics Quarterly* 1:479–98.

———1974. *Representation, Roll Calls, and Constituencies*. Lexington, MA: Heath.

———1977a. "The Case of the Vanishing Marginals: The Bureaucracy Did It." *American Political Science Review* 71:177–81.

———1977b. *Congress: Keystone of the Washington Establishment*. New Haven: Yale University Press.

———1978. "Economic Retrospective Voting in American National Elections: A Microanalysis." *American Journal of Political Science* 22:426–43.

———1981. "Some Problems in Studying the Effects of Resource Allocation in Congressional Elections." *American Journal of Political Science* 25:542–67.

———1996. *Divided Government*. Boston: Allyn and Bacon.

Fiorina, Morris P., David W. Rohde, and Peter Wissel. 1975. "Historical Change in House Turnover." In *Congress in Change*, ed. Norman Ornstein. New York: Praeger.

Fiorina, Morris P., and Kenneth A. Shepsle. 1989. "Is Negative Voting an Artifact?" *American Journal of Political Science* 33:423–39.

Fishel, Jeff. 1971. "Ambition and the Political Vocation: Congressional Challengers in American Politics." *Journal of Politics* 33:25–56.

Follett, Mary Parker. 1896. *The Speaker of the House of Representatives*. New York: Longmans, Green.

Fowler, Linda L. 1980. "Candidate Perceptions of Electoral Coalitions: Limits and Possibilities." Paper delivered during the Conference on Congressional Elections, Rice University and the University of Houston, Houston, TX, January 10–12.

———1993. *Candidates, Congress, and the American Democracy*. Ann Arbor: University of Michigan Press.

Fowler, Linda L., and Robert D. McClure. 1989. *Political Ambition: Who Decides to Run for Congress*. New Haven: Yale University Press.

Fox, Harrison W., Jr., and Susan Webb Hammond. 1977. *Congressional Staffs: The Invisible Force in American Lawmaking*. New York: Free Press.

Frady, Marshall. 1969. *Wallace*. New York: New American Library.

Froman, Lewis A., Jr. 1968a. "The Categorization of Policy Content." In *Political Science and Public Policy*, ed. Austin Ranney. Chicago: Markham.

———1968b. "Organization Theory and the Explanation of Important Characteristics of Congress." *American Political Science Review* 62:518–26.

Froman, Lewis A., Jr., and Randall B. Ripley. 1965. "Conditions for Party Leadership: The Case of the House Democrats." *American Political Science Review* 59:52–63.

Frost, Murray. 1972. "Senatorial Ambition and Legislative Behavior." Ph.D. diss. Michigan State University.

Galloway, George B. 1946. *Congress at the Crossroads*. New York: Crowell.

———1961. *History of the House of Representatives*. New York: Thomas Crowell.

Garand, James C., and Donald Gross. 1984. "Changes in the Vote Margins for Congressional Candidates: A Specification of Historical Trends." *American Political Science Review* 78:17–30.

Gelman, Andrew, and Gary King. 1990. "Estimating Incumbency Advantage Without Bias." *American Journal of Political Science* 34:1142–64.

Gerber, Elisabeth R., and Arthur Lupia. 1996. "Term Limits, Responsiveness, and the Failures of Increased Competition." In *Legislative Term Limits: Public Choice Perspectives*, ed. Bernard Grofman. Boston: Kluwer Academic Publishers.

Gerlich, Peter. 1973. "The Institutionalization of European Parliaments." In *Legislatures in a Comparative Perspective*, ed. Allan Kornberg. New York: McKay.

Gerth, H. H., and C. Wright Mills, eds. 1946. *From Max Weber: Essays in Sociology*. New York: Oxford University Press.

Gertzog, Irwin N. 1970. "The Socialization of Freshman Congressmen: Some Agents of Organizational Continuity." Paper prepared for delivery at the 66th Annual Meeting of the American Political Science Association, Los Angeles.

Gilligan, Thomas, and Keith Krehbiel. 1989. "Asymmetric Information and Legislative Rules with a Heterogeneous Committee." *American Journal of Political Science* 33: 459–90.

Gilmour, John, and Paul Rothstein. 1994. "Term Limitation in a Dynamic Model of Partisan Balance." *American Journal of Political Science* 38:770–96.

Ginsberg, Benjamin, and Alan Stone, eds. 1996. *Do Elections Matter?* 3rd ed. Armonk, NY: M. E. Sharpe.

Glazer, Amihai, and Martin P. Wattenberg. 1996. "How Will Term Limits Affect Legislative Work?" In *Legislative Term Limits: Public Choice Perspectives*, ed. Bernard Grofman. Boston: Kluwer Academic Publishers.

Goffman, Erving. 1959. *The Presentation of Self in Everyday Life*. New York: Doubleday.

Gold, Martin, Michael Hugo, Hyde Murray, Peter Robinson, and A. L. "Pete" Singleton. 1992. *The Book on Congress: Process, Procedure, and Structure*. Washington: Big Eagle Publishing Co.

Goldberg, Arthur. 1969. "Social Determinism and Rationality as Bases of Party Identification." *American Political Science Review* 63:5–25.

Goodman, Marshall, Debra Gross, Thomas Boyd, and Herbert Weisberg. 1986. "Constituency Service as a Legislative Goal." *Polity*. 18:707–19.

Goodwin, George, Jr. 1959. "The Seniority System In Congress." *American Political Science Review* 53:417.

———1970. *The Little Legislatures*. Amherst: University of Massachusetts Press.

Green, Donald P., and Jonathan Krasno. 1988. "Salvation for the Spendthrift Incumbent." *American Journal of Political Science* 32:844–907.

Green, Donald P., and Ian Shapiro. 1994. *Pathologies of Rational Choice Theory*. New Haven: Yale University Press.

Greenstein, Fred I. 1987. *Personality and Politics: Problems of Evidence, Inference and Conceptualization*. Chicago: Markham Publishing.

Greer, Scott. 1955. *Social Organization*. Garden City, NY: Doubleday.

Grenzke, Janet. 1989. "PACs and the Congressional Supermarket: The Currency is Complex." *American Journal of Political Science* 33:1–24.

Grofman, Bernard, and Neil Sutherland. 1996. "The Effect of Term Limits when Competition is Endogenized: A Preliminary Model." In *Legislative Term Limits: Public Choice Perspectives*, ed. Bernard Grofman. Boston: Kluwer Academic Publishers.

Gross, Bertram M. 1953. *The Legislative Struggle: A Study of Social Combat*. New York: McGraw-Hill.

Gross, Neal, Ward S. Mason, and Alexander W. McEachern. 1958. *Explorations in Role Analysis: Studies of the School Superintendency Role*. New York: Wiley.

Guinier, Lani. 1994. *The Tyranny of the Majority: Fundamental Fairness in Representative Democracy*. New York: Free Press.

Hadley, Lisa, and Bernard Grofman. 1994. "The Impact of the Voting Rights Act on Minority Representation: Black Officeholding in Southern State Legislatures and Congressional Delegations." In *Quiet Revolution the the South*, ed. Chandler Davidson and Bernard Grofman. Princeton: Princeton University Press.

Hain, Paul, and Terry Smith. 1973. "Congressional Challengers for the Office of Governor." Paper delivered at the annual meeting of the American Political Science Association, New Orleans, Louisiana.

Haines, Lynn. 1915. *Your Congress*. Washington: National Voters' League.

Hall, Richard H., J. Eugene Haas, and Norman J. Johnson. 1967. "Organizational Size, Complexity, and Formalization." *American Sociological Review* 32:903–12.

Hall, Richard L., 1987. "Participation and Purpose in Committee Decision Making." *American Political Science Review* 81:105–28.

———1996. *Participation in Congress*. New Haven: Yale University Press.

Hall, Richard L., and Bernard Grofman. 1990. "The Committee Assignment Process and the Conditional Nature of Committee Bias." *American Political Science Review* 84:1149–66.

Hall, Richard L., and Robert Van Houweling. 1995. "Avarice and Ambition in Congress: Representatives' Decisions to Run or Retire from the U.S. House." *American Political Science Review*. 89:121–36.

Hall, Richard L., and Frank W. Wayman. 1990. "Buying Time: Moneyed Interests and the Mobilization of Bias in Congressional Committees." *American Political Science Review* 84:797–820.

Hansen, John Mark. 1991. *Gaining Access: Congress and the Farm Lobby*. Chicago: University of Chicago Press.

Harlow, Ralph V. 1917. *The History of Legislative Methods in the Period Before 1825*. New Haven: Yale University Press.

Harris, Fred R. 1993. *Deadlock or Decision: The U.S. Senate and the Rise of National Politics*. New York: Oxford University Press.

Harris, Joseph. 1964. *Congressional Control of Administration*. Washington: Brookings Institution.

Harris, Richard. 1966. *A Sacred Trust*. New York: New American Library.

Hasbrouck, Paul De Witt. 1927. *Party Government in the House of Representatives*. New York: Macmillan.

Hechler, Kenneth. 1940. *Insurgency*. New York: Columbia University Press.

Hedlund, Ronald D. 1985. "Organizational Attributes of Legislative Institutions: Structure, Rules, Norms, Resources." In *Handbook of Legislative Research*, ed. Gerhard Loewenberg, Samuel C. Patterson, and Malcolm E. Jewell. Cambridge, MA: Harvard University Press.

Hermann, Margaret G. 1984. "Personality and Foreign Policy Decision Making: A study of 53 Heads of State." In *Foreign Policy Decision Making*, ed. Donald Sylvan and Steve Chan. New York: Praeger.

Hero, Rodney E., and Caroline J. Tolbert. 1995. "Latinos and Substantive Representation in the U.S. House of Representatives: Direct, Indirect, or Nonexistent?" *American Journal of Political Science* 39:640–52.

Herrick, Rebekah, Michael K. Moore, and John R. Hibbing. 1994. "Unfastening the Electoral Connection: The Behavior of U.S. Representatives when Reelection is No Longer a Factor." *Journal of Politics* 56:214–27.

Herrick, Rebekah, and David L. Nixon. 1994. "Is There Life After Congress?: Patterns and Determinants of Post-Congressional Careers." Paper prepared for the annual meeting of the American Political Science Association.

Herring, Pendleton. 1940. *Presidential Leadership*. New York: Farrar and Rinehart.

Herrnson, Paul S. 1992. "Campaign Professionalism and Fundraising in Congressional Elections." *Journal of Politics* 54:859–70.

——1995. *Congressional Elections: Campaigning at Home and in Washington*. Washington: Congressional Quarterly.

Hibbing, John R. 1988. "Legislative Institutionalization with Illustrations from the British House of Commons." *American Journal of Political Science* 32:681–712.

——1991. *Congressional Careers: Contours of Life in the U.S. House of Representatives*. Chapel Hill, NC: University of North Carolina Press.

Hibbing, John R., and Elizabeth Theiss-Morse. 1995. *Congress as Public Enemy*. Cambridge: Cambridge University Press.

Hill, Andrew, and Anthony Whichelow. 1964. *What's Wrong with Parliament?* Harmondsworth: Penguin.

Hill, Kevin A. 1995. "Does the Creation of Majority Black Districts Aid Republicans? An Analysis of the 1992 Congressional Election in Eight Southern States." *Journal of Politics* 57:384–401.

Hinckley, Barbara. 1970. "Congressional Leadership Selection and Support: A Comparative Analysis." *Journal of Politics* 32:268–87.

——1975. "Policy Content, Committee Membership, and Behavior." *American Journal of Political Science* 19:543–57.

——1994. *Less than Meets the Eye: Foreign Policy Making and the Myth of the Assertive Congress*. Chicago: University of Chicago Press.

Hinds, Asher C. 1907. *Hinds Precedents of the House of Representatives of the United States*. Vol. 4. Washington: Government Printing Office.

——1909. "The Speaker of the House of Representatives." *American Political Science Review* 3:160–61.

Hirsch, Herbert, and Donald Hancock, eds. 1971. *Comparative Legislative Systems: A Reader in Theory and Research*. New York: The Free Press.

Holden, Alice M. 1930. "The Imperial Mandate in the Spanish Cortes in the Middle Ages." *American Political Science Review* 24:886–912.

Homans, George C. 1950. *The Human Group*. New York: Harcourt Brace.

Huber, John. 1992. "Restrictive Legislative Procedures in France and the United States." *American Political Science Review* 86:675–87.

Huitt, Ralph K. 1954. "The Congressional Committee: A Case Study." *American Political Science Review* 48:340–65.

——1961a. "Democratic Party Leadership in the Senate." *American Political Science Review* 55:333–344.

——1961b. "The Outsider in the Senate." *American Political Science Review* 55:566–75.

Huitt, Ralph K., and Robert L. Peabody. 1969. *Congress: Two Decades of Analysis*. New York: Harper and Row.

Huntington, Samuel P. 1965a. "Congressional Response to the Twentieth Century." In *The Congress and America's Future*, 2nd ed., ed. David Truman. Englewood Cliffs, NJ: Prentice-Hall.

——1965b. "Political Development and Political Decay." *World Politics* 17:386–430.

——1968. *Political Order and Changing Societies*. New Haven: Yale University Press.

Hurley, Patricia A. 1989. "Partisan Representation and the Failure of Realignment in the 1980s." *American Journal of Political Science* 33:240–61.

Hurley, Patricia A., and Rick K. Wilson. 1989. "Partisan Voting Patterns in the U.S. Senate, 1877–1986." *Legislative Studies Quarterly* 14:225–50.

Jackson, John E., and John W. Kingdon. 1992. "Ideology, Interest Group Scores, and Legislative Votes." *American Journal of Political Science* 36:805–23.

Jacobson, Gary C. 1978. "The Effects of Campaign Spending in Congressional Elections." *American Political Science Review* 72:469–91.

————1980. *Money in Congressional Elections*. New Haven: Yale University Press.

————1985. "Money and Votes Reconsidered: Congressional Elections, 1972–1982." *Public Choice* 47:7–62.

————1990. *The Electoral Origins of Divided Government*. Boulder, CO: Westview Press.

————1997. *The Politics of Congressional Elections*, 4th ed. New York: Longman.

Jacobson, Gary C., and Samuel Kernell. 1983. *Strategy and Choice in Congressional Elections*, 2nd ed. New Haven: Yale University Press.

————1990. "National Forces in the 1986 U.S. House Elections." *Legislative Studies Quarterly* 15:65–88.

Jewell, Malcolm E. 1962. *Senatorial Politics and Foreign Policy*. Lexington, KY: University of Kentucky Press.

Jewell, Malcolm E., and Marcia Lynn Whicker. 1994. *Legislative Leadership in the American States*. Ann Arbor: University of Michigan Press.

Johannes, John R., and John C. McAdams. 1981. "The Congressional Incumbency Effect: Is it Case Work, Policy Compatibility, or Something Else?" *American Journal of Political Science* 25:512–42.

Johnson, Donald B., and James R. Gibson. 1974. "The Divisive Primary Revisited: Party Activists in Iowa." *American Political Science Review* 68:67–77.

Johnson, Harry M. 1960. *Sociology*. New York: Harcourt Brace.

Jones, Bryan D. 1994. *Reconceiving Decision Making in Democratic Politics*. Chicago: University of Chicago Press.

Jones, Bryan D., Frank R. Baumgartner, and Jeffrey C. Talbert. 1993. "The Destruction of Issue Monopolies in Congress." *American Political Science Review* 87:657–71.

Jones, Charles O. 1961. "Representation in Congress: The Case of the House Agriculture Committee." *American Political Science Review* 55:358–67.

————1964. "Interparty Competition for Congressional Seats." *Western Political Quarterly* 17:461–476.

————1968. "Joseph G. Cannon and Howard W. Smith: A Essay on the Limits of Leadership in the House of Representatives." *Journal of Politics* 30:617–46.

————1970. *The Minority Party in Congress*. Boston: Little, Brown.

————1975. *Clean Air: The Policies and Politics of Pollution Control*. Pittsburgh, PA: University of Pittsburgh Press.

————1994. *The Presidency in a Separated System*. Washington: Brookings Institution.

Kabaker, Harvey. 1969. "Estimating the Normal Vote in Congressional Elections." *Midwest Journal of Political Science* 13:58–83.

Kathlene, Lyn. 1994. "Power and Influence in State Legislative Policymaking: The Interaction of Gender and Position in Committee Hearing Debates." *American Political Science Review* 88:560–76.

————1995. "Alternative Views of Crime: Legislative Policymaking in Gendered Terms." *Journal of Politics* 57:696–723.

Katz, Jonathan N., and Brian R. Sala. 1996. "Careerism, Committee Assignments, and the Electoral Connection." *American Political Science Review* 90:21–33.

Kazee, Thomas A. 1980. "The Decision to Run for the U.S. Congress: Challenger Attitudes in the 1970s." *Legislative Studies Quarterly* 5:79–100.

————1994. *Who Runs for Congress?: Ambition, Context, and Candidate Emergence*. Washington: Congressional Quarterly Press.

Keefe, William J. 1976. *Parties, Politics, and Public Policy in America*, 2nd ed. Hinsdale, IL: Dryden Press.

Kefauver, Estes. 1947. *A Twentieth-Century Congress*. New York: Duell, Sloan, and Pearce.

Kelley, Stanley, Jr. 1956. *Professional Public Relations and Political Power*. Baltimore, MD: The Johns Hopkins University Press.

Kernell, Samuel. 1977. "Toward Understanding Ninteenth-Century Congressional Careers: Ambition, Competition, and Rotation." *American Journal of Political Science* 21:669–93.

————1979. "Congressional Careerism and the Emergence of a Political Career Structure." Paper presented during the meeting of the Social Science History Association, Cambridge, MA.

Kesselman, Mark. 1961. "Presidential Leadership in Congress on Foreign Policy." *Midwest Journal of Political Science* 5:284–89.

———1965. "Presidential Leadership in Congress on Foreign Policy: A Replication of a Hypothesis." *Midwest Journal of Political Science* 9:401–6.

Kessler, Daniel, and Keith Krehbiel. 1996. "Dynamics of Cosponsorship." *American Political Science Review* 90:555–66.

Key, V. O., Jr. 1949. *Southern Politics in State and Nation.* New York: Knopf.

———1966. *The Responsible Electorate.* Cambridge: Harvard University Press.

Kiewiet, D. Roderick, and Mathew D. McCubbins. 1991. *The Logic of Delegation: Congressional Parties and the Appropriations Process.* Chicago: University of Chicago Press.

Kimball, David C., and Samuel C. Patterson. 1997. "Living up to Expectations: Public Attitudes Toward Congress." *Journal of Politics* 59:701–28.

Kinder, Donald R., and R. Roderick Kiewiet. 1981. "Sociotropic Politics: The American Case." *British Journal of Political Science* 11:129–61.

King, Gary. 1991. "Constituency Service and Incumbency Advantage." *British Journal of Political Science* 21:119–28.

King, Gary, Robert O. Keohane, and Sidney Verba. 1994. *Designing Social Inquiry.* Princeton: Princeton University Press.

Kingdon, John W. 1973, 1981, 1989. *Congressmen's Voting Decisions.* First, 2nd, and 3rd ed. New York: Harper and Row.

———1977. "Models of Legislative Voting." *Journal of Politics* 39:563–95.

———1984, 1995. *Agendas, Alternatives, and Public Policies.* Boston: Little Brown (2nd ed, New York: Longman).

Kofmehl, Kenneth. 1962. *Professional Staffs of Congress.* Lafayette, IN: Purdue University Press.

Koford, Kenneth. 1989. "Dimensions in Congressional Voting." *American Political Science Review* 83:949–62.

Kornberg, Allan. 1964. "The Rules of the Game in the Canadian House of Commons." *Journal of Politics* 26:358–80.

———, ed. 1973. *Legislatures in Comparative Perspective.* New York: McKay.

Kostroski, Warren. 1973. "Party Incumbency in Postwar Senate Elections: Trends, Patterns, and Models." *American Political Science Review* 67:1213–34.

Kramer, Gerald H. 1971. "Short-Term Fluctuations in U.S. Voting Behavior, 1896–1964." *American Political Science Review* 65:131–43.

Krasno, Jonathan S. 1994. *Challengers, Competition, and Reelection: Comparing Senate and House Elections.* New Haven: Yale University Press.

Krasno, Jonathan S., and Donald P. Green. 1988. "Preempting Quality Challengers in House Elections." *Journal of Politics* 50:920–36.

Krehbiel, Keith. 1986. "Unanimous Consent Agreements: Going Along in the Senate." *Journal of Politics* 48:541–64.

———1988. "Spatial Models of Legislative Choice." *Legislative Studies Quarterly* 13:259–319.

———1990. "Are Congressional Committees Composed of Preference Outliers?" *American Political Science Review* 84:149–164.

———1991. *Information and Legislative Organization.* Ann Arbor: University of Michigan Press.

———1998. *Pivotal Politics: A Theory of U.S. Lawmaking.* Chicago: University of Chicago Press.

Krehbiel, Keith, and Douglas Rivers. 1988. "The Analysis of Committee Power." *American Journal of Political Science* 32:1151–74.

———1990. "Sophisticated Voting in Congress: A Reconsideration." *Journal of Politics* 52:548–78.

Lacy, Dean. 1998. "Back from Intermission: The 1994 Elections and the Return to Divided Government." In *Great Theatre*, ed. Herbert F. Weisberg and Samuel C. Patterson. New York: Cambridge University Press.

Ladd, Everett C., and Charles P. Hadley. 1975. *Transformations of the American Party System.* New York: William Norton.

Langbein, Laura. 1993. "PACs, Lobbies, and Political Conflict: The Case of Gun Control." *Public Choice* 77:551–72.

Lasswell, Harold D., and Abraham Kaplan. 1950. *Power and Society*. New Haven: Yale University Press.

Leuthold, David. 1968. *Electioneering in a Democracy: Campaigns for Congress*. New York: Wiley.

Libby, Orrin G. 1896. "A Plea for the Study of Votes in Congress." *Annual Report of the American Historical Association* 1:323–34.

Light, Paul C. 1985. *Artful Work: The Politics of Social Security Reform*. New York: Random House.

———1991. *The President's Agenda*. Rev. ed. Baltimore: The Johns Hopkins University Press.

Lijphart, Arend. 1963. "The Analysis of Bloc Voting in the General Assembly: A Critique and a Proposal." *American Political Science Review* 57:902–17.

Loewenberg, Gerhard, Samuel C. Patterson, and Malcolm E. Jewell, eds. 1985. *Handbook of Legislative Research*. Cambridge: Harvard University Press.

Loomis, Burdett. 1981. "The 'Me Decade' and the Changing Context of House Leadership." In *Understanding Congressional Leadership*, ed. Frank H. Mackaman. Washington: Congressional Quarterly Press.

Lowell, A. Lawrence. 1902. "The Influence of Party upon Legislation in England and America." *Annual Report of the American Historical Association for 1901* 1:321–542.

Lowi, Theodore J. 1964. "American Business, Public Policy, Case Studies, and Political Theory." *World Politics* 16:677–715.

Lublin, David. 1997. *The Paradox of Representation*. Princeton: Princeton University Press.

Luce, R. Duncan, and Howard Raiffa. 1957. *Games and Decisions*. New York: Wiley.

Luce, Robert. 1922. *Legislative Procedures*. Boston: Houghton-Mifflin.

Mackaman, Frank H., ed. 1981. *Understanding Congressional Leadership*. Washington: Congressional Quarterly Press.

MacNeil, Neil. 1963. *Forge of Democracy*. New York: David McKay.

MacRae, Duncan. 1958. *Dimensions of Congressional Voting: A Statistical Study of the House of Representatives in the Eighty-First Congress*. Berkeley: University of California Press.

———1967. *Parliament, Parties, and Society in France, 1946–1958*. New York: St. Martin's Press.

———1970. *Issues and Parties in Legislative Voting: Methods of Statistical Analysis*. New York: Harper and Row.

Maltzman, Forrest. 1995. "Meeting Competing Demands: Committee Performance in the Postreform House." *American Journal of Political Science* 39:653–82.

Manley, John F. 1965. "The House Committee on Ways and Means: Conflict Management in a Congressional Committee." *American Political Science Review* 59:927–39.

———1969. "Wilbur D. Mills: A Study in Congressional Influence." *American Political Science Review* 63:442–64.

———1970. *The Politics of Finance*. Boston: Little, Brown.

———1973. "Congressional Control of the Budget." Paper presented at the Study of Congress conference, Washington.

———1977. "The Conservative Coalition in Congress." In *Congress Reconsidered*, ed. Lawrence C. Dodd and Bruce I. Oppenheimer. New York: Praeger.

Mann, Thomas E. 1978. *Unsafe at Any Margin: Interpreting Congressional Elections*. Washington: American Enterprise Institute.

Mann, Thomas E., and Raymond E. Wolfinger. 1980. "Candidates and Parties in Congressional Elections." *American Political Science Review* 74: 617–32.

March, James, and Herbert Simon. 1958. *Organizations*. New York: John Wiley and Sons.

Marmor, Theodore R. 1973. *The Politics of Medicare*. New York: Aldine.

Marvick, Dwaine. 1952. "Congressional Appropriations Politics." Unpublished manuscript. Columbia.

Masters, Nicholas A. 1961. "Committee Assignments in the House of Representatives." *American Political Science Review* 55:345–57.

Matthews, Donald R. 1959. "The Folkways of the U.S. Senate." *American Political Science Review* 53:1064–89.

——1968, 1973. *U.S. Senators and their World*. Chapel Hill: University of North Carolina Press.

——1961. "Can the Outsider's Role Be Legitimate?" *American Political Science Review* 55:882–86.

Matthews, Donald R., and James A. Stimson. 1970. "Decision Making by U.S. Represen-tatives." In *Political Decision Making*, ed. S. Sidney Ulmer. New York: Van Nostrand Reinhold.

——1975. *Yeas and Nays: Normal Decision Making in the U.S. House of Representatives*. New York: Wiley.

Mayhew, David R. 1966. *Party Loyalty Among Congressmen*. Cambridge, MA: Harvard University Press.

——1971. "Congressional Representation: Theory and Practice in Drawing the Districts." In *Reapportionment in the 1970s*, ed. Nelson W. Polsby. Berkeley: University of California Press.

——1974a. *Congress: The Electoral Connection*. New Haven: Yale University Press.

——1974b. "Congressional Elections: The Case of the Vanishing Marginals." *Polity* 6:295–317.

——1991. *Divided We Govern: Party Control, Lawmaking, and Investigations, 1946–1990*. New Haven: Yale University Press.

Mayo, Bernard. 1937. *Henry Clay: Spokesman of the New West*. Boston: Houghton Mifflin.

McAdams, John C., and John R. Johannes. 1987. "Determinants of House Spending by Challengers." *American Journal of Political Science* 31:457–83.

McCall, Samuel W. 1899. *Thaddeus Stevens*. Boston: Houghton-Mifflin.

McConachie, Lauros G. 1898. *Congressional Committees: A Study of the Origins and Development of Our National and Local Legislative Methods*. New York: Thomas Y. Crowell.

McCubbins, Mathew D. 1991. "Party Governance and U.S. Budget Deficits: Divided Government and Fiscal Stalemate." In *Politics and Economics in the Eighties*, ed. Alberto Alesina and Geoffrey Carliner. Chicago: University of Chicago Press.

McCubbins, Mathew D., and Terry Sullivan. 1987. *Congress: Structure and Policy*. Cambridge: Cambridge University Press.

McCurley, Carl, and Jeffery J. Mondak. 1995. "Inspected by #1184063113: The Influence of Incumbents' Competence and Integrity in the U.S. House Elections." *American Journal of Political Science* 39:864–85.

McKelvey, Richard D. 1976. "Intransitivities in Multidimensional Voting Models and Some Implications for Agenda Control." *Journal of Economic Theory* 12:472–82.

Members of Congress, 1945–1970. 1970. Washington: Congressional Quarterly, Inc.

Merton, Robert K. 1949, 1957. *Social Theory and Social Structure*. Glencoe, IL: The Free Press.

Mezey, Michael L. 1970. "Ambition Theory and the Office of Congressman." *Journal of Politics* 32:563–79.

——1985. "The Functions of Legislatures in the Third World." In *Handbook of Legislative Research*, ed. Gerhard Loewenberg, Samuel Patterson, and Malcolm Jewell. Cambridge: Harvard University Press.

——1993. "Legislatures: Individual Purpose and Institutional Performance." In *Political Science: The State of the Discipline II*, ed. Ada Finifter. Washington: American Political Science Association.

Milbrath, Lester M. 1963. *The Washington Lobbyists*. Chicago: Rand McNally.

Miller v. Johnson, 515 U.S. 900 (1995).

Miller, Clem. 1962. *Member of the House: Letters of a Congressman*. ed. John W. Baker. New York: Scribner.

Miller, Warren E. 1964. "Majority Rule and the Representative System of Government." In *Cleavages, Ideologies, and Party Systems*, ed. Erik Allardt and Yrjo Littunen. Helsinki, Distributor: Academic Bookstore.

Miller, Warren E., and Donald E. Stokes. n.d. "Representation and the American Congress." Unpublished manuscript, mimeograph, University of Michigan.

——1963. "Constituency Influence in Congress." *American Political Science Review* 57:45–56.

Miner, John B. 1980. *Theories of Organizational Behavior*. Hinsdale, IL: Dryden Press.

Moncrief, Gary F., Joel A. Thompson, Michael Haddon, and Robert Hoyer. 1992. "For Whom the Bell Tolls: Term Limits and State Legislatures." *Legislative Studies Quarterly* 17:37–47.

Mondak, Jeffery J., Carl McCurley, and Steven R. L. Millman. 1999. "The Impact of Incumbents' Levels of Competence and Integrity in the 1994 and 1996 U.S. House Elections." In *Reelection 1996*, ed. Herbert F. Weisberg and Janet M. Box-Steffensmeier. Chatham, NJ: Chatham House.

Mooney, Booth. 1964. *Mr. Speaker*. Chicago: Follett.

Murphy, James T. 1974. "Political Parties and the Porkbarrel: Party Conflict and Cooperation in the House Public Works Committee." *American Political Science Review* 68: 169–85.

Nelson, Dalmas H. 1953. "The Omnibus Appropriations Act of 1950." *Journal of Politics* 15:274–88.

Nelson, Garrison. 1977. "Partisan Patterns of House Leadership Change 1789–1977." *American Political Science Review* 71:918–39.

Neustadt, Richard. 1960. *Presidential Power*. New York: Wiley.

Newcomb, Theodore M. 1951. *Social Psychology*. New York: H. Holt.

O'Brien, Kevin J. 1994. "Chinese People's Congresses and Legislative Embeddedness: Understanding Early Organizational Development." *Comparative Political Studies* 27:80–107.

Oleszek. Walter J. 1989, 1996. *Congressional Procedures and the Policy Process*. 3rd and 4th ed. Washington: Congressional Quarterly Press.

Opello, Walter C., Jr. 1986. "Portugal's Parliament: An Organizational Analysis of Legislative Performance." *Legislative Studies Quarterly* 11:291–319.

Oppenheimer, Bruce I. 1985. "Changing Time Constraints on the Congress: Historical Perspectives on the Use of Cloture." In *Congress Reconsidered*, 3rd ed., ed. Lawrence C. Dodd and Bruce I. Oppenheimer. Washington: Congressional Quarterly Press.

———1996. "The Representational Experience: The Effect of State Population on Senator-Constituency Linkages." *American Journal of Political Science* 40:1280–99.

Ordeshook, Peter C. 1986. *Game Theory and Political Theory: An Introduction*. Cambridge: Cambridge University Press.

Ornstein, Norman J. 1995. "Prepared Testimony Before Senate Judiciary Committee, Subcommittee on the Constitution." In the *Federal News Service*, 25 January.

Ornstein, Norman J., Thomas E. Mann, and Michael J. Malbin. 1990. *Vital Statistics on Congress, 1989-1990*. Washington: Congressional Quarterly Press.

Overby, L. Marvin, and Kenneth M. Cosgrove. 1996. "Unintended Consequences?: Racial Redistricting and the Representation of Minority Interests." *Journal of Politics* 58:540–50.

Page, Benjamin I., and Robert Y. Shapiro. 1983. "Effects of Public Opinion on Policy." *American Political Science Review* 77:175–90.

Parker, Glenn R. 1985. *Studies of Congress*. Washington: Congressional Quarterly Press.

———1986. *Homeward Bound: Explaining Changes in Congressional Behavior*. Pittsburgh: University of Pittsburgh Press.

Parker, Glenn R., and Roger H. Davidson. 1979. "Why Do Americans Love Their Congressmen So Much More than Their Congress?" *Legislative Studies Quarterly* 4:52–61.

Parker, Glenn R., and Suzanne L. Parker. 1979. "Factions in Committees: The U.S. House of Representatives." *American Political Science Review* 73:85–102.

———1985. *Factions in House Committees*. Knoxville: University of Tennessee Press.

Parkinson, C. Northcote. 1957. *Parkinson's Law*. Boston: Houghton Mifflin.

Parsons, Talcott, and Edward A. Shils, eds. 1951. *Toward a General Theory of Action*. Cambridge: Harvard University Press.

Patterson, Samuel C. 1967. "Congressional Committee Professional Staffing: Capabilities and Constraints." Paper presented at the Planning Conference of the Comparative Administration Group, Legislative Services Project, Planting Fields, NY, December 8–10.

——— 1989. "Party Leadership in the U.S. Senate." *Legislative Studies Quarterly* 14:393–413.

Patterson, Samuel C., and Gregory A. Caldeira. 1988. "Party Voting in the United States Congress." *British Journal of Political Science* 18:111–31.

Patterson, Samuel C., and Joseph Quin Monson. 1999. "Two More Years: Reelecting the Republican Congress." In *Reelection*, ed. Herbert F. Weisberg and Janet M. Box-Steffensmeier. Chatham, NJ: Chatham House.

Patterson, Samuel C., and John C. Wahlke, eds. 1972. *Comparative Legislative Behavior: Frontiers of Research*. New York: Wiley Interscience.

Peabody, Robert L. 1969. "Research on Congress: Coming of Age." In *Congress: Two Decades of Analysis*, ed. Ralph K. Huitt and Robert L. Peabody. New York: Harper and Row.

———1976. *Leadership in Congress: Stability, Succession and Change*. Boston: Little, Brown.

Peabody, Robert L., Norman J. Ornstein, and David W. Rohde. 1976. "The United States Senate as a Presidential Incubator: Many Are Called But Few Are Chosen." *Political Science Quarterly* 91:237–58.

Perkins, Lynette P. 1980. "Influence of Members' Goals on Their Committee Behavior: The House Judiciary Committee." *Legislative Studies Quarterly* 5:373–92.

Peterson, Mark A. 1990. *Legislating Together: The White House and Capitol Hill from Eisenhower to Reagan*. Cambridge: Harvard University Press.

Peterson, Paul. 1970. "Forms of Representation: Participation of the Poor in Community Action Programs." *American Political Science Review* 64:491–501.

Petracca, Mark P. 1992. "Rotation in Office: The History of an Idea." In *Limiting Legislative Terms*, ed. Gerald Benjamin and Michael J. Malbin. Washington: Congressional Quarterly Press.

Petrocik, John R. 1991. "Divided Government: Is It All in the Campaigns?" In *The Politics of Divided Government*, ed. Gary W. Cox and Samuel Kernell. Boulder, CO: Westview Press.

Petrocik, John R., and Joseph Doherty. 1996. "The Road to Divided Government: Paved Without Intention." In *Divided Government: Change, Uncertainty, and the Constitutional Order*, ed. Peter F. Galderisi, with Roberta Q. Herzberg and Peter McNamara. Lanham, MD: Rowman and Littlefield Publishers, Inc.

Pitkin, Hanna F. 1961. "The Theory of Representation." Ph.D. diss. University of California, Berkeley.

——— 1967. *The Concept of Representation*. Berkeley: University of California Press.

Plott, Charles R. 1967. "A Notion of Equilibrium and Its Possibility Under Majority Rule." *American Economic Review* 57:788–806.

Plott, Charles R., and Michael E. Levine. 1978. "A Model of Agenda Influence on Committee Decisions." *American Economic Review* 68:146–60.

Pollock, James K. 1925. "The Seniority Rule in Congress." *North American Review* 222:235, 236.

Polsby, Nelson W. 1963. "Two Strategies of Influence: Choosing a Majority Leader, 1962." In *New Perspectives on the House of Representatives*, ed. Nelson W. Polsby and Robert Peabody. Chicago: Rand McNally.

———1964. *Congress and the Presidency*. New York: Prentice-Hall.

———1968. "The Institutionalization of the House of Representatives." *American Political Science Review* 62:144–68.

———1971. "Goodbye to the Inner Club." In *Congressional Behavior*, ed. Nelson W. Polsby. New York: Random House.

———1975. "Legislatures." In *Handbook of Political Science*, Vol. 5, ed. Fred I. Greenstein and Nelson W. Polsby. Reading, MA.: Addison-Wesley.

Polsby, Nelson W., Miriam Gallaher, and Barry S. Rundquist. 1969. "The Growth of Seniority in the U.S. House of Representatives." *American Political Science Review* 63:787–807.

Poole, Keith T., and Howard Rosenthal. 1997. *Congress: A Political-Economic History of Roll-Call Voting*. New York: Oxford University Press.

Prewitt, Kenneth. 1990. Review of *Political Ambition*, by Linda Fowler and Robert McClure. *American Political Science Review* 84:995–96.

Prewitt, Kenneth, and William Nolan. 1969. "Political Ambitions and the Behavior of Incumbent Politicians." *Western Political Quarterly* 22:298–308.

Price, Charles M., and Charles G. Bell. 1970. "The Rules of the Game: Political Fact or Academic Fancy?" *Journal of Politics* 32:855.

Price, David E. 1978. "Policy Making in Congressional Committees: The Impact of 'Environmental' Factors." *American Political Science Review* 72:548–74.

Price, H. Douglas. 1977. "Careers and Committees in the American Congress." In *The History of Parliamentary Behavior*, ed. William O. Aydelotte. Princeton: Princeton University Press.

Reed, Robert W., and D. Eric Schansberg. 1994. "An Analysis of the Impact of Congressional Term Limits." *Economic Inquiry* 32(1):79–91.

Reeves, Andree E. 1993. *Congressional Committee Chairmen: Three Who Made an Evolution*. Lexington: University of Kentucky Press.

Rice, Stuart A. 1925. "The Behavior of Legislative Groups." *Political Science Quarterly* 40:60–72.

———1928. *Quantitative Methods in Politics*. New York: Knopf.

Rieselbach, Leroy N. 1977. *Congressional Reform in the Seventies*. Morristown, NJ: General Learning.

———, ed. 1978. *Legislative Reform: The Policy Impact*. Lexington, MA: Lexington Books.

———1983. "The Forest for the Trees: Blazing Trails for Congressional Research." In *Political Science: The State of the Discipline*, ed. Ada W. Finifter. Washington: The American Political Science Association.

———1994. *Congressional Reform: The Changing Modern Congress*. Washington: Congressional Quarterly Press.

———1995. "Congressional Change: Historical Perspectives." In *Remaking Congress: Change and Stability in the 1990s*, ed. James A. Thurber and Roger H. Davidson. Washington: Congressional Quarterly Press.

Riker, William H. 1961. "Voting and the Summation of Preferences: An Interpretive Bibliographic Review of Selected Developments During the Last Decade." *American Political Science Review* 55:900–912.

———1962. *The Theory of Political Coalitions*. New Haven: Yale University Press.

———1965. "Arrow's Theorem and Some Examples of the Paradox of Voting." In *Mathematical Applications in Political Science I*, ed. John Claunch. Dallas: Southern Methodist University Press.

———1983. "Political Theory and the Art of Heresthetics. In *Political Science: The State of the Discipline*. ed. Ada W. Finifter. Washington: American Political Science Association.

———1986. *The Art of Political Manipulation*. New Haven: Yale University.

Riker, William H., and Peter C. Ordeshook. 1973. *An Introduction to Positive Political Theory*. Englewood Cliffs, NJ: Prentice-Hall.

Ripley, Randall B. 1964. "The Party Whip Organization in the United States House of Representatives." *American Political Science Review* 58:561–76.

———1967. *Party Leaders in the House of Representatives*. Washington: Brookings Institution.

———1969a. *Majority Party Leadership in Congress*. Boston: Little, Brown.

———1969b. *Power in the Senate*. New York: St. Martin's Press.

Ripley, Randall B., and Grace A. Franklin. 1991. *Congress, the Bureaucracy, and Public Policy*, 5th ed. Pacific Grove, CA: Brooks/Cole.

Ripley, Randall B., and James M. Lindsay, eds. 1993. *Congress Resurgent: Foreign and Defense Policy on Capitol Hill*. Ann Arbor, MI: University of Michigan Press.

Robinson, James. 1963. *The House Rules Committee*. Indianapolis: Bobbs-Merrill.

Rogers, Lindsay. 1941. "The Staffing of Congress." *Political Science Quarterly* 56:1–22.

Rohde, David W. 1979. "Risk-Bearing and Progressive Ambition: The Case of Members of the United States House of Representatives." *American Journal of Political Science* 23:1–26.

———1990. "'The Reports of My Death Are Greatly Exaggerated': Parties and Party Voting in the House of Representatives." In *Changing Perspectives on Congress*, ed. Glenn R. Parker. Knoxville: University of Tennessee Press.

———1991. *Parties and Leaders in the Postreform House*. Chicago: University of Chicago Press.

Rohde, David W., and Kenneth A. Shepsle. 1973. "Democratic Committee Assignments in the House of Representatives: Strategic Aspects of a Social Choice Process." *American Political Science Review* 67:889–905.

Rohde, David W., and Dennis M. Simon. 1985. "Presidential Vetoes and Congressional Response: A Study of Institutional Conflict." *American Journal of Political Science* 29:399–427.

Rosenthal, Alan. 1996. "State Legislative Development." *Legislative Studies Quarterly*, 21:169–98.

Rossiter, Clinton. 1956. *The American Presidency*. New York: New American Library.

Rothenberg, Lawrence S. 1992. *Linking Citizens to Government: Interest Group Politics at Common Cause*. New York: Cambridge University Press.

Rothman, David. 1966. *Politics and Power: The U.S. Senate, 1869–1901*. Cambridge: Harvard University Press.

Rovere, Richard H. 1965. "Letter from Washington." *The New Yorker* 41, 16 October: 233–44.

Rudder, Catherine E. 1977. "Committee Reform and the Revenue Process." In *Congress Reconsidered*, ed. Lawrence C. Dodd and Bruce I. Oppenheimer. New York: Praeger.

Rundquist, Barry S., and Gerald S. Strom. 1987. "Bill Construction in Legislative Committees: A Study of the U.S. House." *Legislative Studies Quarterly* 12:97–113.

Salisbury, Robert H., and Kenneth A. Shepsle. 1981. "Congressional Staff Turnover and the Ties-That-Bind." *American Political Science Review* 75:381–96.

Scammon, Richard, ed. Various Years. *America Votes*. Washington: Congressional Quarterly, Inc.

Schattschneider, E. E. 1935. *Politics, Pressures, and the Tariff*. New York: Arno.

———1960. *The Semisovereign People*. New York: Holt, Rinehart, and Winston.

Scher, Seymour. 1960. "Congressional Committee Members as Independent Agency Overseers: A Case Study." *American Political Science Review* 54:911–20.

Schlesinger, Joseph A. 1966. *Ambition and Politics: Political Careers in the United States*. Chicago: Rand McNally.

Schlesinger, Joseph A. 1972a. "A Comparison of the Relative Positions of Governors." In *The American Governor in a Behavioral Perspective*, ed. Thad Beyle and J. Oliver Williams. New York: Harper and Row.

———1972b. "The Governor's Place in American Politics." In *The American Governor in a Behavioral Perspective*, ed. Thad Beyle and J. Oliver Williams. New York: Harper and Row.

Schneider, Jerrold E. 1979. *Ideological Coalitions in Congress*. Westport, CT: Greenwood.

Searing, Donald D. 1991. "Roles, Rules, and Rationality in the New Institutionalism." *American Political Science Review* 85:1239–60.

Segal, Jeffrey A., and Harold J. Spaeth. 1993. *The Supreme Court and the Attitudinal Model*. New York: Cambridge University Press.

Selznick, Philip. 1953. *TVA and the Grass Roots*. Berkeley: University of California Press.

———1957. *Leadership in Administration*. Evanston: Row, Peterson.

Serra, George, and David Moon. 1994. "Casework, Issue Positions, and Voting in Congressional Elections." *Journal of Politics* 56:200–13.

Shaw v. Reno, 509 U.S. 630 (1993).

Shelley, Mark C., III. 1983. *The Permanent Majority: The Conservative Coalition in the United States Congress*. University, AL: University of Alabama Press.

Sheppard, Burton D. 1985. *Rethinking Congressional Reform*. Cambridge, MA: Schenkman.

Shepsle, Kenneth A. 1972a. "Parties, Voters and the Risk Environment: A Mathematical Treatment of Electoral Competition Under Uncertainty." In *Probability Models of Collective Decision Making*, ed. Richard Niemi and Herbert Weisberg. Columbus, OH: Charles E. Merrill.

———1972b. "The Strategy of Ambiguity: Uncertainty and Electoral Competition." *American Political Science Review* 66:555–68.

———1978. *The Giant Jigsaw Puzzle: Democratic Committee Assignments in the Modern House*. Chicago: University of Chicago Press.

———1979. "Institutional Arrangements and Equilibrium in Multidimensional Voting Models." *American Journal of Political Science* 23:27–59.

———1985. "Prospects for Formal Models of Legislatures." *Legislative Studies Quarterly* 10:5–19.

————1989. "Congressional Institutions and Behavior: The Changing Textbook Congress." In *Can the Government Govern?* ed. John E. Chubb and Paul E. Peterson. Washington: Brookings Institution.

Shepsle, Kenneth A., and Barry R. Weingast. 1981. "Structure-Induced Equilibrium and Legislative Choice." *Public Choice* 37:503–19.

————1987. "The Institutional Foundations of Committee Power." *American Political Science Review* 81:85–104.

————1995. *Positive Theories of Congressional Institutions.* Ann Arbor: University of Michigan Press.

Shull, Steven A., ed. 1991. *The Two Presidencies: A Quarter Century Assessment.* Chicago: Nelson-Hall.

————1997. *Presidential-Congressional Relations.* Ann Arbor: University of Michigan Press.

Silbey, Joel H. 1967. *The Shrine of Party: Congressional Voting Behavior, 1841–1952.* Pittsburgh: University of Pittsburgh Press.

Silverman, Corinne. 1962. "The Little Rock Story." Interuniversity Case Program Series. Reprint. In *Case Studies in American Government,* ed. Edwin A. Bock and Alan K. Campbell. Englewood Cliffs: Prentice-Hall.

Simon, Herbert A. 1954. "Spurious Correlation: A Causal Interpretation." *Journal of the American Statistical Association* 49:467–79.

————1968. "On Judging the Plausibility of Theories." In *Logic, Methodology, and Philosophy of Science, III,* ed. Bob van Rootselaar and J. F. Staal. Amsterdam: North-Holland Publishing Company.

————1969. *The Sciences of the Artificial.* Cambridge: MIT Press.

Sinclair, Barbara. 1977. "Party Realignment and the Transformation of the Political Agenda: The House of Representatives, 1925–1938." *American Political Science Review* 71:940–53.

————1978. "From Party Voting to Regional Fragmentation: The House of Representatives, 1933–1956." *American Politics Quarterly* 6:125–47.

————1982. *Congressional Realignment, 1925–1978.* Austin: University of Texas Press.

————1983. *Majority Leadership in the House.* Baltimore, MD: The Johns Hopkins University Press.

————1989. *The Transformation of the U.S. Senate.* Baltimore: The Johns Hopkins University Press.

————1995. *Legislators, Leaders, and Lawmaking: The U.S. House of Representatives in the Postreform Era.* Baltimore: The Johns Hopkins University Press

————1997. *Unorthodox Lawmaking: New Legislative Processes in the U.S. Congress.* Washington: Congressional Quarterly Press.

Sisson, Richard. 1973. "Comparative Legislative Institutionalization." In *Legislatures in Comparative Perspective,* ed. Allan Kornberg. New York: McKay.

Smith, Richard A. 1984. "Advocacy, Interpretation, and Influence in the U.S. Congress." *American Political Science Review* 78:44–63.

————1995. "Interest Group Influence in the U.S. Congress." *Legislative Studies Quarterly* 20:89–139.

Smith, Steven S. 1988. "An Essay on Sequence, Position, Goals, and Committee Power." *Legislative Studies Quarterly* 13:151–76.

————1989. *Call to Order: Floor Politics in the House and Senate.* Washington: Brookings Institution.

Smith, Steven S., and Christopher J. Deering. 1990. *Committees in Congress.* 2nd ed. Washington: Congressional Quarterly Press.

Smith, Steven S., and Marcus Flathman. 1989. "Managing the Senate Floor: Complex Unanimous Consent Agreements since the 1950s." *Legislative Studies Quarterly* 14:349–74.

Snowiss, Leo. 1966. "Congressional Recruitment and Representation." *American Political Science Review* 60:627–39.

Squire, Peverill. 1992. "Challenger Quality and Voting Behavior in U.S. Senate Elections." *Legislative Studies Quarterly* 17:247–63.

Stealey, Orlando Oscar. 1906. *Twenty Years in the Press Gallery.* New York: Publishers Printing Company.

Stein, Robert M., and Kenneth N. Bickers. 1995. "Perpetuating the Pork Barrel." *Policy Subsystems and American Democracy.* New York: Cambridge University Press.

Steinberg, Alfred. 1975. *Sam Rayburn*. New York: Hawthorn Books.

Steiner, Gilbert Y. 1976. *The Children's Cause*. Washington: Brookings Institution.

Stevens, Arthur G., Daniel P. Mulhollan, and Paul S. Rundquist. 1981. "U.S. Congressional Structure and Representation: The Role of Informal Groups." *Legislative Studies Quarterly* 6:415–37.

Stewart, John G. 1971. "Two Strategies of Leadership: Johnson and Mansfield." In *Congressional Behavior*, ed. Nelson W. Polsby. New York: Random House.

Stimson, James A., Michael B. MacKuen, and Robert S. Erikson. 1995. "Dynamic Representation." *American Political Science Review* 89:543–65.

Stokes, Donald E. 1967. "Parties and the Nationalization of Electoral Forces. In *The American Party Systems*, ed. William N. Chambers and Walter D. Burnham. New York: Oxford University Press.

Stokes, Donald E., and Warren E. Miller. 1962. "Party Government and the Saliency of Congress." *Public Opinion Quarterly* 26:531–46.

Strahan, Randall. 1990. *New Ways and Means: Reform and Change in a Congressional Committee*. Chapel Hill: University of North Carolina Press.

———1992. "Reed and Rostenkowski: Congressional Leadership in Institutional Time." In *The Atomistic Congress: An Interpretation of Congressional Change*, ed. Allen D. Hertzke and Ronald M. Peters, Jr. Armonk, NY: M. E. Sharpe.

———1993. "Dan Rostenkowski: A Study in Congressional Power." In *Congress Reconsidered*, 5th ed., ed. Lawrence C. Dodd and Bruce I. Oppenheimer. Washington: Congressional Quarterly Press.

Strayer, Joseph R. 1970. *On the Medieval Origins of the Modern State*. Princeton, NJ: Princeton University Press.

Sullivan, John L., L. Earl Shaw, Gregory E. McAvoy, and David G. Barnum. 1993. "The Dimensions of Cue-Taking in the House of Representatives: Variation by Issue Area." *Journal of Politics* 55:975–97.

Sullivan, William E. 1975. "Criteria for Selecting Party Leadership in Congress: An Empirical Test." *American Politics Quarterly* 3:25–44.

Sundquist, James L. 1968. *Politics and Policy*. Washington: Brookings Institution.

———1973. *Dynamics of the Party System*. Washington: Brookings Institution.

———1992. *Constitutional Reform and Effective Government*, Rev. ed. Washington: Brookings Institution.

Swain, Carol M. 1993. *Black Faces, Black Interests: The Representation of African Americans in Congress*. Cambridge: Harvard University Press.

Swift, Elaine K. 1996. *The Making of an American Senate: Reconstitutive Change in Congress, 1787–1841*. Ann Arbor: University of Michigan Press.

Swinerton, E. Nelson. 1968. "Ambition and American State Executives." *Midwest Journal of Political Science* 12:538–49.

Tacheron, Donald G., and Morris K. Udall. 1970. *The Job of the Congressman*. Indianapolis: Bobbs-Merrill.

Taylor, Edward E. 1941. *A History of the Committee on Appropriations*. House Document 299. 77th Cong. 1st sess. Washington: Government Printing Office.

Thelen, Kathleen, ed. and Sven Steinmo. 1992. "Historical Institutionalism in Comparative Politics." In *Structuring Politics*, ed. Sven Steinmo, Kathleen Thelen, and Frank Longstreth. Cambridge: Cambridge University Press.

Thibaut, John W., and Harold H. Kelley. 1959. *The Social Psychology of Groups*. New York: Wiley.

Thomas, Sue. 1994. *How Women Legislate*. New York: Oxford University Press.

Tidmarch, Charles M., and Charles M. Sabatt. 1972. "Presidential Leadership Changes and Foreign Policy Roll-Call Voting in the U.S. Senate." *Western Political Quarterly* 25:613–25.

Tiefer, Charles. 1989. *Congressional Practice and Procedure*. Westport, CT: Greenwood Press.

Truman, David B. 1951. *The Governmental Process*. New York: Alfred Knopf.

———1959. *The Congressional Party*. New York: Wiley.

———1965. "Introduction: The Problem and Its Setting." In *The Congress and America's Future*, ed. David Truman. Englewood Cliffs, NJ: Prentice-Hall.

————1966. "The Representative Function in Western Systems." In *Essays in Political Science*, ed. Edward H. Buchrig. Bloomington: Indiana University Press.

Tufte, Edward R. 1973. "The Relation Between Seats and Votes in Two Party Systems." *American Political Science Review* 67:540–54.

————1975. "Determinants of the Outcomes of Midterm Congressional Elections." *American Political Science Review* 69:812–26.

Turner, Julius. 1951a. *Party and Constituency: Pressures on Congress*. Baltimore: The Johns Hopkins University Press.

————1951b. "Responsible Parties: A Dissent From the Floor." *American Political Science Review* 45:143–52.

————1970. *Party and Constituency: Pressures on Congress*. Revised by Edward V. Schneier, Jr. Baltimore: The Johns Hopkins University Press.

Turett, J. Stephen. 1971. "The Vulnerability of American Governors: 1900–1969." *Midwest Journal of Political Science* 15:108–32.

Unekis, Joseph K., and Leroy N. Rieselbach. 1984. *Congressional Committee Politics: Continuity and Change*. New York: Praeger.

U.S. Term Limtis v. Hill, 316 Ark. 251 (1994).

U.S. Term Limits v. Thornton, 514 U.S. 779 (1994).

U.S. Office of Management and Budget. 1987. *Historical Tables: Budget of the United States Government, FY 1988*. Washington: Government Printing Office.

Uslaner, Eric M. 1993. *The Decline of Comity in Congress*. Ann Arbor: University of Michigan Press.

Van Deusen, Glyndon G. 1937. *The Life of Henry Clay*. Boston: Little, Brown.

Van Doren, Peter. 1990. "Can We Learn the Causes of Congressional Decisions from Roll-Call Data?" *Legislative Studies Quarterly* 15:311–40.

Voorhis, Jerry. 1947. *Confessional of a Congressman*. Garden City: Doubleday and Company.

Wahlke, John C., Heinz Eulau, William Buchanan, and Leroy C. Ferguson. 1962. *The Legislative System*. New York: Wiley.

Ward, Daniel S. 1993. "The Continuing Search for Party Influence in Congress: A View from the Committees." *Legislative Studies Quarterly* 18:211–30.

Weaver, R. Kent. 1988. *Automatic Government: The Politics of Indexation*. Washington: Brookings Institution.

Weber, Max. 1947. *The Theory of Social and Economic Organization*. Glencoe: The Free Press.

Weingast, Barry R. 1979. "A Rational Choice Perspective on Congressional Norms." *American Journal of Political Science* 23:245–62.

————1989. "Floor Behavior in the U.S. Congress: Committee Power Under the Open Rule." *American Political Science Review* 83:795–816.

Weisberg, Herbert F. 1968. "Dimensional Analysis of Legislative Roll Calls." Ph.D. diss. University of Michigan.

————1972. "Scaling Models for Legislative Roll-Call Analysis." *American Political Science Review* 66:1306–15.

————1978. "Evaluating Theories of Congressional Roll-Call Voting." *American Journal of Political Science* 22:554–77.

Weisberg, Herbert F., and Samuel C. Patterson, eds. 1998. *Great Theatre: The American Congress in the 1990s*. Cambridge: Cambridge University Press.

Weissberg, Robert. 1978. "Collective and Dyadic Representation in Congress." *American Political Science Review* 72:535–47.

Wesberry v. Sanders, 376 U.S. 1(1964).

Westefield, Louis P. 1974. "Majority Party Leadership and the Committee System in the House of Representatives." *American Political Science Review* 68:1593–1604.

Westlye, Mark C. 1992. *Senate Elections and Campaign Intensity*. Baltimore: The Johns Hopkins University Press.

Whitby, Kenny J. 1997. *The Color of Representation*. Ann Arbor: University of Michigan Press.

White, Theodore H. 1961. *The Making of the President, 1960*. New York: Atheneum.

———1973. *The Making of the President, 1972*. New York: Atheneum.

White, William S. 1956. *Citadel: The Story of the United States Senate*. New York: Harper and Brothers.

Wicker, Tom. 1968. *JFK and LBJ*. New York: William Morrow.

Wilcox, Clyde, and Aage R. Clausen. 1991. "The Dimensionality of Roll-Call Voting Reconsidered." *Legislative Studies Quarterly* 16:393–406.

Wildavsky, Aaron. 1966. "The Two Presidencies." *Trans-Action* 4(December): 7–14.

Will, George F. 1995. "Term Limits Might Be Just What Budget Needs." *Wisconsin State Journal*, 12 February.

Wilson, Woodrow. [1885] 1956. *Congressional Government*. Reprint. New York: Meridian Books, The World Publishing Company.

———[1908] 1961. *Constitutional Government in the United States*. Reprint. New York: Columbia University Press.

Winter, David G., Margaret G. Hermann, Walter Weintraub, and Stephen G. Walker. 1991. "The Personalities of Bush and Gorbachev Measured at a Distance." *Political Psychology* 12:215–43.

Wood, David M. 1968. "Majority vs. Opposition in the French National Assembly, 1956–1965." *American Political Science Review* 62:88–109.

Wright, John R. 1990. "Contributions, Lobbying, and Committee Voting in the U.S. House of Representatives." *American Political Science Review* 84:417–38.

———1996. *Interest Groups and Congress: Lobbying, Contributions, and Influence*. Boston: Allyn and Bacon.

Wright, Sewall. 1920. "Correlation and Causation." *Journal of Agricultural Research* 20:557–85.

Young, Gary, and Joseph Cooper. 1995. "Multiple Referral and the Transformation of House Decision Making." In *Congress Reconsidered*, 5th ed., ed. Lawrence C. Dodd and Bruce I. Oppenheimer. Washington: Congressional Quarterly Press.

Young, James S. 1966. *The Washington Community, 1800–1828*. New York: Columbia University Press.

Young, Roland. 1943. *This Is Congress*. New York: Alfred A. Knopf.

———1956. *Congressional Politics in the Second World War*. New York: Columbia University Press.

Name Index

Subject Index